THE COLLEGE WRITER

A Guide to Thinking, Writing, and Researching

Third Edition

Randall VanderMey
Westmont College

Verne Meyer
Dordt College

John Van Rys
Redeemer University College

Pat Sebranek

HEINLE
CENGAGE Learning

Australia • Brazil • Japan • Korea • Mexico • Singapore • Spain • United Kingdom • United States

HEINLE
CENGAGE Learning

The College Writer: A Guide to Thinking, Writing, and Researching, Third Edition

Randall VanderMey, Verne Meyer, John Van Rys, and Pat Sebranek

Executive Publisher: Patricia Coryell

Senior Marketing Manager:
 Tom Ziolkowski

Discipline Product Manager: Pina Daniel

Development Manager, English:
 Judith Fifer

Senior Project Editor: Aileen Mason

Senior Media Producer: Philip Lanza

Content Manager: Janet Edmonds

Cover Design Manager: Anne S. Katzeff

Senior Photo Editor: Jennifer Meyer Dare

Senior New Title Project Manager:
 Patricia O'Neill

Editorial Associate: Daisuke Yasutake

Marketing Associate, English and Student
 Success: Bettina Chiu

Editorial Assistant, Editorial Production:
 Anne Finley

Sebranek, Inc.: Steve Augustyn, Laura
 Bachman, Ron Bachman, April Barrons,
 Colleen Belmont, Chris Erickson, Mark
 Fairweather, Mariellen Hanrahan,
 Tammy Hintz, Rob King, Lois Krenzke,
 Mark Lalumondier, Kevin Nelson, Mike
 Ramczyk, Janae Sebranek, Lester Smith,
 Jean Varley

Cover image: © Tischenko Irina /
 Shutterstock.com

"A Hanging" from SHOOTING AN
 ELEPHANT AND OTHER ESSAYS by
 George Orwell, copyright 1950 by the
 Estate of Sonia B. Orwell and renewed
 1978 by Sonia Pitt-Rivers, reprinted by
 permission of Cengage Learning.

Credits begin on page 680, which
 constitutes an extension of this
 copyright page.

For product information and technology assistance, contact us at
Cengage Learning Customer & Sales Support, 1-800-354-9706

For permission to use material from this text or product,
submit all requests online at **www.cengage.com/permissions**
Further permissions questions can be emailed to
permissionrequest@cengage.com

Library of Congress Control Number: 2007910087

ISBN-13: 978-0-547-14782-6

ISBN-10: 0-547-14782-1

Heinle
20 Channel Center Street
Boston, MA 02210
USA

Cengage Learning is a leading provider of customized learning solutions with office locations around the globe, including Singapore, the United Kingdom, Australia, Mexico, Brazil, and Japan. Locate your local office at **international.cengage.com/region**

Cengage Learning products are represented in Canada by Nelson Education, Ltd.

To learn more about Heinle, visit **www.cengage.com/heinle**

Purchase any of our products at your local college store or at our preferred online store **www.ichapters.com**

Printed in the United States of America
2 3 4 5 6 7 8 9-DOC-12 11 10 09

Preface

The College Writer, third edition, offers students thorough yet accessible coverage of the writing process; the book's visual format helps them quickly grasp the big picture and easily locate supporting details. In response to reviewers' requests, the authors added new student and professional samples, including new MLA and APA papers, to help students achieve a formal academic voice. In addition, the entire book, as well as audio, video, exercises, models, and weblinks, is available as an e-book or with a separate passkey that permits students to access additional online features.

Key Features of *The College Writer,* Third Edition

- Unique "at-a-glance" format presents each concept in one or two pages.
- Colorful design and visuals reinforce the concepts and aid retention.
- Tabbed sections enable students to find topics quickly.
- Coverage of planning, drafting, revising, editing, and proofreading is thorough, with sample paragraphs and visuals that walk students through the rhetorical situation (identifying purpose, audience, and context).
- Instruction on "Writing with Sources" is integrated into the writing-process chapters in page spreads that explain how to use sources during a given step (e.g., pages 40–41 and 68–69).
- Both student and professional samples of each type of writing are included to offer students writing models appropriate for their needs.
- Coverage of research methods, such as electronic research, includes extensive instruction on how to work with and evaluate sources, integrate them effectively, and document them so as to avoid plagiarism.
- New model MLA and APA papers illustrate a wide variety of research-writing practices, including accessing and documenting online sources.
- A friendly "coaching" tone develops students' self-confidence as learners.
- Cross-curricular writing instruction is offered throughout the text: chapters 2–7 give research-writing tips called "Cross-Curricular Connections"; chapter 9 identifies writing forms and skills emphasized in each discipline; chapters 10–23 include sample papers written in a variety of courses; and chapters 28–33 address research skills.
- Coverage of critical thinking and critical viewing throughout the text helps students learn to analyze and evaluate both written and visual "arguments," such as advertisements and political campaign coverage.
- The end-of-text Handbook covers key points of grammar, mechanics, and punctuation. These topics are reinforced by exercises available on the text's website, **www.thecollegewriter.com/3e.**

 A thematic table of contents supports instructors who employ themes such as community and conscience or ethics and equity.

New to This Edition

Critical Thinking and Reading From cover to cover, *The College Writer* helps students develop and apply critical-thinking skills. For example, chapter 1 explains how to think critically when reading, studying, taking tests, or viewing; chapters 2–8 show how to think critically while working through the writing process; and chapters 10–32 explain how to apply critical-thinking strategies when reading or writing a broad range of literary forms.

Chapter 1 Critical Thinking Through Reading, Viewing, and Writing   **17**

Evaluate an image.

Discussion

Evaluating an image such as this WWII poster aimed at U.S. servicemen reveals its strong stereotypes of both men and women, stereotypes related to the historical period. As with all images, evaluation begins with understanding and interpreting the poster.

In the poster's center is a woman in evening dress, her hair done up, wearing jewels and a corsage. She is seated, at ease, looking at us. Perhaps she represents beauty, both sensual attractiveness and sophistication. The colors used to present her are pale and muted, except for her blue eyes and red lips.

Surrounding the woman are three men, individually dressed in the uniforms of Army, Air Force, and Navy. Drinking and smoking, the men seem to be competing for her attention.

The poster implies that all service personnel were male, which was not true even in WWII, when WACs and WAVEs served in the armed forces. It cautions that these male members of the armed forces should be wary in seemingly innocent social situations, since even a beautiful woman, whom popular stereotypes of the day characterized as "dumb," might not be what she appears. Such a woman could, in fact, be a spy—an idea perhaps inspired by the famous case of Mata Hari. The statement that "careless talk costs lives" is a version of another phrase from the period: "Loose lips sink ships."

Evaluating this poster involves considering its original context within from our current perspective. In the heat of WWII, this poster could a fair piece of military persuasion. Today, however, what is striking stereotypes at work in both image and words. Not only are service p both male and female, in every branch of the armed forces, but they roles, including combat positions. With respect to the men, the ima in social situations (which are assumed to include smoking and drin untrustworthy and apt to boast or compete in the presence of an att With respect to women, the image both denounces and warns, implyi especially attractive women, are cunning and dangerous. Today, su press us to question the quality, truthfulness, and value of the image

93

EDITING AND PROOFREADING

6

In any writing project, there comes a point (like a fast-approaching due date) when you must prepare your writing for submission. At that time you must edit and proofread your revised writing so that it speaks clearly and accurately. When you edit, look first for words, phrases, and sentences that sound awkward, uninteresting, or unclear. When you proofread, check your writing for spelling, mechanics, usage, and grammar errors.

Before you begin, make sure you have the proper tools: handbook, dictionary, thesaurus, computer spell checker, and so on. Also, ask one of your writing peers to help you edit your work. Then prepare your final draft, following the guidelines established by your instructor, and proofread it for errors.

The guidelines and strategies given in this chapter will help you to edit your writing for style and clarity and to proofread it for errors.

New Visuals and Thinking Prompts Each of the first thirty-two chapters begins with a visual that introduces the chapter and concludes with a prompt (called "Visually Speaking") that challenges students to think critically about the nature and function of the visual.

Additional Third-Person Essays Third-person essays, both student and professional, have been added to this edition of the text. Additional student models are available in a new print supplement, *Student Voices: A Sampling of College Writing,* and on the text's companion website.

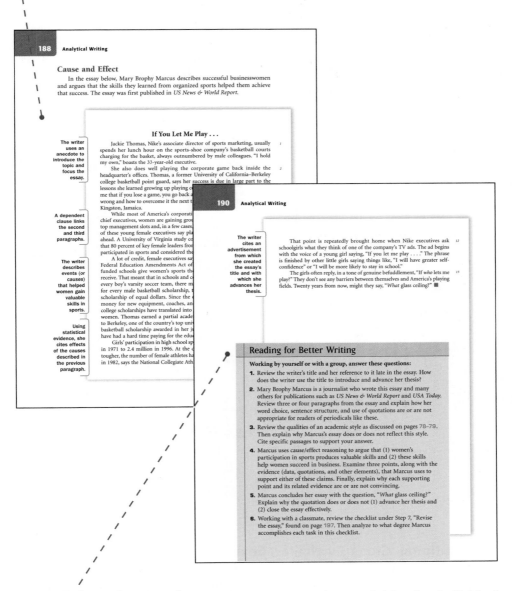

Collaborative Work In addition to providing activities for individual thinking and writing, each chapter also features response topics that promote group discussion and projects that facilitate collaborative learning.

More on Integrating Sources Chapters 2–7 each include a new two-page spread called "Writing with Sources." This feature offers tips on how to work with researched information at each step in the writing process. For example, chapter 2 presents and explains how to do the following:

- Track resources in a working bibliography.
- Use a note-taking system that respects sources.
- Distinguish summaries, paraphrases, and quotations.

Additional coverage of integrating sources is included in section 3, "Research and Writing." (More on avoiding plagiarism and integrating sources can also be found on the student website.)

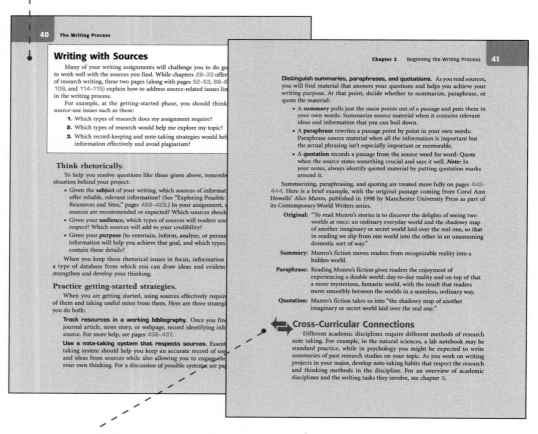

Additional Cross-Curricular Coverage Chapters 2–7 each include a new feature called "Cross-Curricular Connections," an insert explaining research-writing strategies required or emphasized in specific disciplines. Chapter 9, "Forms of College Writing," lists the types of writing and thinking skills emphasized across the curriculum. In addition, chapters 10–23 include instructions for and models of writing done in a variety of courses.

New MLA and APA Papers The third edition of *The College Writer* includes new MLA and APA student sample papers and reflects updates to electronic citation for the APA system. The MLA citations in this text follow the sixth edition of the *MLA Handbook for Writers of Research Papers* pending publication of the seventh edition; visit mla.org for more information.

More Online Supplementation for the Student

The College Writer E-book *The College Writer* is now available as an e-book (electronic book), which offers students online access to the entire text, along with video and audio explanations that enhance the text, writing tutorials, grammar exercises, additional writing models, and links to carefully selected websites.

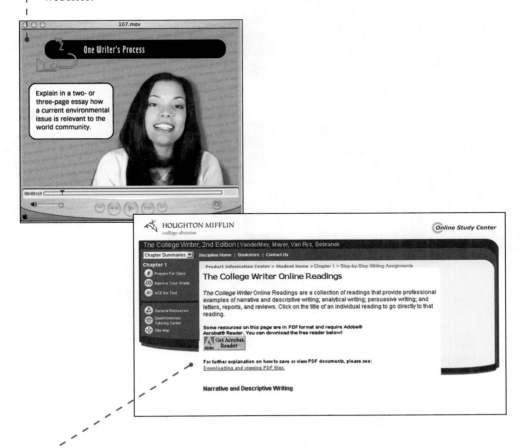

Student Website Students can go to **www.thecollegewriter.com/3e** to find weblinks, visual activities, games, annotated readings, writing assignments, grammar exercises, and more.

Student Voices: A Sampling of College Writing This new 64-page supplement of student papers illustrates each of the modes and provides additional writing formats. This resource can be packaged with the text for only $5.00.

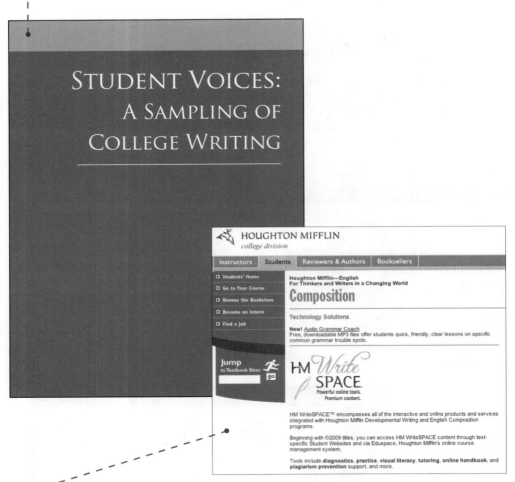

WriteSPACE offers additional premium content that is passkey-protected and is available to be packaged with the text. This content includes all of the features of WriteSPACE with Eduspace, Houghton Mifflin's signature Classroom Management System, but can be used with any CMS. This premium content includes tutorials, grammar exercises, writing assignments, interactive proofreading practice, additional readings, visual activities, games, and music activities.

More Online Supplementation for the Instructor

Instructor's Resource Manual is available in a print version or is downloadable from the instructor's website; the document contains an overview of the course, sample syllabi, chapter summaries, and teaching suggestions.

Instructor's Website, a password-protected site accessed at **www .thecollegewriter.com/3e,** provides the downloadable version of the *Instructor's Resource Manual,* assessment rubrics, learning objectives, and access to all materials in the student website.

WriteSPACE with Eduspace, Cengage Learning's Classroom Management System, provides an integrated, customizable system with a wide variety of content that can be administered as self-paced exercises or gradable exams. WriteSpace delivers exercises, diagnostic tests, assignments, and learning modules, as well as access to CL Assess, a personalized assessment tool that can pinpoint a student's writing problems and track his or her progress.

Acknowledgments

The authors express their gratitude to the following people, who have contributed to the development of this edition of the text or to prior editions and supplements.

Reviewers: Alena Balmforth, *Salt Lake Community College;* Cherrie Bergandi, *Chippewa Valley Technical College;* Michael D. Cook, *Everest College—Phoenix;* Tamera Davis, *Northern Oklahoma College— Stillwater;* Mary Etter, *Davenport University;* Patrick L. Green, *Aiken Technical College;* Jennifer Haber, *St. Petersburg College;* Patricia A. Herb, *North Central State College;* David Jacobsen, *Westmont College;* John L. Liffiton, *Scottsdale Community College;* Molly Luby, *Central Carolina Community College;* Kelly B. McCalla, *Central Lakes College;* Christine A. Miller, *Davenport University;* Nancy W. Noel, *Germanna Community College;* Francie Quaas-Berryman, *Cerritos College;* Christine A. Saxlid, *Wisconsin Indianhead Technical College;* Vicki Scheurer, *Palm Beach Community College;* Catherine Scudder Wolf, *Susssex County Community College;* Susan M. Smith, *Tompkins Cortland Community College;* Donald Stinson, *Northern Oklahoma College;* Christine Szymczak, *Erie Community College*

Instructors: Mary Adams, *Peru State College;* Jim Addison, *Western Carolina University;* Susan Aguila, *Palm Beach Community College;* Cathryn Amdahl, *Harrisburg Area Community College;* Edmund August, *McKendree College;* Richard Baker, *Adams State College;* Thomas G. Beverage, *Coastal Carolina Community College;* Patricia Blaine, *Paducah Community College;* Tammie Bob, *College of DuPage;* Candace Boeck, *San Diego State University;* Charley Boyd, *Genesee Community College;* Deborah Bradford, *Bridgewater State College;* Linda Brender, *Macomb Community College;* Colleen M. Burke, *Rasmussen College;* Vicki Byard, *Northeastern Illinois University;* Susan Callender, *Sinclair Community College;* Sandra Camillo, *Finger Lakes Community College;* Sandy Cavanah, *Hopkinsville Community College;* Annette Cedarholm, *Snead State Community College;* James William Chichetto, *Stonehill College;* Sandra Clark, *Anderson University;* Beth Conomos, *Erie Community College, SUNY;* Keith Coplin, *Colby Community College;* Sue Cornett, *St. Petersburg College;* Debra Cumberland, *Winona State University;* David Daniel,

Newbury College; Sarah Dangelantonio, *Franklin Pierce College;* Rachelle L. Darabi, *Indiana University, Purdue University Fort Wayne;* Judy C. Davidson, *University of Texas, Pan American;* Helen Deese, *University of California, Riverside;* Darren DeFrain, *Wichita State University;* Sarah Dengler, *Franklin Pierce College;* Linda Dethloff, *Prairie State College;* Steven Dolgin, *Schoolcraft College;* Carol Jean Dudley, *Eastern Illinois University;* Chris Ellery, *Angelo State University;* Ernest J. Enchelmayer, *Louisiana State University;* Anne K. Erickson, *Atlantic Cape Community College;* Kelly A. Foth, *University of Dubuque;* Julie Foust, *Utah State University;* Lyneé Lewis Gaillet, *Georgia State University;* Gregory R. Glau, *Arizona State University;* Patricia Glynn, *Middlesex Community College;* Samuel J. Goldstein, *Daytona Beach Community College;* Kim Grewe, *Wor-Wic Community College;* Loren C. Gruber, *Missouri Valley College;* Michael Hammond, *Northeastern Illinois University;* Katona Hargrave, *Troy State University;* Dick Harrington, *Piedmont Virginia Community College;* Karla Hayashi, *University of Hawaii, Hilo;* Anne Christine Helms, *Alamance Community College;* Stan Hitron, *Middlesex Community College;* Karen Holleran, *Kaplan College;* Barbara Dondiego Holmes, *University of Charleston;* Maurice Hunt, *Baylor University;* Barbara Jacobskind, *University of Massachusetts, Dartmouth;* Linda G. Johnson, *Southeast Technical Institute;* Alex M. Joncas, *Estrella Mountain Community College;* Nina B. Keery, *Massachusetts Bay Community College;* Sandra Keneda, *Rose State College;* Margo LaGattuta, *University of Michigan, Flint;* Richard Larschan, *University of Massachusetts, Dartmouth;* Dusty Maddox, *DeVry University;* Bonnie J. Marshall, *Grand Valley State University;* Daphne Matthews, *Mississippi Delta Community College;* Claudia Milstead, *Missouri Valley College;* Kate Mohler, *Mesa Community College;* Meghan Monroe, *Central Michigan University;* Ed Moritz, *Indiana University, Purdue University Fort Wayne;* Linda Morrison, *Niagara University;* Deborah Naquin, *Northern Virginia Community College;* Julie Nichols, *Okaloosa-Walton Community College;* Robert H. Nordell, *Des Moines Area Community College;* Christine Pavesic, *University of Wisconsin, Waukesha;* Sherry Rankin, *Abilene Christian University;* Laura Robbins, *Portland Community College;* Matthew Roudané, *Georgia State University;* Robert E. Rubin, *Wright State University;* Nancy Ruff, *Southern Illinois University, Edwardsville;* Christine M. Ryan, *Middlesex Community College;* Larry W. Severeid, *College of Eastern Utah;* Donna K. Speaker, *Wallace State Community College;* Talbot Spivak, *Edison College;* Joyce Swofford, *Clayton College & State University;* Terry Thacker, *Coastline Community College;* Diane Thompson, *Northern Virginia Community College;* Monica Parrish Trent, *Montgomery College;* Dori Wagner, *Austin Community College;* Shonda Wilson, *Suffolk County Community College;* Frances J. Winter, *Massachusetts Bay Community College;* Kelly Wonder, *University of Wisconsin, Eau Claire;* Benjamin Worth, *Bluegrass Community and Technical College;* Deanna L. Yameen, *Quincy College.*

Students: Lindsi Bittner, *St. Petersburg College;* Danielle Brown, *Oakton Community College;* Marie Burns, *University of Tampa;* Will Buttner, *University of Tampa;* Debra Cotton, *St. Petersburg College;* Jessica de Olivera, *Northeastern Illinois University;* Petra Hickman, *St. Petersburg College;* Anne Hsiao, *Oakton Community College;* Cassie Hull, *St. Petersburg College;* Courtney Langford, *St. Petersburg College;* Sandy Lehrke, *Hillsborough Community College;* Michael Pistorio, *Oakton Community College;* Crystal Smuk, *Triton Junior College;* Marc Sordja, *St. Petersburg College;* Johnny Velez, *Hillsborough Community College;* Anthony Zalud, *Harper Community College;* Omar Zamora, *Northeastern Illinois University.*

Special Thanks: A special thanks goes to Sarah Dangelantonio and Sarah Dengler of *Franklin Pierce College* for their work on the *Instructor's Resource Manual.* Also, thanks to Mark Gallaher, Kelly McGuire, Julie Nash, Dee Seligman, and Janet Young.

Randall VanderMey • Verne Meyer • John Van Rys • Pat Sebranek

Contents

Preface, **iii**

I. Rhetoric: A College Student's Guide to Writing

Reading, Thinking, Viewing, and Writing

The Writing Process

II. Reader: Strategies and Models

Writing Across the Curriculum

Narrative, Descriptive, and Reflective Writing

Special Forms of Writing

III. Research and Writing

Research and Writing

Thematic Table of Contents for Readings

Memory and Tradition

Science and Health

Terror and Our Time

Rhetoric:
A COLLEGE STUDENT'S GUIDE TO WRITING

I

CONTENTS

Reading, Thinking, Viewing, and Writing

The Writing Process

The College Essay

CRITICAL THINKING THROUGH READING, VIEWING, AND WRITING

Audio

In many respects, critical thinking defines your college work. When you think critically, you examine ideas fully and logically, weigh multiple perspectives on issues, and draw reasonable conclusions. In the process, you carry on an in-depth dialogue with information and evidence.

In many of your courses, your instructors will ask you to undertake critical thinking through reading, viewing, and writing. You might have to analyze Flannery O'Connor's short story "Good Country People," identify the comic conventions in the film *Sideways*, or analyze data gathered about the fermentation of ethanol. In all of these assignments, you are being pressed to think critically, using reading, viewing, and writing—connected as they are—to make sense of things. And one goal is that your training in critical thinking will prepare you for work in your profession and in the public square.

Thoughtful reading and viewing, then, lie at the heart of critical thinking and feed into thoughtful writing. These natural reading-viewing-thinking-writing connections are this chapter's focus.

Video

Critical Thinking Through Reading

Reading is basic to writing the way that eating is basic to cooking. Just as creating food worth tasting and digesting is at the heart of cooking, so is making words worth reading at the heart of writing. And while the cook must plan the meal around the tastes of his or her guests, the writer must always develop his or her text with awareness of the readers' perspectives. To appeal to a reader, in other words, the writer must know firsthand what good reading is.

Use a reading strategy: SQ3R.

Obviously, reading a novel, a textbook, and a webpage are all different activities. Nevertheless, all college reading assignments can be approached systematically, especially when your goal is to absorb and engage the text. One such strategy for critical reading, especially of information-rich texts, is called **SQ3R: Survey, Question, Read, Recite,** and **Review.** Here is how SQ3R works.

Survey

The first step in SQ3R is to preview the material. Try to spot main ideas. They will serve as reference points during the reading that follows. Perhaps you've been given questions or a study guide. Read those first. Then read the introductory and concluding paragraphs and glance at each page in between. Pay special attention to headings, chapter titles, illustrations, and boldfaced type. Also check out any graphics—charts, maps, diagrams, illustrations—that visually reinforce key points.

Benefits: Surveying serves three important purposes: (1) It gives you the big picture, (2) it stabilizes and directs your thoughts, and (3) it gets you over the starting hump.

Question

As you survey, begin to ask questions that you hope to answer as you read.

- Turn the headings and subheadings into questions. For example, if the subhead says "Methods," ask, "What methods did the researcher use?"
- Imagine a specific test question covering each major point in your reading. For example, if the reading addresses the media and the ethics of cloning, as shown on page 7, you might imagine this test question: "What can the media do to foster productive public debate on cloning?"
- Be thorough by asking the journalist's questions: *who, what, when, where, why,* and *how.* Examples: *Who are the media? What's the popular understanding of cloning? How have the media presented cloning? Why does the author see the media's treatment of cloning as an ethical issue?*
- Look over any questions found at the end of the text or the chapter.

Benefits: Asking questions will keep you actively thinking about what is coming up and will help you to maintain an appropriate critical distance.

Read

As you encounter facts and ideas, ask these questions: What does this mean? How do the ideas relate to each other and to what I know? What's coming next?

Keep track of your answers by taking notes, annotating the text, mapping, or outlining. (See pages **6–9** for more on these active-reading techniques.) Read difficult parts slowly; reread them if necessary. Look up unfamiliar words or ideas, and use your senses to imagine the events, people, places, or things you are reading about. Imagine talking with the writer. Express agreement, lodge complaints, ask for proof—and imagine the writer's response or look for it in the text.

Benefits: Engaging actively with the text in this way will draw you deeper into the world of the writing. You'll trigger memories and make surprising connections.

Recite

After finishing a page, section, or chapter, recite the key points aloud. Answering *Who? What? When? Where? Why?* and *How?* questions is a quick way of testing yourself on how well you understood what you read. You can also recite the key points by listing them or writing a summary (see page **11**).

Benefits: Reciting tests your comprehension, drives the material deeper into your long-term memory, and helps you connect the content with what you already know.

Review

As soon as you finish reading the material, double-check the questions you posed in the "question" stage of SQ3R. Can you answer them? Glance over any notes you made as well. But don't stop there if the reading is especially important. You will remember the material much better by spacing out your reviews; spend a few minutes reviewing each text over the next few days. Consider the following helpful memory techniques:

- Visualize the concepts in concrete ways. *Example:* If a text discusses media sound bites about cloning, imagine a television panel discussing the topic.
- Draw diagrams or develop clusters. *Example:* See the cluster on page **36**.
- Put the material in your own words. *Example:* See the summary on page **11**.
- Teach it to someone. *Example:* For a text on cloning, explain the main points to a friend or relative—in person, on the phone, or by e-mail.
- Use acronyms or rhymes. *Example:* "*i* before *e* except after *c*."

Benefits: Research shows that reviewing within 24 hours helps considerably to move information from your short-term memory to your long-term memory. You will also improve your memory if you create a network of associations with the information you want to remember, if you link the memory to two or more senses, or if you reorganize the material while still retaining the substance with accuracy.

Reading Actively

Truly active reading requires more than highlighting every line in yellow or pink. Active reading is really *inter*-active, a kind of mental dialogue with the writer. Certain practical techniques will help you stay alert for active reading:

- **Pace yourself.** Read in stretches of thirty to forty-five minutes, followed by short breaks. As you read, slow down in tough spots, respond to the text, ask questions, and note your reactions.
- **Project.** Based on where you've been and where you are in the text, anticipate what will come next and why.
- **Speak the text.** Read difficult parts out loud, or take turns reading aloud with a partner.
- **Track the text.** Record your dialogue with the text through writing strategies such as note taking, annotating, mapping, and outlining (all of which are explored on the following pages).

Take thoughtful notes.

Find a note-taking system that suits you, using legal tablets, note cards, laptop software, or a handheld device. Your system should allow you to distinguish clearly among facts, quotations, paraphrases, summaries, and personal remarks. It is a good idea to include a reference number or topic word at the top of each note to help you organize your notes later.

Although effective note taking is crucial for typical reading assignments in your courses, it's especially important for any research-based writing. On pages 438–441 you'll find more instruction on note-taking systems.

Annotate the text.

Annotating involves marking up the text itself. If you own the book you're reading or if you are reading a photocopy, write notes in the margins. Writing activates your thinking and records your insights. Try these techniques, shown in the sample passage on the next page:

- Write a question—or a simple "?"—next to anything that concerns or puzzles you. See if the text eventually answers your question.
- Link related passages by drawing circles, lines, or arrows, or by making notes such as "see page 36."
- Add personal observations. Keep track of your reactions without worrying about them initially. You can analyze these reactions later.
- Create a marginal index. Write key words in the margin or at the top of the page to identify important themes, names, or patterns. For books, list these key words, with page numbers, on a blank page at the end. By doing so, you'll create an index for future use.

Annotating in Action

The excerpt below is from an article written by Leigh Turner, an academic and medical professional who has studied, worked, and taught in both the United States and Canada. Written in the wake of the first successful animal cloning, of Dolly the sheep, this reading might be assigned in a communication, philosophy, biology, environmental studies, political science, or agriculture course for class discussion, a written response, a test, or a research project. This excerpt shows how a student reader engages the text and comments on key ideas. (The full essay appears on pages 321–325.)

What's the connection?

The Media and the Ethics of Cloning

Who is he? check

If the contemporary debate on cloning has a patron saint, surely it is Andy Warhol. Not only did Warhol assert that everyone would have fifteen minutes of fame—witness the lawyers, philosophers, theologians, and bioethicists who found their expertise in hot demand on the nightly morality plays of network television following Ian Wilmut's cloning of the sheep Dolly—but he also placed "clones," multiple copies of the same phenomenon, at the heart of popular culture. Instead of multiple images of Marilyn Monroe and Campbell's soup cans, we now have cloned sheep. Regrettably, it is Warhol's capacity for hyperbole rather than his intelligence and ironic vision that permeates the current debate on cloning.

see textbook p. 375

good definition of cloning

means extreme exaggeration

It would be unfair to judge hastily written op-ed pieces, popular talk shows, and late-night radio programs by the same standards that one would apply to a sustained piece of philosophical or legal analysis. But the popular media could do more to foster thoughtful public debate on the legal, moral, political, medical, and scientific dimensions of the cloning of humans and nonhuman animals.

media needs to consider cloning thoughtfully

As did many of my colleagues at the Hastings Center, I participated in several interviews with the media following Ian Wilmut's announcement in *Nature* that he had succeeded in cloning Dolly from a mammary cell of an adult sheep. After clearly stating to one Los Angeles radio broadcaster before our interview that I was not a theologian and did not represent a religious organization, I was rather breathlessly asked during the taping what God's view on cloning is and whether cloning is "against creation." Predictably, the broadcaster didn't want to discuss how religious ethicists are contributing to the nascent public discourse about the ethics of cloning. Instead, he . . .

INSIGHT: Underlining or highlighting key words or phrases can be helpful, but don't overdo it. If you're not careful, too much highlighting or underlining becomes a means of evading rather than engaging the text. Excessive highlighting might be your brain saying "I'll learn this later." Moreover, excessive highlighting can make the text difficult to reread and hence tough to review.

Map the text.

If you are visually oriented, you may understand a text best by mapping out its important parts. One way to do so is by "clustering." Start by naming the main topic in a circle at the center of the page. Then branch out using lines and "balloons," where each balloon contains a word or phrase for one major subtopic. Branch out in further layers of balloons to show even more subpoints. If you wish, add graphics, arrows, drawings—anything that helps you visualize the relationships among ideas.

Outline the text.

Outlining is the traditional way of showing all the major parts, points, and subpoints in a text. An outline uses parallel structure to show main points and subordinate points. See pages **48–49** for more on outlines.

SAMPLE OUTLINE FOR "THE MEDIA AND THE ETHICS OF CLONING"

1. Introduction: The debate about cloning is filled with exaggeration.
2. The mass media have confused the debate:
   - Bombarding the public with sound bites
   - Focusing on human cloning and ignoring animal cloning
   - Wrongly stressing that people are products of their genes
   - Promoting the idea that scientific "progress" can't be stopped
3. Thesis: The discussion can be improved in three ways:
   - Scientists and ethicists must learn to understand one another's work.
   - Ethicists need to improve how they communicate to the mass media.
   - Public debate about scientific topics must be expanded to forums and outreach programs.
4. Conclusion: We need more intelligent discussion so that the public is not misled by the mass media.

Evaluate the text.

Critical reading does not mean disproving the text or disapproving of it. It means thoughtfully inspecting, weighing, and evaluating the writer's ideas. To strengthen your reading skills, learn to evaluate texts using the criteria below.

1. Judge the reading's credibility. Where was it published? How reliable is the author? How current is the information? How accurate and complete does it seem to be? In addition, consider the author's tone of voice, attitude, and apparent biases.

Discussion: Leigh Turner, the author of "The Media and the Ethics of Cloning" on pages 321–325, tells us that he was a member of the Hastings Center, a nonprofit research institute. How does this information build or break his credibility? Within the article, how does he build credibility?

2. Put the reading in a larger context. How do the text's ideas match what you know from other sources? Which details of background, history, and social context help you understand this text's perspective? How have things changed or remained the same since the text's publication? Which allusions (references to people, events, and so on) does the writer use? Why?

Discussion: The topic of cloning belongs to the broader subjects of genetic research and ethics. In addition, the topic relates to debates over the nature of human identity, and cloning research has advanced and expanded dramatically since the article's publication. As for allusions, Turner refers to the artist Andy Warhol and the cloning of the sheep Dolly. What else is part of this context?

3. Evaluate the reasoning and support. Is the reasoning clear and logical? Are the examples and other supporting details appropriate and enlightening? Are inferences (what the text implies) consistent with the tone and message? (Look especially for hidden logic and irony that undercut what is said explicitly.)

Discussion: Turner uses examples and illustrations extensively in his article. He analyzes the problem by breaking it down, and he systematically presents a three-part solution. Is his reasoning sound?

4. Reflect on how the reading challenges you. Which of your beliefs and values does the reading call into question? What discomfort does it create? Does your own perspective skew your evaluation?

Discussion: The article may make us feel uncomfortable about several issues: our lack of concern for animals, our inability to see past the media's treatment of cloning, and the application of cloning to several areas of life (including replication of ourselves). What other challenges does the article raise?

 For additional help evaluating texts, see pages 432–435. For information on detecting logical fallacies often used in texts by writers, see pages 267–270.

Responding to a Text

In a sense, when you read a text, you enter into a dialogue with it. Your response expresses your turn in the dialogue. Such a response can take varied forms, from a journal entry to a blog to a discussion-group posting.

Follow these guidelines for response writing.

On the surface, responding to a text seems perfectly natural—just let it happen. But it can be a bit more complicated. A written response typically is not the same as a private diary entry but is instead shared with other readers, whether your instructor or a class. You develop your response keeping in mind your instructor's requirements and the response's role in the course. Therefore, follow these guidelines:

1. **Be honest.** Although you want to remain sensitive to the context in which you will share your response, be bold enough to be honest about your reaction to the text—what it makes you think, feel, and question. To that end, a response usually allows you to express yourself directly using the pronoun "I."

2. **Be fluid.** Let the flow of your thoughts guide you in what you write. Don't stop to worry about grammar, punctuation, mechanics, and spelling. These can be quickly cleaned up before you share or submit your response.

3. **Be reflective.** Generally, the goal of a response is to offer thoughtful reflection as opposed to knee-jerk reaction. Show, then, that you are engaging the text's ideas, relating them to your own experience, looking both inward and outward. Avoid a shallow reaction that comes from skimming the text or misreading it.

4. **Be selective.** By nature, a response must limit its focus; it cannot exhaust all your reactions to the text. So zero in on one or two elements of your response, and run with those to see where they take you in your dialogue with the text.

Sample Response

Here is part of a student's response to Leigh Turner's "The Media and the Ethics of Cloning," on pages 321–325. Note the informality and exploratory tone.

> Turner seems dead right about the treatment of cloning in the media, based on some news stories I've recently heard about food from cloned cows. The media just don't go very deep, especially on science issues, which most people find too tough to understand anyway.
>
> Like most people, I've focused on the (scary?) idea of human cloning, afraid of what it could lead to, but I'm also curious about it. Cloning animals is an issue that hasn't been on my radar screen much. Cloning animals just for the benefit of people, is that right? Would I approve of human cloning if it benefited me, if it helped someone I loved or saved my own life?

INSIGHT: A response does not simply summarize the text. See the next page to understand the difference between a response and a summary.

Summarizing a Text

Writing a summary disciplines you by making you pull only essentials from a reading—the main points, the thread of the argument. By doing so, you not only create a brief record of the text's contents but also exercise your ability to comprehend, analyze, and synthesize information.

Use these guidelines for summary writing.

Writing a summary requires sifting out the least important points, sorting the essential ones to show their logical relationships, and putting those points in your own words. Follow these guidelines:

1. **Skim first; then read closely.** First, get a sense of the whole, including the main idea and strategies for support. Then read carefully, taking notes as you do.

2. **Capture the text's argument.** Review your notes and annotations, looking for main points and clear connections. State these briefly and clearly, in your own words. Include only what is essential, excluding most examples and details. Don't say simply that the text talks about its subject; tell *what it says* about that subject.

3. **Test your summary.** Aim to objectively provide the heart of the text; avoid interjecting your own opinions and presence as a writer. Similarly, don't confuse an objective summary of a text with a response to it (shown on the previous page). Finally, check your summary against the original text for accuracy and consistency.

Sample Summary

Below is a student's summary of Leigh Turner's article, "The Media and the Ethics of Cloning," on pages 321–325. Note how the summary writer includes only main points and phrases them in terms she understands. She departs from the precise order of ideas in the original but communicates their sense accurately.

> Popular media cover the topic of cloning inadequately. They offer unfocused and one-sided coverage, typically ignoring animal cloning, especially the ethics of cloning animals to create "pharmaceutical factories." By stressing "genetic essentialism," the idea that people are simply products of their genes, they ignore the complexity of growth. And last, the media make it sound as though the advance of cloning is unstoppable. How can this problem be resolved? First, through training, scientists and ethicists need to understand one another's work better. Second, ethicists need to be better communicators in the media, especially by publishing in journals that nonscientists can understand. Finally, public institutions need to sponsor debates so that views can be expressed at the grassroots level.

INSIGHT: Writing formal summaries—whether as part of literature reviews or as abstracts—is an important skill, especially in the social and natural sciences. For help, go to **www.thecollegewriter.com/3e.**

Video

Critical Thinking Through Viewing

A flood of visual images—on magazine covers, movie trailers, webpages, and cell phones with flip-up video screens—affect the way we think. Images quicken our work, provoke ideas, and often trigger our emotions. Images convey persuasive ideas, simplify complex concepts, and dramatize important points.

But images have drawbacks, too. They can distort facts, manipulate emotions, and cut reasoning short. As a writer, you must learn to think critically through viewing—to "read" images actively; to interpret what is meant by an image, not just what is shown; and to evaluate the quality and value of an image. These challenges are addressed on the following pages.

Consider these guidelines for actively viewing images.

View with a purpose. Your viewing of an image needs to be guided by your own reading goals. Are you a student seeking to learn something, a citizen seeking insight into social and political issues, or a consumer seeking guidance on a purchase? Also, given where the image has been published and by whom, what is the image meant to do?

- **Arouse curiosity?** Open your imagination, but stay on guard.
- **Entertain?** Look for the pleasure or the joke, but be wary of excess or of ethically questionable material in the image.
- **Inform or educate?** Search for key instruction, noting what's left out.
- **Illustrate?** Relate the image to the words or concept being illustrated: Does the image clarify or distort the meaning?
- **Persuade?** Examine how the image appeals to the viewer's needs, from safety and satisfaction to self-worth. Are the appeals manipulative, clichéd, or fallacious? Do they play on emotions to bypass reason?
- **Summarize?** Look for the essential message in the image: Does that main idea correspond with the written text?

View with a plan. Give your active attention by following this process:

1. **Survey the image.** See the image as a whole so that you can absorb its overall idea. Look for the image's focal point—what your eye is drawn to. Also consider the relationship between the image's foreground and background, its left content and right content, and its various colors.

2. **Inspect the image.** Let your "sight" touch every part of the image, as if you were reading Braille. Hints of its meaning may lurk in the tiny details as well as in the relationship between the image's parts.

3. **Question the image.** Who made the image? What does it show? When was it made? Where does it appear? Why was it placed there?

4. **Relate the image.** Put the image in context by connecting it to surrounding text, to other images, and to your own experience.

View an image.

The use of *minors* as *miners* is no *minor* problem.

Discussion

The illustration and caption above by Chris Krenzke effectively combine humor with instruction. Originally published in a high school writing handbook, the image's aim is to teach students about a specific word-usage problem while also entertaining them. The image is line art in the "comic" genre, using a humorous scene to convey a serious message. Here are some thoughts on how you might actively view this image:

1. **Survey.** The image tells a story of heavily burdened children working under the heavy supervision of an authoritarian male. That story moves from left to right, from breaking rocks to loading rocks to carrying rocks toward a likely distant destination, the destination pointed to by the man. The black-and-white medium accentuates the starkness.

2. **Inspect.** In terms of the illustration's details, each figure is striking. The individual children share a thinness in their bodies and a strain in their faces. The four children in the line are pictured as beasts of burden bent over by bags that dwarf them. The repetition of figures emphasizes the trudging repetition of their work, and each child in line is pressed farther toward the ground. As for the man, his back is straight and his posture tall. His enormous chin, large nose, overly long but skinny arm, and sharply pointed finger suggest a negative authority. His stubbly face and his caveman clothing add to this figure's prehistoric character.

3. **Question.** Who is the artist Chris Krenzke? When did he first create this image? In what book was it published? When? Why did Krenzke use this caveman style? Who or what do "minors," "miners," and "minor" refer to in the illustration?

4. **Relate.** The connection between the sentence and the image becomes clear when the viewer realizes that "minors" are children not of a legal age to work, "miners" refers to an occupation, and "minor" means insignificant. But the image prompts other connections: the history of horrific child-labor practices during the Industrial Revolution as well as continuing child-labor issues in today's global economy. With these allusions, Krenzke succeeds in deepening the instruction offered by his art.

Interpreting an Image

Interpreting an image follows naturally from viewing or "reading" the image. Interpreting means figuring out what the image or design is meant to do, say, or show. If the meaning were fixed, like the number of jellybeans in a jar, interpreting would be easy. But the meaning is something you have to gather for yourself by considering all the evidence.

Understand the elements of interpretation.

Keep in mind the following elements as you interpret an image. The **designer** of the image (for example, a cartoonist or webpage editor) uses an **image** to get some kind of **message** across to a **viewer**. The **image** offers a certain view of a certain **subject** in a certain **medium**. All of this is set in a certain **context**—a page of a textbook, an annual report, or a webpage. When you interpret the image, you consider each of these elements to arrive at an overall sense of meaning.

Understand the complications in interpretation.

Each element in the diagram above may offer special challenges to the reader:

Image: It might be strange, deceiving, very detailed, or highly technical.

Designer: He or she might be unknown or representing someone else, or the image might be designed by a team of people.

Viewer: You might be uninterested in the subject, unfamiliar with the visual "language" used by the designer, or biased toward the subject.

Subject: It might be vague, unfamiliar, complex, or disturbing.

Message: It might be mixed, implied, ironic, unwelcome, or distorted. The content could be literal, stylized, numeric, symbolic, and so on.

Context: It might be disconnected from the image, changing, or multilayered.

Medium: It might be multiple, awkward, or "the message."

INSIGHT: Like words, visuals can be clichés—trite, misleading, or worn-out expressions of concepts or ideas. For example, TV ads for weight-loss drugs commonly picture scantily clad, fit young people, incorrectly suggesting that using the drugs will produce fit, youthful bodies.

Interpret an image.

Discussion

This color photograph shows a multireligious commemoration of the 229,000 victims of the Indian Ocean tsunami of December 26, 2004.

The symbolism is clearly rooted in the points of light created by the candle balloons, where light itself is a cross-cultural symbol of hope, endurance, the human spirit, and God's presence. The skyward angle of the photograph, with the clusters of candle balloons floating up and the people in the lower right of the frame, creates this sense of vertical longing and release, emphasizing perhaps humanity's longing to solve life's mysteries, including death and disaster. Although the large, just-released candle balloons are most prominent, the viewer's eyes are also drawn upward, where clusters of far-off candles become constellations of starlike lights. The mourners in the right of the frame, forming a loose circle, are all gazing skyward, like the viewer. Ordinary people in ordinary clothes, they appear to be clapping and, for some, the clapping shows their hands virtually in a posture of prayer. In this way, the image both mourns the dead and celebrates life.

Designer: Photographer Bazuki Muhammad.

Medium: Digital color photograph.

Subject: Thais release candle balloons during mass prayer for tsunami victims.

Message: Remember those who died; move forward with hope.

Context: Part of a series of photographs provided by Reuters, for inclusion in global newspapers with news stories about the commemoration on January 19, 2005.

Viewer: Anyone around the globe reading a newspaper, magazine article, or web article on this story.

Evaluating an Image

When you encounter an image, you must do more than understand and interpret it: You must assess its quality, truthfulness, and value. In other words, you must evaluate it. When you have done that well, you can fairly say you have thought it through. The following questions will guide your assessment.

Consider the purpose.

What purpose does the visual image best seem to serve?

- **Ornamentation:** Makes the page more pleasing to the eye
- **Illustration:** Supports points made in the accompanying text
- **Revelation:** Gives an inside look at something or presents new data
- **Explanation:** Uses imagery or graphics to clarify a complex subject
- **Instruction:** Guides the viewer through a complex process
- **Persuasion:** Influences feelings or beliefs
- **Entertainment:** Amuses the reader

Evaluate the quality.

Essentially, how good is the image?

- Is the image done with skill? A map, for example, should be accurately and attractively drawn, should use color effectively, and should be complete enough to serve its purpose.
- Does the image measure up to standards of quality? See **www.thecollegewriter.com/3e** for design tips for a variety of visuals.
- Is it backed by authority? Does the designer have a good reputation? Does the publication or institution have good credentials?
- How does the image compare to other images like it? Are clearer or more accurate images available?
- What are its shortcomings? Are there gaps in its coverage? Does it twist the evidence? Does it convey clichéd or fallacious information? (See pages 267–270 for a discussion of logical fallacies.)
- Could you think of a better way to approach the image's subject? If you were to produce the visual, what might you improve?

Determine the value.

What is the image's tangible and intangible worth? Its benefits and drawbacks?

- Is the visual worth viewing? Does it enrich the document by clarifying or otherwise enhancing its message?
- Does the visual appeal to you? Listen to authorities and peers, but also consider your own perspective.

Evaluate an image.

Discussion

Evaluating an image such as this WWII poster aimed at U.S. servicemen reveals its strong stereotypes of both men and women, stereotypes related to the historical period. As with all images, evaluation begins with understanding and interpreting the poster.

In the poster's center is a woman in evening dress, her hair done up, wearing jewels and a corsage. She is seated, at ease, looking at us. Perhaps she represents beauty, both sensual attractiveness and sophistication. The colors used to present her are pale and muted, except for her blue eyes and red lips.

Surrounding the woman are three men, individually dressed in the uniforms of Army, Air Force, and Navy. Drinking and smoking, the men seem to be competing for her attention.

The poster implies that all service personnel were male, which was not true even in WWII, when WACs and WAVEs served in the armed forces. It cautions that these male members of the armed forces should be wary in seemingly innocent social situations, since even a beautiful woman, whom popular stereotypes of the day characterized as "dumb," might not be what she appears. Such a woman might, in fact, be a spy—an idea perhaps inspired by the famous case of WWI spy Mata Hari. The statement that "careless talk costs lives" is a version of another common phrase from the period: "Loose lips sink ships."

Evaluating this poster involves considering its original context while assessing it from our current perspective. In the heat of WWII, this poster could be considered a fair piece of military persuasion. Today, however, what is striking are the gender stereotypes at work in both image and words. Not only are service personnel today both male and female, in every branch of the armed forces, but they fulfill the same roles, including combat positions. With respect to the men, the image implies that in social situations (which are assumed to include smoking and drinking), they are untrustworthy and apt to boast or compete in the presence of an attractive woman. With respect to women, the image both denounces and warns, implying that women, especially attractive women, are cunning and dangerous. Today, such stereotypes press us to question the quality, truthfulness, and value of the image.

Critical Thinking Through Writing

In college, your writing often must show your ability to think critically about topics and issues by analyzing complex processes, synthesizing distinct concepts, weighing the value of opposing perspectives, and practicing new applications of existing principles. To hone your critical-thinking skills, you need to develop sound critical-thinking habits, sharpen your reasoning skills, and distinguish inductive and deductive logic.

Develop sound critical-thinking habits.

Like everything worthwhile, improving your critical-thinking skills takes time and practice. But cultivating the habits below will pay off in sound, thoughtful writing.

1. **Be curious.** Ask "Why?" Cultivate your ability to wonder; question what you see, hear, and read—both inside and outside the classroom.

2. **Be creative.** Don't settle for obvious answers. Look at things in a fresh way, asking "what-if" questions such as "What if Ophelia didn't die in *Hamlet?* How would the play be different?"

3. **Be open to new ideas.** Approach thinking as you would approach a road trip—looking for the unexpected and musing over mysteries.

4. **Value others' points of view.** Look at issues from another person's perspective and weigh that against your own. Honestly examine how the core of her or his perspective compares to the core of your perspective, and how each basis for thought might lead to different conclusions.

5. **Get involved.** Read books, journals, and newspapers. Watch documentaries. Join book clubs, film clubs, or political and social-action activities.

6. **Focus.** Sharpen your concentration, looking for details that distinguish a topic and reveal key questions related to its nature, function, and impact.

7. **Be rational.** Choose logical thinking patterns like those discussed in this chapter, and then work through the steps to deepen and develop your understanding of a topic.

8. **Make connections.** Use writing to explore how and why topics or issues are related. Use comparisons to identify and name these relationships.

9. **Tolerate ambiguity.** Respectfully analyze issues not readily resolved—and acknowledge when your position requires further research or thought.

10. **Test the evidence.** Be properly skeptical about all claims (see pages 262–263). Look for corroboration (or verification) in other sources.

11. **Develop research-based conclusions.** Focus on understanding issues, assessing their history, development, function, and impact. During the process, gather details that lead to and support a reasonable conclusion.

12. Expect results. Consider each paper to be a benchmark that reflects your progress in developing your thinking and writing skills. Save your papers for periodic analyses of your progress and revision of the writing.

For more help with critical-thinking skills such as making and supporting claims, recognizing logical fallacies, and dealing with opposition, see "Strategies for Argumentation and Persuasion," pages 259–274.

Ask probing questions.

Every field uses questions to trigger critical thinking. For example, scientific questions generate hypotheses, sociological questions lead to studies, mathematical questions call for proofs, and literary criticism questions call for interpretations. A good question opens up a problem and guides you all the way to its solution. But not all questions are created equal. Consider the differences:

- "Rhetorical" questions aren't meant to be answered. They're asked for effect. *Example:* Who would want to be caught in an earthquake?
- Closed questions seek a limited response and can be answered with "yes," "no," or a simple fact. *Example:* Would I feel an earthquake measuring 3.0 on the Richter scale?
- Open questions invite brainstorming and discussion. *Example:* How might a major earthquake affect this urban area?
- Theoretical questions call for organization and explanation of an entire field of knowledge. *Example:* What might cause a sudden fracturing of Earth's crust along fault lines?

To improve the critical thinking in your writing, ask better questions. The strategies below will help you think freely, respond to reading, study for a test, or collect your thoughts for an essay.

Ask open questions. Closed questions sometimes choke off thinking. Use open questions to trigger a flow of ideas.

Ask "educated" questions. Compare these questions: (A) What's wrong with television? (B) Does the 16.3 percent rise in televised acts of violence during the past three years signal a rising tolerance for violence in the viewing audience? You have a better chance of expanding the "educated" question—question B—into an essay because the question is clearer and suggests debatable issues.

Keep a question journal. Divide a blank notebook page or split a computer screen. On one side, write down any questions that come to mind regarding the topic that you want to explore. On the other side, write down answers and any thoughts that flow from them.

Write Q & A drafts. To write a thoughtful first draft, write quickly, then look it over. Turn the main idea into a question and write again, answering your question. For example, if your main idea is that TV viewers watch far more violence than they did ten years ago, ask *Which viewers? Why?* and *What's the result?* Go on that way until you find a key idea to serve as the main point of your next draft.

Practice inductive and deductive logic.

Questions invite thinking; reasoning responds to that challenge in an organized way. Will the organization of your thoughts be inductive or deductive? **Inductive logic** reasons from specific information toward general conclusions. **Deductive logic** reasons from general principles toward specific applications. Notice in the diagram below that inductive reasoning starts with specific details or observations (as shown at the base) and then moves "up" to broader ideas and eventually to a concluding generalization. In contrast, deduction starts with general principles at the top and works down, applying the principles to explain particular instances.

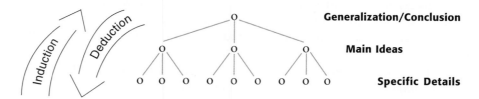

Sentences, paragraphs, and entire essays can be organized either inductively or deductively. Use induction when you want to postpone your conclusions. Use deduction for logical clarity, directness, and strength, or to apply what is already agreed on to what is still under dispute. Narrative or personal essays tend toward inductive organization, whereas analytical essays (particularly those written in the social or natural sciences) typically use both induction and deduction.

Example: Read through the paragraphs below from the student essay "If We Are What We Wear, What Are We?" by Allison Young (**www.thecollegewriter.com/3e**). The first paragraph works deductively, the second paragraph inductively. Note how each approach affects the message.

Deduction: generalization to specific details

The American excuse for owning multiples is that clothing styles change so rapidly. At the end of the '80s, trends in high fashion changed every two and a half months (During 95). Even for those of us who don't keep up with high fashion, styles change often enough that our clothing itself lasts much longer than the current trend. Perhaps this is one of the reasons the average American spent $997 on clothing in 1996 (U.S. Department of Commerce).

Induction: specific details to generalization

While Americans are spending a thousand dollars on clothing a year, people in Ethiopia make an average of only $96 a year, those in Bangladesh $280, and the average Filipino worker makes $1,052 (United Nations Statistics Division). I, on the other hand, made over $5,000 last year, and that job was only part-time. When an American college student can earn more money at her part-time job than three billion people each make for a living, it's time to question our culture and ask, as Alan During did, "How much is enough?"

Practicing Modes of
Thinking in Your Writing

In your various writing assignments, you will need to practice specific modes of thinking. The table below maps out these modes (from elementary to complex) and the tasks each requires. The more complex modes are then fleshed out on the following pages.

When you are asked to _____ , *be ready to* _____ .

Know

define	memorize
identify	name
list	recall
match	recognize

Call to mind what you have learned

- Recall information
- List details
- Define key terms
- Identify main points

Understand

comprehend	interpret
connect	restate
explain	summarize
grasp	

Show what you have learned

- Connect related examples
- Summarize important details
- Explain how something works
- Interpret what something means

Analyze

characterize	contrast
classify	divide
compare	examine

Break down information

- Divide a whole into its parts
- Group things into categories
- Analyze causes and effects
- Examine similarities and differences

Synthesize

assemble	imagine
combine	invent
construct	link
formulate	

Shape information into a new form

- Bring together a body of evidence
- Blend the old with the new
- Predict or hypothesize
- Construct a new way of looking at something

Evaluate

assess	measure
check	monitor
critique	rank
judge	rate

Determine the worth of information

- Point out a subject's strengths and weaknesses
- Evaluate its clarity, accuracy, logic, value, and so on
- Convince others of its value/worth

Apply

anticipate	propose
choose	select
generate	

Use what you have learned

- Propose a better way of doing something
- Generate a plan of action
- Offer solutions to a problem

Think by using analysis.

The word *analyze* literally means "to loosen or undo." When you analyze something, you break it down into parts and examine each part separately. You classify information, compare objects, trace a process, or explain causes.

As you analyze, think about the questions listed below. Note that each type of thinking answers certain kinds of questions. Remember, too, that thinking tasks often require two or more kinds of analysis that support one another.

Composition: What elements does it contain? What is not part of it?

Categories: How are things grouped, divided, or classified?

Structures: What are the parts or elements? How are they related?

**Comparisons/
contrasts:** How are things similar? How are they different?

Causes/effects: Why did this happen? What are the results?

Processes: How does it work or happen? What are the stages?

Example: Read through the passage below, from "Wayward Cells." In the full essay on pages 231–232, student writer Kerri Mertz explains the process by which healthy body cells become cancerous cells. Note how in this excerpt, the writer develops an overall analysis based on a process but also uses compare-contrast and cause-effect thinking within that structure, as well as informal definition.

The writer explains a cellular process and contrasts healthy and cancerous versions.

Most healthy cells reproduce rather quickly, but their reproduction rate is controlled. For example, your blood cells completely die off and replace themselves within a matter of weeks, but existing cells make only as many new cells as the body needs. The DNA codes in healthy cells tell them how many new cells to produce. However, cancer cells don't have this control, so they reproduce quickly with no stopping point, a characteristic called "autonomy" (Braun 3). What's more, all their "offspring" have the same qualities as their messed-up parent, and the resulting overpopulation produces growths called tumors.

The writer explains the three harmful effects of tumor cells (the cause).

Tumor cells can hurt the body in a number of ways. First, a tumor can grow so big that it takes up space needed by other organs. Second, some cells may detach from the original tumor and spread throughout the body, creating new tumors elsewhere. This happens with lymphatic cancer—a cancer that's hard to control because it spreads so quickly. A third way that tumor cells can hurt the body is by doing work not called for in their DNA. For example, a gland cell's DNA code may tell the cell to produce a necessary hormone in the endocrine system. However, if cancer damages or distorts that code, sick cells may produce more of the hormone than the body can use—or even tolerate (Braun 4). Cancer cells seem to have minds of their own, and this is why cancer is such a serious disease.

Examples illustrate the analysis.

Think by using synthesis.

Synthesis is the opposite of analysis. Where analysis breaks things down into parts, synthesis combines elements into a new whole. In your writing, when you pull together things that are normally separate, you are synthesizing. Common ways of synthesizing include predicting, inventing, redesigning, and imagining a whole new way of looking at something.

Working with synthesis involves both reason and imagination. Start by looking closely at two or more items that you want to synthesize, and then think of fresh ways they can be related. Don't be afraid to see your subjects in a new way. In other words, think "sideways" rather than straight ahead. Ask the following questions:

Applying: What can I do with both? What will be the outcome?

Bridging: How can I build a connection between the two?

Combining: How can I connect, associate, or blend the two?

Conflicting: Which is good, better, or best? What strength does each offer the other?

Inventing: What parts could these two play in a drama?

Proposing: What do I suggest doing with both?

Sequencing: Which comes first? Is one an extension of the other?

Projecting: Based on current information, what is the best forecast for what will happen in the near future or the long term?

Example: Read through the passage below, from "In Africa, AIDS Has a Woman's Face," by former United Nations Secretary-General Kofi Annan (see pages 307–309). In the full article, Annan argues that resolving the AIDS crisis in Africa must begin by saving the familial, social, and economic backbones of African cultures—women. In the following passage, Annan synthesizes his discussion by projecting what is necessary for successful solutions.

Pulling together his discussion of the twin tragedies of AIDS and famine in Africa, the writer calls for imaginative, multifaceted solutions.

Because this crisis is different from past famines, we must look beyond relief measures of the past. Merely shipping in food is not enough. Our effort will have to combine food assistance and new approaches to farming with treatment and prevention of H.I.V. and AIDS. It will require creating early-warning and analysis systems that monitor both H.I.V. infection rates and famine indicators. It will require new agricultural techniques, appropriate to a depleted work force. It will require a renewed effort to wipe out H.I.V.-related stigma and silence.

It will require innovative, large-scale ways to care for orphans, with specific measures that enable children in AIDS-affected communities to stay in school. Education and prevention are still the most powerful weapons against the spread of H.I.V. Above all, this new international effort must put women at the center of our strategy to fight AIDS.

Think by using evaluation.

Movies, proposals, arguments—anything can be evaluated. Evaluation measures the value or worth of things. For example, when you express your judgment about an issue or discuss the weak and strong points of what someone else has said, you are evaluating. Many kinds of writing are evaluative.

To evaluate a topic, start by learning as much about it as possible. Then consider which criteria or standards are appropriate. Next, judge how the topic measures up based on those criteria. Support your judgment with concrete details, examples, illustrations, and comparisons. Ask questions like these:

Aspects: What elements of the topic will I evaluate?

Vantage point: What are my experience and my point of view?

Criteria: On which standards will I base my judgment?

Assessment: How does the topic measure up by those standards?

Comparison: How does it compare to and contrast with similar things?

Recommendation: Based on my evaluation, what do I advise?

Example: The passage below is taken from David Blankenhorn's "Fatherless America," on pages 287–291. In the full essay, Blankenhorn examines the causes and effects of the increased fatherlessness within U.S. families—that is, the absence of fathers in many homes. In the following excerpt, he assesses the failures of a society that is losing a healthy sense of fatherhood.

> **The writer establishes a criterion for evaluating a culture's fatherhood models and practices.**
>
> . . . Margaret Mead and others have observed that the supreme test of any civilization is whether it can socialize men by teaching them to be fathers—creating a culture in which men acknowledge their paternity and willingly nurture their offspring. Indeed, if we can equate the essence of the antisocial male with violence, we can equate the essence of the socialized male with being a good father. Thus, at the center of our most important cultural imperative, we find the fatherhood script: the story that describes what it ought to mean for a man to have a child. . . .
>
> **After exploring this criterion in depth (not shown), the writer measures U.S. culture and assesses its failures with respect to fatherhood.**
>
> The stakes on this issue could hardly be higher. Our society's conspicuous failure to sustain or create compelling norms of fatherhood amounts to a social and personal disaster. Today's story of fatherhood features one-dimensional characters, an unbelievable plot, and an unhappy ending. It reveals in our society both a failure of collective memory and a collapse of moral imagination. It undermines families, neglects children, causes or aggravates our worst social problems, and makes individual adult happiness—both male and female—harder to achieve.
>
> Ultimately, this failure reflects nothing less than a culture gone awry: a culture increasingly unable to establish the boundaries, erect the signposts, and fashion the stories that can harmonize individual happiness with collective well-being. In short, it reflects a culture that increasingly fails to "enculture" individual men and women, mothers and fathers.

Think by using application.

Thinking by using application defines the practical implications of something. It involves using what you know to demonstrate, show, relate, or extend ideas in view of their outcomes. For example, using what you have learned about the ecology of forest fires to examine the effects of a particular fire—that's application in action.

Applying involves moving from ideas to possible action. First, understand the information you have. Second, relate this information to a given situation. Third, select those facts and details that clarify and support the application. Fourth, test the application to see whether it has been reasonable.

When applying ideas, let questions like these guide your writing:

Purpose: What is something designed to be or do?

Benefits: What would this idea make clearer, better, or more complete?

Solutions: What problems are solved by application of this idea?

Outcomes: What results can be expected? Where could we go from there?

Example: Read the paragraphs below, from Anna Quindlen's "Uncle Sam and Aunt Samantha" (pages **318–320**). In this essay, Quindlen argues that in the United States, women— as well as men—should be eligible to be drafted for military service. In the passage below, she applies the concept of equal rights to this specific situation.

Using the word "egalitarian" to refer to a key principle, the writer points out the real inequality and argues for a change.

Parents face a series of unique new challenges in this more egalitarian world, not the least of which would be sending a daughter off to war. But parents all over this country are doing that right now, with daughters who enlisted; some have even expressed surprise that young women, in this day and age, are not required to register alongside their brothers and friends. While all involved in this debate over the years have invoked the assumed opposition of the people, even 10 years ago more than half of all Americans polled believed women should be made eligible for the draft. Besides, this is not about comfort but about fairness. My son has to register with the Selective Service this year, and if his sister does not when she turns 18, it makes a mockery not only of the standards of this household but of the standards of this nation.

She backs up her conclusion with historical context and presses readers to agree.

It is possible in Afghanistan for women to be treated like little more than fecund pack animals precisely because gender fear and ignorance and hatred have been codified and permitted to hold sway. In this country, largely because of the concerted efforts of those allied with the women's movement over a century of struggle, much of that bigotry has been beaten back, even buried. Yet in improbable places the creaky old ways surface, the ways suggesting that we women were made of finer stuff. The finer stuff was usually porcelain, decorative and on the shelf, suitable for meals and show. Happily, the finer stuff has been transmuted into the right stuff. But with rights come responsibilities, as teachers like to tell their students . . .

Critical-Thinking Checklist

Use the checklist below to track improvements in critical thinking.

_____ I regularly and effectively practice the SQ3R reading method for important reading assignments for my courses and research projects.

_____ I read actively rather than passively by taking thoughtful notes, annotating texts, mapping, and outlining.

_____ I evaluate the credibility, context, reasoning, and challenges of texts.

_____ As needed, I can generate thoughtful responses to texts and/or objective summaries of textual content.

_____ I can effectively "read" visual images by carefully viewing, interpreting, and evaluating their content and design.

_____ I am developing advanced critical-thinking skills that include curiosity, creativity, reason, and tolerance of complexity and ambiguity—all rooted in asking probing questions.

_____ I can effectively reason using inductive and/or deductive logic.

_____ I am improving my ability to write out of advanced thinking modes: analysis, synthesis, evaluation, and application.

Critical-Thinking and Writing Activities

As directed by your instructor, complete the following critical-thinking and writing activities by yourself or with classmates.

1. Northrop Frye has argued that "[n]obody is capable of free speech unless he [or she] knows how to use language, and such knowledge is not a gift: It has to be learned and worked at." How does Frye's claim relate to the discussions of critical reading, viewing, and writing in this chapter?

2. What thinking, reading, viewing, and writing skills are required in your field of study? Reflect on those possibilities.

3. Choose a subject you know something about. Practice thinking about that subject both inductively and deductively. Then write two paragraphs—one developed inductively and the other developed deductively.

4. Select a sample essay from the "Strategies and Models" section. Read the piece carefully and identify where and how the writer uses different thinking modes. Do the same analysis on a recent sample of your own writing, rating your analysis, synthesis, evaluation, and application.

◀ VISUALLY SPEAKING:

Review the image on page 3 and explain what is suggests about critical thinking and critical viewing. Note: You will find additional visual-literacy activities in each chapter, as well as at **www.thecollegewriter.com/3e**.

BEGINNING THE WRITING PROCESS

College instructors assign writing projects for a variety of reasons. Often they want to encourage you to think more deeply about a topic. For example, writing a paper on climate change helps you sort out the issues, digging into a topic only briefly introduced in class or in a textbook. Your writing helps you get at the complex truth of a topic.

Your instructors may have additional reasons for assigning writing. They may want you to practice the specific thinking habits and forms of writing used in their disciplines. For these reasons, you might be assigned a lab report in biology, a case study in business, or a literary analysis in English.

Finally, your instructors may assign writing so that you learn how to contribute to a learning community. Submitting your paper for graded feedback is a basic contribution, but you might also share your writing with other members of your class or a broader online audience. By sharing your writing, you contribute to research and discussion on your topic.

Video

Web Link

Video

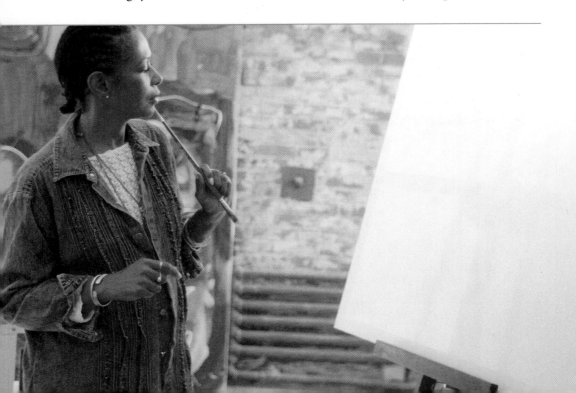

The Writing Process:
From Start to Finish

It's easy to feel overwhelmed by a writing project—especially if the form of writing is new to you, the topic is complex, or the paper must be long. However, using the writing process will relieve some of that pressure by breaking down the task into manageable steps. An overview of those steps is shown below, and key principles are addressed on the next page.

An Overview of the Writing Process

The following flowchart maps out the basic steps in the writing process. As you work on your writing project, periodically review this diagram to keep yourself on task.

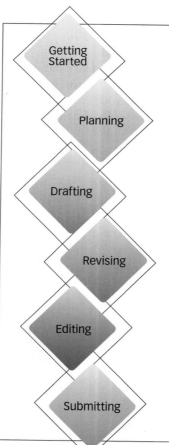

GETTING STARTED
Understanding the assignment
Selecting a subject
Collecting information

PLANNING
Forming a thesis
Using methods of development
Developing a plan or an outline

DRAFTING
Opening your draft
Developing the middle
Ending your draft

REVISING
Improving ideas, organization, and voice
Revising collaboratively

EDITING AND PROOFREADING
Editing for style
Proofreading for correctness

SUBMITTING
Preparing a paper for submission
Checking for page design and documentation

Adapting the Process to Your Project

The writing process shown on the previous page is flexible, not rigid. As a writer, you need to adapt the process to your situation and assignment. To do so, consider these essential principles.

Writing tends not to follow a straight path. While writing begins with an assignment or a need and ends with a reader, the journey in between is often indirect. The steps in the flowchart overlap to show that when you write, you sometimes move back and forth between steps, meaning that the process is recursive. For example, during the revision phase, you may discover that you need to draft a new paragraph or do more research.

Each assignment presents distinct challenges. A personal essay may develop best through clustering or freewriting; a literary analysis through close reading of a story; a lab report through the experimental method; and a position paper through reading of books and journal articles, as well as through careful and balanced reasoning.

Writing can involve collaboration. From using your roommate as a sounding board for your topic choice to working with a group to produce a major report, college writing is not solitary writing. In fact, many colleges have a writing center to help you refine your writing assignments. (See page 89 for more.)

Each writer works differently. Some writers do extensive prewriting before drafting, while others do not. You might develop a detailed outline, whereas someone else might draft a brief list of topics. Experiment with the strategies introduced in chapters 2–7, adopting those that help you.

Good writing can't be rushed. Although some students regard pulling an all-nighter as a badge of honor, good writing takes time. A steady, disciplined approach will generally produce the best results. For example, by brainstorming or reading early in a project, you stimulate your subconscious mind to mull over issues, identify problems, and project solutions—even while your conscious mind is working on other things. Similarly, completing a first draft early enough gives you time to revise objectively.

Different steps call for attention to different writing issues. As you use the writing process, at each stage keep your focus where it belongs:

1. While getting started, planning, and drafting, focus on global issues: ideas, structure, voice, format, and design.

2. During revising, fix big content problems by cutting, adding, and thoroughly reworking material. (Our experience is that students benefit the most from revising—but spend the least time doing it!)

3. While editing and proofreading, pay attention to small, local issues— word choice, sentence smoothness, and grammatical correctness. Worrying about these issues early in the writing process interrupts the flow of drafting and wastes time on material that later is deleted.

Understanding the Rhetorical Situation:
Subject, Audience, and Purpose

Rhetoric is the art of using language effectively. As Aristotle, Quintilian, and others have explained, your language is effective when all aspects of your message (including content and style) fit your **subject,** address the needs of your **audience,** and fulfill your **purpose.** For these reasons, before you put fingers to the keyboard, you must think carefully about all three. By doing so you're analyzing your *rhetorical situation*—the conditions or issues that affect writing decisions, including choosing the best *form* (such as essay or report), the best *medium* (paper or electronic), and the best *organizational strategy* (such as cause/effect or chronological process).

Understand your subject.

Ideas—and the information that relates to them—are the substance of all good writing. Without informative ideas, your writing cannot fulfill the needs of your audience and will not achieve your purpose. Understanding your subject involves gathering and assimilating all relevant details, including its history, makeup, function, and impact on people and culture. Knowing these details will help you decide issues such as what to include in your writing and how to organize it.

Understand your audience.

For any writing task, you must understand your audience in order to develop writing that meets their needs. To assess your audience, answer questions like these:

- Who are my readers: instructor? classmates? web surfers?
- What do they know about my topic, and what do they need to know?
- How well do they understand the terminology, procedures, and technology?
- What are their attitudes toward the topic and toward me?
- How well do they read written English—or visuals such as graphs and charts?
- How will they use my writing (as entertainment or to complete a task)?

Note: Answers to such questions will help you develop meaningful sentences (pages 95–101), choose appropriate words (pages 102–106), and select relevant visuals (page 416).

Understand your purpose.

Knowing your purpose—*why* you are writing—will help you make decisions, such as choosing an organizational strategy. In assignments, key words (especially verbs) either hint at or specify your purpose. For example, an assignment asking you to *analyze* a topic requires that you break the subject into subparts and then explain the relationships among those subparts. Organizational patterns useful for analyzing a topic include classification, definition, and process (pages 62–65).

Understanding the Assignment

Each college instructor has a way of personalizing a writing assignment, but most assignments will spell out (1) the objective, (2) the task, (3) the formal requirements, and (4) suggested approaches and topics. Your first step, therefore, is to read the assignment carefully, noting the options and restrictions that are part of it. The suggestions below will help you do that. (Also see pages 117–121 for one writer's approach.)

Read the assignment.

Certain words in the assignment explain what main action you must perform. Here are some words that signal what you are to do:

Key Words

Analyze:	Break down a topic into subparts, showing how those parts relate.
Argue:	Defend a claim with logical arguments.
Classify:	Divide a large group into well-defined subgroups.
Compare/contrast:	Point out similarities and/or differences.
Define:	Give a clear, thoughtful definition or meaning of something.
Describe:	Show in detail what something is like.
Evaluate:	Weigh the truth, quality, or usefulness of something.
Explain:	Give reasons, list steps, or discuss the causes of something.
Interpret:	Tell in your own words what something means.
Reflect:	Share your well-considered thoughts about a subject.
Summarize:	Restate someone else's ideas very briefly in your own words.
Synthesize:	Connect facts or ideas to create something new.

Options and Restrictions

The assignment often gives you some choice of your topic or approach but may restrict your options to suit the instructor's purpose. Note the options and restrictions in the following short sample assignment:

Reflect on the way a natural disaster or major historical event has altered your understanding of the past, the present, or the future.

Options:	(1) You may choose any natural disaster or historical event.
	(2) You may focus on the past, present, or future.
	(3) You may examine any kind of alteration.
Restrictions:	(1) You must reflect on a change in your understanding.
	(2) The disaster must be natural.
	(3) The historical event must be major.

Relate the assignment to the goals of the course.

1. How much value does the instructor give the assignment? (The value is often expressed as a percentage of the course grade.)

2. What benefit does your instructor want you to receive?
- Strengthen your comprehension?
- Improve your research skills?
- Deepen your ability to explain, prove, or persuade?
- Expand your style?
- Increase your creativity?

3. How will this assignment contribute to your overall performance in the course? What course goals (often listed in the syllabus) does it address?

Relate the assignment to other assignments.

1. Does it build on previous assignments?

2. Does it prepare you for the next assignment?

Relate the assignment to your own interests.

1. Does it connect with a topic that already interests you?

2. Does it connect with work in your other courses?

3. Does it connect with the work you may do in your chosen field?

4. Does it connect with life outside school?

Reflect on the assignment.

1. First impulses: How did you feel when you first read the assignment?

2. Approaches: What's the usual approach for an assignment like this? What's a better way of tackling it?

3. Quality of performance: What would it take to produce an excellent piece of writing?

4. Benefits: What are the benefits to your education? to you personally? to the class? to society?

5. Features: Reflect further on four key features of any writing assignment.
Purpose: What is the overall purpose of the assignment—to inform, to explain, to analyze, to entertain? What is the desired outcome?
Audience: Should you address your instructor? your classmates? a general reader? How much does the reader already know about the topic? What type of language should you use?
Form: What are the requirements concerning length, format, and due date?
Assessment: How will the assignment be evaluated? How can you be sure that you are completing the assignment correctly?

Selecting a Subject

For some assignments, finding a suitable subject (or topic) may require little thinking on your part. If an instructor asks you to summarize an article in a professional journal, you know what you will write about—the article in question. But suppose the instructor asks you to analyze a feature of popular culture in terms of its impact on society. You won't be sure of a specific writing topic until you explore the possibilities. Keep the following points in mind when you conduct a topic search. Your topic must . . .

- meet the requirements of the assignment.
- be limited in scope.
- seem reasonable (that is, be within your means to research).
- genuinely interest you.

Limit the subject area.

Many of your writing assignments may relate to general subject areas you are currently studying. Your task, then, is to select a specific topic related to the general area of study—a topic limited enough that you can treat it with some depth in the length allowed for the assignment. The following examples show the difference between general subjects and limited topics:

General Subject Area: Popular culture
Limited Topic: *The Simpsons* TV show

General Subject Area: Energy sources
Limited Topic: Using wind power

Conduct your search.

Finding a writing idea that meets the requirements of the assignment should not be difficult, if you know how and where to look. Follow these steps:

1. Check your class notes and handouts for ideas related to the assignment.
2. Search the Internet. Type in a keyword or phrase (the general subject stated in the assignment) and see what you can find. You could also follow a subject tree to narrow a subject. (See pages 469–471.)
3. Consult indexes, guides, and other library references. *The Readers' Guide to Periodical Literature*, for example, lists current articles published on specific topics and where to find them. (See pages 458–463.)
4. Discuss the assignment with your instructor or an information specialist.
5. Use one or more of the prewriting strategies described on the following pages to generate possible writing ideas.

Explore for possible topics.

You can generate possible writing ideas by using the following strategies. These same strategies can be used when you've chosen a topic and want to develop it further.

Journal Writing

Write in a journal on a regular basis. Reflect on your personal feelings, develop your thoughts, and record the happenings of each day. Periodically go back and underline ideas that you would like to explore in writing assignments. In the following journal-writing samples, the writer came up with an idea for a writing assignment about the societal impacts of popular culture.

I read a really disturbing news story this morning. I've been thinking about it all day. In California a little girl was killed when she was struck by a car driven by a man distracted by a billboard ad for lingerie featuring a scantily clothed woman. Not only is it a horrifying thing to happen, but it also seems to me all too symbolic of the way that sexually charged images in the media are putting children, and especially girls, in danger. That reminds me of another news story I read this week about preteen girls wanting to wear the kinds of revealing outfits that they see in music videos, TV shows, and magazines aimed at teenagers. <u>Too many of today's media images give young people the impression that sexuality should begin at an early age. This is definitely a dangerous message.</u>

Freewriting

Write nonstop for ten minutes or longer to discover possible writing ideas. Use a key concept related to the assignment as a starting point. You'll soon discover potential writing ideas that might otherwise have never entered your mind. Note in the following example that the writer doesn't stop writing even when he can't think of anything to say. Note also that he doesn't stop to correct typos and other mistakes.

Popular culture. What does that include? Television obviously but thats a pretty boring subject. What else? Movies, pop music, video games. Is there a connection between playing violent video games and acting out violent behavior? Most video players I know would say no but sometimes news reports suggest a connection. Is this something I'd want to write about? Not really. What then? Maybe I could think about this a different way and focus on the positive effects of playing video games. They release tension for one thing and they can really be challenging. Other benefits? They help to kill time, that's for sure, but maybe that's not such a good thing. I would definitely read more if it weren't for video games, tv, etc. Maybe I could write about how all the electronic entertainment that surrounds us today is creating a generation of nonreaders. Or maybe I could focus on whether people aren't getting much physical exercise because of the time they spend with electronic media. Maybe both. At least I have some possibilities to work with.

QUICK GUIDE
▬ Freewriting ▬▬▬▬▬▬▬▬▬▬▬▬▬▬▬▬

Freewriting is the writing you do without having a specific outcome in mind. You simply write down whatever pops into your head as you explore your topic. Freewriting can serve as a starting point for your writing, or it can be combined with any of the other prewriting strategies to help you select, explore, focus, or organize your writing. If you get stuck at any point during the composing process, you can return to freewriting as a way of generating new ideas.

▬ Reminders

- **Freewriting helps you get your thoughts down on paper.**
  (Thoughts are constantly passing through your mind.)
- **Freewriting helps you develop and organize these thoughts.**
- **Freewriting helps you make sense out of things** that you may be studying or researching.
- **Freewriting may seem awkward at times,** but just stick with it.

▬ The Process

- **Write nonstop and record whatever comes into your mind.** Follow your thoughts instead of trying to direct them.
- **If you have a particular topic or assignment to complete, use it as a starting point.** Otherwise, begin with anything that comes to mind.
- **Don't stop to judge, edit, or correct your writing;** that will come later.
- **Keep writing even when you think you have exhausted all of your ideas.** Switch to another angle or voice, but keep writing.
- **Watch for a promising writing idea to emerge.** Learn to recognize the beginnings of a good idea, and then expand that idea by recording as many specific details as possible.

▬ The Result

- **Review your writing and underline the ideas you like.** These ideas will often serve as the basis for future writings.
- **Determine exactly what you need to write about.** Once you've figured out what you are required to do, you may then decide to do a second freewriting exercise.
- **Listen to and read the freewriting of others;** learn from your peers.

Listing

Freely list ideas as they come to mind, beginning with a key concept related to the assignment. (Brainstorming—listing ideas in conjunction with members of a group—is often an effective way to extend your lists.) The following is an example of a student's list of ideas for possible topics on the subject of news reporting:

Aspect of popular culture: News reporting

Sensationalism
Sound bites rather than in-depth analysis
Focus on the negative
Shock radio
Shouting matches pretending to be debates
Press leaks that damage national security, etc.
Lack of observation of people's privacy
Bias
Contradictory health news confusing to readers
Little focus on "unappealing" issues like poverty
Celebration of "celebrity"

Clustering

To begin the clustering process, write a key word or phrase related to the assignment in the center of your paper. Circle it, and then cluster ideas around it. Circle each idea as you record it, and draw a line connecting it to the closest related idea. Keep going until you run out of ideas and connections. The following is a student's cluster on the subject of sports:

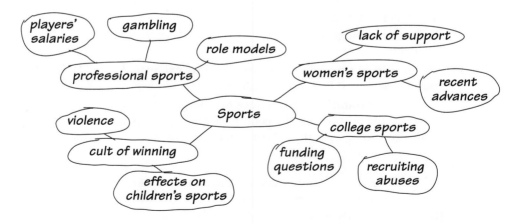

TIP: After four or five minutes of listing or clustering, scan your work for an idea to explore in a freewriting. A writing idea should begin to emerge during this freewriting session. (See pages **34–35**.)

Collecting Information

Writer and instructor Donald Murray said that "writers write with information. If there is no information, there will be no effective writing." How true! Before you can develop a thoughtful piece of writing, you must gain a thorough understanding of your topic; to do so, you must carry out the necessary reading, reflecting, and researching. Writing becomes a satisfying experience once you can speak with authority about your topic. Use the following guidelines when you start collecting information. (Also see "Research and Writing" in this book.)

- Determine what you already know about your topic. (Use the strategies below this bulleted list.)
- Consider listing questions you would like to answer during your research. (See page 38.)
- Identify and explore possible sources of information. (See page 39.)
- Carry out your research following a logical plan. (See page 48–51.)

Find out what you already know.

Use one or more of the following strategies to determine what you already know about a writing topic.

1. **Focused freewriting:** At this point, you can focus your freewriting by (1) exploring your limited topic from different angles or (2) approaching your freewriting as if it were a quick draft of the actual paper. A quick version will tell you how much you know about your topic and what you need to find out.

2. **Clustering:** Try clustering with your topic serving as the nucleus word. Your clustering should focus on what you already know. (See page 36.)

3. **Five W's of writing:** Answer the five W's—*Who? What? When? Where?* and *Why?*—to identify basic information on your subject. Add *How?* to the list for better coverage.

4. **Directed writing:** Write whatever comes to mind about your topic, using one of the modes listed below. (Repeat the process as often as you need to, selecting a different mode each time.)

    Describe it: What do you see, hear, feel, smell, and taste?

    Compare it: What is it similar to? What is it different from?

    Associate it: What connections between this topic and others come to mind?

    Analyze it: What parts does it have? How do they work together?

    Argue it: What do you like about the topic? What you do not like about it? What are its strengths and weaknesses?

    Apply it: What can you do with it? How can you use it?

Ask questions.

To guide your collecting and researching, you may find it helpful to list questions about your topic that you would like to answer. Alternatively, you can refer to the questions below. These questions address problems, policies, and concepts. Most topics will fall under one of these categories. Use those questions that seem helpful as a guide to your research.

	DESCRIPTION	FUNCTION	HISTORY	VALUE
P R O B L E M S	What is the problem? What type of problem is it? What are its parts? What are the signs of the problem?	Who or what is affected by it? What new problems might it cause in the future?	What is the current status of the problem? What or who caused it? What or who contributed to it?	What is its significance? Why? Why is it more (or less) important than other problems? What does it symbolize or illustrate?
P O L I C I E S	What is the policy? How broad is it? What are its parts? What are its most important features?	What is the policy designed to do? What is needed to make it work? What are or will be its effects?	What brought about this policy? What are the alternatives?	Is the policy workable? What are its advantages and disadvantages? Is it practical? Is it a good policy? Why or why not?
C O N C E P T S	What is the concept? What are its parts? What is its main feature? Whom or what is it related to?	Who has been influenced by this concept? Why is it important? How does it work?	When did it originate? How has it changed over the years? How might it change in the future?	What practical value does it have? Why is it superior (or inferior) to similar concepts? What is its social worth?

Identify possible sources.

Finding meaningful sources is one of the most important steps you will take as you prepare to write. Listed below are tips that will help you identify good sources:

1. **Give yourself enough time.** Finding good sources of information may be time-consuming. Books and periodicals you need may be checked out, your computer service may be down, and so on.

2. **Be aware of the limits of your resources.** Print material may be out-of-date. Online information may be more current, but it may not always be reliable. (See pages 432–435 for ways to help you evaluate information.)

3. **Use your existing resources to find additional sources of information.** Pay attention to books, articles, and individuals mentioned in reliable initial sources of information.

4. **Ask for help.** The specialists in your school library can help you find information that is reliable and relevant. These people are trained to find information; don't hesitate to ask for their help. (See page 455.)

5. **Bookmark useful websites.** Include reference works and academic resources related to your major.

Explore different sources of information.

Of course, books and websites are not the only possible sources of information. Primary sources such as interviews, observations, and surveys may lead you to a more thorough and meaningful understanding of a topic. (See pages 449–451.)

PRIMARY SOURCES	SECONDARY SOURCES
Interviews	Articles
Observations	Reference book entries
Participation	Books
Surveys	Websites

Carry out your research.

As you conduct your research, try to use a variety of reliable sources. It's also a good idea to choose an efficient note-taking method before you start. You will want to take good notes on the information you find and record all the publishing information necessary for citing your sources. (See pages 438–441.)

Reserve a special part of a notebook to question, evaluate, and reflect on your research as it develops. The record of your thoughts and actions created during this process will mean a great deal to you—as much as or more than the actual information you uncover. Reflection helps you make sense of new ideas, refocus your thinking, and evaluate your progress.

Writing with Sources

Many of your writing assignments will challenge you to do good research and to work well with the sources you find. While chapters 28–33 offer a full treatment of research writing, these two pages (along with pages 52–53, 68–69, 90–91, 108–109, and 114–115) explain how to address source-related issues linked to each step in the writing process.

For example, at the getting-started phase, you should think through broad source-use issues such as these:

1. Which types of research does my assignment require?
2. Which types of research would help me explore my topic?
3. Which record-keeping and note-taking strategies would help me use source information effectively and avoid plagiarism?

Think rhetorically.

To help you resolve questions like those given above, remember the rhetorical situation behind your project:

- Given the **subject** of your writing, which sources of information would offer reliable, relevant information? (See "Exploring Possible Information Resources and Sites," pages 428–429.) In your assignment, which types of sources are recommended or expected? Which sources should be avoided?
- Given your **audience,** which types of sources will readers understand and respect? Which sources will add to your credibility?
- Given your **purpose** (to entertain, inform, analyze, or persuade), which information will help you achieve that goal, and which types of sources contain those details?

When you keep these rhetorical issues in focus, information sources become a type of database from which you can draw ideas and evidence that help you strengthen and develop your thinking.

Practice getting-started strategies.

When you are getting started, using sources effectively requires keeping track of them and taking useful notes from them. Here are three strategies that will help you do both:

Track resources in a working bibliography. Once you find a useful book, journal article, news story, or webpage, record identifying information for the source. For more help, see pages 436–437.

Use a note-taking system that respects sources. Essentially, your note-taking system should help you keep an accurate record of useful information and ideas from sources while also allowing you to engage those sources with your own thinking. For a discussion of possible systems, see pages 438–441.

Distinguish summaries, paraphrases, and quotations. As you read sources, you will find material that answers your questions and helps you achieve your writing purpose. At that point, decide whether to summarize, paraphrase, or quote the material:

- A **summary** pulls just the main points out of a passage and puts them in your own words: Summarize source material when it contains relevant ideas and information that you can boil down.

- A **paraphrase** rewrites a passage point by point in your own words: Paraphrase source material when all the information is important but the actual phrasing isn't especially important or memorable.

- A **quotation** records a passage from the source word for word: Quote when the source states something crucial and says it well. *Note:* In your notes, always identify quoted material by putting quotation marks around it.

Summarizing, paraphrasing, and quoting are treated more fully on pages 442–444. Here is a brief example, with the original passage coming from Coral Ann Howells' *Alice Munro,* published in 1998 by Manchester University Press as part of its Contemporary World Writers series.

Original: "To read Munro's stories is to discover the delights of seeing two worlds at once: an ordinary everyday world and the shadowy map of another imaginary or secret world laid over the real one, so that in reading we slip from one world into the other in an unassuming domestic sort of way."

Summary: Munro's fiction moves readers from recognizable reality into a hidden world.

Paraphrase: Reading Munro's fiction gives readers the enjoyment of experiencing a double world: day-to-day reality and on top of that a more mysterious, fantastic world, with the result that readers move smoothly between the worlds in a seamless, ordinary way.

Quotation: Munro's fiction takes us into "the shadowy map of another imaginary or secret world laid over the real one."

Cross-Curricular Connections

Different academic disciplines require different methods of research note taking. For example, in the natural sciences, a lab notebook may be standard practice, while in psychology you might be expected to write summaries of past research studies on your topic. As you work on writing projects in your major, develop note-taking habits that respect the research and thinking methods in the discipline. For an overview of academic disciplines and the writing tasks they involve, see chapter 9.

Beginning the Process Checklist

Use this checklist as a guide to help you plan your writing.

The Situation and Assignment *I know the . . .*

_____ subject and form—essay, narrative, or research paper.

_____ audience—who they are, what they know, and what they need.

_____ purpose of the writing—to inform, explain, analyze, or persuade.

_____ main action (key words), restrictions, and options.

_____ connection to personal and course goals.

_____ requirements for length, format, research, and documentation.

_____ assessment method that will be used.

The Topic *I have . . .*

_____ explored possible topics through journal writing, freewriting, listing, clustering, or dialogue.

_____ chosen a limited topic that fits the assignment and spurs my interest.

_____ recorded what I already know and what I need to learn.

_____ developed a research plan and collected information about the topic.

Critical-Thinking and Writing Activities

As directed by your instructor, complete the following critical-thinking and writing activities by yourself or with classmates.

1. Writer Ralph Fletcher shares, "When I write, I am always struck at how magical and unexpected the process turns out to be." Would you describe the writing process you follow as "magical" and "unexpected"? Why or why not? What would it take to make writing this kind of experience for you?

2. Reread one of your recent essays. Does the writing show that you thoroughly understood your *subject*, met the needs of your *audience*, and achieved your writing *purpose*?

3. Below is a list of general subject areas. Select one that interests you and do the following: Using the strategies on pages 33–36, brainstorm possible topics and select one. Then use the strategies on pages 37–39 to explore what you know about that topic and what you need to learn.

Arts/music	Environment	Exercise
Health/medicine	Housing	Work/occupation

◂ VISUALLY SPEAKING

Consider the photo on page 27. In a one- to two-page double-spaced response, reflect on what that image suggests about beginning the writing process.

PLANNING

Video

Planning of almost any type requires careful thinking. When you plan an essay, you have two basic thinking objectives: (1) establish a thesis or focus for your writing, and (2) organize the supporting information. The amount of organization time required depends on the type of writing. For narratives, very little organizing may be required. For most academic essays, however, you will need to identify the method of development—comparison, cause/effect, classification—that best supports your thesis, and then organize your details accordingly. (See pages **46–47**.) At this point, your goal is to establish the general structure of your writing.

Writer and instructor Ken Macrorie offers this important insight about planning: "Good writing is formed partly through plan and partly through accident." In other words, too much early planning can get in the way. Writing at its best is a process of discovery. You never know what new insights or ideas will spring to mind until you put pen to paper or fingers to keyboard.

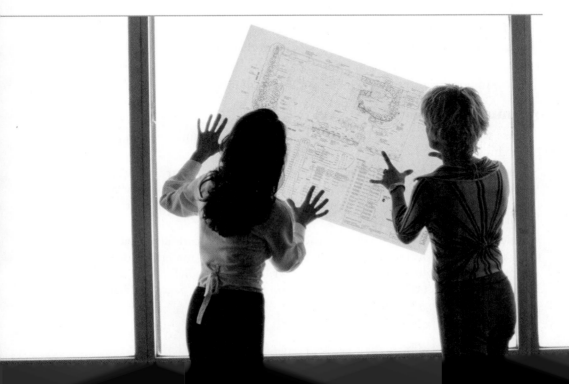

Taking Inventory of Your Thoughts

Suppose you've done some searching, and you've succeeded in discovering some interesting information and perspectives about your subject. Now may be a good time to see how well your findings match up with your topic.

Revisit your rhetorical situation.

After considering the following questions, you should be able to decide whether to move ahead with your planning or reconsider your topic.

Subject

- How much do I already know about this topic?
- Do I need to know more? Is additional information available? Where?
- Have I tried any of the collecting strategies? (See pages 37–39.)
- What help would I need to find information, schedule an interview with a source, and so on?

Audience

- How much does my audience already know about this subject?
- How can I get my audience interested in my idea?
- How can I help them understand related technical terms and concepts?

Purpose

- What are the specific requirements of this assignment?
- Do I have enough time to do a good job with this topic?
- Am I writing to entertain, to inform, to explain, to analyze, or to persuade?
- How important is this assignment, and how will it be assessed?

Continue the process.

Assess whether you need additional information. If you think you do, go back to researching.

Research more deeply. If you need to know more about your topic, continue collecting your own thoughts and/or investigating other sources of information. Remember that it is important to investigate secondary and primary sources of information. (See pages 448–463.)

Review your material. If you are ready to move ahead, carefully review your initial notes. As you read through this material, circle or underline ideas that seem important enough to include in your writing. Then look for ways in which these ideas connect or relate. The activities on the following pages will help you focus your thoughts for writing.

Forming Your Thesis Statement

After you have completed enough research and collecting, you may begin to develop a more focused interest in your topic. If all goes well, this narrowed focus will give rise to a thesis for your writing. A thesis statement identifies your central idea. It usually highlights a special condition or feature of the topic, expresses a specific claim about it, or takes a stand.

State your thesis in a sentence that effectively expresses what you want to explore or explain in your essay. Sometimes a thesis statement develops early and easily; at other times, the true focus of your writing emerges only after you've written your first draft.

Find a focus.

A general subject area is typically built into your writing assignments. Your task, then, is to find a limited writing topic and examine it from a particular angle or perspective. (You will use this focus to form your thesis statement.)

FOCUSING A TOPIC

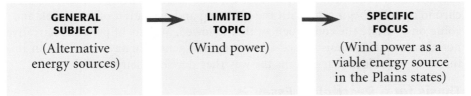

GENERAL SUBJECT	→	**LIMITED TOPIC**	→	**SPECIFIC FOCUS**
(Alternative energy sources)		(Wind power)		(Wind power as a viable energy source in the Plains states)

State your thesis.

You can use the following formula to write a thesis statement for your essay. A thesis statement sets the tone and direction for your writing. Keep in mind that at this point you're writing a *working thesis statement*—a statement in progress, so to speak. You may change it as your thinking on the topic evolves.

A manageable or limited topic (wind power)
+   a specific claim (provides a viable energy source in the Plains states)
=   an effective thesis statement

Thesis Statement: Wind power provides a viable energy source in the Plains states.

THESIS CHECKLIST

_____   Does the thesis statement reflect a limited topic?
_____   Does it clearly state the specific idea you plan to develop?
_____   Is the thesis supported by the information you have gathered?
_____   Does the thesis suggest a pattern of organization for your essay?

Using Methods of Development

An organizing pattern for your essay may be built into your assignment. For example, you may be asked to develop an argument or to write a process paper. When a pattern is not apparent, one may still evolve naturally during the research and information-collecting steps. If this doesn't happen, take a careful look at your thesis statement.

Let your thesis guide you.

An effective thesis will often suggest an organizing pattern. Notice how the thesis statements below provide direction and shape for the writing to follow. (Also see page 21.)

Thesis (Focus) for a Personal Narrative

What began as a simple prank ended up having serious consequences for all of us who were involved.

Discussion: This statement identifies the focus of a personal narrative. It suggests that the essay will recount a personal experience and will most likely be arranged chronologically, beginning with the planning and execution of the prank and then going on to relate the consequences that followed. Writers of personal narratives do not always state a thesis directly, but they will generally have in mind an implied theme or main idea that governs the way they develop their writing.

Thesis for a Descriptive Essay

Although it was no more than an overgrown lot, as children we imagined the property next to my boyhood home to be a forest full of danger and adventure.

Discussion: This statement indicates that the writer will describe a special place from childhood. This description might be organized spatially, moving from the edges of the wooded lot to its interior. A description may be organized thematically, in this case by describing the specific features of the lot through the adventures the children imagined having there.

Thesis for a Cause-and-Effect Essay

Some stress is inescapable, but for their own health and for the well-being of others, people must understand what stress is, as well as its causes and effects.

Discussion: This thesis indicates that the writer is developing a cause-and-effect essay. Essays following this pattern usually begin with one or more causes followed by an explanation of the effects, or they begin with a primary effect followed by an explanation of the causes. To develop this thesis, the writer will follow the first route, exploring the causes of stress before examining its effects. (See pages 185–187 for this essay.)

Thesis for an Essay of Comparison

Bigger in *Native Son* and Alan in *Equus* are both entering adulthood and have come to realize that they are controlled by work, religion, and the media.

Discussion: Comparisons are patterned in two ways: Either you discuss one of the subjects completely and then the other (whole versus whole), or you discuss both subjects at the same time (point by point). The writer of this thesis is comparing two literary characters point by point. (See pages 201–202 for this essay.)

Thesis for an Essay of Classification

There are four main perspectives, or approaches, that readers can use to converse about literature.

Discussion: The writer is writing an essay of classification. Essays following this pattern identify the main parts or categories of a topic and then examine each one. In this thesis, the writer identifies four ways to discuss literature, and he examines each one in turn. (See pages 220–221 for this essay.)

Thesis for a Process Essay

When a cell begins to function abnormally, it can initiate a process that results in cancer.

Discussion: As indicated in this thesis, the writer of this essay will explain how cancer cells multiply and affect the body. Process essays, such as this one, are organized chronologically. Each step is examined in turn to help readers understand the complete process. (See pages 231–232 for this essay.)

Thesis for an Essay of Definition

Strangely, the word *gullible* connects people and birds, relating them to each other by their willingness to "swallow."

Discussion: This essay of definition explores the root meaning of the word *gullible*. To do so, the writer explains the word's meaning by analyzing its etymology (history) and identifying its lingual associations.

Thesis for an Essay Proposing a Solution

The best solution to controlling deer populations is to stay as close to nature's ways as possible, and game management by hunting meets this criterion.

Discussion: The writer of this thesis is developing a problem/solution essay. Essays following this pattern usually begin with a discussion of the problem and its causes and then examine possible solutions. In this essay, the writer presents a problem's history, causes, and effects. He then identifies and dismisses some solutions before arguing for one solution in particular.

Developing a Plan or an Outline

After writing a working thesis and reviewing the methods of development (pages 46–47), you should be ready to organize the information you have collected. A simple listing of main points may work for you, or you may need to outline the information or use a graphic organizer.

- **Basic list:** a brief listing of main points
- **Topic outline:** a more formal arrangement, including main points and essential details (See below.)
- **Sentence outline:** a formal arrangement, including main points and essential details, written as complete sentences (See page 49.)
- **Graphic organizer:** an arrangement of main points and essential details in an appropriate chart or diagram (See pages 49–51.)

Choose an organization method.

If you have a good deal of information to sort and arrange, you may want to use a topic or sentence outline for your planning.

Topic Outline

In a topic outline, you state each main point and essential detail as a word or phrase. Before you start constructing your outline, write your working thesis statement at the top of your paper to help keep you focused on the subject. (Do not attempt to outline your opening and closing paragraphs unless you are specifically asked to do so.)

SAMPLE TOPIC OUTLINE

Thesis: There are four main perspectives, or approaches, that readers can use to converse about literature.

    I. Text-centered approaches
        A. Also called formalist criticism
        B. Emphasis on structure of text and rules of genre
        C. Importance placed on key literary elements
   II. Audience-centered approaches
        A. Also called rhetorical or reader-response criticism
        B. Emphasis on interaction between reader and text
  III. Author-centered approaches
        A. Emphasis on writer's life
        B. Importance placed on historical perspective
        C. Connections made between texts
  IV. Ideological approaches
        A. Psychological analysis of text
        B. Myth or archetype criticism
        C. Moral criticism
        D. Sociological analysis

Sentence Outline

The sample outline below uses complete sentences to explain the main points and essential details that will be covered in the main part of the essay.

SAMPLE SENTENCE OUTLINE

Thesis: There are four main perspectives, or approaches, that readers can use to converse about literature.
  I. A text-centered approach focuses on the literary piece itself.
    A. This approach is often called formalist criticism.
    B. This method of criticism examines text structure and the rules of the genre.
    C. A formalist critic determines how key literary elements reinforce meaning.
  II. An audience-centered approach focuses on the "transaction" between text and reader.
    A. This approach is often called rhetorical or reader-response criticism.
    B. A rhetorical critic sees the text as an activity that is different for each reader.
  III. An author-centered approach focuses on the origin of a text.
    A. An author-centered critic examines the writer's life.
    B. This method of criticism may include a historical look at a text.
    C. Connections may be made between the text and related works.
  IV. The ideological approach applies ideas outside of literature.
    A. Some critics apply psychological theories to a literary work.
    B. Myth or archetype criticism applies anthropology and classical studies to a text.
    C. Moral criticism explores the moral dilemmas in literature.
    D. Sociological approaches include Marxist, feminist, and minority criticism.

Graphic Organizers

If you are a visual person, you might prefer a graphic organizer when it comes to arranging your ideas for an essay or a report. Graphic organizers can help you map out ideas and illustrate relationships among them. Here is a graphic organizer—a line diagram—that was used to organize the ideas for the essay. (Also see pages 50–51.)

SAMPLE GRAPHIC ORGANIZER

Types of Graphic Organizers

The following organizers are related to some of the methods of development discussed on pages **46–47**. Each will help you collect and organize your information. Adapt the organizers as necessary to fit your particular needs or personal style.

CAUSE/EFFECT

COMPARISON/CONTRAST

COMPARISON

CLASSIFICATION

PROCESS ANALYSIS

Subject: _____
(Chronological Order)

Step 1

Step 2

Step 3

PROBLEM/SOLUTION

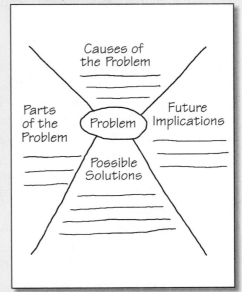

Causes of
the Problem

Parts
of the
Problem

Problem

Future
Implications

Possible
Solutions

DEFINITION

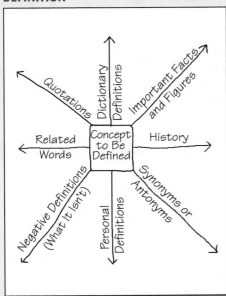

Quotations

Dictionary
Definitions

Important Facts
and Figures

Related
Words

Concept
to Be
Defined

History

Negative Definitions
(What It Isn't)

Personal
Definitions

Synonyms or
Antonyms

EVALUATION

Subject: _____

Points to Evaluate	Supporting Details
1.	
2.	
3.	
4.	
5.	

Writing with Sources

When your writing project involves working with sources, the planning phase will involve a great deal of sorting through and sorting out sources as they relate to your own thinking. To advance your writing toward a first draft, thoughtfully review and order your source notes, using them to stimulate your thinking and planning.

Think rhetorically.

At the beginning of this chapter, you were encouraged to review your subject, audience, and purpose when planning your first draft. For projects that involve research, consider how all three might guide your use of sources:

1. For your **subject,** which sources offer reliable information and analysis that has shaped your thinking and pointed you toward a working thesis?

2. Given your **audience,** which resources will help you create credibility with readers and clarify the topic for them?

3. To achieve your **purpose** (to entertain, inform, analyze, and/or persuade), which resources should be featured in your writing?

When you keep these rhetorical questions in mind, your own thinking will control the sources rather than being controlled by them.

Practice planning strategies.

When you plan your first draft, use the following source-focused strategies to develop a working thesis, choose a method of development, and form an outline. (For more on planning research writing, see pages 424–427.)

Let your research notes speak to you. Read and reread your research notes to let key ideas develop. What discoveries have you made? What conclusions have you reached? What questions have you answered? Those discoveries, conclusions, and answers will point toward a thesis and supporting details.

Consider where to position primary and secondary sources. Different writing projects require different approaches to integrating and balancing primary and secondary sources. (See page 448 for the distinction.) Ask these questions:

• Where and how should I work with primary sources—interviews, surveys, analyses, observations, experiments, and other data I have collected?

• Where and how should I bring in secondary sources—scholarly books, journal articles, and the like?

Example: In a literary analysis, you may rely on primary textual analysis of a novel throughout your paper but support that analysis with secondary-source information from biographical research placed early in your paper.

Order your writing around key sources. Sometimes your writing can take direction specifically from your sources. Consider these options:

- **Make your thesis a response to a specific source.** Did a particular source stand out as especially strong or especially contrary to your own thinking? Shape your thesis as an affirmation of the strong source's authority or as a rebuttal to the contrary source's claims.

- **Structure your paper around a dialogue with sources.** Do your sources offer multiple, divergent, or even contradictory perspectives on your topic? If they do, consider organizing your paper around a dialogue with these sources. This approach works especially well with complex or controversial topics or in papers that need to present multiple dimensions or views.

Put your discussion in context. Often, the early part of your paper establishes a context for your topic. Use sources to present background, explain terms, describe the big picture, or establish a theoretical framework for your discussion.

Example: If your paper will explore the problem of teen homelessness in Atlanta, you might put that analysis in context by supplying information on national trends, general causes of homelessness, or sociological definitions of homelessness.

Clump source material under your supporting points. Once you have developed a thesis and sketched out some supporting points, arrange source material under those points. Depending on the note-taking method you have used, try the following:

- Reorder your notes: For electronic notes, try copy-and-paste. For notes on paper, cut and paste using scissors.

- Code your notes using numbers or letters matching points in your outline.

- With books, articles, and other resources, apply sticky notes to key pages.

Caution: Whatever method you use, make sure that you can still identify source material so as to avoid plagiarism when you draft your paper.

Cross-Curricular Connections

In most disciplines, it is common practice early in the paper to "survey the literature" on the topic. In a literary analysis, you might survey common interpretations of a key concept before you relay your view. In a botany field report, you might situate your own study by first reviewing other studies done on the topic. To conduct such a review, do the following:

1. Based on whether your review must be comprehensive or representative, identify the studies that should be included in the review.

2. Order these studies logically by (1) categorizing them according to their approach, perspective, or essential argument, or (2) arranging them chronologically from earliest to most recent publication (if you need to convey the history of research on your topic).

Planning Checklist

Use this checklist as a guide to help you plan your writing.

Thesis *I have . . .*

_____ reviewed information I've collected up to this point.

_____ identified a specific focus or feature of my topic to develop.

_____ stated a focus in a working thesis statement.

_____ tested the thesis to make sure it is supportable.

Development *I have . . .*

_____ identified a pattern of organization to develop my thesis.

_____ organized my support in a list, an outline, or a graphic organizer.

_____ prepared to write the first draft.

Critical-Thinking and Writing Activities

As directed by your instructor, complete the following critical-thinking and writing activities by yourself or with classmates.

1. Author Ken Macrorie claims that "good writing is formed partly through plan and partly through accident." Do you agree? Why or why not? Relate Macrorie's idea to your own writing experiences. How carefully do you plan? How much do you leave to accident?

2. A number of organizational patterns are discussed on pages 46–47. Choose one of these patterns and select a model essay from chapters 10–20 that follows the pattern. Read the essay, note the thesis, and explain how the writer develops it.

3. Listed below are general subject areas. Do the following for three of these subjects: (1) identify a limited topic, (2) write a working thesis statement, and (3) identify a pattern of organization you could use to develop the thesis.

Afghanistan	Education	Iraq
Agriculture	Entertainment	Medicine
Careers	Exercise	Natural Resources
Communications	Family	Olympics
Community	Freedom	U.S. Courts

◀ VISUALLY SPEAKING

Consider the photo on page 43. Then explain in writing how the photo's "story" parallels the planning stage in writing.

DRAFTING

Video

The early twentieth-century French novelist Anatole France is reported to have said that one of his first drafts could have been written by any schoolboy, his next draft by a bright upper-level student, his third draft by a superior graduate, his fourth draft by a seasoned professional, and his final draft "only by Anatole France." Even if that report is exaggerated, the point is well taken: The first draft is not the one that will distinguish you as a writer. It's a way of getting material together, starting out, connecting your ideas. A first draft gives you something to work with—verbal wet clay—that will later, through revising and editing, result in a polished piece of writing.

This section provides information and advice about drafting a college-level essay. Our special focus is on the sorts of "moves" that may occur at each major stage of the draft. If you know in advance what moves to make, you'll be in a better position to develop a thoughtful and complete draft.

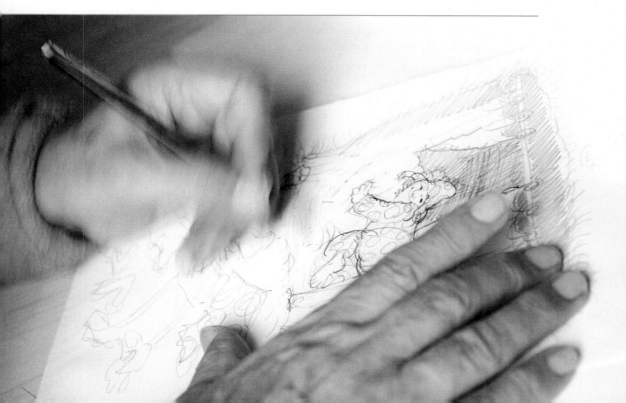

Writing Your First Draft

The American novelist Kurt Vonnegut once laughingly divided writers into two categories: swoopers and bashers. Swoopers write seventeen drafts at high speed before they're done; bashers won't move to sentence number two until they have polished sentence number one. When you draft your next paper, you'll strike a better balance between carelessness and care if you focus on the essentials of your rhetorical situation: audience, purpose, and subject.

Reconsider your audience.

Review who your readers are, including their knowledge of and attitude toward your topic. Then get ready to talk with them, person to person.

Reconsider your purpose.

Briefly review (1) what you want your writing to do (your task), (2) what you want it to say (your thesis), and (3) how you want to say it (list of ideas or outline).

Focus on your subject.

As you develop your first draft, these strategies can help you keep your subject in focus.

- Use your outline or writing plan as a general guide. Try to develop your main points, but allow new ideas to emerge naturally.
- Write freely without being too concerned about neatness and correctness. Concentrate on developing your ideas, not on producing a final copy.
- Include as much detail as possible, continuing until you reach a logical stopping point.
- Use your writing plan or any charts, lists, or diagrams you've produced, but don't feel absolutely bound by them.
- Complete your first draft in one or two sittings.
- Use the most natural voice you can so that the writing will flow smoothly. If your voice is too formal during drafting, you'll be tempted to stop and edit your words.
- Quote sources accurately by using your word-processing program's copy-and-paste features or by handwriting or typing quotations carefully.

INSIGHT: If you have trouble getting started, think of your writing as half of a conversation with a reader you invent. Talk to your silent partner. Think about what you've already said and let that help you decide what you should say next.

Basic Essay Structure:
Major Moves

The following chart lists the main writing moves that occur during the development of a piece of writing. Use it as a general guide for all of your drafting. Remember to keep your purpose and audience in mind throughout the drafting process.

Opening

Engage your reader.
Stimulate and direct the reader's attention.

Establish your direction.
Identify the topic and put it in perspective.

Get to the point.
Narrow your focus and state your thesis.

Middle

Advance your thesis.
Provide background information and cover your main points.

Test your ideas.
Raise questions and consider alternatives.

Support your main points.
Add substance and build interest.

Build a coherent structure.
Start new paragraphs and arrange the support.

Use different levels of detail.
Clarify and complete each main point.

Ending

Reassert the main point.
Remind the reader of the purpose and rephrase the thesis.

Urge the reader.
Gain the reader's acceptance and look ahead.

Opening Your Draft

The opening paragraph is one of the most important elements in any composition. It should accomplish at least three essential things: (1) engage the reader; (2) establish your direction, tone, and level of language; and (3) introduce your line of thought.

Advice: The conventional way of approaching the first paragraph is to view it as a kind of "funnel" that draws a reader in and narrows to a main point. Often, the final sentence explicitly states your thesis.

Cautions: • Don't feel bound by the conventional pattern, which may sound stale if not handled well.

• Don't let the importance of the first paragraph paralyze you. Relax and write.

The information on the next two pages will help you develop your opening. You can refer to the sample essays in the handbook for ideas.

Engage your reader.

Your reader will be preoccupied with other thoughts until you seize, stimulate, and direct his or her attention. Here are some effective ways to "hook" the reader:

- Mention little-known facts about the topic.
- Pose a challenging question.
- Offer a thought-provoking quotation.
- Tell a brief, illuminating story.
- Introduce your angle or focus on the topic.

Establish your direction.

The direction of your line of thought should become clear in the opening part of your writing. Here are some moves you might make to set the right course:

- **Identify the topic (issue).** Show a problem, a need, or an opportunity.
- **Deepen the issue.** Connect the topic, showing its importance.
- **Acknowledge other views.** Tell what others say or think about the topic.

Web Link

INSIGHT: Your opening affects the direction and line of thinking of your entire piece of writing. If you don't like the first or second attempt, keep trying. You'll know when you hit the right version because it will help you visualize the rest of your draft.

Get to the point.

You may choose to state your main point up front, or you may wait until later to introduce your thesis. For example, you could work inductively by establishing an issue, a problem, or a question in your opening and then build toward the answer—your thesis—in your conclusion. (See page 20 for more on inductive reasoning.) Sometimes, in fact, your thesis may simply be implied. In any case, the opening should at least hint at the central issue or thesis of your paper. Here are three ways to get to the point:

1. **Narrow your focus.** Point to what interests you about the topic.

2. **Raise a question.** Answer the question in the rest of the essay.

3. **State your thesis.** If appropriate, craft a sentence that boils down your thinking to a central claim. You can use the thesis sentence as a "map" for the organization of the rest of the essay. (See pages 45–47, 118–121, and 424–425.)

Weak Opening

Although the opening below introduces the topic, the writing lacks interesting details and establishes no clear focus for the essay.

> I would like to tell you about the TV show *The Simpsons*. It's about this weird family of five people who look kind of strange and act even stranger. In fact, the characters aren't even real—they're just cartoons.

Strong Opening

In the essay opener below, the writer uses his first paragraph to get his readers' attention and describe his subject. He uses the second paragraph to raise a question that leads him to a statement of his thesis (underlined).

> The Simpsons, stars of the TV show by the same name, are a typical American family, or at least a parody of one. Homer, Marge, Bart, Lisa, and Maggie Simpson live in Springfield, U.S.A. Homer, the father, is a boorish, obese oaf who works in a nuclear power plant. Marge is an overprotective, nagging mother with an outrageous blue hairdo. Ten-year-old Bart is an obnoxious, "spiky-haired demon." Lisa is eight and a prodigy on the tenor saxophone and in class. The infant Maggie never speaks but only sucks on her pacifier.
>
> What is the attraction of this yellow-skinned family that stars on a show in which all of the characters have pronounced overbites and only four fingers on each hand? Viewers see a little bit of themselves in everything the Simpsons do. <u>The world of Springfield is a parody of the viewer's world, and Americans can't get enough of it.</u> Viewers experience this parody in the show's explanations of family, education, workplace, and politics.

INSIGHT: Note how, after stating the thesis, the writer forecasts the method of supporting that thesis.

Developing the Middle

The middle of an essay is where you do the "heavy lifting." In this part you develop the main points that support your thesis statement.

Advice: As you write, you will likely make choices that were unforeseen when you began. Use "scratch outlines" (temporary jottings) along the way to show where your new ideas may take you.

Cautions: • Writing that lacks effective detail gives only a vague image of the writer's intent.

• Writing that wanders loses its hold on the essay's purpose.

For both of these reasons, always keep your thesis in mind when you develop the main part of your writing. Refer to the guidelines on the next two pages for help. You can refer to the sample essays in this book for ideas.

Advance your thesis.

If you stated a thesis in the opening, you can advance it in the middle paragraphs by covering your main points and supporting them in these ways.

Explain: Provide important facts, details, and examples.

Narrate: Share a brief story or re-create an experience to illustrate an idea.

Describe: Tell in detail how someone appears or how something works.

Define: Identify or clarify the meaning of a specific term or idea.

Analyze: Examine the parts of something to better understand the whole.

Compare: Provide examples to show how two things are alike or different.

Argue: Use logic and evidence to prove that something is true.

Reflect: Express your thoughts or feelings about something.

Cite authorities: Add expert analysis or personal commentary.

Test your ideas.

When you write a first draft, you're testing your initial thinking about your topic. You're determining whether your thesis is valid and whether you have enough compelling information to support it. Here are ways to test your line of thinking as you write:

Raise questions. Try to anticipate your readers' questions.

Consider alternatives. Look at your ideas from different angles; weigh various options; reevaluate your thesis.

Answer objections. Directly or indirectly deal with possible problems that a skeptical reader might point out.

Build a coherent structure.

Design paragraphs as units of thought that develop and advance your thesis clearly and logically. For example, look at the brief essay below, noting how each body paragraph presents ideas with supporting details that build on and deepen the main idea.

The writer introduces the topic, suggests his organizational pattern (comparison/contrast), and states his thesis.

Making a transition into his discussion, the writer starts with a basic explanation of how the two types of lightbulbs function differently; details show how.

The writer shifts his attention to weaknesses of compact bulbs.

Using "On the other hand" as a transition, he next explains the strengths of compacts.

He acknowledges that compacts cost more, but he then justifies the cost.

The writer rephrases his thesis as a challenge.

Seeing the Light

All lightbulbs make light, so they're all the same, right? Not quite. You have many choices regarding how to light up your life. Two types of bulbs are the traditional incandescent and the newer, more compact fluorescent. By checking out how they're different, you can better choose which one to buy.

While either incandescent or compact fluorescent bulbs can help you read or find the bathroom at night, each bulb makes light differently. In an incandescent bulb, electricity heats up a tungsten filament (thin wire) to 450 degrees, causing it to glow with a warm, yellow light. A compact fluorescent is a glass tube filled with mercury vapor and argon gas. Electricity causes the mercury to give off ultraviolet radiation. That radiation then causes phosphors coating the inside of the tube to give off light.

Both types of bulbs come in many shapes, sizes, and brightnesses, but compacts have some restrictions. Because of their odd shape, compacts may not fit in a lamp well. Compacts also may not work well in very cold temperatures, and they can't be used with a dimmer switch.

On the other hand, while compact fluorescents are less flexible than incandescents, compacts are four times more efficient. For example, a 15-watt compact produces as many lumens of light as a 60-watt incandescent! Why? Incandescents turn only about 5 percent of electricity into light and give off the other 95 percent as heat.

But are compacts less expensive than incandescents? In the short run, no. A compact costs about $15 while an incandescent costs only a dollar. However, because compacts burn less electricity—and last 7 to 10 times longer—in the long run, compacts are less expensive.

Now that you're no longer in the dark about lightbulbs, take a look at the lamp you're using to read this essay. Think about the watts (electricity used), lumens (light produced), efficiency, purchase price, and lamplife. Then decide how to light up your life in the future.

Arrange supporting details.

Organizing information in a logical pattern within a paragraph strengthens its coherence. The following pages explain and illustrate ten organizational strategies. (See also page 483.)

Analogy

An analogy is a comparison that a writer uses to explain a complex or unfamiliar phenomenon (how the immune system works) in terms of a familiar one (how mall security works).

The human body is like a mall, and the immune system is like mall security. Because the mall has hundreds of employees and thousands of customers, security guards must rely on photo IDs, name tags, and uniforms to decide who should be allowed to open cash registers and who should have access to the vault. In the same way, white blood cells and antibodies need to use DNA cues to recognize which cells belong in a body and which do not. Occasionally security guards make mistakes, wrestling Kookie the Klown to the ground while DVD players "walk" out of the service entrance, but these problems amount only to allergic reactions or little infections. If security guards become hypervigilant, detaining every customer and employee, the situation is akin to leukemia, in which white blood cells attack healthy cells. If security guards become corrupt, letting thieves take a "five-finger discount," the situation is akin to AIDS. Both systems—mall security and human immunity—work by correctly differentiating friend from foe.

—Rob King

Cause and Effect

Cause-and-effect organization shows how events are linked to their results. If you start with effects, follow with specific causes; if you begin with causes, follow with specific effects. The example below discusses the effects of hypothermia on the human body.

Even a slight drop in the normal human body temperature of 98.6 degrees Fahrenheit causes hypothermia. Often produced by accidental or prolonged exposure to cold, the condition forces all bodily functions to slow down. The heart rate and blood pressure decrease. Breathing becomes slower and shallower. As the body temperature drops, these effects become even more dramatic until it reaches somewhere between 86 and 82 degrees Fahrenheit and the person lapses into unconsciousness. When the temperature reaches between 65 and 59 degrees Fahrenheit, heart action, blood flow, and electrical brain activity stop. Normally such a condition would be fatal. However, as the body cools down, the need for oxygen also slows down. A person can survive in a deep hypothermic state for an hour or longer and be revived without serious complications.

—Laura Black

Chronological Order

Chronological (time) order helps you tell a story or present steps in a process. For example, the following paragraph describes how cement is made. Notice how the writer explains every step and uses transitional words to lead readers through the process.

> The production of cement is a complicated process. The raw materials that go into cement consist of about 60 percent lime, 25 percent silica, and 5 percent alumina. The remaining 10 percent is a varying combination of gypsum and iron oxide (because the amount of gypsum determines the drying time of the cement). First, this mixture is ground up into very fine particles and fed into a kiln. Cement kilns, the largest pieces of moving machinery used by any industry, are colossal steel cylinders lined with firebricks. They can be 25 feet in diameter and up to 750 feet long. The kiln is built at a slant and turns slowly as the cement mix makes its way down from the top end. A flame at the bottom heats the kiln to temperatures of up to 3,000 degrees Fahrenheit. When the melted cement compound emerges from the kiln, it cools into little marble-like balls called clinker. Finally, the clinker is ground to a consistency finer than flour and packaged as cement.
>
> —Kevin Maas

Classification

When classifying a subject, place the subject in its appropriate category and then show how this subject is different from other subjects in the same category. In the following paragraph, a student writer uses classification to describe the theory of temperament.

> Medieval doctors believed that "four temperaments rule man kind wholly." According to this theory, each person has a distinctive temperament or personality (sanguine, phlegmatic, melancholy, or choleric) based on the balance of four elements in the body, a balance peculiar to the individual. The theory was built on Galen's and Hippocrates' notion of "humors," which stated that the body contains blood, phlegm, black bile, and yellow bile—four fluids that maintain the balance within the body. The sanguine person was dominated by blood, associated with fire: Blood was hot and moist, and the person was fat and prone to laughter. The phlegmatic person was dominated by phlegm (associated with earth) and was squarish and slothful—a sleepy type. The melancholy person was dominated by cold, black bile (connected with the element of water) and as a result was pensive, peevish, and solitary. The choleric person was dominated by hot, yellow bile (air) and thus was inclined to anger.
>
> —Jessica Radsma

Compare-Contrast

To compare and contrast, show how two or more subjects are similar and different. See models on pages 201–211.

Climax

Climax is a method in which you first present details and then provide a general climactic statement or conclusion drawn from the details.

> The cockroach is unhonored and unsung. It walks about with downcast eyes. Its head hangs dejectedly between its knees. It lives on modest fare and in humble circumstances. It is drab-colored and inconspicuous. But don't let that Uriah Heep exterior fool you. For there you have Superbug, himself!
>
> —Edwin Way Teale, *The Lost Woods*

Definition

A definition provides the denotation (dictionary meaning) and connotation (feeling) of a given term. It often provides examples, gives anecdotes, and offers negative definitions—what the thing is not. In the paragraph below, the writer begins his definition by posing a question.

> First of all, what is the grotesque—in visual art and in literature? A term originally applied to Roman cave art that distorted the normal, the grotesque presents the body and mind so that they appear abnormal— different from the bodies and minds that we think belong in our world. Both spiritual and physical, bizarre and familiar, ugly and alluring, the grotesque shocks us, and we respond with laughter and fear. We laugh because the grotesque seems bizarre enough to belong only outside our world; we fear because it feels familiar enough to be part of it. Seeing the grotesque version of life as it is portrayed in art stretches our vision of reality. As Bernard McElroy argues, "The grotesque transforms the world from what we 'know' it to be to what we fear it might be. It distorts and exaggerates the surface of reality in order to tell a qualitative truth about it."
>
> —John Van Rys

Illustration

An illustration supports a general idea with specific reasons, facts, and details.

> As the years passed, my obsession grew. Every fiber and cell of my body was obsessed with the number on the scale and how much fat I could pinch on my thigh. No matter how thin I was, I thought I could never be thin enough. I fought my sisters for control of the TV and VCR to do my exercise programs and videos. The cupboards were stacked with cans of diet mixes, the refrigerator full of diet drinks. Hidden in my underwear drawer were stacks of diet pills that I popped along with my vitamins. At my worst, I would quietly excuse myself from family activities to turn on the bathroom faucet full blast and vomit into the toilet. Every day I stood in front of the mirror, a ritual not unlike brushing my teeth, and scrutinized my body. My face, arms, stomach, buttocks, hips, and thighs could never be small enough.
>
> —Paula Treick

Narration

In the paragraph below, the writer uses narration and chronological order to relate an anecdote—a short, illustrative story.

> When I was six or seven years old, growing up in Pittsburgh, I used to take a precious penny of my own and hide it for someone else to find. It was a curious compulsion; sadly, I've never been seized by it since. For some reason I always "hid" the penny along the same stretch of sidewalk up the street. I would cradle it at the roots of a sycamore, say, or in a hole left by a chipped-off piece of sidewalk. Then I would take a piece of chalk, and, starting at either end of the block, draw huge arrows leading up to the penny from both directions. After I learned to write I labeled the arrows: surprise ahead or money this way. I was greatly excited, during all this arrow-drawing, at the thought of the first lucky passer-by who would receive in this way, regardless of merit, a free gift from the universe. But I never lurked about. I would go straight home and not give the matter another thought, until, some months later, I would be gripped again by the impulse to hide another penny.
>
> —Annie Dillard, *Pilgrim at Tinker Creek*

Process

In the paragraph that follows, a student writer describes the process of entering the "tube," or "green room," while surfing.

> At this point you are slightly ahead of the barreling part of the wave, and you need to "stall," or slow yourself, to get into the tube. There are three methods of stalling used in different situations. If you are slightly ahead of the tube, you can drag your inside hand along the water to stall. If you are a couple of feet in front of the barrel, apply all your weight onto your back foot and sink the tail of the board into the water. This is known as a "tail stall" for obvious reasons, and its purpose is to decrease your board speed. If you are moving faster than the wave is breaking, you need to do what is called a "wrap-around." To accomplish this maneuver, lean back away from the wave while applying pressure on the tail. This shifts your forward momentum away from the wave and slows you down. When the wave comes, turn toward the wave and place yourself in the barrel.
>
> —Luke Sunukjian, "Entering the Green Room"

TIP: Choose an organizational pattern that most clearly advances your thesis for your specific audience. For example, to explain anorexia to readers unfamiliar with the condition, Paula Treick illustrates its effects (see page 64).

Web Link

Ending Your Draft

Closing paragraphs can be important for tying up loose ends, clarifying key points, or signing off with the reader. In a sense, the entire essay is a preparation for an effective ending; the ending helps the reader look back over the essay with new understanding and appreciation. Many endings leave the reader with fresh food for thought.

Advice: Because the ending can be so important, draft a variety of possible endings. Choose the one that flows best from a sense of the whole.

Cautions:
- If your thesis is weak or unclear, you will have a difficult time writing a satisfactory ending. To strengthen the ending, strengthen the thesis.

- You may have heard this formula for writing an essay: "Say what you're going to say, say it, then say what you've just said." Remember, though, if you need to "say what you've just said," say it in new words.

The information on the next two pages will help you develop your ending. You can refer to the sample essays elsewhere in this book for ideas.

Reassert the main point.

If an essay is complicated, the reader may need reclarification at the end. Show that you are fulfilling the promises you made in the beginning.

Remind the reader. Recall what you first set out to do; check off the key points you've covered; or answer any questions left unanswered.

Rephrase the thesis. Restate your thesis in light of the most important support you've given. Deepen and expand your original thesis.

Urge the reader.

Your reader may still be reluctant to accept your ideas or argument. The ending is your last chance to gain the reader's acceptance. Here are some possible strategies:

Show the implications. Follow further possibilities raised by your train of thought; be reasonable and convincing.

Look ahead. Suggest other possible connections.

List the benefits. Show the reader the benefits of accepting or applying the things you've said.

INSIGHT: When your writing comes to an effective stopping point, conclude the essay. Don't tack on another idea.

Complete and unify your message.

Your final paragraphs are your last opportunity to refocus, unify, and otherwise reinforce your message. Draft the closing carefully, not merely to finish the essay but to further advance your purpose and thesis.

Weak Ending

The ending below does not focus on and show commitment to the essay's main idea. Rather than reinforcing this idea, the writing leads off in a new direction.

> So the bottom line is that Mom's photo showed how much I liked my little stream. Of course, I have lots of other good childhood memories as well, like the times Dad would read to me before bedtime. I loved those books. How about you? Do you have good childhood memories?

Strong Endings

Below are final paragraphs from two essays in this book. Listen to their tone, watch how they reconsider the essay's ideas, and note how they offer further food for thought. (The first example is a revision of the weak paragraph above.)

> Sometimes, I want to go back there, back into that photo. I want to step into a time when life seemed safe, and a tiny stream gave us all that we needed. In that picture, our smiles last, our hearts are calm, and we hear only quiet voices, forest sounds, and my bubbling stream. Bitter words are silenced and tears held back by the click and whir of a camera.
>
> I've been thinking about making the journey again past the hunter's fort, under the stand of cedars, through the muck and mire, and over the rocky rise. But it's been a long summer, and the small seasonal stream running out of the overflow of the pond has probably dried up.

(See the full essay on pages 167–168.)

> I still wish I could cure cancer with a magic miracle liquid in a medicine bottle. But today I understand that cancer is a complicated disease. My grandparents died from three types of the disease—multiple myeloma, prostate cancer, and lung cancer. If it hadn't been for cancerous tumors taking over their bodies, my grandparents might still be alive, and I'd have many more memories of them. Maybe I'd even be sharing with them stories about my first year at college. On the other hand, perhaps this paper is a cure of a different type—while it can't change what happened, it can help me understand it.

(See the full essay on pages 217–219.)

INSIGHT: Think about your document's opening and closing as a type of contract that you make with your reader. Whereas the opening explains what you intend to do, the closing reviews and confirms what you have done.

Writing with Sources

Writing a first draft often involves exploring your own thinking in relation to the ideas and information you have discovered through research. Use creativity and care—the creativity to see connections and to trace lines of thinking, and the care to respect ideas and information from sources. (See pages 484–487 for drafting strategies for research papers.)

Think rhetorically.

Decide which sources aid your *purpose* (to entertain, to inform, to persuade) and help you connect with your *audience*. Also focus on your role as the writer. In a research paper, you are not only using sources to support your own ideas, but are also conversing with those sources. While showing respect for your sources, you want to avoid being intimidated by them.

Practice drafting strategies.

To work with sources during your drafting, try these strategies:

Keep your sources handy. While drafting, keep source material at your fingertips, whether in paper or electronic form, so that you can integrate summaries, paraphrases, and quotations without disrupting the flow of your drafting.

Start your draft with a strong source reference. Could something from a source get your paper off to an engaging start? Consider these powerful beginnings:

- A pithy, thought-provoking, or startling quotation
- A problematic or controversial statement or fact from a source
- An anecdote (a brief example, story, or case study) that makes the issue concrete

Take care not to overwhelm your draft with source material. As you draft, keep the focus on your own ideas:

- Avoid strings of references and chunks of source material with no discussion, explanation, or interpretation on your part in between.
- Don't offer entire paragraphs of material from a source (whether paraphrased or quoted) with a single in-text citation at the end. When you do so, your thinking disappears.
- Be careful not to overload your draft with complex information and dense data lacking explanation.
- Resist the urge to simply copy and paste big chunks from sources. Even if you document the sources, your paper will quickly become a patchwork of source material with a few weak stitches (your contribution) holding it together.

Advance and deepen your thesis with reliable reasons and evidence. A typical supporting paragraph starts with a topic sentence and elaborates it with detailed evidence and careful reasoning. Note this pattern in the paragraph below:

SAMPLE PARAGRAPH SHOWING INTEGRATION OF SOURCE MATERIAL

Topic sentence: idea elaborating and supporting thesis

Development of idea through reasoning

Support of idea through reference to source material

Concluding statement of idea

> Antibiotics are effective only against infections caused by bacteria and should never be used against infections caused by viruses. Using an antibiotic against a viral infection is like throwing water on a grease fire—water may normally put out fires but will only worsen the situation for a grease fire. In the same way, antibiotics fight infections, but they cause the body harm only when they are used to fight infections caused by viruses. Viruses cause the common cold, the flu, and most sore throats, sinus infections, coughs, and bronchitis. Yet antibiotics are commonly prescribed for these viral infections. The New England Journal of Medicine reports that 22.7 million kilograms (25,000 tons) of antibiotics are prescribed each year in the United States alone (Wenzel and Edmond 1962). Meanwhile, the CDC reports that approximately 50 percent of those prescriptions are completely unnecessary ("Antibiotic Overuse" 25). "Every year, tens of millions of prescriptions for antibiotics are written to treat viral illnesses for which these antibiotics offer no benefits," says the CDC's antimicrobial resistance director David Bell, M.D. (qtd. in Bren 30). Such mis-prescribing is simply bad medical practice that contributes to the problem of growing bacterial infection.

Save the best for last. Consider using an especially thought-provoking or summarizing statement, quotation, or detail in your conclusion. Doing so clinches your point and leaves your reader with provocative food for thought.

Track borrowed material in your draft. As you bring source material into your draft, track those summaries, paraphrases, and quotations by marking them clearly with codes, highlighting, brackets, or other symbols that will allow you to identify that material as you revise, edit, and polish your paper.

Cross-Curricular Connections

Referring to sources is handled differently from one discipline to the next. In humanities disciplines, a reference might give the author's name and credentials and the source's title; by contrast, a reference in the social or natural sciences might give the year that the study was done or published.

Drafting Checklist

Use this checklist as a guide when you develop a first draft for an essay. (To see drafting in action, turn to pages 122–129.)

Opening *The opening of my paper . . .*

———— engages the reader.

———— establishes a focus and states a main point.

Middle *The middle of my paper . . .*

———— advances my thesis by developing and testing my ideas.

———— has a clear, logical order and includes needed supporting details.

Closing *The closing of my paper . . .*

———— reasserts the main point and emphasizes the topic's relevance.

———— completes and unifies the message.

Critical-Thinking and Writing Activities

As directed by your instructor, complete the following critical-thinking and writing activities by yourself or with classmates.

1. Patricia T. O'Connor says, "All writing begins life as a first draft, and first drafts are never any good. They're not supposed to be." Is this claim true? Why or why not? What do you hope to accomplish with a first draft?

2. Study the chart on page 57. Based on other material you have read or written, add another writing move for each of the three main parts of the essay: opening, middle, and ending. Name the move, explain it, and tell what types of writing it might appear in.

3. Read the final paragraphs of any three essays included in this book. Write a brief analysis of each ending based on the information on pages 66–67.

4. Imagine that you are a journalist who has been asked to write an article about a wedding, a funeral, or another significant event you have experienced. Choose an event and sketch out a plan for your article. Include the main writing moves and the type of information at each stage of your writing.

◄ VISUALLY SPEAKING ────────────

Consider the photo on page 55. In a one- to two-page double-spaced response, reflect on what the photo suggests about drafting a piece of writing.

REVISING

5

Video

Revising takes courage. Once you have your first draft on paper, the piece may feel finished. The temptation then is to be satisfied with a quick "spell check" before turning in the paper. A word to the wise: Avoid this temptation.

Good writing almost always requires revising and, in some cases, substantial rework. During this step in the writing process, you make changes in the content of your first draft until it says exactly what you mean. To get started, assess the overall quality of the ideas, organization, and voice in your writing. Then be prepared to tinker with your writing until it effectively carries your message. It's also a good idea to share your draft with your instructor, a peer, or a tutor. All writers benefit from sincere, constructive advice during the revision process. This chapter will introduce you to valuable revising guidelines and strategies to use in all of your writing.

Addressing Whole-Paper Issues

When revising, first look at the big picture. Take it all in. Determine whether the content is interesting, informative, and worth sharing. Note any gaps or soft spots in your line of thinking. Ask yourself how you can improve what you have done so far. The information that follows will help you address whole-paper issues such as these.

Revisit your rhetorical situation.

Remember why you are writing—your purpose. Are you entertaining readers, sharing information, recalling an experience, explaining a process, or arguing a point? Does your writing achieve that purpose? Also, consider your readers. How much do they know about the subject? What else do they need to know? Finally, revisit the subject. Has your draft addressed the topic fully and clearly?

Consider your overall approach.

Sometimes it's better to start fresh if your writing contains stretches of uninspired ideas. Consider a fresh start if your first draft shows one of these problems:

The topic is worn-out. An essay titled "Lead Poisoning" may not sound very interesting. Unless you can approach it with a new twist ("Get the Lead Out!"), consider cutting your losses and finding a fresh topic.

The approach is stale. If you've been writing primarily to get a good grade, finish the assignment, or sound cool, start again. Try writing to learn something, prompt real thinking in readers, or touch a chord.

Your voice is predictable or fake. Avoid the bland "A good time was had by all" or the phony academic "When one studies this significant problem in considerable depth . . . " Be real. Be honest.

The draft sounds boring. Maybe it's boring because you pay an equal amount of attention to everything and hence stress nothing. Try condensing less important material and expanding what's important.

The essay is formulaic. In other words, it follows the "five-paragraph" format. This handy organizing frame may prevent you from doing justice to your topic and thinking. If your draft is dragged down by rigid adherence to a formula, try a more original approach.

TIP: To energize your writing, try these strategies:
- Freewrite to find a new angle or approach to the topic.
- Review your research notes for additional interesting details.
- List and respond to arguments opposed to your thesis.

Revising Your First Draft

Revising helps you turn your first draft into a more complete, thoughtful piece of writing. The following information will help you do that.

Prepare to revise.

Once you've finished a first draft, set it aside (ideally for a few days) until you can look at the draft objectively and make needed changes. If you drafted on paper, photocopy the draft. If you drafted on a computer, print your paper (double-spaced). Then make changes with a good pencil or colored pen. If you prefer revising on the computer, consider using your software editing program. In all cases, save your first draft for reference.

Think globally.

When revising, focus on the big picture—the overall strength of the ideas, organization, and voice.

Ideas: Check your thesis, focus, or theme. Has your thinking on your topic changed? Also think about your readers' most pressing questions concerning this topic. Have you answered these questions? Finally, consider your reasoning and support. Are both complete and sound?

Organization: Check the overall design of your writing, making sure that ideas move smoothly and logically from one point to the next. Does your essay build effectively? Do you shift directions cleanly? Fix structural problems in one of these ways:

- Reorder material to improve the sequence.
- Cut information that doesn't support the thesis.
- Add details where the draft is thin.
- Rewrite parts that seem unclear.
- Improve links between points by using transitions.

Voice: Voice is your personal presence on the page, the tone and attitude that others hear when reading your work. In other words, voice is the between-the-lines message your readers get (whether you want them to or not). When revising, make sure that the tone of your message matches your purpose, whether it is serious, playful, or satiric.

INSIGHT: Don't pay undue attention to spelling, grammar, and punctuation at this early stage in the process. Otherwise, you may become distracted from the task at hand: improving the content of your writing. Editing and proofreading come later.

Revising for Ideas and Organization

As you review your draft for content, make sure the ideas are fully developed and the organization is clear. From your main claim or thesis to your reasoning and your evidence, strengthen your thinking and sequencing.

Examine your ideas.

Review the ideas in your writing, making sure that each point is logical, complete, and clear. To test the logic in your writing, see pages 267–270.

Complete Thinking

Have you answered readers' basic questions? Have you supported the thesis? The original passage below is too general; the revision is clearly more complete.

Original Passage (Too general)

As soon as you receive a minor cut, the body's healing process begins to work. Blood from tiny vessels fills the wound and begins to clot. In less than 24 hours, a scab forms.

Revised Version (More specific)

As soon as you receive a minor cut, the body's healing process begins to work. In a simple wound, the first and second layers of skin are severed along with tiny blood vessels called capillaries. As these vessels bleed into the wound, minute structures called platelets help stop the bleeding by sticking to the edges of the cut and to one another, forming a plug. The platelets then release chemicals that react with certain proteins in the blood to form a clot. The blood clot, with its fiber network, begins to join the edges of the wound together. As the clot dries out, a scab forms, usually in less than 24 hours.

Clear Thesis

Make sure that your writing centers on one main issue or thesis. Although this next original passage lacks a thesis, the revision has a clear one.

Original Passage (Lacks a thesis)

Teen magazines are popular with young girls. These magazines contain a lot of how-to articles about self-image, fashion, and boy-girl relationships. Girls read them to get advice on how to act and how to look. Girls who don't really know what they want are the most eager readers.

Revised Version (Identifies a specific thesis statement)

Adolescent girls often see teen magazines as handbooks on how to be teenagers. These magazines influence the ways they act and the ways they look. For girls who are unsure of themselves, these magazines can exert an enormous amount of influence. Unfortunately, the advice these magazines give about self-image, fashion, and boys may do more harm than good.

Examine your organization.

Good writing has structure. It leads readers logically and clearly from one point to the next. When revising for organization, consider four areas: the overall plan, the opening, the flow of ideas, and the closing.

Overall Plan

Look closely at the sequence of ideas or events that you share. Does that sequence advance your thesis? Do the points build effectively? Are there gaps in the support or points that stray from your original purpose? If you find such problems, consider the following actions:

- Refine the focus or emphasis by rearranging material within the text.
- Fill in the gaps with new material. Go back to your planning notes.
- Delete material that wanders away from your purpose.
- Use an additional (or different) method of organization. For example, if you are comparing two subjects, add depth to your analysis by contrasting them as well. If you are describing a complex subject, show the subject more clearly and fully by distinguishing and classifying its parts. (See pages 62–65 for more on organizational methods.)

INSIGHT: What is the best method of organization for your essay? The writing you are doing will usually determine the choice. As you know, a personal narrative is often organized by time. Typically, however, you combine and customize methods to develop a writing idea. For example, within a comparison essay you may do some describing or classifying. See pages 46–47 and 118 for more on the common methods of development.

Opening Ideas

Reread your opening paragraph(s). Is the opening organized effectively? Does it engage readers, establish a direction for your writing, and express your thesis or focus? The original opening below doesn't build to a compelling thesis statement, but the revised version engages the reader and leads to the thesis.

Original Opening (Lacks interest and direction)

The lack of student motivation is a common subject in the news. Educators want to know how to get students to learn. Today's higher standards mean that students will be expected to learn even more. Another problem in urban areas is that large numbers of students are dropping out. How to interest students is a challenge.

Revised Version (Effectively leads readers into the essay)

How can we motivate students to learn? How can we get them to meet today's rising standards of excellence? How can we, in fact, keep students in school long enough to learn? The answer to these problems is quite simple. Give them money. Pay students to study and learn and stay in school.

Flow of Ideas

Look closely at the beginnings and endings of each paragraph. Have you connected your thoughts clearly? (See page 85 for a list of transition words.) The original opening words of the paragraph sequence below, from an essay of description, offer no links for readers. The revised versions use strong transitions indicating spatial organization (order by location).

Original First Words in the Four Middle Paragraphs

There was a huge, steep hill . . .
Buffalo Creek ran . . .
A dense "jungle" covering . . .
Within walking distance from my house . . .

Revised Versions (Words and phrases connect ideas)

Behind the house, there was a huge, steep hill . . .
Across the road from the house, Buffalo Creek ran . . .
On the far side of the creek bank was a dense "jungle" covering . . .
Up the road, within walking distance from my house . . .

INSIGHT: Review "Supporting Your Claims" (pages 264–266) and use those strategies to strengthen weak or unconvincing passages.

Closing Ideas

Reread your closing paragraph(s). Do you offer an effective summary, reassert your main point in a fresh way, and provide readers with food for thought as they leave your writing? Or is your ending abrupt, repetitive, or directionless? The original ending below is uninspiring; it adds little to the main part of the writing. The revision summarizes the main points in the essay and then urges the reader to think again about the overall point of writing.

Original Ending (Sketchy and flat)

Native Son deals with a young man's struggle against racism. It shows the effects of prejudice. Everyone should read this book.

Revised Version (Effectively ends the writing)

Native Son deals with a young man's struggle in a racist society, but also with so much more. It shows how prejudice affects people, how it closes in on them, and what some people will do to find a way out. Anyone who wants to better understand racism in the United States should read this book.

TIP: To generate fresh ideas for your closing, freewrite answers to questions like these: Why is the topic important to me? What should my readers have learned? Why should this issue matter to readers? What evidence or appeal (pages 272–273) will help readers remember my message and act on it? How does the topic relate to broader issues in society, history, or life?

Revising for Voice and Style

Generally, readers more fully trust writing that speaks in an informed voice and a clear, natural style. To develop an informed voice, make sure that your details are correct and complete; to develop a clear style, make sure that your writing is well organized and unpretentious. Check the issues below. (For a definition of voice, see page **73**.)

Check the level of commitment.

Consider how and to what degree your writing shows that you care about the topic and reader. For example, note how the original passage below lacks a personal voice, revealing nothing about the writer's connection to—or interest in—the topic. In contrast, the revision shows that the writer cares about the topic.

Original Passage (Lacks voice)

Cemeteries can teach us a lot about history. They make history seem more real. There is an old grave of a Revolutionary War veteran in the Union Grove Cemetery. . . .

Revised Version (Personal, sincere voice)

I've always had a special feeling for cemeteries. It's hard to explain any further than that, except to say history never seems quite as real as it does when I walk among many old gravestones. One day I discovered the grave of a Revolutionary War veteran. . . .

Check the intensity of your writing.

All writing—including academic writing—is enriched by an appropriate level of intensity, or even passion. In the original passage below, the writer's concern for the topic is unclear because the piece sounds neutral. In contrast, the revised version exudes energy.

Original Passage (Lacks feeling and energy)

Motz blames Barbie dolls for all the problems that women face today. Instead, one should look to romance novels, fashion magazines, and parental training for causes of these societal problems.

Revised Version (Expresses real feelings)

In other words, Motz uses Barbie as a scapegoat for problems that have complex causes. However, a girl's interest in romance is no more Barbie's fault than the fault of books like *On the Shores of Silver Lake*. Fashion magazines targeted at adolescents are the cause of far more anorexia than is Barbie. And mothers who encourage daughters to find security in men teach female dependency, but Barbie doesn't.

INSIGHT: To develop your personal writing voice, begin each writing assignment by freely recording your thoughts and feelings about the topic.

Develop an academic style.

Most college writing requires an academic style. Such a style isn't stuffy; you're not trying to impress readers with ten-dollar words. Rather, you are using language that facilitates a thoughtful, engaged discussion of the topic. To choose the best words for such a conversation, consider the issues that follow.

Personal Pronouns

In some academic writing, personal pronouns are acceptable. Such is the case in informal writing, such as reading responses, and in personal essays involving narration, description, and reflection. In addition, *I* is correctly used in academic writing rooted in personal research, sometimes called an *I-search paper.*

Generally, however, avoid using *I, we,* and *you* in traditional academic writing. The concept, instead, is to focus on the topic itself and let your attitude be revealed indirectly. As E. B. White puts it, "To achieve style, begin by affecting none—that is, begin by placing yourself in the background."

No: I really think that the problem of the homeless in Chicago is serious, given the number of people who are dying, as I know from my experience where I grew up.

Yes: Homelessness in Chicago often leads to death. This fact demands the attention of more than lawmakers and social workers; all citizens must address the problems of their suffering neighbors.

> **TIP:** Use the pronoun *one* carefully in academic prose. When it means "a person," *one* can lead to a stilted style if overused. In addition, the pronoun *their* (a plural pronoun) should not be used with *one* (a singular pronoun).

Technical Terms and Jargon

Technical terms and jargon—"insider" words—can be the specialized vocabulary of a subject, a discipline, a profession, or a social group. As such, jargon can be difficult to read for "outsiders." Follow these guidelines:

- Use technical terms to communicate with people within the profession or discipline as a kind of shorthand. However, be careful that such jargon doesn't devolve into meaningless buzzwords and catchphrases.
- Avoid jargon when writing for readers outside the profession or discipline. Use simpler terms and define technical terms that must be used.

Technical: Bin's Douser power washer delivers 2200 psi p.r., runs off standard a.c. lines, comes with 100 ft. h.d. synthetic-rubber tubing, and features variable pulsation options through three adjustable s.s. tips.

Simple: Bin's Douser power washer has a pressure rating of 2200 psi (pounds per square inch), runs off a common 200-volt electrical circuit, comes with 100 feet of hose, and includes three nozzles.

Level of Formality

Most academic writing (especially research papers, literary analyses, lab reports, and argumentative essays) should meet the standards of formal English. **Formal English** is characterized by a serious tone; careful attention to word choice; longer and more complex sentences reflecting complex thinking; strict adherence to traditional conventions of grammar, mechanics, and punctuation; and avoidance of contractions.

> Formal English, modeled in this sentence, is worded correctly and carefully so that it can withstand repeated readings without seeming tiresome, sloppy, or cute.

You may write other papers (personal essays, commentaries, journals, and reviews) in which informal English is appropriate. **Informal English** is characterized by a personal tone, the occasional use of popular expressions, shorter sentences with slightly looser syntax, contractions, and personal references (*I, we, you*), but it still adheres to basic conventions.

> Informal English sounds like one person talking to another person (in a somewhat relaxed setting). It's the type of language you are reading now. It sounds comfortable and real, not affected or breezy.

> **TIP:** In academic writing, generally avoid slang—words considered outside standard English because they are faddish, familiar to few people, and sometimes insulting.

Unnecessary Qualifiers

Using qualifiers (such as *mostly, often, likely,* or *tends to*) is an appropriate strategy for developing defendable claims in argumentative writing. (See pages 262–263.) However, when you "overqualify" your ideas or add intensifiers (*really, truly*), the result is insecurity—the impression that you lack confidence in your ideas. The cure? Say what you mean, and mean what you say.

> **Insecure:** I totally and completely agree with the new security measures at sporting events, but that's only my opinion.

> **Secure:** I agree with the new security measures at sporting events.

 Each academic discipline has its own vocabulary and its own vocabulary resources. Such resources include dictionaries, glossaries, or handbooks. Check your library for the vocabulary resources in your discipline. Use them regularly to deepen your grasp of that vocabulary.

Know when to use the passive voice.

Most verbs can be in either the active or the passive voice. When a verb is active, the sentence's subject performs the action. When the verb is passive, the subject is acted upon.

> **Active:** If you *can't attend* the meeting, *notify* Richard by Thursday.
>
> **Passive:** If a meeting *can't be attended* by you, Richard *must be notified* by Thursday.

Weaknesses of Passive Voice: The passive voice tends to be wordy and sluggish because the verb's action is directed backward, not ahead. In addition, passive constructions tend to be impersonal, making people disappear.

> **Passive:** The sound system *can* now *be used* to listen in on sessions in the therapy room. Parents *can be helped* by having constructive one-on-one communication methods with children modeled by therapists.
>
> **Active:** Parents *can* now *use* the sound system to listen in on sessions in the therapy room. Therapists *can help* parents by modeling constructive one-on-one communication methods with children.

Strengths of Passive Voice: Using the passive voice isn't wrong. In fact, the passive voice has some important uses: (1) when you need to be tactful (say, in a bad-news letter), (2) if you wish to stress the object or person acted upon, and (3) if the actual actor is understood, unknown, or unimportant.

> **Active:** Our engineers determined that you *bent* the bar at the midpoint.
>
> **Passive:** Our engineers determined that the bar *had been bent* at the midpoint. (tactful)
>
> **Active:** Congratulations! We *have approved* your scholarship for $2,500.
>
> **Passive:** Congratulations! Your scholarship for $2,500 *has been approved*. (emphasis on receiver; actor understood)

TIP: Avoid using the passive voice unethically to hide responsibility. For example, an instructor who says, "Your assignments could not be graded because of scheduling difficulties," might be trying to evade the truth: "I did not finish grading your assignments because I was watching *CSI*."

Addressing Paragraph Issues

While drafting, you may have constructed paragraphs that are loosely held together, poorly developed, or unclear. When you revise, take a close look at your paragraphs for focus, unity, and coherence (pages 82–84).

Remember the basics.

A paragraph should be a concise unit of thought. Revise a paragraph until it . . .

- Is organized around a controlling idea—often stated in a topic sentence.
- Consists of supporting sentences that develop the controlling idea.
- Concludes with a sentence that summarizes the main point and prepares readers for the next paragraph or main point.
- Serves a specific function in a piece of writing—opening, supporting, developing, illustrating, countering, describing, or closing.

SAMPLE PARAGRAPH

Topic sentence ----- Tumor cells can hurt the body in a number of ways. First, a tumor can grow so big that it takes up space needed by other organs. Second, some cells may detach from the original tumor and spread throughout the body, creating new tumors elsewhere. This happens with lymphatic cancer—a cancer that's hard to control because it spreads so quickly. A third way that **Supporting sentences** tumor cells can hurt the body is by doing work not called for in their DNA. For example, a gland cell's DNA code may tell the cell to produce a necessary hormone in the endocrine system. However, if cancer damages or distorts that code, sick cells may produce more of the hormone than the body can **Closing sentence** use—or even tolerate (Braun 4). Cancer cells seem to have minds of their own, and this is why cancer is such a serious disease.

Keep the purpose in mind.

Use these questions to evaluate the purpose and function of each paragraph:

- What function does the paragraph fulfill? How does it add to your line of reasoning or the development of your thesis?
- Would the paragraph work better if it were divided in two—or combined with another paragraph?
- Does the paragraph flow smoothly from the previous paragraph, and does it lead effectively into the next one?

Check for unity.

A unified paragraph is one in which all the details help to develop a single main topic or achieve a single main effect. Test for unity by following these guidelines.

Topic Sentence

Very often the topic of a paragraph is stated in a single sentence called a "topic sentence." Check whether your paragraph needs a topic sentence. If the paragraph has a topic sentence, determine whether it is clear, specific, and well focused. Here is a formula for writing good topic sentences:

> **Formula:** A topic sentence = a limited topic + a specific feeling or thought about it.
>
> *Example:* The fear that Americans feel (limited topic) comes partly from the uncertainty related to this attack (a specific thought).

Placement of the Topic Sentence

Normally the topic sentence is the first sentence in the paragraph. However, it can appear elsewhere in a paragraph.

Middle Placement: Place a topic sentence in the middle when you want to build up to and then lead away from the key idea.

> During the making of *Apocalypse Now,* Eleanor Coppola created a documentary about the filming called *Hearts of Darkness: A Filmmaker's Apocalypse.* In the first film, the insane Colonel Kurtz has disappeared into the Cambodian jungle. As Captain Willard searches for Kurtz, the screen fills with horror. **However, as *Hearts of Darkness* relates, the horror portrayed in the fictional movie was being lived out by the production company.** For example, in the documentary, actor Larry Fishburne shockingly says, "War is fun. . . . Vietnam must have been so much fun." Then toward the end of the filming, actor Martin Sheen suffered a heart attack. When an assistant informed investors, the director exploded, "He's not dead unless I say he's dead."

End Placement: Place a topic sentence at the end when you want to build to a climax, as in a passage of narration or persuasion.

> When sportsmen stop to reflect on why they find fishing so enjoyable, most realize that what they love is the feel of a fish on the end of the line, not necessarily the weight of the fillets in their coolers. Fishing has undergone a slow evolution over the last century. While fishing used to be a way of putting food on the table, most of today's fishermen do so only for the relaxation that it provides. The barbed hook was invented to increase the quantity of fish a man could land so that he could better feed his family. **This need no longer exists, so barbed hooks are no longer necessary.**

Supporting Sentences

All the sentences in the body of a paragraph should support the topic sentence. The closing sentence, for instance, will often summarize the paragraph's main point or emphasize a key detail. If any sentences shift the focus away from the topic, revise the paragraph in one of the following ways:

- Delete the material from the paragraph.
- Rewrite the material so that it clearly supports the topic sentence.
- Create a separate paragraph based on the odd-man-out material.
- Revise the topic sentence so that it relates more closely to the support.

Consistent Focus

Examine the following paragraph about fishing hooks. The original topic sentence focuses on the point that some anglers prefer smooth hooks. However, the writer leaves this initial idea unfinished and turns to the issue of the cost of new hooks. In the revised version, unity is restored: The first paragraph completes the point about anglers who prefer smooth hooks; the second paragraph addresses the issue of replacement costs.

Original Paragraph (Lacks unity)

According to some anglers who do use smooth hooks, their lures perform better than barbed lures as long as they maintain a constant tension on the line. Smooth hooks can bite deeper than barbed hooks, actually providing a stronger hold on the fish. Some people have argued that replacing all of the barbed hooks in their tackle would be a costly operation.

Revised Version (Unified)

According to some anglers who do use smooth hooks, their lures perform better than barbed lures as long as the anglers maintain a constant tension on the line. Smooth hooks can bite deeper than barbed hooks, actually providing a stronger hold on the fish. These anglers testify that switching from barbed hooks has not noticeably reduced the number of fish that they are able to land. In their experience, and in my own, enjoyment of the sport is actually heightened by adding another challenge to playing the fish (maintaining line tension).

Some people have argued that replacing all of the barbed hooks in their tackle would be a costly operation. While this is certainly a concern, barbed hooks do not necessarily require replacement. With a simple set of pliers, the barbs on most conventional hooks can be bent down, providing a cost-free method of modifying one's existing tackle. . . .

Paragraphs that contain unrelated ideas lack unity and are hard to follow. As you review each paragraph for unity, ask yourself these questions: Is the topic of the paragraph clear? Does each sentence relate to the topic? Are the sentences organized in the best possible order?

Check for coherence.

When a paragraph is coherent, the parts stay together. A coherent paragraph flows smoothly because each sentence is connected to others by patterns in the language such as repetition and transitions. To strengthen the coherence in your paragraphs, check for the issues discussed below.

Effective Repetition

To achieve coherence in your paragraphs, consider using repetition—repeating words or synonyms where necessary to remind readers of what you have already said. You can also use parallelism—repeating phrase or sentence structures to show the relationships among ideas. At the same time, you will add a unifying rhythm to your writing.

Ineffective: The floor was littered with discarded soda cans, newspapers that were crumpled, and wrinkled clothes.

Effective: **The floor was littered with discarded soda cans, crumpled newspapers, and wrinkled clothes.** (Three parallel phrases are used.)

Ineffective: Reading the book was enjoyable; to write the critique was difficult.

Effective: **Reading the book was enjoyable; writing the critique was difficult.** (Two similar structures are repeated.)

Clear Transitions

Linking words and phrases like "next," "on the other hand," and "in addition" connect ideas by showing the relationship among them. There are transitions that show location and time, compare and contrast things, emphasize a point, conclude or summarize, and add or clarify information. (See page **85** for a list of linking words and phrases.) Note the use of transitions in the following examples:

- The paradox of Scotland is that violence had long been the norm in this now-peaceful land. In fact, the country was born, bred, and came of age in war. (The transition is used to emphasize a point.)

- The production of cement is a complicated process. First, the mixture of lime, silica, alumina, and gypsum is ground into very fine particles. (The transition is used to show time or order.)

INSIGHT: Another way to achieve coherence in your paragraphs is to use pronouns effectively. A pronoun forms a link to the noun it replaces and ties that noun (idea) to the ideas that follow. As always, don't overuse pronouns or rely too heavily on them in establishing coherence in your paragraphs.

Transitions and Linking Words

The words and phrases below can help you tie together words, phrases, sentences, and paragraphs.

WORDS USED TO SHOW LOCATION:

above	behind	down	on top of
across	below	in back of	onto
against	beneath	in front of	outside
along	beside	inside	over
among	between	into	throughout
around	beyond	near	to the right
away from	by	off	under

WORDS USED TO SHOW TIME:

about	during	next	today
after	finally	next week	tomorrow
afterward	first	second	until
as soon as	immediately	soon	when
at	later	then	yesterday
before	meanwhile	third	

WORDS USED TO COMPARE THINGS (SHOW SIMILARITIES):

also	in the same way	likewise
as	like	similarly

WORDS USED TO CONTRAST THINGS (SHOW DIFFERENCES):

although	even though	on the other hand	still
but	however	otherwise	yet

WORDS USED TO EMPHASIZE A POINT:

again	for this reason	particularly	to repeat
even	in fact	to emphasize	truly

WORDS USED TO CONCLUDE OR SUMMARIZE:

all in all	finally	in summary	therefore
as a result	in conclusion	last	to sum up

WORDS USED TO ADD INFORMATION:

additionally	and	equally important	in addition
again	another	finally	likewise
along with	as well	for example	next
also	besides	for instance	second

WORDS USED TO CLARIFY:

for instance	in other words	put another way	that is

Note: Use transitions to link, expand, or intensify an idea, but don't add elements carelessly, creating run-on or rambling sentences (pages 651–652).

Check for completeness.

The sentences in a paragraph should support and expand on the main point. If your paragraph does not seem complete, you will need to add information.

Supporting Details

If some of your paragraphs are incomplete, they may lack details. There are numerous kinds of details, including the following:

facts	anecdotes	analyses	paraphrases
statistics	quotations	explanations	comparisons
examples	definitions	summaries	analogies

Add details based on the type of writing you are engaged in.

Describing: Add details that help readers see, smell, taste, touch, or hear it.

Narrating: Add details that help readers understand the events and actions.

Explaining: Add details that help readers understand what it means, how it works, or what it does.

Persuading: Add details that strengthen the logic of your argument.

Specific Details

The original paragraph below fails to answer fully the question posed by the topic sentence. In the revised paragraph, the writer uses an anecdote to answer the question.

Original Paragraph (Lacks completeness)

So what is stress? Actually, the physiological characteristics of stress are some of the body's potentially good self-defense mechanisms. People experience stress when they are in danger. In fact, stress can be healthy.

Revised Version (Full development)

So what is stress? Actually, the physiological characteristics of stress are some of the body's potentially good self-defense mechanisms. Take, for example, a man who is crossing a busy intersection when he spots an oncoming car. Immediately his brain releases a flood of adrenaline into his bloodstream. As a result, his muscles contract, his eyes dilate, his heart pounds faster, his breathing quickens, and his blood clots more readily. Each one of these responses helps the man leap out of the car's path. His muscles contract to give him exceptional strength. His eyes dilate so that he can see more clearly. His heart pumps more blood and his lungs exchange more air—both to increase his metabolism. If the man were injured, his blood would clot faster, ensuring a smaller amount of blood loss. In this situation and many more like it, stress symptoms are good (Curtis 25–26).

INSIGHT: If a paragraph is getting long, divide it at a natural stopping point. The topic sentence can then function as the thesis for that part of your essay or paper.

Revising Collaboratively

Web Link

Every writer can benefit from feedback from an interested audience, especially one that offers constructive and honest advice during a writing project. Members of an existing writing group already know how valuable it is for writers to share their work. Others might want to start a writing group to experience the benefits. Your group might collaborate online or in person. In either case, the information on the next two pages will help you get started.

Know your role.

Writers and reviewers should know their roles and fulfill their responsibilities during revising sessions. Essentially, the writer should briefly introduce the draft and solicit honest responses. Reviewers should make constructive comments in response to the writing.

Provide appropriate feedback.

Feedback can take many forms, including the three approaches described here.

Basic Description: In this simple response, the reviewer listens or reads attentively and then simply describes what she or he hears or sees happening in the piece. The reviewer offers no criticism of the writing.

Ineffective: "That was interesting. The piece was informative."

Effective: "First, the essay introduced the challenge of your birth defect and how you have had to cope with it. Then in the next part you . . ."

Summary Evaluation: Here the reviewer reads or listens to the piece and then provides a specific evaluation of the draft.

Ineffective: "Gee, I really liked it!" or "It was boring."

Effective: "Your story at the beginning really pulled me in, and the middle explained the issue strongly, but the ending felt a bit flat."

Thorough Critique: The reviewer assesses the ideas, organization, and voice in the writing. Feedback should be detailed and constructive. Such a critique may also be completed with the aid of a review sheet or checklist. As a reviewer, be prepared to share specific responses, suggestions, and questions. But also be sure to focus your comments on the writing, rather than the writer.

Ineffective: "You really need to fix that opening! What were you thinking?"

Effective: "Let's look closely at the opening. Could you rewrite the first sentence so it grabs the reader's attention? Also, I'm somewhat confused about the thesis statement. Could you rephrase it so it states your position more clearly?"

Respond according to a plan.

Using a specific plan or scheme like the following will help you give clear, helpful, and complete feedback.

OAQS Method: Use this simple four-step scheme—**Observe, Appreciate, Question,** and **Suggest**—to respond to your peers' writing.

1. **Observe** means to notice what another person's essay is designed to do and say something about its design or purpose. For example, you might say, "Even though you are writing about your boyfriend, it appears that you are trying to get a message across to your parents."

2. **Appreciate** means to praise something in the writing that impresses or pleases you. You can find something to appreciate in any piece of writing. For example, you might say, "You make a very convincing point" or "With your description, I can actually see his broken tooth."

3. **Question** means to ask whatever you want to know after you've read the essay. You might ask for background information, a definition, an interpretation, or an explanation. For example, you might say, "Can you tell us what happened when you got to the emergency room?"

4. **Suggest** means to give helpful advice about possible changes. For example, you might say, "With a little more physical detail—especially more sounds and smells—your third paragraph could be the highlight of the whole essay. What do you think?"

ASKING THE WRITER QUESTIONS

Reviewers should ask the following types of questions while reviewing a piece of writing:

- **To help writers reflect on their purpose and audience . . .**
  Why are you writing this?
  Who will read this, and what do they need to know?

- **To help writers focus their thoughts . . .**
  What message are you trying to get across?
  Do you have more than one main point?
  What are the most important examples?

- **To help writers think about their information . . .**
  What do you know about the subject?
  Does this part say enough?
  Does your writing cover all of the basics (*Who? What? Where? When? Why?* and *How?*)?

- **To help writers with their openings and closings . . .**
  What are you trying to say in the opening?
  How else could you start your writing?
  How do you want your readers to feel at the end?

Using the Writing Center

A college writing center or lab is a place where a trained adviser will help you develop and strengthen a piece of writing. You can expect the writing center adviser to do certain things; other things only you can do. For quick reference, refer to the chart below.

Web Link

ADVISER'S JOB	**YOUR JOB**
Make you feel at home	Be respectful
Discuss your needs	Be ready to work
Help you choose a topic.	Decide on a topic
Discuss your purpose and audience.	Know your purpose and audience
Help you generate ideas.	Embrace the best ideas
Help you develop your logic	Consider other points of view; stretch your own perspective
Help you understand how to research your material	Do the research
Read your draft.	Share your writing
Identify problems in organization, logic, expression, and format	Recognize and fix problems
Teach ways to correct weaknesses	Learn important principles
Help you with grammar, usage, diction, vocabulary, and mechanics	Correct all errors

---

TIPS for getting the most out of the writing center

- Visit the center at least several days before your paper is due.
- Take your assignment sheet with you to each advising session.
- Read your work aloud, slowly.
- Expect to rethink your writing from scratch.
- Do not defend your wording—if it needs defense, it needs revision.
- Ask questions. (No question is "too dumb.")
- Request clarification of anything you don't understand.
- Ask for examples or illustrations of important points.
- Write down all practical suggestions.
- Ask the adviser to summarize his or her remarks.
- Rewrite as soon as possible after—or even during—the advising session.
- Return to the writing center for a response to your revisions.

Writing with Sources

When your writing project involves working with sources, test your first draft for effective use of researched material. You can do this by examining how well references to sources advance your thesis and enrich your ideas.

Think rhetorically.

At the beginning of this chapter, you were instructed to revisit your project's rhetorical situation: your purpose, your audience, and your subject. When revising your paper, consider how well your sources help you achieve that purpose, reach that audience, and thoroughly address that subject. Specifically, assess your first draft by asking questions like these:

- Will readers accept my sources and how I used them, or will they question my reasoning and evidence? What alternatives, objections, or questions might they raise?
- Does my writing encourage readers to think thoroughly about my topic? Do I need to add more background details, definitions, and contextual information?
- Do my sources get at essential, deep truths about my subject, or do they simply offer basic data or common knowledge?

Depending on your answers to these questions, you may have to reread your notes and sources, or you may have to look for additional information.

Practice revising strategies.

To improve source use in your paper as you revise, try strategies like these:

Test the balance of reasoning and support. Examine the big picture of how you have used source material—summaries, paraphrases, and quotations—in relation to your own discussion of the issue. If your draft is thin on the support side (filled with big claims that lack adequate support), you need to either scale back your claims or beef up the support with more information and evidence.

Conversely, your draft may be dominated by source material, not your own thinking. If your paper reads like a series of source summaries or loosely stitched together quotations, if it contains big patches of copy-and-paste material, if your paragraphs all seem to start and end with source material, or if your writing is dense with detailed but almost incomprehensible data, you may need to deepen your own contribution to the paper. Do so by trying the following:

1. Before diving into source material within a paragraph or section of your paper, flesh out your thinking more fully. Offer reasoning that elaborates the claim and effectively leads into the evidence.
2. As you present evidence from source material, build on it by explaining what it means. Evidence doesn't typically speak for itself: through

analysis, synthesis, illustration, contrast, and other means, you need to show how or why your sources advance your thesis.

3. After you have presented evidence that elaborates on and supports your idea, extend your thoughts by addressing the reader's "So what?" or "Why does this matter?" skepticism.

Test your evidence. Review your draft by examining how well your researched information expands on and backs up your points or claims. That evidence should be solid enough to encourage readers to accept your ideas; weak evidence will lead readers to reject your analysis or argument. Specifically, the evidence should be

- **accurate:** The information is all correct.
- **precise:** The data are concrete and specific, not vague and general.
- **substantial:** The amount of evidence reaches a critical mass—enough to convey the idea and convince readers of its validity.
- **authoritative:** The evidence comes from a reliable source. Moreover, the information is as close to the origin as possible; it is not a report conveying thirdhand or fourthhand information.
- **representative:** The information fairly represents the range of data on the issue. Your presentation of evidence is balanced.
- **fitting:** Given your purpose, the topic, and your reader, the evidence is appropriate and relevant for the question or issue you are discussing.

Test the flow of information. Generally, your writing with source material should follow the known/new principle. Because readers "build" meaning as they proceed through your writing, your paper's overall structure, its sections, and its paragraphs should all be built so that new information emerges gradually and is linked to information the reader already knows. Make sure your draft unfolds this way.

Test for plagiarism. Going back to your notes and sources as needed, check that you have clearly indicated which material in your draft is summarized, paraphrased, or quoted from a source. In particular, check that your attributive phrases and citations set off all source material except for common knowledge. (For more help with this issue, see pages 486–489.)

Cross-Curricular Connections

Different disciplines treat evidence differently; in fact, each field values certain types of evidence and reasoning more highly than other types. For example, humanities disciplines might value close interpretations of texts and documents, social sciences might prefer statistics and case studies, and natural sciences would value quantitative evidence gathered through the scientific method in lab experiments and in field work. As you write papers for your major, make sure that you use types of evidence and methods of analysis that this research community accepts and respects.

Revising Checklist

Use this checklist as a guide when you revise your writing. (To see revising in action, turn to pages 124–127.)

Ideas

_____ My writing has a clear thesis, focus, or theme.

_____ I have fully developed and supported that thesis with relevant, accurate, well-researched details.

Organization

_____ My writing follows a clear pattern of organization that advances the main idea.

_____ I have added, cut, reordered, and rewritten material as needed.

_____ All of the paragraphs are unified, coherent, and complete.

Voice

_____ The tone is matched to the assignment, the reader, and the purpose.

_____ The style is clear, genuine, and appropriately academic.

_____ My voice sounds energetic and interested.

Critical-Thinking and Writing Activities

As directed by your instructor, complete the following critical-thinking and writing activities by yourself or with classmates.

1. Doris Lessing has stated that when it comes to writing, "The more a thing cooks, the better." In what sense is revision a crucial stage in that cooking process? Using Lessing's cooking metaphor as a starting point, explore how revision should function in your own writing.

2. Review the opening and closing paragraphs of one of your essays. Then come up with fresh and different approaches for those paragraphs using the information on pages 75–76 as a guide.

3. For your current writing assignment, ask a peer to provide detailed feedback using the information in this chapter as a guide. Then take a fresh copy of your paper to the writing center and work through your draft with an adviser. Revise the draft as needed.

◄ VISUALLY SPEAKING

Review the photograph on page 71. Then explain in writing how the potter's work shown in the picture might be similar to (or different from) your work when revising an essay.

EDITING AND PROOFREADING

Video

In any writing project, there comes a point (like a fast-approaching due date) when you must prepare your writing for submission. At that time you must edit and proofread your revised writing so that it speaks clearly and accurately. When you edit, look first for words, phrases, and sentences that sound awkward, uninteresting, or unclear. When you proofread, check your writing for spelling, mechanics, usage, and grammar errors.

Before you begin, make sure you have the proper tools: handbook, dictionary, thesaurus, computer spell checker, and so on. Also, ask one of your writing peers to help you edit your work. Then prepare your final draft, following the guidelines established by your instructor, and proofread it for errors.

The guidelines and strategies given in this chapter will help you to edit your writing for style and clarity and to proofread it for errors.

Editing Your Revised Draft

When you have thoroughly revised your writing, you need to edit it so as to make it clear and concise enough to present to readers. Use the editing guidelines below to check your revised draft.

Review the overall style of your writing.

1. Read your revised writing aloud. Better yet, have a writing peer read it aloud to you. Highlight any writing that doesn't read smoothly and naturally.

2. Check that your style fits the rhetorical situation.

> **Goal:** Does your writing sound as if you wrote it with a clear aim in mind? Do the sentence style and word choice match the goal?
>
> **Reader:** Is the tone sincere? Does the writing sound authentic and honest?
>
> **Subject:** Does the writing suit the subject and your treatment of it in terms of seriousness or playfulness, complexity or simplicity?

3. Examine your sentences. Check them for clarity, conciseness, and variety. Replace sentences that are wordy or rambling; combine or expand sentences that are short and choppy. Also, vary the beginnings of your sentences and avoid sentence patterns that are too predictable. (See pages 95–101.)

Consider word choice.

1. Avoid redundancy. Be alert for words or phrases that are used together but mean nearly the same thing.

> repeat again   red in color   refer back

2. Watch for repetition. When used appropriately, repetition can add rhythm and coherence to your writing. When used ineffectively, however, it can be a real distraction.

> **The man** looked as if he were in his late seventies. **The man** was dressed in an old suit. I soon realized that **the man** was homeless. . . .

3. Look for general nouns, verbs, and modifiers. Specific words are much more effective than general ones. (See page 102.)

> The girl moved on the bench. (general)
>
> Rosie slid quietly to the end of the park bench. (specific)

4. Avoid highly technical terms. Check for jargon or technical terms that your readers will not know or that you haven't adequately explained. (See page 103.)

> As the **capillaries** bleed, **platelets** work with **fibrinogens** to form a clot.

5. Use fair language. Replace words or phrases that are biased or demeaning. (See pages 104–106.)

Combining Sentences

Effective sentences often contain several basic ideas that work together to show relationships and make connections. Here are five basic ideas followed by seven examples of how they can be combined into effective sentences.

1. The longest and largest construction project in history was the Great Wall of China.

2. The project took 1,700 years to complete.

3. The Great Wall of China is 1,400 miles long.

4. It is between 18 and 30 feet high.

5. It is up to 32 feet wide.

Edit short, simplistic sentences.

Combine your short, simplistic sentences into longer, more detailed sentences. Sentence combining is generally carried out in the following ways:

- Use a **series** to combine three or more similar ideas.

  The Great Wall of China is **1,400 miles long,** between **18 and 30 feet high,** and up to **32 feet wide.**

- Use a **relative pronoun** (*who, whose, that, which*) to introduce subordinate (less important) ideas.

  The Great Wall of China, **which is 1,400 miles long and between 18 and 30 feet high,** took 1,700 years to complete.

- Use an **introductory phrase** or **clause**.

  Having taken 1,700 years to complete, the Great Wall of China was the longest construction project in history.

- Use a **semicolon** (and a conjunctive adverb if appropriate).

  The Great Wall took 1,700 years to complete**;** it is 1,400 miles long and up to 30 feet high and 32 feet wide.

- Repeat a **key word** or phrase to emphasize an idea.

  The Great Wall of China was the longest construction **project** in history, a **project** that took 1,700 years to complete.

- Use **correlative conjunctions** (*either, or; not only, but also*) to compare or contrast two ideas in a sentence.

  The Great Wall of China is **not only** up to 30 feet high and 32 feet wide, **but also** 1,400 miles long.

- Use an **appositive** (a word or phrase that renames) to emphasize an idea.

  The Great Wall of China—**the largest construction project in history**—is 1,400 miles long, 32 feet wide, and up to 30 feet high.

Expanding Sentences

Expand sentences when you edit so as to connect related ideas and make room for new information. Length has no value in and of itself: The best sentence is still the shortest one that says all it has to say. An expanded sentence, however, is capable of saying more—and saying it more expressively.

Use cumulative sentences.

Modern writers often use an expressive sentence form called the cumulative sentence. A cumulative sentence is made of a general "base clause" that is expanded by adding modifying words, phrases, or clauses. In such a sentence, details are added before and after the main clause, creating an image-rich thought. Here's an example of a cumulative sentence, with the base clause or main idea in boldface:

In preparation for her Spanish exam, **Julie was studying** at the kitchen table, completely focused, memorizing a list of vocabulary words.

Discussion: Notice how each new modifier adds to the richness of the final sentence. Also notice that each of these modifying phrases is set off by a comma. Here's another sample sentence:

With his hands on his face, **Tony was laughing** half-heartedly, looking puzzled and embarrassed.

Discussion: Such a cumulative sentence provides a way to write description that is rich in detail, without rambling. Notice how each modifier changes the flow or rhythm of the sentence.

Expand with details.

Here are seven basic ways to expand a main idea:

1. with **adjectives and adverbs:** *half-heartedly, once again*

2. with **prepositional phrases:** *with his hands on his face*

3. with **absolute phrases:** *his head tilted to one side*

4. with **participial (-ing or -ed) phrases:** *looking puzzled*

5. with **infinitive phrases:** *to hide his embarrassment*

6. with **subordinate clauses:** *while his friend talks*

7. with **relative clauses:** *who isn't laughing at all*

INSIGHT: To edit sentences for more expressive style, it is best to (1) know your grammar and punctuation (especially commas); (2) practice tightening, combining, and expanding sentences using the guidelines in this chapter; and (3) read carefully, looking for models of well-constructed sentences.

Checking for Sentence Style

Writer E. B. White advised young writers to "approach sentence style by way of simplicity, plainness, orderliness, and sincerity." That's good advice from a writer steeped in style. It's also important to know what to look for when editing your sentences. The information on this page and the following four pages will help you edit your sentences for style and correctness.

Avoid these sentence problems.

Always check for and correct the following types of sentence problems. Turn to the pages listed below for guidelines and examples when attempting to fix problems in your sentences.

Short, Choppy Sentences: Combine or expand any short, choppy sentences; use the examples and guidelines on page 95.

Flat, Predictable Sentences: Rewrite any sentences that sound predictable and uninteresting by varying their structures and expanding them with modifying words, phrases, and clauses. (See pages 98–100.)

Incorrect Sentences: Look carefully for fragments, run-ons, and comma splices and correct them accordingly. (See pages 651–652.)

Unclear Sentences: Edit any sentences that contain unclear wording, misplaced modifiers, dangling modifiers, or incomplete comparisons. (See pages 653–654.)

Unacceptable Sentences: Change sentences that include nonstandard language, double negatives, or unparallel construction. (See page 655.)

Unnatural Sentences: Rewrite sentences that contain jargon, clichés, or flowery language. (See page 103.)

Review your writing for sentence variety.

Use the following strategy to review your writing for variety in terms of sentence beginnings, lengths, and types.

- In one column on a piece of paper, list the opening words in each of your sentences. Then decide if you need to vary some of your sentence beginnings.
- In another column, identify the number of words in each sentence. Then decide if you need to change the lengths of some of your sentences.
- In a third column, list the kinds of sentences used (exclamatory, declarative, interrogative, and so on). Then, based on your analysis, use the instructions on the next two pages to edit your sentences as needed.

Vary sentence structures.

To energize your sentences, vary their structures using one or more of the methods shown on this page and the next.

1. Vary sentence openings. Move a modifying word, phrase, or clause to the front of the sentence to stress that modifier. However, avoid creating dangling or misplaced modifiers. (See page **653**.)

The norm:	We apologize for the inconvenience this may have caused you.
Variation:	For the inconvenience this may have caused you, we apologize.

2. Vary sentence lengths. Short sentences (ten words or fewer) are ideal for making points crisply. Medium sentences (ten to twenty words) should carry the bulk of your information. When well crafted, occasional long sentences (more than twenty words) can develop and expand your ideas.

Short:	Welcome back to Magnolia Suites!
Medium:	Unfortunately, your confirmed room was unavailable last night when you arrived. For the inconvenience this may have caused you, we apologize.
Long:	Because several guests did not depart as scheduled, we were forced to provide you with accommodations elsewhere; however, for your trouble, we were happy to cover the cost of last night's lodging.

3. Vary sentence kinds. The most common sentence is declarative—it states a point. For variety, try exclamatory, imperative, interrogative, and conditional statements.

Exclamatory:	Our goal is providing you with outstanding service!
Declarative:	To that end, we have upgraded your room at no expense.
Imperative:	Please accept, as well, this box of chocolates as a gift to sweeten your stay.
Interrogative:	Do you need further assistance?
Conditional:	If you do, we are ready to fulfill your requests.

INSIGHT: In creative writing (stories, novels, plays), writers occasionally use fragments to vary the rhythm of their prose, emphasize a point, or create dialogue. Avoid fragments in academic or business writing.

4. **Vary sentence arrangements.** Where do you want to place the main point of your sentence? You make that choice by arranging sentence parts into loose, periodic, balanced, or cumulative patterns. Each pattern creates a specific effect.

Loose Sentence

The Travel Center offers an attractive flight-reservation plan for students, one that allows you to collect bonus miles and receive $150,000 in life insurance per flight.

Analysis: This pattern is direct. It states the main point immediately (bold), and then tacks on extra information.

Periodic Sentence

Although this plan requires that you join the Travel Center's Student-Flight Club and pay the $10 admission fee, **in the long run you will save money!**

Analysis: This pattern postpones the main point (bold) until the end. The sentence builds to the point, creating an indirect, dramatic effect.

Balanced Sentence

Joining the club in your freshman year will save you money over your entire college career; in addition, **accruing bonus miles over four years will earn you a free trip to Europe!**

Analysis: This pattern gives equal weight to complementary or contrasting points (bold); the balance is often signaled by a comma and a conjunction (*and, but*) or by a semicolon. Often a conjunctive adverb (*however, nevertheless*) or a transitional phrase (*in addition, even so*) will follow the semicolon to further clarify the relationship.

Cumulative Sentence

Because the club membership is in your name, **you can retain its benefits** as long as you are a student, even if you transfer to a different college or go on to graduate school.

Analysis: This pattern puts the main idea (bold) in the middle of the sentence, surrounding it with modifying words, phrases, and clauses.

5. **Use positive repetition.** Although you should avoid needless repetition, you might use emphatic repetition to repeat a key word to stress a point.

Repetitive Sentence

Each year, more than a million young people who read poorly leave high school unable to read well, functionally illiterate.

Emphatic Sentence

Each year, more than a million young people leave high school functionally illiterate, so **illiterate** that they can't read daily newspapers, job ads, or safety instructions.

Use parallel structure.

Coordinated sentence elements should be parallel—that is, they should be written in the same grammatical forms. Parallel structures save words, clarify relationships, and present the information in the correct sequence. (See page 650.4.) Follow these guidelines.

1. For words, phrases, or clauses in a series, keep elements consistent.

> **Not parallel:** I have tutored students in Biology 101, also Chemistry 102, not to mention my familiarity with Physics 200.

> **Parallel:** I have tutored students in *Biology 101, Chemistry 102,* and *Physics 200.*

> **Not parallel:** I have volunteered as a hospital receptionist, have been a hospice volunteer, and as an emergency medical technician.

> **Parallel:** I have done volunteer work as *a hospital receptionist, a hospice counselor,* and *an emergency medical technician.*

2. Use both parts of correlative conjunctions *(either, or; neither, nor; not only, but also; as, so; whether, so; both, and)* so that both segments of the sentence are balanced (see pages 635.3 and 635.5).

> **Not parallel:** *Not only* did Blake College turn 20 this year. Its enrollment grew by 16 percent.

> **Parallel:** *Not only* did Blake College turn 20 this year, *but* its enrollment *also* grew by 16 percent.

3. Place a modifier correctly so that it clearly indicates the word or words to which it refers.

> **Confusing:** MADD promotes *severely* punishing and eliminating drunk driving because this offense leads to a *great number* of deaths and sorrow.

> **Parallel:** MADD promotes eliminating and *severely* punishing drunk driving because this offense leads to *many* deaths and *untold* sorrow.

4. Place contrasting details in parallel structures (words, phrases, or clauses) to stress a contrast.

> **Weak contrast:** The average child watches 24 hours of television a week and reads for 36 minutes.

> **Strong contrast:** Each week, the average child *watches television for 24 hours but reads for only about half an hour.*

Avoid weak constructions.

Avoid constructions (like those below) that weaken your writing.

Nominal Constructions

The nominal construction is both sluggish and wordy. Avoid it by changing the noun form of a verb (*description or instructions*) to a verb (*describe or instruct*). At the same time, delete the weak verb that preceded the noun.

NOMINAL CONSTRUCTIONS (NOUN FORM UNDERLINED)	STRONG VERBS
Tim gave a <u>description</u> . . . Lydia provided <u>instructions</u> . . .	Tim *described* . . . Lydia *instructed* . . .

Sluggish: John *had a discussion* with the tutors regarding the incident. They gave him their *confirmation* that similar developments had occurred before, but they had not *provided* submissions of their reports.

Energetic: John *discussed* the incident with the tutors. They *confirmed* that similar problems had developed before, but they hadn't *submitted* their reports.

Expletives

Expletives such as "it is" and "there is" are fillers that serve no purpose in most sentences—except to make them wordy and unnatural.

Sluggish: *It is* likely that Nathan will attend the Communication Department's Honors Banquet. *There is* a journalism scholarship that he might win.

Energetic: Nathan will likely attend the Communication Department's Honors Banquet and might win a journalism scholarship.

Negative Constructions

Sentences constructed upon the negatives *no, not, neither/nor* can be wordy and difficult to understand. It's simpler to state what *is* the case.

Negative: During my four years on the newspaper staff, *I have not been* behind in making significant contributions. My editorial skills *have* certainly *not deteriorated*, as I have *never failed* to tackle challenging assignments.

Positive: During my four years on the newspaper staff, *I have made* significant contributions. My editorial skills have steadily *developed* as *I have tackled* difficult assignments.

Web Link

Avoiding Imprecise, Misleading, and Biased Words

As you edit your writing, check your choice of words carefully. The information on the next five pages will help you edit for word choice.

Substitute specific words.

Replace vague nouns and verbs with words that generate clarity and energy.

Specific Nouns

Make it a habit to use specific nouns for subjects. General nouns *(woman, school)* give the reader a vague, uninteresting picture. More specific nouns *(actress, university)* give the reader a better picture. Finally, very specific nouns *(Meryl Streep, Notre Dame)* are the type that can make your writing clear and colorful.

GENERAL TO SPECIFIC NOUNS

Person	Place	Thing	Idea
woman	school	book	theory
actor	university	novel	scientific theory
Meryl Streep	Notre Dame	*Pride and Prejudice*	relativity

Vivid Verbs

Like nouns, verbs can be too general to create a vivid word picture. For example, the verb *looked* does not say the same thing as *stared, glared, glanced,* or *peeked.*

- Whenever possible, use a verb that is strong enough to stand alone without the help of an adverb.

  Verb and adverb: John fell down in the student lounge.
  Vivid verb: John **collapsed** in the student lounge.

- Avoid overusing the "be" verbs *(is, are, was, were)* and helping verbs. Often a main verb can be made from another word in the same sentence.

  A "be" verb: Cole is someone who follows international news.
  A stronger verb: Cole **follows** international news.

- Use active rather than passive verbs. (Use passive verbs only if you want to downplay who is performing the action in a sentence. See page 80.)

  Passive verb: Another provocative essay was submitted by Kim.
  Active verb: Kim **submitted** another provocative essay.

- Use verbs that show rather than tell.

  A verb that tells: Dr. Lewis is very thorough.
  A verb that shows: Dr. Lewis **prepares** detailed, interactive lectures.

Replace jargon and clichés.

Replace language that is overly technical or difficult to understand. Also replace overused, worn-out words.

Understandable Language

Jargon is language used in a certain profession or by a particular group of people. It may be acceptable to use if your audience is that group of people, but to most ears jargon will sound technical and unnatural.

Jargon: The bottom line is that our output is not within our game plan.

Clear: Production is not on schedule.

Jargon: I'm having conceptual difficulty with these academic queries.

Clear: I don't understand these review questions.

Jargon: Pursuant to our conversation, I have forwarded you a remittance attached herewith.

Clear: As we discussed, I am mailing you the check.

Fresh and Original Writing

Clichés are overused words or phrases. They give the reader no fresh view and no concrete picture. Because clichés spring quickly to mind (for both the writer and the reader), they are easy to write and often slip by.

an axe to grind	piece of cake
as good as dead	planting the seed
beat around the bush	rearing its ugly head
between a rock and a hard place	stick your neck out
burning bridges	throwing your weight around
easy as pie	up a creek

Purpose and Voice

Other aspects of your writing may also be tired and overworked. Be alert to the two types of clichés described below.

Clichés of Purpose:

- Sentimental papers gushing about an ideal friend or family member, or droning on about a moving experience
- Overused topics with recycled information and predictable examples

Clichés of Voice:

- Writing that assumes a false sense of authority: "I have determined that there are three basic types of newspapers. My preference is for the third."
- Writing that speaks with little or no sense of authority: "I flipped when I saw *Viewpoints*."

Change biased words.

When depicting individuals or groups according to their differences, you must use language that implies equal value and respect for all people.

Words Referring to Ethnicity

Acceptable General Terms	*Acceptable Specific Terms*
American Indians, Native Americans	**Cherokee people, Inuit people,** and so forth
Asian Americans (not *Orientals*)	**Chinese Americans, Japanese Americans,** and so forth
Latinos, Latinas, Hispanics	**Mexican Americans, Cuban Americans,** and so forth

African Americans, blacks
"African American" has come into wide acceptance, though the term "black" is preferred by some individuals.

Anglo Americans (English ancestry), **European Americans**
Use these terms to avoid the notion that "American," used alone, means "white."

ADDITIONAL REFERENCES

Not Recommended	*Preferred*
Eurasian, mulatto	**person of mixed ancestry**
nonwhite	**person of color**
Caucasian	**white**
American (to mean U.S. citizen)	**U.S. citizen**

Words Referring to Age

Age Group	*Acceptable Terms*
up to age 13 or 14	**boys, girls**
between 13 and 19	**youth, young people, young men, young women**
late teens and 20s	**young adults, young women, young men**
30s to age 60	**adults, men, women**
60 and older	**older adults, older people** (not *elderly*)
65 and older	**seniors** (**senior citizens** also acceptable)

INSIGHT: Whenever you write about a person with a disability, an impairment, or other special condition, give the person and your readers the utmost respect. Nothing is more distracting to a reader than an insensitive or outdated reference.

Words Referring to Disabilities or Impairments

In the recent past, some writers were choosing alternatives to the term *disabled,* including *physically challenged, exceptional,* or *special.* However, it is not generally held that these new terms are precise enough to serve those who live with disabilities. Of course, degrading labels such as *crippled, invalid,* and *maimed,* as well as overly negative terminology, must be avoided.

Not Recommended	*Preferred*
handicapped	**disabled**
birth defect	**congenital disability**
stutter, stammer, lisp	**speech impairment**
an AIDS victim	**person with AIDS**
suffering from cancer	**person who has cancer**
mechanical foot	**prosthetic foot**
false teeth	**dentures**

Words Referring to Conditions

People with various disabilities and conditions have sometimes been referred to as though they *were* their condition (*quadriplegics, depressives, epileptics*) instead of people who simply happen to have a particular disability. As much as possible, remember to refer to the person first, the disability second.

Not Recommended	*Preferred*
the disabled	**people with disabilities**
cripples	**people who have difficulty walking**
the retarded	**people with a developmental disability**
dyslexics	**students with dyslexia**
neurotics	**patients with neuroses**
subjects, cases	**participants, patients**
quadriplegics	**people who are quadriplegic**
wheelchair users	**people who use wheelchairs**

Additional Terms

Make sure you understand the following terms that address specific impairments:

hearing impairment	=	partial hearing loss, hard of hearing (not *deaf,* which is total loss of hearing)
visual impairment	=	partially sighted (not *blind,* which is total loss of vision)
communicative disorder	=	speech, hearing, and learning disabilities affecting communication

Words Referring to Gender

- Use parallel language for both sexes:

  The **men** and the **women** rebuilt the school together.

  Hank and **Marie**

  Mr. Robert Gumble, Mrs. Joy Gumble

  Note: The courtesy titles *Mr., Ms., Mrs.,* and *Miss* ought to be used according to the person's preference.

- Use nonsexist alternatives to words with masculine connotations:

  humanity (not *mankind*)   **synthetic** (not *man-made*)

  artisan (not *craftsman*)

- Do not use masculine-only or feminine-only pronouns *(he, she, his, her)* when you want to refer to a human being in general:

  A politician can kiss privacy good-bye when **he** runs for office.
  (not recommended)

  Instead, use *he or she,* change the sentence to plural, or eliminate the pronoun:

  A politician can kiss privacy good-bye when **he or she** runs for office.

  Politicians can kiss privacy good-bye when **they** run for office.

  A politician can kiss privacy good-bye when running for office.

- Do not use gender-specific references in the salutation of a business letter when you don't know the person's name:

  Dear Sir: Dear Gentlemen: (neither is recommended)

  Instead, address a position:

  Dear Personnel Officer:

  Dear Members of the Economic Committee:

Occupational Issues

Not Recommended	*Preferred*
chairman	**chair, presiding officer, moderator**
salesman	**sales representative, salesperson**
mailman	**mail carrier, postal worker, letter carrier**
insurance man	**insurance agent**
fireman	**firefighter**
businessman	**executive, manager, businessperson**
congressman	**member of Congress, representative, senator**
steward, stewardess	**flight attendant**
policeman, policewoman	**police officer**

Proofreading Your Writing

The following guidelines will help you check your revised writing for spelling, mechanics, usage, grammar, and form. Also refer to the Handbook in this book for additional help. (See pages 569–679.)

Web Link

Review punctuation and mechanics.

1. **Check for proper use of commas** before coordinating conjunctions in compound sentences, after introductory clauses and long introductory phrases, between items in a series, and so on. (See pages 571–575.)

2. **Look for apostrophes** in contractions, plurals, and possessive nouns. (See pages 587–588.)

3. **Examine quotation marks** in quoted information, titles, or dialogue. (See pages 582–583.)

4. **Watch for proper use of capital letters** for first words in written conversation and for proper names of people, places, and things. (See pages 589–592.)

Look for usage and grammar errors.

1. **Look for misuse of any commonly mixed-up words:** *there/their/they're; accept/except.* (See pages 607–618.)

2. **Check for verb use.** Subjects and verbs should agree in number: Singular subjects go with singular verbs; plural subjects go with plural verbs. Verb tenses should be consistent throughout. (See pages 627–628.)

3. **Review for pronoun/antecedent agreement problems.** A pronoun and its antecedent must agree in number. (See page 649.)

Check for spelling errors.

1. **Use a spell checker.** Your spell checker will catch most errors.

2. **Check each spelling you are unsure of.** Especially check those proper names and other special words your spell checker won't know.

3. **Consult your Handbook.** Use the list of commonly misspelled words in the Handbook (pages 601–605), as well as an up-to-date dictionary.

Check the writing for form and presentation.

1. **Note the title.** A title should be appropriate and lead into the writing.

2. **Examine any quoted or cited material.** Are all sources of information properly presented and documented? (See pages 493–534 and 535–566.)

3. **Look over the finished copy of your writing.** Does it meet the requirements for a final manuscript? (See page 134.)

Writing with Sources

When you edit and proofread your writing, you sweat the small stuff—sentence style and word choice, grammatical correctness and punctuation, usage and spelling. When you are writing with sources, you need to sweat additional stuff—documentation, for example. For help, follow the guidelines below.

Think rhetorically.

As noted on page 30, when editing you need to consider the rhetorical situation: your writing's goal, your audience, and your subject. Correctly cited sources smoothly integrated into your writing establish your authority with the *subject*, build credibility with your *reader*, and help you achieve your writing *goal*.

Practice editing and proofreading strategies.

For a full treatment of editing issues related to sources, see chapters 32 and 33. However, to get started on a close edit for proper treatment of sources in your writing, check your paper for these issues.

Respect for Sources: Your draft needs to show respect for sources and for your reader. Test your writing for lapses, especially when you disagree with a source or press your reader to accept a position. And when the evidence itself is contradictory, incomplete, or uncertain, signal those limits with qualifiers such as *possibly, usually,* and *might.* (See pages 262–263 for more.)

Weak: The arguments that such slaves of the oil companies use to attack climate change are completely ignorant of the overwhelming evidence.

Strong: While researchers are right to be cautious about interpreting the climate-change evidence, the arguments used to question climate change are flawed.

Correct Summaries, Paraphrases, and Quotations: Check your use of sources for accuracy. Are summaries and paraphrases true to the original? Are your quotations word-for-word the same as the original? Have you attributed source material to the right source, with the author's name spelled correctly? Is the page number correct?

Correct Use of Historical Present Tense: Even though the sources you are using were written in the past, in a sense they still "speak" in the present. That's the logic behind what's called the historical present tense. Unless you are emphasizing the pastness of a source or its publication date in relation to other sources, use the present tense when conveying what an author says in the source.

Example: In his review of Alice Munro's 1996 *Selected Stories,* John Updike **offers** [not *offered*] the following assessment of the composite heroine at the heart of Munro's work: "She is neither virtuous nor a victim; what she is is vital" (11).

Correct Grammar with Quotations and Citations: Quotations need to be integrated into your sentences so that the syntax and punctuation are correct. Check especially for these issues:

- Proper use of commas and colons before source material, as well as end punctuation after source material
- Proper pronoun reference (When using a quotation in a sentence, make sure the pronouns in the quotation match the nouns and pronouns in the rest of the sentence.)
- Proper content, format, and punctuation for citations (For MLA rules, see pages 496–497; for APA rules, see page 538.)

Incorrect: As she explores her spiritual attraction to monasteries, Kathleen Norris clarifies that: "I am not a monk, although I have a formal relationship with the Benedictines as an oblate." (page 17)

Correct: As she explores her spiritual attraction to monasteries, Kathleen Norris states, "I am not a monk, although I have a formal relationship with the Benedictines as an oblate" (17).

Acknowledgment of Changes to and Errors in Quotations: Sometimes, you need to signal changes that you have made to quotations, changes that do not seriously change the meaning of the original but may be needed for clarity and conciseness. Brackets [] signal changes to words and letters; ellipses [. . .] signal that you have omitted words from the original; and the Latin [sic] signals that the preceding word contains an error (e.g., spelling) that was in the original source, not in your own writing. See page 489 for more details.

Example: As she explores her spiritual attraction to monasteries, Kathleen Norris clarifies that "[she is] not a monk, although [she has] a formal relationship with the Benedictines as an oblate . . . of a community of about sixty-five monks" (17).

Cross-Curricular Connections

Some editing issues related to writing with sources are discipline-specific. That is, different disciplines and their preferred documentation systems refer to sources differently, using different conventions, formats, and punctuation practices. For example, note the differences between the MLA and APA in-text citations below:

MLA: Some child prodigies "are not necessarily retarded or autistic—there have been itinerant calculators of normal intelligence as well" (Sacks 191).

APA: Some child prodigies "are not necessarily retarded or autistic—there have been itinerant calculators of normal intelligence as well" (Sacks, 1995, p. 191).

Editing and Proofreading Checklist

Use this checklist as a guide when you edit and proofread your writing. To see editing and proofreading in action, turn to pages 128–129.

Sentence Structure

_____ Sentences are clear, complete, and correct.

_____ Sentences flow smoothly and vary in terms of their lengths, beginnings, kinds (exclamatory, declarative), and arrangements (loose, periodic).

Word Choice

_____ The writing is free of vague words, jargon, and clichés.

_____ The language is unbiased and fair.

Correctness

_____ Spelling, punctuation, and mechanics are correct.

_____ Verb tenses are correct.

_____ Subjects agree with their verbs; pronouns agree with their antecedents.

_____ Research documentation is punctuated correctly.

_____ Formatting and design follow assigned instructions.

Critical-Thinking and Writing Activities

As directed by your instructor, complete the following activities.

1. The nineteenth-century British writer Matthew Arnold offers this advice to writers about refining their writing: "Have something to say and say it as clearly as you can. That is the only secret of style." Does your own writing clearly communicate a meaningful message? Explain why or why not.

2. Choose a writing assignment that you have recently completed. Edit the sentences in this writing for style and correctness using pages 94–101 as a guide. Then use pages 102–107 in this chapter to edit the piece of writing for vague words, jargon, clichés, and biased language.

3. Combine some of the following ideas into longer, more mature sentences. Write at least four sentences, using page 95 as a guide.

Dogs can be difficult to train. The necessary supplies include a leash and treats. Patience is also a necessity. Dogs like to please their owners. Training is not a chore for dogs. A well-trained dog is a pleasure to its owner.

➤ VISUALLY SPEAKING

The photograph on page 93 represents editing and proofreading. Reflect in writing on that image, relating it to the writing process and your own practices.

SUBMITTING WRITING AND CREATING PORTFOLIOS

Video

Submitting a final paper is the driving force behind writing. Doing so explains why you may have spent so much time planning, drafting, revising, and editing an essay or a paper in the first place—to share a finished piece of writing that effectively expresses your thoughts and feelings. Often, the most immediate and important form of submitting is sharing a finished piece of writing with your instructor and writing peers. As writer Tom Liner states, "You learn ways to improve your writing by seeing its effect on others."

You can also submit a piece of writing to a newspaper, journal, or website—or simply place it in your writing portfolio. This chapter will help you prepare your writing for virtually any audience or publication.

Formatting Your Writing

A good page design makes your writing clear and easy to follow. Keep that in mind when you produce a final copy of your writing.

Strive for clarity in page design.

Examine the following design elements, making sure that each is appropriate and clear in your project and in your writing.

Format and Documentation

Keep the design clear and uncluttered. Aim for a sharp, polished look in all your assigned writing.

Use the designated documentation form. Follow all the requirements outlined in the MLA (pages 493–534) or APA (pages 535–566) style guides.

Typography

Use an easy-to-read serif font for the main text. *Serif* type, like this, has "tails" at the tops and bottoms of the letters. For most types of writing, use a 10- or 12-point type size.

Consider using a sans serif font for the title and headings. *Sans serif* type, like this, does not have "tails." Use larger, perhaps 18-point, type for your title and 14-point type for any headings. You can also use boldface for headings if they seem to get lost on the page. (Follow your instructor's formatting guidelines.)

 Because most people find a sans serif font easier to read on screen, consider a sans serif font for the body and a serif font for the titles and headings in any writing you publish online.

Spacing

Follow all requirements for indents and margins. This usually means indenting the first line of each paragraph five spaces, maintaining a one-inch margin around each page, and double-spacing throughout the paper.

Avoid widows and orphans. Avoid leaving headings, hyphenated words, or single lines of new paragraphs alone at the bottom of a page. Also avoid single words at the bottom of a page or carried over to the top of a new page.

Graphic Devices

Create bulleted or numbered lists to highlight important points. But, be selective; your writing should not include too many lists.

Include charts or other graphics. Graphics should neither be so small that they get lost on the page, nor so large that they overpower the page.

Submitting Writing and Creating Portfolios

Once you have formatted and proofread your final draft, you should be ready to share your writing. For college assignments, you will often simply turn in your paper to your instructor. However, you should also think about sharing your writing with other audiences, including those who will want to see your writing portfolio.

Consider potential audiences.

You could receive helpful feedback by taking any of the following steps:

- Share your writing with peers or family members.
- Submit your work to a local publication or an online journal.
- Post your writing on an appropriate website, including your own.
- Turn in your writing to your instructor.

Select appropriate submission methods.

There are two basic methods for submitting your work.

- **Paper submission:** Print an error-free copy on quality paper.
- **Electronic submission:** If allowed, send your writing as an e-mail attachment.

Use a writing portfolio.

There are two basic types of writing portfolios: (1) a *working portfolio* in which you store documents at various stages of development, and (2) a *showcase portfolio* with which you share appropriate finished work. For example, you could submit a portfolio to complete course requirements or to apply for a scholarship, graduate program, or job. The documents below are commonly included in a showcase portfolio:

- A table of contents listing the pieces included in your portfolio
- An opening essay or letter detailing the story behind your portfolio (how you compiled it and why it features the qualities expected by the intended reader)
- A specified number of—and types of—finished pieces
- A cover sheet attached to each piece of writing, discussing the reason for its selection, the amount of work that went into it, and so on
- Evaluation sheets or checklists charting the progress or experience you want to show related to issues of interest to the reader

Writing with Sources

For your writing project, submitting your paper and adding it to your portfolio clearly mark the end of the writing process. However, in a larger sense, these steps are simply mile markers on your writing journey. This is also the case when you are writing with sources: Sharing and collecting your writing signals your deepening participation in the world of research and research writing. To make this process productive, follow the guidelines below.

Think rhetorically.

Sharing your writing and building your portfolio are activities closely related to your rhetorical situation: your goals, your readers, and your subjects. For example, getting feedback from real *readers* helps you know whether you have achieved your *goals*, whether those goals are to entertain, to inform, to analyze, or to persuade. Similarly, adding a paper to your portfolio helps you see the range of *subjects* that you have addressed. When your writing is research-based, you should think about the following issues:

- **Your Goals:** How have submitting this paper and adding it to your portfolio helped you achieve specific aims as a researcher and a writer? Have you strengthened certain research skills, become familiar with important research tools, or learned about key resources? Have you improved your ability to think and write with researched information? Have you become more familiar with a specific form of research writing (e.g., literary interpretation, historical analysis, field report)?

- **Your Readers:** How has sharing your research writing deepened your participation in your major? How have you entered into or continued a dialogue with a specific research community (e.g., others in the discipline, experts on your topic, students on your campus, people looking for information on the web)?

- **Your Subjects:** How has writing on your topic added to the range of subjects on which you have written? How has researching this topic modified your understanding of other topics you have researched? Has this research project piqued your interest in conducting further research into this topic? Did you come across other interesting topics during research—topics you might research and write about in the future?

Practice submission and portfolio strategies.

When you submit research papers and add them to your writing portfolio, pay attention to helpful strategies such as these.

Follow submission guidelines. Double-check your assignment description to make sure that your paper meets your instructor's expectations. Have you followed all the format and citation rules of the system you are using (e.g., MLA, APA)? For example, are all of your in-text citations or notes properly keyed to entries in your bibliography? Finally, turn in print and/or electronic copies as directed by your instructor, and, if required, run your paper through a plagiarism detector such as www.Turnitin.com.

Analyze feedback on your paper. Your writing doesn't stop with submitting the paper and placing it in a portfolio. Study all the feedback you can get: your instructor's marginal notes and concluding comments, peer discussion of your research and thinking, responses to your online posting or website. What do these responses tell you about what you did well, what you need to work on, and what it means to participate in this research community?

Reflect on your research in a cover sheet. Instead of just placing a final copy of your paper in your portfolio, take time to reflect on what went well in your research and writing and what needs to be improved. Reflect on the project as a process of discovery and dialogue. Save these reflections and revisit them at the start of your next research project.

Save and track resources you used. Keep more of your research project than just the final copy of the paper. For comparison purposes, hold onto the first draft: That way, you can revisit which major changes you had to make. Moreover, keep a full bibliography of resources on the topic, including key reference works, books, journal articles, and web pages. In fact, if you have hard copies, printouts, and electronic copies of sources, collect them in folders (paper and/or electronic). You can use such bibliographies and folders not only to create a record of your research, but also to establish a resource that might prove useful for future research and writing.

Cross-Curricular Connections

When you turn in research writing in your major and when you add that writing to a portfolio, you achieve important goals in your discipline.

1. By writing a paper that carefully follows the format and documentation guidelines used in your major (e.g., MLA or APA style, business case study or chemistry lab report), you

   • work within your role as a scholar in the discipline.

   • show respect for your discipline's research methods.

   • participate in your discipline's research community.

2. When you add your paper to a portfolio, you

   • show the range of discipline-specific subjects with which you are becoming familiar through in-depth research and analysis.

   • generate a foundation of research writing on which to build in future projects, such as a senior thesis.

   • add to the writing samples that you can use for professional preparation, for an application for advanced training, or for a job search.

Submissions and Portfolio Checklist

Use the checklist below to review details regarding submitting your writing and building your portfolio.

_____ The submission method (such as an essay given to an instructor or posted on a website) is appropriate for my assignment, program, and career goals.

_____ The publishing process tests and develops my skills as a writer and scholar.

_____ The document's format (e.g., parts, headings, layout, margins, typography, and documentation) conforms to all of the instructor's guidelines.

_____ My portfolio documents address the types of topics and show the level of research and scholarship expected by my readers.

_____ The voice and style of my portfolio documents are appropriate for the kinds of writing done in the program or job for which I am applying.

_____ The portfolio includes an engaging essay or cover letter that clearly explains the portfolio's design, purpose, and focus.

Critical-Thinking and Writing Activities

As directed by your instructor, complete the following critical-thinking and writing activities by yourself or with classmates.

1. Catherine Drinker Bowen has argued the following: "Writing is not apart from living. Writing is a kind of double living." As you think about sharing your own writing and adding it to your writing portfolio, does this claim ring true? Why or why not?

2. Choose one of your recent writing assignments and use the instructions on page 112 to assess the quality of your formatting and page design. Edit and redesign the paper as needed.

3. For the class in which you are using this book, begin two working portfolios: (1) an electronic portfolio on your computer and (2) a paper portfolio in a sturdy folder or binder. In the electronic portfolio, store all drafts of your assignments, as well as all related electronic correspondence with your instructor. In your paper portfolio, store all printed drafts of your work, including copies that show your instructor's notations and grades.

◀ VISUALLY SPEAKING

The photograph on page 111 pictures a writer's sharing his or her writing in book form. How is this sharing similar to your submitting an assigned essay or portfolio?

ONE WRITER'S PROCESS

Audio

An essay is an attempt to understand a topic more deeply and clearly. That's one of the reasons this basic form of writing is essential in many college courses. It's a tool for both discovering and communicating.

How do you move from an assignment to a finished, polished essay? The best strategy is to take matters one step at a time, from understanding the assignment to submitting the final draft. Don't try to churn out the essay the night before it's due.

This chapter shows up close how student writer Angela Franco followed the writing process outlined in chapters 2 through 7.

Video

Audio

Angela's Assignment and Response

In this chapter you will follow student Angela Franco as she writes an assigned essay for her Environmental Policies class. Start by carefully reading the assignment and discussion below, noting how she thinks through the assignment's purpose, audience, form, and assessment method.

Angela examined the assignment.

Angela carefully read her assignment and responded with the notes below.

"Explain in a two- to three-page essay how a recent environmental issue is relevant to the world community. Using *The College Writer* as your guide, format the paper and document sources in APA style, but omit the title page and abstract. You may seek revising help from a classmate or from the writing center."

Subject

- *The subject is a recent environmental issue.*

Purpose

- *My purpose is to explain how the issue is relevant to all people. That means I must show how this issue affects my audience— both positively and negatively.*

Audience

- *My audience will be people like me—neighbors, classmates, and community members.*
- *I'll need to keep in mind what they already know and what they need to know.*

Form

- *I need to write a two- to three-page essay—that sounds formal.*
- *I'll need to include a thesis statement, as well as references to my sources using APA style.*

Assessment

- *I'll use the guidelines and checklists in the handbook to evaluate and revise my writing.*
- *I'll get editing feedback from Jeanie and from the writing center.*

TIP: For each step in the writing process, choose strategies that fit your writing situation. For example, a personal essay in an English class might require significant time getting started, whereas a lab report in a chemistry class might require little or none.

Video

Angela explored and narrowed her assignment.

Angela explored her assignment and narrowed its focus by clustering and freewriting.

Angela's Cluster

When she considered environmental issues, Angela first thought of water pollution as a possible topic for her essay. After writing the phrase in the center of her page, she drew from memories, experiences, and readings to list related ideas and details. Notice how she used three different-colored inks to distinguish the topic (blue) from ideas (red) and details (green).

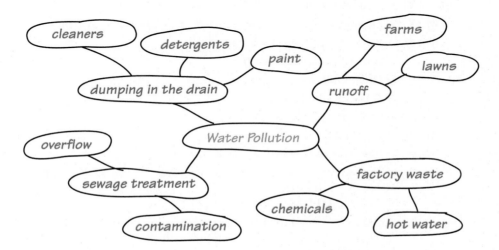

Angela's Freewriting

Angela decided to freewrite about the water pollution caused a few years earlier by improper sewage treatment in a small Canadian town.

I remember reading an article about problems in a small Canadian town. People actually died. The water they drank was contaminated. This is becoming a problem in developed countries like ours. I thought for a long time this was a problem only in developing countries. So who is responsible for sewage treatment? Who guarantees the safety of our drinking water? How does water get contaminated? Are there solutions for every kind of contamination: mercury, PCBs, sewage?

Angela's Narrowed Assignment

Based on her freewriting, Angela rephrased her assignment to narrow its focus.

Explain in a two- to three-page essay how a recent water pollution problem in a small Canadian town is relevant to the world community.

Angela's Planning

Angela reviewed her narrowed assignment and reassessed her topic.

Narrowed Writing Assignment

Explain in a two- to three-page essay how a recent water pollution problem in a small Canadian town is relevant to the world community.

Angela focused her topic.

To focus her topic, Angela answered the journalistic questions (five Ws and H).

Topic: Water pollution in a small Canadian town

Who?	*- Farm operators, wastewater officials, Walkerton residents*
What?	*- Water supply contaminated*
	- Spread bacteria (E. coli)
	- Caused disease
	- Clean, fresh water depleted
Where?	*- Walkerton, Ontario*
When?	*- May 2000*
Why?	*- Improper regulation; human error*
How?	*- Groundwater from irrigation, untreated sewage, and runoff*

Angela researched the topic.

Angela then did some research to check her information and collect more details for her paper. She recorded all the essential data on each source and then listed the specific details related to her topic. Here's one source:

Nikiforuk, Andrew. (2000, June 12) "When Water Kills." Maclean's. pp. 18–21.

- *Factory farms hold as many as 25,000 cattle*
- *Manure contains things like heavy metals (from mineral-rich feed), nutrients, and pathogens (E. coli)*
- *8,000 hogs can produce as much waste as 240,000 people*
- *Six rural Ontario counties had high E. coli 0157 levels in 1990 and 1995*

> **TIP:** During your research, take time to create or copy visuals (charts, graphs, or photos) that clarify details about which you're writing. If you copy an item, be sure to correctly record the source as well. To create your own graphic, gather the data that you want to present, and then choose the type of graphic (table, pie graph, bar graph) that best displays your point.

Angela decided how to organize her writing.

With a focus selected, Angela used the three guidelines below to choose the best organizational pattern for her writing.

Guidelines

1. Review your assignment and record your response.

Assignment: Explain in a two- to three-page essay how a recent environmental issue is relevant to the world community.

Response: *My assignment clearly states that I need to explain my topic, so I have a general idea of how my paper will be organized.*

2. Decide on your thesis statement and think about your essay's possible content and organization.

Thesis Statement: The water pollution incident in Walkerton, Ontario, had a devastating effect that every town should learn from.

Reflection: *After reading my thesis statement, it's obvious that I'm going to be writing about a problem and its causes.*

3. Choose an overall method and reflect on its potential effectiveness.

Reflection: *Looking at the list of methods, I see that I can use cause/ effect or problem/solution. After making two quick lists of my main points using both approaches, I decided to use a problem/ solution approach. I will still talk about causes and effects in my essay—they just won't be front and center.*

With problem/solution, I need to first present the problem clearly so that readers can fully understand it and see why it's important. Then I need to explore solutions to the problem—maybe what they did in Walkerton and what we all need to do to make water safe.

TIP: Many essays you write will be organized according to one basic method or approach. However, within that basic structure you may want to include other methods. For example, while developing a comparison essay you may do some describing or classifying. In other words, you should choose methods of development that (1) help you understand the topic and (2) help your readers understand your message.

Audio

Angela's First Draft

After composing her opening, middle, and closing paragraphs, Angela put together her first draft. She then added a working title.

Video

The writer uses a series of images to get the reader's attention.

The thesis statement (boldfaced) introduces the subject.

Video

The writer describes the cause of the problem.

The writer indicates some of her source material with a citation.

Water Woes

It's a hot day. Several people just finished mowing their lawns. A group of bicyclists—more than 3,000—have been passing through your picturesque town all afternoon. Dozens of Little Leaguers are batting, running, and sweating. What do all these people have in common? They all drinks lots of tap water, especially on hot summer days. They also take for granted that the water is clean and safe. But in reality, the water they drink could be contaminated and pose a serious health risk. **That's just what happened in Walkerton, Ontario, where a water pollution incident had a devastating effect that every town can learn from.**

What happened in Walkerton Ontario? Heavy rains fell on May 12. It wasn't until May 21 that the townspeople were advised to boil their drinking water. The rains washed cattle manure into the town well. The manure contained E coli, a type of bacteria. E coli is harmless to cattle. It can make people sick. Seven days after the heavy rains, people began calling public health officials. The warning came too late. Two people had already died (Wickens, 2000).

Once Walkerton's problem was identified, the solutions were known. The government acted quickly to help the community and to clean the water supply. One Canadian newspaper reported that a $100,000 emergency fund was set up to help families with expenses. Bottled water for drinking and containers of bleach for sanitizing and cleaning were donated by local businesses.

1

2

3

So what messed up Walkerton? Basically, people screwed up! According to one news story, a flaw in the water treatment system allowed the bacteria-infested water to enter the well. The manure washed into the well, but the chlorine should have killed the deadly bacteria. In Walkerton, the PUC group fell asleep at the wheel. ⁴

The writer covers the solutions that were used to resolve the problem.

At last, the Provincial Clean Water Agency restored the main water and sewage systems by flushing out all of the town's pipes and wells. The ban on drinking Walkerton's water was finally lifted seven months after the water became contaminated. ⁵

The concluding paragraph stresses the importance of public awareness.

Could any good come from Walkerton's tragedy? Does it have a silver lining? It is possible that more people are aware that water may be contaminated. Today people are beginning to take responsibility for the purity of the water they and their families drink. In the end, more and more people will know about the dangers of contaminated water—without learning it the hard way. ⁶

Video

Angela kept a working bibliography.

As she researched her topic, Angela kept a working bibliography—a list of resources that she thought might offer information helpful to her essay. During the writing process, she deleted some resources, added others, and edited the document that became the references page on page 133.

Working References

Wickens, Barbara. (2000, June 5), Tragedy in Walkerton.
     Macleans' 113 (23): 34–36.
Phone interview with Alex Johnson, Walkerton Police
     Department, 23 September 2007.
Blackwell, Thomas (2001, January 9). Walkerton doctor defends
     response. *The Edmonton Journal.*
     http://edmontonjournal.com.

Video

Audio

Angela's First Revision

After finishing the first draft, Angela set it aside. When she was ready to revise it, she looked carefully at global issues—ideas, organization, and voice. She wrote notes to herself to help keep her thoughts together.

Angela's comments

Water Woes

an unusually Saturday afternoon ☺

It's ~~a~~ hot ~~day~~. Several people just finished mowing their lawns. A group of bicyclists— ~~more than 3,000—have been~~ *pedal up the street* ~~passing through your picturesque town all afternoon~~. Dozens of Little Leaguers are batting, running, and sweating. What do all these people have in common? They all drink lots of tap water, especially on hot summer days. They also take for granted that the water is clean and safe. But in reality, the water they drink could be contaminated and pose a serious health risk. That's just what happened in Walkerton, Ontario, where a water pollution incident had a devastating effect that every town can learn from.

What happened in Walkerton, Ontario? Heavy rains fell on May 12. [It wasn't until May 21 that the townspeople were advised to boil their drinking water.] The rains washed cattle manure into the town well. The manure contained E coli, a type of bacteria. E coli is harmless to cattle. It can make people sick. Seven days after the heavy rains, people began calling public health officials. The warning came too late. Two people had already died (Wickens, 2000).

Once Walkerton's problem was identified, the solutions were known. The government acted quickly to help the community and to clean the water supply. One Canadian newspaper reported that a $100,000 emergency fund was set up to help families with expenses. Bottled water for drinking and containers of bleach for sanitizing and cleaning were donated by local businesses.

I need to give my opening more energy.

Does my thesis still fit the paper?— Yes.

Using time sequence, put this paragraph in better order.

Move this paragraph—it interrupts the discussion of causes.

1

2

3

*My voice
here is too
informal.*

went wrong in

So what ~~messed up~~ Walkerton? ~~Basically, people screwed~~ **4**

Human error was a critical factor.

First,

~~up!~~ According to one news story, a flaw in the water treatment

system allowed the bacteria-infested water to enter the well. The

Even after

manure washed into the well, ~~but~~ the chlorine should have killed

the deadly bacteria. In Walkerton, the ~~PUC group fell asleep at~~

*Explain "fell
asleep."
Move para-
graph three
here and
combine.*

~~the wheel.~~

In addition,

~~At last,~~ the Provincial Clean Water Agency restored the **5**

main water and sewage systems by flushing out all of the

town's pipes and wells. The ban on drinking Walkerton's

water was finally lifted seven months after the water became

contaminated.

Could any good come from Walkerton's tragedy? ~~Does it~~ **6**

Cut the clichés.

~~have a silver lining?~~ It is possible that more people are aware

that water may be contaminated. Today people are beginning to

take responsibility for the purity of the water they and their

families drink. In the end, more and more people will know

about the dangers of contaminated water—without learning it

the hard way.

*Public Utilities Commission was responsible for overseeing
the testing and treating of the town's water, but they
failed to monitor it properly. Apparently, shortcuts were
taken when tracking the water's chlorine level, and as a
result, some of the water samples were mislabeled. There
was also a significant delay between the time that the
contamination was identified and the time it was reported.*

Video

Angela's Second Revision

Next, Angela asked a peer to review her work. His comments are in the margin. Angela used them to make additional changes, including writing a new opening and closing.

Reviewer's comments

Angela's changes

Water Woes

Could you make the opening more relevant and urgent?

1 *WARNING: City tap water is polluted with animal waste. Using the water for drinking, cooking, or bathing could cause sickness or death.*

2 *According to the Seirra Club, run-off pollutants from farm cites are steadily seeping into our streams, lakes, reservoirs and wells. Because much of our drinking water comes from these resources, warnings like the one above are already posted in a number of U.S. and Canadian communities, and many more postings will be needed (Sierra Club, 2005). As the Seirra Club argues, the pollution and related warnings are serious, and failure to take them seriously could be deadly. For example, a few years ago the citizens of Walkerton Ontario learned that the water that they believed to be clean was actually poisoned.*

Could you clarify your focus on the topic?

– –

3 *The events*
~~What happened~~ in Walkerton, ~~Ontario? Heavy rains fell~~ *began*
2000, when heavy rains
on May 12, ~~The rains~~ washed cattle manure into the town well. The manure contained E coli, a type of bacteria. E coli is harmless to cattle. It can make people sick. Seven days after
to complain of nausea and diarrhea ⊙
the heavy rains, people began calling public health officials. It wasn't until May 21 that the townspeople were advised to boil their drinking water. The warning came too late. Two people had
, and more than 2,000 were ill
already died (Wickens, 2000).

Add the year and other specific details.

4 *Several factors contributed to the terrible tragedy in Walkerton,*
~~So what went wrong in Walkerton? Human error was a~~
including human error.
The Edmonton Journal
~~critical factor.~~ First, according to ~~one news story,~~ a flaw in the water treatment system allowed the bacteria-infested water to
(Blackwell, 2001) ⊙
enter the well. Even after the manure washed into the well, the chlorine should have killed the deadly bacteria. In Walkerton, the Public Utilities Commission was responsible for overseeing

Make sure you document all source material— you have just one citation in your draft.

the testing and treating of the town's water, but it failed to monitor it properly. Apparently, shortcuts were taken when tracking the water's chlorine level, and as a result, some of the water samples were mislabeled. There was also a significant delay between the time that the contamination was identified and the time it was reported.

Use active voice.

Once Walkerton's problem was identified, the ~~solutions were known.~~ The government acted quickly to help the community and ~~to clean the water supply.~~ *The Edmonton Journal* ~~One Canadian newspaper~~ reported a $100,000 emergency fund was set up to help families with expenses. *Local businesses donated* Bottled water for drinking and containers of bleach for basic sanitizing and cleaning ~~were donated by local businesses.~~ In addition, the Provincial Clean Water Agency restored the main water and sewage systems by flushing out all of the town's pipes and wells. The ban on drinking Walkerton's water was finally lifted seven months after the water became contaminated.

Consider adding details— maybe an entire paragraph— calling readers to action, and stating your thesis clearly.

As the Sierra Club warned and the citizens of Walkerton learned, water purity is a life-and-death issue. Fortunately, both the United States and Canada have been addressing the problem. For example, since 2001, more states and provinces are tightening their clean-water standards, more communities have begun monitoring their water quality, and more individuals have been using water-filtration systems, bottled water, or boiled tap water. However, a tragedy like that in Walkerton could happen again. To avoid such horror, all of us must get involved by demanding clean tap water in our communities and by promoting the polices and procedures needed to achieve that goal.

Video

Audio

Angela's Edited Draft

When Angela began editing, she read each of her sentences aloud to check for clarity and smoothness. **The first page of Angela's edited copy is shown below.**

The writer revises the title.

Water Woes ∧ *in Walkerton*

> *Warning: City tap water is polluted with animal waste. Using the water for drinking, cooking, or bathing could cause sickness or death.*

According to the Seirra Club, run-off pollutants from farm cites are steadily seeping into our streams, lakes, reservoirs∧and wells. Because much of our drinking water comes from these resources, warnings like the one above are already posted in a number of U.S. and Canadian communities, and many more

She qualifies her statement, replacing "will" with "might"

postings ~~will~~ *might* be needed∧ *in the future* (Sierra Club, 2005). As the Seirra Club argues, the pollution and related warnings are serious, and failure to take them seriously could be deadly. For example, a few years ago the citizens of Walkerton Ontario learned that the water that they believed to be clean was∧ *tragically* ~~actually~~ poisoned.

1

The events in Walkerton began on May 12, 2000, when heavy rains washed cattle manure into the town well. The manure

She rewrites and combines several choppy sentences.

contained ~~E coli. a~~ *commonly called* bacteria. ∧ *While E coli* E coli∧is harmless to cattle∧It can make people sick. Seven days after the heavy rains, people began calling public health officials to complain of nausea and diarrhea. It wasn't until May 21 that the townspeople were advised to boil their drinking water. The warning came too late. Two people had already died, and more than 2,000 were ill (Wickens, 2000).

2

Angela deletes unnecessary words.

Several factors contributed to the ~~terrible~~ tragedy in Walkerton, including human error. First, according to *The Edmonton Journal*, a flaw in the water treatment system allowed the ~~bacteria~~-infested water to enter the well (Blackwell, 2001). Even after the manure washed into the well, the chlorine . . .

3

Video

Angela's Proofread Draft

Angela reviewed her edited copy for punctuation, agreement issues, and spelling. **The first page of Angela's proofread essay is shown below.**

Water Woes in Walkerton

> *Warning: City tap water is polluted with animal waste. Using the water for drinking, cooking, or bathing could cause sickness or death.*

The writer corrects errors that the spell checker did not pick up.

According to the Sierra Club, run-off pollutants from farm sites are steadily seeping into our streams, lakes, reservoirs, and wells. Because much of our drinking water comes from these resources, warnings like the one above are already posted in a number of U.S. and Canadian communities, and many more postings might be needed in the future (Sierra Club, 2005). As the Sierra Club argues, the pollution and related warnings are serious, and failure to take them seriously could be deadly.

She adds a comma between the city and province.

For example, a few years ago the citizens of Walkerton, Ontario, learned that the water that they believed to be clean was tragically poisoned.

The events in Walkerton began on May 12, 2000, when heavy rains washed cattle manure into the town well. The manure contained bacteria commonly called *E. coli*. While *E. coli* is harmless to cattle, it can make people sick. Seven days after the heavy rains, people began calling public health officials to complain of nausea and diarrhea. It wasn't until May 21 that the townspeople were advised to boil their drinking water. The warning came too late. Two people had already died, and more than 2,000 were ill (Wickens, 2000).

She adds periods and italicizes "E. coli" to show that it is a scientific term.

Several factors contributed to the tragedy in Walkerton, including human error. First, according to *The Edmonton Journal*, a flaw in the water treatment system allowed the infested water to enter Walkerton's well (Blackwell, 2001). Even after the manure washed ~~into the well,~~ *into Walkerton's well* the chlorine should have . . .

She adds a word for clarity.

1

2

3

Video

Audio

Angela's Finished Essay

After proofreading and formatting her essay, Angela added a heading and page numbers. She also added more documentation and a references page at the end. As assigned, she omitted the title page and abstract.

Clean Water Is Everyone's Business 1

Angela Franco

Professor Kim Van Es

English 101

October 10, 2008

Clean Water Is Everyone's Business

Complete details are supplied in the heading.

> Warning: City tap water is polluted with animal waste. Using the water for drinking, cooking, or bathing could cause sickness or death.

The title is changed. The warning is emphasized with red print.

According to the Sierra Club, run-off pollutants from farm sites are steadily seeping into our streams, lakes, reservoirs, and wells. Because much of our drinking water comes from these resources, warnings like the one above are already posted in a number of U.S. and Canadian communities, and many more postings might be needed in the future (Sierra Club, 2005). As the Sierra Club argues, the pollution and related warnings are serious, and failure to take them seriously could be deadly. For example, a few years ago the citizens of Walkerton, Ontario, learned that the water that they believed to be clean was tragically poisoned.

An appropriate font and type size are used.

The events in Walkerton began on May 12, 2000, when heavy rains washed cattle manure into the town well. The

1

2

Title and page number are used on each page.

manure contained the bacteria commonly called *E. coli*. While *E. coli* is harmless to cattle, it can make people sick. Seven days after the heavy rains, people began calling public health officials to complain of nausea and diarrhea. It wasn't until May 21 that the townspeople were advised to boil their drinking water. The warning came too late. Two people had already died, and more than 2,000 were ill (Wickens, 2000).

Each claim or supporting point is backed up with reasoning and evidence.

Several factors contributed to the tragedy in Walkerton, including human error. First, according to *The Edmonton Journal*, a flaw in the water treatment system allowed the infested water to enter Walkerton's well (Blackwell, 2001). Even after the manure washed into Walkerton's well, the chlorine should have killed the deadly bacteria. In Walkerton, the Public Utilities Commission was responsible for overseeing the testing and treating of the town's water, but it failed to monitor the procedure properly ("Walkerton's water-safety," 2000). Apparently, shortcuts were taken when tracking the water's chlorine level, and as a result, some of the water samples were mislabeled. There was also a significant delay between the time that the contamination was identified and the time it was reported.

The writer continues to give credit throughout the essay.

Once Walkerton's problem was identified, the government acted quickly to help the community. In its December 7, 2000, edition, *The Edmonton Journal* reported that a $100,000 emergency fund was set up to help families with expenses. Local businesses donated bottled water for drinking and containers of bleach for basic sanitizing and cleaning. In addition, the Provincial

Clean Water Is Everyone's Business 3

Clean Water Agency restored the main water and sewage systems by flushing out all of the town's pipes and wells. Seven months after the water became contaminated, the ban on drinking Walkerton's water was finally lifted.

As the Sierra Club warns and the citizens of Walkerton learned, water purity is a life-and-death issue. Fortunately, both the United States and Canada have been addressing the problem. For example, since 2001, more states and provinces have been tightening their clean-water standards, more communities have been monitoring their water quality, and more individuals have been using water-filtration sytems, bottled water, or boiled tap water. However, a tragedy like that in Walkerton could happen again. To avoid such horror, all of us must get involved by demanding clean tap water in our communities and by promoting the policies and procedures needed to achieve that goal.

The writer restates her thesis in the last sentence.

5

Clean Water Is Everyone's Business 4

References

Blackwell, T. (2001, January 9). Walkerton doctor defends
response. *The Edmonton Journal*. Retrieved September 22,
2008, from <http://edmontonjournal.com>.

Sierra Club. (n.d.) Water sentinels: Keeping it clean around the
U.S.A. Retrieved September 24, 2008, from <http://
sierraclub.org/watersentinels/>.

Walkerton's water-safety tests falsified regularly, utility
official admits. (2000, December 7). *The Edmonton
Journal*. Retrieved April 2, 2005, from <http://
edmontonjournal.com>.

Wickens, B. (2000, June 5). Tragedy in Walkerton. *Maclean's*,
113(23), 34–36.

Sources used are listed correctly, in alphabetical order.

Each entry follows APA rules for content, format, and punctuation.

Critical-Thinking and Writing Activities

Complete these activities by yourself or with classmates.

1. Scott Russell Sanders suggests that "essays are experiments in making sense of things." Does Sanders' statement ring true? What makes such experiments flop or succeed? What kinds of "sense" do essays create?

2. Review Angela's writing process. How does it compare with your own writing process on a recent assignment?

3. Review the peer-editing instructions in "Revising Collaboratively" (pages 87–88). Then reread the reviewer's comments in the margins of Angela's second revision (pages 126–127). Do the comments reflect the instructions? Explain.

◀ VISUALLY SPEAKING ───────────

Revisit the photograph on page 117. Then explain what the picture suggests about Angela's writing process shown in this chapter—and your own writing process.

Effective Writing Checklist

Check your finished work using these traits or standards as a guide.

Stimulating Ideas *The writing . . .*

_____ presents interesting and important information.

_____ maintains a clear focus or purpose—centered on a thesis, theme, concern, or question.

_____ develops the focus through a line of thought or reasoning elaborated with sufficient details or evidence.

_____ holds the reader's attention (and answers her or his questions).

Logical Organization

_____ includes a clear beginning, middle, and ending.

_____ contains specific details, arranged in an order that builds understanding with readers.

_____ uses transitions to link sentences and paragraphs.

Engaging Voice

_____ speaks in a sincere, natural way that fits the writing situation.

_____ shows that the writer really cares about the subject.

Appropriate Word Choice

_____ contains specific, clear words.

_____ uses a level of language appropriate for the type of writing and the audience.

Overall Fluency

_____ flows smoothly from sentence to sentence.

_____ displays varied sentence beginnings and lengths.

_____ follows a style that fits the situation (e.g., familiar versus academic).

Correct, Accurate Copy

_____ adheres to the rules of grammar, spelling, and punctuation.

_____ follows established documentation guidelines.

Reader-Friendly Design

_____ exhibits a polished, professional design in terms of overall format, page layout, and typographical choices.

_____ makes the document attractive and easy to read.

_____ is formatted correctly in MLA or APA style.

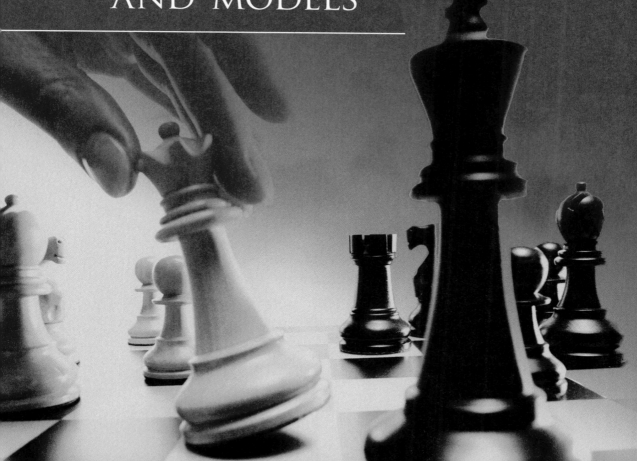

Reader:
STRATEGIES
AND MODELS

CONTENTS

▬ Writing Across the Curriculum

FORMS OF COLLEGE WRITING

Video

In college, professors in nearly all departments give writing assignments. Why? Because they know that writing helps you in two ways: (1) to learn course content and (2) to learn how to carry on a written dialogue with others in your field. In other words, writing will help you learn course material today, but it will also help you use that information in subsequent college courses and in the workplace.

The purpose of this chapter is to show you three important things about writing across the curriculum:

- How a college curriculum and faculty are organized
- What kinds of writing you can expect to do in your courses
- How writing and thinking skills required in one class are linked to writing and thinking skills required in another class

The chapter begins by showing the big picture: the three divisions into which most college curricula are divided, and the academic departments that constitute each division. The chapter then presents more specific information about academic departments, including the topics students study, the forms of writing teachers assign, and the traits of those forms.

Three Curricular Divisions

Based on each department's area of study and focus, the college curriculum is generally divided into three groups: humanities, social sciences, and natural and applied sciences. These groups are then subdivided into specific departments, such as biology, chemistry, and physics. Below you will find an explanation of each division, along with its more common departments.

Humanities

Scholars within this division study human culture, both past and present. They examine topics such as the history of civilization, cultural institutions and trends, religious beliefs and practices, languages and their use, and artwork and performance skills. Some departments in this division include the following:

Archeology	Ethnic Studies	Modern Languages	Theater Arts
Asian Studies	Film Studies	Music	Theology
Dance	Graphic Design	Philosophy	Visual Arts
English	History	Religion	Women's Studies

Social Sciences

Scholars in this division study human behavior and societies using research strategies adapted from the natural sciences. For example, a researcher may develop a hypothesis regarding a topic or phenomenon, and then devise an experiment to test that hypothesis. Students study economic systems, correctional programs, and personality disorders. Departments in this division include the following:

Anthropology	Economics	Geophysics	Psychology
Business	Education	Government	Social Work
Communication	Genetics	Health & Phys. Ed.	Sociology
Criminology	Geography	Political Science	Urban Planning

Natural and Applied Sciences

The natural sciences (such as biology, zoology, and chemistry) focus on specific aspects of nature, such as animal life, plant life, and molecular structures. In contrast, the applied sciences (such as mathematics, computer science, and engineering) consider how to use science-based information to understand concepts and develop artifacts. Here are some of the departments in this division:

Agriculture	Biology	Environment	Physics
Agronomy	Botany	Forestry	Physiology
Anatomy	Chemistry	Mathematics	Public Health
Architecture	Computer Science	Nutrition	Space Science
Astronomy	Engineering	Oceanography	Zoology

Types of Writing in Each Division

Listed below are the types of writing commonly assigned in the three academic divisions. Often instructors in different divisions will assign the same type of essay—but with a different purpose, audience, or focus. When an assigned form differs from the one shown in the book, adapt the guidelines in the book to the form stated in the assignment.

Humanities

Anecdotes (147–148)
Application Writing (390–396)
Cause and Effect (183–198)
Classification (215–228)
Comparison and Contrast (199–214)
Definition (243–256)
Describing a Process (229–242)
Description and Reflection (165–180)
Essay Test (377–382)
Interview Report (331–338)

Literary Analysis (355–372)
Narration and Description (145–164)
Oral Presentations (409–418)
Personal Essay (145–180)
Persuading Readers to Act (295–312)
Proposing a Solution (313–328)
Research Paper (493–534)
Taking a Position (275–294)
Test Taking (383–384)
Web Writing (397–408)

Social Sciences

Abstracts/Summaries (442–444)
Application Writing (390–396)
Cause and Effect (183–198)
Classification (215–228)
Comparison and Contrast (199–214)
Definition (243–256)
Describing a Process (229–242)
Description and Reflection (165–180)
Field Report (347–352)
Interview Report (331–338)

Literary Analysis (355–372)
Oral Presentations (409–418)
Personal Essay (145–180)
Persuading Readers to Act (295–312)
Proposing a Solution (313–328)
Surveys (449–451)
Taking a Position (275–294)
Test Taking (383–384)
Web Writing (397–408)

Natural and Applied Sciences

Abstracts/Summaries (442–444)
Application Writing (390–396)
Cause and Effect (183–198)
Classification (215–228)
Comparison and Contrast (199–214)
Definition (243–256)
Describing a Process (229–242)
Experiment Report (343–346)
Field Report (347–352)
Interview Report (331–338)

Lab Report (340–342)
Personal Essay (145–180)
Persuading Readers to Act (295–312)
Proposing a Solution (313–328)
Research Paper (475–490)
Surveys (449–451)
Test Taking (383–384)
Web Writing (397–408)

Traits of Writing Across the Curriculum

Listed below are the more common writing tasks in each of the three divisions, along with seven traits that distinguish good writing for each task.

Humanities

Idea: **Personal writing:** Explores the writer's ideas, experiences, and feelings
Organization: Usually chronological
Voice: Engaging, fits the story, honest, direct
Word Choice: Words are precise and fit the writer's topic, purpose, audience, and characters
Sentences: Appropriate for dialogue and description; others use varied forms
Correctness: Documentation (where necessary) follows MLA or CMS style
Design: Designed as an essay with proper formatting and typeface

---

Idea: **Analysis of a work of art:** Describes the work and analyzes its parts and how they function
Organization: Appropriate for the work and the writer's focus
Voice: Objective appraisal and analysis, supported by evidence
Word Choice: Appropriate for the art form; technical terms explained
Sentences: Varied in length and structure, with clear transitions
Correctness: Documentation follows MLA or CMS style
Design: Designed as an essay with proper formatting and typeface

---

Idea: **Argument supporting a claim:** Persuades reader regarding the point's meaning, importance, and truth
Organization: Order fits the topic and purpose: cause/effect, compare/contrast, and so on
Voice: Informed, impartial, inviting
Word Choice: Precise, with scholarly terms used in the discipline
Sentences: Tend to be longer; complexity fits the topic and audience
Correctness: Documentation follows MLA or CMS style
Design: Designed as an essay with proper formatting and typeface

---

Idea: **Analysis of a phenomenon:** Explains its meaning in relation to its historical, social, and/or natural context (e.g., Marxism)
Organization: Often combines cause/effect, compare/contrast, and examples
Voice: Scholarly, fair, informed, balanced
Word Choice: Precise, often including scholarly terms used in the discipline
Sentences: Tend to be longer; complexity fits the topic and audience
Correctness: Documentation follows MLA or CMS style
Design: Designed as an essay with proper formatting, typeface, and graphics

Social Sciences

Idea: **Case study:** Describes and analyzes the topic, identifies methodology, gives results

Organization: Gives overview, presents steps chronologically, analyzes outcome

Voice: Impartial reporting; respectful, thoughtful analysis

Word Choice: Precise statistics and discipline-related terms

Sentences: Medium-length sentences with clear transitions

Correctness: Documentation follows APA or CMS style

Design: Formatted as a report for easy reading and in accordance with the discipline's or department's style guide

---

Idea: **Literature review:** Summarizes and evaluates journal articles (usually research based) on a topic

Organization: Each article discussed separately followed by conclusions

Voice: Unbiased reporting, formal tone, logical analysis

Word Choice: Includes precise technical terms and statistics

Sentences: Shorter sentences and paragraphs with clear transitions

Correctness: Documentation follows APA or CMS style

Design: Formatted as a report for easy reading and in accordance with the discipline's or department's style guide

---

Idea: **Policy or project analysis:** Analyzes the topic, its history, and its effects

Organization: Analysis often uses cause/effect, classification, and compare/contrast

Voice: Impartial, informed, concerned, thoughtful

Word Choice: Includes precise technical terms and statistics

Sentences: Sentences are varied in length and structure, with clear transitions

Correctness: Documentation follows APA or CMS style

Design: Formatted as a report for easy reading and in accordance with the discipline's or department's style guide

---

Idea: **Process description:** Describes materials, steps in the process, and the importance of the process

Organization: Usually states topic and outcome, gives steps chronologically

Voice: Objective, yet concerned about effectiveness and safety

Word Choice: Precise, often including technical terms

Sentences: Description of a process—sentences tend to be short, direct, and in parallel form

Correctness: Documentation follows APA or CMS style

Design: Formatted as a report for easy reading and in accordance with the discipline's or department's style guide, or as workplace instructions with numbered steps and graphics

Natural and Applied Sciences

Idea: **Lab or experiment report:** Includes clear data, logical analysis, unbiased reporting

Organization: States issues and hypothesis, methods with procedure, results with data, discusses results

Voice: Interested, curious, impartial, logical, meticulous

Word Choice: Precise, often including scientific and technical terms

Sentences: Medium length, logical, passive voice only when needed

Correctness: Documentation and format follow CSE or APA style

Design: Formatted as a report in accordance with the discipline's style guide; graphics (such as tables, charts) are clear

---

Idea: **Field report:** Includes clear data and unbiased reporting

Organization: States focus and issues, methods with procedure, results with data, discusses results

Voice: Interested, curious, logical, meticulous

Word Choice: Precise, often including scientific and technical terms

Sentences: Medium length, logical, passive voice only when needed

Correctness: Documentation and format follow CSE or APA style

Design: Formatted as a report in accordance with the discipline's style guide; graphics (such as tables, photos) are strong

---

Idea: **Literature review:** Summarizes and compares journal articles (usually research based)

Organization: Each article discussed separately, followed by conclusions

Voice: Equitable reporting, formal tone, logical, clear analysis

Word Choice: Includes technical scientific words and concepts; first person rarely used

Sentences: Shorter sentences and paragraphs with clear transitions

Correctness: Documentation and format follow CSE or APA style

Design: Formatted as a report with proper spacing and typeface

---

Idea: **Process explanation:** Describes each step in a process

Organization: Usually states topic, gives steps chronologically, closes

Voice: Impartial, concerned about effectiveness and safety

Word Choice: Precise, often including scientific and technical terms

Sentences: Description of a process—sentences vary depending on the form; instructions—short, direct

Correctness: Description follows CSE or APA style

Design: Formatted as an essay or workplace instructions

Research and Documentation Websites

MLA Modern Language Association **www.mla.org**

APA American Psychological Association **www.apa.org**

CMS Chicago Manual of Style **www.press.uchicago.edu**

CSE Council of Science Editors **councilscienceeditors.org**

Note: CSE has replaced CBE *(Council of Biology Editors)*

NARRATIVE, DESCRIPTIVE, AND REFLECTIVE WRITING

Chapters 10 and 11 offer instruction in writing personal essays, pieces that focus on experience, especially the writer's experience—whether of places, people, or events—with the goal of vividly sharing that experience with readers. To that end, personal essays tend to be informal in voice and style, freely using personal pronouns such as "I" and "we." Note, too, that such writing depends on strategies of narration, description, and reflection. While virtually all personal essays blend the three techniques, chapter 10 focuses on the combination of narration and description, and chapter 11 focuses on the combination of description and reflection.

As with all forms of writing, you should develop your personal essays using whatever strategies fit your writing situation: your subject, audience, and purpose. For examples, watch how the authors of the essays in chapters 10 and 11 use not only the strategies narration, description, and reflection (commonly associated with personal writing), but also the strategies cause/effect, compare/contrast, and definition (often associated with analytical writing).

CONTENTS
Narrative, Descriptive, and Reflective Writing

NARRATION AND DESCRIPTION

10

A personal narrative is a story—a story that mirrors you and your experiences. In a narrative, you may tell about a time when you were afraid, lost something (or someone), found joy, learned a tough lesson, or discovered some secret. Whatever the topic, your story should help readers see, hear, touch, and taste those details that make your experience come alive. To do that, you must carefully describe key aspects of the experience.

As you prepare to share your story with others, get ready to relive it yourself—to reexperience all that you felt, thought, or sensed during the original event. But get ready also to learn something new about the event, about others, and even about yourself. That's what writing a personal narrative can do.

Audio

Video

Video

Web Link

Overview
Writing Narration and Description

Writer's Goal

Your goal is to write a personal narrative about something significant that has happened to you. Write in a way that allows your readers to vividly relive the experience and to learn something about you and about themselves.

Keys for Success

Be passionate. Choose an experience from your life, anchored in your memory, that still makes you feel happy, angry, humble, afraid, or some other strong emotion.

Include characters. Make the people in your narrative come to life. Let your story unfold through their actions and words. Above all, show how you—and these other people—react to the experience.

Create memorable descriptions. Choose details that create pictures in your readers' minds. First, use your senses to trigger the readers' senses. What did you see? What did you hear? Next, choose strong nouns and active verbs. Finally, show what happened—don't tell about it.

Topics to Consider

Memorable experiences can be categorized in a number of ways. Understanding these categories may help you identify possible subjects for your narratives. *Remember:* Your personal narratives should show something significant about you and about human nature in general.

- **Initiation:** Think of a time when you had to prove yourself, test your abilities, or "grow up." Share this "test" with your readers.

- **Loss:** Explore a time when you lost someone or something that was important to you.

- **Run-In:** Consider an unavoidable confrontation with another person. How did you react to the situation? What did you learn about yourself?

- **Arrival:** Recall when you were the new kid on the block or in school. How did the experience change your life? Or remember a time when someone new arrived in your life. How did this person affect you?

- **Occasion:** Focus on a revealing get-together, celebration, holiday, party, or vacation experience. What did you learn from the experience?

> **Next Step** Read the model essays and perform the activities that follow. As you read, think of "defining experiences" in your life. How did each shape you? Would your readers find something of value for themselves in your experiences? Would they sense the importance of your experience?

Personal Narrative

A common personal narrative is the anecdote—a short, direct story that adds spark to your writing while introducing a topic or illustrating an idea. Below and on the following page are three anecdotes taken from essays in this book.

The story gets our attention and shows some causes and effects of stress.

The transition links the anecdote and the thesis.

Anecdote introducing a topic:

It was 8:00 a.m.; her husband, Lance, had left for work without filling the tank on the Mazda; and her daughter, Gina, had gotten on the school bus without her show-and-tell bunny. "Great!" thought Jan, "now I have to get gas at Demler's, stop by Gina's school, and drop Alex off at day care—all before my 9:30 class!" Quickly she grabbed the diaper bag, picked up the baby, and headed for the door. At 9:35, with her heart pounding and hands sweating, she scrambled into the classroom, found an open seat, and was hurriedly pulling out her psych notes when the prof asked, "So . . . precisely what does Jung mean by 'collective unconscious'—Jan?"   *1*

"Uh . . . what was the question?" she responded.   *2*

Does the scene sound familiar—too much work, too little time, and too much stress?   *3*

From "Life-Threatening Stress," page **185**

The transition tells why the anecdote is used.

The quote and description show how a dementia patient feels.

The transition shifts the focus.

Anecdote illustrating a point:

Steve is a good example. When he entered the nursing home just six months ago, he was experiencing the early stages of dementia. Today, however, his illness is much more advanced. The stress of moving into this new environment and leaving his wife at home alone affected Steve deeply. When he first arrived, Steve often cried and begged to be taken home. "I'll give you $20—please just take me home," he'd plead.   *1*

Painfully, I would explain, "Steve, this is your home." After some time, the situation got so bad that he would not sleep or eat. He was depressed, and he cried often, thinking that no one cared about him. Eventually, Steve was given stronger drugs to help with the depression. For a few months, the medication seemed to work—he laughed at jokes and occasionally told one himself. But then Steve's dementia returned. Soon he was asking his same sad questions: "Where am I?" and "Do you know what I'm doing here?"   *2*

So what is the best "medication" for people with dementia?   *3*

From "Understanding Dementia," page **247**

Anecdote illustrating character traits:

> The writer describes how Jackie Thomas's competitive drive helps her excel in both basketball and business.

Jackie Thomas, Nike's associate director of sports marketing, usually *1* spends her lunch hour on the sports-shoe company's basketball courts charging for the basket, always outnumbered by male colleagues. "I hold my own," boasts the 33-year-old executive.

She also does well playing the corporate game back inside the *2* headquarter's offices. Thomas, a former University of California-Berkeley college basketball point guard, says her success is due in large part to the lessons she learned growing up playing competitive team sports. "It's taught me that if you lose a game, you go back afterward and figure out what went wrong and how to overcome it the next time," says the former tomboy from Kingston, Jamaica.

> The writer then argues that the same trait is helping other women succeed in business.

While most of America's corporations are still commanded by male *3* chief executives, women are gaining ground, winning vice-presidential and top management slots and, in a few cases, the highest leadership roles. Many of these young female executives say playing team sports helped them get ahead. A University of Virginia study conducted in the late 1980s showed that 80 percent of key female leaders from *Fortune* 500 companies said they participated in sports and considered themselves tomboys.

From "If You Let Me Play . . . ," page **188**

Reading for Better Writing

Working by yourself or with a group, answer these questions:

1. Reread the three models and explain the qualities of an effective anecdote.

2. How does each transitional sentence link the story to the rest of the essay?

3. Find the introductory anecdotes on pages **185**, **188**, and **247**; explain why each does or does not effectively introduce the topic and focus the essay.

Narration and Description

In this essay, student writer Jacqui Nyangi Owitti recalls an important personal experience in her life that taught her the pain of loss.

Mzee Owitti

The opening sets the scene and gives background information.

I am about 12 years old. We are en route from Nairobi, the capital city, to the rural area of Kisumu on the eastern shores of Lake Victoria in western Kenya, where my grandparents live. My five brothers and I are traveling with Mum on the overnight train. I am not particularly sad, though I know what has happened. I base my reactions on my mother's, and since she appears to be handling the whole thing well, I am determined to do the same. You see, my grandfather has died. My dad's dad.

We reach the town of my ancestry just as dawn lazily turns into early morning. We buy snacks and hire a car for the last leg of the journey. We then meander through a bewildering maze of mud huts, sisal scrub, and sandy clay grassland, until we come within sight of my grandfather's land, the place where my father grew up.

The narrator describes what she sees and how she feels.

The first thing I notice is a crude "tent" made by sticking four poles in the ground, crisscrossing the top with long branches, and covering that with thatch. Despite the early hour, the place is filled with dignitaries, guests, and people like my mother's parents, who have traveled far to honor our family. I am struck by the stillness and all-pervading silence. Everything seems frozen. Time itself seems to mourn, and even the wind is still. The car stops a short distance from the property, and we sit motionless and quiet.

Verbs in present tense describe the action.

I turn to my mother, questioning. But she has drawn a handkerchief from somewhere and is climbing out of the car. Almost as an actor on the stage, she releases a sound I have never heard before. It is a moan, a scream, and a sob that is deep-throated, guttural, and high-pitched all at the same time. This sudden transformation from a calm, chipper person to a stricken stranger strikes in me a fear that I will long remember. Holding her handkerchief to her face, she breaks into a shuffling run. I sit in the car petrified, watching the drama unfold.

Out of seemingly nowhere, wailing answers my mother's cry. Other women appear at a run, heading for my mother, hands fluttering from the tops of their heads, to their waists, to their feet. Their heads are thrown back and from side to side in restless anguish. Their bodies are half-bent forward, and their feet are in constant motion even though no distance is covered. My aunts and close female relatives weep, letting loose high-pitched, ululating moaning in support of my mother. As the wife of the first child and only son, she commands a high place, and she must not grieve alone.

The last sentence explains the women's actions.

In the confusion, one lady is knocked down, and she seems to rock with her legs separated in a way that in other circumstances would be inappropriate and humiliating. Oddly, the people in the tent, mostly male, appear to have seen and heard nothing. They continue silent and still. The whole scene seems unreal. Seeing my fear and confusion, the driver talks soothingly, explaining what is going on.

A paragraph describes one segment of the ceremony.

The wailing and mourning continue intermittently for a couple of days. Then the time comes for my grandfather to be taken from the mortuary in Kisumu to his final resting place. We all travel to the mortuary. He is dressed in his best suit and then taken to church, where his soul is committed to God. Afterward, the procession starts for home. On the way we are met by the other mourners, who, according to tradition, will accompany the hearse on foot, driving along the cows that are a symbol of wealth in life and a testament to a good life, respectability, and honor in death. Being city kids unable to jog for an hour with the mourners and cows, we ride in a car.

A transition word indicates a shift.

Finally, we are back at the homestead. My grandfather is put in the house where he spent the latter part of his life. The crying and mourning are now nearly at a feverish pitch, and the sense of loss is palpable. However, before people may enter the house to pay their last respects, one—they call him "Ratego"—must lead the way to say his good-byes. Suddenly, there is a commotion, and I stare in disbelief as a big bull, taller than my tall-for-my-age twelve-year-old height and wider than the doorway, is led toward my grandfather's house. Long, thick horns stick out of the colossal head. The

Precise words tell what the narrator sees and smells.

body, pungent with an ammonia-laced, grassy smell, is a mosaic of black and brown—an odorous, pulsing mountain.

The bull's wild, staring eyes seem fixed on me. An old, barefoot man, dressed in a worn, too-short jacket and dusty black pants, leads this bull with a frayed rope. He waves his rod, yelling and leaping in syncopation with the bull's snorting and pawing. Dust puffs dance around their feet. The bull is a symbol of high honor for my grandfather, and only the largest bull in the land can embody this deep respect. Although I do not fully comprehend its significance, I know that it is the biggest animal I have ever seen. I step back as people try to get the bull into the house to pay its respects to my grandfather. After much yelling, shoving, and cries of pain from those whose feet the bull steps on, the effort is abandoned. Ratego is much too big.

The narrative approaches its climax.

As the bull is led away into the *boma*, people enter the room that has been emptied of furniture. I squeeze through the heaving, weeping mass, almost suffocating in the process. The room is surprisingly cool and dim, unlike the hot and bright sun outside. I approach curiously and cautiously, not knowing what to expect. At last I stand before the casket and look at my grandfather. He does not look dead. In fact, he is smiling! He looks like the person I remember, who always had a smile and an unshared secret lurking in the depths of his eyes.

A flashback adds depth to the present.

I peer into his face, recalling a time when I was four and he caught me *11* doing something that deserved a reprimand. I had thought no one had seen me. However, my grandfather, on one of his rare visits to the city, had seen. Standing in front of his casket, I again hear him laugh. I remember how his kind, brown eyes had twinkled, and his white mustache, white teeth, and rich bitter-chocolate face had broken into an all-knowing, but-you-can-trust-me smile. I remember how the deep love that radiated from him assured me that I was his no matter what. And I remember how I had responded to his love by laughing happily and then skipping away, his answering laugh reverberating in my ears.

The narrator describes a pivotal point in the story.

That is my grandfather. Death cannot possibly touch him! Then I look *12* closer and realize that the white streak breaking up his face is not the white teeth I remember. It is, instead, cotton stuffed into his mouth, as white as his teeth had been, making a mockery of my memories. At that moment, my granddaddy dies.

The last sentence offers a powerful image.

Until this point, the whole has been a drama played out before my *13* stunned, wide-eyed gaze. Rich in ancestry and tradition, its very nature and continuity are a celebration of life rather than death, fostering in me a keen sense of identity and a strong desire to keep the ancestral torch burning brightly, fiercely, and with pride. Now, however, Grandpa is dead. It is now that I cry. I am grieving. My granddaddy is gone, and the weighted arrow of sorrow pierces home. The pain is personal, unrelenting, and merciless. I stare at him and cannot tear myself away. I weep, saying over and over that he is smiling, he is smiling. My heartbreak and tears echo the refrain. He is smiling—a radiant, unforgettable smile. ■

Reading for Better Writing

Working by yourself or with a group, answer these questions:

1. The writer uses verbs in the present tense to tell her story. How does this choice affect (a) the clarity of the plot, (b) the tension in the episode about the bull, and (c) your empathy with the narrator in the closing?

2. Choose a paragraph containing a particularly vivid description. How do the word choice, sentence structure, and punctuation affect your ability to sense the action?

3. In a conversation with an editor of this book, Jacqui Nyangi Owitti described her love for her grandfather and her pride in her heritage. Does the story reflect that love and pride? Explain.

Narration and Description

James C. Schaap is a writer and college professor. In this essay he describes the place that he took his writing students on a particularly memorable day. The essay was first published in the *Des Moines Register*.

That Morning on the Prairie

The writer introduces the setting.

On some beautiful early fall days out here on the emerald cusp of the Great Plains, it's hard to believe that we are where we are. Warm southern breezes swing up from Texas, the sun smiles with a gentleness not seen since June, and the spacious sky reigns over everything in azure glory. *1*

Early on exactly that kind of fall morning, I like to take my writing classes to a ghost town, Highland, Iowa, ten miles west and two south, as they say out here on the square-cut prairie. Likely as not, Highland fell victim to a century-old phenomenon in the Upper Midwest: 100 years ago, land was cut into 160-acre chunks, most had homesteads, and small towns thrived. Today, when the portions are ten times bigger, fewer people live out here, and many towns have died out. *2*

He details the location.

What's left of Highland is a stand of pines circled around no more than twenty gravestones, and an old carved sign with hand-drawn figures detailing what was home for some people—a couple of Protestant churches, a couple of horse barns, and a blacksmith shop, little else. The town of Highland once flourished atop this swell of land at the confluence of a pair of nondescript gravel roads that still float out in four distinct directions like dusky ribbons over undulating prairie. But mostly, today, it's gone. *3*

He explains why he takes students to Highland— and how they respond.

I like to take my students to Highland because what's not there never fails to silence them. Maybe it's the emaciated cemetery; maybe it's the south wind's low moan through that stand of pines, a sound you don't hear often on the plains; maybe it's some variant of culture shock—they stumble sleepily out of their cubicle dorm rooms and wake up suddenly in a place with no walls. *4*

I'm lying. I know why they fall into psychic shock. It's the sheer immensity of the land that unfurls before them, the horizon only seemingly there where earth weaves effortlessly into sky; it's the vastness of rolling landscape William Cullen Bryant once claimed looked like an ocean stopped in time. It seems as if there's nothing here, and everything, and that's what stuns them into silence. That September morning, on those gravel roads, no cars passed. We were alone—twenty of us, all alone and vulnerable on a high-ground swath of prairie once called Highland, surrounded by nothing but startling openness. *5*

The topic sentence indicates a transition.

That's where I was—and that's where they were—on September 11, 2001. We left for Highland about the same time Mohamed Atta and his friends were commandeering American Airlines Flight 11 into the north *6* tower of the World Trade Center, so we knew absolutely nothing about what had happened until we returned. While the rest of the world watched in horror, my students, notebooks and pens in hand, looked over a landscape so immense only God could live there—and were silent.

They found it hard to leave, but then no one can stay on retreat forever, so when we returned we heard the horrible news. All over campus and all over town, TVs blared. 7

I like to think that maybe on our campus that morning my students were best prepared for the horror everyone felt—prepared, not by having been warned, but by having been awed. 8

> The writer reflects on the trip's impact on students.

Every year it's a joy for me to sit at Highland with a new group of students, all of us trying to define and describe the beauty of what seems characterless prairie. But this year our being there on the morning of September 11 was more than a joy—it was also a kind of blessing. ■ 9

Reading for Better Writing

Working by yourself or with a group, answer these questions:

1. In the first three paragraphs of his essay, the writer describes Highland. Cite passages that do or do not help you see the setting. What mood or feeling does the description evoke?

2. James C. Schaap, himself a writer, takes his students to Highland, where he asks them to use the setting as a writing prompt. What could students learn from the experience? Why?

3. Schaap concludes the essay by saying that his students' presence in Highland on September 11 was "a kind of blessing." What does he mean?

4. What do you think the writer is trying to say in the last several lines?

Narration and Description

Eric Arthur Blair, better known as George Orwell, was a British author who wrote political and cultural commentary in the 1930s and 1940s. Some of his best-known works include the novels *Animal Farm* and *1984* and essays such as this one.

A Hanging

The writer starts in the middle of the scene so that we have to keep reading to learn what is happening.

It was in Burma, a sodden morning of the rains. A sickly light, like yellow tinfoil, was slanting over the high walls into the jail yard. We were waiting outside the condemned cells, a row of sheds fronted with double bars, like small animal cages. Each cell measured about ten feet by ten and was quite bare within except for a plank bed and a pot for drinking water. In some of them brown, silent men were squatting at the inner bars, with their blankets draped round them. These were the condemned men, due to be hanged within the next week or two.

The word *caressing* is an unexpected choice to describe the handling of the prisoner.

One prisoner had been brought out of his cell. He was a Hindu, a puny wisp of a man, with a shaven head and vague liquid eyes. He had a thick sprouting mustache, absurdly too big for his body, rather like the mustache of a comic man on the films. Six tall Indian warders were guarding him and getting him ready for the gallows. Two of them stood by with rifles and fixed bayonets, while the others handcuffed him, passed a chain through his handcuffs and fixed it to their belts, and lashed his arms tight to his sides. They crowded very close about him, with their hands always on him in a careful, caressing grip, as though all the while feeling him to make sure he was there. It was like men handling a fish which is still alive and may jump back into the water. But he stood quite unresisting, yielding his arms limply to the ropes, as though he hardly noticed what was happening.

Eight o'clock struck and a bugle call, desolately thin in the wet air, floated from the distant barracks. The superintendent of the jail, who was standing apart from the rest of us, moodily prodding the gravel with his stick, raised his head at the sound. He was an army doctor, with a grey toothbrush mustache and a gruff voice. "For God's sake, hurry up, Francis," he said irritably. "The man ought to have been dead by this time. Aren't you ready yet?"

The writer offers few details about the characters and event, building our curiosity.

Francis, the head jailer, a fat Dravidian in a white drill suit and gold spectacles, waved his black hand. "Yes sir, yes sir," he bubbled. "All iss satisfactorily prepared. The hangman iss waiting. We shall proceed."

"Well, quick march, then. The prisoners can't get their breakfast till this job's over."

We set out for the gallows. Two warders marched on either side of the prisoner, with their rifles at the slope; two others marched close against him, gripping him by arm and shoulder, as though at once pushing and

A surprise adds interest and contrast.

supporting him. The rest of us, magistrates and the like, followed behind. Suddenly, when we had gone ten yards, the procession stopped short without any order or warning. A dreadful thing had happened—a dog, come goodness knows whence, had appeared in the yard. It came bounding among us with a loud volley of barks and leapt round us wagging its whole body, wild with glee at finding so many human beings together. It was a large woolly dog, half Airedale, half pariah. For a moment it pranced around us, and then, before anyone could stop it, it had made a dash for the prisoner, and jumping up tried to lick his face. Everybody stood aghast, too taken aback even to grab the dog.

The quotation enlivens the scene.

"Who let that bloody brute in here?" said the superintendent angrily. "Catch it, someone!"   7

A warder detached from the escort, charged clumsily after the dog, but it danced and gambolled just out of his reach, taking everything as part of the game. A young Eurasian jailer picked up a handful of gravel and tried to stone the dog away, but it dodged the stones and came after us again. Its yaps echoed from the jail walls. The prisoner, in the grasp of the two warders, looked on incuriously, as though this was another formality of the hanging. It was several minutes   8

The writer offers a specific detail.

before someone managed to catch the dog. Then we put my handkerchief through its collar and moved off once more, with the dog still straining and whimpering.

It was about forty yards to the gallows. I watched the bare brown back of the prisoner marching in front of me. He walked clumsily with

> *This man was not dying, he was alive . . .*   9

his bound arms, but quite steadily, with that bobbing gait of the Indian who never straightens his knees. At each step his muscles slid neatly into place, the lock of hair on his scalp danced up and down, his feet printed themselves on the wet gravel. And once, in spite of the men who gripped him by each shoulder, he stepped lightly aside to avoid a puddle on the path.

Multiple details show that the man "was alive just as we are alive."

It is curious; but till that moment I had never realized what it means   10
to destroy a healthy, conscious man. When I saw the prisoner step aside to avoid the puddle, I saw the mystery, the unspeakable wrongness, of cutting a life short when it is in full tide. This man was not dying, he was alive just as we are alive. All the organs of this body were working—bowels digesting food, skin renewing itself, nails growing, tissues forming—all toiling away in solemn foolery. His nails would still be growing when he stood on the drop, when he was falling through the air with a tenth-of-a-second to live. His eyes saw the yellow gravel and the grey walls, and his brain still remembered, foresaw, reasoned—even about puddles. He and we were a party of men walking together, seeing, hearing, feeling, understanding the same world; and in two minutes, with a sudden snap, one of us would be gone—one mind less, one world less.

Details help us to picture the scene.

The gallows stood in a small yard, separate from the main grounds of the prison, and overgrown with tall prickly weeds. It was a brick erection like three sides of a shed, with planking on top, and above that two beams and a crossbar with the rope dangling. The hangman, a greyhaired convict in the white uniform of the prison, was waiting beside his machine. He greeted us with a servile crouch as we entered. At a word from Francis the two warders, gripping the prisoner more closely than ever, half led, half pushed him to the gallows and helped him clumsily up the ladder. Then the hangman climbed up and fixed the rope around the prisoner's neck.   *11*

Details about sounds and sights add tension and suspense.

We stood waiting, five yards away. The warders had formed in a rough circle round the gallows. And then, when the noose was fixed, the prisoner began crying out to his god. It was a high, reiterated cry of "Ram! Ram! Ram! Ram!" not urgent and fearful like a prayer or cry for help, but steady, rhythmical, almost like the tolling of a bell. The dog answered the sound with a whine. The hangman, still standing on the gallows, produced a small cotton bag like a flour bag and drew it down over the prisoner's face. But the sound, muffled by the cloth, still persisted, over and over again: "Ram! Ram! Ram! Ram!"   *12*

The writer contrasts the super-intendent's musings with the spectators' desire that the man die quickly so order can be restored.

The hangman climbed down and stood ready, holding the lever. Minutes seemed to pass. The steady, muffled crying from the prisoner went on and on, "Ram! Ram! Ram!" never faltering for an instant. The superintendent, his head on his chest, was slowly poking the ground with his stick; perhaps he was counting the cries, allowing the prisoner a fixed number—fifty, perhaps, or a hundred. Everyone had changed colour. The Indians had gone grey like bad coffee, and one or two of the bayonets were wavering. We looked at the lashed, hooded man on the drop, and listened to his cries—each cry another second of life; the same thought was in all our minds; oh, kill him quickly, get it over, stop that abominable noise!   *13*

> *The Indians had gone grey like bad coffee . . .*

Suddenly the superintendent made up his mind. Throwing up his head he made a swift motion with his stick. "Chalo!" he shouted almost fiercely.   *14*

There was a clanking noise, and then dead silence. The prisoner had vanished, and the rope was twisting on itself. I let go of the dog, and it galloped immediately to the back of the gallows; but when it got there it stopped short, barked, and then retreated into a corner of the yard, where it stood among the weeds, looking timorously out at us. We went round the gallows to inspect the prisoner's body. He was dangling with his toes pointed straight downwards, very slowly revolving, as dead as a stone.   *15*

"*He's* all right" is an unexpected, ironic remark.

The superintendent reached out with his stick and poked the bare brown body; it oscillated slightly. "*He's* all right," said the superintendent. He backed out from under the gallows, and blew out a deep breath. The moody look had gone out of his face quite suddenly. He glanced at his   *16* wrist-watch. "Eight minutes past eight. Well, that's all for this morning, thank God."

The warders unfixed bayonets and marched away. The dog, sobered and conscious of having misbehaved itself, slipped after them. We walked out of the gallows yard, past the condemned cells with their waiting prisoners, into the big central yard of the prison. The convicts, under the command of warders armed with lathis, were already receiving their breakfast. They squatted in long rows, each man holding a tin pannikin, while two warders with buckets marched around ladling out rice; it seemed quite a homely, jolly scene, after the hanging. An enormous relief had come upon us now that the job was done. One felt an impulse to sing, to break into a run, to snigger. All at once everyone began chattering gaily. ■

17

The closing describes an orderly, upbeat scene.

Reading for Better Writing

Working by yourself or with a group, answer these questions:

1. Orwell's title, "A Hanging," summarizes the plot and forecasts the closing. Would the climax of the piece shift if the hanging were a surprise? How and why?

2. What effect does the writer create by beginning the essay in the middle of the action, without explaining what led up to the hanging?

3. We anticipate that a hanging will take place, so the event itself is no surprise. However, some characters' actions do surprise us. Cite examples and explain their effects.

4. What do we learn about the narrator by what is—and is not—included in his retelling of events? For example, how do you respond to his summary of the hanging as a "job" and a "relief"? Why do you think the prisoner "vanishes" from the narrative after the hanging?

5. Throughout the piece, the narrator carefully describes the setting while offering few details about characters' emotional responses to the hanging. Why?

Narration and Description

Bel Kaufman is known as the author of *Up the Down Staircase* and as a scholar and a teacher. In this piece she explores what happens when an academic couple encounters a bully in the park.

Sunday in the Park

In the essay, highlight narrative passages. In the margin, note how each passage distinguishes a character or develops the essay's ideas.

It was still warm in the late-afternoon sun, and the city noises came muffled through the trees in the park. She put her book down on the bench, removed her sunglasses, and sighed contentedly. Morton was reading the *Times Magazine* section, one arm flung around her shoulder; their three-year-old son, Larry, was playing in the sandbox; a faint breeze fanned her hair softly against her cheek. It was five-thirty of a Sunday afternoon, and the small playground, tucked away in a corner of the park, was all but deserted. The swings and seesaws stood motionless and abandoned, the slides were empty, and only in the sandbox two little boys squatted diligently side by side. *How good this is*, she thought, and almost smiled at her sense of well-being. They must go out in the sun more often; Morton was so city-pale, cooped up all week inside the gray factorylike university. She squeezed his arm affectionately and glanced at Larry, delighting in the pointed little face frowning in concentration over the tunnel he was digging. The other boy suddenly stood up and with a quick, deliberate swing of his chubby arm threw a spadeful of sand at Larry. It just missed his head. Larry continued digging; the boy remained standing, shovel raised, stolid and impassive. 1

"No, no, little boy." She shook her finger at him, her eyes searching for the child's mother or nurse. "We mustn't throw sand. It may get in someone's eyes and hurt. We must play nicely in the nice sandbox." The boy looked at her in unblinking expectancy. He was about Larry's age but perhaps ten pounds heavier, a husky little boy with none of Larry's quickness and sensitivity in his face. Where was his mother? The only other people left in the playground were two women and a little girl on roller skates leaving now through the gate, and a man on a bench a few feet away. He was a big man, and he seemed to be taking up the whole bench as he held the Sunday comics close to his face. She supposed he was the child's father. He did not look up from his comics, but spat once deftly out of the corner of his mouth. She turned her eyes away. 2

At that moment, as swiftly as before, the fat little boy threw another spadeful of sand at Larry. This time some of it landed on his hair and forehead. Larry looked up at his mother, his mouth tentative; her expression would tell him whether to cry or not. 3

Her first instinct was to rush to her son, brush the sand out of his hair, and punish the other child, but she controlled it. She always said that she wanted Larry to learn to fight his own battles. 4

"Don't *do* that, little boy," she said sharply, leaning forward on the 5
bench. "You mustn't throw sand!"

The man on the bench moved his mouth as if to spit again, but instead 6
he spoke. He did not look at her, but at the boy only.

"You go right ahead, Joe," he said loudly. "Throw all you want. This 7
here is a *public* sandbox."

She felt a sudden weakness in her knees as she glanced at Morton. He 8
had become aware of what was happening. He put his *Times* down carefully
on his lap and turned his fine, lean face toward the man, smiling the shy,
apologetic smile he might have offered a student in pointing out an error
in his thinking. When he spoke to the man, it was with his usual
reasonableness.

"You're quite right," he said pleasantly, 9
"but just because this is a public place. . . ."

The man lowered his funnies and looked 10
at Morton. He looked at him from head to foot,
slowly and deliberately. "Yeah?" His insolent
voice was edged with menace. "My kid's got
just as good right here as yours, and if he feels
like throwing sand, he'll throw it, and if you
don't like it, you can take your kid the hell out of here."

> *His insolent voice was edged with menace.*

The children were listening, their eyes and mouths wide open, their 11
spades forgotten in small fists. She noticed the muscle in Morton's jaw
tighten. He was rarely angry; he seldom lost his temper. She was suffused
with a tenderness for her husband and an impotent rage against the man for
involving him in a situation so alien and so distasteful to him.

"Now, just a minute," Morton said courteously, "you must realize. . . ." 12

"Aw, shut up," said the man. 13

Her heart began to pound. Morton half rose; the *Times* slid to the 14
ground. Slowly the other man stood up. He took a couple of steps toward
Morton, then stopped. He flexed his great arms, waiting. She pressed her
trembling knees together. Would there be violence, fighting? How dreadful,
how incredible. . . . She must do something, stop them, call for help. She
wanted to put her hand on her husband's sleeve, to pull him down, but for
some reason she didn't.

Morton adjusted his glasses. He was very pale. "This is ridiculous," 15
he said unevenly. "I must ask you. . . ."

"Oh, yeah?" said the man. He stood with his legs spread apart, rocking 16
a little, looking at Morton with utter scorn. "You and who else?"

For a moment the two men looked at each other nakedly. Then Morton 17
turned his back on the man and said quietly, "Come on, let's get out of
here." He walked awkwardly, almost limping with self-consciousness, to the
sandbox. He stooped and lifted Larry and his shovel out.

At once Larry came to life; his face lost its rapt expression and he began to kick and cry. "I don't *want* to go home, I want to play better, I don't want any supper, I don't *like* supper. . . ." It became a chant as they walked, pulling their child between them, his feet dragging on the ground. In order to get to the exit gate they had to pass the bench where the man sat sprawling again. She was careful not to look at him. With all the dignity she could summon, she pulled Larry's sandy, perspiring little hand, while Morton pulled the other. Slowly and with head high she walked with her husband and child out of the playground. 18

Her first feeling was one of relief that a fight had been avoided, that no one was hurt. Yet beneath it there was a layer of something else, something heavy and inescapable. She sensed that it was more than just an unpleasant incident, more than defeat of reason by force. She felt dimly it had something to do with her and Morton, something acutely personal, familiar, and important. 19

> *Yet beneath it there was a layer of something else . . .*

Suddenly Morton spoke. "It wouldn't have proved anything." 20

"What?" she asked. 21

"A fight. It wouldn't have proved anything beyond the fact that he's bigger than I am." 22

"Of course," she said. 23

"The only possible outcome," he continued reasonably, "would have been—what? My glasses broken, perhaps a tooth or two replaced, a couple of days' work missed—and for what? For justice? For truth?" 24

"Of course," she repeated. She quickened her step. She wanted only to get home and to busy herself with her familiar tasks; perhaps then the feeling, glued like heavy plaster on her heart, would be gone. *Of all the stupid, despicable bullies*, she thought, pulling harder on Larry's hand. The child was still crying. Always before she had felt a tender pity for his defenseless little body, the frail arms, the narrow shoulders with sharp, winglike shoulder blades, the thin legs, unsure, but now her mouth tightened in resentment. 25

"Stop crying," she said sharply. "I'm ashamed of you!" She felt as if all three of them were tracking mud along the street. The child cried louder. 26

If there had been an issue involved, she thought, *if there had been something to fight for. . . . But what else could he possibly have done? Allow himself to be beaten? Attempt to educate the man? Call a policeman? "Officer, there's a man in the park who won't stop his child from throwing sand on mine. . . ."* The whole thing was as silly as that, and not worth thinking about. 27

"Can't you keep him quiet, for Pete's sake?" Morton asked irritably.   *28*

"What do you suppose I've been trying to do?" she said. Larry pulled   *29*
back, dragging his feet.

"If you can't discipline this child, I will," Morton snapped, making   *30*
a move toward the boy.

But her voice stopped him. She was shocked to hear it, thin and cold   *31*
and penetrating with contempt. "Indeed?" she heard herself say. "You and
who else?" ■

Reading for Better Writing

Working by yourself or with a group, answer these questions:

1. Reread the first paragraph. How does Kaufman's description make the
setting seem first idyllic and then suddenly menacing?

2. Why isn't the woman given a name?

3. Notice that Morton is reading the *Times* whereas the other man is
reading the "funnies." What does Kaufman suggest about each man by
noting what he is reading?

4. How might the overall effect of the essay differ if it were told from
Morton's perspective?

5. Notice the use of contrast and repetition in this piece: repeated
references to the contrasting newspapers; repeated contrasts between
the way the woman had previously felt and the way she feels now;
repeated physical contrasts between Morton and the man, or Larry and
the boy; and repeated contrasts in the tone and diction of Morton and
the man. In what ways does this contrast and repetition accentuate the
significance of the woman's final question?

Model

Guidelines
Writing Narration and Description

1. **Select a topic.** Think about your own experiences. Sort through the stories you recall and choose one that is important enough to share with others. Think of a way to approach this experience in a personal narrative.

> **TIP:** If you can't think of an interesting story, try writing in response to the following statement: *Remember a time when you first discovered that the world was (a) stranger, (b) more wonderful, or (c) more complex than you had thought as a child.* Think about how that experience prepared you to be who you are today.

2. **Narrow your focus.** Once you have chosen an experience to write about, begin to narrow your topic by focusing on a specific moment or outcome. The following questions can help you find a clear focus:
   - What is the key moment—the significant point or climax— in the story?
   - What led up to this key moment? What resulted from it?
   - What was really going on?
   - How did others experience the event?
   - What has time taught you about this experience?
   - What would you have changed?

3. **Determine your purpose and audience.** After you have a specific focus, decide why you are telling your story and who might read the story. Personal narratives can serve one of many purposes and appeal to many audiences. Consider these purposes:
   - To entertain
   - To warn
   - To challenge
   - To celebrate
   - To illustrate
   - To persuade
   - To remind
   - To gain sympathy
   - To encourage

4. **Gather details.** Gather material that will serve your purpose. Try sorting through photo albums, home videos, and letters. Interview someone who shared your experience or saw you through it. Consult your journal or diary.

5. **Collaborate.** Tell someone your story; then ask for comments and questions. Based on the feedback you receive, create a basic writing plan. Your plan can be anything from a simple list to a detailed outline.

6. **Write your first draft.** As you write, keep in mind your specific focus and your overall purpose for telling this story. Use the following strategies as you create your first draft:

    - **Set the stage.** Show where things happened. Describe the atmosphere, the people, and the events by using precise details that appeal to the five senses. If appropriate, use comparisons and metaphors to make the descriptions vivid.
    - **Include dialogue.** To infuse your narrative with a sense of reality, recall and create conversations between the people in your story.

    > **TIP:** Use dialogue to enhance a key scene or to explain the relationship between people. But be selective—don't let dialogue dribble on for its own sake.

    - **Build the plot.** Arouse and sustain interest by establishing conflict, building suspense, highlighting the main point, and showing the outcome.
    - **Express your feelings.** It may help to include both past and present thoughts and feelings—those you had during the experience and those you have now, looking back on the past.
    - **Use transitions.** Words like *as, before, meanwhile,* and *later* show where your story is leading. (See page 85.)
    - **Select verbs carefully.** Verbs affect the movement and voice of your story. Choose strong, active verbs, and make sure tenses accurately reflect time sequences and relationships.

7. **Share your story.** Show your draft to someone. What main point does this reader see in your story? What suggestions or questions does the reader have?

8. **Revise your writing.** Carefully review and revise your writing. Remember that your goal is to re-create an interesting incident or event for your readers. Ask yourself the following questions:

    - Does the writing focus on a specific incident or event?
    - Does the writing contain effective details, descriptions, and dialogue?
    - Does the narrative effectively state or imply a theme, thesis, or point of significance?
    - Does the writing sound sincere and natural?
    - Will readers appreciate the way the story is told?

9. **Edit and proofread.** (See the checklist on page 110.)

10. **Prepare your final copy.** Use an appropriate type font and size. Leave the right margin ragged (uneven). Place photographs or drawings close to the text they illustrate. Print your final copy on quality paper.

Writing Checklist

Use these seven traits to check the quality of your writing; then revise as needed:

_____ The **ideas** focus on a specific experience or event and present an engaging picture of the action and people involved.

_____ The **organization** pattern adds to the clarity of the piece and includes a clear beginning that pulls readers in.

_____ The **voice** shows that the writer is truly interested in the subject by speaking knowledgeably and enthusiastically.

_____ The **words** *show* instead of *tell about*; they appeal to the senses and evoke pictures in the reader's mind.

_____ The **sentences** are clear, varied in structure, and smooth.

_____ The **copy** includes no errors in spelling, mechanics, punctuation, or grammar.

_____ The **design** follows assigned guidelines for format. Photographs and drawings are clear and well placed.

Interactive

Critical-Thinking and Writing Activities

As directed by your instructor, complete the following activities alone or with a group.

1. Review "Mzee Owitti" and "Sunday in the Park," observing how the writers help you share their experiences by presenting vivid details in an open, honest way. List a few of your own experiences that you would like to explore and share. Then choose one that would be an appropriate subject for a personal narrative. Write the narrative, perhaps using some of the same organizational strategies employed in these models.

2. Review the ways in which Bel Kaufman uses dialogue, physical description, and personal objects/possessions to contrast two characters in "Sunday in the Park." Draft or revise a narrative in which you shape characters through distinctive dialogue, physical description, and personal possessions.

3. Review "A Hanging" and "Sunday in the Park," noting how the authors of both essays portray certain characters in a negative light without making direct comments to that effect. Draft or revise a portrayal of a person in which you show (rather than tell) your feelings about the individual.

◄ VISUALLY SPEAKING

Review the image on page **145**, looking for its "story." Imagine what has happened and what is happening. Then write a brief narrative relating what happens next.

DESCRIPTION AND REFLECTION

11

Audio

Video

It is human nature to reflect. On this score, eighteenth-century poet Robert Burns thought mice luckier than people. In his poem "To a Mouse," Burns noted that mice worry only about the present, whereas humans worry about past, present, and future woes. Whether or not reflecting on the past is unique to humans, we do know that this trait brings joy, regret, and a thousand variations of those feelings to humans both young and old.

A personal reflection is often written to draw wisdom from past experiences. Accordingly, you may want to explore an earlier time in your life and reflect on why you felt as you did when you suffered a stinging setback or won a glorious victory.

In this chapter, you'll find topics to consider, model essays, and guidelines that will help you describe and reflect on a memorable experience. In the process, you will likely gain insight not only into your past experience, but also into its links to your present and future.

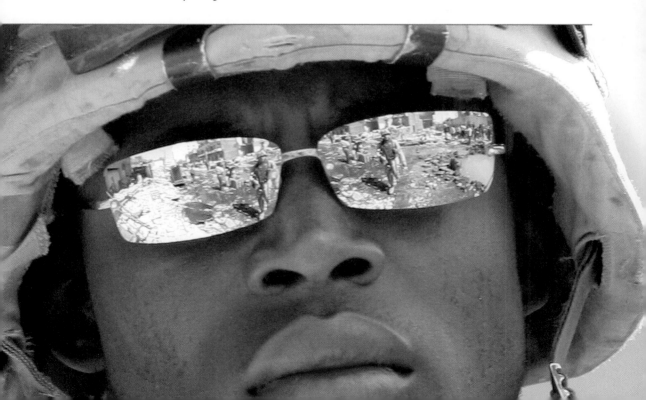

Overview
Writing Description and Reflection

Writer's Goal

Your goal is to write an essay in which you carefully describe one or more past experiences and reflect on their importance in your life.

Keys for Success

Recall precise details. To understand and appreciate your reflections, readers first have to grasp exactly what you experienced. For that reason, you must describe those key details (sights, smells, tastes) that make the experience memorable to you—and worth reflecting on. Often you will find these details in the hardly-noticed-at-the-time part of your memory.

Probe the topic. The mind-searching aspect of writing this essay happens while asking *so-why* questions: *So why does this picture still make me smile?* or *Why does his comment still hurt?* or *Why did I do that when I knew better?*—or *Did I know better?* Your answers will help explain why this memory is important to you.

Reveal what you find. Your readers need to experience what you experienced, so don't hide what's embarrassing, painful, or still unclear. Show them the details clearly, explain your insights honestly, and then trust readers to respond with sensitivity, appreciation, and respect.

Topics to Consider

The most promising topics are experiences that gave you insights into yourself, and possibly into others as well. Often such an experience will have led you or others to change patterns of thinking, feeling, or behavior. To identify such topics, consider the categories below and then list whatever experiences come to mind:

* Times when you felt *secure, hopeful, distraught, appreciated, confident, frightened, exploited,* or *misunderstood.*
* Times when you made a decision about *lifestyles, careers, education, politics, religion, leaving home,* or *getting an education.*
* Events that tested your *will, patience, self-concept,* or *goals.*
* Events that changed or confirmed your assessment of a *person, a group, an institution, a religious belief, a political conviction,* or a *philosophical worldview.*

> **Next Step** Read the model essays and perform the activities that follow. As you read, note how the writers help you grasp what they experienced and why their experiences are important.

Description and Reflection

Nicole Suurdt is a student from Ontario, Canada. In this essay, she describes a time and place that she loved as a child and yearns for as an adult.

The Stream in the Ravine

Behind my childhood home is a small ravine, and through it runs the seasonal overflow of a little pond deep within the woods. It's a noisy stream, just narrow enough for an eight-year-old to take one stretching step across and reach the other side with dry shoes. And when I was eight, this stream was everything to me. *1*

The writer introduces the topic and then gives background information.	You see, for most of my childhood, I lived on a small hobby farm in Ontario, Canada, where rolling pasture and croplands surrounded my home. The pasture fenced in Scottish Highland cattle with terrifying horns, unbroken horses with skittish hooves, and one half-blind, unpredictable donkey. These creatures separated me from the woods just beyond the pasture. But when I was little, it wasn't simply my fear of these fitful animals that penned me in on my side of the fence—it was a fear of what lay beyond the shadowy barrier of maples and pines. *2*
Description of the visits builds tension.	It's not that I'd never been to the woods before. I had, twice. The first time, my brother took me in search of the tallest tree in the forest and got us lost for a couple of hours. My second visit was a dark winter journey. Dad dragged the family into the woods late one night in search of a missing cow. We found her half-devoured body lying in bloodstained snow, packed down by wolves' paws. *3*
A transition signals a shift in the action.	But eventually, curiosity overpowered my fears. One spring day when I was eight, armed with a staff, I skirted the pasture and headed for the forest. I approached the fence that my dad had put up to ward off the woods. Quickly I scaled the fence, but then stood some time holding on to its boards, figuring that if a wolf came along, I could scramble back to the other side. However, after five minutes passed and no wolf appeared, I calmed down, let go of the fence, and stepped into the forest—lured on by the sound of chipmunks, birds, wind through trees, and snapping twigs. *4*
	Drawn forward, I discovered rocky burrows of unknown creatures. I chased chipmunks. I sang. I passed a hunter's fort perched high in a pine, deserted after last fall's deer-hunting season. I passed under an archway of tall cedars. I waded through the muck and mire surrounding a small swamp and plodded my mud-caked shoes up a small rise, thick with the faded, crumbled leaves of last year's fall. One particular sound kept pulling me forward—the gurgle of running water. *5*
The writer describes the stream and shares its personal importance.	Standing at the peak of the rise, with brown leaves stuck to my muddy sneakers, I found the source. Below me, within its shallow bed, ran a tiny stream, little more than a trickle, really. But to me it was a beautiful, rushing *6*

brook, my own source of clear, cold water protected by oak, maple, and pine sentries. That day I spent hours scooping decaying leaves out of my stream's bed and sitting by her side to watch the water spill over the rocks and roots. She was my own discovery, my own territory, my own secret place. From that day on, the little stream past the hunter's fort, under the cedar archway, through the muck and the mire, and over the rocky rise became my quiet, private place.

The picture shows the father, the daughter, and their bridge.

But I never could keep a secret for long. During dinner one Sunday, I told my parents about my stream. I figured that it needed a bridge, something only Dad could help me build. And so, that afternoon, I led Mom and Dad over the fence, into the woods, and up to my secret stream. Together, we built a bridge using the fallen branches lying about. Mom took a picture of Dad and me sitting on our homemade, lopsided bridge, the water washing over the toes of the big rubber boots that she had insisted we wear.   7

My parents separated eight years after that picture was taken, and I haven't gone back to my stream since, though I think of it often. Somewhere, tucked away in Mom's photo albums, is the picture of a little girl in her dreamland, her dad beside her, his big feet hanging near her small ones. Her mom stands in the water just a few feet away behind the camera lens.   8

The writer yearns for life as shown in the photo.

Sometimes, I want to go back there, back into that photo. I want to step into a time when life seemed safe, and a tiny stream gave us all that we needed. In that picture, our smiles last, our hearts are calm, and we hear only quiet voices, forest sounds, and my bubbling stream. Bitter words are silenced and tears held back by the click and whir of a camera.   9

I've been thinking about making the journey again past the hunter's fort, under the stand of cedars, through the muck and mire, and over the rocky rise. But it's been a long summer, and the small, seasonal stream running out of the overflow of the pond has probably dried up. ■   10

Reading for Better Writing

Working by yourself or with a group, answer these questions:

1. Three times in the essay, the writer mentions four sites (hunter's fort, cedar archway, muck and mire, rocky rise) along her route. What do the references to these sites contribute to the description?

2. How does the writer organize her description? Identify the strategies used and discuss their effectiveness.

3. Review the references to the photograph taken by the mother, and describe what the photo shows. What does the writer mean when she says, "Sometimes, I want to go back there, back into that photo"?

4. Reread the opening and closing paragraphs, comparing how the writer describes the stream in each paragraph. Are the details and voices of the two passages different? Give examples.

Description and Reflection

Randall VanderMey is a college professor and writer who based this essay on the observations he recorded while waiting for a bus in a Greyhound station. As you will see, the essay is much more than an as-it-happened record of what the writer saw and heard. It is also a brief documentary of a particular slice of American life.

"Scab!"

1

The opening establishes a tense context and tone.

The driver of the airport shuttle bus had to drop me off on the street so as not to cross the line of Greyhound drivers marching with their picket signs in the dusk. The picketers were angry. Had he turned in at the driveway to the terminal, they would have spat on him and yelled "Scab!" or "Strikebreaker!" Newspapers and TV had carried stories of rocks and bottles being thrown at passenger-filled buses by disgruntled Greyhound drivers whose demands for decent wages had not been heard. Most of the drivers in other unions were honoring the picket lines. Someday, they knew, they might be in the same fix.

2

The writer locates himself in the scene.

Inside the terminal I sat with my feet on my suitcase. I didn't want to pay four quarters for a storage box and didn't want to turn my back on my belongings. In the strange, tense atmosphere of the bus depot, I wondered if I was better off there or on a bus. Writing notes became my shield.

3

Switching to present tense, he describes what he senses.

A Hispanic couple behind me plays Spanish music for everyone in the terminal to hear. Men go in the men's room and stay there for a strangely long time, punching the button on the electric blow dryer over and over as if to cover up their talk. Near me an old man in a blue baseball cap and blue nylon jacket mumbles to himself as he paces the floor slowly. I hear him say, "My children is all grown up." Another man in a white yachting cap strides around the terminal making a sliding, streaking sound with a metal heel protector that's working its way loose. He seems to like the sound because he keeps walking around on the hard tile floors, over to the video-game room, over to the cafeteria, over to the bathroom, over to the ticket window, around and around in the open spaces in front of the nuns, college kids, young black girls with children, and Texas farmers waiting for their bus to Dallas. I know where the man in the yachting cap is without even looking up.

4

A tiny boy, curiosity in a red sweater, is twirling around. Everybody who sees him smiles. A while ago I saw an older man teasing him, saying "Hey, I'm gonna get you" and trying to slip a ten-gallon straw cowboy hat over his ears.

5

He describes the terminal and the people, including snippets of dialogue.

A policeman with his hair shaved off all over his round, bumpy head takes his drawn nightstick into the men's room and brings out, by the elbow, a young black man who doesn't seem to know where he is. He cradles a radio in his arm that blasts its music to everyone's discomfort. The cop says,

"Didn't I throw you out of here last night? Come on with me."

The guy looks dazed and says, "Where we going?" 6

The cop says, "We're just going to have a little talk." Turning off the 7
blaring radio, he walks the young man toward the entrance.

He records what he sees, hears, and smells.

Something weird is in the air, as if drugs are being dealt in the 8
bathrooms, though the place remains calm and well lit. The odor of french
fries and cleaning solutions fills the air.

The Hispanic music plays much more softly now, and I hear the dyed- 9
blond lady break out of her Spanish to say to her husband or boyfriend,
"Thang you very mush."

The writer briefly reflects on the scene.

The iron screen benches are starting to lay a print in my back and rear 10
end, so I shift and squirm. When I bought my ticket at the front counter, I
asked the lady who took my money what I'd have to do for two hours and a
half. She had laughed and said, "Look at the walls," and she had been right.

The man in the blue baseball cap is mumbling again. But now I see 11
that he's reading the newspaper and seems not to be able to read unless he
pronounces the words aloud. I hear him say, "That's a liquidation sale."

Contrasting details create rich impressions.

The man with the metal heel protector is back again, clicking and 12
shrieking across the tile floor, carrying a blue nylon satchel. Out of the
video-game room come noises like echoes in a long hollow pipe. A kid
behind the cash register in the cafeteria has neatly combed hair and glasses.
He keeps smiling all the time, looking comfortingly sane. Overhead in there,
the ceiling-fan blades turn hardly faster than the second hand on a clock.

Reflecting on his experience, the writer relates it to crossing a picket line.

It has taken me some time to realize fully how I felt on that hard metal 13
bench for two and a half hours among so many different kinds of people
harboring so many different purposes. I said not a word to anyone. Only
wrote and wrote. With my eyes and ears I broke into their lives while giving
nothing of myself. I got in and got away without any real contact.

I hope the drivers get their money. But I'm not sure my being there 14
helped. I felt like a scab. ■

Reading for Better Writing

Working by yourself or with a group, answer these questions:

1. This personal essay is filled with tension. What is the source of this tension, and how does it create a theme for the essay?

2. Locate where the writer shifts verb tenses from past to present, and then to past again. What is the effect of these shifts?

3. How does the writer make his observations vivid? Trace sights, sounds, smells, textures, and tastes. Do these details create patterns or themes?

4. The writer is both present in and separate from the scene. Explore the strengths and limitations of the writer's uneasy position.

Description and Reflection

Mary Seymour reflects on her experiences with bipolar disorder, which is sometimes called manic depression.

Call Me Crazy, But I Have to Be Myself

The writer labels herself "mentally ill."

Nearly every day, without thinking, I say things like "So-and-so is driving me crazy" or "That's nuts!" Sometimes I catch myself and realize that I'm not being sensitive toward people with mental illness. Then I remember I'm one of the mentally ill. If I can't throw those words around, who can?   1

Being a functional member of society and having a mental disorder is an intricate balancing act. Every morning I send my son to junior high school, put on professional garb, and drive off to my job as alumni-magazine editor at a prep school, where I've worked for six years. Only a few people at work know I'm manic-depressive, or bipolar, as it's sometimes called.   2

An example illustrates the extent of the illness.

Sometimes I'm not sure myself what I am. I blend in easily with "normal" people. You'd never know that seven years ago, fueled by the stress of a failing marriage and fanned by the genetic inheritance of a manic-depressive grandfather, I had a psychotic break. To look at me, you'd never guess I once ran naked through my yard or shuffled down the hallways of a psychiatric ward. To hear me, you'd never guess God channeled messages to me through my computer. After my breakdown at 36, I was diagnosed as bipolar, a condition marked by moods that swing between elation and despair.   3

More examples show the difficulties the writer faces.

It took a second, less-severe psychotic episode in 1997, followed by a period of deep depression, to convince me I truly was bipolar. Admitting I had a disorder that I'd have to manage for life was the hardest thing I've ever done. Since then, a combination of therapy, visits to a psychiatrist, medication, and inner calibration have helped me find an even keel. Now I manage my moods with the vigilance of a mother hen, nudging them back to center whenever they wander too far. Eating wisely, sleeping well, and exercising regularly keep me balanced from day to day. Ironically, my disorder has taught me to be healthier and happier than I was before.   4

Most of the time, I feel lucky to blend in with the crowd. Things that most people grumble about—paying bills, maintaining a car, working 9 to 5—strike me as incredible privileges. I'll never forget gazing through the barred windows of the psychiatric ward into the parking lot, watching people come and go effortlessly, wondering if I'd ever be like them again. There's nothing like a stint in a locked ward to make one grateful for the freedoms and burdens of full citizenship.   5

Yet sometimes I feel like an impostor. Sometimes I wish I could sit at the lunch table and talk about lithium and Celexa instead of *Will & Grace*.   6

> **Each sentence begins with a similar phrase that reveals the writer's feelings.**

While everyone talks about her fitness routine, I want to brag how it took five orderlies to hold me down and shoot me full of sedatives when I was admitted to the hospital, and how for a brief moment I knew the answers to every infinite mystery of the blazingly bright universe. I yearn for people to know me—the real me—in all my complexity, but I'm afraid it would scare the bejesus out of them.

Every now and then, I feel like I'm truly being myself. Like the time the school chaplain, in whom I'd confided my past, asked me to help counsel a severely bipolar student. This young woman had tried to commit suicide, had been hospitalized many times, and sometimes locked herself in her dorm room to keep the "voices" from overwhelming her. I walked and talked with her, sharing stories about medication and psychosis. I hoped to show by example that manic-depression did not necessarily mean a diminished life. At commencement, I watched her proudly accept her diploma; despite ongoing struggles with her illness, she's continuing her education. 7

> **An extended example illustrates the point.**

I'm able to be fully myself with my closest friends, all of whom have similar schisms between private and public selves. We didn't set out to befriend each other—we just all speak the same language, of hardship and spiritual discovery and psychological awareness. 8

What I yearn for most is to integrate both sides of myself. I want to be part of the normal world but I also want to own my identity as bipolar. I want people to know what I've been through so I can help those traveling a similar path. Fear has kept me from telling my story: fear of being stigmatized, of making people uncomfortable, of being reduced to a label. But hiding the truth has become more uncomfortable than letting it out. It's time for me to own up to who I am, complicated psychiatric history and all. Call me crazy, but I think it's the right thing to do. ■ 9

> **The final line echoes the title.**

Reading for Better Writing

Working by yourself or with a group, answer these questions:

1. What purpose does Seymour identify for writing the essay? What other purposes might be served by publishing this piece for *Newsweek*'s readers?

2. The writer starts with one category label for herself ("mentally ill") and then quickly adds another ("functional member of society"). How does the second label redefine the first?

3. Description is used to support many other kinds of writing, including the types of analytical and persuasive writing outlined here in *The College Writer*. In what other chapters could this essay have been included, and how do you know?

4. Review the "Editing and Proofreading" section of this book (pages 93–110), especially the portion on biased words. Why does Seymour use the phrase "call me crazy"? Is her use of the word biased or insulting? Explain.

Description and Reflection

At the age of six, K. Oanh Ha fled Vietnam as a refugee and came to the United States, where she has become an accomplished journalist. In this essay, Ha reflects on experiences through which she developed her Asian American identity. (Note: By typing the writer's name in your browser, you can peruse her website, blog, and sample publications.)

American Dream Boat

As you read this essay, highlight key descriptive and reflective passages. Then, in the margin, note what each contributes to the essay.

1   The wedding day was only two weeks away when my parents called with yet another request. In accordance with Vietnamese custom, they fully expected Scott Harris, my fiancé, and his family to visit our family on the morning of the wedding, bearing dowry gifts of fruit, candies, jewelry, and a pig, in an elaborate procession.

2   "But it's not going to mean anything to Scott or his family. They're not Vietnamese!" I protested. My parents were adamant: "Scott's marrying a Vietnamese. If he wants to marry you, he'll honor our traditions."

3   Maybe there's no such thing as a stress-free wedding. Small or large, there's bound to be pressure. But our February 12 wedding was a large do-it-yourselfer that required a fusion of Vietnamese and American traditions—a wedding that forced me and my parents to wrestle with questions about our identities, culture, and place in America. After nearly twenty years here, my family, and my parents in particular, were determined to have a traditional Vietnamese wedding of sorts, even if their son-in-law and Vietnam-born, California-raised daughter are as American as they can be.

4   And so I grudgingly called Scott that night to describe the wedding procession and explain the significance of the ritual. It's a good thing that he is a patient, easygoing man. "I'll bring the pig," he said, "but I'm worried it'll make a mess in the car."

5   "Oh! It's a roasted pig," I told him, laughing.

6   I was six years old when my family fled Vietnam in July 1979, just one family among the thousands who collectively became known as the "boat people," families who decided it was better to risk the very real possibility of death at sea than to live under Communist rule. But, of course, I never understood the politics then. I was just a child following my parents.

7   My memories are sketchy. There was the time that Thai pirates wielding saber-like machetes raided our boat. Two years ago, I told my mother, Kim Hanh Nguyen, how I remembered a woman dropping a handful of jewelry into my porridge during the raid with the instruction to keep eating. "That was no woman," my mother said. "That was me!" When we reached the refugee camp in Kuala Lumpur, my mother used the wedding ring and necklace to buy our shelter.

In September 1980, we arrived in Santa Ana, California, in Orange   *8*
County, now home to the largest Vietnamese community outside of
Vietnam. Those who had left in 1975, right after the end of the war and the
American withdrawal, had been well educated, wealthy, and connected with
military. My family was part of the wave of boat people—mostly middle-
class and with little education—who sought refuge in America.

For nearly a year after we arrived,   *9*
we crowded into the same three-bedroom
apartment—all thirteen of us: brothers,
sisters, cousins, uncles, aunts, sisters-in-law,
and my father's mother. There were only
four of us children in my immediate family
then, three born in Vietnam and one born
shortly after our resettlement in the U.S.

> *We started school
> and watched Mr.
> Rogers on PBS in
> the afternoons,
> grew to love*   *10*
> *hamburgers and
> ketchup, and
> longed to lose our
> accents.*

We started school and watched Mr.
Rogers on PBS in the afternoons, grew to
love hamburgers and ketchup, and longed
to lose our accents. We older kids did lose
our accents—and those who came later
never had accents to begin with because
they were born here. When we first came, I
was the oldest of three children, all born in
Vietnam. Now I have seven siblings, twenty-two years separating me from
my youngest brother, who will start kindergarten in the fall.

In some ways, I was the stereotypical Asian nerd. I took honors classes,   *11*
received good grades, played the violin and cello. But there was a part of
me that also yearned to be as American as my blond-haired neighbors
across the street. I joined the school's swim and tennis teams, participated
in speech competitions (which were attended by mostly white students)
and worshipped Esprit and Guess. My first serious boyfriend was white,
but most of my friends were Asians who were either born in the U.S. or
immigrated when they were very young. None of us had accents, and we
rarely spoke our native languages around one another. The last thing we
wanted was to be mistaken for FOBs—fresh off the boat. I even changed my
name to Kyrstin, unaware of its Nordic roots.

I wanted so badly to be a full-fledged American, whatever that meant.   *12*
At home, though, my parents pushed traditional Vietnamese values. I spent
most of my teenage years babysitting and had to plead with my then overly
strict parents to let me out of the house. "Please, please. I just want to be
like any other American kid."

My parents didn't understand. "You'll always be Vietnamese. No one's   *13*
going to look at you and say you're an American," was mother's often-heard
refrain.

I saw college as my escape, the beginning of the trip I would undertake *14* on my own. We had come to America as a family but it was time I navigated alone. College was my flight from the house that always smelled of fish sauce and jasmine tea.

At UCLA, I dated the man who would become my husband. Though he's *15* seventeen years older than I am, my parents seemed to be more concerned with the cultural barriers than our age difference. "White Americans are fickle. They don't understand commitment and family responsibility like we Asians do," I was told.

Soon after I announced my engagement, my father, Minh Phu Ha, and *16* I had a rare and intimate conversation. "I'm just worried for you," he said. "All the Vietnamese women I know who have married whites are divorced from them. Our cultures are too far apart."

My father, I think, is worried that none of his kids will marry Vietnamese. *17* My sisters are dating non-Vietnamese Asians while my brother is dating a white American. "It's just that with a Vietnamese son-in-law, I can talk to him," my father explained to me one day. "A Vietnamese son-in-law would call me 'Ba' and not by my first name."

Although my parents have come to terms with having Scott as their son-in-law and to the prospect of grandchildren who will be racially mixed, there are still times when Scott comes to visit that there are awkward silences. There are still many cultural barriers. *18*

I still think of what it all means to marry a white American. I worry that my children won't be able to speak Vietnamese and won't appreciate that part of their heritage. I also wonder if somehow this is the ultimate fulfillment of a latent desire to be "American." *19*

Vietnamese-Americans, like Chinese-Americans, Indian-Americans, and other assimilated immigrants, often speak of leading hyphenated lives, of feet that straddle both cultures. I've always been proud of being Vietnamese. As my family *20*

> *Vietnamese-Americans, like Chinese-Americans, Indian-Americans, and other assimilated immigrants, often speak of leading hyphenated lives, of feet that straddle both cultures.*

and I discussed and heatedly debated what the wedding event was going to look like, I began to realize just how "American" I had become.

And yet there was no denying the pull of my Vietnamese roots. Four *21* months before the wedding, I traveled back to Vietnam for the second time since our family's escape. It was a trip I planned for more than a year. I was in Saigon, the city of my birth, to research and write a novel that loosely mirrors the story of my own family and our journey from Vietnam. The novel is my tribute to my family and our past. I'm writing it for myself as much as for my younger siblings, so they'll know what our family's been through.

I returned to Vietnam to connect with something I can't really name but know I lost when we left twenty years ago. I was about to start a new journey with the marriage ahead, but I needed to come back to the place where my family's journey began.

Scott came along for the first two weeks and met my extended family. They all seemed to approve, especially when he showed he could eat pungent fish and shrimp sauce like other Vietnamese.

> *I returned to Vietnam to connect with something I can't really name but know I lost when we left twenty years ago.*

During my time there I visited often with family members and talked about the past. I saw the hospital where I was born, took a walk through our old house, chatted with my father's old friends. The gaps in the circle of my hyphenated life came closer together with every new Vietnamese word that I learned, with every Vietnamese friend that I made.

I also chose the fabric for the tailoring of the ao dai, the traditional Vietnamese dress of a long tunic over flowing pants, which I would change into at the reception. I had my sisters' bridesmaid gowns made. And I had a velvet ao dai made for my eighty-eight-year-old maternal grandmother, B Ngoai, to wear to the wedding of her oldest grandchild. "My dream is to see you on your wedding day and eat at your wedding feast," she had told me several times.

B Ngoai came to the U.S. in 1983, three years after my family landed in Orange County as war refugees. As soon as we got to the United States, my mother filed immigration papers for her. B Ngoai nurtured and helped raise her grandchildren.

I had extended my stay in Vietnam. Several days after my original departure date, I received a phone call. B Ngoai had died. I flew home carrying her ao dai. We buried her in it.

In Vietnamese tradition, one is in mourning for three years after the loss of a parent or grandparent. Out of respect and love for the deceased, or hieu, decorum dictates that close family members can't get married until after the mourning period is over. But my wedding was only a month and a half away.

On the day we buried my grandmother, my family advised me to burn the white cloth headband that symbolized my grief. By burning it, I ended my official mourning.

Through my tears I watched the white cloth become wispy ashes. My   *30*
family was supportive. "It's your duty to remember and honor her," my
father told me. "But you also need to move forward with your life."

On the morning of our wedding, Scott's family stood outside our house   *31*
in a line bearing dowry gifts. Inside the house, Scott and I lighted incense in
front of the family altar. Holding the incense between our palms, we bowed
to my ancestors and asked for their blessings. I looked at the photo of B
Ngoai and knew she had to be smiling. ■

Reading for Better Writing

Working by yourself or with a group, answer these questions:

1. What is the writer's thesis or main idea? Explain why you do or do not
   find the idea relevant to your history, culture, or identity.

2. Identify all passages in the essay in which the writer describes or reflects
   on her wedding. How does she use those passages to develop her main
   idea? How are the early references different from the later references?
   Which passages include more description or reflection? Why?

3. In the opening of the essay, the writer and her parents disagree
   regarding a specific wedding tradition. What are their arguments? Do
   the details regarding the family's history help you understand why they
   have different views? Explain.

4. In paragraph 22, the writer says, "I returned to Vietnam to connect
   with something I can't really name but know I lost when we left twenty
   years ago." What does she mean? Review what she does and learns on
   this trip, and then explain how her research and writing might help her
   identify and regain what she lost.

5. Review the writer's description of her grandmother's funeral (paragraphs
   29–30). Explain how the wedding and funeral ceremonies affect the
   family. In what ways are the impacts of both similar or different?

6. How do the wedding and the funeral help the writer "connect with
   something I can't really name but know I lost when we left [Vietnam]
   twenty years ago"?

7. If you were to describe and reflect upon your own cultural heritage,
   which images, elements, moments, conflicts, and/or themes would come
   to mind?

Guidelines
Writing Description and Reflection

1. **Select a topic.** Choose an experience or experiences that influenced you in some key way—either confirming what you thought or planned at that time or changing those thoughts or plans. (Revisit "Topics to Consider" on page **166** for additional ideas.)

> **TIP:** If you can't think of any experiences, try listing topics in response to the following statement: *Reflect on times when you first discovered that the world was one of the following—strange, wonderful, complex, frightening, boring, small, uncaring, like you, unlike you, full, or empty.* How did these experiences affect who you are today?

2. **Get the big picture.** Once you have chosen one or more experiences to write about, gather your thoughts by reflecting on the questions below through brainstorming or by freewriting.
   - What are the key moments—the pivotal points—in your experiences?
   - What led to those key moments? Why? What resulted from them?
   - What was going on from your perspective?
   - How did others experience the events?
   - What did you learn from these experiences?
   - Did these experiences end as you had hoped? Why or why not?
   - What themes, conflicts, and insights arose from these experiences?
   - How do your feelings now differ from your feelings then?

   > **TIP:** To find out more details about the event or people involved, sort through photo albums and home videos to trigger memories; talk to someone who shared your experiences or saw you through them; or consult your journal, diary, old letters, and saved e-mail.

3. **Get organized.**
   - Review your brainstorming or freewriting, and highlight key details, quotations, or episodes that you want to include in your writing.
   - Draft a brief outline that shows where key information fits into the big picture.
   - List the main events in chronological order, or use a cluster to help you gather details related to your experiences.

   > **TIP:** To help you decide which details to include and how to organize your information, consider what your audience needs to understand and appreciate your story.

4. **Write the first draft.** Review your outline and rough out the first draft in one sitting. Then test your reflection for its significance. Does it answer these questions: What happened? How did the experience affect you? How do you feel about it now?

5. **Review and revise.** After drafting the essay, take a break. Then read your paper again for accuracy and completeness. Look first at the entire piece. Does it say what you wanted to say? Does it include any gaps or weak spots? Check your outline to make sure all key details are covered and in the right sequence. (See the checklist on page 92.)

6. **Test your reflection.** Review what you say about the experiences:
    *   Does the tone—whether sarcastic, humorous, regretful, or meditative—fit the content of the reflection?
    *   Have you established a viewpoint, and is the reflection built on this point of view?
    *   Will the intended readers appreciate the treatment of the subject?

7. **Get feedback.** Ask a classmate or someone in the writing center to read your paper, looking for the following:
    *   An opening that pulls the reader into the reflection
    *   Experiences that are portrayed clearly and vividly
    *   An explanation of how you've changed that is woven naturally into the experiences
    *   Transitions that connect paragraphs effectively
    *   A conclusion that restates the point of the reflection clearly and succinctly

8. **Edit and proofread your essay.** Once you have revised the content, organization, and voice of your personal reflection, polish it. Carefully check your choice of words; the clarity of your sentences; and your grammar, usage, and mechanics.

9. **Publish your writing by doing one or more of the following:**
    *   Share your essay with friends and family.
    *   Publish it in a journal or on a website.
    *   Make copies of your writing, read it to your class, and discuss their responses.
    *   Place a copy in your professional portfolio.
    *   Submit a copy to your instructor.

Writing Checklist

Use these seven traits to check the quality of your writing; then revise as needed:

_____ The **ideas** (the topic being reflected on) provide the reader with an interesting look at your experience.

_____ The **organization** pattern effectively blends description and reflection.

_____ The **voice** is thoughtful, and characters and events are treated respectfully.

_____ The **words** are precise and clear; descriptions help the reader experience what you experienced.

_____ The **sentences** are smooth and natural.

_____ The **copy** is free of errors in grammar, punctuation, and mechanics.

_____ The **design** uses a format, page layout, and typography fitting for your assignment.

Interactive

Critical-Thinking and Writing Activities

As directed by your instructor, complete the following activities.

1. Writing reflectively requires sharing personal thoughts and feelings about experiences and events—a task that can be difficult to do effectively. Review Mary Seymour's piece, "Call Me Crazy, But I Have To Be Myself" noting the places where she uses phrases similar to "I think" and "I feel," along with an example or comparison to make her perspective clear to her readers. Draft or revise a reflection in which you use these strategies to clarify your own point of view.

2. In "American Dream Boat," K. Oanh Ha describes and reflects on a time in her life during which she sought clarity regarding who she was as a Vietnamese American. Think about a time in your life when you needed clarity regarding an issue related to your identity: nationality, cultural heritage, family legacy, faith life, career path, health challenge, and so forth. Then describe that time in your life, probe its impact on you, and reflect on its value.

◖ VISUALLY SPEAKING

Review the photograph at the opening of this chapter. What thoughts or feelings does the picture elicit? What does the picture suggest about the relationship between descriptive details and reflective thought?

ANALYTICAL WRITING

Chapters 12 through 16 introduce the traditional modes of analytical writing: cause-effect, comparison-contrast, classification, process, and definition. All of these modes are analytical in the sense that they involve mentally "breaking down" a topic in an effort to reveal structures and logical relationships. Often called expository writing, such modes seek to clearly explain to readers the logical workings of a given topic—from stress to dog food to dementia.

Note, however, that virtually any piece of analytical writing blends these distinctive modes. For example, you might use compare-contrast as the primary organizational strategy for an entire essay, but you also might use another mode (such as definition) to organize a specific paragraph within that essay. In all of your writing, you should choose the writing strategy that best fits your subject, audience, and purpose.

CONTENTS
Analytical Writing

CAUSE AND EFFECT

12

Now, why did that happen? We ask this question every day at home, in college, and on the job. But why do we ask, "Why?"

We ask it to understand and cope with things that happen in our lives. For example, knowing why our car overheated will help us avoid that problem in the future. Knowing what causes a disease such as diabetes—or knowing its effects—helps us understand and control the condition. In other words, cause-effect reasoning helps us deal with everyday issues.

In a cause-effect essay, the writer develops the thesis through cause-effect reasoning. That is, he or she analyzes and explains the causes, the effects, or both the causes and the effects of a phenomenon.

Are you ready to write—to analyze and explain the causes and/or effects of one of life's "happenings"? This chapter will help you do so.

Audio

Video

Web Link

Overview
Writing a Cause-Effect Essay

Writer's Goal

Your goal is to analyze and explain the causes, the effects, or both the causes and the effects of some phenomenon (fact, occurrence, or circumstance).

Keys for Success

Know your readers. Consider what your readers know and think about your subject. Are they aware of the cause-effect connection associated with it? Do they accept it? Why or why not? If they deny that the connection exists or is relevant, which arguments support their position? Are these arguments strong?

Think logically. Linking cause to effect, or vice versa, requires clear, logical thinking supported by strong evidence. To practice this kind of reasoning, (1) research the topic for evidence connecting a specific cause and/or effect to a specific phenomenon, (2) draft a working thesis stating that connection, and (3) explain the connection in language that your readers will understand.

Test your thinking. Check your main points for clarity, your supporting points for relevance, and your overall argument for logic. Use the list of logical fallacies to identify common weaknesses. (See pages 267–270, especially "False Cause" on page 269.)

Topics to Consider

Choose a topic that you care about. Begin by thinking about categories such as those listed below. Then brainstorm a list of phenomena related to each category. From this list, choose a topic and prove its causes, its effects, or both.

- **Family life:** adult children living with parents, increasing number of stay-at-home dads, families choosing to simplify their lifestyles, more people squeezed by needs of children and parents, older women having babies
- **Politics:** decreasing number of student voters, increasing support for oil exploration, increased interest in third-party politics, tension between political action groups
- **Society:** nursing shortage, security concerns, nursing-care facilities, immigrant-advocacy groups, shifting ethnic balances
- **Environment:** common water pollutants, new water-purification technology, effects of a community's recycling program
- **Workplace:** decreasing power of unions, more businesses providing child-care services, need for on-the-job training in technology

> **Next Step** Read the model essays and do the activities that follow. As you read, note how the writers develop their theses using cause-effect reasoning.

Cause and Effect

In the essay below, student writer Tiffany Boyett analyzes the causes and effects of stress in our lives.

Life-Threatening Stress

The writer uses an anecdote to introduce the topic.

It was 8:00 a.m.; her husband, Lance, had left for work without filling the tank on the Mazda, and her daughter, Gina, had gotten on the school bus without her show-and-tell bunny. "Great," thought Jan, "now I have to get gas at Demler's, stop by Gina's school, and drop Alex off at day care—all before my 9:30 class!" Quickly she grabbed the diaper bag, picked up the baby, and headed for the door. At 9:35, with her heart pounding and hands sweating, she scrambled into the classroom, found an open seat, and was hurriedly pulling out her psych notes when the prof asked, "So . . . precisely what does Jung mean by 'collective unconscious'—Jan?"

"Uh . . . what was the question?" she responded.

Does the scene sound familiar—too much work, too little time, and too much stress? Actually, periods of excessive stress are just part of life in college—or out of college, for that matter. Normally, stress (the response to a perceived threat) is a powerful, life-saving force, but when stress becomes excessive, it is a life-threatening condition. So what should people do—simply accept stress as one more cost of living?

She states the thesis.

While accepting some stress is inescapable, for their own health and for the well-being of others, people must do more. They have to understand what stress is—both its causes and its effects. In addition, to avoid the negative effects, they have to learn how to manage the stress in their lives.

She explains the symptoms of stress with an example.

So what is stress? Actually, the physiological characteristics of stress are some of the body's potentially good self-defense mechanisms. Take, for example, a man who is crossing a street when he spots an oncoming car. Immediately his brain signals his adrenal glands to release a flood of adrenaline into his bloodstream. As a result, his muscles contract, his eyes dilate, his heart pounds faster, his breathing quickens, and his blood clots more readily. Each one of these responses helps the man leap out of the car's path. His muscles contract to give him exceptional strength. His eyes dilate so that he can see more clearly. His heart pumps more blood and his lungs exchange more air—both to increase his metabolism. If the man were injured, his blood would clot faster, ensuring a smaller amount of blood loss. In this situation and many more like it, stress symptoms are good (Curtis 25–26).

A question indicates a transition.

So when is stress dangerous? The danger comes when stress responses are triggered too frequently in a short period of time, or when they are triggered constantly over a longer period of time. While everyday stressors are not life-threatening by themselves, when these stressors happen so frequently that the body lacks time to relax, the normal effects of stress become compounded. One result is that certain body hormones, such as adrenaline and cortisol, are elevated. If the levels of these two hormones are elevated over an extended period of time, several life-threatening conditions can result.

An effect of prolonged stress is described.

One of the most immediate results of prolonged stress is a decrease   7
in the body's natural immune function. The release of cortisol into the bloodstream inhibits a protective hormone released during the immune response and thereby suppresses immune reactions. During periods of stress, the immune system becomes compromised, and the body experiences increased susceptibility to disease (Dombrowski 128). For example, some studies have proven that when medical students prepare for board exams, they experience more stress and get sick more often than when they prepare for less stressful exams.

The writer explains the effects of elevated stress.

How do elevated stress levels affect one's health? According to the U.S.   8
Census Bureau, the most common cause of death in the United States is heart disease (90). Elevated levels of adrenaline and cortisol in the bloodstream trigger the release of fatty acids, triglycerides, and cholesterol. These substances contribute to the blockage of arteries in the heart, and the blockages lead to heart attacks (Dombrowski 126). Excessive production of cortisol also produces a sustained level of elevated blood pressure or hypertension. If a person is under stress for a long period of time, his or her blood pressure will remain high, forcing the heart to work harder and, consequently, wear out sooner (Wickrama 527).

She shows that stress is linked to specific illnesses.

But stress-induced illnesses include more than head colds, flu, and   9
heart disease. The U.S. Census Bureau reports that the second most common cause of death in the United States is cancer (90). Recent studies have linked stress with an increased risk of developing cancer. Increased levels of cortisol associated with stress reduce the efficacy of the immune system, allowing cancer cells to multiply more easily and, therefore, lead to full-blown cancer (Eysenck 223).

According to the U.S. Census Bureau, the third most common cause   10
of death in the United States is stroke (90). A new study released by the University of Michigan claims that stress is linked to increased risk of stroke in middle-aged white men (Chande 1771). Increased blood pressure from higher adrenaline levels, along with the blood's increased clotting ability associated with stress, results in a higher risk that blood clots will develop in the brain and cause a stroke.

Another example is given.

Diabetes is another illness that has recently been linked to stress.   11
Adrenaline in the bloodstream causes the liver to release glucose, the increased glucose raises the level of blood sugar, and increased blood sugar causes the pancreas to secrete insulin. In addition, because cortisol released into the bloodstream actually decreases the effectiveness of insulin, the pancreas must release even greater amounts of insulin. As a result of the high insulin levels, the insulin receptors become less sensitive to insulin,

making it harder for the cells to take up sugar, even when there are no stressors. This decrease in the receptors' sensitivity is the basis for type II diabetes (Dombrowski 127).

> **The writer inserts a qualifier to refine the focus of the sentence.**

Excessive stress is dangerous not only because of its link to serious illnesses, but also because of its very nature. In other words, stress is a nonspecific response: Although stress may vary in degree, its nature is the same no matter what sort of threat is perceived. In fact, the threat doesn't even have to be real! As long as a person perceives a threat, he or she will experience stress. For example, someone who is afraid of poisonous spiders may undergo great stress even when in the presence of a harmless spider. In addition, the nonspecific nature of stress works the other way: Someone who is in real danger, but doesn't perceive the danger, will experience no stress. Finally, stress's nonspecific nature makes stress particularly dangerous for those people who perceive threats very readily. These individuals experience stress more commonly—and often more intensely—than others. *12*

> **She reuses her opening illustration to close and unify the essay.**

Because stress is so common, many people fail to recognize its potential danger. For example, Jan, the student described earlier, was certainly aware that she experienced stress while bustling through her busy morning. However, if she is like most college students, she wasn't aware that excessive stress could lead to serious illness and early death. Learning about stress's causes and effects is an important first step that they must take. After that, they will be ready for the second step—learning how to manage life-threatening stress. ■ *13*

> *Note:* The Works Cited page is not shown. For sample pages, see MLA (pages **532–533**) and APA (page **564**).

Reading for Better Writing

Working by yourself or with a group, answer these questions:

1. The writer uses an anecdote to open and close the essay. Explain why the illustration is or is not effective.

2. List the causes of stress described in the essay. Are they described objectively? Cite examples to support your answer.

3. The writer distinguishes between—and describes the effects of—three forms of stress: normal stress, prolonged stress, and elevated (or excessive) stress. Examine the thinking she uses to link each form to specific effects. Is the logic clear? Is it believable? Why or why not?

4. The writer states her purpose as follows: "They have to understand what stress is—both its causes and its effects." Does she convince you that understanding and managing stress are important? Cite examples to support your answer.

Cause and Effect

In the essay below, Mary Brophy Marcus describes successful businesswomen and argues that the skills they learned from organized sports helped them achieve that success. The essay was first published in *US News & World Report*.

If You Let Me Play . . .

The writer uses an anecdote to introduce the topic and focus the essay.

Jackie Thomas, Nike's associate director of sports marketing, usually spends her lunch hour on the sports-shoe company's basketball courts charging for the basket, always outnumbered by male colleagues. "I hold my own," boasts the 33-year-old executive.   1

She also does well playing the corporate game back inside the headquarter's offices. Thomas, a former University of California–Berkeley college basketball point guard, says her success is due in large part to the lessons she learned growing up playing competitive team sports. "It's taught me that if you lose a game, you go back afterward and figure out what went wrong and how to overcome it the next time," says the former tomboy from Kingston, Jamaica.   2

A dependent clause links the second and third paragraphs.

While most of America's corporations are still commanded by male chief executives, women are gaining ground, winning vice-presidential and top management slots and, in a few cases, the highest leadership roles. Many of these young female executives say playing team sports helped them get ahead. A University of Virginia study conducted in the late 1980s showed that 80 percent of key female leaders from *Fortune* 500 companies said they participated in sports and considered themselves tomboys.   3

The writer describes events (or *causes*) that helped women gain valuable skills in sports.

A lot of credit, female executives say, has to go to Title IX, part of the Federal Education Amendments Act of 1972. It mandated that federally funded schools give women's sports the same treatment as men's games receive. That meant that in schools and colleges across the United States, for every boy's varsity soccer team, there must be a girl's varsity soccer team; for every male basketball scholarship, there must be a female basketball scholarship of equal dollars. Since the early 1970s, the law has increased money for new equipment, coaches, and travel for women's teams. More college scholarships have translated into more diplomas and better jobs for women. Thomas earned a partial academic scholarship when she applied to Berkeley, one of the country's top universities, but without an additional basketball scholarship awarded in her junior and senior years, she would have had a hard time paying for the education.   4

Using statistical evidence, she cites effects of the causes described in the previous paragraph.

Girls' participation in high school sports has spiked from about 300,000 in 1971 to 2.4 million in 1996. At the college level, where competition is tougher, the number of female athletes has increased to 123,832 from 80,040 in 1982, says the National Collegiate Athletic Association.   5

A quotation supports the writer's thesis: Skills learned in sports help one succeed in business.

"No other experience I know of can prepare you for the high-level competition of business," says Anh Ngyuen, 25, a former Carnegie Mellon University varsity soccer star. She should know. Now she battles Microsoft as a product manager for Netscape Communications. "My colleagues can't believe how aggressive I am," she says.

Sports helped these women master the interpersonal skills, like teamwork, that many men take for granted. "I've seen firsthand hundreds and hundreds of times that one person can't win a soccer or softball game," says Maria Murnane, a 28-year-old senior account executive for a San Francisco public-relations firm. "Same goes for work. You have to learn to trust the people on your team, let them run with projects," the former Northwestern soccer center midfielder says. Her boss, William Harris, the president of Strategy Associates, agrees: "We don't want Lone Rangers. She's a team player—a captain and cheerleader."

Playing team sports helps with the little things, too. Women learn to speak in sports metaphors as many men do. Lisa Delpy, professor of sports management at George Washington University in Washington, D.C., also notes that in many companies a lot of business is conducted on the golf course, at ballgames, or at other sports events. Women who know the difference between a slide tackle and a sweeper at a World Cup soccer match can fit right in.

The writer supports her thesis with an anecdote.

Stephanie Delaney, now 31, captained the varsity soccer team at Franklin and Marshall College in Lancaster, Pennsylvania, when it won the Mid-Atlantic Conference championship her senior year. Now the sales manager for the Caribbean and Latin American division of ConAgra's Lamb-Weston, one of the world's largest frozen-French-fry producers, she was the only woman to play a game of basketball with potential clients at a big food conference last year in Jamaica. "I was the high scorer," she notes.

A lively quotation offers interesting details.

And yes, it helped sell french fries. "I didn't close the deal on the court, but afterward when we were hanging out drinking water and shooting the breeze, they agreed to test my product. Now we have Kentucky Fried Chicken's business in Jamaica," says Delaney.

The dash links the word power to the defining clause that follows.

Female executives say that Title IX had another subtle, but important, effect. For the first time, many boys, coaches, and parents opened their eyes to the fact that their sisters and daughters could be just as strong, fast, and nimble on the field as their brothers and sons. Likewise, girls whose talents had formerly gone unnoticed under driveway basketball nets and on back lots began realizing their own power—that they could compete with boys and win. "When my girlfriends and I formed a softball team back in college, we were dreadful—like the Keystone Kops," recalls Penny Cate, 45, now a vice president at Quaker Oats. "There'd be four of us in the outfield and the ball would go through our legs. But after a few years, we became very good. It built my confidence, made me realize I could accomplish anything in sports or out," she says.

The writer cites an advertisement from which she created the essay's title and with which she advances her thesis.

That point is repeatedly brought home when Nike executives ask schoolgirls what they think of one of the company's TV ads. The ad begins with the voice of a young girl saying, "If you let me play . . . ." The phrase is finished by other little girls saying things like, "I will have greater self-confidence" or "I will be more likely to stay in school."   *12*

The girls often reply, in a tone of genuine befuddlement, "If *who* lets me play?" They don't see any barriers between themselves and America's playing fields. Twenty years from now, might they say, "*What* glass ceiling?" ■   *13*

Reading for Better Writing

Working by yourself or with a group, answer these questions:

1. Review the writer's title and her reference to it late in the essay. How does the writer use the title to introduce and advance her thesis?

2. Mary Brophy Marcus is a journalist who wrote this essay and many others for publications such as *US News & World Report* and *USA Today*. Review three or four paragraphs from the essay and explain how her word choice, sentence structure, and use of quotations are or are not appropriate for readers of periodicals like these.

3. Review the qualities of an academic style as discussed on pages 78–79. Then explain why Marcus's essay does or does not reflect this style. Cite specific passages to support your answer.

4. Marcus uses cause-effect reasoning to argue that (1) women's participation in sports produces valuable skills and (2) these skills help women succeed in business. Examine three points, along with the evidence (data, quotations, and other elements), that Marcus uses to support either of these claims. Finally, explain why each supporting point and its related evidence are or are not convincing.

5. Marcus concludes her essay with the question, "*What* glass ceiling?" Explain why the quotation does or does not (1) advance her thesis and (2) close the essay effectively.

6. Working with a classmate, review the checklist under Step 7, "Revise the essay," found on page 197. Then analyze to what degree Marcus accomplishes each task in this checklist.

Cause and Effect

Christy Haubegger is the founder of *Latina* magazine. This essay was originally published in the July 12, 1999, issue of *Newsweek* magazine.

The Legacy of Generation Ñ

About 20 years ago, some mainstream observers declared the 1980s the "decade of the Hispanic." The Latino population was nearing 15 million! (It's since doubled.) However, our decade was postponed—a managerial oversight, no doubt—and eventually rescheduled for the '90s. What happens to a decade deferred? It earns compounded interest and becomes the next hundred years. The United States of the 21st century will be undeniably ours. Again.

1

It's Manifest *Destino*. After all, Latinos are true Americans, some of the original residents of the *Américas*. Spanish was the first European language spoken on this continent. Which is why we live in places like *Los Angeles, Colorado,* and *Florida* rather than The Angels, Colored, and Flowered. Now my generation is about to put a Latin stamp on the rest of the culture—and that will ultimately be the Ñ legacy.

2

We are not only numerous; we are also growing at a rate seven times that of the general population. Conservative political ads notwithstanding, this growth is driven by natural increase (births over deaths) rather than immigration. At 30, I may be the oldest childless Latina in the United States. More important, however, while our preceding generation felt pressure to assimilate, America has now generously agreed to meet us in the middle. Just as we become more American, America is simultaneously becoming more Latino.

3

This quiet *revolución* can perhaps be traced back to the bloodless coup of 1992, when salsa outsold ketchup for the first time. Having toppled the leadership in the condiment category, we set our sights even higher. Fairly soon, there was a congresswoman named Sanchez representing Orange County, a taco-shilling Chihuahua became a national icon, and now everyone is *loca* for Ricky Martin.

4

We are just getting started. Our geographic concentration and reputation for family values are making us every politician's dream constituency. How long can New Hampshire, with just four Electoral College votes—and probably an equal number of Hispanic residents—continue to get so much attention from presidential candidates? Advertisers will also soon be begging for our attention. With a median age of 26 (eight years younger than the general market), Latinos hardly exist outside their coveted 18–34 demographic. Remember, we may only be 11 percent of the country, but we buy 16 percent of the lipliner.

5

A metaphor helps to make the writer's point.

The writer lists examples that illustrate her claim.

Examples from pop culture connect with readers and help to make the writer's ideas memorable.

The writer transitions to the anticipated effects of the population growth she has described.

The media will change as well, especially television, where we now appear to be rapidly approaching extinction. Of the 26 new comedies and dramas appearing this fall [1999] on the four major networks, not one has a Latino in a leading role. The Screen Actors Guild released employment statistics for 1998 showing that the percentage of roles going to Hispanic actors actually declined from the previous year. But, pretty soon, the cast of "Friends" will need to find some amigos. Seeing as they live in New York City, and there's almost 2 million of us in the metropolitan area, this shouldn't prove too difficult.

Shifting to future tense ("will") marks these statements as predictions.

Face it: This is going to be a bilingual country. Back in 1849, the California Constitution was written in both Spanish and English, and we're headed that way again. If our children speak two languages instead of just one, how can that not be a benefit to us all? The re-Latinization of this country will pay off in other ways as well. I, for one, look forward to that pivotal moment in our history when all American men finally know how to dance. Latin music will no longer be found in record stores under "Foreign," and romance will bloom again. Our children will ask us what it was like to dance without a partner.

The paragraph begins with the word *dawn* and ends with *mañana* and *morning*.

"American food" will mean low-fat enchiladas and hamburgers served with rice and beans. As a result, the American standard of beauty will necessarily expand to include a female size 12, and anorexia will be found only in medical-history books. Finally, just in time for the baby boomers' senescence, living with extended family will become hip again. *Simpsons* fans of the next decade will see Grandpa moving back home. We'll all go back to church together.

At the dawn of a new millennium, America knows Latinos as entertainers and athletes. But, someday very soon, all American children can dream of growing up to be writers like Sandra Cisneros, astronauts like Ellen Ochoa, or judges like Jose Cabranes of the Second Circuit Court of Appeals. To put a Latin spin on a famous Anglo phrase: It is truly *mañana* in America. For those of you who don't know it (yet), that word doesn't just mean tomorrow; *mañana* also means morning. ■

Reading for Better Writing

Working by yourself or with a group, answer these questions:

1. In one sentence, summarize the cause(s) and effect(s) of the changes described in this essay.

2. Writers must make their claims using words that convey an appropriate level of certainty. Is Haubegger's use of "will" (versus "may") appropriate in paragraphs 7 and 8? Why?

3. Review paragraph 9. What is the writer's point? Do you agree?

4. The writer published this essay in 1999. Cite examples showing that the changes she described are continuing.

Cause and Effect

Anna Quindlen's 1992 *New York Times* column "Public and Private" won the Pulitzer Prize for commentary. She now writes a regular column for *Newsweek* magazine, where the piece below was originally published in 2001.

Our Tired, Our Poor, Our Kids

As you read this essay, highlight passages that help advance Quindlen's cause-effect argument. In the margin, note why each passage is effective.

Six people live here, in a room the size of the master bedroom in a modest suburban house. Trundles, bunk beds, dressers side by side stacked with toys, clothes, boxes, in tidy claustrophobic clutter. One woman, five children. The baby was born in a shelter. The older kids can't wait to get out of this one. Everyone gets up at 6 a.m., the little ones to go to day care, the others to school. Their mother goes out to look for an apartment when she's not going to drug-treatment meetings. "For what they pay for me to stay in a shelter I could have lived in the Hamptons," Sharanda says.

Here is the parallel universe that has flourished while the more fortunate were rewarding themselves for the stock split with SUVs and home additions. There is a boom market in homelessness. But these are not the men on the streets of San Francisco holding out cardboard signs to the tourists. They are children, hundreds of thousands of them, twice as likely to repeat a grade or be hospitalized and four times as likely to go hungry as the kids with a roof over their heads. Twenty years ago New York City provided emergency shelter for just under a thousand families a day; last month it had to find spaces for 10,000 children on a given night. Not since the Great Depression have this many babies, toddlers, and kids had no place like home.

> *They are children, hundreds of thousands of them . . .*

Three mothers sit in the living room of a temporary residence called Casa Rita in the Bronx and speak of this in the argot of poverty. "The landlord don't call back when they hear you got EARP," says Rosie, EARP being the Emergency Assistance Rehousing Program. "You get priority for Section 8 if you're in a shelter," says Edna, which means federal housing programs will put you higher on the list. Edna has four kids, three in foster care; she arrived at Casa Rita, she says, "with two bags and a baby." Rosie has three, they share a bathroom down the hall with two other families. Sharanda's five range in age from thirteen to just over a year. Her eldest was put in the wrong grade when he changed schools. "He's humiliated, living here," his mother says.

All three women are anxious to move on, although they appreciate this place, where they can get shelter, get sober, and keep their kids at the same time. They remember the Emergency Assistance Unit, the city office that is the gateway to the system, where hundreds of families sit every day surrounded by their bags, where children sleep on benches until they are shuffled off dull-eyed for one night in a shelter or a motel, only to return as supplicants again the next day.

In another world, middle-class Americans have embraced new-home   5
starts, the stock market, and the Gap. But in the world of these displaced families, problems ignored or fumbled or unforeseen during this great period of prosperity have dovetailed into an enormous subculture of children who think that only rich people have their own bedrooms. Twenty years ago, when the story of the homeless in America became a staple of news reporting, the solution was presented as a simple one: affordable housing. That's still true, now more than ever. Two years ago the National Low Income Housing Coalition calculated that the hourly income necessary to afford the average two-bedroom apartment was around $12. That's more than twice the minimum wage.

The result is that in many cities police officers and teachers cannot afford to live where they work, that in Las Vegas old motels provide housing for casino employees, that in shelters now there is a contingent of working poor who get up off their cots and go off to their jobs. The result is that if you are evicted for falling behind on your rent, if there is a bureaucratic foul-up in your welfare check, or the factory in which you work shuts down, the chances of finding another place to live are very small indeed. You're one understanding relative, one paycheck, one second chance from the street. And so are your kids.

> *[P]olice officers and teachers cannot afford to live where they work . . .*   6

So-called welfare reform, which emphasizes cutbacks and make-work,   7
has played a part in all this. A study done in San Diego in 1998 found that a third of homeless families had recently had benefits terminated or reduced, and that most said that was how they had wound up on the street. Drugs, alcohol, and domestic abuse also land mothers with kids in the shelter system or lead them to hand their children over to relatives or foster homes. Today the average homeless woman is younger than ever before, may have been in foster care or in shelters herself, and so considers a chaotic childhood the norm. Many never finished high school, and have never held a job.

Ralph Nunez, who runs the organization Homes for the Homeless, says   8
that all this calls for new attitudes. "People don't like to hear it, but shelters are going to be the low-income housing of the future," he says. "So how do we enrich the experience and use the system to provide job training and education?" Bonnie Stone of Women in Need, which has eight other residences along with Casa Rita, says, "We're pouring everything we've got into the nine months most of them are here—nutrition, treatment,

budgeting. By the time they leave, they have a subsidized apartment, day care and, hopefully, some life skills they didn't have before."

But these organizations are rafts in a rising river of need that has roared through this country without most of us ever even knowing. So now you know. There are hundreds of thousands of little nomads in America, sleeping in the back of cars, on floors in welfare offices, or in shelters five to a room. What would it mean, to spend your childhood drifting from one strange bed to another, waking in the morning to try to figure out where you'd landed today, without those things that confer security and happiness: a familiar picture on the wall, a certain slant of light through a curtained window? "Give me your tired, your poor," it says on the base of the Statue of Liberty, to welcome foreigners. Oh, but they are already here, the small refugees from the ruin of the American dream, even if you cannot see them. ■

9

Reading for Better Writing

Working by yourself or with a group, answer these questions:

1. In one sentence, state the cause/effect relationship that Quindlen outlines in "Our Tired, Our Poor, Our Kids."

2. In writing, an *allusion* is an indirect reference to another text. What allusions can you identify in this piece? Why does the writer use allusions in this essay?

3. Use a pencil or sticky notes to distinguish portions of the essay where Quindlen addresses the cause(s) and the effect(s) of the problem. What is the approximate ratio of space given to each? How are the cause-effect sections arranged? How do these factors affect the essay's message?

4. Notice that Quindlen occasionally begins sentences with conjunctions such as *but* or *and*. Where, and why? Where might this strategy be appropriate in your writing?

Model

Guidelines
Writing a Cause-Effect Essay

1. **Select a topic.** Look again at the list of facts, occurrences, or circumstances mentioned under "Topics to Consider" on page 184. Expand the list by jotting down additional items for each category, or listing new categories along with related items. From this finished list, choose a topic and prove its causes, its effects, or both.

    > **TIP:** If your professor approves, you could write an essay contradicting the logic in another writer's cause-effect essay. For an example, see "An Apology for the Life of Ms. Barbie D. Doll" on pages 277–278.

2. **Narrow and research the topic.** Write down or type your topic. Below it, brainstorm a list of related causes and effects in two columns. Next, do preliminary research to expand the list and distinguish primary causes and effects from secondary ones. Revise your topic as needed to address only primary causes and/or effects that research links to a specific phenomenon.

Cause/Effect Topic: _____	
Causes (Because of)	**Effects** (this results)
1._____	1._____
2._____	2._____
3._____	3._____
4._____	4._____

3. **Draft and test your thesis.** Based on your preliminary research, draft a working thesis (you may revise it later) that introduces the topic, along with the causes and/or effects you intend to discuss. Limit your argument to only those points you can prove.

4. **Gather and analyze information.** Research your topic, looking for clear evidence that links specific causes to specific effects. At the same time, avoid arguments mistaking a coincidence for a cause-effect relationship. Use the list of logical fallacies (see pages 267–270) to weed out common errors in logic. For example, finding chemical pollutants in a stream running beside a chemical plant does not "prove" that the plant caused the pollutants.

5. **Get organized.** Develop an outline that lays out your thesis and argument in a clear pattern. Under each main point asserting a cause-effect connection, list details from your research that support the connection.

    Thesis: _____

Point 1	*Point 2*	*Point 3*
• Supporting details	• Supporting details	• Supporting details
• Supporting details	• Supporting details	• Supporting details
• Supporting details	• Supporting details	• Supporting details

6. **Use your outline to draft the essay.** Try to rough out the essay's overall argument before you attempt to revise it. As you write, show how each specific cause led to each specific effect, citing examples as needed. To show those cause-effect relationships, use transitional words like the following:

accordingly	for this purpose	since	therefore
as a result	for this reason	so	thus
because	hence	such as	to illustrate
consequently	just as	thereby	whereas

7. **Revise the essay.** Whether your essay presents causes, effects, or both, use the checklist below to trace and refine your argument.

   _____ The thesis and introduction clearly identify the causes and/or effects.

   _____ All major causes and/or effects are addressed.

   _____ Statements regarding the causes and/or effects are sufficiently limited and focused.

   _____ Supporting details are researched, relevant, and strong.

   _____ Links between causes and effects are clear and logical.

   _____ The conclusion restates the main argument and unifies the essay.

8. **Get feedback.** Ask a peer reviewer or someone from the college's writing center to read your essay for the following:
   - An engaging opening
   - A clear and logical thesis
   - Clear and convincing reasoning that links specific causes to specific effects
   - A closing that wraps up the argument, leaving no loose ends

9. **Edit the essay for clarity and correctness.** Check for the following:
   - Precise, appropriate word choice
   - Complete, smooth sentences
   - Clear transitions between paragraphs
   - Correct names, dates, and supporting details
   - Correct mechanics, usage, and grammar

10. **Publish your essay.** Share your writing with others as follows:
    - Submit it to your instructor.
    - Post it on the class's or department's website.
    - Submit the essay for presentation at an appropriate conference.
    - Send it as a service to relevant nonprofit agencies.
    - Share the essay with family and friends.

Writing Checklist

Use these seven traits to check the quality of your writing and revise as needed:

_____ The **ideas** explain the causes and/or effects of the topic in a clear, well-reasoned argument supported by credible information.

_____ The **organization** helps the reader understand the cause-effect relationship. The links between the main points and the supporting points are clear.

_____ The **voice** is informed, polite, and professional.

_____ The **words** are precise and clear. Technical or scientific terms are defined. Causes are linked to effects with transitional words and phrases such as _therefore, as a result,_ and _for this reason._

_____ The **sentences** are clear, varied in structure, and smooth.

_____ The **copy** is correct and clear.

_____ The **design** follows the assigned guidelines and format.

Interactive

Critical-Thinking and Writing Activities

As directed by your instructor, complete the following activities.

1. In "Life-Threatening Stress," the writer describes a health problem experienced by many college students. List their other common health problems, choose one, and write an essay proving its causes and/or effects.

2. Draft an essay in which you support your claim with cause-effect reasoning.

3. One way to instill coherence in an essay is to make direct or indirect connections between the opening and closing of the piece. Review Anna Quindlen's "Our Tired, Our Poor, Our Kids," noting the connections between the title and the concluding paragraph. Revise one of your essays by linking the language and ideas of the opening and closing sections.

4. Choose a phenomenon that is related to your program or major and that is discussed in the news media. Write an essay that analyzes and explains its causes, its effects, or both. Consider submitting the essay to your adviser, asking for feedback, and then polishing the piece for inclusion in your professional portfolio.

◀ Visually Speaking

Review the photograph on the opening page of this chapter. What concepts or ideas does the picture convey? How might cause-effect reasoning be used to develop and advance these ideas? Explain.

COMPARISON AND CONTRAST

Audio

Video

In his plays, William Shakespeare creates characters, families, and even plot lines that mirror each other. As a result, we see Hamlet in relation to Laertes and the Montagues in relation to the Capulets. In the process, we do precisely what the writer wants us to do—we compare and contrast the subjects. The result is clarity and insight: By thinking about both subjects, we understand each one more clearly.

In this chapter, four writers use compare-and-contrast organization: one to analyze two literary characters, another to explain two views of a river, a third to assess two patterns of dress for Iranian women, and a fourth to describe ethnic groups. Elsewhere in this book, you will find writers working in the natural sciences, the social sciences, and the humanities—all comparing and contrasting two or more subjects with the goal of helping their readers understand the topics.

What's the point? Comparing and contrasting is a writing-and-thinking strategy used across the curriculum and in the workplace. You are about to write an essay using this strategy. What you learn in the process will help you succeed both in other courses and in your postcollege career.

Overview
Writing a Comparison-Contrast Essay

Writer's Goal

Your goal is to write an essay that (1) sets two or more subjects side by side, (2) shows the reader how they are similar and/or different, and (3) draws conclusions or makes some point based on what you have shown.

Keys for Success

Think about your readers. What do they know about the subject? What should they know? Why should they care? Answering these questions will help you understand both your readers and your purpose for writing.

Know your purpose. What do you want your essay to do? Inform? Explain? Persuade? Some combination of these? Knowing your purpose will help you decide what to include (and not include) in the essay, how to organize it, and how to help readers use the information.

Be logical. Comparing and contrasting is a logical process that helps you understand your subjects more fully and explain them more clearly. Begin by determining the basis of your comparison: How are the subjects related? Then decide whether to compare, to contrast, or both. When *comparing* subjects, show how they are similar. When *contrasting* them, show how they are different. When *comparing* and *contrasting* subjects, show how they are both similar and different. To choose which of the three patterns to follow, think about your purpose. Which pattern will help your essay accomplish what you want it to?

Topics to Consider

Choose subjects that are related in some important way. To get started, think about pairs of objects, events, places, processes, people, ideas, beliefs, and so on. For more inspiration, read the four models in this chapter and scan the models listed below. Each of these essays uses strategies to compare and contrast. List topics similar to those in the models.

- "Three Family Cancers," pages 217–219
- "Four Ways to Talk About Literature," pages 220–221
- "No Wonder They Call Me a Bitch," pages 222–225

> **Next Step** Read the model essays and perform the activities that follow. As you read, note whether the writer compares, contrasts, or both. Also note the pattern used to organize the essay: subject by subject, trait by trait, and so on.

Comparison

In this essay, Janae Sebranek compares the fate of two tragic literary characters, Bigger in *Native Son* and Alan in *Equus*. The student writer makes a trait-by-trait comparison, exploring how work, religion, and the media affect the characters.

Beyond Control

The writer introduces her topic, main points of comparison, and thesis.

Most children, no matter what their personal or family situation, lead more or less controlled lives. As they grow, they begin to sense the pressure of controlling factors in their lives, and start struggling to take control themselves. This can be a difficult process. In the works *Native Son* and *Equus*, Richard Wright and Peter Shaffer, respectively, create two characters who must deal with this struggle. Bigger in *Native Son* and Alan in *Equus* are both entering adulthood and have come to realize that they are controlled by work, religion, and the media. In the midst of these characters' efforts to gain control, each character falls into a tragic situation. *1*

She describes one of the traits of the first character.

We find Alan experiencing the pressure of working as a clerk at Bryson's appliance store. The customers are demanding, and the many products and brand names are confusing. He finds that he cannot function in this work environment. Later, under hypnosis, he admits to Dr. Dysart that his "foes" are the myriad of brand names he is challenged to locate and explain to the customers—"The Hosts of Hoover. The Hosts of Philco. Those Hosts of Pifco. The House of Remington and all its tribe!" (73). However, by recognizing the demands of this job, Alan attempts to take some control over his life. *2*

Alan exercises further control when he decides to look for another job. He likes being around horses, so he pursues and lands a job with Mr. Dalton, a stable owner. He enjoys his job and begins to deal more effectively with the whole concept of work. *3*

She describes a parallel trait of the second character and then contrasts the traits.

Bigger must also struggle with the pressure and anxiety of his first job. Because of his family's desperate financial situation, he is forced to take the one job he is offered, coincidentally, by a Mr. Dalton. He works as a chauffeur for Mr. Dalton's wealthy suburban family. Bigger cannot relate to them. He sees himself as a foreigner, forced to live and work among the privileged. The Daltons tell him where, when, and even how to drive. Bigger struggles; but, like Alan, he cannot deal with the extreme discomfort he is feeling. He quits after only two days on the job. Unlike Alan, however, he does not have the option of getting a job that interests him. *4*

Alan and Bigger also find religion to be a controlling factor in their lives. Alan's mother, Dora, "doses [religion] down the boy's throat" as she whispers "that Bible to him hour after hour, up there in his room" (33). Obviously, Alan's mother believes that he needs the controlling force of religion in his life, so she preaches to him every night. For a time, he is fascinated by the Bible's imagery and ideas. Eventually, though, this fascination begins to fade. *5*

She notes a contrast.

Bigger's mother does not push the issue of religion to the extreme that Alan's mother does. Instead, she tries to make her son see its value with daily comments such as "You'll regret how you living someday" (13). She offers her advice by singing religious songs from behind a curtain in their one-room apartment. She tries to show Bigger that religion is a valid way of dealing with a world out of control. But Bigger refuses to accept her religion, and he is left with no spiritual footing or direction.

6

She introduces her last point of comparison.

Finally, we find the media playing a tormenting, controlling role in both Alan's and Bigger's lives. Alan's father calls television a "dangerous drug" (27) that can control the mind. Alan still manages to watch television, but only because his mother "used to let him slip off in the afternoons to a friend next door" (31) to watch. Later, while he is under psychiatric care, he watches television every night and eventually finds himself becoming controlled by the medium.

7

Bigger, in a more tragic way, is also controlled by the media. He reads about himself in the newspapers and begins to believe certain things that have no valid basis. He is referred to as a "Negro killer" who looks "as if about to spring upon you at any moment" (260). The papers remark that Bigger "seems a beast utterly untouched" (260) by and out of place in the white man's world. Unfortunately, Bigger has no control over what is printed or over what other people believe about him.

8

She summarizes her argument and restates the thesis.

Bigger's ultimate fate is clearly beyond his control. He is falsely accused of raping and killing a woman, and he cannot convince anyone of the truth. Bigger's identity is too closely linked with the descriptions given in the newspapers. And this identity tragically leads to his death. Alan's fate is different, although tragic in its own right. While in the psychiatric ward, he gains a certain control with the help of therapy and medication. However, he loses his passion for life: "Passion, you see, can be destroyed by a doctor. It cannot be created" (108). This is Alan's personal tragedy.

9

Ultimately, both Alan and Bigger fail to gain real control over the outside forces in their lives. Alan forfeits his interest in life, and Bigger forfeits life itself. They, like so many people, become victims of the world in which they live. ■

10

Note: The Works Cited page is not shown. For sample pages, see MLA (page 532–533) and APA (page 564).

Reading for Better Writing

1. Do the opening paragraphs adequately introduce the topic and the thesis? Why or why not?

2. This essay is organized trait by trait. Is this strategy used effectively?

3. Does the writer focus on similarities, differences, or both? Is her choice effective?

Comparison and Contrast

Mark Twain is best known for his novels *The Adventures of Tom Sawyer* and *The Adventures of Huckleberry Finn*. In this excerpt from his 1883 memoir, *Life on the Mississippi,* Twain contrasts his mindset as an apprentice with his perspective as a steamboat pilot.

Two Views of the River

The writer starts the sentence with the contrasting conjunction but.

Now when I had mastered the language of this water, and had come to know every trifling feature that bordered the great river as familiarly as I knew the letters of the alphabet, I had made a valuable acquisition. But I had lost something, too. I had lost something which could never be restored to me while I lived. All the grace, the beauty, the poetry, had gone out of the majestic river! I still keep in mind a certain wonderful sunset which I witnessed when steamboating was new to me. A broad expanse of the river was turned to blood; in the middle distance the red hue brightened into gold, through which a solitary log came floating black and conspicuous; in one place a long, slanting mark lay sparkling upon the water; in another the surface was broken by boiling, tumbling rings that were as many-tinted as an opal; where the ruddy flush was faintest, was a smooth spot that was covered with graceful circles and radiating lines, ever so delicately traced; the shore on our left was densely wooded, and the somber shadow that fell from this forest was broken in one place by a long, ruffled trail that shone like silver; and high above the forest wall a clean-stemmed dead tree waved a single leafy bough that glowed like a flame in the unobstructed splendor that was flowing from the sun. There were graceful curves, reflected images, woody heights, soft distances; and over the whole scene, far and near, the dissolving lights drifted steadily, enriching it every passing moment with new marvels of coloring.

The sunset is described in a long, one-sentence list of sensory details.

I stood like one bewitched. I drank it in, in a speechless rapture. The world was new to me, and I had never seen anything like this at home. But as I have said, a day came when I began to cease from noting the glories and the charms which the moon and the sun and the twilight wrought upon the river's face; another day came when I ceased altogether to note them. Then, if that sunset scene had been repeated, I should have looked upon it without rapture, and should have commented upon it, inwardly, after this fashion: "This sun means that we are going to have wind tomorrow; that floating log means that the river is rising, small thanks to it; that slanting mark on the water refers to a bluff reef which is going to kill somebody's steamboat one of these nights, if it keeps on stretching out like that, those tumbling 'boils' show a dissolving bar and a changing channel there; the lines and circles in the slick water over yonder are a warning that that troublesome place

Again a sentence begins with but.

Another long, one-sentence list counters the earlier description of the river.

is shoaling up dangerously; that silver streak in the shadow of the forest is the 'break' from a new snag, and he has located himself in the very best place he could have found to fish for steamboats; that tall dead tree, with a single living branch, is not going to last long, and then how is a body ever going to get through this blind place at night without the friendly old landmark?"

No, the romance and beauty were all gone from the river. All the value any feature of it had for me now was the amount of usefulness it could furnish toward compassing the safe piloting of a steamboat. Since those days, I have pitied doctors from my heart. What does the lovely flush in a beauty's cheek mean to a doctor but a "break" that ripples above some deadly disease? Are not all her visible charms sown thick with what are to him the signs and symbols of hidden decay? Does he ever see her beauty at all, or doesn't he simply view her professionally, and comment upon her unwholesome condition all to himself? And doesn't he sometimes wonder whether he has gained most or lost most by learning his trade? ■

3

> **The paragraph ends with a series of interrelated questions.**

Reading for Better Writing

Working by yourself or with a group, answer these questions:

1. The purpose for comparing and contrasting two things is to make a point. What two specific things is Twain comparing and contrasting, and what is the point he is making? How do you know?

2. Twain first describes one way of looking at the river, then another. How else might he have organized the ideas in this passage? Make an argument for the organizational pattern that you think is most effective.

3. At two points in the passage, Twain begins sentences with the conjunction *but*. Why doesn't he simply combine these sentences with those that precede them?

4. Find examples of short, average, and long sentences in this passage. Where are they located, and why does Twain vary his sentence length in this way?

5. This passage ends with a series of rhetorical questions—questions that are intended to provoke thought but not an expressed answer. What clues suggest that Twain is expecting thought rather than actual answers? Why might he use this strategy?

Comparison and Contrast

Gelareh Asayesh grew up in Iran before moving to Florida. She writes about her experiences in *Saffron Sky: A Life Between Iran and America*. The article below first appeared in the *New York Times* in November 2001.

Shrouded in Contradiction

Two contrasting scenes appear in the first sentence.

I grew up wearing the miniskirt to school, the veil to the mosque. In the Tehran of my childhood, women in bright sundresses shared the sidewalk with women swathed in black. The tension between the two ways of life was palpable. As a schoolgirl, I often cringed when my bare legs got leering or contemptuous glances. Yet, at times, I long for the days when I could walk the streets of my country with the wind in my hair. When clothes were clothes. In today's Iran, whatever I wear sends a message. If it's a chador, it embarrasses my Westernized relatives. If it's a skimpy scarf, I risk being accused of stepping on the blood of the martyrs who died in the war with Iraq. Each time I return to Tehran, I wait until the last possible moment, when my plane lands on the tarmac,

> *As a schoolgirl, I often cringed when my bare legs got leering or contemptuous glances.*

Italics distinguish *hijab* as a non-English word.

to don the scarf and long jacket that many Iranian women wear in lieu of a veil. To wear *hijab*—Islamic covering—is to invite contradiction. Sometimes I hate it. Sometimes I value it.

Most of the time, I don't even notice it. It's annoying, but so is wearing pantyhose to work. It ruins my hair, but so does the humidity in Florida, where I live. For many women, the veil is neither a symbol nor a statement. It's simply what they wear, as their mothers did before them. Something to dry your face with after your ablutions before prayer. A place for a toddler to hide when he's feeling shy. Even for a woman like me, who wears it with a hint of rebellion, *hijab* is just not that big a deal.

Notice the one-sentence paragraph.

Except when it is.

"Sister, what kind of get-up is this?" a woman in black, one of a pair, asks me one summer day on the Caspian shore. I am standing in line to ride a gondola up a mountain, where I'll savor some ice cream along with vistas of sea and forest. Women in chadors stand wilting in the heat, faces gleaming with sweat. Women in makeup and clunky heels wear knee-length jackets with pants, their hair daringly exposed beneath sheer scarves.

None have been more daring than I. I've wound my scarf into a turban, leaving my neck bare to the breeze. The woman in black is a government employee paid to police public morals. "Fix your scarf at once!" she snaps.   5

"But I'm hot," I say.   6

"You're hot?" she exclaims. "Don't you think we all are?"   7

I start unwinding my makeshift turban. "The men aren't hot," I mutter.   8

Her companion looks at me in shocked reproach. "Sister, this isn't about men and women," she says, shaking her head. "This is about Islam."   9

Contradictory feelings are pushed together in a compact list.

I want to argue. I feel like a child. Defiant, but powerless. Burning with injustice, but also with a hint of shame. I do as I am told, feeling acutely conscious of the bare skin I am covering. In policing my sexuality, these women have made me more aware of it.   10

The writer offers definitions of *passion* reflecting three different perspectives.

The veil masks erotic freedom, but its advocates believe *hijab* transcends the erotic— or expands it. In the West, we think of passion as a fever of the body, not the soul. In the East, Sufi poets used earthly passion as a metaphor; the beloved they celebrated was God. Where I come from, people are more likely to find delirious passion in the mosque than in the bedroom.   11

> *The veil masks erotic freedom, but its advocates believe "hijab" transcends the erotic—or expands it.*   11

There are times when I feel a hint of this passion. A few years after my encounter on the Caspian, I go to the wake of a family friend. Sitting in a mosque in Mashhad, I grip a slippery black veil with one hand and a prayer book with the other. In the center of the hall, there's a stack of Koranic texts decorated with green-and-black calligraphy, a vase of white gladioluses and a large photograph of the dearly departed. Along the walls, women wait quietly.   12

From the men's side of the mosque, the mullah's voice rises in lament. His voice is deep and plaintive, oddly compelling. I bow my head, sequestered in my veil while at my side a community of women pray and weep with increasing abandon. I remember from girlhood this sense of   13

> **The writer uses terms of limited certainty, such as *perhaps* and *all I know.***

being exquisitely alone in the company of others. Sometimes I have cried as well, free to weep without having to offer an explanation. Perhaps they are right, those mystics who believe that physical love is an obstacle to spiritual love; those architects of mosques who abstained from images of earthly life, decorating their work with geometric shapes that they believed freed the soul to slip from its worldly moorings. I do not aspire to such lofty sentiments. All I know is that such moments of passionate abandon, within the circle of invisibility created by the veil, offer an emotional catharsis every bit as potent as any sexual release.

> **The final line summarizes the contradictions described in the passage.**

Outside, the rain pours from a sullen sky. I make my farewells and walk *14* toward the car, where my driver waits. My veil is wicking muddy water from the sidewalk. I gather up the wet and grimy folds with distaste, longing to be home, where I can cast off this curtain of cloth that gives with one hand, takes away with the other. ■

Reading for Better Writing

Working by yourself or with a group, answer these questions:

1. Sometimes writers use comparison-contrast organization to take a position on an issue—in some cases to show that one side is better than the other, but in others, to show the difficulty of choosing one side over the other. What do you think is Asayesh's position on *hijab*, and why?

2. Find Asayesh's one-sentence paragraph (paragraph 3). Why might the writer have constructed the paragraph in this way? How would this excerpt differ if that sentence had been part of either the preceding or the following paragraph?

3. What contrasts are listed in paragraph 4? How does the writer use sentence structure and punctuation to mark the contrasts?

4. Why does Asayesh use words that indicate limited certainty, such as *perhaps* and *all I know*?

5. In what ways are the opening and closing sentences alike? How are these similarities significant for readers?

Comparison and Contrast

Author Gary Soto describes falling in love against his family's advice with a woman who is not Mexican. In doing so, he draws a number of comparisons.

In the text, highlight elements of comparison and contrast that you find interesting or engaging. Then in the margin, explain your response.

Like Mexicans

My grandmother gave me bad advice and good advice when I was in my early teens. For the bad advice, she said that I should become a barber because they made good money and listened to the radio all day. "Honey, they don't work como burros," she would say every time I visited her. She made the sound of donkeys braying. "Like that, Honey!" For good advice, she said that I should marry a Mexican girl. "No Okies, hijo"—she would say—"Look, my son. He marry one and they fight every day about I don't know what and I don't know what." For her, everyone who wasn't Mexican, black, or Asian was an Okie. The French were Okies, the Italians in suits were Okies. When I asked about Jews, whom I had read about, she asked for a picture. I rode home on my bicycle and returned with a calendar depicting the important races of the world. "Pues si, son Okies también!" she said, nodding her head. She waved the calendar away and we went to the living room, where she lectured me on the virtues of the Mexican girl: first, she could cook and, second, she acted like a woman, not a man, in her husband's home. She said she would tell me about a third when I got a little older.

I asked my mother about it—becoming a barber and marrying Mexican. She was in the kitchen. Steam curled from a pot of boiling beans, the radio was on, looking as squat as a loaf of bread. "Well, if you want to be a barber—they say they make good money." She slapped a round steak with a knife, her glasses slipping down with each strike. She stopped and looked up. "If you find a good Mexican girl, marry her, of course." She returned to slapping the meat, and I went to the backyard where my brother and David King were sitting on the lawn feeling the insides of their cheeks.

"This is what girls feel like," my brother said, rubbing the inside of his cheek. David put three fingers inside his mouth and scratched. I ignored them and climbed the back fence to see my best friend, Scott, a second-generation Okie. I had called him, and his mother pointed to the side of the house where his bedroom was, a small aluminum trailer, the kind you gawk at when they're flipped over on the freeway, wheels spinning in the air. I went around to find Scott pitching horseshoes.

I picked up a set of rusty ones and joined him. While we played, we talked about school and friends and record albums. The horseshoes scuffed up dirt, sometimes ringing the iron that threw out a meager shadow like a sundial. After three argued-over games we pulled two oranges apiece from his tree and started down the alley still talking school and friends and record

1

2

3

4

albums. We pulled more oranges from the alley and talked about who we would marry. "No offense, Scott," I said with an orange slice in my mouth, "but I would never marry an Okie." We walked in step, almost touching, with a sled of shadows dragging behind us. "No offense, Gary," Scott said, "but I would *never* marry a Mexican." I looked at him: a fang of orange slice showed from his munching mouth. I didn't think anything of it. He had his girl and I had mine. But our seventh-grade vision was the same: to marry, get jobs, buy cars and maybe a house if we had money left over.

We talked about our future lives until, to our surprise, we were on   5
the downtown mall, two miles from home. We bought a bag of popcorn at Penneys and sat on a bench near the fountain watching Mexican and Okie girls pass. "That one's mine," I pointed with my chin when a girl with eyebrows arched into black rainbows ambled by. "She's cute," Scott said about a girl with yellow hair and mouthful of gum. We dreamed aloud, our chins busy pointing out girls. We agreed that we couldn't wait to become men and lift them onto our laps.

But the woman I married was not Mexican but Japanese. It was a   6
surprise to me. For years, I went about wide-eyed in my search for the brown girl in a white dress at a dance. I searched the playground at the baseball diamond. When the girls raced for grounders, their hair bounced like something that couldn't be caught. When they sat together in the lunchroom, heads pressed together, I knew they were talking about us Mexican guys. I saw them and dreamed them. I threw my face into my pillow, making up sentences that were as good as in the movies.

> *For years, I went about wide-eyed in my search for the brown girl in a white dress at a dance.*

But when I was twenty, I fell in love with   7
this other girl who worried my mother, who had my grandmother asking once again to see the calendar of the Important Races of the World. I told her I had thrown it away many years before. I took a much-glanced-at snapshot from my wallet. We looked at it together, in silence. Then Grandma reclined in her chair, lit a cigarette, and said, "Es pretty." She blew and asked with all her worry pushed up to her forehead: "Chinese?"

I was in love and there was no looking back. She was the one. I told   8
my mother, who was slapping hamburger into patties. "Well, sure, if you want to marry her," she said. But the more I talked, the more concerned she became. Later I began to worry. Was it all a mistake? "Marry a Mexican girl," I heard my mother say in my mind. I heard it at breakfast. I heard it over math problems, between Western Civilization and cultural geography. But then one afternoon while I was hitchhiking home from school, it struck me like a baseball in the back: My mother wanted me to marry someone of

my own social class—a poor girl. I considered my fiancee, Carolyn, and she didn't look poor, though I knew she came from a family of farm workers and pull-yourself-up-by-your-bootstraps ranchers. I asked my brother who was marrying Mexican poor that fall, if I should marry a poor girl. He screamed "Yeah" above this terrible guitar playing in his bedroom. I considered my sister, who had married Mexican. Cousins were dating Mexicans. Uncles were remarrying poor women. I asked Scott, who was still my best friend, and he said, "She's too good for you, so you better not."

I worried about it until Carolyn took me home to meet her parents. We drove in their Plymouth until the houses gave way to farms and ranches and finally her house fifty feet from the highway. We pulled into the drive; I panicked and begged Carolyn to make a U-turn and go back so we could talk about it over a soda. She pinched my cheek, calling me a "silly boy." I felt better, though, when I got out of the car and saw the house: the chipped paint, a cracked window, boards for a walk to the back door. There were rusting cars near the barn. A tractor with a net of spiderwebs under a mulberry. A field. A bale of barbed wire like children's scribbling leaning against an empty chicken coop. Carolyn took my hand and pulled me to my future mother-in-law, who was coming out to greet us.

9

> *She pinched my cheek, calling me a "silly boy."*

We had lunch: sandwiches, potato chips, and iced tea. Carolyn and her mother talked mostly about neighbors and the congregation at the Japanese Methodist Church in West Fresno. Her father, who was in khaki work clothes, excused himself with a wave that was almost a salute and went outside. I heard a truck start, a dog bark, and then the truck rattle away.

10

Carolyn's mother offered another sandwich, but I declined with a shake of my head and a smile. I looked around when I could, when I was not saying over and over that I was a college student, hinting that I could take care of her daughter. I shifted my chair. I saw newspapers piled in corners, dusty cereal boxes and vinegar bottles in corners. The wallpaper was bubbled from rain that had come in from a bad roof. Dust. Dust lay on lamp shades and windowsills. These people are just like Mexicans, I thought. Poor people.

11

Carolyn's mother asked me through Carolyn if I would like a sushi. A plate of black and white things was held in front of me. I took one, wide-eyed, and turned it over like a foreign coin. I was biting into one when I saw a kitten crawl up the window screen over the sink. I chewed and the kitten opened its mouth of terror as she crawled higher, wanting to paw the leftovers from our plates. I looked at Carolyn, who said that the cat was just showing off. I looked up in time to see it fall. It crawled up, then fell again.

12

We talked for an hour and had apple pie and coffee, slowly. Finally, we *13*
got up with Carolyn taking my hand. Slightly embarrassed, I tried to pull
away, but her grip held me. I let her have her way as she led me down the
hallway with her mother right behind me. When I opened the door, I was
startled by a kitten clinging to the screen door, its mouth screaming "cat
food, dog biscuits, *sushi* . . . . " I opened the door and the kitten, still holding
on, whined in the language of hungry animals. When I got into Carolyn's car,
I looked back: The cat was still clinging. I asked Carolyn if it were possibly
hungry, but she said the cat was being silly. She started the car, waved to her
mother, and bounced over the rain-poked drive, patting my thigh for being
her lover baby. Carolyn waved again. I looked back, waving, then gawking at
a window screen where there were now three kittens clawing and screaming
to get in. Like Mexicans, I thought. I remembered the Molinas and how the
cats clung to their screens—cats they shot down with squirt guns. On the
highway, I felt happy, pleased by it all. I patted Carolyn's thigh. Her people
were like Mexicans, only different. ∎

Reading for Better Writing

1. Briefly explain what the title, "Like Mexicans," signifies.

2. List the items the writer either directly or indirectly compares (for
example, two kitchens, two mothers). Do these comparisons add to
or detract from the essay's main point? Explain your answer.

3. Explain how the essay is organized. Is the organization effective?
Why or why not?

4. The writer describes cats three times. How is the climbing of cats on
screens related to his main point?

Model

Guidelines
Writing a Comparison-Contrast Essay

1. **Select a topic.** List subjects that are similar and/or different in ways that you find interesting, perplexing, disgusting, infuriating, charming, or informing. Then choose two subjects whose comparison and/or contrast gives the reader some insight into who or what they are. For example, you could explain how two chemicals that appear to be similar are actually different—and how that difference makes one more explosive, poisonous, or edible.

2. **Get the big picture.** Using a computer or a paper and pen, create three columns as shown below. Brainstorm a list of traits under each heading. (Also see the Venn diagram on page 50.)

   Traits of Subject 1   Shared Traits   Traits of Subject 2

3. **Gather information.** Review your list of traits, highlighting those that could provide insight into one or both subjects. Research the subjects, using hands-on analysis when possible. Consider writing your research notes in the three-column format shown above.

4. **Draft a working thesis.** Review your expanded list of traits and eliminate those that now seem unimportant. Write a sentence stating the core of what you learned about the subjects and whether you are comparing, contrasting, or both. If you're stuck, try completing the sentence below. (Switch around the terms "similar" and "different" if you wish to stress similarities.)

   While _____ and _____ seem similar, they are different in several ways, and the differences are important because _____.

5. **Get organized.** Decide how to organize your essay. Generally, *subject by subject* works best for short, simple comparisons. *Trait by trait* works best for longer, more complex comparisons.

6. **Draft the essay.** Review your outline and write your first draft in one sitting if possible. Check your outline for details and integrate them into the text.

Subject by Subject:

Introduction
Subject 1
• Trait A
• Trait B
• Trait C
Subject 2
• Trait A
• Trait B
• Trait C

Trait by Trait:

Introduction
Trait A
• Subject 1
• Subject 2
Trait B
• Subject 1
• Subject 2
Trait C
• Subject 1
• Subject 2

Subject-by-subject pattern:

- **Opening**—get readers' attention and introduce the subjects and thesis.
- **Middle**—describe one "package" of traits representing the first subject and a parallel set of traits representing the second subject.
- **Conclusion**—point out similarities and/or differences, note their significance, and restate your main point.

Trait-by-trait pattern:

- **Opening**—get readers' attention and introduce the subjects and thesis.
- **Middle**—compare and/or contrast the two subjects trait by trait (include transitions that help readers look back and forth between the two subjects).
- **Conclusion**—summarize the key relationships, note their significance, and restate your main point.

7. **Revise the essay.** Check the essay for the following:
   - Balanced comparisons and contrasts of comparable traits
   - Complete and thoughtful treatment of each subject
   - Genuine and objective voice
   - Clear, smooth sentences with varied structure
   - Title and introduction that spark interest
   - Thoughtful, unifying conclusion

8. **Get feedback.** Ask a classmate or someone in the writing center to read your paper, looking for the following:
   - A clear, interesting thesis
   - An engaging and informative introduction
   - A middle that compares and/or contrasts significant, parallel traits
   - Ideas that offer insight into the subject
   - A conclusion that restates the main point and unifies the essay

9. **Edit your essay.** Look for the following:
   - Transitions that signal comparisons and link paragraphs: *on the other hand, in contrast, similarly, also, both, even though, in the same way*
   - Correct quotations and documentation
   - Correct spelling, punctuation, usage, and grammar

10. **Publish your essay.** Share your writing with others:
    - Submit it to your instructor.
    - Share it with other students or publish it on a website.

Writing Checklist

Use these seven traits to check the quality of your writing; then revise as needed:

_____ The **ideas** (points made or conclusions drawn from comparing and contrasting) provide insight into who or what both subjects are and why they are important. The basis for comparison is clear.

_____ The **organization** pattern (subject by subject, trait by trait) helps readers grasp the similarities and differences between the subjects.

_____ The **voice** is informed, involved, and genuine.

_____ The **words** are precise and clear. Technical or scientific terms are defined. Links between subjects are communicated with transitions such as these:

Although	Either one	In contrast	Neither
As a result	For this reason	In the same way	On the other hand
Both	However	Likewise	Therefore

_____ The **sentences** are clear, well reasoned, varied in structure, and smooth.

_____ The **copy** is correct and clean.

_____ The **design** includes proper formatting, and graphics such as photos or drawings are clear and well placed.

Interactive

Critical-Thinking and Writing Activities

As directed by your instructor, complete the following activities.

1. Review the way in which Mark Twain makes his point in "Two Views of the River" by comparing and contrasting two perspectives of the Mississippi River. Revise or draft a passage of your own in which you use comparison and contrast to emphasize a point.

2. Review Gelareh Asayesh's essay "Shrouded in Contradiction," noting how she uses comparison-contrast strategies so as to take a position. Draft or revise an essay in which you use comparison-contrast strategies to develop or support a position.

3. In "Like Mexicans," Gary Soto compares two ethnic groups who are part of his family. List related pairs that are part of your life (siblings, uncles, homes, family conflicts, educational experiences, teachers, neighbors, and so on). Write an essay in which you compare and/or contrast the subjects to share insight into your life.

◄ VISUALLY SPEAKING

Study the photograph on page 199. What does the picture compare or contrast? What ideas or feelings does the comparison/contrast elicit? Could an essay addressing the same topic elicit the same response? Explain.

CLASSIFICATION

Audio

Video

Classification is an organizational strategy that helps writers make sense of large or complex sets of things. A writer who is using this strategy looks at a topic and then breaks it into components that can be sorted into clearly distinguishable subgroups. For example, if he or she is writing about the types of residents who live in assisted-care facilities, a nursing student might classify possible residents according to various physical and/or mental limitations.

By sorting the residents in this way, the writer can discuss them as individuals, as representatives of a subgroup, or as members of the group as a whole. By using an additional strategy such as compare/contrast, he or she can show both similarities and differences between one subgroup and another, or between individuals within a subgroup. By using classification, the writer helps readers understand both individual components of the topic and relationships among the components.

For help as you write a classification essay, read the instructions and models in this chapter.

Overview
Writing a Classification Essay

Writer's Goal

Your goal is to divide a group of people, places, things, or concepts into subgroups, and then to write an essay that helps readers understand each component, the subgroups, and the topic as a whole.

Keys for Success

Choose classification criteria that fit the topic. Use classification criteria to distinguish one subgroup from another. For example, to explain her family's experience with cancer, student writer Kim Brouwer examines three types of cancer (*type* is a basis for classification). Because cancer is a complex illness, grouping by type fits her subject (see "Three Family Cancers," pages 217–219).

Choose classification criteria that fit your purpose. Use criteria that help you achieve your goal. For example, Ann Hodgman wants to assess the quality of dog-food products (her purpose). To achieve this goal, she measures their color, texture, taste, smell, and nutritional value—suitable criteria for assessing levels of quality (see "No Wonder They Call . . . ," pages 222–225).

Follow classification principles. Sort items into subgroups according to the following principles:

- **Consistency:** Use the same criteria in the same way when deciding which individual items to place in which subgroups. For example, Hodgman measures the quality of all dog-food products with the same criteria: color, taste, and so on.
- **Exclusivity:** Establish distinct subgroups so that each one differs from the others. For example, in "Three Family Cancers," the writer explains three distinct—or exclusive—types of cancer. Although the three types share some traits, each type is distinct.

Topics to Consider

To choose a topic, start by writing a half-dozen general headings like the academic headings below; then list two or three related topics under each heading. Finally, pick a topic that can best be explained by breaking it into subgroups.

Engineering	**Biology**	**Social Work**	**Education**
Machines	Whales	Child welfare	Learning styles
Bridges	Fruits	Organizations	Testing methods

Next Step Read the model essays and do the activities that follow. As you read, note how the classification strategy helps writers address complex topics.

Classification

Kim Brouwer's essay below is what professor Ken Macrorie calls an *I-search paper*—a piece that one writes "to find something he needs to know for his own life." Kim's conversational tone and use of personal pronouns are appropriate elements in such a document.

Audio

Three Family Cancers

The writer introduces the topic with an anecdote.

One day back in fourth grade, my teacher said, "Use your imagination and make an invention—something new and useful." I grumped all the way home from school. An invention? For what, I thought. What could I invent that we could use? "What about a cure for cancer?" Mom asked.   *1*

A few weeks earlier my family had learned that Grandpa DeRonde had cancer, so I went to work imagining my very own miracle cure. I drew a picture of a medicine bottle, similar to a bottle of cough syrup, with a drop of liquid coming out of it. I called my masterpiece, "The Cure for Cancer."   *2*

She gives her criterion for classifying ("different forms") and identifies subgroups.

I can remember those school days pretty well, but I can't say the same for three of my grandparents—Grandma and Grandpa DeRonde and Grandpa Vernooy. Before I could grow up and get to know them, their lives were invaded, taken over, and destroyed by different forms of cancer—multiple myeloma, prostate cancer, and lung cancer. Now, years later, I am a college freshman, faced with another assignment that gives me a chance to think about cancer: What is it, and what causes it? And what were these illnesses like for my grandparents? To get some answers, I researched cancer and talked with my mother.   *3*

She explains what all forms of cancer have in common.

Cancer, as my family learned firsthand, is a serious killer. In fact, it's the second leading cause of death in the United States. Each year, the disease kills about 500,000 Americans, and doctors discover more than one million new cases (Microsoft Encarta). Cancer is so powerful because it's not one illness, but rather many diseases attacking many parts of the body. All cancers are basically body cells gone crazy—cells that develop abnormally. These cells then clone themselves using an enzyme called telomerase. As they multiply like creatures in a sci-fi horror movie, the cells build into tumors, which are tissues that can "invade and destroy other tissues" (Microsoft Encarta).   *4*

The writer categorizes carcinogens.

Researchers aren't exactly sure what triggers these cancerous growths, but they think that 80 percent of cancers happen because people come into regular contact with carcinogens—cancer-causing agents. Carcinogens are classified into three groups: chemicals, radiation, and viruses (Compton's). People can be exposed to these carcinogens in many ways and situations. One study showed that 5 percent of cancers could be traced to environmental pollution, including carcinogens in the workplace. Radiation, for example, devastated the population of Chernobyl, Russia, after the nuclear power plant meltdown. But carcinogens don't cause cancer overnight—even from   *5* exposure in a terrible accident. The cancer may take thirty to forty years to develop (Compton's).

She describes the first subgroup.

I don't know what carcinogens attacked my Grandma DeRonde, but I do know the result: She developed multiple myeloma. For a multiple-myeloma patient, the average period of survival is twenty months to ten years (Madden 108). When I talked with my mother, she said that my family doesn't really know when Grandma came down with multiple myeloma, but she lived for two years after learning that she had it. For two years, she suffered through radiation and chemotherapy treatments, and life seemed measured by the spaces between appointments to check her white-blood cell count.

She gives distinguishing details.

What causes multiple myeloma remains a mystery, though its effects are well known. This cancer involves a malignant growth of cells in the bone marrow that makes holes in the skeleton. The holes develop mostly in the ribs, vertebrae, and pelvis. Because the holes make the bones brittle, the patient cannot do simple things like driving and cooking. In the end, patients fracture bones and die from infection and pneumonia (Madden 108). It was this weakening of the bones, along with the chemotherapy treatments, that made my grandmother suffer.

She describes the second subgroup.

My Grandpa DeRonde was diagnosed with prostate cancer several years after my grandma died. The doctors began radiation therapy right away, and my family was hopeful because the cancer was caught in its early stages. At first, the cancer seemed to go into remission, but cancer cells were actually invading other sites in his body. Because the cancer spread, the doctors couldn't treat all of it through radiation or surgery. Grandpa lived for only two years after learning he was ill, and during that time he had many chemotherapy treatments and spent a lot of time in the hospital. On his death certificate, the doctor wrote that Grandpa died of cardiac arrest and carcinoma of the lung, with metastasis.

She provides distinguishing details.

Like multiple myeloma, prostate cancer is a powerful killer. Even though many technological changes help doctors catch this cancer at an early stage, the number of deaths per year is still going up. Prostate cancer is the second most common cancer in the United States, and experts believe that it can be found in about 25 million men over the age of fifty (Fintor).

Prostate cancer is a tumor (called a carcinoma) lining the inside of the prostate gland. Many factors trigger this form of cancer: age, diet, environmental conditions, or maybe just having a cancer-prone family ("Prostate Cancer Trends" 183). A survey of more than 51,000 American men showed that eating a lot of fat, found mostly in red meat, can lead to advanced prostate cancer. On the other hand, researchers concluded that fats from vegetables, fish, and many dairy products are probably not linked to the growth of a carcinoma (Cowley 77).

She describes the third subgroup.

My second grandfather died from a different carcinoma—lung cancer. Doctors found a tumor in the lower lobe of Grandpa Vernooy's right lung, recommended surgery, and removed the lung. The next winter, he weakened, got pneumonia, and died. His doctors believed that his smoking habit caused the cancer. Smoking, in fact, remains the most important factor in developing lung cancer ("Family Ties" 109). The truth is that cigarette smoking causes almost half of all cancer cases, even though only one out of ten smokers actually comes down with this disease (Compton's).

She cites distinguishing details.

One study concluded that genetics may play a role in whether a person 12 develops lung cancer. Research suggests that if a person is missing positive genes called tumor-suppressor genes, it's bad news. If these genes weren't inherited, or if smoking destroyed them, then cancer-related genes are free to do their damage (Edwards 358). Another study identified a special gene that is inherited from one or both parents and that metabolizes chemicals from cigarette smoke. In this case, if the gene is there, the cancer risk goes up, especially for smokers ("Family Ties" 109).

She closes by reviewing the subgroups and reflecting on the opening anecdote.

I still wish I could cure cancer with a magic miracle liquid in a 13 medicine bottle. But today I understand that cancer is a complicated disease. My grandparents died from three types of the disease—multiple myeloma, prostate cancer, and lung cancer. If it hadn't been for cancerous tumors taking over their bodies, my grandparents might still be alive, and I'd have many more memories of them. Maybe I'd even be sharing with them stories about my first year at college. On the other hand, perhaps this paper is a cure of a different type—while it can't change what happened, it can help me understand it. ■

> **Note:** The Works Cited page is not shown. For sample pages, see MLA (page 532–533) and APA (page 564).

Reading for Better Writing

Working by yourself or in a group, do the following:

1. The writer opens and closes the essay with a personal anecdote. Explain why this story does or does not strengthen the essay.

2. For each subgroup (type of cancer), the writer uses a grandparent as an example. Explain how her use of examples does or does not help clarify the subject.

3. Where in the essay does the writer compare and contrast different forms of cancer? Is the comparison and contrast effective? Why or why not?

4. Writing about a scientific topic like cancer nearly always requires technical terminology. Cite two such terms used in this essay, and explain how the writer clarifies each term's meaning.

Classification

In this essay John Van Rys, a college professor, classifies four basic approaches to literary criticism. His essay is intended to help college freshmen interpret literature.

Four Ways to Talk About Literature

The writer introduces the topic and criterion for creating four subgroups.

Have you ever been in a conversation in which you suddenly felt lost—out of the loop? Perhaps you feel that way in your literature class. You may think a poem or short story means one thing, and then your instructor suddenly pulls out the "hidden meaning." Joining the conversation about literature—in class or in an essay—may indeed seem daunting, but you can do it if you know what to look for and what to talk about. There are four main perspectives, or approaches, that you can use to converse about literature.   1

He describes the first subgroup and gives an example.

Text-centered approaches focus on the literary piece itself. Often called *formalist criticism,* such approaches claim that the structure of a work and the rules of its genre are crucial to its meaning. The formalist critic determines how various elements (plot, character, language, and so on) reinforce the meaning and unify the work. For example, the formalist may ask the following questions concerning Robert Browning's poem "My Last Duchess": How do the main elements in the poem—irony, symbolism, and verse form—help develop the main theme (deception)? How does Browning use the dramatic monologue genre in this poem?   2

He describes the second subgroup and gives an example.

Audience-centered approaches focus on the "transaction" between text and reader—the dynamic way the reader interacts with the text. Often called *rhetorical* or *reader-response criticism,* these approaches see the text not as an object to be analyzed, but as an activity that is different for each reader. A reader-response critic might ask these questions of "My Last Duchess": How does the reader become aware of the duke's true nature if it's never actually stated? Do men and women read the poem differently? Who were Browning's original readers?   3

He describes the third subgroup and gives examples.

Author-centered approaches focus on the origins of a text (the writer and the historical background). For example, an author-centered study examines the writer's life—showing connections, contrasts, and conflicts between his or her life and the writing. Broader historical studies explore social and intellectual currents, showing links between an author's work and the ideas, events, and institutions of that period. Finally, the literary historian may make connections between the text in question and earlier and later literary works. The author-centered critic might ask these questions of "My Last Duchess": What were Browning's views of marriage, men and women, art, class, and wealth? As an institution, what was marriage like in Victorian England (Browning's era) or Renaissance Italy (the duke's era)? Who was the historical Duke of Ferrara?   4

He describes the fourth approach and gives examples of each subgroup in it.

The fourth approach to criticism applies ideas outside of literature to literary works. Because literature mirrors life, argue these critics, disciplines that explore human life can help us understand literature. Some critics, for example, apply psychological theories to literary works by exploring dreams, symbolic meanings, and motivation. Myth or archetype criticism uses insights from psychology, cultural anthropology, and classical studies to explore a text's universal appeal. Moral criticism, rooted in religious studies and ethics, explores the moral dilemmas literary works raise. Marxist, feminist, and minority criticism are, broadly speaking, sociological approaches to interpretation. While the Marxist examines the themes of class struggle, economic power, and social justice in texts, the feminist critic explores the just and unjust treatment of women as well as the effect of gender on language, reading, and the literary canon. The critic interested in race and ethnic identity explores similar issues, with the focus shifted to a specific cultural group.

5

He cites sample questions.

Such ideological criticism might ask a wide variety of questions about "My Last Duchess": What does the poem reveal about the duke's psychological state and his personality? How does the reference to Neptune deepen the poem? What does the poem suggest about the nature of evil and injustice? In what ways are the duke's motives class-based and economic? How does the poem present the duke's power and the duchess's weakness? What is the status of women in this society?

6

The closing presents qualities shared by all four approaches.

If you look at the variety of questions critics might ask about "My Last Duchess," you see both the diversity of critical approaches and the common ground between them. In fact, interpretive methods actually share important characteristics: (1) a close attention to literary elements such as character, plot, symbolism, and metaphor; (2) a desire not to distort the work; and (3) a sincere concern for increasing interest and understanding in a text. In actual practice, critics may develop a hybrid approach to criticism, one that matches their individual questions and concerns about a text. Now that you're familiar with some of the questions defining literary criticism, exercise your own curiosity (and join the ongoing literary dialogue) by discussing a text that genuinely interests you. ■

7

Reading for Better Writing

Working by yourself or with a group, do the following:

1. Explain how the writer introduces the subject and attempts to engage the reader. Is this strategy effective? Why or why not?

2. The writer uses one poem to illustrate how each of the four critical approaches works. Explain why this strategy is or is not effective.

3. Review the last paragraph and explain why it does or does not unify the essay.

Classification

This piece was first printed in *Spy* magazine, an engaging periodical that ceased publication in 1998. In its time, the magazine was known for pieces that were both humorous and research based. Ann Hodgman was a food editor for *Spy*.

Working with one or two classmates, read the article and note how Hodgman uses categories to organize her analysis of dog food. Then discuss how the categories help direct and clarify her study.

No Wonder They Call Me a Bitch

1 I've always wondered about dog food. Is a Gaines-burger really like a hamburger? Can you fry it? Does dog food "cheese" taste like real cheese? Does Gravy Train actually make gravy in the dog's bowl, or is that brown liquid just dissolved crumbs? And exactly what *are* by-products?

2 Having spent the better part of a week eating dog food, I'm sorry to say that I now know the answers to these questions. While my dachshund, Shortie, watched in agonies of yearning, I gagged my way through can after can of stinky, white-flecked mush and bag after bag of stinky, fat-drenched nuggets. And now I understand exactly why Shortie's breath is so bad.

3 Of course, Gaines-burgers are neither mush nor nuggets. They are, rather, a miracle of beauty and packaging—or at least that's what I thought when I was little. I used to beg my mother to get them for our dogs, but she always said they were too expensive. When I finally bought a box of cheese-flavored Gaines-burgers—after 20 years of longing—I felt deliciously wicked.

4 "Dogs love real beef," the back of the box proclaimed proudly. "That's why Gaines-burgers is the only beef burger for dogs with real beef and no meat by-products!" The copy was accurate: Meat by-products did not appear in the list of ingredients. Poultry by-products did, though—right there next to preserved animal fat.

5 One Purina spokesman told me that poultry by-products consist of necks, intestines, undeveloped eggs, and other "carcass remnants," but not feathers, heads, or feet. When I told him I'd been eating dog food, he said, "Oh, you're kidding! Oh no!" (I came to share his alarm when, weeks later, a second Purina spokesman said that Gaines-burgers *do* contain poultry heads and feet—but *not* undeveloped eggs).

6 Up close my Gaines-burger didn't much resemble chopped beef. Rather, it looked—and felt—like a single long, extruded piece of redness that had been chopped into segments and formed into a patty. You could make one at home if you had a Play-Doh Fun Factory.

7 I turned on the skillet. While I waited for it to heat up I pulled out a shred of cheese-colored material and palpated it. Again, like Play-Doh, it was quite malleable. I made a little cheese bird out of it; then I counted to three and ate the bird.

8 There was a horrifying rush of cheddar taste, followed immediately by the dull tang of soybean flour—the main ingredient in Gaines-burgers.

Next I tried a piece of red extrusion. The main difference between the meat-flavored and cheese-flavored extrusions is one of texture. The "cheese" chews like fresh Play-Doh, whereas the "meat" chews like Play-Doh that's been sitting out on a rug for a couple of hours.

Frying only turned the Gaines-burger black. There was no melting, no sizzling, no warm meat smells. A cherished childhood illusion was gone. I flipped the patty into the sink, where it immediately began leaking rivulets of red dye. *9*

As alarming as the Gaines-burgers were, their soy meal began to seem like an old friend when the time came to try some *canned* dog foods. I decided to try the Cycle foods first. When I opened them, I thought about how rarely I use can openers these days, and I was suddenly visited by a long-forgotten sensation of can-opener distaste. *This* is the kind of unsavory place can openers spend their time when you're not watching! Every time you open a can of, say, Italian plum tomatoes, you infect them with invisible particles of by-product. *10*

I had been expecting to see the usual homogeneous scrapple inside, but each can of Cycle was packed with smooth, round, oily nuggets. As if someone at Gaines had been tipped off that a human would be tasting the stuff, the four Cycles really were different from one another. Cycle-1, for puppies, is wet and soyish, Cycle-2, for adults, glistens nastily with fat, but it's passably edible—a lot like some canned Swedish meatballs I once got in a care package at college. Cycle-3, the "lite" one, for fatties, had no specific flavor, it just tasted like dog food. But at least it didn't make me fat. *11*

Cycle-4, for senior dogs, had the smallest nuggets. Maybe old dogs can't open their mouths as wide. This kind was far sweeter than the other three Cycles—almost like baked beans. It was also the only one to contain "dried beef digest," a mysterious substance that the Purina spokesman defined as "enzymes" and my dictionary defined as "the products of digestion." *12*

Next on the menu was a can of Kal-Kan Pedigree with Chunky Chicken. Chunky chicken? There were chunks in the can, certainly—big, purplish-brown chunks. I forked one chunk out (by now I was becoming more callous) and found that while it had no discernible chicken flavor, it wasn't bad except for its texture—like meat loaf with ground-up chicken bones. *13*

In the world of canned dog food, a smooth consistency is a sign of low quality—lots of cereal. A lumpy, frightening, bloody, stringy horror is a sign of high quality—lots of meat. Nowhere in the world of wet dog foods was this demonstrated better than in the fanciest I tried—Kal Kan's Pedigree Select Dinners. These came not in a can but in a tiny foil packet with a picture of an imperious Yorkie. When I pulled open the container, juice spurted all over my hand, and the first chunk I speared was trailing a long gray vein. I shrieked and went instead for a plain chunk, which I was able to swallow only after taking a break to read some suddenly fascinating office *14* equipment catalogs. Once again, though, it tasted no more alarming than, say, canned hash.

Still, how pleasant it was to turn to *dry* dog food! Gravy Train was the 15 first I tried, and I'm happy to report that it really does make a "thick, rich, real beef gravy" when you mix it with water. Thick and rich, anyway. Except for a lingering rancid-fat flavor, the gravy wasn't beefy, but since it tasted primarily like tap water, it wasn't nauseating either.

My poor dachshund just gets plain old Purina Dog Chow, but Purina 16 also makes a dry food called Butcher's Blend that comes in Beef, Bacon & Chicken flavor. Here we see dog food's arcane semiotics at its best: a red triangle with a *T* stamped into it is supposed to suggest beef; a tan curl, chicken; and a brown *S*, a piece of bacon. Only dogs understand these messages. But Butcher's Blend does have an endearing slogan: "Great Meaty Tastes—without bothering the Butcher!" *You know, I wanted go buy some meat, but I just couldn't bring myself to bother the butcher. . . .*

Purina O.N.E. ("Optimum Nutritional Effectiveness") is targeted at 17 people who are unlikely ever to worry about bothering a tradesperson. "We chose chicken as a primary ingredient in Purina O.N.E. for several reasonings," the long, long essay on the back of the bag announces. Chief among these reasonings, I'd guess, is the fact that chicken appeals to people who are—you know—*like us*. Although our dogs do nothing but spend 18-hour days alone in the apartment, we still want them to be *premium* dogs. We want them to cut down on red meat, too. We also want dog food that comes in a bag with an attractive design, a subtle typeface, and no kitschy pictures of slobbering golden retrievers.

Besides that, we want a list of the Nutritional Benefits of our dog 18 food—and we get it on O.N.E. One thing I especially like about this list is its constant references to a dog's "hair coat," as in "Beef tallow is good for the dog's skin and hair coat." (On the other hand, beef tallow merely provides palatability, while the dried beef digest in Cycle provides palatability *enhancement.*)

I hate to say it, but O.N.E. was pretty palatable. Maybe that's because 19 it has about 100 percent more fat than, say, Butcher's Blend. Or maybe I'd been duped by the packaging; that's been known to happen before.

As with people food, dog snacks taste much better than dog meals. 20 They're better-looking, too. Take Milk-Bone Flavor Snacks. The loving-hands-at-home prose describing each flavor is colorful; the writers practically choke on their own exuberance. Of bacon they say, "It's so good, your dog will think it's hot off the frying pan." Of liver: "The only taste your dog wants more than liver—is even more liver!" Of poultry: "All those farm fresh flavors deliciously mixed in one biscuit. Your dog will bark with delight!" And of vegetable: "Gardens of taste! Specially blended to give your dog that vegetable flavor he wants—but can rarely get!"

Well, I may be a sucker, but advertising *this* emphatic just doesn't 21 convince me. I lined up all seven flavors of Milk-Bone Flavor Snacks on the floor. Unless my dog's palate is a lot more sensitive than mine—and considering that she steals dirty diapers out of the trash and eats them, I'm loath to think it is—she doesn't detect any more difference in the seven flavors than I did when I tried them.

I much preferred Bonz, the hard-baked, bone-shaped snack stuffed 22 with simulated marrow. I liked the bone part, that is; it tasted almost exactly like the cornmeal it was made of. The mock-marrow inside was a bit more problematic: in addition to looking like the sludge that collects in the treads of my running shoes, it was bursting with tiny hairs.

I'm sure you have a few dog food questions of your own. To save us 23 time, I've answered them in advance.

Q. *Are those little cans of Mighty Dog actually branded with the sizzling* 24 *word* **BEEF**, *the way they show in the commercials?*

A. You should know by now that that kind of thing never happens. 25

Q. *Does chicken-flavored dog food taste like chicken-flavored cat food?* 26

A. To my surprise, chicken cat food was actually a little better—more 27 chickeny. It tasted like inferior canned pâté.

Q. *Was there any dog food that you just couldn't bring yourself to try?* 28

A. Alas, it was a can of Mighty Dog called Prime Entree with Bone 29 Marrow. The meat was dark, dark brown, and it was surrounded by gelatin that was almost black. I knew I would die if I tasted it, so I put it outside for the raccoons. ■

Reading for Better Writing

Working by yourself or with a group, answer these questions:

1. Why does Hodgman claim to taste-test dog food and then report on her findings in writing? Can you think of other texts written for similar purposes?

2. What criteria does Hodgman use to divide her subject into categories? Where and how does she indicate that she is shifting her discussion from one category to the next?

3. The title grabs our attention with the word *bitch*, a word rarely used in titles. Does the word use serve additional purposes?

4. This piece is based on primary-source research. Review chapter 29, "Conducting Primary and Library Research," especially the portion on conducting primary research. What other research strategies could the author have used to explore her topic? Which would be most effective for her *Spy* audience? How would she need to change her tactics if her audience were a scientific journal? A magazine for dog enthusiasts?

Model

Guidelines
Writing a Classification Essay

1. **Select a topic.** Review the list of headings and topics that you developed in response to "Topics to Consider" on page 216. Choose a topic that you find interesting and can explain well using classification strategies. If you need more choices, develop a new list of headings and topics.

2. **Look at the big picture.** Conduct preliminary research to get an overview of your topic. Review your purpose (to explain, persuade, inform, and so on), and consider which classification criteria will help you divide the subject into distinct, understandable subgroups.

3. **Choose and test your criterion.** Choose a criterion for creating subgroups. Make sure it produces subgroups that are consistent (all members fit the criterion), exclusive (subgroups are distinct—no member of the group fits into more than one subgroup), and complete (each member fits into a subgroup with no member left over).

   > **TIP:** To better visualize how you are dividing your topic and classifying its members, take a few minutes to fill out a graphic organizer like the one shown below. (Also see the graphic organizer on page 50.)

4. **Gather and organize information.** Gather information from library and web resources, as well as interviews. To take notes and organize your information, consider using a classification grid like the one shown below. Set up the grid by listing the classification criteria down the left column and listing the subgroups in the top row of the columns. Then fill in the grid with appropriate details. (The following grid lists the classification criterion and subgroups used in "Four Ways to Talk About Literature," pages 220–221.)

Classification Criteria	Subgroup 1	Subgroup 2	Subgroup 3	Subgroup 4
	Text-centered approach	*Audience-centered approach*	*Author-centered approach*	*Ideas outside literature*
focus of the critical approach	• Trait 1 • Trait 2 • Trait 3	• Trait 1 • Trait 2 • Trait 3	• Trait 1 • Trait 2 • Trait 3	• Trait 1 • Trait 2 • Trait 3

   Note: If you do not use a grid similar to this one, construct an outline to help organize your thoughts (see pages 48–49).

5. **Draft a thesis.** Draft a working thesis (you can revise it later as needed) that states your topic and main point. Include language introducing your criteria for classifying subgroups.

6. **Draft the essay.** Write your first draft, using either the organizational pattern in the classification grid or an outline.

   Opening: Get the readers' attention, introduce the subject and thesis, and give your criteria for dividing the subject into subgroups.

   Middle: Develop the thesis by discussing each subgroup, explaining its traits, and showing how it is distinct from the other subgroups. For example, in the middle section of "Four Ways to Talk About Literature," the writer first shows the unique focus of each of the four approaches to literary criticism, and then illustrates each approach by applying it to the same poem, "My Last Duchess."

   Closing: While the opening and the middle of the essay separate the subject into components and subgroups, the closing brings the components and subgroups back together. For example, in "Four Ways to Talk About Literature," the writer closes by identifying three characteristics that the four subgroups have in common (see pages 220–221).

7. **Get feedback.** Ask a classmate or someone from the writing center to read your essay, looking for the following:

   - An engaging opening that introduces the subject, thesis, and criteria for classification
   - A well-organized middle that distinguishes subgroups, shows why each subgroup is unique, and includes adequate details
   - A clear closing that reaches some sort of conclusion

8. **Revise the essay.** Check the essay for the following:

   - Subgroups that are consistent, exclusive, and complete
   - Organization that helps the reader understand the subject
   - Appropriate examples that clarify the nature and function of each subgroup
   - A unifying conclusion

9. **Edit the essay.** Check for the following:

   - An informed, reader-friendly voice
   - Clear, complete sentences
   - Unified paragraphs linked with appropriate transitions
   - Correct usage, grammar, punctuation, and spelling

10. **Publish the essay.** Share your writing by doing the following:

    - Offer copies to classmates and friends.
    - Publish it in a journal or on a website.
    - Place a copy in your professional portfolio.

Writing Checklist

Use these seven traits to check the quality of your writing; then revise as needed:

_____ The **ideas** in the classification criteria are logical and clear. The criteria result in subgroups that are consistent, exclusive, and complete.

_____ The **organization** of the essay helps the reader understand the components, the subgroups, and the subject as a whole. Paragraphs form cohesive units of thought.

_____ The **voice** is informed, courteous, and professional.

_____ The **words** are precise, descriptive, and appropriate for the subject. Terms used in classifications are employed in the same way throughout the essay.

_____ The **sentences** are complete, varied, and easy to read. Appropriate transitions link sentences and paragraphs.

_____ The **copy** has correct punctuation, grammar, and mechanics.

_____ The **design** follows assigned formatting instructions.

Interactive

Critical-Thinking and Writing Activities

As directed by your instructor, complete the following activities.

1. Kim Brouwer wrote "Three Family Cancers" to better understand a series of painful experiences in her family's life. List painful (or pleasant) experiences in your family's life, and select a topic that you can clarify by classifying. Write an essay using classification strategies that explain the topic.

2. "Four Ways to Talk About Literature" examines four approaches to reading and understanding a piece of literature. Identify a similar group of approaches to analysis or problem solving in your program or major. Write an essay in which you break your topic into subgroups, sort the subgroups, and explain the topic to the reader.

3. Review the ways in which Ann Hodgman incorporates primary-source research into her essay, "No Wonder They Call Me a Bitch." Employ this strategy in your draft or revision of an essay.

4. Develop a list of social, economic, or political topics in the news. Choose one, research it, classify its components, and then write an essay that explains the topic.

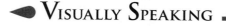

◀ VISUALLY SPEAKING

Working with a classmate, look again at the photograph on page 215. Then discuss what the picture suggests about why one might classify things and what challenges are part of the process.

PROCESS WRITING 15

Process writing is practical writing that answers the kinds of questions we face every day at home, in college, or on the job: "How do I remove these ugly stains?" or "How does cancer spread?" or "How do I install this software?" Writing that answers these types of questions analyzes the process in which we're interested, breaks it down into steps, and shows how the process works.

The three basic forms of process writing include *describing* a process, *explaining* a process, and giving *instructions*. This chapter distinguishes these forms and shows how to write each. In addition, the chapter includes models showing how writers have used the forms to accomplish their writing goals.

Study this chapter for tips that will help you choose a topic, break it into steps, and explain it clearly in writing.

Audio

Video

Web Link

Overview
Writing About a Process

Writer's Goal

Your goal is to analyze a process, break it into specific steps, and write about it using one of the following forms: a *description* of a process, an *explanation* of the process, or *instructions* on how to carry out the process.

Keys for Success

Think logically. To write one of these forms, you must study the process until you understand it, and then write clearly about it. In other words, you must know—and show—how each step leads *logically* to the next, and how all the steps together complete the process.

Know your purpose and your audience. Decide what your writing should do and choose the form that fits your purpose and audience:

- To inform a broad audience how something happens, *describe* the process in an essay that tells how the process unfolds—for example, how cancer cells multiply (pages 231–232) or how interracial marriage has become common (pages 238–239).

- To help readers who want to know how something is done or made, *explain* the process in an essay that tells how someone would complete each step— for example, how to deal with campus racism (pages 234–237).

- To help readers who wish to perform the process themselves, provide how-to information in brief, clear *instructions*—for example, how to download photos onto your computer (page 233).

  Note: While descriptions and explanations are usually formatted as essays, instructions are formatted somewhat differently. Instructions include a summary of the process, a list of materials and tools, and a numbered list of steps organized chronologically and stated using clear, imperative verbs.

Consider *all* of your readers. Regardless of the form that you choose, make your writing accessible to all of your readers by addressing the reader who knows the least about your topic. Include all the information that this person needs to have, and use language that everyone can understand.

Topics to Consider

- A course-related process
- A process that keeps you healthy
- A process that you've mastered

- A process in the news
- A process that helps you get a job
- A process in your planned occupation

Next Step Read the model essays and perform the activities that follow. As you read, observe how each writer approaches the task of explaining, describing, or instructing.

Process: Description

Student writer Kerri Mertz wrote this essay to help nonscientists understand how cancer cells multiply and affect the body.

Audio

Wayward Cells

The writer uses the title and an analogy to introduce the topic.

Imagine a room containing a large group of people all working hard toward the same goal. Each person knows his or her job, does it carefully, and cooperates with other group members. Together, they function efficiently and smoothly—like a well-oiled machine.

Then something goes wrong. One guy suddenly drops his task, steps into another person's workstation, grabs the material that she's working with, and begins something very different—he uses the material to make little reproductions of himself, thousands of them. These look-alikes imitate him—grabbing material and making reproductions of themselves. Soon the bunch gets so big that they spill into other people's workstations, getting in their way, and interrupting their work. As the number of look-alikes grows, the work group's activity slows, stutters, and finally stops.

She uses a simile to explain the analogy.

A human body is like this room, and the body's cells are like these workers. If the body is healthy, each cell has a necessary job and does it correctly. For example, right now red blood cells are running throughout your body carrying oxygen to each body part. Other cells are digesting that steak sandwich that you had for lunch, and others are patching up that cut on your left hand. Each cell knows what to do because its genetic code—or DNA—tells it what to do. When a cell begins to function abnormally, it can initiate a process that results in cancer.

She describes the first step in the process and cites a potential cause.

The problem starts when one cell "forgets" what it should do. Scientists call this "undifferentiating"—meaning that the cell loses its identity within the body (Pierce 75). Just like the guy in the group who decided to do his own thing, the cell forgets its job. Why this happens is somewhat unclear. The problem could be caused by a defect in the cell's DNA code or by something in the environment, such as cigarette smoke or asbestos (German 21). Causes from inside the body are called genetic, whereas causes from outside the body are called carcinogens, meaning "any substance that causes cancer" (Neufeldt and Sparks 90). In either case, an undifferentiated cell can disrupt the function of healthy cells in two ways: by not doing its job as specified in its DNA and by not reproducing at the rate noted in its DNA.

She describes the next step and its result.

Most healthy cells reproduce rather quickly, but their reproduction rate is controlled. For example, your blood cells completely die off and replace themselves within a matter of weeks, but existing cells make only as many new cells as the body needs. The DNA codes in healthy cells tell them how many new cells to produce. However, cancer cells don't have this control, so they reproduce quickly with no stopping point, a characteristic called "autonomy" (Braun 3). What's more, all their "offspring" have the same qualities as their messed-up parent, and the resulting overpopulation produces growths called tumors.

She describes the third step—how tumors damage the body.

Tumor cells can hurt the body in a number of ways. First, a tumor can grow so big that it takes up space needed by other organs. Second, some cells may detach from the original tumor and spread throughout the body, creating new tumors elsewhere. This happens with lymphatic cancer—a cancer that's hard to control because it spreads so quickly. A third way that tumor cells can hurt the body is by doing work not called for in their DNA. For example, a gland cell's DNA code may tell the cell to produce a necessary hormone in the endocrine system. However, if cancer damages or distorts that code, sick cells may produce more of the hormone than the body can use—or even tolerate (Braun 4). Cancer cells seem to have minds of their own, and this is why cancer is such a serious disease.

6

A transition signals a shift in focus from the illness to treatments.

Fortunately, there is hope. Scientific research is already helping doctors do amazing things for people with cancer. One treatment that has been used for some time is chemotherapy, or the use of chemicals to kill off all fast-growing cells, including cancer cells. (Unfortunately, chemotherapy can't distinguish between healthy and unhealthy cells, so it may cause negative side effects such as damaging fast-growing hair follicles, resulting in hair loss.) Another common treatment is radiation, or the use of light rays to kill cancer cells. One of the newest and most promising treatments is gene therapy—an effort to identify and treat chromosomes that carry a "wrong code" in their DNA. A treatment like gene therapy is promising because it treats the cause of cancer, not just the effect. Year by year, research is helping doctors better understand what cancer is and how to treat it.

7

The writer reuses the analogy to review main points.

Much of life involves dealing with problems like wayward workers, broken machines, or dysfunctional organizations. Dealing with wayward cells is just another problem. While the problem is painful and deadly, there is hope. Medical specialists and other scientists are making progress, and some day they will help win the battle against wayward cells. ■

8

Note: The Works Cited page is not shown. For sample pages, see MLA (pages 532–533) and APA (page 564).

Reading for Better Writing

1. Review the opening four-paragraph analogy used to introduce and describe the process. Explain why the analogy is or is not effective.

2. Review the three steps cited by the writer, and note the transitions used to lead into and out of each step. Are the transitions effective?

3. Review the guidelines on page 240 to identify and list traits of a *description* of a process. Explain why this essay does or does not exemplify these traits.

Process: Instructions

These instructions, like those for many technical devices, include both written and visual elements.

Opening
Use a descriptive title. Note or list materials needed.

Middle
State steps in chronological order and parallel form.

Add graphics (such as the arrow) to create a quick visual cue.

Boldface words that need special attention.

To show an object's size, use a reference (such as the fingers).

Use only well-focused photographs.

Closing
Note common problems.

Downloading Photographs from the MC-150 Digital Camera

Note: MC-150 software must be loaded on your computer to download photographs from the camera.

1. Turn your computer on.

2. Plug the camera's USB cable into your computer.

3. Turn the camera's mode dial to the **data transfer setting** (Figure 1).

4. Open the camera's flash-card door and plug the other end of the USB cable into the **camera port** (Figure 2).

Figure 1: Data Transfer Setting

5. Select USB transfer from the camera screen menu. The MC-150 software will then launch on your computer.

6. Follow the instructions on the computer screen to download all of your photos or specific photos.

Figure 2: Camera Port

7. When your download is complete, turn the camera off and unplug the USB cable from the camera and the computer.

Note: If the MC-150 software doesn't launch, disconnect the camera (step 7), and then restart the computer and continue on from step 2. ■

Process: Explanation

Nikki Giovanni is an acclaimed poet and essayist; you can learn more about her work by visiting her webpage at http://nikki-giovanni.com/index.shtml. In this piece, first published in *Essence* in 1991, Giovanni advises African American students on how to succeed in colleges where the majority of students are white.

Campus Racism 101

The title reminds us of the names of college courses.

There is a bumper sticker that reads: *TOO BAD IGNORANCE ISN'T PAINFUL*. I like that. But ignorance is. We just seldom attribute the pain to it or even recognize it when we see it. Like the postcard on my corkboard. It shows a young man in a very hip jacket smoking a cigarette. In the background is a high school with the American flag waving. The caption says: "Too cool for school. Yet too stupid for the real world." Out of the mouth of the young man is a bubble enclosing the words "Maybe I'll start a band." There could be a postcard showing a jock in a uniform saying, "I don't need school. I'm going to the NFL or NBA." Or one showing a young man or woman studying and a group of young people saying, "So you want to be white." Or something equally demeaning. We need to quit it.

The writer identifies problems that prompt her to write this essay.

Where can you go and what can you do that frees you from interacting with the white American mentality?

The writer raises a question and then provides a list of answers.

I am a professor of English at Virginia Tech. I've been here for four years, though for only two years with academic rank. I am tenured, which means I have a teaching position for life, a rarity on a predominantly white campus. Whether from malice or ignorance, people who think I should be at a predominantly Black institution will ask, "Why are you at Tech?" Because it's here. And so are Black students. But even if Black students weren't here, it's painfully obvious that this nation and this world cannot allow white students to go through higher education without interacting with Blacks in authoritative positions. It is equally clear that predominantly Black colleges cannot accommodate the numbers of Black students who want and need an education.

The series of questions contributes to a conversational tone.

Is it difficult to attend a predominantly white college? Compared with what? Being passed over for promotion because you lack credentials? Being turned down for jobs because you are not college-educated? Joining the armed forces or going to jail because you cannot find an alternative to the streets? Let's have a little perspective here. Where can you go and what can you do that frees you from interacting with the white American mentality?

You're going to interact; the only question is, will you be in some control of yourself and your actions, or will you be controlled by others? I'm going to recommend self-control.

What's the difference between prison and college? They both prescribe your behavior for a given period of time. They both allow you to read books and develop your writing. They both give you time alone to think and time with your peers to talk about issues. But four years of prison doesn't give you a passport to greater opportunities. Most likely that time only gives you greater knowledge of how to get back in. Four years of college gives you an opportunity not only to lift yourself but to serve your people effectively. What's the difference when you are called nigger in college from when you are called nigger in prison? In college you can, though I admit with effort, follow procedures to have those students who called you nigger kicked out or suspended. You can bring issues to public attention without risking your life. But mostly, college is and always has been the future. We, neither less nor more than other people, need knowledge. There are discomforts attached to attending predominantly white colleges, though no more so than living in a racist world. Here are some rules to follow that may help: 4

Go to class. No matter how you feel. No matter how you think the professor feels about you. It's important to have a consistent presence in the classroom. If nothing else, the professor will know you care enough and are serious enough to be there.   5

Meet your professors. Extend your hand (give a firm handshake) and tell them your name. Ask them what you need to do to make an A. You may never make an A, but you have put them on notice that you are serious about getting good grades.   6

Do assignments on time. Typed or computer-generated. You have the syllabus. Follow it, and turn those papers in. If for some reason you can't complete an assignment on time, let your professor know before it is due and work out a new due date—then meet it.   7

Go back to see your professor. Tell him or her your name again. If an assignment received less than an A, ask why, and find out what you need to do to improve the next assignment.   8

Yes, your professor is busy. So are you. So are your parents who are working to pay or help with your tuition. Ask early what you need to do if you feel you are starting to get into academic trouble. Do not wait until you are failing.   9

Understand that there will be professors who do not like you; there may even be professors who are racist or sexist or both. You must discriminate among your professors to see who will give you the help you need. You may not simply say, "They are all against me." They aren't. They mostly don't   10

Repeated use of *you* also adds to the conversational feel.

After a paragraph addressed to *you*, the writer shifts to *we*.

Each rule is discussed in a new paragraph and is marked with italics.

The writer anticipates arguments and counters them.

care. Since you are the one who wants to be educated, find the people who want to help.

Don't defeat yourself. Cultivate your friends. Know your enemies. You cannot undo hundreds of years of prejudicial thinking. Think for yourself and speak up. Raise your hand in class. Say what you believe no matter how awkward you may think it sounds. You will improve in your articulation and confidence. 11

Participate in some campus activity. Join the newspaper staff. Run for office. Join a dorm council. Do something that involves you on campus. You are going to be there for four years, so let your presence be known, if not felt. 12

You will inevitably run into some white classmates who are troubling because they often say stupid things, ask stupid questions—and expect an answer. Here are some comebacks to some of the most common inquiries and comments: 13

Q: What's it like to grow up in a ghetto? 14

A: I don't know. 15

Q (from the teacher): Can you give us the Black perspective on Toni Morrison, Huck Finn, slavery, Martin Luther King, Jr., and others? 16

A: I can give you my perspective. (Do not take the burden of 22 million people on your shoulders. Remind everyone that you are an individual, and don't speak for the race or any other individual within it.) 17

Q: Why do all the Black people sit together in the dining hall? 18

A: Why do all the white students sit together? 19

Q: Why should there be an African-American studies course? 20

A: Because white Americans have not adequately studied the contributions of Africans and African-Americans. Both Black and white students need to know our total common history. 21

Q: Why are there so many scholarships for "minority" students? 22

A: Because they wouldn't give my great-grandparents their forty acres and the mule. 23

Q: How can whites understand Black history, culture, literature, and so forth? 24

A: The same way we understand white history, culture, literature, and so forth. That is why we're in school: to learn. 25

Q: Should whites take African-American studies courses? 26

A: Of course. We take white-studies courses, though the universities don't call them that. 27

Comment: When I see groups of Black people on campus, it's really intimidating. 28

Imperative statements begin with verbs, while supporting explanations begin with *you*.

The question-and-answer format deals efficiently with a large number of problem situations.

Question-answer sets are grouped in one cluster; comment-comeback sets in another.

The comebacks flip the intent of language from the original comments.

Comeback: I understand what you mean. I'm frightened when I see   *29*
white students congregating.

Comment: It's not fair. It's easier for you guys to get into college than   *30*
for other people.

Comeback: If it's so easy, why aren't there more of us?   *31*

Comment: It's not our fault that America is the way it is.   *32*

Comeback: It's not our fault, either, but both of us have a responsibility   *33*
to make changes.

The final line uses the positive word *chance*.

It's really very simple. Educational progress is a national concern;   *34*
education is a private one. Your job is not to educate white people; it is to
obtain an education. If you take the racial world on your shoulders, you will
not get the job done. Deal with yourself as an individual worthy of respect,
and make everyone else deal with you the same way. College is a little like
playing grown-up. Practice what you want to be. You have been telling your
parents you are grown. Now is your chance to act like it. ■

Reading for Better Writing

Working by yourself or with a group, answer these questions:

1. Summarize Giovanni's key points. What details suggest that this essay
was highly relevant when it was first published in 1991? Why might
textbook and anthology editors continue to republish this essay?

2. *Essence* magazine (in which this essay was first published) has been
described by its editors as the "preeminent lifestyle magazine for today's
African American woman." How does the *Essence* audience differ from
the target audience for texts such as *The College Writer?* In what ways
does Giovanni's essay speak to multiple audiences? In what ways might
the piece have relevance for you and your campus?

3. Comment on the essay's title: Why might Giovanni have chosen it?
How effective is it, and why?

4. Describe the tone of the essay. How does the writer achieve this tone,
and what is the effect for you as a reader? Imagine the piece with a tone
that contrasts starkly with the existing feel. How might this change the
effect of the piece, and when/where might such a tone be appropriate?

5. The writer gives direct instructions to readers through the final two-
thirds of the essay. Why isn't the last line an imperative or command?

Process Writing

Nicholas D. Kristof, a Pulitzer Prize-winning journalist, describes how interracial marriages have become common in the United States.

Love and Race

Highlight information indicating that interracial marriages are common and beneficial. In the margin, note whether the information is convincing.

1 In a world brimming with bad news, here's one of the happiest trends. Instead of preying on people of different races, young Americans are falling in love with them.

2 Whites and blacks can be found strolling together as couples even at the University of Mississippi, once a symbol of racial confrontation.

3 "I will say that they are always given a second glance," acknowledges C. J. Rhodes, a black student at Ole Miss. He adds that there are still misgivings about interracial dating, particularly among black women and a formidable number of "white Southerners who view this race-mixing as abnormal, frozen by fear to see Sarah Beth bring home a brotha."

4 Mixed-race marriages in the U.S. now number 1.5 million and are roughly doubling each decade. About 40 percent of Asian-Americans and 6 percent of blacks have married whites in recent years.

5 Still more striking, one survey found that 40 percent of Americans had dated someone of another race.

6 In a country where racial divisions remain deep, all this love is an enormously hopeful sign of progress in bridging barriers. Scientists who study the human genome say that race is mostly a bogus distinction reflecting very little genetic difference, perhaps one-hundredth of 1 percent of our DNA.

7 Skin color differences are recent, arising over only the last 100,000 years or so, a twinkling of an evolutionary eye. That's too short a period for substantial genetic differences to emerge, and so there is perhaps 10 times more genetic differences within a race than there is between races. Thus we should welcome any trend that makes a superficial issue like color less central to how we categorize each other.

8 The rise in interracial marriage reflects a revolution in attitudes. As recently as 1958, a white mother in Monroe, N.C., called the police after her little girl kissed a black playmate on the cheek; the boy, Hanover Thompson, 9, was then sentenced to 14 years in prison for attempted rape. (His appeals failed, but he was released later after an outcry.)

9 In 1963, 59 percent of Americans believed that marriage between blacks and whites should be illegal. At one time or another 42 states banned interracial marriages, although the Supreme Court finally invalidated these laws in 1967.

10 Typically, the miscegenation laws voided any interracial marriages, making the children illegitimate, and some states included penalties such as enslavement, life imprisonment, and whippings. My wife is Chinese-American, and our relationship would once have been felonious.

At every juncture from the 19th century on, the segregationists warned that granting rights to blacks would mean the start of a slippery slope, ending with black men marrying white women. The racists were prophetic.   *11*

"They were absolutely right," notes Randall Kennedy, the Harvard Law School professor and author of a dazzling new book, *Interracial Intimacies* . . . . "I do think [interracial marriage] is a good thing. It's a welcome sign of thoroughgoing desegregation. We talk about desegregation in the public sphere; here's desegregation in the most intimate sphere."   *12*

These days, interracial romance can be seen on the big screen, on TV shows, and in the lives of some prominent Americans. Former Defense Secretary William Cohen has a black wife, as does Peter Norton, the software guru. The Supreme Court justice Clarence Thomas has a white wife.   *13*

I find the surge in intermarriage to be one of the most positive fronts in American race relations today, building bridges and empathy. But it's still in its infancy.   *14*

I was excited to track down interracial couples at Ole Miss, thinking they would be perfect to make my point about this hopeful trend: But none were willing to talk about the issue on record.   *15*

"Even if people wanted to marry [interracially], I think they'd keep it kind of quiet," explained a minister on campus.   *16*

For centuries, racists warned that racial equality would lead to the "mongrelization" of America. Perhaps they were right in a sense, for we're increasingly going to see a blurring of racial distinctions. But these distinctions acquired enormous social resonance without ever having much basis in biology. ■   *17*

Reading for Better Writing

Working by yourself or with a group, do the following:

1. Review the opening paragraph and explain why the passage does or does not effectively introduce the topic and focus the essay.

2. Kristof argues that the popularity of interracial marriages is a process that has developed over time. Cite key events or stages in that process and explain why they indicate progress.

3. "Love and Race" was written for a broad audience. How might the content and style of the essay be different if it were written as a research paper for a college course in sociology?

4. Review the last paragraph and explain why you do or do not find it a strong closing.

Model

Guidelines
Writing About a Process

1. **Select a topic.** Choose a topic from the list that you generated under "Topics to Consider" on page 230. If you're stuck, review your notes and textbooks to generate more course-related topics.

2. **Review the process.** Use your knowledge of the topic to fill out an organizer like the one on the right. List the subject at the top, each of the steps in chronological order, and the outcome at the bottom. Review the organizer to find issues you need to research.

PROCESS ANALYSIS
Subject:
• Step 1
• Step 2
• Step 3
Outcome:

3. **Research as needed.** Find information that spells out the process: what it is, what steps are required, what order the steps should follow, how to do the steps, what outcome the process should produce, and what safety precautions are needed. If possible, observe the process in action or perform it yourself. Carefully record correct names, materials, tools, and safety or legal issues.

4. **Organize information.** After conducting your research, revise the organizer by adding or reordering steps as needed. Then develop an outline, including steps listed in the organizer, as well as supporting details from your research.

5. **Draft the document.** Write the document using the guidelines below.

DESCRIBING A PROCESS	EXPLAINING A PROCESS	WRITING INSTRUCTIONS
Opening: Introduce the topic, stating its importance and giving an overview of the steps. **Middle:** Describe each step clearly (usually in separate paragraphs), and link steps with transitions like *first, second, next, finally,* and *while.* Describe the outcome and its importance. **Closing:** Describe the process as a whole and restate key points.	**Opening:** Introduce the topic and give an overview of the process. **Middle:** Explain what each step involves and how to do it (typically using a separate paragraph for each). Use transitions such as *first, second,* and *next* to link the steps. Explain the outcome. **Closing:** Explain follow-up activity and restate key points.	**Opening:** Name the process in the title; summarize the process and list any materials and tools needed. **Middle:** Present each step in a separate— usually one- or two-sentence—paragraph. Number the steps and state them as commands in parallel form (see page 100). **Closing:** In a short paragraph, explain any follow-up action.

6. **Revise the writing.** Check for the following and revise as needed:
   - A clear opening that identifies the process
   - Steps that are stated clearly and in the correct order
     For explanations and instructions:
     - Clear details explaining how to perform each step
     - A closing that includes necessary follow-up activity
     For instructions:
     - Clear and correct safety cautions in boldface type

7. **Test the writing.** Read the writing for organization and completeness. For *explanations* and *instructions,* perform the process yourself using the writing as a guide. For each step, do only *what* you're told to do and *how* you're told to do it. Note where the writing is incomplete, out of order, and/or lacking adequate safety precautions. Revise as needed.

8. **Get feedback.** Ask a classmate who is unfamiliar with the process to read the writing for clarity, completeness, and correctness. For *instructions,* have the person use the writing as a guide to perform the process, noting where details are incomplete or unclear, and noting where word choice is either imprecise or too technical. Use the feedback to guide further revision.

9. **Edit the writing by looking for the following:**
   - Word choice appropriate for your least-informed reader
   - Clear transitions between steps
   - Consistent verb tense in all steps
   - For *instructions*—verbs that give clear commands (imperative mood)
   - Correct, consistent terminology
   - Informed, respectful voice
   - Proper format (particularly for *instructions*—adequate white space)

10. **Publish the essay.** Share your writing with others:
    - Offer it to instructors or students working with the process.
    - Offer explanations and instructions to people on campus or at nonprofit agencies who can use the writing to do their work.
    - Post the writing on a suitable website.

INSIGHT: The *mood* of a verb (see **629.2**) indicates the tone or attitude with which a statement is made. For instructions, writers use the imperative mood (or command form) to communicate a firm, direct, and informed tone.

Writing Checklist

Use these seven traits to check your essay; then revise as needed:

_____ The **ideas** describe or explain the process clearly and completely.

_____ The **organization** sequence helps clarify the process. In explanations and instructions, the organization is chronological and helps the reader work through the process.

_____ The **voice** matches the writer's purpose. Cautions regarding safety or legal issues sound serious but are not alarming.

_____ The **words** are precise, and technical terms are defined.

_____ The **sentences** are smooth, varied in structure, and engaging. In instructions, sentences are shaped as clear, brief, no-nonsense commands stated in parallel form.

_____ The **copy** includes no errors in grammar, punctuation, and spelling.

_____ The page **design** and format are appropriate for an essay or a set of instructions.

Interactive

Critical-Thinking and Writing Activities

As directed by your instructor, complete the following activities.

1. Review the topics that you listed under "Topics to Consider" on page 230. Choose a topic and write about it, letting the writing take any one of these forms: *description, explanation,* or *instructions*.

2. Review the "Wayward Cells" and "Love and Race" models. List similar natural sciences or social sciences processes that interest you. Choose one and write about it as a *description*.

3. Review the process instructions titled "Downloading Photographs from the MC-150 Digital Camera," considering how the written and visual elements on the page work together. Draft or revise a piece in which visual elements are essential to effectively communicate your ideas. Integrate relevant, high-quality visuals (photos, illustrations, diagrams) that will help readers to better understand your ideas.

4. Using Giovanni's "Campus Racism 101" as a model, write a process essay based on your own experience in which you give advice about how to succeed in a difficult situation.

◀ Visually Speaking

Study the photograph on page 229 and identify the ceremony taking place. Then select one person in the crowd and write a two-page essay describing the process that led him or her to participate. Create details as needed.

Definition

16

Whether you're writing a persuasive essay, a lab report, or a project proposal, defining key terms helps you distinguish the boundaries of your subject.

Audio

In most writing situations, you will include short definitions of terms consisting of one or two sentences or one or two paragraphs. Although this chapter includes information (see pages 245–246 and 250) that will enable you to write such brief definitions, its main purpose is to help you write longer, essay-length pieces sometimes called *extended definitions*.

When you write an extended definition, study this chapter, which will guide you through every step in the writing process—from choosing the term to refining the definition. When reading the model essays, look closely at the strategies that each writer uses "to peel the onion"—that is, to unfold and examine each layer of a word's meaning until finally reaching the core.

Web Link

Overview
Writing a Definition Essay

Writer's Goal

Your goal is to choose a word or phrase that interests you, explore what it means (and doesn't mean), and write an essay that helps readers better understand, appreciate, and use that term.

Keys for Success

Know your purpose. Decide what you want your writing to do: entertain, inform, explain, persuade readers to act, or a combination of these.

Choose appropriate writing strategies. Select strategies that help you accomplish your purpose. For example, the writers whose documents are included in this chapter make the following choices:

- In the excerpt from the research paper, "Economic Disparities Fuel Human Trafficking," Shon Bogar defines *human trafficking* in part by distinguishing it from related practices.
- To show readers how to treat patients with *dementia*, Sarah Anne Morelos defines the term using anecdotes and details gathered through both primary and library research.
- To entertain and instruct people listening to his radio program, David Schelhaas examines the word *deft* by first sharing a personal anecdote, and then comparing and contrasting the definitions and etymologies of *deft* and *daft*.
- To describe her mother and herself, Cynthia Ozick offers two distinct definitions of *excellence,* each clarified with precise, colorful details.

Present fresh information. Choose details that help readers understand the word's denotations (literal meanings) as well as its connotations (associated meanings). For example, one denotation of *cute* is *attractive*. Depending on the context, however, associations with this word may be positive or negative.

Topics to Consider

Beneath headings like the following, list words that you'd like to explore.

Words	Words	Words	Words	Words
that are related to an art or a sport	that are (or should be) in the news	that are overused, unused, or abused	that make you chuckle, frown, or fret	that do— or do not— describe you

Next Step Read the model essays and notice the writing strategies these writers use; think about how you might use them in your own essays.

Definition

The excerpt below comes from a research paper by student writer Shon Bogar. The paper focuses on the problems of human trafficking and slavery as phenomena associated with current trends in globalization. After reviewing global economic trends since the end of the Cold War, Bogar defines the key terms that readers must understand if they are to appreciate the problem. (For more on research writing, see chapters 28–33.)

At the end of the introduction, the writer transitions to the extended definition.

An informal definition of the broader concept of slavery prefaces the extended definition.

The main term is distinguished from related terms using reliable source material.

Economic Disparities Fuel Human Trafficking

1 . . . . These great economic disparities, from extreme poverty to fabulous wealth, have helped fuel the international trade in human cargo, as those people with nothing seek a better life serving those with excess.

2 The buying, selling, and forced exploitation of people—slavery—is not a new phenomenon. Most nations and most cultures have, at one time or another, enslaved others and been themselves enslaved in turn. The pattern continues today; in fact, slavery exists far beyond the developing world and reaches into the comfortable First World of the United States, Europe, Japan, and Australia. However, examining current trends in the trade of human cargo shows that trafficking and slavery are extremely difficult to define and understand, and that they coexist with and are codependent upon each other. These problems, moreover, have a variety of complex causes and too few solutions that offer a realistic possibility of ending this global abomination.

3 Human trafficking, in particular, is a term that is difficult to define properly, but it must first be clarified if the problem itself is to be addressed. To begin, migration, human smuggling, and human trafficking are distinct but related phenomena, and incorrect definitions would put different groups of people in the wrong category, with potentially dire consequences. For example, the Trafficking Victims Prevention Act (TVPA), which came into law in 2000, requires the U.S. government to ensure that victims of trafficking are not jailed or "otherwise penalized solely for unlawful acts as a direct result of being trafficked" (U.S. Department of State, 2004), whereas illegal immigrants are still subject to deportation and criminal proceedings. The U.S. State Department recognizes the potentially "confusing" difference between smuggling and human trafficking, so it defines human smuggling as "the procurement or transport for profit of a person for illegal entry in a country" (2004). However, even if the smuggling involves "dangerous or degrading conditions," the act is still considered smuggling, not human trafficking, and so smuggling is considered an immigration matter, not necessarily a human rights issue (2004).

4 What distinguishes trafficking from smuggling is the element of exploitation, including but not limited to "fraud, force, or coercion" (U.S.

The writer offers a formal definition of the key term "human trafficking" by going to official sources.

Department of State, 2004). With this distinction in mind, the United Nations Convention Against Transnational Organized Crime has developed this standard definition of human trafficking: "the recruitment, transportation, transfer, harbouring or receipt of persons, by means of the threat or use of force or other forms of coercion, of abduction, of fraud, of deception, of the abuse of power, or of a position of vulnerability or of the giving or receiving of payments or benefits to achieve the consent of a person having control over another person, for the purpose of exploitation" (U.N. Resolution 25, 2001).

The writer restates a complex legal definition in terms readers will understand.

To unravel the U.N. legalese, human trafficking involves any use of force, coercion, fraud, or deception by those with power so as to exploit people, primarily by moving them into some form of slavery. Under this definition, smuggling can become trafficking if the smugglers have used any means of deception. Unfortunately, the requirement that the smuggler/trafficker be aware of the "victim's final circumstances" makes distinguishing between smuggling and trafficking an inexact science (U.S. Department of State, 2004), and it creates a new set of problems in combating trafficking apart from smuggling. Nevertheless, this definition of human trafficking is a helpful starting point from which the United Nations and governments around the globe can start to fight the trafficking and eventual enslavement of people.

While admitting a difficulty in the definition, the writer stresses the definition's usefulness.

All difficulties of definition aside, human trafficking and slavery are real problems—historical problems that have taken new shapes due to globalization. In fact, today human trafficking is linked to millions of people experiencing multiple forms of slavery, from traditional "chattel slavery" to sexual slavery to debt bondage. . . . ■   5

Note: The Works Cited page is not shown. For sample pages, see MLA (pages 532–533) and APA (page 564).

Reading for Better Writing

Working by yourself or with a group, answer these questions:

1. Without looking back at the model, define "human trafficking" in a sentence or two.

2. Examine each of the three main paragraphs of Bogar's extended definition. What does each paragraph accomplish? How do the paragraphs build on each other?

3. Identify the strategies that the author uses to argue that the definition is necessary. Is the reasoning compelling? Why or why not?

4. Look again at the sources that the writer uses to develop the necessary definitions. Why are these sources appropriate for the terms in question? Which other types of sources might be useful?

5. Examine how the writer transitions into and out of the extended definition. Are these transitions effective? Why or why not?

Definition

In her sociology course, Sarah Anne Morelos was asked to use her personal experience and knowledge to write an essay that helps readers understand a health issue discussed in class. In response, she wrote the following essay that defines a class (or group) of illnesses known as dementia. (Note that Morelos's personal voice and use of personal pronouns are appropriate for her assignment.)

Understanding Dementia

The writer uses the title and an anecdote to introduce the topic.

"Hello, Jenny! It's Sarah . . . I'm going to clean your room." Saying her name assured her that I knew who she was and that I was friendly. As I made her bed, I asked, "How are you doing this morning, Jenny?"

"Oh, I'm good," she said. Then, after a pause, she added, "My husband, Charlie, died in this room, you know."

I looked in her face and saw the familiar tears. "I'm so sorry, Jenny," I answered. Then I held her hand and listened to the same details of Charlie's death that I had heard every week for the past year. Suddenly Jenny stopped her story, looked up, and asked, "Who are you?" She didn't even remember my entering her room.

Jenny has dementia, a disease that affects many people over eighty years old. When I first started work as a nursing-home housekeeper, the patients experiencing this illness frightened me. I didn't understand their words or behavior. Now that I understand more about the patients and their illness, I am better able to respond to them in a helpful way.

"You took it! You rotten thief!" she screamed.

She defines the word and distinguishes the class (dementia) from illnesses within that class.

It is now estimated that more than half of the nursing-home residents in the United States have dementia. But what, exactly, is this disease? Dementia is a broad term that refers to a number of health problems, including Alzheimer's disease, brain tumors, and arteriosclerosis, the hardening of arteries to the heart. The outward symptoms of dementia are often disturbing, as this disease affects both the language skills and the behavior of the patient.

She describes symptoms.

The most common and noticeable symptom is memory loss. Patients in the early stages of dementia first experience short-term memory loss; as the illness advances, they also experience long-term memory loss. For example, Jenny demonstrated short-term loss. While she could remember countless details about Charlie's death, an event that had happened ten years earlier, she could not remember my name—or even that I had entered the room. Another sign of memory loss is repetitiveness: Patients like Jenny retell their stories over and over.

1

2

3

4

5

6

She uses
another
anecdote.

In addition to forgetting information and repeating stories, people *7* with dementia may express strange beliefs or fears. At one point, a resident named Wilma accused me of stealing from her. "You took it! You rotten thief!" she screamed.

"What are you missing, Wilma?" I asked. She started to tell me, but *8* then couldn't remember. Soon she had forgotten the episode altogether, although she was still flustered and very angry. This irrationality may be caused by bouts of schizophrenia.

Another symptom of dementia is diminished language skills. While *9* adults with healthy minds easily recall thousands of vocabulary words, patients with dementia struggle to name even the most common things and most familiar people in their lives. For example, a woman in the middle stages of the illness may recognize her son, but not be able to recall his name. However, as the illness advances, she will lose the ability to recognize his face as well.

For each
symptom,
the writer
provides
examples
and/or
anecdotes.

Patients with dementia also show behavioral changes. One common change is forgetting how to do simple tasks like washing dishes. Another change is forgetting to do basic things like shutting off the stove. Other behavioral changes signal a shift in personality. For example, fifteen years ago, Wilma was my friendly next-door neighbor who occasionally brought my family cookies. Today, Wilma is one of the dementia patients whom I take care of. As a neighbor, she was mild-mannered, but as a patient she gets very angry with anyone who enters her room. "Get out of here!" she yells with arms flailing. "You're not allowed in here!"

> *"Get out of* *10*
> *here!" she*
> *yells with*
> *arms flailing.*

Not surprisingly, dementia can also leave people unable to care for *11* themselves. They may have trouble dressing, bathing, or even using the bathroom. This level of neediness causes two problems. First, the individual cannot do the activity, and second, he or she often suffers from related depression.

A question
signals a
transition.

What's the solution to dementia? Sadly, there is no cure. While nursing- *12* home staff can help patients with activities, and medication helps them cope with depression, nothing can stop the illness. Both the disease and its symptoms get worse.

The writer
gives
another
example.

Steve is a good example. When he entered the nursing home just *13* six months ago, he was experiencing the early stages of dementia. Today, however, his illness is much more advanced. The stress of moving into this new environment and leaving his wife at home alone affected Steve deeply. When he first arrived, Steve often cried and begged to be taken home. "I'll give you $20—please just take me home," he'd plead.

Painfully, I would explain, "Steve, this is your home." After some time, *14* the situation got so bad that he would not sleep or eat. He was depressed, and he cried often, thinking that no one cared about him. Eventually, Steve was given stronger drugs to help with the depression. For a few months, the medication seemed to work—he laughed at jokes and occasionally told one himself. But then Steve's dementia advanced again. Soon he was asking his same sad questions: "Where am I?" and "Do you know what I'm doing here?"

So what is the best "medication" for people with dementia? While no *15* treatment can stop the illness, understanding the disease and its symptoms is the key to helping people cope. Doctors who understand the science of dementia can prescribe medicine. However, all of us who understand the heartbreaking symptoms and effects of the disease can provide another, possibly more effective treatment. We can respond to the victim of dementia with patience, kindness, and love. ■

> She closes by encouraging readers to show understanding and kindness.

Reading for Better Writing

Working by yourself or with a group, do the following:

1. Describe how the writer introduces the topic, and explain why the introduction is or is not effective.

2. Describe how the writer distinguishes the class (dementia) from specific illnesses within that class. How are illnesses within the class defined and explained?

3. The writer extends her definition by focusing largely on the symptoms of the disease. Examine her strategies for doing so, and explain whether you find them effective.

4. Review how the writer closes with an appeal to readers. Is the closing fitting? Why or why not?

5. The conversational voice and personal tone of this essay are appropriate for the writer's assignment described in the introduction to this essay. List ways in which the text and voice might be different if the assignment required writing that (a) was based on secondary sources (see page **448**) and (b) followed the academic style described on pages **78–79**.

Definition

Professor David Schelhaas delivered the following definition on his weekly radio program, *What's the Good Word?*

Deft or Daft

The writer introduces the topic with an anecdote.

The other day, my wife, watching our son-in-law with his large hands gracefully tie the shoelaces of his little daughter, remarked, "You really are deft." Ever the cynic, I remarked, "He's not only deft, he's daft." I talk that sort of nonsense frequently, but as I said this, I began to wonder. What if *deft* and *daft* come from the same root and once meant the same thing? A quick trip to the dictionary showed that, indeed, they did once mean the same thing (though my wife thought me daft when I first suggested it).

He describes the history of daft.

Let me see if I can explain the original meaning and also how *daft* and *deft* came to part company. *Daft* originally meant mild or gentle. The Middle English *dafte* comes from the Old English *gadaefte*, which has as its underlying sense *fit* or *suitable*. Quite likely, mild or gentle people were seen as behaving in a way that was fit and suitable.

Gradually, however, the mild, gentle meaning descended in connotation to mean crazy or foolish. First, animals were described as daft—that is, without reason—and eventually people also. The word *silly*, which once meant happy or blessed, slid down the same slope. So that explains where *daft* got its present meaning.

He compares and contrasts the two words.

But how does *deft*, meaning skillful or dexterous, fit into the picture? Again, if we start with the Old English meaning of *fit* or *suitable*, we can see a connection to skillful. In fact, the root of *gadaefte*, which is *dhabh*, to fit, carries with it the sense of a joiner or an artisan, someone who skillfully made the ends or corners of a cupboard or piece of furniture fit neatly together. From *fit* to *skillful* to *dexterous*. Thus we see how one root word meaning *fit* or *suitable* went in two different directions—one meaning crazy, the other meaning skillful.

He closes with a reflection and his usual sign-off.

These days it is usually considered much better to be deft than to be daft. But don't be too sure. It is good to remind ourselves that one person's deftness might very well appear as daftness to another.

This is David Schelhaas asking, "What's the Good Word?" ■

Reading for Better Writing

Working by yourself or with a group, answer these guidelines:

1. Explain how the opening attempts to engage the reader. In what ways does it succeed?
2. Describe how the writer shows that the meanings of the words have changed. Is his explanation clear? Why or why not?
3. Describe the writer's tone. Is it effective for a radio program? Explain.

Definition

Cynthia Ozick is an American writer known for her fiction, poetry, and essays on Jewish American life. In 2005, she was nominated for the Man Booker International Prize for lifetime achievement in literature.

Working with classmates, read the essay and note how Ozick defines *excellence* in part by comparing and contrasting her mother's qualities with others' qualities. Highlight these passages in the text. Then discuss how each passage helps define *excellence*.

On *Excellence*

In my Depression childhood, whenever I had a new dress, my cousin Sarah would get suspicious. The nicer the dress was, and especially the more expensive it looked, the more suspicious she would get. Finally she would lift the hem and check the seams. This was to see if the dress had been bought or if my mother had sewed it. Sarah could always tell. My mother's sewing had elegant outsides, but there was something catch-as-catch-can about the insides. Sarah's sewing, by contrast, was as impeccably finished inside as out; not one stray thread dangled.

My uncle Jake built meticulous grandfather clocks out of rosewood; he was a perfectionist and sent to England for the clockworks. My mother built serviceable radiator covers and a serviceable cabinet, with hinged doors, for the pantry. She built a pair of bookcases for the living room. Once, after I was grown and in a house of my own, she fixed the sewer pipe. She painted ceilings, and also landscapes; she reupholstered chairs. One summer she planted a whole yard of tall corn. She thought herself capable of doing anything, and did everything she imagined. But nothing was perfect. There was always some clear flaw, never visible head-on. You had to look underneath where the seams were. The corn thrived, though not in rows. The stalks elbowed one another like gossips in a dense little village.

"Miss Brrrroooobaker," my mother used to mock, rolling her Russian *r*'s, whenever I crossed a *t* she had left uncrossed, or corrected a word she had misspelled, or became impatient with a *v* that had tangled itself up in a *w* in her speech. ("Vvventriloquist," I would say. "Vventriloquist," she would obediently repeat. And the next time it would come out "wiolinist.") Miss Brubaker was my high school English teacher, and my mother invoked her name as an emblem of raging finical obsession. "Miss Brrrroooobaker," my mother's voice hoots at me down the years, as I go on casting and recasting sentences in a tiny handwriting on monomaniacally uniform paper. The loops of my mother's handwriting—it was the Palmer Method—were as big as hoops, spilling generous splashy ebullience. She could pull off, at five minutes' notice, a satisfying dinner for ten concocted out of nothing more than originality and panache. But the napkin would be folded a little off-center, and the spoon might be on the wrong side of the knife. She was an optimist who ignored trifles; for her, God was not in the details but in the intent. And all these culinary and agricultural efflorescences were extracurricular, accomplished in the crevices and niches of a fourteen-hour business day. When she scribbled out her family memoirs, in heaps of dog-eared notebooks or on the backs of old bills or on the margins of last year's calendar, I would resist typing them; in the speed of the chase she often omitted words like "the," "and," "will." The same flashing and bountiful hand fashioned and fired ceramic pots, and painted brilliant autumn views and vases of imaginary flowers and ferns, and decorated ordinary Woolworth platters with lavish enameled gardens. But bits of the painted petals would chip away.

Lavish: my mother was as lavish as nature. She woke early and saturated the hours with work and inventiveness, and read late into the night. She was all profusion, abundance, fabrication. Angry at her children, she would run after us whirling the cord of the electric iron, like a lasso or a whip; but she never caught us. When, in the seventh grade, I was afraid of failing the Music Appreciation final exam because I could not tell the difference between "To a Wild Rose" and "Barcarolle," she got the idea of sending me to school with a gauze sling rigged up on my writing arm, and an explanatory note that was purest fiction. But the sling kept slipping off. My mother gave advice like mad—she boiled over with so much passion for the predicaments of strangers that they turned into permanent cronies. She told intimate stories about people I had never heard of.

Despite the gargantuan Palmer loops (or possibly because of them), I have always known that my mother's was a life of—intricately abashing word!—excellence: insofar as excellence means ripe generosity. She burgeoned, she proliferated; she was endlessly leafy and flowering. She wore red hats and called herself a gypsy. In her girlhood she marched with the suffragettes and for Margaret Sanger and called herself a Red. She made me laugh, she was so varied: like a tree on which lemons, pomegranates, and prickly pears absurdly all hang together. She had the comedy of prodigality.

My own way is a thousand times more confined. I am a pinched perfectionist, the ultimate fruition of Miss Brubaker; I attend to crabbed minutiae and am self-trammeled through taking pains. I am a kind of human snail, locked in and condemned by my own nature. The ancients believed that the moist track left by the snail as it crept was the snail's own essence, depleting its body little by little; the farther the snail toiled, the smaller it became, until it finally rubbed itself out. That is how perfectionists are. Say to us "Excellence," and we will show you how we use up our substance and wear ourselves away, while making scarcely any progress at all. The fact that I am an exacting perfectionist in a narrow strait only, and nowhere else, is hardly to the point, since nothing matters to me so much as a comely and muscular sentence. It is my narrow strait, this snail's road: the track of the sentence I am writing now; and when I have eked out the wet substance, ink or blood, that is its mark, I will begin the next sentence. Only in reading out sentences am I perfectionist; but then there is nothing else I know how to do, or take much interest in. I miter every pair of abutting sentences

4

5

6

as scrupulously as Uncle Jake fitted one strip of rosewood against another. My mother's worldly and bountiful hand has escaped me. The sentence I am writing is my cabin and my shell, compact, self-sufficient. It is the burnished horizon—a merciless planet where flawlessness is the single standard, where even the inmost seams, however hidden from a laxer eye, must meet perfection. Here "excellence" is not strewn casually from a tipped cornucopia, here disorder does not account for charm, here trifles rule like tyrants.

I measure my life in sentences, and my sentences are superior to my mother's, pressed out, line by line, like the lustrous ooze on the underside of the snail, the snail's secret open seam, its wound, leaking attar. My mother was too mettlesome to feel the force of a comma. She scorned minutiae. She measured her life according to what poured from the horn of plenty, which was her ample, cascading, elastic, susceptible, inexact heart. My narrower heart rides between the tiny horns of the snail, dwindling as it goes.

And out of this thinnest thread, this ink-wet line of words, must rise a visionary fog, a mist, a smoke, forging cities, histories, sorrows, quagmires, entanglements, lives of sinners, even the life of my furnace-hearted mother: so much wilderness, waywardness, plentitude on the head of the precise and impeccable snail, between the horns. ■

Reading for Better Writing

Working by yourself or with a group, answer these questions:

1. What words and phrases does Ozick use to define *excellence?* How does contrasting her mother's life with her own enable Ozick to further define *excellence?* What point(s) is she making about *excellence?*

2. One way to write a definition is to use words and phrases that have similar meanings to the word you wish to define. What other techniques does Ozick use to define *excellence?* What additional strategies could be used to define a term?

3. Writing a good definition is challenging because it requires the use of precise words to shed light on the meaning of another word that has its own precise meaning(s). Find instances where Ozick lists one term or idea after another to build precision into a definition. How would her meaning change if she had used only one word from the list?

4. Find examples of words that have especially positive or negative connotations. How do these connotations help Ozick to make her main point(s)?

Model

Guidelines
Writing a Definition Essay

1. **Select a topic.** Review the words that you listed under "Topics to Consider" on page 244, and choose one that you want to explore. If you're stuck, list words similar to those defined in the four models.

> **TIP:** The best topics are abstract nouns (*totalitarianism, individualism,* or *terrorism*), complex terms (*dementia, spousal abuse,* or *Italian opera*), or adjectives connected to a personal experience (like the words defined in the models—*human trafficking, excellence, deft* and *daft*).

2. **Identify what you know.** To discern what you already know about the topic, write freely about the word, letting your writing go where it chooses. Explore both your personal connections and your academic connections with the word.

3. **Gather information.** To find information about the word's history, usage, and grammatical form, use such strategies as the following:

   - Consult a general dictionary, including an unabridged dictionary; list both denotative (literal) and connotative (associated) meanings for the word.
   - Consult specialized dictionaries that define words from specific disciplines or occupations: music, literature, law, medicine, and so on.
   - When appropriate, interview experts or students on your topic.
   - Check reference books such as *Bartlett's Famous Quotations* to see how famous speakers and writers have used the word.
   - Research the word's etymology and usage by consulting appropriate web sources such as dictionary.com, m-w.com, or xrefer.com.
   - Do a general search on the web to see where the word pops up in titles of songs, books, or films; company names, products, and ads; nonprofit organizations; and news topics.
   - List synonyms (words meaning the same—or nearly the same) and antonyms (words meaning the opposite).

4. **Compress what you know.** Based on your freewriting and research, try writing a formal, one-sentence definition that satisfies the following equation:

   Equation: **Term = larger class + distinguishing characteristics**

   Examples: **Swedish pimple** = fishing lure + silver surface, tubular body, three hooks

   melodrama = stage play + flat characters, contrived plot, moralistic theme

   Alzheimer's = dementia + increasing loss of memory, hygiene, social skills

5. **Get organized.** To organize the information that you have, and to identify details that you may want to add, fill out a graphic organizer like the one on page 51.

> **TIP:** Although you can draft your essay directly from the organizer, you may save time by writing a traditional outline that lists your main points, subpoints, and supporting details.

6. **Draft the essay.** Review your outline as needed to write the first draft.

   Opening: Get the reader's attention and introduce the term. If you are organizing the essay from general to specific, consider using an anecdote, an illustration, or a quotation to set the context for what follows. If you are organizing it from specific to general, consider including an interesting detail from the word's history or usage. Wherever you use a dictionary definition, do so with a new slant and avoid the dusty phrase "According to *Webster's* . . . "

   Middle: Show your reader precisely what the word does or does not mean. Build the definition in unified paragraphs, each of which addresses distinct aspects of the word: common definitions, etymology, usage by professional writers, and so on. Link paragraphs so that the essay unfolds the word's meaning one layer after another.

   Closing: Review your main point and close your essay. (You might, for example, conclude by encouraging readers to use—or not use—the word.)

7. **Get feedback.** Ask a classmate or someone from the college's writing center to read your essay for the following:

   - **Engaging opening**—Does the introduction identify the word and set the context for what follows?
   - **Clarity**—Is each facet of the definition clear, showing precisely what the word does and does not mean?
   - **Continuity**—Is each paragraph unified, and is each one linked to the paragraphs that precede and follow it? Is the essay focused and unified?
   - **Completeness**—Is the definition complete, telling the reader all that she or he needs to know to understand and use the word?
   - **Fitting closing**—Does the conclusion wrap up the message and refocus on the word's core meaning?

8. **Revise and edit the essay.** Use the feedback to revise the essay. If necessary, do additional research to find information to answer your reader's questions. Edit the essay by looking for clear sentences; correct quotations; specific, appropriate words; and correct grammar, spelling, usage, and punctuation.

9. **Publish the essay.** Share your writing with interested readers, including friends, family, and classmates. Submit the essay to your instructor.

Writing Checklist

Use these seven traits to check your essay; then revise as needed:

_____ The **ideas** in the definition clearly distinguish what the word does and does not mean. Supporting details help strengthen main points.

_____ The **organizational** pattern is logical and appropriate for the definition's content. Paragraphs are unified and ordered to build a clear pattern of thought.

_____ The **voice** is informed, engaging, and courteous.

_____ The **words** are precise and appropriate, and complex or technical terms are defined. Transitional words and phrases link paragraphs smoothly and logically.

_____ The **sentences** are complete, clear, varied in structure, and readable.

_____ The **copy** includes no errors in spelling, punctuation, or grammar.

_____ The page **design** is attractive and properly formatted.

Interactive

Critical-Thinking and Writing Activities

As directed by your instructor, complete the following activities.

1. Review the definition excerpted from "Economic Disparities Fuel Human Trafficking," noting that at the end the writer transitions to a discussion of slavery. Research and draft an extended definition of "slavery" that would pick up where student writer Shon Bogar left off after defining "human trafficking." Tip: to gather your ideas, use the definition diagram on page **51**.

2. Review "Deft or Daft" and choose a pair of words that similarly mirror each other's meaning. Research the words, and write an essay comparing and contrasting their etymologies and meanings.

3. Review "On *Excellence*" by Cynthia Ozick, concentrating on the way Ozick uses lists of words, phrases, and ideas to build precise definitions. Experiment with this strategy for definition in an essay that you draft or revise.

4. Write an essay defining a word or phrase that is understood by people in a particular field of study but not by "outsiders." Write for the audience of outsiders.

◀ Visually Speaking

Revisit the photograph on page **243**. Then reflect on what the image might suggest about the nature of definitions and definition writing.

PERSUASIVE WRITING

"Convince me!" is the reader's cry that lies behind all persuasive writing. Whether you are taking a position on an issue (chapter 18), persuading readers to take action (chapter 19), or proposing a solution to a vexing problem (chapter 20), you are arguing a point in an attempt to persuade readers to accept your claims, with the result that they change their own thinking and perhaps even their actions. In other words, even though each of these forms has a distinctive rhetorical emphasis, all three rely on foundational strategies for argumentation and persuasion (chapter 17): from making and supporting claims effectively to avoiding logical fallacies.

Carefully study the four chapters in this section, noting the strategies discussed in each. Then, when you're writing a persuasive essay, use those strategies that best address your writing situation: your subject, audience, and purpose.

CONTENTS

■ Persuasive Writing

STRATEGIES FOR ARGUMENTATION AND PERSUASION

17

"I wasn't convinced." "I just didn't buy it." Maybe you've said something similar while watching a political debate, viewing a TV ad, or discussing an issue in class or at work. You simply didn't find the argument logical, believable, or persuasive.

In a sense, college is a place where big issues get argued out. Your courses aim to strengthen your reasoning abilities so that you can construct persuasive arguments. Your goal as a persuasive writer is to reason effectively with your readers or listeners and to motivate them to believe, change, or act.

This chapter is a resource on reasoning. It explains the foundations of argumentation and persuasion, from making claims to using fitting appeals. The three chapters that follow introduce, explain, and model three related forms of argumentative writing: taking a position, persuading readers to act, and proposing a solution.

Audio

Video

Web Link

Building Persuasive Arguments

What is an argument?

Formally, an *argument* is a series of statements arranged in a logical sequence, supported with sound evidence, and expressed powerfully so as to sway your reader or listener. Arguments appear in a variety of places:

- A research paper about e-mail surveillance by the FBI
- An analysis of "Good Country People" (short story) or *War of the Worlds* (film)
- A debate about the ethics of transferring copyrighted music over the Internet

How do you build a persuasive argument?

Step 1: Prepare your argument.

- **Identify your audience and purpose.** Who is your audience and what is your goal? Do you want to take a position, persuade readers to act, or offer a solution?
- **Generate ideas and gather solid evidence.** You can't base an argument on opinions. Find accurate, pertinent information about the issue and uncover all viewpoints on it.
- **Develop a line of reasoning.** To be effective, you need to link your ideas in a clear, logical sequence.

Step 2: Make and qualify your claim.

- **Draw reasonable conclusions from the evidence.** State your claim (a debatable idea) as the central point for which you will argue. For example, you might assert that something is true, has value, or should be done.
- **Add qualifiers.** Words such as "typically" and "sometimes" soften your claim, making it more reasonable and acceptable.

Step 3: Support your claim.

- **Support each point** in your claim with solid evidence.
- **Identify logical fallacies.** Test your thinking for errors in logic. (See pages 267–270.)

Step 4: Engage the opposition.

- **Make concessions,** if needed, by granting points to the opposition.
- **Develop rebuttals** that expose the weaknesses of the opposition's position, whenever possible.
- **Use appropriate appeals**—emotional "tugs" that ethically and logically help readers see your argument as convincing.

Preparing Your Argument

An argument is a reason or chain of reasons used to support a claim. To use argumentation well, you need to know how to draw logical conclusions from sound evidence. Preparing an effective argument involves a number of specific steps, starting with those discussed below.

Consider the situation.

- **Clearly identify your purpose and audience.** This step is essential for all writing, but especially true when building an argument. (See page 30.)
- **Consider a range of ideas** to broaden your understanding of the issue and to help focus your thinking on a particular viewpoint. (See page 44.)
- **Gather sound evidence** to support your viewpoint. (See pages 264–266.)

Develop a line of reasoning.

Argumentative writing requires a clear line of reasoning with each point logically supporting your argument. Develop the line of reasoning as you study the issue, or use either of the following outlines as a guide.

SAMPLE ARGUMENTATIVE OUTLINES

Outline 1: **Present your supporting arguments, then address counterarguments, and conclude with the strongest argument.**
   Introduction: question, concern, or claim
   1. Strong argument-supporting claim
      • Discussion and support
   2. Other argument-supporting claims
      • Discussion of and support for each argument
   3. Objections, concerns, and counterarguments
      • Discussion, concessions, answers, and rebuttals
   4. Strongest argument-supporting claim
      • Discussion and support
   Conclusion: argument consolidated—claim reinforced

Outline 2: **Address the arguments and counterarguments point by point.**
   Introduction: question, concern, or claim
   1. Strong argument-supporting claim
      • Discussion and support
      • Counterarguments, concessions, and rebuttals
   2. Other argument-supporting claims
      • For each argument, discussion and support
      • For each argument, counterarguments, concessions, and rebuttals
   3. Strongest argument-supporting claim
      • Discussion and support
      • Counterarguments, concessions, and rebuttals
   Conclusion: argument consolidated—claim reinforced

Making and Qualifying Claims

An argument centers on a claim—a debatable statement. That claim is the thesis, or key point you wish to explain and defend so well that readers agree with it. A strong claim has the following traits:

- **It's clearly arguable**—it can be vigorously debated.
- **It's defendable**—it can be supported with sufficient arguments and evidence.
- **It's responsible**—it takes an ethically sound position.
- **It's understandable**—it uses clear terms and defines key words.
- **It's interesting**—it is challenging and worth discussing, not bland and easily accepted.

Distinguish claims from facts and opinions.

A claim is a conclusion drawn from logical thought and reliable evidence. A fact, in contrast, is a statement that can be checked for accuracy. An opinion is a personally held taste or attitude. A claim can be debated, but a fact or an opinion cannot.

> **Fact:** *The Fellowship of the Ring* is the first book in J. R. R. Tolkien's trilogy *The Lord of the Rings.*

> **Opinion:** I liked the movie almost as much as the book.

> **Claim:** While the film version of *The Fellowship of the Ring* does not completely follow the novel's plot, the film does faithfully capture the spirit of Tolkien's novel.

Note: While the fact's accuracy can easily be checked, the opinion statement simply offers a personal feeling. Conversely, the claim states an idea that can be supported with reasoning and evidence.

Distinguish three types of claims.

Truth, value, and policy—these types of claims are made in an argument. The differences among them are important because each type has a distinct goal.

Claims of truth state that something is or is not the case. As a writer, you want readers to accept your claim as trustworthy.

- The Arctic ice cap will begin to disappear as early as 2050.
- The cholesterol in eggs is not as dangerous as previously feared.

> **Comment:** Avoid statements that are (1) obviously true or (2) impossible to prove. Also, truth claims must be argued carefully because accepting them (or not) can have serious consequences.

> **Sample Essay:** "An Apology for the Life of Ms. Barbie D. Doll," pages 277–278.

Claims of value state that something does or does not have worth. As a writer, you want readers to accept your judgment.

- Volunteer reading tutors provide a valuable service.
- Many music videos fail to present positive images of women.

> **Comment:** Claims of value must be supported by referring to a known standard or by establishing an agreed-upon standard. To avoid a bias, base your judgments on the known standard, not on your feelings.

Sample Essay: "Apostles of Hatred . . . , " pages 279–280

Claims of policy state that something ought or ought not to be done. As a writer, you want readers to approve your course of action.

- Special taxes should be placed on gas-guzzling SUVs.
- The developer should not be allowed to fill in the pond where the endangered tiger salamander lives.

> **Comment:** Policy claims focus on action. To arrive at them, you must often first establish certain truths and values; thus an argument over policy may include both truth and value claims.

Sample Essay: "Pornography," pages 281–286

Develop a supportable claim.

An effective claim balances confidence with common sense. Follow these tips:

Avoid all-or-nothing, extreme claims. Propositions using words that are overly positive or negative—such as *all, best, never,* and *worst*—may be difficult to support. Statements that leave no room for exceptions are easy to attack.

> **Extreme:** All people charged even once for DUI should never be allowed to drive again.

Make a truly meaningful claim. Avoid claims that are obvious, trivial, or unsupportable. None is worth the energy needed to argue the point.

> **Obvious:** College athletes sometimes receive special treatment.

> **Trivial:** The College Rec Center is a good place to get fit.

> **Unsupportable:** Athletics are irrelevant to college life.

Use qualifiers to temper your claims. Qualifiers are words or phrases that make claims more reasonable. Notice the difference between these two claims:

> **Unqualified:** Star athletes take far too many academic shortcuts.

> **Qualified:** Some star athletes take improper academic shortcuts.

Note: The "qualified" claim is easier to defend because it narrows the focus and leaves room for exceptions. Use qualifier words like these:

almost	many	often	tends to
frequently	maybe	probably	typically
likely	might	some	usually

Supporting Your Claims

A claim stands or falls on its support. It's not the popular strength of your claim that matters, but rather the strength of your reasoning and evidence. To develop strong support, consider how to select and use evidence.

Gather evidence.

Several types of evidence can support claims. To make good choices, review each type, as well as its strengths and weaknesses.

Observations and anecdotes share what people (including you) have seen, heard, smelled, touched, tasted, and experienced. Such evidence offers an "eyewitness" perspective shaped by the observer's viewpoint, which can be powerful but may also prove narrow and subjective.

- Most of us have closets full of clothes: jeans, sweaters, khakis, T-shirts, and shoes for every occasion.

Statistics offer concrete numbers about a topic. Numbers don't "speak for themselves," however. They need to be interpreted and compared properly—not slanted or taken out of context. They also need to be up-to-date, relevant, and accurate.

- Pennsylvania spends $30 million annually in deer-related costs.
- Wisconsin has an estimated annual loss of $37 million for crop damage alone.

Tests and experiments provide hard data developed through the scientific method, data that must nevertheless be carefully studied and properly interpreted.

- According to the two scientists, the rats with unlimited access to the functional running wheel ran each day and gradually increased the amount of running; in addition, they started to eat less.

Graphics provide information in visual form—from simple tables to more complex charts, maps, drawings, and photographs. When poorly done, however, graphics can distort the truth. See the line graph in the experiment report on page 345 and the photographs in "Downloading Photographs . . ." on page 233.

Analogies compare two things, creating clarity by drawing parallels. However, every analogy breaks down if pushed too far.

- It is obvious today that America has defaulted on this promissory note insofar as her citizens of color are concerned. Instead of honoring this sacred obligation, America has given the Negro people a bad check; a check which has come back marked "insufficient funds." But we refuse to believe that the bank of justice is bankrupt.

—Martin Luther King, Jr.

Expert testimony offers insights from an authority on the topic. Such testimony always has limits: Experts don't know it all, and they work from distinct perspectives, which means that they can disagree.

■ One specialist opposed to drilling is David Klein, a professor at the Institute of Arctic Biology at the University of Alaska–Fairbanks. Klein argues that if the oil industry opens up the ANWR for drilling, the number of caribou will likely decrease because the calving locations will change.

Illustrations, examples, and demonstrations support general claims with specific instances, making such statements seem concrete and observable. Of course, an example may not be your best support if it isn't familiar.

■ Think about how differently one can frame Rosa Parks' historic action. In prevailing myth, Parks—a holy innocent—acts almost on whim. . . . The real story is more empowering: It suggests that change is the product of deliberate, incremental action.

Analyses examine parts of a topic through thought patterns—cause/effect, compare/contrast, classification, process, or definition. Such analysis helps make sense of a topic's complexity, but muddles the topic when poorly done.

■ A girl's interest in romance is no more Barbie's fault than the fault of books like *On the Shores of Silver Lake.* Fashion magazines targeted at adolescents are the cause of far more anorexia cases than is Barbie.

Predictions offer insights into possible outcomes or consequences by forecasting what might happen under certain conditions. Like weather forecasting, predicting can be tricky. To be plausible, a prediction must be rooted in a logical analysis of present facts.

■ While agroterrorist diseases would have little direct effect on people's health, they would be devastating to the agricultural economy, in part because of the many different diseases that could be used in an attack.

Use evidence.

Finding evidence is one thing; using it well is another. To marshal evidence in support of your claim, follow three guidelines:

1. Go for quality and variety, not just quantity. More evidence is not necessarily better. Instead, support your points with sound evidence in different forms. Quality evidence is . . .

- *accurate:* correct and verifiable in each detail.
- *complete:* filled with pertinent facts.
- *concrete:* filled with specifics.
- *relevant:* clearly related to the claim.
- *current:* reliably up-to-date.
- *authoritative:* backed by expertise, training, and knowledge.
- *appealing:* able to influence readers.

2. Use inductive and deductive patterns of logic. Depending on your purpose, use inductive or deductive reasoning. (See page 20.)

Induction: Inductive reasoning works from the particular toward general conclusions. In a persuasive essay using induction, look at facts first, find a pattern in them, and then lead the reader to your conclusion.

For example, in "To Drill or Not to Drill," Rebecca Pasok first details specific threats to the environment before arriving at her claim that drilling for oil in an Alaskan wilderness refuge is not our best option. (See pages 297–299.)

Deduction: Deductive reasoning—the opposite of inductive reasoning—starts from accepted truths and applies them to a new situation so as to reach a conclusion about it. For deduction to be sound, be sure the starting principles or facts are true, the new situation is accurately described, and the application is logical.

For example, Martin Luther King opened his 1963 "I Have a Dream" speech by noting that more than one hundred years earlier, the Emancipation Proclamation promised African Americans justice and freedom. He then described the continuing unjust treatment of African Americans, deducing that the promises in the Proclamation remained unfulfilled. (See pages 300–303.)

3. Reason using valid warrants. To make sense, claims and their supporting reasons must have a logical connection. That connection is called the *warrant*—the often unspoken thinking used to relate the reasoning to the claim. If warrants are good, arguments hold water; if warrants are faulty, then arguments break down. In other words, beware of faulty assumptions.

Check the short argument outlined below. Which of the warrants seem reasonable and strong, and which seem weak? Where does the argument fail?

Reasoning: If current trends in water usage continue, the reservoir will be empty in two years.

Claim: Therefore, Emeryville should immediately shut down its public swimming pools.

Unstated Warrants or Assumptions:

- It is not good for the reservoir to be empty.
- The swimming pools draw significant amounts of water from the reservoir.
- Emptying the pools would help raise the level of the reservoir.
- No other action would better prevent the reservoir from emptying.
- It is worse to have an empty reservoir than an empty swimming pool.

INSIGHT: Because an argument is no stronger than its warrants, you must make sure that your reasoning clearly and logically supports your claims.

Identifying Logical Fallacies

Fallacies are false arguments—that is, bits of fuzzy, dishonest, or incomplete thinking. They may crop up in your own thinking, in your opposition's thinking, or in such public "arguments" as ads, political appeals, and talk shows. Because fallacies may sway an unsuspecting audience, they are dangerously persuasive. By learning to recognize fallacies, however, you may identify them in opposing arguments and eliminate them from your own writing. In this section, logical fallacies are grouped according to how they falsify an argument.

Distorting the Issue

The following fallacies falsify an argument by twisting the logical framework.

Bare Assertion The most basic way to distort an issue is to deny that it exists. This fallacy claims, "That's just how it is."

- The private ownership of handguns is a constitutional right. (*Objection:* The claim shuts off discussion of the U.S. Constitution or the reasons for regulation.)

Begging the Question Also known as circular reasoning, this fallacy arises from assuming in the basis of your argument the very point you need to prove.

- We don't need a useless film series when every third student owns a DVD player or VCR. (*Objection:* There may be uses for a public film series that private video viewing can't provide. The word "useless" begs the question.)

Oversimplification This fallacy reduces complexity to simplicity. Beware of phrases like "It's a simple question of." Serious issues are rarely simple.

- Capital punishment is a simple question of protecting society.

Either/Or Thinking Also known as black-and-white thinking, this fallacy reduces all options to two extremes. Frequently, it derives from a clear bias.

- Either this community develops light-rail transportation or the community will not grow in the future. (*Objection:* The claim ignores the possibility that growth may occur through other means.)

Complex Question Sometimes by phrasing a question a certain way, a person ignores or covers up a more basic question.

- Why can't we bring down the prices that corrupt gas stations are charging? (*Objection:* This question ignores a more basic question— "Are gas stations really corrupt?")

Straw Man In this fallacy, the writer argues against a claim that is easily refuted. Typically, such a claim exaggerates or misrepresents the opponents' position.

- Those who oppose euthanasia must believe that the terminally ill deserve to suffer.

Sabotaging the Argument

These fallacies falsify the argument by twisting it. They destroy reason and replace it with something hollow or misleading.

Red Herring This strange term comes from the practice of dragging a stinky fish across a trail to throw tracking dogs off the scent. When a person puts forth a volatile idea that pulls readers away from the real issue, readers become distracted. Suppose the argument addresses drilling for oil in the Arctic National Wildlife Refuge (ANWR) of Alaska, and the writer begins with this statement:

■ In 1989, the infamous oil spill of the *Exxon Valdez* led to massive animal deaths and enormous environmental degradation of the coastline.
(*Objection:* Introducing this notorious oil spill distracts from the real issue—how oil drilling will affect the ANWR.)

Misuse of Humor Jokes, satire, and irony can lighten the mood and highlight a truth; when humor distracts or mocks, however, it undercuts the argument. What effect would the mocking tone of this statement have in an argument about tanning beds in health clubs?

■ People who use tanning beds will just turn into wrinkled old prunes or leathery sun-dried tomatoes!

Appeal to Pity This fallacy engages in a misleading tug on the heartstrings. Instead of using a measured emotional appeal, an appeal to pity seeks to manipulate the audience into agreement.

■ Affirmative action policies ruined this young man's life. Because of them, he was denied admission to Centerville College.

Use of Threats A simple but unethical way of sabotaging an argument is to threaten opponents. More often than not, a threat is merely implied: "If you don't accept my argument, you'll regret it."

■ If we don't immediately start drilling for oil in the ANWR, you will soon face hour-long lines at gas stations from New York to California.

Bandwagon Mentality Someone implies that a claim cannot be true because a majority of people are opposed to it, or it must be true because a majority support it. (History shows that people in the minority have often had the better argument.) At its worst, such an appeal manipulates people's desire to belong or be accepted.

■ It's obvious to intelligent people that cockroaches live only in the apartments of dirty people. (*Objection:* Based on popular opinion, the claim appeals to a kind of prejudice and ignores scientific evidence about cockroaches.)

Appeal to Popular Sentiment This fallacy consists of associating your position with something popularly loved: the American flag, baseball, apple pie. Appeals to popular sentiment sidestep thought to play on feelings.

■ Anyone who has seen *Bambi* could never condone hunting deer.

Drawing Faulty Conclusions from the Evidence

This group of fallacies falsifies the argument by short-circuiting proper logic in favor of assumptions or faulty thinking.

Appeal to Ignorance This fallacy suggests that because no one has proven a particular claim, it must be false; or, because no one has disproven a claim, it must be true. Appeals to ignorance unfairly shift the burden of proof onto someone else.

- Flying saucers are real. No scientific explanation has ruled them out.

Hasty or Broad Generalization Such a claim is based on too little evidence or allows no exceptions. In jumping to a conclusion, the writer may use intensifiers such as *all, every,* or *never.*

- Today's voters spend too little time reading and too much time being taken in by 30-second sound bites. (*Objection:* Quite a few voters may, in fact, spend too little time reading about the issues, but it is unfair to suggest that this is true of everyone.)

False Cause This well-known fallacy confuses sequence with causation: If *A* comes before *B*, *A* must have caused *B*. However, *A* may be one of several causes, or *A* and *B* may be only loosely related, or the connection between *A* and *B* may be entirely coincidental.

- Since that new school opened, drug use among young people has skyrocketed. Better that the school had never been built.

Slippery Slope This fallacy argues that a single step will start an unstoppable chain of events. While such a slide may occur, the prediction lacks evidence.

- If we legalize marijuana, it's only a matter of time before hard drugs follow and America becomes a nation of junkies and addicts.

Misusing Evidence

These fallacies falsify the argument by abusing or distorting the evidence.

Impressing with Numbers In this case, the writer drowns readers in statistics and numbers that overwhelm them into agreement. In addition, the numbers haven't been properly interpreted.

- At 35 ppm, CO levels factory-wide are only 10 ppm above the OSHA recommendation, which is 25 ppm. Clearly, that 10 ppm is insignificant in the big picture, and the occasional readings in some areas of between 40 and 80 ppm are aberrations that can safely be ignored. (*Objection:* The 10 ppm may be significant, and higher readings may indicate real danger.)

Half-Truths A half-truth contains part of but not the whole truth. Because it leaves out "the rest of the story," it is both true and false simultaneously.

- The new welfare bill is good because it will get people off the public dole. (*Objection:* This may be true, but the bill may also cause undue suffering for some truly needy individuals.)

Unreliable Testimonial An appeal to authority has force only if the authority is qualified in the proper field. If he or she is not, the testimony is irrelevant. Note that fame is not the same thing as authority.

■ On her talk show, Alberta Magnus recently claimed that most pork sold in the United States is tainted. (*Objection:* Although Magnus may be an articulate talk show host, she is not an expert on food safety.)

Attack Against the Person This fallacy directs attention to a person's character, lifestyle, or beliefs rather than to the issue.

■ Would you accept the opinion of a candidate who experimented with drugs in college?

Hypothesis Contrary to Fact This fallacy relies on "if only" thinking. It bases the claim on an assumption of what would have happened if something else had, or had not, happened. Being pure speculation, such a claim cannot be tested.

■ If only multiculturalists hadn't pushed through affirmative action, the United States would be a united nation.

False Analogy Sometimes a person will argue that *X* is good (or bad) because it is like *Y.* Such an analogy may be valid, but it weakens the argument if the grounds for the comparison are vague or unrelated.

■ Don't bother voting in this election; it's a stinking quagmire. (*Objection:* Comparing the election to a "stinking quagmire" is unclear and exaggerated.)

Misusing Language

Essentially, all logical fallacies misuse language. However, three fallacies falsify the argument, especially by the misleading use of words.

Obfuscation This fallacy involves using fuzzy terms like *throughput* and *downlink* to muddy the issue. These words may make simple ideas sound more profound than they really are, or they may make false ideas sound true.

■ Through the fully functional developmental process of a streamlined target-refractory system, the U.S. military will successfully reprioritize its data throughputs. (*Objection:* What does this sentence mean?)

Ambiguity Ambiguous statements can be interpreted in two or more opposite ways. Although ambiguity can result from unintentional careless thinking, writers sometimes use ambiguity to obscure a position.

■ Many women need to work to support their children through school, but they would be better off at home. (*Objection:* Does *they* refer to *children* or *women?* What does *better off* mean? These words and phrases can be interpreted in opposite ways.)

Slanted Language By choosing words with strong positive or negative connotations, a writer can draw readers away from the true logic of the argument. Here is an example of three synonyms for the word *stubborn* that the philosopher Bertrand Russell once used to illustrate the bias in slanted language:

■ I am firm. You are obstinate. He is pigheaded.

Engaging the Opposition

Think of an argument as an intelligent, lively dialogue with readers. Anticipate their questions, concerns, objections, and counterarguments. Then follow these guidelines.

Make concessions.

By offering concessions—recognizing points scored by the other side—you acknowledge your argument's limits and the truth of other positions. Paradoxically, such concessions strengthen your overall argument by making it seem more credible. Concede your points graciously, using words such as the following:

Admittedly	Granted	I agree that	I cannot argue with
It is true that	You're right	I accept	No doubt
Of course	I concede that	Perhaps	Certainly it's the case

■ Granted, Barbie's physical appearance isn't realistic. As Motz explains . . .

Develop rebuttals.

Even when you concede a point, you can often answer that objection by rebutting it. A good rebuttal is a small, tactful argument aimed at a weak spot in the opposing argument. Try these strategies:

1. **Point out the counterargument's limits** by putting the opposing point in a larger context. Show that the counterargument leaves something important out of the picture.

2. **Tell the other side of the story.** Offer an opposing interpretation of the evidence, or counter with stronger, more reliable, more convincing evidence.

3. **Address logical fallacies** in the counterargument. Check for faulty reasoning or emotional manipulation. For example, if the counterargument forces the issue into an either/or straightjacket, show that other options exist.

    ■ Granted, Barbie's physical appearance isn't realistic. As Motz explains . . . I say, so what? While the only "real" version of Barbie's body would be a long-limbed 13-year-old with breast implants, who cares? Arguing that Barbie's body isn't realistic and that the lack of realism hurts girls' self-esteem is weak logic. Children have had dolls for ages. For example . . .

Consolidate your claim.

After making concessions and rebutting objections, you may need to regroup. Restate your claim so carefully that the weight of your whole argument can rest on it.

■ Playing with Barbies need not be an unimaginative, antisocial activity that promotes conformity, materialism, and superficial ideals.

Using Appropriate Appeals

For your argument to be persuasive, it must not only be logical, but also "feel right." It must treat readers as real people by appealing to their common sense, hopes, pride, and notion of right and wrong. How do you appeal to all these concerns? Do the following: (1) build credibility, (2) make logical appeals, and (3) focus on readers' needs.

Build credibility.

A persuasive argument is credible—so trustworthy that readers can change their minds painlessly. To build credibility, observe these rules:

Be thoroughly honest. Demonstrate integrity toward the topic—don't falsify data, spin evidence, or ignore facts. Document your sources and cite them wherever appropriate.

Make realistic claims, projections, and promises. Avoid emotionally charged statements, pie-in-the-sky forecasts, and undeliverable deals.

Develop and maintain trust. From your first word to your last, develop trust—in your attitude toward the topic, your treatment of readers, and your respect for opposing viewpoints.

Make logical appeals.

Arguments stand or fall on their logical strength, but your readers' acceptance of those arguments is often affected more by the emotional appeal of your ideas and evidence. To avoid overly emotional appeals, follow these guidelines:

Engage readers positively. Appeal to their better natures—to their sense of honor, justice, social commitment, altruism, and enlightened self-interest. Avoid appeals geared toward ignorance, prejudice, selfishness, or fear.

Use a fitting tone. Use a tone that is appropriate for the topic, purpose, situation, and audience.

Aim to motivate, not manipulate, readers. While you do want them to accept your viewpoint, it's not a win-at-all-costs situation. Avoid bullying, guilt-tripping, and exaggerated tugs on heartstrings.

Don't trash-talk the opposition. Show tact, respect, and understanding. Focus on issues, not personalities.

Use arguments and evidence that readers can understand and appreciate. If readers find your thinking too complex, too simple, or too strange, you've lost them.

INSIGHT: Remember the adage: The best argument is so clear and convincing that it sounds like an explanation.

Focus on readers' needs.

Instead of playing on readers' emotions, connect your argument with readers' needs and values. Follow these guidelines:

Know your real readers. Who are they—peers, professors, or fellow citizens? What are their allegiances, their worries, their dreams?

Picture readers as resistant. Accept that your readers, including those inclined to agree with you, need convincing. Think of them as alert, cautious, and demanding—but also interested.

Use appeals that match needs and values. Your argument may support or challenge readers' needs and values. To understand those needs, study the table below, which is based loosely on the thinking of psychologist Abraham Maslow. Maslow's hierarchy ranks people's needs on a scale from the most basic to the most complex. The table begins at the bottom with *having necessities* (a basic need) and ends at the top with *helping others* (a more complex need). For example, if you're writing to argue for more affordable housing for the elderly, you'd argue differently to legislators (whose focus is on *helping others*) than to the elderly who need the housing (whose focus is on *having necessities*). Follow these guidelines:

- Use appeals that match the foremost needs and values of your readers.
- If appropriate, constructively challenge those needs and values.
- Whenever possible, phrase your appeals in positive terms.
- After analyzing your readers' needs, choose a persuasive theme for your argument—a positive benefit, advantage, or outcome that readers can expect if they accept your claim. Use this theme to help readers to care about your claims.

READER NEEDS . . .	USE PERSUASIVE APPEALS TO . . .
To make the world better by • *helping others*	values and social obligations
To achieve by • *being good at something* • *getting recognition*	self-fulfillment, status appreciation
To belong by • *being part of a group*	group identity, acceptance
To survive by • *avoiding threats* • *having necessities*	safety, security physical needs

Critical-Thinking and Writing Activities

As directed by your instructor, complete the following activities alone or with a group.

1. Select an essay from chapters 18–20, "Taking a Position," "Persuading Readers to Act," or "Proposing a Solution." Read the essay carefully. Then describe and evaluate the argumentative strategies used by the writer, answering the specific questions below:

- *What is the writer's main claim? Is it a claim of truth, value, or policy?*
- *Is the claim arguable—that is, is it supportable, appropriately qualified, and effectively phrased?*
- *What arguments does the writer develop in support of the claim? Are these arguments logical?*
- *What types of evidence does the writer provide to support her or his discussion? Is the evidence valid, sufficient, and accurate?*
- *Does the writer effectively address questions, alternatives, objections, and counterarguments?*

2. Examine the essay that you read for the first activity, and then answer the following questions:

- *Describe the writer's tone. Does it effectively engage readers?*
- *Does the argument seem credible and authoritative? Explain.*
- *Identify ways that the writer connects with readers' needs and values. How does he or she develop a persuasive theme that appeals to those needs and stresses reader benefits?*

3. Working with a classmate, examine an ad in a newspaper or magazine, on TV, or on the Internet. What kind of persuasive appeals (pages 272–273) does the ad use? Are they used effectively and appropriately? For example, using the instructions on "Critical Thinking Through Viewing" (pages 12–17), explain how the visuals aim to persuade viewers.

4. Find a letter to the editor on a current controversial issue. Examine the strengths and weaknesses of the writer's argument, and construct your own argument on this issue in the form of a letter to the same editor.

5. What are some of the key academic journals in your field of study? With help from a librarian or an instructor in your discipline, find a quality article in a respected journal. Read the article and then answer these questions: What forms of reasoning, appeals, and evidence does the author use? What forms does she or he avoid?

◀ VISUALLY SPEAKING

Photographs are commonly used with writing to support an argument. How might you use the photograph on page 259 to make a point? Explain.

TAKING A POSITION 18

Audio

Video

Sometimes you just have to take a stand. An issue comes up that evokes strong feeling and challenges your thinking. In response, you say, "Okay, this is what I believe, and this is why I believe it."

Writing a position paper gives you the opportunity to take a stand. It's a chance, in other words, to refine what you think and feel, to clarify and deepen your perspective on an issue that you find meaningful—from scientific experiments on animals to regulating pornography. The list of debate-worthy issues is endless. In fact, each discipline in college has its own controversial issues that press scholars and students to test one another's positions.

Because a position paper articulates what you profess to believe about an issue, such writing requires commitment. Use the position paper, then, as an opportunity to take a stand, to debate those who hold different positions, and to explore what you are willing to risk.

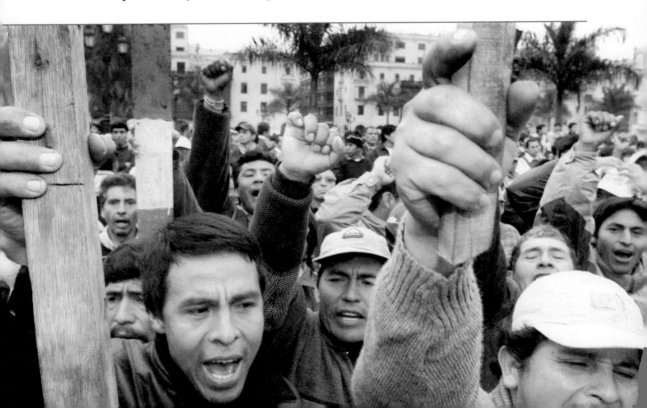

Overview
Taking a Position

Writer's Goal

Your goal is to take a stand on a controversial issue. Aim to explain what you believe and why you believe it. Be thoughtful but bold, encouraging readers to respect and even adopt your position.

Keys for Success

Explore all positions. Before settling firmly on a position, study the pluses and minuses of all possible stands that could be taken on the issue.

Go beyond pure opinion. Opinions and positions are different. Whereas an opinion may be uninformed and inherited, you *think* your way into a position. A position carries weight because of tested reasoning and reliable evidence. The writing shows mature thinking—thinking that is lively and concrete, not clichéd.

Take a measured stance. Instead of taking a defend-at-all-costs approach, be reasonable. Concede points to your opponents, and address objections to your view. If necessary, soften your stance with qualifiers. Let the evidence weigh in favor of your position—not verbal aggression, bluster, or the fever of your feelings.

Topics to Consider

Which topics work well for a position paper? Debatable ones, of course—ideas about which thoughtful people can reasonably disagree.

- **Current Affairs:** Explore recent trends, new laws, major changes, and emerging controversies discussed in the news media, journals, or online discussion groups.
- **Burning Issues:** Which issues related to family, work, education, recreation, technology, the environment, or popular culture do you care about? Which issue do you want to confront?
- **Dividing Lines:** What dividing lines characterize the communities to which you belong—which issues set people against one another? Religion, gender, money, class, sports? Think about these broad subjects, and then identify a focused issue in one of them.
- **Fresh Fare:** Sometimes an unexpected topic, like barbed versus smooth fishing hooks, offers the most potential. Avoid tired issues unless you can revive them with a fresh perspective.

> **Next Step** Read the model essays and perform the activities that follow. As you read, think of similar issues on which you could take a stand. What position would you take, and how would you defend it?

Taking a Position

Rita Isakson was asked to use logic and her personal experience to critique an article in which the writer asserted that Barbie dolls harm young girls' development. In her essay below, Isakson analyzes the article and builds a counterargument.

An Apology for the Life of Ms. Barbie D. Doll

The writer states her opponent's arguments and disagrees with them.

Barbie's boobs and spacious mansion helped cause the decay of today's youth, supposed experts say. For example, in her article, "'I Want to Be a Barbie Doll When I Grow Up': The Cultural Significance of the Barbie Doll," Marilyn Ferris Motz argues the following: Barbie dolls encourage young girls to be conformists focused on "leisure activities, personal appearance, popularity, and the consumption of materials" (125). Barbie's skinny waist, huge bosom, and narrow hips entice girls into poor diets and eating disorders. Barbie-play trains girls to depend on Ken-figures (or other males) to achieve self-worth. Barbie's all-American-girl values teach conformity; and Barbie's racy cars, plush houses, and chic outfits cause materialism (128–132). But I don't buy Motz's "reasons." They sound fake—like the theories of somebody who lacks first-hand experience. I had Barbie dolls—twelve of them, in fact, and the Barbie Mansion and Soda Shop to boot—but I don't consider myself an anorexic, dependent, conforming, materialistic girl, at least no more than I would be had I foregone the Barbie experience. *1*

Her tone is forceful and playful, but thoughtful.

She concedes a point but rebuts the argument.

Granted, Barbie's physical appearance isn't realistic. As Motz explains, "If Barbie stood five feet nine inches tall, her bust measurement would be 33 inches, her waist a meager 18 inches, and her hips only 28 1/2 inches" (128). In addition, Motz says, "Barbie's arms are extremely thin and her hands disproportionately small. Her legs are much too long . . ." (128–129). I say, so what? While the only "real" version of Barbie's body would be a long-limbed 13-year-old with breast implants, who cares? Arguing that Barbie's unrealistic body hurts girls' self-esteem is weak logic. Children have had dolls for ages. For example, in Pompeii, the preserved remains of a 3,000-year-old doll are displayed. That doll has an egghead, and a body that looks like a thick, shapeless rock. If Barbie's proportions hurt modern girls' self-esteem, I pity antiquity's girls, who had these lumps for models! *2*

Her own experience adds support.

Motz says that the average age of girls who play with Barbie is six, and that girls this age imitate the doll's values, like her preoccupation with appearance (127). However, while I was about six when I played with Barbie, I didn't imitate her. At age seven, I had a bowl haircut that was constantly snarled because I wouldn't take time to brush it. I didn't care about my own appearance, while fixing Barbie's was fun. I didn't fuss over my own hair and weight until I was in high school, and fashion mags were scripture. In other words, Motz's theory—that girls' preoccupation with Barbie's appearance leads to later preoccupation with their own—simply doesn't reflect my experience. Nor does her theory reflect the experiences of many other girls, including my two roommates. *3*

The writer rebuts each point in turn, often quoting directly from the article.

In response to Motz's idea that Barbies make girls dependent on males, I say, "Phooey." I played with Barbies until every last cow came home, and I am now a happy single girl. In fact, I have often been single, free from all romantic attachments. True, I've had boyfriends, but I never felt compelled to sacrifice my needs or identity to keep a boyfriend. And I am not an exception to Motz's rule! I know many girls whose primary concerns are their friends, family, and/or schoolwork. Admittedly, there is probably an equal number of girls who live only for their beaus; however, their behavior doesn't prove that Barbie causes female dependency. For example, my own interest in boys was prompted most by "good" TV shows and books—like Laura Ingalls Wilder's *On the Shores of Silver Lake.* It was stories like these—about teenage girls in love—that encouraged me to crave romance.

4

She summarizes her disagreement and offers alternative explanations.

In other words, Motz uses Barbie as a scapegoat for problems that have complex causes. For example, a girl's interest in romance is no more Barbie's fault than the fault of books like *On the Shores of Silver Lake.* Fashion magazines targeted at adolescents are the cause of far more anorexia cases than is Barbie. Mothers who encourage daughters to find security in men teach female dependency, but Barbie doesn't. In fact, Motz herself points out that when "the Barbie doll was created, many parents hailed the doll as a model of wholesome teenage behavior and appearance" (130). I would add that today many parents still hail Barbie as a model for wholesome behavior. But it is more the manner in which parents give toys to their children—the parents' ideas and instructions about how to play—that determine whether Barbie-play is good or bad.

5

Speaking directly to the opposition, the writer shares an anecdote and restates her counterclaim.

To Motz and similar "experts," I say this: Some of my finest childhood memories are of my best friend, Solara, coming over to my house with her pink carry-on suitcase stuffed with Barbies and their accoutrements. For hours we would play with them, giving haircuts, filling mixing bowls to make swimming pools, and creating small "campfires" so Barbie could make s'mores. Sometimes we dressed her in store-bought clothes, and sometimes we designed clothing for her. Other times we turned Barbie into the heroines in our books, and she helped us act out the plots. Playing with Barbies need not be an unimaginative, antisocial activity that promotes conformity, materialism, and superficial ideals. I played with Barbies and I'm fine. Take that, Motz! ■

6

Reading for Better Writing

Working by yourself or with a group, answer these questions:

1. The word *apology* can mean *defense,* as well as a statement of regret for wrongdoing. Is the use of the word fitting in the title? Why or why not?

2. This essay is a counterargument that relies heavily on logic and personal experience for support. How does the writer treat the original source? How do concessions and rebuttals function in the argument?

Taking a Position

Pulitzer Prize-winning political commentator Leonard Pitts, Jr., writes a syndicated column for the *Miami Herald*. This column was published in March 2005, shortly after news sources reported that a teen from Minnesota's Red Lake Reservation had posted messages to a neo-Nazi website before killing himself and nine others.

Apostles of Hatred Find It Easy to Spread Their Message

The phrase "I learned" introduces the ideas posted on the website.

1   I just visited the website that fascinated Jeff Weise, the 16-year-old who shot up his high school last week on the Red Lake Reservation in Minnesota.

2   There, I learned that the tribes of humanity must be separated or risk destruction by assimilation. That Jews are a "fanatical religious-ethnic" group conspiring to control communications media. And that for all the dubious talk about a "Holocaust," you never hear about the good things Adolf Hitler did.

3   I also read the posts that Weise left on the site's bulletin board. I was particularly interested in the one asking if the group would accept him, given that he was a Chippewa Indian. Weise was friendless, his father was dead, his mother in a nursing home, so there was something poignant and needy in the asking.

4   In all, I spent half an hour on nazi.org. It gave me a headache.

The writer notes that his friend is white and implies that he is black.

5   Used to be easier to laugh this stuff off. Once, when I was in college, a man in a "White Power" T-shirt came into the bookstore where I worked. My friend Cathy, who was white, promptly plopped herself in my lap, pecked me on the cheek, and asked loudly when I might be "home" for dinner.

6   Mr. White Power glared at us, then beat a quick retreat.

7   Thirty years later, it's harder to respond to the apostles of organized hatred. Not just because the Internet gives them a reach no guy in a T-shirt could match but because many have refined their message, made it slicker, given it a patina of reason.

The writer justifies giving attention to only one side of the issue.

8   The people behind nazi.org, for instance, would want you to know they don't consider themselves white supremacists. To the contrary, they are open to anyone—black, Asian, Indian—who believes blacks, Asians, and Indians should confine themselves to their own countries—and that Jews are "vicious," "parasitic," "liars," and "hypocrites."

9   I won't subject you to a treatise on why these people are abhorrent. If you don't already know, you need more help than anyone can give you in a few inches of newsprint. No, I am only here to note the sad incongruity of an American Indian boy asking admission to their ranks.

A clarification is offered.

Perhaps when you heard that, you concluded that it spoke to the self-hatred that is sometimes inculcated among minority communities. But Weise's complaint wasn't that he hated Indians but, rather, that too many of his people were not "Indian" enough, that their culture was diluted by exposure to others. He was especially offended by those Native youth who are fans of hip-hop. He saw them as more black than Native.   *10*

It's a painful reminder that building a society where different cultures are welcomed and interaction valued is a difficult task. Some of us see it as the onerous burden of a politically correct era; others, as a clear and present danger to the status quo. The latter intuit, correctly, that when one culture is exposed to another, both are likely to be changed.   *11*

The words *us* and *we* show the writer identifying with his readers.

The difference between those people and the rest of us is that we aren't scared of change. We recognize that while change is a challenge, it is also a condition of life. The trick—difficult, to be sure, but also rewarding—is to hold on to what is good, yet incorporate what is new.   *12*

For some people, that's an accomplishment beyond achieving or even attempting.   *13*

We don't know what role Weise's Nazi beliefs played in his decision to kill nine people before taking his own life. But it seems obvious he needed what the Nazis provided—the illusion that culture can be made orderly and change put on hold.   *14*

The writer explains how quotations from the opposing view can be used to support his own claim.

Yet what did his Nazi friends have to say after the massacre? That they would not "wring hands" over a "tragedy," the last word in quotes to indicate that it wasn't tragic at all. Makes you sorrow for the boy even in the midst of your anger at him.   *15*

Weise wanted so badly to belong to something. Obviously, he never did. ■   *16*

Reading for Better Writing

Working by yourself or with a group, answer these questions:

1. On which issue is Pitts taking a position, and what is his view? In what ways is the topic controversial (or not), and how might this affect the ways in which various readers might respond to the piece?

2. In paragraph 2, Pitts states that he "learned" a number of things from the website. What do you think he means by his use of the word "learned," and why?

3. Writers are often encouraged to explore multiple views of an issue before taking a position. Why doesn't Pitts offer a detailed explanation about why he finds the nazi.org website "abhorrent"? What do you think about this choice?

4. Where does Pitts quote from the website in question, and why?

Taking a Position

Canadian author Margaret Atwood is well known for her ability to address feminist concerns in a wide range of genres. Her novels *The Handmaid's Tale* and *The Blind Assassin* (a winner of the 2000 Booker Prize) are especially well known. This essay was first published in 1983.

The topic is clearly stated in the title.

Pornography

When I was in Finland a few years ago for an international writers' conference, I had occasion to say a few paragraphs in public on the subject of pornography. The context was a discussion of political repression, and I was suggesting the possibility of a link between the two. The immediate result was that a male journalist took several large bites out of me. Prudery and pornography are two halves of the same coin, said he, and I was clearly a prude. What could you expect from an Anglo-Canadian? Afterward, a couple of pleasant Scandinavian men asked me what I had been so worked up about. All "pornography" means, they said, is graphic depictions of whores, and what was the harm in that?

The writer summarizes another person's comments about her to introduce and clarify her position.

Not until then did it strike me that the male journalist and I had two entirely different things in mind. By "pornography," he meant naked bodies and sex. I, on the other hand, had recently been doing the research for my novel *Bodily Harm,* and was still in a state of shock from some of the material I had seen, including the Ontario Board of Film Censors' "outtakes." By "pornography," I meant women getting their nipples snipped off with garden shears, having meat hooks stuck into their vaginas, being disemboweled; little girls being raped; men (yes, there are some men) being smashed to a pulp and forcibly sodomized. The cutting edge of pornography, as far as I could see, was no longer simple old copulation, hanging from the chandelier or otherwise: it was death, messy, explicit, and highly sadistic. I explained this to the nice Scandinavian men. "Oh, but that's just the United States," they said. "Everyone knows they're sick." In their country, they said, violent "pornography" of that kind was not permitted on television or in movies; indeed, excessive violence of any kind was not permitted. They had drawn a clear line between erotica, which earlier studies had shown did not incite men to more aggressive and brutal behavior toward women, and violence, which later studies indicated did.

She distinguishes between two terms: *erotica* and *violence*.

Some time after that I was in Saskatchewan, where, because of the scenes in *Bodily Harm,* I found myself on an open-line radio show answering questions about "pornography." Almost no one who phoned in was in favor of it, but again they weren't talking about the same stuff I was, because they hadn't seen it. Some of them were all set to stamp out bathing suits and negligees, and, if possible, any depictions of the female body whatsoever. God, it was implied, did not approve of female bodies, and sex of any kind, including that practiced by bumblebees, should be shoved back into the dark, where it belonged. I had more than a suspicion that *Lady Chatterley's*

1

2

3

Lover, Margaret Laurance's *The Diviners,* and indeed most books by most serious modern authors would have ended up as confetti if left in the hands of these callers.

For me, these two experiences illustrate the two poles of the emotionally   *4*
heated debate that is now thundering around this issue. They also underline the desirability and even the necessity of

> The writer acknowledges a range of views about how to define pornography.

defining the terms. "Pornography" is now one of those catchalls, like "Marxism" and "feminism," that have become so broad they can mean almost anything, ranging from certain verses in the Bible, ads for skin lotion, and sex texts for children to the contents of *Penthouse,* Naughty '90s postcards, and films with titles containing the word *Nazi* that show

> *"Pornography" is now one of those catchalls . . .*

vicious scenes of torture and killing. It's easy to say that sensible people can tell the difference. Unfortunately, opinions on what constitutes a sensible person vary.

> A list illustrates a range of arguments that are made for censoring pornography.

But even sensible people tend to lose their cool when they start talking   *5*
about this subject. They soon stop talking and start yelling, and the name-calling begins. Those in favor of censorship (which may include groups not noticeably in agreement on other issues, such as some feminists and religious fundamentalists) accuse the others of exploiting women through the use of degrading images, contributing to the corruption of children, and adding to the general climate of violence and threat in which both women and children live in this society; or, though they may not give much of a hoot about actual women and children, they invoke moral standards and God's supposed aversion to "filth," "smut," and deviated *perversion,* which may mean ankles.

> Another list points to a range of people who may make arguments against censoring pornography.

The camp in favor of total "freedom of expression" often comes out   *6*
howling as loud as the Romans would have if told they could no longer have innocent fun watching the lions eat up Christians. It too may include segments of the population who are not natural bedfellows: those who proclaim their God-given right to freedom, including the freedom to tote guns, drive when drunk, drool over chicken porn, and get off on videotapes of women being raped and beaten, may be waving the same anticensorship banner as responsible liberals who fear the return of Mrs. Grundy, or gay groups for whom sexual emancipation involves the concept of "sexual theater." *Whatever turns you on* is a handy motto, as is *A man's home is his castle* (and if it includes a dungeon with beautiful maidens strung up in chains and bleeding from every pore, that's his business).

> Yet another list represents the questions that people raise about the causes and effects of pornography.

Meanwhile, theoreticians theorize and speculators speculate. Is   *7*
today's pornography yet another indication of the hatred of the body, the deep mind–body split, which is supposed to pervade Western Christian society? Is it a backlash against the women's movement by men who are threatened by uppity female behavior in real life, and so like to fantasize

about women done up like outsize parcels, being turned into hamburger, kneeling at their feet in slavelike adoration, or sucking off guns? Is it a sign of collective impotence, of a generation of men who can't relate to real women at all but have to make do with bits of celluloid and paper? Is the current flood just a result of smart marketing and aggressive promotion by the money men in what has now become a multibillion-dollar industry? If they were selling movies about men getting their testicles stuck full of knitting needles by women with swastikas on their sleeves, would they do as well, or is this penchant somehow peculiarly male? If so, why? Is pornography a power trip rather than a sex one? Some say that those ropes, chains, muzzles, and other restraining devices are an argument for the immense power female sexuality still wields

> *Is pornography a power trip rather than a sex one?*

in the male imagination: You don't put these things on dogs unless you're afraid of them. Others, more literary, wonder about the shift from the 19th-century Magic Woman or Femme Fatale image to the lollipoplicker, airhead, or turkey-carcass treatment of women in porn today. The proporners don't care much about theory: They merely demand product. The antiporners don't care about it in the final analysis either: There's dirt on the street, and they want it cleaned up, now.

The writer labels two camps: proporners and antiporners.

It seems to me that this conversation, with its *You're-a-prude/You're-a-pervert* dialectic, will never get anywhere as long as we continue to think of this material as just "entertainment." Possibly we're deluded by the packaging, the format: magazine, book, movie, theatrical presentation. We're used to thinking of these things as part of the "entertainment industry," and we're used to thinking of ourselves as free adult people who ought to be able to see any kind of "entertainment" we want to. That was what the First Choice pay-TV debate was all about. After all, it's only entertainment, right? Entertainment means fun, and only a killjoy would be antifun. What's the harm? 8

She cites an impasse.

This is obviously the central question: *What's the harm?* If there isn't any real harm to any real people, then the antiporners can tsk-tsk and/or throw up as much as they like, but they can't rightfully expect more legal controls or sanctions. However, the no-harm position is far from being proven. 9

The writer identifies a key point.

(For instance, there's a clear-cut case for banning—as the federal government has proposed—movies, photos, and videos that depict children engaging in sex with adults: Real children are used to make the movies, and hardly anybody thinks this ethical. The possibilities for coercion are too great.) 10

To shift the viewpoint, I'd like to suggest three other models for looking at "pornography"—and here I mean the violent kind. 11

A transition sentence predicts the organization of ideas that will follow.

Those who find the idea of regulating pornographic materials repugnant   *12*
because they think it's Fascist or Communist or otherwise not in accordance
with the principles of an open democratic society should consider that Canada
has made it illegal to disseminate material that
may lead to hatred toward any group because of
race or religion. I suggest that if pornography of

> *The human
> brain is to a
> certain extent
> a computer:
> garbage in,
> garbage out.*

the violent kind depicted these acts being done
predominantly to Chinese, to blacks, to Catholics,
it would be off the market immediately, under
the present laws. Why is hate literature illegal?
Because whoever made the law thought that
such material might incite real people to do real
awful things to other real people. The human
brain is to a certain extent a computer: garbage
in, garbage out. We only hear about the extreme cases (like that of American
multimurderer Ted Bundy) in which pornography has contributed to the
death and/or mutilation of women and/or men. Although pornography is not
the only factor involved in the creation of such deviance, it certainly has upped
the ante by suggesting both a variety of techniques and the social acceptability
of such actions. Nobody knows yet what effect this stuff is having on the
less psychotic.

> The nature
> and effects
> of porn are
> compared
> to those of
> hate crimes.

Studies have shown that a large part of the market for all kinds of porn,   *13*
soft and hard, is drawn from the 16-to-21-year-old population of young men.
Boys used to learn about sex on the street, or (in Italy, according to Fellini
movies) from friendly whores, or, in more genteel surroundings, from girls,
their parents, or, once upon a time, in school, more or less. Now porn has
been added, and sex education in the schools is rapidly being phased out. The
buck has been passed, and boys are being taught that all women secretly like
to be raped and that real men get high on scooping out women's digestive
tracts.

> References
> to studies
> lend
> scientific
> authority
> to the
> argument.

Boys learn their concept of masculinity from other men: Is this what most   *14*
men want them to be learning? If word gets around that rapists are "normal"
and even admirable men, will boys feel that in order to be normal, admirable,
and masculine they will have to be rapists? Human beings are enormously
flexible, and how they turn out depends a lot on how they're educated, by
the society in which they're immersed as well as by their teachers. In a society
that advertises and glorifies rape or even implicitly condones it, more women
get raped. It becomes socially acceptable. And at a time when men and the
traditional male role have taken a lot of flak and men are confused and casting
around for an acceptable way of being male (and, in some cases, not getting
much comfort from women on that score), this must be at times a pleasing
thought.

It would be naïve to think of violent pornography as just harmless   *15*
entertainment. It's also an educational tool and a powerful propaganda

Two models
are identified
with labels.

device. What happens when boy educated on porn meets girl brought up on Harlequin romances? The clash of expectations can be heard around the block. She wants him to get down on his knees with a ring; he wants her to get down on all fours with a ring in her nose. Can this marriage be saved?

A
comparison
to regulated
substances
helps
support an
argument for
regulating
pornography.

Pornography has certain things in common with such addictive substances as alcohol and drugs: For some, though by no means for all, it induces chemical changes in the body, which the user finds exciting and pleasurable. It also appears to attract a "hard core" of habitual users and a penumbra of those who use it occasionally but aren't dependent on it in any way. There are also significant numbers of men who aren't much interested in it, not because they're undersexed but because real life is satisfying their needs, which may not require as many appliances as those of users.

16

For the "hard core," pornography may function as alcohol does for the alcoholic: Tolerance develops, and a little is no longer enough. This may account for the short viewing time and fast turnover in porn theatres. Mary Brown, chairwoman of the Ontario Board of Film Censors, estimates that for every one mainstream movie requesting entrance to Ontario, there is one porno flick. Not only the quantity consumed but the quality of explicitness must escalate, which may account for the growing violence: Once the big deal was breasts, then it was genitals, then copulation, then that was no longer enough and the hard users had to have more. The ultimate kick is death, and after that, as the Marquis de Sade so boringly demonstrated, multiple death.

17

> *The ultimate kick is death, and after that . . . multiple death.*

After out-
lining three
alternative
models,
the writer
reviews
her main
question.

The existence of alcoholism has not led us to ban social drinking. On the other hand, we do have laws about drinking and driving, excessive drunkenness, and other abuses of alcohol that may result in injury or death to others.

18

She
proposes a
direction for
further study.

This leads us back to the key question: What's the harm? Nobody knows, but this society should find out fast, before the saturation point is reached. The Scandinavian studies that showed a connection between depictions of sexual violence and increased impulse toward it on the part of male viewers would be a starting point, but many more questions remain to be raised as well as answered. What, for instance, is the crucial difference between men who are users and men who are not? Does using affect a man's relationship with actual women, and, if so, adversely? Is there a clear line between erotica and violent pornography, or are they on an escalating continuum? Is this a "men versus women" issue, with all men secretly siding with the proporners and all women secretly siding against? (I think not; there *are* lots of men who don't think that running their true love through the Cuisinart is the best way they can think of to spend a Saturday night,

19

and they're just as nauseated by films of someone else doing it as women are.) Is pornography merely an expression of the sexual confusion of this age or an active contributor to it?

Nobody wants to go back to the age of official repression, when even piano legs were referred to as "limbs" and had to wear pantaloons to be decent. Neither do we want to end up in George Orwell's *1984*, in which pornography is turned out by the State to keep the proles in a state of torpor, sex itself is considered dirty and the approved practice it only for reproduction. But Rome under the emperors isn't such a good model either. *20*

If all men and women respected each other, if sex were considered joyful and life-enhancing instead of a wallow in germ-filled glop, if everyone were in love all the time, if, in other words, many people's lives were more satisfactory for them than they appear to be now, pornography might just go away on its own. But since this is obviously not happening, we as a society are going to have to make some informed and responsible decisions about how to deal with it. ■ *21*

> The limits of the two extreme views are reviewed.

> The writer states an ideal as well as a position grounded in reality.

Reading for Better Writing

Working by yourself or with a group, answer these questions:

1. What views on pornography does Atwood examine before detailing her own view?

2. Skilled writers often "make a space" for their arguments by demonstrating the limits or shortcomings of others' ideas and then showing how their own ideas fill the gaps. How (and where) does Atwood do this?

3. Atwood proposes three alternative models for thinking about pornography. What are they? How could the piece be edited to include signal words (such as headings or numbers) to make these three models more readily apparent?

4. Besides stating her opinion, what does the writer do to support her position?

5. In what ways does (or doesn't) Atwood succeed in taking a measured stance that may appeal to readers on both sides of the debate?

Taking a Position

In the essay below, David Blankenhorn argues that America is losing its understanding of and appreciation for fatherhood.

Blankenhorn builds his argument by making and supporting a series of bold claims. Working with one or two classmates, highlight key writing strategies and note in the margin how each strategy does or does not advance the thesis.

Fatherless America

The United States is becoming an increasingly fatherless society. A generation ago, an American child could reasonably expect to grow up with his or her father. Today, an American child can reasonably expect not to. Fatherlessness is now approaching a rough parity with fatherhood as a defining feature of American childhood.

This astonishing fact is reflected in many statistics, but here are the two most important. Tonight, about 40 percent of American children will go to sleep in homes in which their fathers do not live. Before they reach the age of eighteen, more than half of our nation's children are likely to spend at least a significant portion of their childhoods living apart from their fathers. Never before in this country have so many children been voluntarily abandoned by their fathers. Never before have so many children grown up without knowing what it means to have a father.

Fatherlessness is the most harmful demographic trend of this generation. It is the leading cause of declining child well-being in our society. It is also the engine driving our most urgent social problems, from crime to adolescent pregnancy to child abuse to domestic violence against women. Yet, despite its scale and social consequences, fatherlessness is a problem that is frequently ignored or denied. Especially within our elite discourse, it remains largely a problem with no name.

If this trend continues, fatherlessness is likely to change the shape of our society. Consider this prediction. After the year 2000, as people born after 1970 emerge as a large proportion of our working-age adult population, the United States will be a nation divided into two groups, separate and unequal. The two groups will work in the same economy, speak a common language, and remember the same national history. But they will live fundamentally divergent lives. One group will receive basic benefits—psychological, social, economic, educational, and moral—that are denied to the other group.

The primary fault line dividing the two groups will not be race, religion, class, education, or gender. It will be patrimony. One group will consist of those adults who grew up with the daily presence and provision of fathers. The other group will consist of those who did not. By the early years of the next [twenty-first] century, these two groups will be roughly the same size.

Surely a crisis of this scale merits a response. At a minimum, it requires a serious debate. Why is fatherhood declining? What can be done about it?

Can our society find ways to invigorate effective fatherhood as a norm of male behavior? Yet, to date, the public discussion on this topic has been remarkably weak and defeatist. There is a prevailing belief that not much can—or even should—be done to reverse the trend.

When the crime rate jumps, politicians promise to do something about it. When the unemployment rate rises, task forces assemble to address the problem. As random shootings increase, public health officials worry about the preponderance of guns. But when it comes to the mass defection of men from family life, not much happens. 7

There is debate, even alarm, about specific social problems. Divorce. Out-of-wedlock childbearing. Children growing up in poverty. Youth violence. Unsafe neighborhoods. Domestic violence. The weakening of parental authority. But in these discussions, we seldom acknowledge the underlying phenomenon that binds together these otherwise disparate issues: the flight of males from their children's lives. In fact, we seem to go out of our way to avoid the connection between our most pressing social problems and the trend of fatherlessness. 8

We avoid this connection because, as a society, we are changing our minds about the role of men in family life. As a cultural idea, our inherited understanding of fatherhood is under siege. Men in general, and fathers in particular, are increasingly viewed as superfluous to family life: either as expendable or as part of the problem. Masculinity itself, understood as anything other than a rejection of what it has traditionally meant to be male, is typically treated with suspicion and even hostility in our cultural discourse. Consequently, our society is now manifestly unable to sustain, or even find reason to believe in, fatherhood as a distinctive domain of male activity. 9

The core question is simple: Does every child need a father? Increasingly, our society's answer is "no" or at least "not necessarily." Few idea shifts in this century are as consequential as this one. At stake is nothing less than what it means to be a man, who our children will be, and what kind of society we will become. 10

This [essay] is a criticism not simply of fatherlessness but of a culture of fatherlessness. For, in addition to losing fathers, we are losing something larger: our idea of fatherhood. Unlike earlier periods of father absence in our history, we now face more than a physical loss affecting some homes. We face a cultural loss affecting every home. For this reason, the most important absence our society must confront is not the absence of fathers but the absence of our belief in fathers. 11

In a larger sense, this [essay] is a *cultural* criticism because fatherhood, much more than motherhood, is a cultural invention. Its meaning for the 12 individual man is shaped less by biology than by cultural script or story—a societal code that guides, and at times pressures, him into certain ways of acting and of understanding himself as a man.

Like motherhood, fatherhood is made up of both a biological and a social dimension. Yet in societies across the world, mothers are far more successful than fathers at fusing these two dimensions into a coherent parental identity. Is the nursing mother playing a biological or social role? Is she feeding or bonding? We can hardly separate the two, so seamlessly are they woven together.   *13*

But fatherhood is a different matter. A father makes his sole biological contribution at the moment of conception—nine months before the infant enters the world. Because social paternity is only indirectly linked to biological paternity, the connection between the two cannot be assumed. The phrase "to father a child" usually refers only to the act of insemination, not to the responsibility for raising a child. What fathers contribute to their offspring after conception is largely a matter of cultural devising.   *14*

Moreover, despite their other virtues, men are not ideally suited to responsible fatherhood. Although they certainly have the capacity for fathering, men are inclined to sexual promiscuity and paternal waywardness. Anthropologically, human fatherhood constitutes what might be termed a necessary problem. It is necessary because, in all societies, child well-being and societal success hinge largely upon a high level of paternal investment: the willingness of adult males to devote energy and resources to the care of their offspring. It is a problem because adult males are frequently—indeed, increasingly—unwilling or unable to make that vital investment.   *15*

Because fatherhood is universally problematic in human societies, cultures must mobilize to devise and enforce the father role for men, coaxing and guiding them into fatherhood through a set of legal and extralegal pressures that require them to maintain a close alliance with their children's mother and to invest in their children. Because men do not volunteer for fatherhood as much as they are conscripted into it by the surrounding culture, only an authoritative cultural story of fatherhood can fuse biological and social paternity into a coherent male identity.   *16*

For exactly this reason, Margaret Mead and others have observed that the supreme test of any civilization is whether it can socialize men by teaching them to be fathers—creating a culture in which men acknowledge their paternity and willingly nurture their offspring. Indeed, if we can equate the essence of the antisocial male with violence, we can equate the essence of the socialized male with being a good father. Thus, at the center of our most important cultural imperative, we find the fatherhood script: the story that describes what it ought to mean for a man to have a child.   *17*

Just as the fatherhood script advances the social goal of harnessing male behavior to collective needs, it also reflects an individual purpose. That purpose, in a word, is happiness. Anthropologists have long understood that the genius of an effective culture is its capacity to reconcile individual happiness with collective well-being. By situating individual lives within a social narrative, culture endows private behavior with larger meaning. By linking the self to moral purposes larger than the self, an effective culture tells us a story in which individual fulfillment transcends selfishness, and personal satisfaction transcends narcissism. *18*

In this respect, our cultural script is not simply a set of imported moralisms, exterior to the individual and designed only to compel self-sacrifice. It is also a pathway—indeed, our only pathway—to what the founders of the American experiment called the pursuit of happiness. *19*

The stakes on this issue could hardly be higher. Our society's conspicuous failure to sustain or create compelling norms of fatherhood amounts to a social and personal disaster. Today's story of fatherhood features one-dimensional characters, an unbelievable plot, and an unhappy ending. It reveals in our society both a failure of collective memory and a collapse of moral imagination. It undermines families, neglects children, causes or aggravates our worst social problems, and makes individual adult happiness—both male and female—harder to achieve. *20*

Ultimately, this failure reflects nothing less than a culture gone awry: a culture increasingly unable to establish the boundaries, erect the sign-posts, and fashion the stories that can harmonize individual happiness with collective well-being. In short, it reflects a culture that increasingly fails to "enculture" individual men and women, mothers and fathers. *21*

In personal terms, the end result of this process, the final residue from what David Gutmann calls the "deculturation" of paternity, is narcissism: a me-first egotism that is hostile not only to any societal goal or larger moral purpose but also to any save the most puerile understanding of personal happiness. In social terms, the primary results of decultured paternity are a decline in children's well-being and a rise in male violence, especially against women. In a larger sense, the most significant result is our society's steady fragmentation into atomized individuals, isolated from one another and estranged from the aspirations and realities of common membership in a family, a community, a nation, bound by mutual commitment and shared memory. *22*

[A good father] is a cultural model, or what Max Weber calls an ideal social type—an anthropomorphized composite of cultural ideas about the meaning of paternity. I call him the Good Family Man. As described by one of the fathers [I] interviewed . . . , a good family man "puts his family first." *23*

A good society celebrates the ideal of the man who puts his family   *24*
first. Because our society is now lurching in the opposite direction, I see the
Good Family Man as the principal casualty of today's weakening fatherhood
script. And because I cannot imagine a good society without him, I offer
him as the protagonist in the stronger script that I believe is both necessary
and possible. ■

Reading for Better Writing

Working by yourself or with a group, answer these questions:

1. What is Blankenhorn's thesis, and how does he introduce that idea? Which key claims and supporting evidence develop the thesis?

2. Choose five paragraphs and analyze their structure (e.g., topic sentence, supporting details, sentence structure, and transitions linking paragraphs). Then explain how these elements do or do not help present a clear message.

3. Working with a classmate, choose seven logical fallacies explained on pages 267–270. Then discuss why you believe that Blankenhorn's argument does or does not include these fallacies. Share your ideas with the class.

4. In paragraph 9, Blankenhorn makes the following claim: "Masculinity itself, understood as anything other than a rejection of what it has traditionally meant to be male, is typically treated with suspicion and even hostility in our cultural discourse." Explain what he means and why you find it a strong or weak claim.

5. Analyze three passages in which the writer uses data to support a point. Then explain why that use of data is or is not effective.

6. In paragraph 17, Blankenhorn says, "Margaret Mead and others have observed that the supreme test of any civilization is whether it can socialize men by teaching them to be fathers—creating a culture in which men acknowledge their paternity and willingly nurture their offspring." Explain what the quotation means and why it does or does not support the writer's thesis.

7. In paragraph 22, the writer says, "In personal terms, the end result of this process, the final residue from what David Gutmann calls the 'deculturation' of paternity, is narcissism." Define *narcissism* and explain how Blankenhorn's use of the term does or does not develop his argument.

Guidelines
Taking a Position

Note: For in-depth help on developing persuasive arguments, see pages 260–273.

1. **Select and narrow a topic.** Through reading, viewing, or surfing the Internet, explore current issues on which people can take different, well-reasoned positions. Select an issue that you care about, and identify one facet of the topic that you could address in an essay.

2. **Take stock.** Before you dig into your topic, assess your starting point. What is your current position on the topic? Why? What evidence do you have?

3. **Get inside the issue.** To take a defensible position, study the issue carefully. The following strategies will help you measure and develop what you know:
   - Investigate all possible positions on the issue. Through brainstorming and research, think through all arguments and issues on all sides.
   - Consider doing firsthand research that will help you speak with authority and passion.
   - Write your position at the top of a page. Below it, set up "Pro" and "Con" columns. List arguments in each column.
   - Develop a line of reasoning supporting your position. Then test that reasoning for two things:

     First, no logical fallacies, such as broad generalization, either/or thinking, oversimplification, or slanted language. (See pages 267–270.)

     Second, an effective range of support: statistics, observations, expert testimony, comparisons, experiences, and analysis. (See pages 264–266.)

4. **Refine your position.** By now, you may have sharpened or radically changed your starting position. Before you organize and draft your essay, clarify your position. If it helps, use this formula:

   I believe this to be true about _____ :

   _____ .

5. **Organize your development and support.** Now you've committed yourself to a position. Before drafting, review these organizational options:
   - **Traditional pattern:** Introduce the issue, state your position, support it, address and refute opposition, and restate your position.
   - **Blatant confession:** Place your position statement in the first sentence—boldly displayed for your reader to chew on.
   - **Delayed gratification:** In the first part of your essay, explore the various positions available on the topic; compare and contrast them, and then state and defend your position.

- **Changed mind:** If your research changed your mind on the topic, build that shift into the essay itself. Readers may respond well to such honesty.
- **Winning over:** If your readers may strongly oppose your position, then focus on that opposition. Defend your position by anticipating and answering each question, concern, and objection.

6. **Write your first draft.** If helpful, set aside your notes and get your position and support down on paper. If you prefer, work closely from your outline. Here are some possible strategies:

   Opening: Seize the reader's imagination. Raise concern for the issue with a dramatic story, a pointed example, a vivid picture, a thought-provoking question, or a personal confession. Supply background information that readers need to understand the issue.

   Development: Deepen, clarify, and support your position statement, using solid logic and reliable support. A clear, well-reasoned defense will help readers accept your position.

   Closing: End on a lively, thoughtful note that stresses your commitment. If appropriate, make a direct or indirect plea to readers to adopt your position.

   Title: Choose a bold title that offers a choice or stresses a stand.

7. **Share your position.** At this point, feedback from a peer or a tutor in the writing center might help. Does your reviewer accept your position? Why or why not?

8. **Revise your writing.** Consider your reviewer's comments and review the draft yourself. Cut, change, and/or add material with the following questions in mind:

   - Is the position clearly stated? Is it effectively qualified and refined?
   - Have you shown how your stand affects yourself and others?
   - Are the reasoning and support sound and complete?
   - Does the essay show awareness of questions, concerns, and other positions?
   - Do the ideas flow smoothly?
   - Is the tone confident and sincere, not bullying, cocky, or apologetic?

9. **Edit and proofread.** See pages 107 and 110 for guidelines, but check especially that your writing is free of slogans, clichés, platitudes, insults, and mystifying jargon. Make your language lively, concrete, and energetic.

10. **Prepare and publish your final essay.** Submit your position paper according to your instructor's requirements. In addition, seek a forum for your position—with peers in a discussion group, with relatives, or online.

Writing Checklist

Use these seven traits to check your essay; then revise as needed:

_____ The **ideas** establish and defend a stand on a debatable issue. The essay provides sound reasoning and support that help the reader understand and appreciate the position.

_____ The **organization** includes an engaging opening that raises the issue, a carefully sequenced development and defense of the position, and a reflective closing.

_____ The **voice** is thoughtful, measured, committed, convincing, and knowledgeable. The feelings expressed are appropriately strong.

_____ The **words** used are precise, concrete, and lively. Jargon, clichés, platitudes, and insults are avoided.

_____ The **sentences** flow smoothly. Their lengths are varied: Short sentences make snappy points and longer sentences develop thoughtful points.

_____ The **copy** follows rules of grammar, punctuation, and mechanics.

_____ The **design** and format are appropriate and attractive.

Interactive

Critical-Thinking and Writing Activities

As directed by your instructor, complete the following activities by yourself or with a group.

1. Take a position on a hot topic in your major. Check textbooks, talk to professors or other experts, and review journals in the field for controversial issues.

2. Review the column "Apostles of Hatred . . . ," noting how Leonard Pitts includes quotations that oppose his view and then presents counter-arguments that support his own claim. Apply this strategy as you draft or revise a position statement on a controversial issue.

3. Review Margaret Atwood's essay "Pornography," paying special attention to the way that she "makes a space" for her argument by demonstrating the limits or shortcomings of others' ideas and then "fills the gaps" with her own. Draft or revise a position statement using these strategies.

4. Choose one of the essays in this chapter and consider how visuals might strengthen the writer's argument. Then find, develop, or describe one or more visuals that would add persuasive power to the piece.

◄● VISUALLY SPEAKING

Review the photograph on page 275. Then explain how publicly demonstrating on an issue is similar to or different from writing an essay on the issue.

PERSUADING READERS TO ACT

19

Persuasion is a challenging task, requiring that you convince readers to believe you, rethink their own perspectives, and take a concrete step. In the end, you want them to change their minds and their actions.

In an essay persuading readers to act, you seek to change readers' opinions on a debatable, complex, and timely issue about which you care deeply, such as wise energy policies or the problem of racism. In addition, your essay presses for the next logical step—motivating readers to act. You achieve that goal with sound logic, reliable support, and fitting appeals. In a sense, you say to readers, "Come, let us reason together."

What do you feel strongly about, and which actions do you want to influence? This chapter will help you write in a way that stirs people to action.

Audio

Video

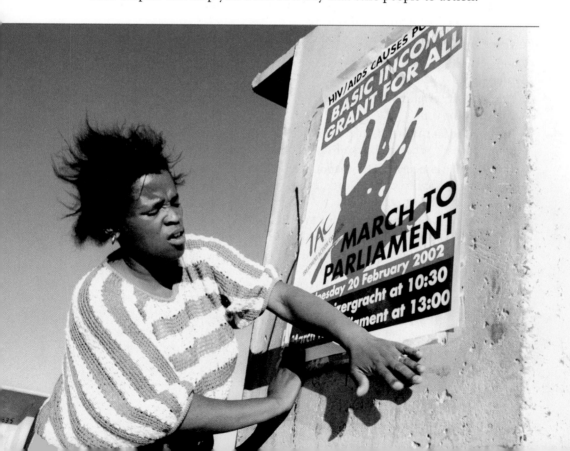

Overview
Persuading Readers to Act

Writer's Goal

Your goal is to urge individual readers to change their behavior or to take action on an issue. To accomplish this goal, you need to change the minds of those who disagree with you, and give encouragement to those who do agree with you.

Keys for Success

Know your audience. When you seek to persuade, you assume that your reader will have some opposition or resistance to your viewpoint. To motivate resistant readers to act, you must know who they are—whether they are peers, professors, the college community, or your nation. Consider their knowledge of and attitudes toward the topic so that you can address their concerns.

Promote your cause—not a quarrel. Your goal is to motivate your readers to act, not to manipulate them so that you win an argument. Study the topic from all sides. Bottom line: Know your subject.

Be reasonable. Make logical claims about your topic, testing them to make sure that they can be supported with sufficient evidence. Review your thinking to identify any logical fallacies as well. Moreover, fine-tune the essay's voice until it is passionate, thoughtful, and sincere.

Topics to Consider

Choose a debate-worthy, timely issue that you care about. Consider topics in these categories:

- **Personal experiences:** Which personal experiences have raised questions or concerns for you?
- **Personal ideas:** Which issues often occupy your mind? What do you stew about or fear? What makes you say, "Something should be done"?
- **Community concerns:** Think about the different "communities" to which you belong—family, college, race, ethnic group, or gender. Which issues concern each group, and why?
- **National or international affairs:** Which national or global issues are discussed in your circle of friends, your college community, or the news?
- **"No comment" topics:** Consider issues about which you don't have an opinion. Would you like to develop a strong stance on one of those topics?

Next Step Read the model essays and perform the activities that follow. As you read, think of parallel issues that interest you. Why do these issues intrigue you? How could you communicate that interest to readers and challenge them to take action?

Persuading Readers to Act

Rebecca Pasok is an environmental studies major who wrote this ecological essay to persuade readers to support lifestyle choices and energy policies that do not require drilling for oil in the Arctic National Wildlife Refuge.

To Drill or Not to Drill

The opening provides background information before raising the controversial position.

Known as "America's Last Frontier," the Arctic National Wildlife Refuge (ANWR) is located in the northeast corner of Alaska, right along the Beaufort Sea. President Dwight D. Eisenhower established the refuge in 1960, and today its 19 million acres make it one of the biggest refuges in the United States and home to a wide variety of wildlife such as eagles, wolves, moose, grizzly bears, polar bears, and caribou. During the last few years, however, the security of that home has been threatened by those who want to use one section of the ANWR to drill for oil. That section—named Area 1002—encompasses 1.5 million acres of pristine land near the coast.

The writer starts with a strong argument against drilling but then maps out why others support it.

One of the strongest arguments against oil drilling anywhere in the refuge is that the environmental impact of drilling conflicts with the very purpose of the ANWR. The primary mandate for the ANWR, as laid out by the U.S. Fish and Wildlife Service that administers the refuge, is "to protect the wildlife and habitats of the area for the benefit of people now and in the future." The question then is whether drilling for oil supports, or is in conflict with, this mandate. President George W. Bush and others argue that oil drilling does not conflict with the mandate because new oil-drilling techniques cause only minimal damage to the environment. These techniques include drilling fewer wells, placing wells closer together, and building pipelines above ground so as not to disturb the animals (McCarthy).

Some environmental experts support the argument that the new techniques will not hurt wildlife. While these individuals acknowledge that some land disturbance will result, they argue that animals such as caribou will not suffer. One expert taking this position is Pat Valkenberg, a research coordinator with the Alaska Department of Fish and Game; he maintains that the caribou population is thriving and should continue to thrive. To support this point, Valkenberg notes that between 1997 and 2000, the caribou population actually grew from 19,700 to 27,128 (*Petroleum News*).

She counters the position with expert testimony for the other side.

Other experts challenge those statistics with information about the caribou's birthing patterns. These experts point to herds like the porcupine caribou that live in the ANWR and move along the coast of the Beaufort Sea in the United States and also into Canada. A majority of the females in this herd wear radio collars that have been tracked to Area 1002 during calving season. Experts who argue against drilling note that the calves born on ANWR's coastal plain have a greater chance of surviving than those that are born in the foothills, where many of their predators live (*U.S. Fish and Wildlife*). This difference in survival ratios, argue antidrilling experts, may not be accounted for in the statistics used by prodrilling advocates like Valkenberg.

One specialist opposed to drilling is David Klein, a professor at the Institute of Arctic Biology at the University of Alaska Fairbanks. Klein argues that if the oil industry opens up the ANWR for drilling, the number of caribou will likely decrease because the calving locations would change. He points out that oil-industry work in the Prudhoe oil field (also in Alaska) has already split up the Central Arctic herd of caribou, so it is likely that drilling in Area 1002 will similarly affect the porcupine herd (McCarthy). [5]

But caribou are not the only wildlife that would be affected by drilling in Area 1002. Musk oxen, polar bears, and grizzly bears could be driven out of the refuge and possibly into regions where people live, thereby threatening both the animals' and people's safety. Clearly, the bottom line in this debate is that drilling in Area 1002 will destroy at least some of the ecological integrity that makes ANWR a natural treasure. Environmentalists say that "just as there is no way to be half-pregnant, there is no 'sensitive' way to drill in a wilderness" (McCarthy). They are right. [6]

However, oil drilling in ANWR will hurt more than the environment and wildlife; the drilling also will hurt at least one of the two Inuit tribes living in Alaska—the Inupiat Eskimos and the Gwich'in Indians. The Inupiat is the larger group, and they favor drilling. Money generated by the oil industry, say the Inupiat, will help them improve a variety of tribal services such as education and health care. On the other hand, the Gwich'in tribe depends on the porcupine caribou for food. As a result, if oil drilling displaces such animals, the people will suffer. Not only do they need the caribou to survive, but they also need them to retain the tribe's dignity and way of life. In other words, while oil drilling in ANWR may give some residents more money, others clearly will pay a price. [7]

So if oil drilling in ANWR would have so many negative effects, what is driving the argument for drilling? Unfortunately, nothing more than a shortsighted, ill-informed effort to satisfy America's excessive appetite for oil: To continue using too much, we want to produce more. But is drilling in the ANWR the answer to our consumption problem? [8]

At best, getting more oil from Alaska is a shortsighted solution: ANWR's reserves are simply too small to provide a long-term solution. A 1998 study by the U.S. Geological Survey concluded that the total amount of accessible oil in the ANWR is 5.7 to 16 billion barrels, with an expected amount of 10.4 billion barrels (*Arctic Power*). While these figures are considered the official estimate, the National Resources Defense Council (a group of lawyers, scientists, and environmentalists) disagrees. It estimates the accessible amount to be 3.2 billion barrels—a resource the United States would use up in just six months! In the meantime, using the ANWR oil [9]

The writer strongly states her thesis— that she agrees with opponents of drilling.

By looking at effects on people, the writer expands her opposition.

A question serves as a transition to a key counter-argument.

would do nothing to ease our dependence on Middle Eastern countries for oil. There has to be a better choice.

The writer redirects the discussion to the root of the problem.

And there is. The question is not whether drilling should take place in the ANWR, but how to provide energy for everyone, now and in the future. A poll taken by the *Christian Science Monitor* shows that voters believe that the best option for Americans is to develop new technologies (Dillan). Finding new energy sources, they say, is more important than finding new oil reserves.   10

There are two main problems with relying primarily on oil for our energy: Oil supplies are limited, and oil use pollutes. Democratic Representative Rosa DeLauro of Connecticut made this point well when she said the following: 11

A closing quotation focuses and supports the writer's objections; the quotation is indented ten spaces.

We need a serious energy policy in the United States. Drilling in the Arctic National Wildlife Refuge is not the solution. We should look to increase domestic production while balancing our desire for a cleaner environment. We must also look at ways to reduce our dependency on fossil fuels themselves, a smart and necessary step that will lead to a cleaner environment. (qtd. in Urban)   12

While reducing our use of fossil fuels will not be easy, it is possible if we do two things: (1) develop energy-saving technologies, and (2) make lifestyle choices that conserve energy. Unlike the short-term (and shortsighted) solution of drilling in the ANWR, these strategies will help save the environment. In addition, the strategies will help people both now and in the future. ■   13

> *Note:* The Works Cited page is not shown. For sample pages, see MLA (page 532–533) and APA (page 564).

Reading for Better Writing

Working by yourself or with a group, answer these questions:

1. The writer describes both positions on drilling before stating her opposition explicitly. Is this strategy effective?

2. The writer uses the testimony of experts extensively. Why?

3. What does the writer do to acknowledge, concede points to, and refute support for drilling?

4. Review pages 264–266 about types of support. Then trace the types of evidence provided in this essay. Evaluate the quality and completeness of the evidence.

5. Does the last paragraph offer an effective closing to the writer's argument? Why or why not?

Persuading Readers to Act

Dr. Martin Luther King, Jr., was a leader in the Civil Rights Movement during the 1950s and 1960s. On August 28, 1963, he delivered this persuasive speech to a crowd of 250,000 people gathered at the Lincoln Memorial in Washington, D.C.

I Have a Dream

King starts with a tragic contrast.

Five score years ago, a great American, in whose symbolic shadow we stand, signed the Emancipation Proclamation. This momentous decree came as a great beacon light of hope to millions of Negro slaves who had been seared in the flames of withering injustice. It came as a joyous daybreak to end the long night of captivity.

He uses figurative language to describe the present situation.

But one hundred years later, we must face the tragic fact that the Negro is still not free. One hundred years later, the life of the Negro is still sadly crippled by the manacles of segregation and the chains of discrimination. One hundred years later, the Negro lives on a lonely island of poverty in the midst of a vast ocean of material prosperity. One hundred years later, the Negro is still languishing in the corners of American society and finds himself an exile in his own land. So we have come here today to dramatize an appalling condition.

An analogy clarifies the problem.

In a sense we have come to our nation's Capitol to cash a check. When the architects of our republic wrote the magnificent words of the Constitution and the Declaration of Independence, they were signing a promissory note to which every American was to fall heir. This note was a promise that all men would be guaranteed the unalienable rights of life, liberty, and the pursuit of happiness.

It is obvious today that America has defaulted on this promissory note insofar as her citizens of color are concerned. Instead of honoring this sacred obligation, America has given the Negro people a bad check; a check which has come back marked "insufficient funds." But we refuse to believe that the bank of justice is bankrupt. We refuse to believe that there are insufficient funds in the great vaults of opportunity of this nation. So we have come to cash this check—a check that will give us upon demand the riches of freedom and the security of justice. We have also come to this hallowed spot to remind America of the fierce urgency of *now*. This is no time to engage in the luxury of cooling off or to take the tranquilizing drug of gradualism. *Now* is the time to make real the promises of Democracy. *Now* is the time to rise from the dark and desolate valley of segregation to the sunlit path of racial justice. *Now* is the time to open the doors of opportunity to all of God's children. *Now* is the time to lift our nation from the quicksands of racial injustice to the solid rock of brotherhood.

Repeated words and phrases create urgency.

It would be fatal for the nation to overlook the urgency of the moment and to underestimate the determination of the Negro. This sweltering summer of the Negro's legitimate discontent will not pass until there is an

1

2

3

4

5

invigorating autumn of freedom and equality. 1963 is not an end, but a beginning. Those who hope that the Negro needed to blow off steam and will now be content will have a rude awakening if the nation returns to business as usual. There will be neither rest nor tranquility in America until the Negro is granted his citizenship rights. The whirlwinds of revolt will continue to shake the foundations of our nation until the bright day of justice emerges.

King addresses specific audiences in turn.

But there is something I must say to my people who stand on the warm threshold which leads into the palace of justice. In the process of gaining our rightful place we must not be guilty of wrongful deeds. Let us not seek to satisfy our thirst for freedom by drinking from the cup of bitterness and hatred. We must forever conduct our struggle on the high plane of dignity and discipline. We must not allow our creative protest to degenerate into physical violence. Again and again we must rise to the majestic heights of meeting physical force with soul force. The marvelous new militancy which has engulfed the Negro community must not lead us to a distrust of all white people, for many of our white brothers, as evidenced by their presence here today, have come to realize that their destiny is tied up with our destiny and their freedom is inextricably bound to our freedom. We cannot walk alone.

6

He responds to the arguments of opponents.

And as we talk, we must make the pledge that we shall march ahead. We cannot turn back. There are those who are asking the devotees of civil rights, "When will you be satisfied?" We can never be satisfied as long as the Negro is the victim of the unspeakable horrors of police brutality. We can never be satisfied as long as our bodies, heaving with the fatigue of travel, cannot gain lodging in the motels of the highways and the hotels of the cities. We cannot be satisfied as long as the Negro's basic mobility is from a smaller ghetto to a larger one. We can never be satisfied as long as a Negro in Mississippi cannot vote and a Negro in New York believes he has nothing for which to vote. No, no, we are not satisfied, and we will not be satisfied until justice rolls down like waters and righteousness like a mighty stream.

7

Appropriate emotional appeals are used in the context of suffering.

I am not unmindful that some of you have come here out of great trials and tribulations. Some of you have come fresh from narrow jail cells. Some of you have come from areas where your quest for freedom left you battered by the storms of persecution and staggered by the winds of police brutality. You have been the veterans of creative suffering. Continue to work with the faith that unearned suffering is redemptive.

8

Go back to Mississippi, go back to Alabama, go back to South Carolina, go back to Georgia, go back to Louisiana, go back to the slums and ghettos of our northern cities, knowing that somehow this situation can and will be changed. Let us not wallow in the valley of despair.

9

I say to you today, my friends, that in spite of the difficulties and frustrations of the moment I still have a dream. It is a dream deeply rooted in the American dream.

10

I have a dream that one day this nation will rise up and live out the true meaning of its creed: "We hold these truths to be self-evident; that all men are created equal." 11

I have a dream that one day on the red hills of Georgia the sons of former slaves and the sons of former slaveowners will be able to sit down together at the table of brotherhood. 12

The repetition of key phrases becomes a persuasive refrain.

I have a dream that the state of Mississippi, a desert state sweltering with the heat of injustice and oppression, will be transformed into an oasis of freedom and justice. 13

I have a dream that my four little children will one day live in a nation where they will not be judged by the color of their skin but by the content of their character. 14

I have a dream today. 15

I have a dream that the state of Alabama, whose governor's lips are presently dripping with the words of interposition and nullification, will be transformed into a situation where little black boys and black girls will be able to join hands with little white boys and girls and walk together as sisters and brothers. 16

I have a dream today. 17

King's vision offers hope and motivates readers to change society.

I have a dream that one day every valley shall be exalted, every hill and mountain shall be made low, the rough places will be made plain, and the crooked places will be made straight, and the glory of the Lord shall be revealed, and all flesh shall see it together. 18

This is our hope. This is the faith with which I return to the South. With this faith we will be able to hew out of the mountain of despair a stone of hope. With this faith we will be able to transform the jangling discords of our nation into a beautiful symphony of brotherhood. With this faith we will be able to work together, to pray together, to struggle together, to go to jail together, to stand up for freedom together, knowing that we will be free one day. 19

This will be the day when all God's children will be able to sing with new meaning. 20

He appeals to ideals and to humanity's better nature, ending with a vision of a just society.

My country 'tis of thee 21
Sweet land of liberty,
    Of thee I sing,
Land where my fathers died,
Land of the pilgrims' pride,
From every mountainside
    Let freedom ring.

And if America is to be a great nation this must become true. So let freedom ring from the prodigious hilltops of New Hampshire. Let freedom ring from the mighty mountains of New York. Let freedom ring from the heightening Alleghenies of Pennsylvania! 22

Let freedom ring from the snow-capped Rockies of Colorado! 23

Let freedom ring from the curvaceous peaks of California! 24

But not only that; let freedom ring from Stone Mountain of Georgia! 25

Let freedom ring from Lookout Mountain of Tennessee! 26

Let freedom ring from every hill and molehill of Mississippi! From 27
every mountainside, let freedom ring.

When we let freedom ring, when we let it ring from every village and 28
every hamlet, from every state and every city, we will be able to speed up
that day when all of God's children, black men and white men, Jews and
Gentiles, Protestants and Catholics, will be able to join hands and sing in
the words of the old Negro spiritual, "Free at last! Free at last! Thank God
almighty, we are free at last!" ■

The closing urges readers to work for a better future.

Reading for Better Writing

Working by yourself or with a group, answer these questions:

1. King is actually speaking to several audiences at the same time. Who are these different audiences? How does King address each?

2. For what specific changes does King call? What does he want his listeners to do?

3. Explore the writer's style. How does he use religious imagery, comparisons, and analogies? How does repetition function as a persuasive technique?

4. In a sense, King's speech addresses a gap between reality and an ideal. How does he present this gap?

Persuading Readers to Act

This essay is by Jack G. Shaheen, Professor Emeritus of Mass Communication at Southern Illinois University at Carbondale, whose work on media portrayals of Arabs has earned recognition and awards. Some of his books include *Reel Bad Arabs* and *Arab and Muslim Stereotyping in American Pop Culture.*

The Media's Image of Arabs

The piece opens with a series of claims, moving from a broad statement to more specific claims.

America's bogyman is the Arab. Until the nightly news brought us TV pictures of Palestinian boys being punched and beaten, almost all portraits of Arabs seen in America were dangerously threatening. Arabs were either billionaires or bombers—rarely victims. They were hardly ever seen as ordinary people practicing law, driving taxis, singing lullabies, or healing the sick. Though TV news may portray them more sympathetically now, the absence of positive media images nurtures suspicion and stereotype. As an Arab-American, I have found that ugly caricatures have had an enduring impact on my family. *1*

The writer gives background about his own history with the topic.

I was sheltered from prejudicial portraits at first. My parents came from Lebanon in the 1920s; they met and married in America. Our home in the steel city of Clairton, Pa., was a center for ethnic sharing—black, white, Jew, and gentile. There was only one major source of media images then, at the State movie theater where I was lucky enough to get a part-time job as an usher. But in the late 1940s, Westerns and war movies were popular, not Middle Eastern dramas. Memories of World War II were fresh, and the screen heavies were the Japanese and the Germans. True to the cliché of the times, the only good Indian was a dead Indian. But when I mimicked or mocked the bad guys, my mother cautioned me. She explained that stereotypes blur our vision and corrupt the imagination. "Have compassion for all people, Jackie," she said. "This way, you'll learn to experience the joy of accepting people as they are, and not as they appear in films. Stereotypes hurt." *2*

This paragraph, like many others, begins with a short, simple sentence.

Mother was right. I can remember the Saturday afternoon when my son, Michael, who was seven, and my daughter, Michele, six, suddenly called out: "Daddy, Daddy, they've got some bad Arabs on TV." They were watching that great American morality play, TV wrestling. Akbar the Great, who liked to hear the cracking of bones, and Abdullah the Butcher, a dirty fighter who liked to inflict pain, were pinning their foes with "camel locks." From that day on, I knew I had to try to neutralize the media caricatures. *3*

Quotation marks set apart others' words and phrases from those of the author.

It hasn't been easy. With my children, I have watched animated heroes Heckle and Jeckle pull the rug from under "Ali Boo-Boo, the Desert Rat," and Laverne and Shirley stop "Sheik Ha-Mean-Ie" from conquering "the U.S. and the world." I have read comic books like the *Fantastic Four* and *G.I. Combat* whose characters have sketched Arabs as "lowlifes" and "human hyenas." Negative stereotypes were everywhere. A dictionary informed my *4* youngsters that an Arab is a "vagabond, drifter, hobo, and vagrant." Whatever happened, my wife wondered, to Aladdin's good genie?

To a child, the world is simple: good versus evil. But my children and others with Arab roots grew up without ever having seen a humane Arab on the silver screen, someone to pattern their lives after. Is it easier for a camel to go through the eye of a needle than for a screen Arab to appear as a genuine human being?

Hollywood producers must have an instant Ali Baba kit that contains scimitars, veils, sunglasses, and such Arab clothing as *chadors* and *kufiyahs*. In the mythical "Ay-rabland," oil wells, tents, mosques, goats, and shepherds prevail. Between the sand dunes, the camera focuses on a mock-up of a palace from *Arabian Nights*—or a military air base. Recent movies suggest that Americans are at war with Arabs, forgetting the fact that out of 21 Arab nations, America is friendly with 19 of them. And in *Wanted Dead or Alive*, a movie that starred Gene Simmons, the leader of the rock group Kiss, the war comes home when an Arab terrorist comes to the United States dressed as a rabbi and, among other things, conspires with Arab Americans to poison the people of Los Angeles. The movie was released last year.

The Arab remains American culture's favorite whipping boy. In his memoirs, Terrel Bell, Ronald Reagan's first secretary of education, writes about an "apparent bias among mid-level, right-wing staffers at the White House" who dismissed Arabs as "sand niggers." Sadly, the racial slurs continue. At a recent teacher's conference, I met a woman from Sioux Falls, South Dakota, who told me about the persistence of discrimination. She was in the process of adopting a baby when an agency staffer warned her that the infant had a problem. When she asked whether the child was mentally ill, or physically handicapped, there was silence. Finally, the worker said: "The baby is Jordanian."

To me, the Arab demon of today is much like the Jewish demon of yesterday. We deplore the false portrait of Jews as a swarthy menace. Yet a similar portrait has been accepted and transferred to another group of Semites—the Arabs. Print and broadcast journalists have started to challenge this stereotype. They are now revealing more humane images of Palestinian Arabs, a people who traditionally suffered from the myth that Palestinian equals terrorist. Others could follow that lead and retire the stereotypical Arab to a media Valhalla.

> *To me, the Arab demon of today is much like the Jewish demon of yesterday.*

It would be a step in the right direction if movie and TV producers developed characters modeled after real-life Arab Americans. We could then see a White House correspondent like Helen Thomas, whose father came from Lebanon, in *The Golden Girls*, a heart surgeon patterned after

---

The writer makes claims related to his main thesis and then supports them with examples drawn from public and personal sources.

The writer compares the present situation with the past.

The writer states the actions that he wishes to persuade various groups to take.

Dr. Michael DeBakey on *St. Elsewhere,* or a Syrian-American playing tournament chess like Yasser Seirawan, the Seattle grandmaster.

Politicians, too, should speak out against the cardboard caricatures. *10* They should refer to Arabs as friends, not just as moderates. And religious leaders could state that Islam, like Christianity and Judaism, maintains that all mankind is one family in the care of God. When all imagemakers rightfully begin to treat Arabs and all other minorities with respect and dignity, we may begin to unlearn our prejudices. ■

Reading for Better Writing

Working by yourself or with a group, answer these questions:

1. Shaheen's essay was first published in 1988. To what extent is his argument still relevant? Give current examples that show how media images of Arabs have or have not changed.

2. Working with a classmate, review the section in chapter 17 about "Making and Qualifying Claims" (pages 262–263). Make notes in the margins of Shaheen's essay, labeling facts, opinions, and claims. For each claim that you identify, label the type of claim that is being made (for example, claims of truth, value, or policy). Look over your margin notes. What observations can you make about Shaheen's essay, and why are they significant?

3. Review the section in chapter 17 titled "Supporting Your Claims" (pages 264–266). Which kinds of evidence does Shaheen use to support his claims? Which types of evidence do you think are most or least effective in this piece? Why?

4. How might the meaning of paragraph 4 in this essay be changed if the author had omitted the quotation marks?

5. Part of Shaheen's style in this essay is to open many of his paragraphs with short, simple sentences. How does he vary the sentence length and structure throughout the remainder of each of these paragraphs? What is the effect of this variation for readers?

Persuading Readers to Act

Kofi A. Annan, the recent Secretary-General of the United Nations, wrote the essay below to urge readers worldwide to help address the suffering caused by AIDS and famine in Africa.

In Africa, AIDS Has a Woman's Face

Working with one or two classmates, note in the margin writing strategies that help the writer build a clear, forceful argument. Then assess why each strategy is or is not effective.

A combination of famine and AIDS is threatening the backbone of *1* Africa—the women who keep African societies going and whose work makes up the economic foundation of rural communities. For decades, we have known that the best way for Africa to thrive is to ensure that its women have the freedom, power, and knowledge to make decisions affecting their own lives and those of their families and communities. At the United Nations, we have always understood that our work for development depends on building a successful partnership with the African farmer and her husband.

Study after study has shown that there is no effective development *2* strategy in which women do not play a central role. When women are fully involved, the benefits can be seen immediately: Families are healthier; they are better fed; their income, savings, and reinvestment go up. And, what is true of families is true of communities and, eventually, of whole countries.

But today, millions of African women are threatened by two simultaneous catastrophes: famine and AIDS. More than 30 million people are now at risk of starvation in southern Africa and the Horn of Africa. All of these predominantly agricultural societies are also battling serious AIDS epidemics. This is no coincidence: AIDS and famine are directly linked. *3*

> *But today, millions of African women are threatened by two simultaneous catastrophes: famine and AIDS.*

Because of AIDS, farming skills are being lost, agricultural development *4* efforts are declining, rural livelihoods are disintegrating, productive capacity to work the land is dropping, and household earnings are shrinking—all while the cost of caring for the ill is rising exponentially. At the same time, H.I.V. infection and AIDS are spreading dramatically and disproportionately among women. A United Nations report released last month shows that women now make up 50 percent of those infected with H.I.V. worldwide— and in Africa that figure is now 59 percent. Today, AIDS has a woman's face.

AIDS has already caused immense suffering by killing almost 2.5 million Africans this year alone. It has left 11 million African children orphaned since the epidemic began. Now it is attacking the capacity of these countries to resist famine by eroding those mechanisms that enable populations to fight back—the coping abilities provided by women. **5**

In famines before the AIDS crisis, women proved more resilient than men. Their survival rate was higher, and their coping skills were stronger. Women were the ones who found alternative foods that could sustain their children in time of drought. Because droughts happened once a decade or so, women who had experienced previous droughts were able to pass on survival techniques to younger women. Women are the ones who nurture social networks that can help spread the burden in times of famine. **6**

But today, as AIDS is eroding the health of Africa's women, it is eroding the skills, experience, and networks that keep their families and communities going. Even before falling ill, a woman will often have to care for a sick husband, thereby reducing the time she can devote to planting, harvesting, and marketing crops. When her husband dies, she is often deprived of credit, distribution networks, or land rights. When she dies, the household will risk collapsing completely, leaving children to fend for themselves. The older ones, especially girls, will be taken out of school to work in the home or the farm. These girls, deprived of education and opportunities, will be even less able to protect themselves against AIDS. **7**

Because this crisis is different from past famines, we must look beyond relief measures of the past. Merely shipping in food is not enough. Our effort will have to combine food assistance and new approaches to farming with treatment and prevention of H.I.V. and AIDS. It will require creating early-warning and analysis systems that monitor both H.I.V. infection rates and famine indicators. It will require new agricultural techniques, appropriate to a depleted work force. It will require a renewed effort to wipe out H.I.V.-related stigma and silence. **8**

> *Because this crisis is different from past famines, we must look beyond relief measures of the past.*

It will require innovative, large-scale ways to care for orphans, with specific measures that enable children in AIDS-affected communities to stay in school. Education and prevention are still the most powerful weapons against the spread of H.I.V. Above all, this new international effort must put women at the center of our strategy to fight AIDS. **9**

Experience suggests that there is reason to hope. The recent United   *10*
Nations report shows that H.I.V. infection rates in Uganda continue to
decline. In South Africa, infection rates for women under 20 have started to
decrease. In Zambia, H.I.V. rates show signs of dropping among women in
urban areas and younger women in rural areas. In Ethiopia, infection levels
have fallen among young women in the center of Addis Ababa.

We can and must build on those successes and replicate them   *11*
elsewhere. For that, we need leadership, partnership, and imagination from
the international community and African governments. If we want to save
Africa from two catastrophes, we would do well to focus on saving Africa's
women. ■

Reading for Better Writing

Working by yourself or with a group, answer these questions:

1. How does Annan introduce the topic and focus the essay? Explain why these strategies are or are not effective.

2. Outline the essay by stating the writer's thesis and main supporting points. Then explain why you do or do not find the argument clear, well organized, and convincing.

3. Annan wants his readers to do something. What, precisely, does he ask them to do? Is his request sufficiently clear, complete, and doable? Explain.

4. Annan supports his argument with a variety of information, including data, historical details, anecdotes, examples, and emotional appeals. Choose a paragraph that you find convincing and explain why.

5. Review the logical fallacies explained on pages 267–270. Do you find any of these weaknesses in Annan's argument? Support your answer with details.

6. In the closing paragraph, the writer uses the pronoun "we" four times. Why does he do this? Replace each "we" with "you" and explain how the changes alter the tone and effectiveness of the writer's effort to convince readers to act.

Model

Guidelines
Persuading Readers to Act

Note: For in-depth help on developing persuasive arguments, see pages 260–273.

1. **Select a topic.** List issues about which you feel passionately, issues where you see a need for change. (See "Topics to Consider" on page 296.) Then choose a topic that meets these criteria: The topic is debatable, significant, current, and manageable.

Not Debatable	*Debatable*
Statistics on spending practices	The injustice of consumerism
The existence of racism	Solutions to racism

2. **Choose and analyze your audience.** Think about who your readers are. Make a list of words and phrases describing their perspectives on the issue.

3. **Narrow your focus and determine your purpose.** Consider what you can achieve within the assignment's constraints. Should you focus on one aspect of the issue or all of it? Which patterns of thinking and behavior can you try to change? With these readers, which actions can you call for?

4. **Generate ideas and support.** Use prewriting strategies like those below to develop your thinking and gather support:
   - Set up "opposing viewpoints" columns. In one column, take one side; in the other column, take the other side.
   - Construct a dialogue between two people—yourself and someone who doesn't support your position.
   - Talk to others about the issue. How do peers, friends, coworkers, and relatives respond to your ideas?
   - Research the issue to find current, reliable sources from a variety of perspectives. Consider interviewing an expert.
   - Consider what outcome or results you want.

5. **Organize your thinking.** Get your thoughts organized so that you can step confidently into your first draft. Consider the following strategies:
   - Make a sharp claim about the issue, a claim that points toward action. Try this basic pattern:

     On the issue of _____ , I believe _____ .

     Therefore, we must change _____ .
   - Review the evidence, and develop your line of reasoning by generating an outline or using a graphic organizer. (See pages 50–51.)

Simple Outline: **Introduction: claim**
          Supporting point 1
          Supporting point 2
          Supporting point 3
          Conclusion: call to action

6. Write your first draft. As you write, remember your persuasive goal and your specific readers. Here are some possible strategies:

Opening: Gain the readers' attention, raise the issue, help the readers care about it, and state your claim.

Development: Follow your outline but feel free to explore new ideas that arise. Decide where to place your most persuasive supporting argument: first or last. Anticipate readers' questions and objections, and use appropriate logical and emotional appeals to overcome their resistance.

Closing: Do one or more of the following: Restate your claim, summarize your support, encourage readers to take the action you want.

Title: Develop a thoughtful, energetic working title that stresses a vision or change. (For ideas, scan the titles of the sample essays in this chapter.)

7. Share your essay. Try out your thinking and persuasive appeals with a reader. Does he or she find your argument convincing? Why or why not?

8. Revise your writing. Think about your reviewer's comments, and then ask these questions of your draft:

- Does your argument flow effectively? Consider shuffling points to make the sequence more persuasive. Add transitions if necessary.
- Is the evidence credible and persuasive? Does your logic have gaps? Do you need to qualify some points and strengthen others?
- Do images, examples, and analogies help readers understand and identify with your cause? Do these elements urge readers to act?
- Is the voice fitting—energetic but controlled, confident but reasonable? Will your tone persuade readers or start a quarrel?

9. Edit and proofread. See pages 107–110 for guidelines, but check especially for appropriate word choice and clear sentences. Avoid clichés and jargon.

10. Prepare and publish your final essay. Submit your essay according to your instructor's format and documentation requirements. If appropriate, "publish" your essay and solicit feedback from your audience—perhaps on a website, in the school newspaper, or with an appropriate discussion group.

TIP: Consider how one or more well-placed visuals (graph, photograph, and so on) might strengthen your argument. See pages 14–17 for more on visuals and pages 272–273 for more on appeals.

Writing Checklist

Use these seven traits to check the quality of your essay; then revise as needed:

_____ The **ideas** in your essay prompt readers to change their thinking and behavior. The essay has a clear opinion statement, effective reasoning, good support, and a clear call to action.

_____ The **organization** is logical and includes an engaging opening that raises the issue, a clearly sequenced argument, and a convincing conclusion focused on change and action.

_____ The **voice** is thoughtful, caring, and convincing.

_____ The **words** are precise, concrete, and easily understood (or defined as needed). The language is free of clichés and glib phrases.

_____ The **sentences** flow smoothly, with effective transitions and logical connections.

_____ The **copy** includes no errors in mechanics, usage, grammar, or punctuation.

_____ The **design** is correctly formatted and features the text, making reading easy.

Interactive

Critical-Thinking and Writing Activities

As directed by your instructor, complete the following activities.

1. The four essays in this chapter address significant social issues. List other significant social issues, choose one, and then write an essay that persuades readers to do something related to the issue.

2. If you are a natural sciences major, consider debatable issues that are central to studying and applying the sciences—environmental, medical, biotechnical, and agricultural issues, for example. If you are a social sciences or humanities major, do the same brainstorming in your area.

3. Consider the workplace. Which issues have come up in your job? Contemplate issues such as pay equity, equal opportunity, management policies, and unsafe work conditions. Then write a persuasive report to a decision maker or to fellow employees.

4. Review the discussion of critical viewing (pages 14–17) and the principles of argumentation (pages 260–266). Then explain how you could strengthen one of this chapter's essays by integrating one or more visuals.

◖ VISUALLY SPEAKING

Imagine that the woman pictured on page 295 is one of the women whom Kofi A. Annan describes in his essay on page 307. Then write a two- or three-page paper describing who she is, what she is doing, and why. Create details as needed.

PROPOSING A SOLUTION

20

Proposals are prescriptions for change. As such, they challenge readers to care about a problem, accept a solution, and act on it. A strong proposal offers a logical, practical, and creative argument that leads toward positive change, whether it's defending against terrorism, requiring both men and women to register for the military draft, or adding to the debate on cloning.

Proposal writers argue for such remedies in all areas of life. In your college courses, you'll be challenged to map out solutions to many difficult problems. In your community, you may participate in policy making and civic development. In the workplace, you may write proposals that justify expenditures, sell products, or troubleshoot problems. In each situation, you'll be challenged to clearly explain the problem, offer a solution, and argue for adopting that solution.

This chapter will walk you through the challenge of writing such proposals, from selecting a problem to submitting your plan.

Note: Some problem-solution writing can be explanatory rather than persuasive.

Audio

Video

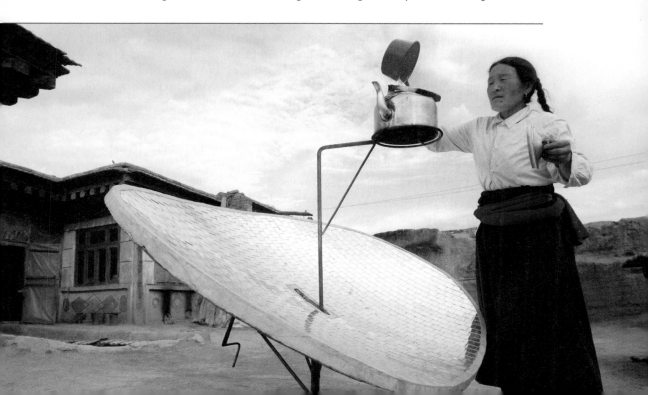

Overview
Proposing a Solution

Writer's Goal

Your goal is to argue for a positive change, convincing readers to accept and contribute to that change. To accomplish this goal, aim to describe a problem, analyze its causes and effects, argue for one solution among several options, defend that solution against objections, and prove the solution both feasible and desirable.

Keys for Success

Show passion for change. Proposal writing requires a willingness to challenge the status quo and a mind that is open to creative possibilities. Dare to ask, "What's really wrong here, and how can we fix it?"

Avoid cosmetic solutions. Whatever solution you choose, base it on a concrete and personal understanding of the problem and a bold exploration of all possible solutions. Choose the best solution only after weighing each option against sensible criteria for solving the problem, comparing and contrasting its strengths and weaknesses. Consider especially how well solutions attack root causes, bring about real benefits, and prove workable.

Know your readers. Who can bring about the change you envision—specific decision makers (the city council, college administrators, a department manager) or a broader community affected by the problem? What are their allegiances and alliances? Knowing your readers will help you speak convincingly to them, build a spirit of teamwork, and persuasively challenge readers to change.

Conduct quality research. Your proposal will stand or fall on the quality of both your reasoning and its support. To build that quality, conduct primary research (observations and interviews, for example), but also check journals, books, and Internet sources to understand the problem, explore possible solutions, and garner support for the solution you choose.

Problems to Consider

- **People problems:** Consider generations—your own or a relative's. What problems does this generation face?
- **College problems:** List the top ten problems faced by college students. In your major, which problems are experts trying to solve?
- **Social problems:** Which problems do our communities and country face? Where do you see suffering, injustice, waste, or harm?
- **Workplace problems:** What challenges do you encounter at work?

> **Next Step** Read the model essays and perform the activities that follow. As you read, consider the problems presented and the solutions offered. What similar problems do you care about?

Proposing a Solution

In this essay, student writer Brian Ley defines agroterrorism, predicts that it could become a serious problem, and proposes a multifaceted solution.

Preparing for Agroterror

The writer opens by illustrating the problem.

An al-Qaeda terrorist in Africa obtains a sample of fluid from a cow infected with foot-and-mouth disease, and he sends the fluid to an accomplice in a small, rural American town. This terrorist takes the sample around the country, stopping at several points to place small amounts of the fluid on objects that animals are likely to touch. When he is finished, he drives to the nearest airport and leaves the country unnoticed.   *1*

Cows, pigs, and sheep then come into contact with this highly contagious disease. Over the next few days, farmers see blisters on the feet and mouths of their animals. Thinking that the animals have a bacterial infection, the farmers administer antibiotics and wait for improvement. However, because antibiotics can't kill a virus, the animals get sicker. Meanwhile, the virus is spreading by means of wind and the movement of animals and humans. Within a few weeks, the virus is out of control.   *2*

While the story above is hypothetical, it is also very possible. People used to think of terrorists as men in ski masks blowing up embassies and taking hostages. But after the events of September 11, 2001, and the subsequent anthrax scares, it is clear that more kinds of terrorism are possible.   *3*

He defines the problem and presents expert testimony.

One type rarely considered is agroterrorism, which involves using diseases as weapons to attack a country's agriculture industry in order to attack the country itself. The agroterrorist's weapons of choice are those diseases that affect plants, animals, and even humans. Professor Peter Chalk of the RAND Corporation, an expert on transnational terrorism, believes that agroterrorism should be a huge concern for Americans because it has many advantages from a terrorist's point of view (37).   *4*

He analyzes why the problem could become serious.

First of all, an attack on the agricultural sector of the United States would be quite easy. The diseases needed to kill large populations of animals can be obtained with little difficulty; the most devastating ones are ready for use in their natural form. These samples pose little risk to the terrorist because many of the diseases are harmless to humans.   *5*

In addition, doing agroterrorism is less risky in terms of getting caught and getting punished. Agroterrorism is hard to trace, especially because Americans have assumed that all animal epidemics are natural in origin and that American livestock contract such diseases only by accident. Consequences for those caught inflicting a disease on animals are also less severe than for terrorists who harm humans. In fact, because agroterrorism first affects the health of plants and animals rather than humans, terrorists using this strategy can even escape some guilt for their actions.   *6*

Using specific details, he outlines the problem's potential effects.

However, while agroterrorist diseases would have little direct effect on people's health, they would be devastating to the agricultural economy, in part because of the many different diseases that could be used in an attack. One of the most devastating is foot-and-mouth disease. This illness hurts all infected animals by impeding their weight gain, and it hurts dairy cows in particular by decreasing their milk production. Because the disease is highly contagious, all infected animals, along with any cloven-hoofed animals within about 50 miles of the infection site, must be killed.

While foot-and-mouth disease is not dangerous to humans, other animal diseases are. One of these is bovine spongiform encephalopathy, better known as mad-cow disease ("Mad Cow"). This illness is not easily spread, but a few cases in the United States would send people into a panic. Meat consumption would drop sharply, and the agricultural economy would be deeply shaken.

Another disease that could be used as a weapon is West Nile encephalitis. This virus can be spread by insects and can even cross species, affecting horses, birds, pigs, and humans. It is a fatal illness without a vaccination or a cure. These diseases are likely candidates for use in an agroterrorist attack (Smith 249).

The agricultural community is particularly susceptible to a terrorist attack. Unlike "typical" terrorist targets in metropolitan areas, farms do not have sophisticated security systems to protect against intruders. The average farmer's security system includes a mean dog and a shotgun: the dog for humans and the gun for animal pests. If terrorists wanted to infect a dairy, swine operation, or even a large-scale cattle-finishing operation, they would encounter few obstacles. The terrorists merely have to place a piece of infected food in an area with livestock. This single action could start an epidemic.

The writer proposes a multifaceted solution.

Agroterrorism is a threat that demands a response. Several actions can be taken to discourage terrorism as well as to deal with its consequences. One of the first steps is convincing all citizens—farmers and nonfarmers alike—that agroterrorism could happen, and that it could cause horrific consequences. Farmers must realize that they are susceptible to an attack even though they may live far from large metropolitan areas. Nonfarmers must realize how an attack could affect them. If nonfarmers know that an attack could create panic, drive up food prices, and possibly eliminate food sources, they will look out for suspicious activity and report it.

Preventive action on farms is needed to ensure the safety of the food supply. For example, the South Dakota Animal Industry Board recently published a newsletter outlining several precautions that farmers can take. Farms should have better security, especially in areas where animals are kept. These security measures include allowing only authorized persons to have access to farm buildings and animals and keeping all key farm buildings locked ("Precautions").

7

8

9

10

11

12

Farmers also need training to detect the diseases that terrorists might   *13*
use and to know what actions can contain and decontaminate an infected
area. For example, if a farmer discovers that cows have blisters on their
tongues and noses, and that they are behaving abnormally, the owner should
immediately call a veterinarian to assess the situation. Because the disease
might be foot-and-mouth, no cattle should leave the farm until a diagnosis
has been made.

In addition, public authorities need a plan for responding to an   *14*
identified agroterrorism attack. For example, thousands of animals may
have to be killed and disposed of—an action with significant environmental
concerns. Moreover, public money should be used for continued research of
the diseases that may be spread by agroterrorists. Vaccines and treatments
may be produced that would stop diseases or limit them from becoming
epidemic.

**The closing
stresses the
problem's
seriousness
and calls
for action.**

Agroterrorism has not yet been used on a large scale anywhere on the   *15*
globe. However, its use seems inevitable. The United States is a prime target
for terrorism of this sort because the country has the largest, most efficiently
raised food supply in the world. Destroying part of this supply would affect
not only the United States but also all those countries with whom it trades.
Because the United States is a prime target, it must act now to develop its
defenses against agroterrorism. If the country waits until an attack happens,
people may become ill, the overall economy could be damaged, and the
agricultural economy may never recover. ■

Note: The Works Cited page is not shown. For sample pages, see MLA (page
532–533) and APA (page **564**).

Reading for Better Writing

Working by yourself or with a group, answer these questions:

1. This essay predicts that a problem may develop. Is the writer's prediction
persuasive? Why or why not?

2. What tactics does the writer use to get readers concerned about the
problem? Are these strategies successful?

3. The solution proposed is multifaceted. Briefly list who must do what.
Is this solution persuasive? Is it workable? Does it get at root causes?

4. A strong proposal provides convincing evidence about both the problem
and the solution. Trace the evidence used in this essay. Are the types of
evidence convincing? Do any gaps need to be filled?

Proposing a Solution

Anna Quindlen's *New York Times* column "Public and Private" won the 1992 Pulitzer Prize for commentary. She now writes a regular column for *Newsweek*, where "Uncle Sam and Aunt Samantha" was originally published in 2001.

Uncle Sam and Aunt Samantha

Each of the first five paragraphs is one sentence long.

One out of every five new recruits in the United States military is female. *1*

The Marines gave the Combat Action Ribbon for service in the Persian Gulf to 23 women. *2*

Two female soldiers were killed in the bombing of the *USS Cole*. *3*

The Selective Service registers for the draft all male citizens between the ages of 18 and 25. *4*

What's wrong with this picture? *5*

The writer identifies the problem that she wants solved.

As Americans read and realize that the lives of most women in this country are as different from those of Afghan women as a Cunard cruise is from maximum-security lockdown, there has nonetheless been little attention paid to one persistent gender inequity in U.S. public policy. An astonishing anachronism, really: While women are represented today in virtually all fields, including the armed forces, only men are required to register for the military draft that would be used in the event of a national-security crisis. *6*

She provides background about the source and history of the problem.

Since the nation is as close to such a crisis as it has been in more than sixty years, it's a good moment to consider how the draft wound up in this particular time warp. It's not the time warp of the Taliban, certainly, stuck in the worst part of the 13th century, forbidding women to attend school or hold jobs or even reveal their arms, forcing them into sex and marriage. Our own time warp is several decades old. The last time the draft was considered seriously was twenty years ago, when registration with the Selective Service was restored by Jimmy Carter after the Soviet invasion of, yep, Afghanistan. The president, as well as the Army chief of staff, asked at the time for the registration of women as well as men. *7*

Amid a welter of arguments—women interfere with esprit de corps, women don't have the physical strength, women prisoners could be sexually assaulted, women soldiers would distract male soldiers from their mission—Congress shot down the notion of gender-blind registration. So did the Supreme Court, ruling that since women were forbidden to serve in combat positions and the purpose of the draft was to create a combat-ready force, it made sense not to register them. *8*

But that was then, and this is now. Women have indeed served in combat positions, in the Balkans and the Middle East. More than 40,000 managed to serve in the Persian Gulf without destroying unit cohesion or failing because of upper-body strength. Some are even now taking out *9* targets in Afghanistan from fighter jets, and apparently without any male soldier's falling prey to some predicted excess of chivalry or lust.

Talk about cognitive dissonance. All these military personnel, male and female alike, have come of age at a time when a significant level of parity was taken for granted. Yet they are supposed to accept that only males will be required to defend their country in a time of national emergency. This is insulting to men. And it is insulting to women. Caroline Forell, an expert on women's legal rights and a professor at the University of Oregon School of Law, puts it bluntly: "Failing to require this of women makes us lesser citizens."

> **A quotation helps to explain why the writer understands the situation to be a problem.**

Neither the left nor the right has been particularly inclined to consider this issue judiciously. Many feminists came from the antiwar movement and have let their distaste for the military in general and the draft in particular mute their response. In 1980 NOW [National Organization for Women] released a resolution that buried support for the registration of women beneath opposition to the draft, despite the fact that the draft had been redesigned to eliminate the vexing inequities of Vietnam, when the sons of the working class served and the sons of the Ivy League did not. Conservatives, meanwhile, used an equal-opportunity draft as the linchpin of opposition to the Equal Rights Amendment, along with the terrifying specter of unisex bathrooms. (I have seen the urinal, and it is benign.) The legislative director of the right-wing group Concerned Women for America once defended the existing regulations by saying that most women "don't want to be included in the draft." All those young men who went to Canada during Vietnam and those who today register with fear and trembling in the face of the Trade Center devastation might be amazed to discover that lack of desire is an affirmative defense.

> **The writer anticipates and addresses counter-arguments to her position.**

Parents face a series of unique new challenges in this more egalitarian world, not the least of which would be sending a daughter off to war. But parents all over this country are doing that right now, with daughters who enlisted; some have even expressed surprise that young women, in this day and age, are not required to register alongside their brothers and friends. While all involved in this debate over the years have invoked the assumed opposition of the people, even ten years ago more than half of all Americans polled believed women should be made eligible for the draft. Besides, this is not about comfort but about fairness. My son has to register with the Selective Service this year, and if his sister does not when she turns 18, it makes a mockery not only of the standards of this household but of the standards of this nation.

> **She supports her position with statistics as well as personal anecdotes and comparisons to other situations.**

Yet they are supposed to accept that only males will be required to defend their country . . .

10

11

12

It is possible in Afghanistan for women to be treated like little more   *13*
than fecund pack animals precisely because gender fear and ignorance and
hatred have been codified and permitted to hold sway. In this country,
largely because of the concerted efforts of those allied with the women's
movement over a century of struggle, much of
that bigotry has been beaten back, even buried.
Yet in improbable places the creaky old ways
surface, the ways suggesting that we women were
made of finer stuff. The finer stuff was usually
porcelain, decorative and on the shelf, suitable
for meals and show. Happily, the finer stuff has
been transmuted into the right stuff. But with
rights come responsibilities, as teachers like to tell
their students. This is a responsibility that should
fall equally upon all, male and female alike. If
the empirical evidence is considered rationally, if the decision is divested of
outmoded stereotypes, that's the only possible conclusion to be reached. ∎

> The writer appeals to the reader's logic and ethics.

> *This is a responsibility that should fall equally upon all, male and female alike.*

Reading for Better Writing

Working by yourself or with a group, answer these questions:

1. Which problem(s) does Quindlen identify? Which solution(s) does she propose? To what extent would the proposed solution(s) solve the problem(s) Quindlen discusses?

2. Review the section in chapter 17 about "Identifying Logical Fallacies" (see pages 267–270). Quindlen's opponents might accuse her of "either/or thinking," pointing out that instead of addressing only two options, she could also have argued to end the draft for everyone. Which other logical fallacies might Quindlen's opponents accuse her of making? Would you agree with them? Why or why not?

3. Which strategies does Quindlen use to try to convince readers that the situation she describes is problematic?

4. Why does the writer acknowledge that there may be opposition to her description of the problem and to her proposed solution? How does she respond to these counterarguments?

5. Why does the essay open with a series of one-sentence paragraphs? How might the effect of the essay differ if these sentences had been combined into one paragraph?

Proposing a Solution

Leigh Turner worked at the Hastings Center, a nonprofit research institute in Garrison, New York. In the following essay, he explains why the current debate on cloning is a problem and he proposes a three-part solution.

Working with a classmate, read Leigh Turner's essay, noting how he first describes a problem and then proposes a three-part solution. In the margin, identify his key organizational strategies and explain how they do or do not clarify his argument.

The Media and the Ethics of Cloning

If the contemporary debate on cloning has a patron saint, surely it is Andy Warhol. Not only did Warhol assert that everyone would have fifteen minutes of fame—witness the lawyers, philosophers, theologians, and bioethicists who found their expertise in hot demand on the nightly morality plays of network television following Ian Wilmut's cloning of the sheep Dolly—but he also placed "clones," multiple copies of the same phenomenon, at the heart of popular culture. Instead of multiple images of Marilyn Monroe and Campbell's soup cans, we now have cloned sheep. Regrettably, it is Warhol's capacity for hyperbole rather than his intelligence and ironic vision that permeates the current debate on cloning.

It would be unfair to judge hastily written op-ed pieces, popular talk shows, and late-night radio programs by the same standards that one would apply to a sustained piece of philosophical or legal analysis. But the popular media could do more to foster thoughtful public debate on the legal, moral, political, medical, and scientific dimensions of the cloning of humans and nonhuman animals.

As did many of my colleagues at the Hastings Center, I participated in several interviews with the media following Ian Wilmut's announcement in *Nature* that he had succeeded in cloning Dolly from a mammary cell of an adult sheep. After clearly stating to one Los Angeles radio broadcaster before our interview that I was not a theologian and did not represent a religious organization, I was rather breathlessly asked during the taping

Instead of multiple images of Marilyn Monroe and Campbell's soup cans, we now have cloned sheep.

what God's view on cloning is and whether cloning is "against creation." Predictably, the broadcaster didn't want to discuss how religious ethicists are contributing to the nascent public discourse about the ethics of cloning. Instead, he wanted me to provide a dramatic response that would get the radio station's phones ringing with calls from atheists, agnostics, and religious believers of all stripes.

In addition to inundating the public with hyperbolic sound bites and their print equivalents, the media have overwhelmingly emphasized the issues involved in cloning humans, paying almost no attention to the moral implications of cloning nonhuman animals. While the ethics of cloning humans clearly need to be debated, the cloning of nonhuman animals has already taken place and deserves to be treated as a meaningful moral concern.

Although I suspect that a compelling argument for the cloning of animals can be made, we should not ignore the difference between actually formulating such arguments and merely presuming that nonhuman cloning is altogether unproblematic. Admittedly, humans already consider nonhuman animals as commodities in many ways, including as a source of food. Yet perhaps cloning animals with the intent of using them as "pharmaceutical factories" to produce insulin and other substances to treat human illnesses should raise questions about how far such an attitude ought to extend. What moral obligations should extend to humans' use of other species? Do the potential medical benefits for humans outweigh the dangers of encouraging people to think of nonhuman animals as machines to be manipulated to fulfill human goals? These kinds of questions deserve to be part of the public discussion about cloning. Given some people's concerns about the use of traps to catch wild animals, the living conditions of farm animals, and the treatment of animals used in medical and pharmaceutical research, I find this gap in public discourse perplexing.

But perhaps the most significant problem with the media hyperbole concerning cloning is the easy assumption that humans simply are a product of their genes—a view usually called "genetic essentialism." Television hosts and radio personalities have asked whether it would be possible to stock an entire basketball team with clones of Michael Jordan. In response, philosophers, theologians, and other experts have reiterated wearily that, although human behavior undeniably has a genetic component, a host of other factors—including uterine environment, family dynamics, social setting, diet, and other personal history—play important roles in an individual's development. Consequently, a clone produced from the DNA of an outstanding athlete might not even be interested in sports.

While this more sophisticated message has received some media attention, we continue to see stories emphasizing that the wealthy might some day be able to produce copies of themselves, or that couples with a dying infant might create an identical copy of the child. The popular media seem to remain transfixed by what Dorothy Nelkin, the New York University sociologist of science, refers to as "DNA as destiny."

What's more, the cloning issue reveals the way in which the mass media foster attitudes of technological and scientific determinism by implying that scientific "progress" cannot be halted. Of course, many scientists share these attitudes, and, too often, they refuse to accept moral responsibility for their participation in research that may contribute to human suffering. But scientists should not merely ply their craft, leaving moral reasoning to others. They should participate in public debates about whether certain scientific projects are harmful and should not be allowed to continue because they have unjustifiable, dehumanizing implications. A good model is the outspoken criticism of nuclear weapons by many nuclear physicists, who have helped limit research intended to produce more effective nuclear devices.

Scientists are not riding a juggernaut capable of crushing everything in its path simply because mass cloning of animals, and possibly eventually humans, may be technically possible. There is no reason to think that scientific research has a mandate that somehow enables it to proceed outside the web of moral concerns that govern all other human endeavors; it does not exist above the law or outside the rest of society. To think otherwise is to succumb to a technological determinism that denies the responsibilities and obligations of citizenship.

Despite the media's oversimplifications, citizens have an obligation to scrutinize carefully all of the issues involved and, if necessary, to regulate cloning through laws, professional codes of behavior, and institutional policies. I want to suggest three ways that scholars, policy makers, and concerned citizens can, in fact, work to improve public debate about ethical issues related to new developments in science and technology.

Recognize Moral Implications

First, scientists and ethicists need a fuller understanding of each other's work. Scientists must recognize the moral implications of their research and address those implications when they discuss the research in public. The formal education of most scientists does not encourage them to consider ethical issues. Whereas courses in bioethics are now found in most schools of medicine and nursing, graduate students in such disciplines as human genetics, biochemistry, and animal physiology are not encouraged to grapple with the ethical aspects of their research. Similarly, most ethicists have very little knowledge of science, although many of them feel perfectly entitled to comment on the moral issues of new scientific discoveries.

This gap in understanding fosters an inaccurate, unrealistic conception of what the most pressing ethical issues are. For example, the real challenges for researchers today involve the cloning of nonhuman animals for use in developing pharmaceutical products. Sustained study of nonhuman clones will be needed before researchers can even begin to seriously consider research involving human subjects. Rather than encouraging the media's interest in cloning humans, ethicists more knowledgeable about the science involved might have been able to shift the public debate toward the moral questions raised by cloning sheep, pigs, and other animals, questions that need immediate public debate.

Thus, we need to include more courses in various scientific   *13*
departments on the ethics of contemporary scientific research; offer courses
for ethicists on the basics of human genetics, anatomy, and physiology;
and establish continuing-education courses and forums that bring together
scientists and scholars in the humanities.

Present Concerns of Ethicists

Second, ethicists need to do a better job of presenting their concerns in   *14*
the popular media. Scientific journals written for a popular audience—such
as *Scientific American, New Scientist, Discover,* and *The Sciences*—provide
excellent popular accounts of scientific research and technological
developments, but they rarely specifically address the moral implications
of the discoveries they report. Regrettably, most of the academic journals
that do address the ethical aspects of scientific topics—such as the *Hastings
Center Report,* the *Journal of Medical Ethics,* and the *Cambridge Quarterly
of Healthcare Ethics*—lack the broad readership of the popular-science
magazines. Right now, perhaps the best "popular" source of sustained
ethical analysis of science, medicine, and health care is the *New York Times
Magazine.*

If ethicists hope to reach larger audiences with more than trivial sound   *15*
bites, they need to establish and promote appropriate outlets for their
concerns. For example, Arthur Caplan, director of the Center for Bioethics
at the University of Pennsylvania, wrote a regular weekly newspaper column
for the *St. Paul Pioneer Press* when he directed a bioethics center at the
University of Minnesota. His column addressed the ethical implications
of medical and scientific research. Other scholars have yet to follow his
example—perhaps, in part, because many academics feel that writing for
the mass media is unworthy of their time. They are wrong.

One way of improving public debate on these important issues is for   *16*
universities to encourage their faculty members to write for newspapers,
popular magazines, and even community newsletters. Such forms of
communication should be viewed as an important complement to other
forms of published research. Leon Kass's writing on cloning in *The New
Republic* and Michael Walzer's and Michael Sandel's writing on assisted
suicide in the same publication should not be considered any less significant
simply because the work appears in a magazine intended for a wide
audience. After all, if universities are to retain their public support, they
must consistently be seen as important players in society, and one easy way
to do this is to encourage their faculty members to contribute regularly to
public discussion.

Expand Public Debate

Finally, we need to expand public debate about ethical issues in science   *17*
beyond the mass media. To complement the activities of the National

Bioethics Advisory Commission and the projects on ethics at universities and research centers, we should create forums at which academics and citizens from all walks of life could meet to debate the issues. Instead of merely providing a gathering place for scholars pursuing research projects, institutions such as the Hastings Center, Georgetown University's Kennedy Institute of Ethics, and the University of Pennsylvania's Center for Bioethics need to foster outreach programs and community-discussion groups that include nonspecialists. My experience suggests that members of civic organizations and community-health groups, such as the New York Citizens' Committee on Health Care Decisions, are quite eager to discuss the topic of cloning.

What we need are fewer commentaries by self-promoting experts 18 on network television, and more intelligent discussions by scholars and citizens in local media, including local public-television stations. We need creative alternatives to the onslaught of talking heads, all saying much the same thing (as though they themselves were clones) to docile, sheep-like audiences waiting for others to address the most pressing moral issues of the day. ■

Reading for Better Writing

Working by yourself or with a group, answer these questions:

1. The writer introduces the topic by using Andy Warhol as an analogy. Explain why the analogy is or is not effective.

2. Reread the first two pages, in which the writer states and explains the problem. Summarize what he says, and explain why his presentation is or is not clear.

3. Summarize the author's three-part solution, and explain why this part of the essay is or is not effective.

4. Reread the conclusion, and explain whether it effectively unifies the essay.

Model

Guidelines
Proposing a Solution

Note: For in-depth help on developing persuasive arguments, see pages 260–273.

1. **Select and narrow a topic.** Choose a problem from "Problems to Consider" on page 314, or search for one in periodicals, on news programs, or on the Internet. Then test your topic:
   - Is the problem real, serious, and fairly complex? Does it show brokenness, danger, or disadvantage? Does it predict future harm?
   - Do you care about this problem and believe that it must be solved?
   - Can you offer a workable solution? Should you narrow the focus to part of the problem or a local angle?

2. **Identify and analyze your audience.** Potentially, you could have three audiences: decision makers with the power to deliver change, people affected by the problem, and a public that needs to learn about the problem and get behind a solution. Once you've determined your audience, study them:
   - What do they know about the problem? What are their attitudes toward it, their likely questions, and their potential concerns?
   - Why might they accept or resist change? Would they prefer a specific solution?
   - Does the problem affect them directly or indirectly? What can and can't they do about the problem?
   - What arguments and evidence would convince them to agree that the problem exists, to care about it, and to take action?
   - What common ground do you and your readers share?

3. **Probe the problem.** If helpful, use the graphic organizer on page 51.
   - **Define the problem.** What is it, exactly? What are its parts or dimensions?
   - **Determine the problem's seriousness.** Why should it be fixed? Who is affected and how? What are its immediate, long-term, and potential effects?
   - **Analyze causes.** What are its root causes and contributing factors?
   - **Explore context.** What is the problem's background, history, and connection to other problems? What solutions have been tried in the past? Who, if anyone, benefits from the problem's existence?
   - **Think creatively.** Take a look at the problem from other perspectives —other states and countries, both genders, different races and ethnic groups, and other generations.

4. **Brainstorm possible solutions.** List all imaginable solutions—both modest and radical fixes. Then evaluate the alternatives:
   - List criteria that any solution should meet. (These measurements indicate a solution's effectiveness at resolving the problem: *The solution must . . .*)
   - Compare and contrast alternatives by examining strengths, weaknesses, and workability.

5. **Choose the best solution and map out support.** In a sentence, state the solution that best solves the problem—a workable plan that attacks causes and treats effects. Try this pattern for your thesis: "Given [the problem—its seriousness, effects, or causes], we must [the solution]." Next, identify support for your solution. Compared with alternatives, why is it preferable? Is it more thorough, beneficial, and practical?

6. **Outline your proposal and complete a first draft.** A proposal's structure is quite simple: Describe the problem, offer a solution, and defend the solution. However, what you do in each section can become complicated. Choose strategies that fit your purpose and audience.
   - **The problem:** Consider whether readers understand the problem and accept its seriousness. Inform and/or persuade them about the problem by using appropriate background information, cause/effect analysis, examples, analogies, parallel cases, visuals, and expert testimony.
   - **The solution:** If necessary, first argue against alternative solutions. Then present your solution. State clearly what should happen, who should be involved, and why. For a complex solution, lay out the different stages.
   - **The support:** Show how the solution solves the problem. Use facts and analysis to argue that your solution is feasible and to address objections. You may choose to accept some objections while refuting others.

7. **Get feedback and revise the draft.** Share your draft with a peer or a tutor in the writing center, getting answers to the following questions:
   - Does the solution fit the problem? Is the proposal precise, well reasoned, realistic, and complete? Does it address all objections?
   - Is the evidence credible, compelling, clear, and well documented?
   - Does the voice fit the problem and treat the opposition tactfully?
   - Is the opening engaging? Is the closing thoughtful, forceful, and clear?

8. **Edit and proofread.** Check for accurate word choice and helpful definitions; smooth, energetic sentences; and correct grammar, spelling, and format.

9. **Prepare and share your final essay.** Submit your proposal to your instructor, but also consider posting it on the web.

Writing Checklist

Use these seven traits to check your essay; then revise as needed:

_____ The **ideas** show a thorough understanding of the problem and present a workable solution. The proposal uses strong reasoning and well-researched evidence.

_____ The **organization** convincingly moves from problem to solution to support. Each part is effectively ordered using strategies such as cause/effect, compare/contrast, and process.

_____ The **voice** is positive, confident, objective, and sensitive to opposing viewpoints. The tone fits the seriousness of the problem.

_____ The **words** are precise and effectively defined.

_____ The **sentences** read and flow smoothly, with effective variations and logical transitions.

_____ The **copy** includes no errors in grammar, spelling, or punctuation.

_____ The **design** is attractive and features the text.

Interactive

Critical-Thinking and Writing Activities

As directed by your instructor, complete the following activities.

1. "Preparing for Agroterror" predicts that a problem may develop. Thinking about current conditions and trends, forecast a problem, and write a proposal explaining how to prepare for or prevent it.

2. Review the section in chapter 17 about "Engaging the Opposition" (page 271). Also review how Anna Quindlen engages her opposition in "Uncle Sam and Aunt Samantha." Then consider a persuasive piece that you are drafting or revising. How might you engage the opposition to your arguments? Revise your writing as needed.

3. Review the section in chapter 17 about "Identifying Logical Fallacies" (pages 267–270). Write a humorous essay in which you make an argument by relying on a number of obvious logical fallacies. A challenge: How effectively can you make serious points by combining these strategies?

4. What are some challenges facing the planet Earth and the human race in the foreseeable future? Find a focused challenge and write a proposal.

5. Select an essay from this chapter and find or develop visuals that support the writer's argument.

VISUALLY SPEAKING

Explain why the "solution" pictured on page 313 is both creative and logical. Then explain which essay in this chapter proposes a solution that best illustrates the same qualities.

REPORT WRITING

It's tempting to suggest that the contents of reports include "just the facts." Whether they focus on interviews (chapter 21) or scientific research (chapter 22), reports at first glance seek only to share with readers the objective results of primary research. However, a more careful reading of reports reveals that they do much more. For example, the reports in this section not only describe their topics, but also use analytical strategies (such as cause/effect) to interpret or explain the activities that they describe.

As you read the various types of reports in this section, note both the research methods and organizational strategies used by each writer. Then, as you write your own report, choose research methods and writing strategies that fit your rhetorical situation: your audience, your purpose, and your subject.

CONTENTS

Report Writing

INTERVIEW REPORT

The idea of an interview is simple. You talk with someone—an expert on a topic, a client, or a case-study subject—to gain insights into the topic and/or person. As a question-and-answer session, an interview can generate primary information to supplement other research, or it can provide the information and focus for an entire piece of writing such as an interview report.

The idea of an interview may be simple, but conducting a good interview and writing a good report can be challenging. A good interview must be carefully planned and executed to become a productive conversation. Planning gives you background information and helps you develop questions that produce solid data, vivid details, and lively quotations. Poor interviewing leads to flat facts, irrelevant tangents, and bland generalities.

This chapter focuses on developing meaningful interview reports. The overview, guidelines, and model that follow will help you carry out your interviews and write your reports.

Audio

Video

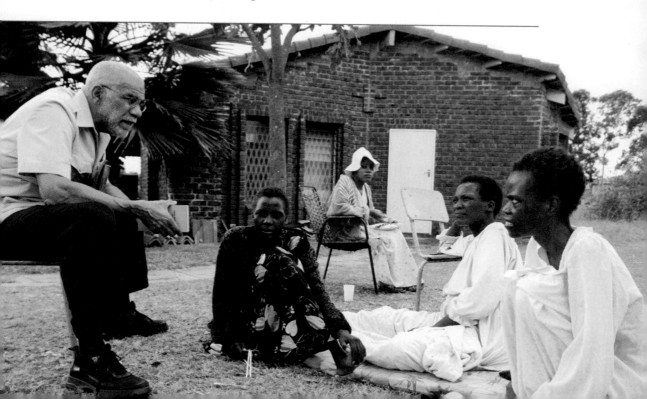

Overview
Writing an Interview Report

Writer's Goal

Your goal is to gain insights by interviewing someone and then sharing those revelations with readers. Aim to ask the right questions, record answers accurately, and report results clearly.

Keys for Success

Plan carefully. An interview needs to be properly prepared, conducted, and processed. Give yourself enough time, and respect your interviewee by being on time, efficient, informed, and courteous.

Ask clear, relevant questions. Clear questions yield useful information—insights into the topic or person that peek below the factual surface. Getting quality information depends on the art of interviewing—planning relevant questions, listening well, following up with sensible responses, and being open to surprises.

Respect the interviewee's voice. Know the person's identity, story, and values. In the interview, listen much more than you talk. In the report, present the person's words and thoughts clearly and honestly. Consider sharing the report with the interview subject before you "go public."

Analyze and synthesize the results. Analysis helps you understand pieces of information, and synthesis helps you pull together separate facts to show relationships. To write an interview report, you must both analyze and synthesize the results of your interview to discover a meaningful theme. Shape the discussion so that the report hangs together, means something, and goes somewhere.

People to Consider

Choose an interviewee from one of the following categories:

- **The expert:** Who is an authority on your topic? Could you find such an expert in your college or community, through local organizations or businesses, or on the Internet?

- **The experienced:** Who has had unique, direct experiences with the topic? Who has participated in, witnessed, or been affected by the situation?

- **The person:** If your purpose is to focus on a person rather than a topic, choose someone intriguing—someone from a particular background, generation, ethnicity, nationality, or occupation.

Next Step Read the model essay and perform the activities that follow. As you read, think about the interview subject chosen and the strategies used to report on the interview. Consider how to use similar strategies.

Audio

Interview Report

Because of a disturbing childhood experience, college student Benjamin Meyer toured a funeral home and interviewed the director. In the following essay, Benjamin reports on what he learned.

The Dead Business

The writer starts with background information that creates a personal theme.

"You're going to tour a what?"   *1*

"A funeral home."   *2*

My friends were shocked. They laughed while describing scenes from   *3*
Night of the Living Dead and *The Shining.*

But their stories didn't frighten me—I feared something else. When I   *4*
was ten, my grandmother died, and my family drove to the funeral home to
view the body. As we entered the place, I noticed the funeral director standing
in the corner, looking like a too-eager-to-please salesman who'd made a deal
he didn't deserve. The guy's thin-lipped smile seemed unnatural—almost
glib. Like a ghoul in a business suit, he didn't seem to care that a stroke had
stopped my grandmother's beating heart midway through the doxology that
concluded the Sunday-evening church service. He didn't seem to care that
she and I would share no more cookies, no more coloring books, no more
Rook games, no more laughing, no more. I was ten, very sad, and he didn't
seem to care.

Freely using "I," the writer tells the story of his visit and interview.

Now a college student, I wanted to tour a different funeral home to   *5*
work through my earlier experience. While I no longer feared ghouls, I was
still nervous while driving to the Vander Ploeg Furniture Store/Funeral
Home. I remembered the thin-lipped smile.

I walked inside not knowing what to expect. Suddenly, a man   *6*
from behind a desk hopped out of his chair and said, "Hi, I'm Howard
Beernink."

I looked at the tall, smiling guy, paused a moment, and glanced back   *7*
at the door. His partner had stepped in front of the exit while scribbling on
tags that dangled from Lazy Boy rockers. I realized that this interview was
something I had to do . . . like getting a tetanus shot.

He describes the setting.

Howard led me into a room full of furniture where he found a soft,   *8*
purple couch. We sat down, and he described how the business started.

He relates the early history of the business.

In 1892, pioneers established the town of Sioux Center, Iowa. Winter   *9*
storms and disease pummeled the tiny community, and soon residents
needed someone to bury the dead. A funeral director wasn't available, but
a furniture maker was. The furniture maker was the only person with the
tools, hardwood, and knowledge to build coffins. As a result, the Vander
Ploeg Furniture Store/Funeral Home was born.

The writer summarizes, paraphrases, and quotes from the interview.

Today, starting a funeral home isn't that easy. For example, a funeral home requires the services of an embalmer, and an embalmer must be certified by the state. To get a certificate, the person must complete two years of college, one year of embalming school, and one year of apprentice work. After that, the individual must pass a state exam every year to retain certification. *10*

"But why a funeral home director?" I was baffled. Why would anyone embalm dead bodies for a living? *11*

"Because it's a family business." Howard smiled as if he expected my question. "Vander Ploegs and Beerninks have run this place for generations. Today it's difficult to start a funeral home because there are so many of them with long histories and good reputations." *12*

After he answered the rest of my questions, Howard asked if I wanted to see the embalming room. *13*

"Okay," I said, tentatively. *14*

He narrates what happened during the interview.

He led me through doors, down hallways, up a staircase, and into a well-lighted display room containing several coffins. Finally, we entered a small, cold room containing a row of cupboards, a large ceramic table, and a small machine that resembled a bottled-water cooler. *15*

"We like to keep the room cold when we're not using it," Howard said. *16*

"What is all this stuff?" I asked. *17*

Howard described why embalming is done and what it involves. The purpose of embalming is to extend the period for viewing the body, and the process includes replacing body fluids with embalming fluid. He opened a cupboard, pulled out a bottle of fluid and said, "Here . . . smell." *18*

"Smells like Pepto-Bismol," I replied. *19*

The writer shares surprises and what he learned.

After he embalms the body, Howard applies makeup so the face appears "more natural." He gets his cosmetics (common powders and tints) from the local Avon lady. *20*

"But sometimes we also have to use this," Howard said, pulling out another bottle. *21*

"Tissue builder?" I asked, squinting at the label. *22*

"It's like silicon implants," he answered. "We inject it into sunken cheeks, like the cheeks of cancer victims." *23*

When the body is ready for burial, the funeral director must show a price list to the family of the deceased. The Funeral Rule, adopted in 1984 by the Federal Trade Commission, requires that a price list be shown to the family before they see caskets, cement boxes, and vaults. The purpose of the Funeral Rule is to prevent unethical funeral directors from manipulating customers with comments like, "But that's a pauper's casket; you don't want to bury your mother in that. Bury her in this beauty over here." *24*

Unfortunately, only a third of the country's 22,000 funeral homes abide by the Funeral Rule.

"After showing customers where the caskets are, I step away so they can talk among themselves," said Howard. "It's unethical to bother the family at this difficult time." *25*

Before burying a casket, Howard and his partner place it in either a cement box or a vault. A cement box is a container that's neither sealed nor waterproofed, whereas a vault is both sealed and waterproofed. Howard explained, "Years ago, cemeteries began to sink and cave in on spots, so state authorities demanded containers. Containers make the cemetery look nicer." *26*

After the tour, I asked Howard, "How has this job affected your life?" *27*

He glanced at the ceiling, smiled, and said, "It's very fulfilling. My partner and I comfort people during a stressful time in their lives, and it strengthens our bond with them." *28*

As I drove back to the college, I thought again about Howard's comment, and about my childhood fear. Howard was right. He doesn't exploit people. Instead, he comforts them and helps them move on. And while I still fear the pain of saying good-bye to someone I love, I don't fear funeral directors anymore. They're just people who provide services that a community needs. ■ *29*

He ends the report with a strong quotation and personal reflection.

Reading for Better Writing

Working by yourself or with a group, answer these questions:

1. This report centers on the writer's own story, reflections, and needs. Discuss how these elements are woven into the report. Are they effective? Why or why not?

2. Examine the opening and the closing of the essay. Do they work well together? Do they effectively share a theme for the report? Explain.

3. Describe how the writer organizes the interview's results. Is the organization effective? Explain.

4. Look carefully at the writer's use of summary and paraphrase on the one hand and quotation on the other hand. Are the strategies effective? Explain.

Guidelines
Writing an Interview Report

1. **Choose a person to interview.** Review "People to Consider" on page 332 to find an interviewee. Also consider a community or campus leader.

2. **Plan the interview.** As soon as possible, take care of the details:
   - Determine your goal—what you want the interview to accomplish and what information and insights you want to gather.
   - Choose a sensible recording method (pen and paper, recorder) and a medium (face-to-face, telephone, e-mail).
   - Consider what you know about the topic and the interviewee. Then figure out what you must know to ask meaningful questions. If necessary, do some research on the interview subject.
   - Contact the interviewee and politely request an interview. Explain who you are, why you need the interview, and how you will use it. Schedule a time and place convenient for the interviewee. If you wish to record the interview, ask permission.
   - Gather and test tools and equipment: a notebook, pens, and perhaps recording equipment (tape, video, digital camera).

3. **Prepare questions.** Do the following to help you structure the interview:
   - Consider types of questions to ask—the five *W's* and *H* (*who, what, when, where, why,* and *how*).
   - Understand open and closed questions. Closed questions ask for simple, factual answers; open questions ask for detailed explanations.
     Closed: How many months did you spend in Vietnam?
     Open: Can you describe your most vivid memory of Vietnam?
   - Avoid slanted questions that pressure a person to give a specific answer.
     Slanted: Aren't you really angry that draft dodgers didn't do their duty?
     Neutral: How do you feel about those who avoided the draft?
   - Think about specific topics to cover and write questions for each one. Start with a simple question that establishes rapport and groundwork. Plan target questions—ones that you must ask.
   - Put questions on the left side of the page with room for notes on the right. Rehearse your questions, visualizing how the interview should go.

4. **Conduct the interview.** Arrive on time and be professional:
   - Introduce yourself, reminding the interviewee why you've come.
   - If you have permission to record the interview, set up equipment off to the side so that it doesn't interfere with the conversation. However, even if you're recording, take notes on key facts and quotations.

- Listen actively by including nods and eye contact. Pay attention to the interviewee's body language.
- Be flexible. If the person looks puzzled by a question, rephrase it or ask another. Ask one of these questions if an answer needs to be amplified:

  Clarifying: "Do you mean this or that?"

  Explanatory: "What do you mean by that?"

  Detailing: "What happened exactly? Can you describe that?"

  Analytical: "What were the causes? The outcomes?"

  Probing: "What do you think that meant?"

  Comparative: "Did that remind you of anything?"

  Contextual: "What else was going on then? Who else was involved?"

  Summarizing: "Overall, what was your response? What was the net effect?"
- Be tactful. If the person avoids a question, politely rephrase it. Don't react negatively or forcefully invade the interviewee's private territory.
- Listen "between the lines" for what the interviewee seems to want to say.
- Expect important points to come up late in the interview, and give the interviewee a chance to add any final thoughts.

5. **Follow up.** As soon as possible, review your notes and fill in the blanks. By phone or in writing, clarify points and thank the interviewee.

6. **Organize and draft the report.** Shape the opening to seize interest, the middle to sustain interest, and the closing to reward interest:
   - Analyze and interpret the interview results. Locate the heart or theme of your report, and then develop an outline supporting the theme.
   - Start with background, along with a point that grabs readers' interest.
   - Summarize and paraphrase material from the interview. (See pages 442–444.) Use quotations selectively to share the interviewee's character or stress a point.
   - If appropriate, weave your thoughts and reflections into the report.

7. **Get feedback and revise the report.** Ask someone to answer these questions: Does the report supply complete, satisfying insights? Is the organization effective, with an engaging opening and closing? Is the writing lively, fair, and respectful?

8. **Edit and proofread.** Review your report for precise word choice, smooth sentences, and correct grammar. In particular, make sure that quotations are integrated smoothly. (See page 487.)

9. **Prepare a final copy.** Submit a clean copy to your instructor (and perhaps the interviewee), but also look for ways to publish your report—as a webpage with digital photos and sound clips, or as a presentation for classmates.

Writing Checklist

Use these seven traits to check the quality of your writing; then revise as needed:

_____ The **ideas** share the heart of the interview—the interviewee's insights—through summary, paraphrase, and quotation.

_____ The **organization** centers on a theme and then creates, sustains, and rewards interest.

_____ The **voice** sounds genuine and interested. The interviewee's voice is understood and respected.

_____ The **words** are precise and understandable. Quotations reflect the interviewee's ideas and personality.

_____ The **sentences** are smooth, with quotations effectively integrated. Transitional words link sentences and sections.

_____ The **copy** has no errors in grammar, punctuation, usage, and spelling.

_____ The **design** is attractive, features the text, and uses photographs or graphics effectively.

Critical-Thinking and Writing Activities

As directed by your instructor, complete the following activities.

1. Generate a list of people who understand the challenges and opportunities related to the career you want to pursue. Then follow the guidelines for a personal interview on page 332 and write a report.

2. "The Dead Business" recounts the writer's exploration of a topic that caused him discomfort and sadness. What similar issues affect you? Would an interview help you work through the issue? Write your own reflective interview report.

3. Do you know someone who has led a fascinating life? Someone who on the surface seems to have led an ordinary life? Someone serving others in inspiring ways? Write that person's life story—an extended biography.

4. Is there a particular issue in your community that concerns you—a public debate, a college problem, a program being cut back? Who has insights into the issue? Who are people on different sides? Whose lives are affected? Who has the power to change things? Select one or more people to interview, and then write a report on the issue.

◄ VISUALLY SPEAKING ────────────

Award-winning CBS correspondent Ed Bradley is shown on page 331. What does the picture suggest about his understanding of journalism and the interview process?

LAB, EXPERIMENT, AND FIELD REPORTS

Audio

Video

Good science writing is rooted in good science—the careful study of phenomena through observation and experiment. Social scientists seek to understand human behavior and societies, whereas natural scientists investigate the physical world.

As a student, you may be asked to conduct scientific research in a range of courses. In labs and in the field, you may perform experiments, gather data, and interpret results, and then share your insights with fellow students and members of the scientific community. Such experiences provide valuable preparation for a variety of careers in the sciences.

When you complete a scientific study, you share your research story. Whether you are studying the nature of hydrochloric acid or the factors affecting fermentation rates in ethanol, your report shares what you did, why you did it, and what you learned. This chapter will help you put your experiments and field research into writing—and your good writing into science.

Web Link

Overview
Writing Lab, Experiment, and Field Reports

Writer's Goal

Your goal is to accurately record and thoughtfully interpret the results of a scientific study or experiment so clearly that others could repeat your experiment.

Keys for Success

Follow the scientific method. Science focuses on measured observations aimed at understanding. Experiments are set up to test hypotheses about why things happen. However, experiments don't prove hypotheses correct: Experimental results can merely "agree with" or disprove a hypothesis. Overall, the method moves from observation to explanation as you do the following:

1. Observe something interesting (often while looking for something else).
2. Check whether other scientists have explained the same observation.
3. Summarize your observations and turn that generalization into a testable hypothesis—a working theory explaining the phenomenon.
4. Design research to test the hypothesis, paying attention to variables and controls.
5. Based on the results of your experiment, accept, reject, or modify your hypothesis.
6. Repeat steps 3 through 5 until you understand the phenomenon. Then write up your research so that others can respond to your work.

Follow the standard format. To model scientific thinking, lab and field reports include an introduction establishing the problem, a methods section detailing procedures, a results section providing the data, and a discussion that interprets the data.

Distinctions to Consider

Whatever your assignment, you need to understand these distinctions:

- **Distinguish facts from possibilities.** Facts are the data you collect. Possibilities are your interpretations of the data. Don't confuse the two.
- **Distinguish experiments from studies.** Experiments test hypotheses by manipulating variables. Studies observe what's there—by counting, measuring, sampling, and so on. In this chapter, the report on fermentation is an experiment, whereas the field report on cockroaches is a study.

> **Next Step** Read the model reports and perform the activities that follow. As you read, examine how the reports follow the scientific method so you can use that method in your own reports.

Lab Report

Student Coby Williams wrote the basic lab report below to describe a chemical compound and inform readers about its nature.

Audio

Working with Hydrochloric Acid

Overview and Purpose *1*
The goal in writing this report is to educate others on the dangers of using and storing hydrochloric acid in the lab (HCl) and in the home (muriatic acid). In addition, this report will list appropriate ways to protect against burns when using HCl as well as ways to dispose of it properly.

Characteristics *2*
Hydrochloric acid (HCl), which is made from hydrogen gas and chlorine gas, is a clear, colorless to slightly yellow, fuming liquid with a sharp, irritating odor. HCl is a strong, highly corrosive acid, soluble in water and alcohol. Other characteristics include the following:

✔ The chemical reaction is: $H_2 + Cl_2 = 2HCl$.

✔ Its molecular weight is 36.45.

✔ Its boiling point is 85°C.

✔ Its specific gravity is 1.16.

Hydrochloric acid is commercially known as muriatic acid, a substance used to *3* manufacture dyes and plastics or to acidize (activate) petroleum wells. It is also used in the food processing of corn, syrup, and sodium glutamate, and is an ingredient in many household and industrial cleaners.

Safety Procedures
Hydrochloric acid is highly corrosive and can severely burn skin. Whenever HCl *4* is used, it must be handled according to the following precautions:

Storage *5*
• Keep hydrochloric acid in tightly capped bottles back from the edge of the shelf or table.
• Keep bottles away from metals. Contact will corrode metals and could release hydrogen gas, which is highly explosive.

Protection *6*
• Always wear safety glasses to protect your eyes.
• Wear latex gloves and old clothes when using concentrated HCl—not short-sleeved shirts, shorts, or sandals.
• Do not breathe the fumes, which can cause fainting.

The writer identifies the chemical compound and states its nature.

He organizes details in distinct categories.

• If acid spills on skin or splashes in someone's eyes, rinse the area with water for five minutes. Treat burns appropriately. In each case, get medical help immediately.

Usage   *7*

In the lab, hydrochloric acid is either diluted or titrated.

• When diluting, always pour the acid into the water. Doing the reverse can cause boiling, splashing, and burning.
• When titrating, carefully measure the HCl needed. Then react the HCl with a sample that has a base such as sodium hydroxide to get an accurate measurement of the base in the sample.

Disposal   *8*

• To dispose of HCl, neutralize it by mixing the acid with a sodium-hydroxide solution. Flush the neutralized solution down the drain.
• If you spill HCl, cover the spill with baking soda. After the fizzing stops, sweep up the soda and flush it down the drain. ■

> **Information is accurate and terms are precise.**

Reading for Better Writing

Working by yourself or with a group, answer these questions:

1. Who would be the main audience for this type of report? What evidence can you point to that supports your analysis?

2. List the strategies used to organize the report. Are these strategies effective? Explain.

3. How does this report demonstrate scientific thinking?

Experiment Report

In this report, student writer Andrea Pizano shares the results of a lab experiment she completed to explore how different factors affect fermentation.

The Effects of Temperature and Inhibitors on the Fermentation Process for Ethanol

Andrea Pizano
January 29, 2008

Introduction

The opening creates context and explains concepts.

Alcoholic liquids were made and used for centuries before scientists fully understood the process by which alcohol developed. An Egyptian papyrus dated 3500 B.C.E. mentions wine making, although production of alcoholic spirits like gin and brandy started only about a thousand years ago. From beverages such as beer and wine to fuel additives such as ethanol, alcohol has been used by people for recreation, religious rites, medical purposes, energy, and industry. Even today people are surprised to learn that it is ethanol—a by-product of yeast growth—that makes bread smell good. Studying the process by which alcohol is made can help make the process more efficient and successful.

Generally, alcohol can be made by fermenting different types of sugars, including sucrose, glucose, and fructose. Fermentation is a process that creates heat and changes the properties of a substance through a leavening or fermenting agent. For the fermentation process to succeed, certain enzymes must function as catalysts. These enzymes are present in yeast, the fermenting agent. While useful as catalysts, these enzymes are sensitive to temperature changes and inhibitors.

The writer describes the experiment and states her hypotheses.

In this experiment, ethanol—a specific type of alcohol—was synthesized from sucrose in the presence of yeast. The effects of extreme temperatures and of inhibitors on the rate of fermentation were tested quantitatively. The factors below were tested, and the outcomes below were anticipated. First, extremely high temperatures denature enzymes. Therefore, fermentation in the sample was expected to stop. Second, extremely cool temperatures reduce the kinetic energy of molecules. Therefore, the reaction rate in the sample was expected to drastically slow. Third, sodium fluoride can inhibit one of the enzymes needed in the fermentation process. Therefore, the presence of sodium fluoride was expected to effectively stop the reaction. Fourth, normal fermentation usually delivers a maximum of up to 15% ethanol. Through distillation, a 95% concentration of ethanol can be obtained. However, the presence of concentrated ethanol kills the yeast cells and also acts as a negative feedback

1

2

3

mechanism to the enzymes necessary for the fermentation process. Therefore, concentrated ethanol was expected to effectively stop the reaction.

Method

To test each of these hypotheses, the following procedure was followed   4
in this experiment:

She details the procedure using numbered steps and precise terms.

1. 200 mg of yeast were mixed with 1.25 mL of warm water in a 5-mL round-bottomed, long-necked flask. The mixture was shaken until the yeast was well distributed.

2. 9 mg of disodium hydrogen phosphate, 1.30 g sucrose, and 3.75 mL warm water were added to the flask. This mixture was left for 15 minutes—until the fermentation was proceeding at a vigorous rate.

3. The fermentation mixture was then divided equally into 5 reaction tubes.

   • To tube 1, 1.0 mL of water was added.

   • To tube 2, 1.0 mL of 95% ethanol was added.

   • To tube 3, 1.0 mL of 0.5 M sodium fluoride solution was added.

   • To each of tubes 4 and 5, 1.0 mL of water was added.

The writer uses passive voice to focus on the action and receiver— not the person doing the action.

4. The bubbles produced in a reaction tube filled with water were counted. A septum was first fit over the neck of each reaction tube. Then some polyethylene tubing was connected from the septum to the water-filled reaction tube. In this way, the reaction rate could be quantitatively measured by counting the number of gas bubbles that were released into the water each minute for 5 minutes.

5. Test tube 4 was heated for 5 minutes in boiling water. Then it was cooled to room temperature, and the fermentation rate was measured as explained in step 4.

6. Test tube 5 was put on ice for 5 minutes, and then the fermentation rate was measured as explained in step 4, while the reaction tube was kept on ice to maintain the low temperature.

7. After the experiment was completed, the solutions were washed down the drain as waste.

Results

The reaction rates of the 5 reaction conditions are plotted on Figure   5
1 below.

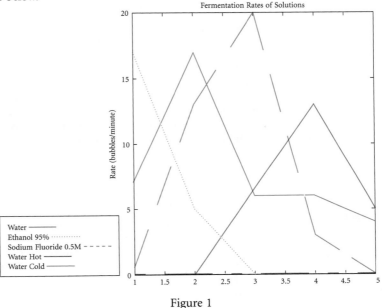

Figure 1

With the sample containing water at room temperature, the fermentation   6
rate peaked at 13 bubbles/minute at minute 4. The fermentation rate of
the sample with 95% ethanol started at 17 bubbles/minute, but within
2 minutes the rate quickly slowed to 5 bubbles/minute. By 3 minutes,
the rate was 0 bubbles/minute. In the sample with sodium fluoride, the
fermentation increased to 20 bubbles/minute after 3 minutes, but then
quickly reached 0 bubbles/minute after 5 minutes. In the sample that was
boiled, the fermentation rate was consistently 0 bubbles/minute. In the
sample placed on ice, the fermentation rate increased to 17 bubbles/minute
after 2 minutes, but then gradually slowed to 4 bubbles/minute after
5 minutes.

Discussion

Many different factors affect fermentation rates. For example, when   7
ethanol concentration is very high, yeast usually dies. So when 95% ethanol
is added to a fermenting sugar and yeast mixture, one would expect the
fermentation rate to decline sharply. The experiment's data support this
hypothesis. After 3 minutes, the fermentation had completely stopped.

In addition, sodium fluoride inhibits the action of a specific enzyme   8
in yeast, an enzyme needed for the fermentation process. Therefore, when

sodium fluoride is added to a fermenting mixture, one would expect a halted fermentation rate. However, the reaction rate initially increased to 20 bubbles/minute when sodium fluoride was added. This increase may have occurred because not all of the enzymes were inhibited at first. Perhaps the fermentation rate declined to 0 bubbles/minute only when the sodium fluoride became evenly distributed. This measurement occurred after 5 minutes.

She explores possible explanations for unexpected results and suggests further research.

Temperature is a third factor affecting fermentation. On the one hand, high temperatures denature many enzymes; therefore, when a fermenting mixture is placed in boiling water for 5 minutes, one would expect the fermentation rate to stop because no enzymes are present at that point to carry out the fermentation process. This hypothesis is supported by the data, as no fermentation occurred in the hot mixture. On the other hand, cold temperatures reduce the kinetic energy of molecules. As a result, the speed decreases, and the likelihood of the enzymes making contact with the substrate decreases exponentially in relation to the temperature. One would expect that the reaction rate would slow down drastically after the mixture has been cooled. This hypothesis is somewhat supported by the data. After an initial increase in the reaction rate to 17 bubbles/minute, the reaction rate slowed to 4 bubbles/minute after 5 minutes. A repeat of the experiment would be needed to clarify this result. Moreover, because the measuring method was somewhat unsophisticated (as indicated by the spikes in the line graph), perhaps a new experiment could be designed to measure fermentation-rate changes more sensitively.

9

The closing summarizes the experiment's value.

This experiment helped quantify the effects that various factors such as temperature, inhibitors, and high ethanol concentration have on fermentation rates. Even though the measuring apparatus was fairly basic, the experiment largely supported the hypotheses. Such data are helpful for determining methods of efficient and successful fermentation. Further research testing other factors and other inhibitors would add to this knowledge. ■

10

Reading for Better Writing

Working by yourself or with a group, answer these questions:

1. Where does the writer discuss the experiment's purpose and value? Are her efforts convincing?

2. In the "Method" section, which strategies does the writer use to ensure that the experiment can be repeated?

3. In the "Results" section, what is the relationship between the line graph and the paragraph?

4. In the "Discussion" section, the writer addresses results that did and did not support the hypotheses. Are her interpretations and conclusions sound?

Field Report

In the following workplace report, a team of writers investigates the causes and effects of cockroach infestation in an apartment complex. In the study, they use their findings to recommend solutions.

SOMMERVILLE DEVELOPMENT CORPORATION

Date: September 20, 2008

To: Bert Richardson, VP of Tenant Relations

From: Hue Nguyen, Cherryhill Complex Manager
Sandra Kao, Building Superintendent
Roger Primgarr, Tenant Relations
Juan Alexander, Tenant Representative

The subject line functions as a title.

Subject: Investigation of Cockroach Infestation at 5690 Cherryhill

The opening clarifies the study's purpose and goals.

During the month of July 2008, 26 tenants of the 400-unit building at 5690 Cherryhill informed the building superintendent that they had found cockroaches in their units. On August 8, the management-tenant committee authorized us to investigate these questions:
1. How extensive is the cockroach infestation?
2. How can the cockroach population best be controlled?

We monitored this problem from August 9 to September 8, 2008. This report contains a summary, an overview of our research methods, and findings, conclusions, and recommendations.

SUMMARY

The summary focuses on outcomes.

The 5690 Cherryhill building has a moderate infestation of German cockroaches. Only an integrated control program can manage this infestation. Pesticide fumigations address only the symptoms, not the causes. We recommend that Sommerville adopt a comprehensive program that includes (1) education, (2) cooperation, (3) habitat modification, (4) treatment, and (5) ongoing monitoring.

RESEARCH METHODS AND FINDINGS

Overview of Research

Research methods are described.

We researched the problem in the following ways:

1. Contacted the Department of Agriculture, the Ecology Action Center, and Ecological Agriculture Projects.
2. Consulted three exterminators.
3. Inspected the 5690 Cherryhill building, from ground to roof.
4. Placed pheromone traps in all units to monitor the cockroach population.

The Cockroach Population

Results are categorized logically.

Pheromone traps revealed German cockroaches, a common variety. Of the 400 units, 112 units (28 percent) showed roaches. Based on the numbers, the infestation is rated as moderate.

The German Cockroach

Research shows that these roaches thrive in apartment buildings.

- Populations thrive when food, water, shelter, and migration routes are available. They prefer dark, humid conditions near food sources.
- The cockroach seeks shelter in spaces that allow its back and underside to remain in constant contact with a solid surface.

Methods of Control

Findings are presented clearly and concisely.

Sources we consulted stressed the need for an integrated program of cockroach control involving sanitation, habitat modification, and non-toxic treatments that attack causes. Here are the facts:

- The German cockroach is immune to many chemicals.
- Roaches detect most pesticides before direct contact.
- Spot-spraying simply causes roaches to move to unsprayed units.
- Habitat modification through (1) eliminating food and water sources, (2) caulking cracks and crevices, (3) lowering humidity, and (4) increasing light and airflow makes life difficult for cockroaches.

CONCLUSIONS

Conclusions follow logically from the findings.

Based on our findings, we conclude the following:

1. A single method of treatment, especially chemical, will be ineffective.
2. A comprehensive program of sanitation, habitat modification, and nontoxic treatments will eliminate the German cockroach.

4

5

6

7

8

RECOMMENDATIONS

Recommend-ations apply what was learned in the study.

We recommend that Sommerville Development adopt an Integrated Program of Cockroach Prevention and Control for its 5690 Cherryhill building. Management would assign the following tasks to appropriate personnel: 9

Education: (1) Give tenants information on sanitation, prevention, and home remedies; and (2) hold tenant meetings to answer questions.   10

Habitat Modification: Revise the maintenance program and renovation schedule to give priority to the following: 11

- Apply residual insecticides before sealing cracks.
- Caulk cracks and crevices (baseboards, cupboards, pipes, sinks). Insert steel wool in large cavities (plumbing, electrical columns).
- Repair leaking pipes and faucets. Insulate pipes to eliminate condensation.
- Schedule weekly cleaning of common garbage areas.

Treatment: In addition to improving sanitation and prevention through education, attack the roach population through these methods: 12

- Use home remedies, traps, and hotels.
- Use borax or boric acid powder formulations as residual, relatively nontoxic pesticides.
- Use chemical controls on an emergency basis.
- Ensure safety by arranging for a Health Department representative to make unannounced visits to the building.

Monitoring: Monitor the cockroach population in the following ways: 13

1. Every six months, use traps to check on activity in all units.
2. Keep good records on the degree of occurrence, population density, and control methods used.

The closing stresses the value and benefits of the study.

We believe that this comprehensive program will solve the cockroach problem. We recommend that Sommerville adopt this program for 5690 Cherryhill and consider implementing it in all its buildings.   14

Reading for Better Writing

Working by yourself or with a group, answer these questions:

1. Examine the report's format and organizational strategies. How is this workplace report similar to and different from the other lab and experiment reports in this chapter?

2. Describe the tone of the report. What does this tone accomplish?

3. This report depends extensively on cause/effect thinking. Where do the writers use cause/effect thinking, and how effective is it?

Model

Guidelines
Writing Lab, Experiment, and Field Reports

1. **Review the lab manual and any handouts.** In most science courses, studies and experiments are assigned through textbooks, manuals, and handouts. Study those materials to understand what you must do and why. Read background information on the topic in textbooks and other sources.

2. **Use a field or lab notebook.** Accurate, complete recordkeeping is crucial to doing good scientific research. Use the notebook to plan research, record what you do, collect data, make drawings, and reflect on results. For each notebook entry, record the date and your goal.

3. **Plan and complete your study or experiment.** For a productive study, do the following:
   - Develop your key research questions. If you are conducting an experiment (not just a study), then state your hypotheses and design procedures for testing them.
   - Gather the proper tools, equipment, and materials required to conduct your study.
   - Carefully conduct your tests and perform your observations.
   - Take copious notes, being especially careful to record data accurately, clearly, and completely. If helpful, use a data-collection sheet.

4. **Relying on your notebook, draft the report.** Wrestle with your data. What do they mean? Were results expected or unexpected? Which factors could explain those results? What further research might be necessary? Once you have conducted this analysis, draft parts of the report in the sequence outlined below:
   - **Methods:** Start by explaining what you did to study the topic or test the hypothesis. Supply essential details, factors, and explanations. Be so clear that someone else could repeat the steps you took.
   - **Results:** Using two strategies, present the data you collected. First, share data in graphical forms—as tables, line charts, bar graphs, photographs, and so on. While the correct design of graphics and the proper presentation of statistical data are beyond the scope of this book, follow this basic rule: Make your graphic independent of the written text by giving it a descriptive title, clear headings and labels, units of measurement, and footnotes. Readers should be able to study your graphics and see the "story" of your study. Second, draw attention to the major observations and key trends available in the data. However, do not interpret the data in your results or give your reactions to them.

- **Discussion:** Interpret the results by relating the data to your original questions and hypotheses, offering conclusions, and supporting each conclusion with details. Essentially, answer the question, "What does it all mean?" Explain which hypotheses were supported, and why. Also explore unexpected results, and suggest possible explanations. Conclude by reemphasizing the value of what you learned.

- **Introduction:** Once you have mapped out the methods, results, and discussion, write an introduction that creates a framework for the report. Explain why you undertook the study, provide background information and any needed definitions, and raise your key questions and/or hypotheses.

- **Summary or abstract:** If required, write a summary of your study's purpose, methods, results, and conclusions. An abstract is a one-paragraph summary that allows readers to (1) get the report in a nutshell and (2) determine whether or not to read the study.

- **Title:** Develop a precise title that captures the "story" of your study. Worry less about the length of the title and more about its clarity.

- **Front and end matter:** If so required, add a title page, references page, and appendixes.

5. **Share and revise the draft.** Once you have roughed out the report, show it to a peer or a tutor in the writing center. Ask these questions:
   - Are the report's purpose, hypotheses, conclusions, and support clear and complete?
   - Is the traditional structure of a lab or field report followed effectively?
   - Is the voice objective, curious, and informed?

6. **Edit and proofread.** Carefully examine the style of your report, checking for these conventions of science writing:
   - **Measured use of passive voice:** Generally, use the passive voice only when needed—usually to keep the focus on the action and the receiver, not the actor. (See page 80.)
   - **Past and present tenses of verbs:** Generally, use the past tense in your report. However, present tense may be appropriate when discussing published work, established theories, and your conclusions.
   - **Objectivity:** Make sure that your writing is precise (not ambiguous), specific (not vague), and concise (not wordy).
   - **Mechanics:** Follow the conventions in the discipline with respect to capitalization, abbreviations, numbers, and symbols.

7. **Prepare and share your report.** Following the format and documentation conventions of the discipline, submit a polished report to your instructor. Also find ways to share your study with the scientific community.

Writing Checklist

Use these seven traits to check your report; then revise as needed:

_____ The **ideas** provide scientifically sound conclusions about accurate data.

_____ The **organization** effectively follows the standard structure: introduction, methods, results, and discussion.

_____ The **voice** demonstrates interest and curiosity, yet remains objective.

_____ The **words** are used accurately. The language of the specific discipline is used precisely.

_____ The **sentences** flow smoothly from point to point. Passive voice constructions are used only when necessary.

_____ The **copy** has no errors in grammar, punctuation, usage, and spelling.

_____ The **design's** use of headings, white space, and graphics feature or clarify the message.

Critical-Thinking and Writing Activities

As directed by your instructor, complete the following activities.

1. The report on hydrochloric acid describes a chemical compound. In your discipline, what are the main objects of study? Write a report that introduces that topic to students new to the discipline.

2. The lab experiment report on fermentation describes careful research that should be repeatable. With appropriate supervision, repeat the lab experiment and compare your results with the student writer's results.

3. The field report objectively researches the problem of cockroach infestation. Which campus or community problems could you research in a similar manner? Develop a research plan, get approval from your instructor, and complete your study.

4. Which issues, problems, or puzzles exist in your area of study? With help from an instructor in your major, write a proposal to conduct a lab experiment or field research.

◀ VISUALLY SPEAKING

Study the graph on page 345 and explain how it clarifies the report's message. Then review the field report on pages 347–349 and suggest visual elements (e.g., graphs, photographs) that might help communicate its message.

SPECIAL FORMS OF WRITING

Chapters 23 through 27 focus on special writing occasions—or rhetorical situations. These chapters explain how to develop a variety of writing forms: a literary analysis, an essay test, a resumé, a webpage, and an oral presentation.

As you read the model pieces, note each writer's strategies for organizing and presenting her or his message. Analyze how and why those strategies are (or are not) effective for the writer's audience, purpose, and subject. Then consider how you might address a similar writing situation.

CONTENTS
■ Special Forms of Writing

WRITING ABOUT LITERATURE AND THE ARTS

23

Audio

Video

In one way or another, people respond to the arts. Audiences may applaud a dancer, gripe about a film or play, or give a standing ovation to a musician. Often writers are moved to respond even more precisely, by analyzing one actor's portrayal while criticizing another's performance, or by praising a film's script but questioning camera angles or lighting.

Because the arts are complex, writing about them requires careful listening, reading, and/or viewing. For example, you might analyze a film or play in terms of the acting, the casting, or the directing. Similarly, you might analyze a poem or story by looking at its form, its diction, or the insights it provides. In other words, to write effectively about the arts, you need a good ear, a keen eye, and an open mind.

This chapter includes model essays, guidelines, literary terms, and assignments to help you evaluate a variety of art forms.

Web Link

Overview
Writing About Literature and the Arts

Writer's Goal

Your goal is to experience an artwork or a performance, understand its elements, and then write an essay analyzing and perhaps evaluating the work.

Keys for Success

Know your subject. Read the poem, view the film or painting, or listen to the concert more than once, if possible. Be sure you understand what the artist/ writer is trying to do, noting specific choices and their effects.

Analyze the work's key elements. In works of fiction, for example, consider issues of point of view, plot, character, setting, and theme. (See the list of literary terms on pages 368–370 for other elements to think about.)

Compare it. If this work of art reminds you of some other piece, review the second work and note similarities and differences.

Form your own insights and opinions. If others have written about this work of art, do not read what they wrote until you have experienced the work yourself and developed your own insights and opinions.

Topics to Consider

Choose a piece of literature, a film, a concert, or a play that has meaning for you or has aroused your curiosity.

- **Poems:** You could choose one of thousands of great poems from literature or poetry anthologies. Poems from literary magazines, college classmates, relatives, or a website may also be analyzed if they merit your time and your readers' attention.
- **Short stories:** Like poems, short stories from literature anthologies, literary or popular magazines, or websites are easy to access.
- **Films:** While you could write about a current big-name film, consider analyzing a classic film or a film never shown in your area theaters. Choosing a film on video will enable you to replay the entire film or just specific scenes.
- **Concerts:** You could write about a major concert in your city or on campus, but consider analyzing the music played by lesser-known artists performing in student recitals or backstreet theaters.
- **Plays:** Any play may invite an analysis (big-name touring shows, for instance), but consider writing about campus productions or plays staged in your community. You might also analyze a play based on your reading of it.

> **Next Step** Read the model essays and perform the activities that follow, noting strategies that help you understand an artwork and write about it.

Writing About a Short Story

In the essay below, student writer Anya Terekhina analyzes the characters and ideas in Flannery O'Connor's short story "Good Country People."

"Good Country People":
Broken Body, Broken Soul

The writer provides background for understanding the characters in O'Connor's stories.

Flannery O'Connor's short stories are filled with characters who are bizarre, freakish, devious, and sometimes even murderous. Every short story, according to O'Connor in *Mystery and Manners: Occasional Prose*, should be "long in depth" and meaning (94). To achieve this, O'Connor develops characters with heavily symbolic attributes and flaws, and "it is clearly evident that boldly outlined inner compulsions are reinforced dramatically by a mutilated exterior self" (Muller 22). In "Good Country People," Joy-Hulga is a typical O'Connor character—grotesque yet real. Her realness comes from her many flaws and, ironically, her flaws are a self-constructed set of illusions. Throughout the story, O'Connor carefully links Joy-Hulga's physical impairments with deeper handicaps of the soul; then, at the closing, she strips Hulga of these physical flaws while helping her realize that her corresponding beliefs are flawed as well.

O'Connor first introduces her character as Joy Hopewell, a name of optimism. However, we soon understand that her chosen name, Hulga, is more fitting. The new name distresses her mother, Mrs. Hopewell, who is "certain that she [Joy] had thought and thought until she had hit upon the ugliest name in any language" (O'Connor 1943). Hulga has connotations of "hull = hulk = huge = ugly" (Grimshaw 51), and all of these are accurate descriptions of her. Far from having a sweet temperament, Hulga stomps and sulks around the farm, "constant outrage . . . [purging] every expression from her face" (1942).

Although Hulga's demeanor could be blamed on her physical impairments, she devises her own rationalizations for behaving as she does. Ironically, each rationale is symbolized by one of her physical disabilities, yet she doesn't recognize the handicaps for what they imply.

The writer begins listing the protagonist's physical disabilities and explains how each one symbolizes a deeper problem in her soul.

One of Hulga's many ailments is her weak heart, which will likely limit her life span. Hulga blames this affliction for keeping her on the Hopewell farm, making it plain that "if it had not been for this condition, she would be far from these red hills and good country people" (1944). Having a Ph.D. in philosophy, Hulga claims to want work as a university professor, lecturing to people at her intellectual level. Hulga's weak heart functions as more than a dream-crusher; it "symbolizes her emotional detachment—and inability to love anyone or anything" (Oliver 233). She exhibits no compassion or love for anything, not even "dogs or cats or birds or flowers or nature or nice young men" (1944–45).

1

2

3

4

Hulga also suffers from poor vision. Without her eyeglasses, she is helpless. Strangely though, her icy blue eyes have a "look of someone who has achieved blindness by an act of will and means to keep it" (1942). Her self-induced blindness symbolizes her blindness to reality. She is indeed intelligent, but she has packed her brain full of ideas and thoughts that only obscure common sense, let alone truth. Because of Hulga's extensive education and her focus on philosophical reasoning, she considers herself superior to everyone around her. For example, she yells at her mother, "Woman! . . . Do you ever look inside and see what you are not? God!" (1944). [5]

Hulga's last and most noticeable physical impairment is her missing leg, which was "literally blasted off" (1944) in a hunting accident when she was ten years old. In *Mystery and Manners*, O'Connor stresses that the wooden leg operates interdependently at a literal and a symbolic level, which means "the wooden leg continues to accumulate meaning" throughout the story (99). Hulga's biggest physical handicap symbolizes her deepest affliction: her belief in nothing. [6]

She points out the root of the protagonist's problems: her lack of belief in anything.

Hulga's philosophical studies did focus on the study of nothing, particularly on the arguments of the French philosopher Nicolas Malebranche. O'Connor describes Hulga as believing "in nothing but her own belief in nothing" (*Mystery* 99). Over time, Hulga's belief in nothing develops into more than just academic study. Her nihilism becomes her religion—suitable for a woman who considers herself superior and despises platitudes. As she explains to Manley Pointer, "We are all damned . . . but some of us have taken off our blindfolds and see that there's nothing to see. It's a kind of salvation" (1952). Hulga's religious terms suggest that she uses faith in nothingness to find the meaning that she can't find elsewhere. [7]

Her nihilism becomes her religion— suitable for a woman who considers herself superior and despises platitudes.

Hulga's nihilism is symbolized by her wooden leg, which is the only thing she tends to with care: "She took care of it as someone else would his soul, in private and almost with her own eyes turned away" (1953). This limb is wooden and corresponds to Hulga's wooden soul. Whereas she believes she worships Nothing, what she actually worships is an "artificial leg and an artificial belief" (Oliver 235). [8]

The writer demonstrates how the protagonist's flaws lead her to make distorted judgments.

Not realizing that her false leg and false religion cripple her both physically and spiritually, Hulga considers seducing Manley Pointer, the Bible salesman. She delightfully imagines that she will have to help him deal with his subsequent remorse, and then she will instruct him into a "deeper understanding of life" (1950). Of course, her intellectual blindness keeps [9] her from realizing that her superiority is only an illusion. Instead, she views Manley as "a vulnerable innocent, a naïve Fundamentalist, and she wishes to seduce him to prove that her sophisticated textbook nihilism is superior to his simpleminded faith" (Di Renzo 76).

In classic O'Connor fashion, the characters and situation reverse dramatically at the end of the story. Hulga and Manley are alone in a hayloft and begin embracing. At first, Hulga is pleased with her reaction to kissing as it aligns well with Malebranche's teachings: "it was an unexceptional experience and all a matter of the mind's control" (1951). Soon, however, she realizes that she is enjoying the first human connection of her life. At this point, the *innocent* Bible salesman has already stripped Hulga of her first physical impairment: her weak heart.

She revisits the protagonist's physical disabilities, showing how the Bible salesman exploits each one.

Hulga hardly notices when Manley takes advantage of her next impairment: "when her glasses got in his way, he took them off of her and slipped them into his pocket" (1952). With her heart opened and her intellectual perspective fuzzy, Hulga swiftly descends into what she despises—platitudes. Hulga and Manley exchange clichéd mumblings of love, and this leads Manley to ask if he can remove her artificial leg. After brief hesitation, Hulga agrees because she feels he has touched and understood a central truth inside her. She considers it a complete surrender, "like losing her own life and finding it again, miraculously, in his" (1953).

> *With her heart opened and her intellectual perspective fuzzy, Hulga swiftly descends into what she despises— platitudes.*

As soon as the artificial leg is off, Manley whips out one of his Bibles, which is hollow. Inside are whiskey, obscene playing cards, and contraceptives. In only moments, Hulga loses control: As each of her physical handicaps is exploited, pieces of her world view crumble, leaving her confused and weak.

The writer reflects on the change in both characters.

In an ironic reversal, Hulga becomes the naïf and Manley becomes the cynic. Hulga pleads in disbelief, "Aren't you . . . just good country people?" (1954). She knows that she has reverted to her mother's platitudes: "If the language is more sophisticated than any at Mrs. Hopewell's command, it is no less trite, and the smug self-deception underlying it . . . is, if anything, greater" (Asals 105). Manley assumes a startling, haughty air, exclaiming, "'I hope you don't think . . . that I believe in that crap! I may sell Bibles but I know which end is up and I wasn't born yesterday and I know where I'm going!'" (1954). Although they exchange roles, both characters use clichés to express their immature, yet authentic, worldviews.

10

11

12

13

Manley runs off with Hulga's wooden leg, leaving her vulnerable and dependent, two things she previously despised. But "Hulga's artificial self—her mental fantasy of her own perfection—has gone out the door with her artificial limb. She is stuck in the hayloft with her actual self, her body, her physical and emotional incompleteness" (Di Renzo 79). 14

In one brief morning of delusional seduction, Hulga learns more about herself and her world than she learned in all her years of university. Forced to acknowledge her physical, emotional, and spiritual disabilities, Hulga begins to realize what she is not—neither a wise intellectual for whom there is *hope*, nor "good country people" who merely *hope well*. ■ 15

> The closing explains how Hulga finally acknowledges the truth about herself.

Note: The Works Cited page is not shown. For sample pages, see MLA (pages 532–533) and APA (page 564).

Reading for Better Writing

Working by yourself or with a group, answer these questions:

1. In her opening paragraph, Terekhina cites Flannery O'Connor's view that every short story should be "long in depth" and meaning. Does Terekhina adequately explore that depth and meaning? Why?

2. In her second paragraph, Terekhina analyzes Hulga Hopewell's first name; in the last paragraph, she comments on the last name. Does Terekhina's attention to names help you understand Hulga's character and the story's themes? How?

3. A writer's thesis is a type of "contract" that he or she makes with readers, spelling out what the essay will do. Review Terekhina's thesis (last sentence, first paragraph) and assess how effectively she fulfills that contract. Cite supporting details.

4. Flannery O'Connor has received strong acclaim for her clearly developed, complex characters. Does Terekhina adequately explore that complexity? Explain.

5. Many praise O'Connor for the challenging philosophical or ethical questions raised in her fiction. What questions does Terekhina identify in "Good Country People," and does she effectively discuss them?

6. What does Terekhina say about the story's plot, symbols, and diction? Does she effectively analyze these elements? Why?

Audio

Writing About a Poem

In the essay on the following two pages, student writer Sherry Van Egdom analyzes the form and meaning of the poem below, "Let Evening Come," by American poet Jane Kenyon. Born in 1947 and raised on a farm near Ann Arbor, Michigan, Kenyon settled in New Hampshire at Eagle Pond Farm after she married fellow poet Donald Hall. During her life, Kenyon struggled with her faith, with depression, and with cancer. At the time of her death in 1995 from leukemia, she was the poet laureate of New Hampshire.

Before you read the student writer's analysis, read the poem aloud to enjoy its sounds, rhythm, images, diction, and comparisons. Then read the piece again to grasp more fully how the poem is structured, what it expresses, and how its ideas might relate to your life. Finally, read Van Egdom's analysis and answer the questions that follow it.

Let Evening Come

Let the light of late afternoon
Shine through chinks in the barn, moving
up the bales as the sun moves down.

Let the crickets take up chafing
as a woman takes up her needles
and her yarn. Let evening come.

Let dew collect on the hoe abandoned
in long grass. Let the stars appear
and the moon disclose her silver horn.

Let the fox go back to its sandy den.
Let the wind die down. Let the shed
go black inside. Let evening come.

To the bottle in the ditch, to the scoop
in the oats, to air in the lung
let evening come.

Let it come, as it will, and don't
be afraid. God does not leave us
comfortless, so let evening come.

"Let Evening Come":
An Invitation to the Inevitable

by Sherry Van Egdom

The writer introduces the poet and her poetry.

Narrowing her focus to the specific poem, the writer states her thesis.

She begins her analysis by explaining the stanza structure and progression.

The writer shows attention to the poem's fine details and to secondary sources on the poem.

She advances her reading of the poem by exploring images, comparisons, and symbols: the poem's "imaginative logic."

The work of American poet Jane Kenyon is influenced primarily by the circumstances and experiences of her own life. She writes carefully crafted, deceptively simple poems that connect both to her own life and to the lives of her readers. Growing out of her rural roots and her struggles with illness, Kenyon's poetry speaks in a still voice of the ordinary things in life in order to wrestle with issues of faith and mortality (Timmerman 163). One of these poems is "Let Evening Come." In this poem, the poet takes the reader on a journey into the night, but she points to hope in the face of that darkness.

That movement toward darkness is captured in the stanza form and in the progression of stanzas. Each three-line stanza offers a self-contained moment in the progress of transition from day to night. The first stanza positions the reader in a simple farm setting. Late afternoon fades into evening without the rumble of highways or the gleam of city lights to distract one's senses from nature, the peace emphasized by the alliteration of "l" in "Let the light of late afternoon." As the sun sinks lower on the horizon, light seeps through cracks in the barn wall, moving up the bales of hay. In the second stanza, the crickets get busy with their nighttime noises. Next, a forgotten farm hoe becomes covered with dew drops, and the silvery stars and moon appear in the sky. In the fourth stanza, complete blackness arrives as a fox returns to its empty den and the silent wind rests at close of day. The alliteration of "d" in "den" and "die down" gives a sinking, settling feeling (Timmerman 176). In the fifth stanza, a bottle and scoop keep still, untouched in their respective places, while sleep comes upon the human body. In the final stanza, Kenyon encourages readers to meet this emerging world of darkness without fear.

Within this stanza progression, the journey into the night is intensified by strong images, figures of speech, and symbols. The natural rhythm of work and rest on the farm is symbolized by the light that rises and falls in the first stanza (Timmerman 175). The simile comparing the crickets taking up their song to a woman picking up her knitting suggests a homespun energy and conviction. The moon revealing her "silver horn" implies that the moon does not instantly appear with brightness and beauty but rather reveals her majesty slowly as the night comes on. The den, the wind, and the shed in stanza four stress a kind of internal, hidden darkness. Then stanza five focuses on connected objects: the thoughtlessly discarded bottle resting in the ditch, oats and the scoop for feeding, human lungs and the air that fills them. Kenyon mentions the air in the lung *after* the bottle, ditch, scoop, and oats in order to picture humanity taking its position among the established natural rhythm of the farm (Harris 31).

The writer compares possible interpretations of a central, repeated statement in the poem.

The refrain, "let evening come," is a powerful part of the poem's   4
journey toward darkness, though critics interpret the line differently. Judith Harris suggests that it symbolizes an acceptance of the inevitable: Darkness will envelop the world, and night will surely come, just as mortality will certainly take its toll in time. This acceptance, in turn, acts as a release from the confinement of one's pain and trials in life. Rather than wrestle with something that cannot be beaten or worry about things that must be left undone, Kenyon advises herself and her readers to let go (31). Night intrudes upon the work and events of the day, perhaps leaving them undone just as death might cut a life short and leave it seemingly unfinished.

By contrast, John Timmerman argues that "let" is used twelve times in   5
a supplicatory, prayer-like manner (176). The final two lines, in turn, act as a benediction upon the supplications. The comfort of God is as inevitable as the evening, so cling to faith and hope and let evening come. Although the Comforter is mentioned only in the last two lines, that statement of faith encourages readers to find a spiritual comfort in spite of the coming of the night.

In her conclusion, the writer offers the poet's explanation of the poem's origin and then expands on the thesis.

When asked how she came to write "Let Evening Come," Jane Kenyon   6
replied that it was a redemptive poem given to her by the Holy Ghost. When there could be *nothing*—a great darkness and despair, there is a great *mystery* of love, kindness, and beauty (Moyers 238). In the poem's calm journey into the night, Kenyon confronts darkness and suffering with a certain enduring beauty and hope (Timmerman 161). Death will come, but there remains divine comfort. "Let Evening Come" encourages readers to release their grip on the temporary and pay attention to the Comforter who reveals Himself both day *and* night. ■

Note: The Works Cited page is not shown. For sample pages, see MLA (pages 532–533) and APA (page 564).

Reading for Better Writing

Working by yourself or with a group, answer these questions:

1. Review the opening and closing paragraphs of the essay. How do they create a framework for the writer's analysis of the poem?

2. On which elements of the poem does the writer focus? Does this approach make sense for her analysis? Explain.

3. In her essay, the writer refers to the poet's life and to ideas from secondary sources. Do these references work well with her analysis? Why or why not?

4. Read the essay "Four Ways to Talk About Literature" on pages 220–221. Which approach does the student writer use to analyze Kenyon's poem? Does this approach make sense? How might another approach interpret the poem differently?

Writing About a Performance

In the essay below, student writer Annie Moore reviews the performance of a rock music group, Sigur Ros. She praises several qualities of their experimental music.

Sigur Ros, *Agaetis Byrjun*

The writer states the accomplishments of the group.

Sigur Ros, an experimental noise quartet hailing from Reykjavik, is the biggest thing since Bjork. Those Icelandic folk must know something we don't. Never before has a rock/pop album captured the beauty and quiet strength that pervades *Agaetis Byrjun,* the band's sophomore release.

1

She describes the quality of their sound.

The album flows seamlessly as a single stream of consciousness. Jonsi Birgisson's ethereal vocals are divine as his falsetto effortlessly rides the sweeping melodies. Tension builds from the delicate intros, gathers fury, and then explodes in a burst of percussion and crashing guitars hammered by violin bow. The storm ends, a quiet lull follows, and then the cycle begins again. Added pianos, muted horns, and the strings of the Icelandic Symphony Orchestra give the songs of *Agaetis Byrjun* the essence of a twentieth-century classic.

2

She describes their effect on the audience.

Although the lyrics are impossibly cryptic, written entirely in Icelandic, they are sung with an emotion and urgency so intense they are not merely perceived, but *felt.* The full force of the music resonates deep in the souls of listeners. It is exactly this "inarticulate speech of the heart," of which Van Morrison once spoke, that gives *Agaetis Byrjun* its heart-wrenching sense of sincerity.

3

With impeccable musicianship and a skillful mix of the traditional and innovative, Sigur Ros will change the world of music. Or perhaps they already have. ■

4

Reading for Better Writing

Working by yourself or with a group, answer these questions:

1. Which characteristics of the vocalists does the writer cite? Why?

2. Which other instrumental sounds does she cite?

3. Why does she tell us of the effect on the audience?

Writing About a Film

In the film review below, David Schaap analyzes Stephen Spielberg's film *War of the Worlds* by asking key questions about the filmmaker's strategies and their effects.

Terror on the Silver Screen: Who Are the Aliens?

The writer introduces the filmmaker and film; he then describes a pivotal scene.

In Steven Spielberg's 2005 movie, *War of the Worlds,* Ray Ferrier and his two children flee their New Jersey home in a stolen minivan. To escape outer-space aliens who are destroying houses and killing people from their enormous three-legged machines, this father, son, and daughter lurch through scene after scene of 9/11-type destruction. At one point, the daughter surveys the violence, panics, and shrieks, "Is it the terrorists?"

He cites an important quotation and explores its significance.

The girl's question nudges the audience to ask the same question, "Are the aliens terrorists?" That would make sense. Often filmmakers will play off members of the audience's real-life emotions to give them a sensational imaginary experience as well as a glimpse at their real world. In this case, by suggesting that the aliens' imaginary attack resembles Al Qaeda's 9/11 attack, Spielberg could be doing two things: (1) heightening fear of the alien characters and (2) suggesting a political theme.

Two questions focus the writer's analysis.

But is Spielberg's *War of the Worlds* this type of film? First, does the film inspire fear by suggesting that the aliens' attack is similar to Al Qaeda's attack? And second, does the film's alien attack represent a future terrorist invasion of the United States?

He answers the first question and offers supporting details.

The answer to the first question is *yes.* Spielberg inspires fear of his outer-space aliens by emphasizing their resemblance to 9/11 terrorists. In a series of scenes, he shows a crashed airliner like the ones used on 9/11, a wall covered with posters of missing loved ones, and mobs of ash- and dust-covered characters like those escaping the collapsing World Trade Center. Because the film takes place in the United States, viewers subconsciously further fear the aliens' violence.

He answers the second question by explaining the film's focus.

However, do the aliens invading the United States represent Al Qaeda fighters? Not really. The aliens are Spielberg's universal stand-in for whatever strikes fear into viewers' hearts. This film does not examine the political, psychological, or cultural roots of any problem. The film's focus is on the *effect* of violence, not the *identity* of the perpetrators. *War of the Worlds* is about *terror,* not *terrorists.* ■

Model

Guidelines
Writing About Literature and the Arts

1. **Select a topic.** Choose an art form or a type of performance with which you are familiar or you are willing to learn about. For ideas, review "Topics to Consider" on page 356.

2. **Understand the work.** Experience it thoughtfully (two or three times, if possible), looking carefully at its content, form, and overall effect.
    -   For plays and films, examine the plot, setting, characters, dialogue, lighting, costumes, sound effects, music, acting, and directing.
    -   For novels and short stories, focus on point of view, plot, setting, characters, style, diction, and theme. (See pages 368–370.)
    -   For poems, examine diction, simile, tone, sound, figures of speech, symbolism, irony, form, and theme. (See page 371.)
    -   For music, focus on harmonic and rhythmic qualities, dynamics, melodic lines, lyrics, and interpretation.

3. **Gather information.** Take notes on what you experience, using the list above to guide your thoughts. Seek to understand the whole work before you analyze the parts. Consider freewriting briefly on one or more aspects of the work to explore your response and to dig more deeply into the work. If you are analyzing a written text, annotate it.

4. **Organize your thoughts.** Review the notes that you took as you analyzed the work. What key insight about the work has your analysis led you to see? Make that insight or judgment your thesis, and then organize supporting points logically in a scratch or full outline.

5. **Write the first draft.**
    Opening: Use ideas like the following to gain your readers' attention, identify your topic, narrow the focus, and state your thesis:
    -   Summarize your subject briefly. Include the title, the author, and the literary form or performance.

        Example: In her poem **"Let Evening Come,"** Jane Kenyon points to hope in the face of death.
    -   Start with a quotation from the film, story, or poem and then comment on its importance.
    -   Explain the artist's purpose and how well she or he achieves it.
    -   Open with a general statement about the artist's style or aesthetic process. (See page 362.)

        Example: The work of American poet Jane Kenyon is influenced primarily by the circumstances and experiences of her own life.

- Begin with a general statement about the plot or performance. (See page 365.)

    Example: In Stephen Spielberg's movie *War of the Worlds*, Ray Ferrier and his two children flee from their New Jersey home in a stolen minivan.

- Assert your thesis. State the key insight about the work that your analysis has revealed—the insight your essay will seek to support.

Middle: Develop or support your focus by following this pattern:

- State the main points, relating them clearly to the focus of your essay.
- Support each main point with specific details or direct quotations.
- Explain how these details prove your point.

Conclusion: Tie key points together to focus your analysis. Assert your thesis or evaluation in a fresh way, leaving readers with a sense of the larger significance of your analysis.

6. **Review and revise.** Once you have a first draft written, relax for a time, and then reread your essay for its logic and completeness. Check whether you have supported each of your observations with evidence from the poem, story, film, or other artwork. Test your analysis with questions like these:

   - Did you fully understand the performance, the reasons for the acting or costuming, the lyrics of the song, or whatever is central to the work?
   - Did you explore the ironies, if present, or any important images, vocal nuances, dramatic action, shift in setting, or symbolism?
   - Did you bring your analysis to a clear conclusion?

7. **Get feedback.** Ask a knowledgeable classmate, friend, or tutor to read your essay, looking for the following:

   - _____ An analytical thesis statement supported by evidence
   - _____ Key insights into both content or meaning on the one hand and form or style on the other hand
   - _____ Clear transitions between sentences and paragraphs
   - _____ A tone that is respectful and honest

8. **Edit and proofread.** Once you have revised your essay, clarified your transitions, and checked your evidence, polish the phrasing and diction. Make certain your paper is free of awkward syntax or errors in usage, punctuation, spelling, or grammar. In particular, check that you have used the special terms of the literary genre or art form clearly and accurately.

9. **Publish your essay.**
   - Share your essay with friends and family.
   - Publish it in a journal or on a website.
   - Place a copy in your personal or professional portfolio.

Literary Terms

Your analysis of novels, poems, plays, and films will be deeper and more sophisticated if you understand the most common literary terms.

Allusion is a reference to a person, a place, or an event in history or literature.

Analogy is a comparison of two or more similar objects, suggesting that if they are alike in certain respects, they will probably be alike in other ways, too.

Anecdote is a short summary of an interesting or humorous, often biographical incident or event.

Antagonist is the person or thing actively working against the protagonist, or hero, of the work.

Climax is the turning point, an intense moment characterized by a key event.

Conflict is the problem or struggle in a story that triggers the action. There are five basic types of conflict:

Person versus person: One character in a story is in conflict with one or more of the other characters.

Person versus society: A character is in conflict with some element of society: the school, the law, the accepted way of doing things, and so on.

Person versus self: A character faces conflicting inner choices.

Person versus nature: A character is in conflict with some natural happening: a snowstorm, an avalanche, the bitter cold, or any other element of nature.

Person versus fate: A character must battle what seems to be an uncontrollable problem. Whenever the conflict is a strange or unbelievable coincidence, the conflict can be attributed to fate.

Denouement is the outcome of a play or story. See **Resolution**.

Diction is an author's choice of words based on their correctness or effectiveness.

Archaic words are old-fashioned and no longer sound natural when used, such as "I believe thee not" for "I don't believe you."

Colloquialism is an expression that is usually accepted in informal situations and certain locations, as in "He really grinds my beans."

Heightened language uses vocabulary and sentence constructions that produce a stylized effect unlike that of standard speech or writing, as in much poetry and poetic prose.

Profanity is language that shows disrespect for someone or something regarded as holy or sacred.

Slang is the everyday language used by group members amongst themselves.

Trite expressions lack depth or originality, or are overworked or not worth mentioning in the first place.

Vulgarity is language that is generally considered common, crude, gross, and, at times, offensive. It is sometimes used in fiction, plays, and films to add realism.

Exposition is the introductory section of a story or play. Typically, the setting, main characters, and themes are introduced, and the action is initiated.

Falling action is the action of a play or story that follows the climax and shows the characters dealing with the climactic event or decision.

Figure of speech is a literary device used to create a special effect or to describe something in a fresh way. The most common types are *antithesis, hyperbole, metaphor, metonymy, personification, simile,* and *understatement.*

Antithesis is an opposition, or contrast, of ideas.
> "It was the best of times, it was the worst of times, it was the age of wisdom, it was the age of foolishness . . ."
> — Charles Dickens, *A Tale of Two Cities*

Hyperbole (hi-pur′ ba-lee) is an extreme exaggeration or overstatement.
> "I have seen this river so wide it had only one bank."
> —Mark Twain, *Life on the Mississippi*

Metaphor is a comparison of two unlike things in which no word of comparison (*as* or *like*) is used: "Life is a banquet."

Metonymy (ma-ton′a-mee) is the substituting of one term for another that is closely related to it, but not a literal restatement.
> "Friends, Romans, countrymen, lend me your ears." (The request is for the *attention* of those assembled, not literally their *ears*.)

Personification is a device in which the author speaks of or describes an animal, object, or idea as if it were a person: "The rock stubbornly refused to move."

Simile is a comparison of two unlike things in which *like* or *as* is used.
> "She stood in front of the altar, shaking like a freshly caught trout."
> —Maya Angelou, *I Know Why the Caged Bird Sings*

Understatement is stating an idea with restraint, often for humorous effect. Mark Twain described Aunt Polly as being "prejudiced against snakes." (Because she hated snakes, this way of saying so is *understatement.*)

Genre refers to a category or type of literature based on its style, form, and content. The mystery novel is a literary *genre.*

Imagery refers to words or phrases that a writer uses to appeal to the reader's senses.
> "The sky was dark and gloomy, the air was damp and raw, the streets were wet and sloppy."
> —Charles Dickens, *The Pickwick Papers*

Irony is a deliberate discrepancy in meaning or in the way something is understood. There are three kinds of irony:

Dramatic irony, in which the reader or the audience sees a character's mistakes or misunderstandings, but the character does not.

Verbal irony, in which the writer says one thing and means another ("The best substitute for experience is being sixteen").

Irony of situation, in which there is a great difference between the purpose of a particular action and the result.

Mood is the feeling that a piece of literature arouses in the reader: *happiness, sadness, peacefulness, anxiety,* and so forth.

Paradox is a statement that seems contrary to common sense yet may, in fact, be true: "The coach considered this a good loss."

Plot is the action or sequence of events in a story. It is usually a series of related incidents that build upon one another as the story develops. There are five basic elements in a plot line: *exposition, rising action, climax, falling action,* and *resolution.*

Point of view is the vantage point from which the story unfolds.
In the **first-person** point of view, the story is told by one of the characters: "I stepped into the darkened room and felt myself go cold."
In the **third-person** point of view, the story is told by someone outside the story: "He stepped into the darkened room and felt himself go cold."
Third-person narrations can be *omniscient,* meaning that the narrator has access to the thoughts of all the characters, or *limited,* meaning that the narrator focuses on the inner life of one central character.

Protagonist is the main character or hero of the story.

Resolution (or denouement) is the portion of the play or story in which the problem is solved. The resolution comes after the climax and falling action and is intended to bring the story to a satisfactory end.

Rising action is the series of conflicts or struggles that build a story or play toward a fulfilling climax.

Satire is a literary tone used to ridicule or make fun of human vice or weakness, often with the intent of correcting, or changing, the subject of the satiric attack.

Setting is the time and place in which the action of a literary work occurs.

Structure is the form or organization a writer uses for her or his literary work. A great number of possible forms are used regularly in literature: parable, fable, romance, satire, farce, slapstick, and so on.

Style refers to how the author uses words, phrases, and sentences to form his or her ideas. Style is also thought of as the qualities and characteristics that distinguish one writer's work from the work of others.

Symbol is a person, a place, a thing, or an event used to represent something else. For example, the dove is a symbol of peace.

Theme is the statement about life that a particular work shares with readers. In stories written for children, the theme is often spelled out clearly at the end. In more complex literature, the theme will often be more complex and will be implied, not stated.

Tone is the overall feeling, or effect, created by a writer's use of words. This feeling may be serious, mock-serious, humorous, satiric, and so on.

Poetry Terms

Alliteration is the repetition of initial consonant sounds in words such as "rough and ready." An example of alliteration is underlined below:

"Our gang paces the pier like an old myth . . . "
—Anne-Marie Oomen, "Runaway Warning"

Assonance is the repetition of vowel sounds without the repetition of consonants.

"My words like silent rain drops fell . . . "—Paul Simon, "Sounds of Silence"

Blank verse is an unrhymed form of poetry. Each line normally consists of ten syllables in which every other syllable, beginning with the second, is stressed. As blank verse is often used in very long poems, it may depart from the strict pattern from time to time.

Consonance is the repetition of consonant sounds. Although it is very similar to alliteration, consonance is not limited to the first letters of words:

" . . . and high school girls with clear-skin smiles . . . "
—Janis Ian, "At Seventeen"

Foot is the smallest repeated pattern of stressed and unstressed syllables in a poetic line. (See **Verse**.)

Iambic: an unstressed followed by a stressed syllable (re-peat´)
Anapestic: two unstressed followed by a stressed syllable (in-ter-rupt´)
Trochaic: a stressed followed by an unstressed syllable (old´-er)
Dactylic: a stressed followed by two unstressed syllables (o´-pen-ly)
Spondaic: two stressed syllables (heart´-break´)
Pyrrhic: two unstressed syllables (Pyrrhic seldom appears by itself.)

Onomatopoeia is the use of a word whose sound suggests its meaning, as in *clang*, *buzz*, and *twang*.

Refrain is the repetition of a line or phrase of a poem at regular intervals, especially at the end of each stanza. A song's refrain may be called the *chorus*.

Rhythm is the ordered or free occurrences of sound in poetry. Ordered or regular rhythm is called *meter*. Free occurrence of sound is called *free verse*.

Stanza is a division of poetry named for the number of lines it contains:

Couplet: two-line stanza	**Sestet:** six-line stanza
Triplet: three-line stanza	**Septet:** seven-line stanza
Quatrain: four-line stanza	**Octave:** eight-line stanza
Quintet: five-line stanza	

Verse is a metric line of poetry. It is named according to the kind and number of feet composing it: *iambic pentameter, anapestic tetrameter,* and so on. (See **Foot**.)

Monometer: one foot	**Pentameter:** five feet
Dimeter: two feet	**Hexameter:** six feet
Trimeter: three feet	**Heptameter:** seven feet
Tetrameter: four feet	**Octometer:** eight feet

Writing Checklist

Use these seven traits to check your writing; then revise as needed:

_____ The **ideas** offer insight into what the literature or art means and how it communicates.

_____ The **organization** of the essay flows logically and provides an easy-to-follow pattern.

_____ The **voice** is positive, confident, objective, and sensitive to opposing viewpoints. The tone fits the literature or art being discussed.

_____ The **words** are precise and effectively defined.

_____ The **sentences** read and flow smoothly, with effective variations and logical transitions.

_____ The **copy** has no errors in spelling, punctuation, mechanics, or grammar.

_____ The page **design** is attractive and follows appropriate formatting rules.

Critical-Thinking and Writing Activities

As directed by your instructor, complete the following activities.

1. Get a copy of "Good Country People," read the story, write your own analysis, and share the essay with your class.

2. Choose a poem or film that you find meaningful and write an essay in which you analyze how and why the work is strong.

3. Attend a concert. Respond to the style of the music, to the performance of the singer or group, and to the content of the lyrics. Note also the age of the audience, its response, and the way in which the performance is or is not affected by that response. Explain your own response as well.

4. Visit an art gallery. Find an exhibit that engages you. Explain what in this exhibit you find appealing or intriguing. Also explain what value this exhibit might have to society or to you personally, and why.

◀ VISUALLY SPEAKING

The short story, film, and poem reviewed in this chapter all include these literary elements: setting, mood, plot, and characters. Does the photograph on page 355 also include these elements? Explain.

TAKING ESSAY TESTS

24

There is nothing more disheartening than sitting down to take a test for which you're not prepared. The results are predictable—and they're not pretty. Conversely, there is nothing more exhilarating than walking out of a classroom after nailing a test. This is especially true in a college setting, where tests count for so much and second chances and extra credit are rare.

Many of the writing skills that you've already developed should serve you well in taking essay tests. Read the instructions for an essay test carefully, and you'll find requests for describing, analyzing, classifying, persuading, and more.

This chapter will help you write better essay answers. As a bonus, it suggests a variety of other helpful ways to improve your test-taking skills.

Audio

Video

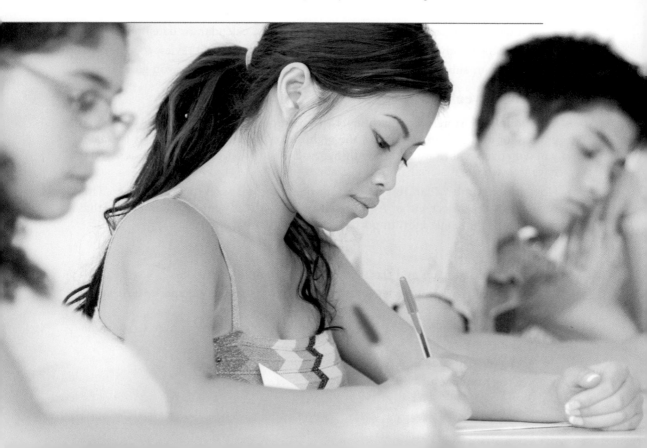

Reviewing for Tests

Do you consider yourself a "bad" test taker? Do you know the material, yet somehow perform poorly on tests? Do you feel overwhelmed by all the information you have to cover when studying for a test? Does even the thought of studying so much material make you nervous? What you need is a positive mental attitude—and good study habits. Together they can make the difference between "spacing" during a test and "acing" an exam.

Perform daily reviews.

Why daily? Begin your reviews on the first day of class; if you miss a day, dust yourself off and keep going. Daily reviews are especially good because you tend to forget new information rapidly. Reviewing while the material is fresh in your mind helps to move it from your short-term memory into your long-term memory.

How much time? Even spending five or ten minutes on your review before or after each class will pay big dividends. Depending on the day's class, you may read through (or talk through) your notes, look over the headings in a reading assignment, skim any summaries you have, or put information into graphic organizers.

What to Do

- Put "Daily review of . . ." on your "To Do" list, calendar, or date book.
- Use the buddy system. Make a pact with a classmate and review together.
- Put your subconscious to work by reviewing material before you go to sleep.

Perform weekly reviews.

Why weekly? More than anything else, repetition helps anchor memory. You can cram a lot of data into your brain the night before an exam, but a day or two later you won't remember much of anything. And when final exam time comes, you'll have to learn the material all over again.

How much time? Plan to spend about one hour per week for each class. (This review can take place either by yourself or with a study group.) Remember that repetition is the single most important factor in learning anything.

What to Do

- Make mind maps and flash cards of important information.
- Practice answering review questions by saying them aloud and by writing out short answers.
- Test your understanding of a subject by teaching or explaining it to someone else.
- Organize a study group. (See page 375.)
- Create mnemonics. (See page 376.)

Forming a Study Group

A study group can keep you interested in a subject, force you to keep up with classwork, and increase your retention of study material. Group energy can be more powerful than individual energy. You will hear other points of view and other ways to approach a subject that you may never have thought of on your own. If you use a chat room, you can meet via a computer. To get started, follow these guidelines.

1. **Find five to six people.**
   - Consider people who seem highly motivated and collaborative.
   - Ask your instructor to inform the class about the opportunity.

2. **Consider a chat room.**
   - Check first with your instructor and student services about the availability of chat rooms on your campus network.
   - Go to any search engine (Yahoo!, Google, Excite, and so on) and enter the term "chat room." For example, Yahoo! provides both private and public chat rooms ("clubs") free of charge.

3. **Arrange a time and place.**
   - Plan one session. (It may become obvious at the first meeting that your group won't work out.)
   - Agree on a time limit for the initial session.
   - Choose somebody in the group to keep everyone on task (or rotate this duty) and agree to accept any prodding and nudging with good humor.

4. **Set realistic goals and decide on a plan of action.**
   - Discuss what the group needs to accomplish and what your goals are.
   - Agree to practice "people skills" (listening, observing, cooperating, responding, and clarifying).
   - Decide which parts of the coursework you will review (lectures? labs? texts? exam questions?).

5. **Evaluate at the end of the first session.**
   - Honestly and tactfully discuss any problems that arose.
   - Ask who wants to continue.
   - Choose a time (and place) for your next session.
   - Determine an agenda for the next session.
   - Exchange necessary information such as phone numbers, e-mail addresses, chat room passwords, and so forth.

Using Mnemonics and Other Memory Guides

Mnemonics is the art of improving memory by using key words, formulas, or other aids to create "file tabs" in your brain that help you pull out hard-to-remember information.

Acronyms Use the first letter in each word to form a new word. Everyone learns a few acronyms during their school years, but feel free to make up your own.

HOMES (the Great Lakes—Huron, Ontario, Michigan, Erie, Superior)

Acrostics Form a phrase or silly sentence in which the first letter of each word helps you remember the items in a series.

Zoe **C**ooks **C**howder **I**n **P**ink **P**ots **I**n **M**iami. (essential minerals—**z**inc, **c**alcium, **c**hromium, **i**ron, **p**otassium, **p**hosphorus, **i**odine, **m**agnesium)

Categories Organize your information into categories for easier recall.

Types of joints in body

immovable: skull sutures, teeth in sockets . . .
slightly movable: between vertebrae, junction at front of pelvis . . .
freely movable: shoulder, elbow, hip, knee, ankle . . .

Peg words Create a chain of associations with objects in a room, a sequence of events, or a pattern with which you are familiar (such as the player positions on a baseball diamond).

To remember a sequence of Civil War battles, you might "peg" them to the positions on a baseball field—for example, Shiloh to home plate (think of the "high" and "low" balls); the Battle of Bull Run to the pitcher's mound (think of the pitcher's battle for no runs); and so on.

Rhymes Make up rhymes or puns.

Brown v. Board of Education / ended public-school segregation.

TIPS to improve your memory

- **Intend to remember.** Scientists say that our brains never forget anything: It's our recall that is at fault. Who forgets that they have tickets to a concert? We remember the things that are important to us.
- **Link new information** to things you already know.
- **Organize your material.** Understand the big picture and then divide the information you need to know into smaller, more manageable categories.
- **Review new material as soon as possible.** The sooner you review, the more likely you'll remember.

Taking the Essay Test

Your teachers expect you to include all the right information, and they expect you to organize it in a clear, well-thought-out way. In addition, they expect you to evaluate, synthesize, predict, analyze, and write a worthwhile answer.

Look for key words.

Key words help you define your task. Pay special attention to them when you read questions. Key words tell you how to present all the information you'll need to write an essay answer.

Following is a list of key terms, along with a definition and an example of how each is used. Studying these terms carefully is the first step in writing worthwhile answers to essay questions.

Analyze To analyze is to break down a larger problem or situation into separate parts of relationships.

> Analyze the major difficulties found at urban housing projects.

Classify To classify is to place persons or things (especially animals and plants) together in a group because they share similar characteristics. Science uses a special classification or group order: phylum, class, order, family, genus, species, and variety.

> Classify three kinds of trees found in the rainforests of Costa Rica.

Compare To compare is to use examples to show how things are similar and different, placing the greater emphasis on similarities.

> Compare the vegetation in the rainforests of Puerto Rico with the vegetation in the rainforests of Costa Rica.

Contrast To contrast is to use examples to show how things are different in one or more important ways.

> Contrast the views of George Washington and Harry S Truman regarding the involvement of the United States in world affairs.

Compare and contrast To compare and contrast is to use examples that show the major similarities and differences between two things (or people, events, ideas, and so forth). In other words, two things are used to clarify each other.

> Compare and contrast people-centered leadership with task-centered leadership.

Define To define is to give the meaning for a term. Generally, defining involves identifying the class to which a term belongs and explaining how it differs from other things in that class.

> Define the term "emotional intelligence" as it pertains to humans.

Describe To describe is to give a detailed sketch or impression of a topic.

> Describe how the Euro tunnel (the Chunnel) was built.

Diagram To diagram is to explain with lines or pictures—a flowchart, map, or other graphic device. Generally, a diagram will label the important points or parts.

> Diagram the parts of a DNA molecule.

Discuss To discuss is to review an issue from all sides. A discussion answer must be carefully organized to stay on track.

> Discuss how Rosa Parks's refusal to move to the back of the bus affected the civil rights movement.

Evaluate To evaluate is to make a value judgment by giving the pluses and minuses along with supporting evidence.

> Evaluate the efforts of midsized cities to improve public transportation services.

Explain To explain is to bring out into the open, to make clear, and to analyze. This term is similar to *discuss* but places more emphasis on cause/effect relationships or step-by-step sequences.

> Explain the effects of global warming on a coastal city like New Orleans.

Justify To justify is to tell why a position or point of view is good or right. A justification should be mostly positive—that is, the advantages are stressed over the disadvantages.

> Justify the use of antilock brakes in automobiles.

Outline To outline is to organize a set of facts or ideas by listing main points and subpoints. A good outline shows at a glance how topics or ideas fit together or relate to one another.

> Outline the events that caused the United States to enter World War II.

Prove To prove is to bring out the truth by giving evidence to back up a point.

> Prove that Atticus Finch in *To Kill a Mockingbird* provided an adequate defense for his client.

Review To review is to reexamine or to summarize the key characteristics or major points of the topic. Generally speaking, a review presents material in the order in which it happened or in decreasing order of importance.

> Review the events since 1976 that have led to the current hip-hop culture.

State To state is to present a concise statement of a position, fact, or point of view.

> State your reasons for voting in the last national election.

Summarize To summarize is to present the main points of an issue in a shortened form. Details, illustrations, and examples are usually omitted.

> Summarize the primary responsibilities of a school in a democracy.

Trace To trace is to present—in a step-by-step sequence—a series of facts that are somehow related. Usually the facts are presented in chronological order.

> Trace the events that led to the fall of the Union of Soviet Socialist Republics.

Plan and write the essay-test answer.

In addition to a basic understanding of the key words, you must understand the process of writing the essay answer.

1. Reread the question several times. (Pay special attention to any key words used in the question.)

2. Rephrase the question into a topic sentence/thesis statement with a clear point.

> **Question:** Explain why public housing was built in Chicago in the 1960s.

> **Thesis statement:** Public housing was built in Chicago because of the Great Migration, the name given to the movement of African Americans from the South to the North.

3. Outline the main points you plan to cover in your answer. Time will probably not allow you to include all supporting details in your outline.

4. Write your essay (or paragraph). Begin with your thesis statement (or topic sentence). Add whatever background information may be needed, and then follow your outline, writing as clearly as possible.

One-Paragraph Answer

If you feel that only one paragraph is needed to answer the question, use the main points of your outline as supporting details for your thesis statement.

Question: Explain why public housing was built in Chicago in the 1960s.

Topic sentence ----- Public housing was built in Chicago because of the Great Migration, the name given to the movement of African Americans from the South to the North. The mechanical cotton picker, introduced in the 1920s, replaced field hands in the cotton fields of the South. At that time Chicago's factories and stockyards were hiring workers. In addition, Jim Crow laws caused hardships and provided reasons for African Americans to move north. Finally, some African Americans had family and relatives in Chicago who had migrated earlier and who, it was thought, could provide a home base for the new migrants until they could get work and housing. According to the U.S. Census

Supporting details ----- Reports, there were 109,000 African Americans in Chicago in 1920. By 1960, there were more than 800,000. However, this increase in population could have been handled except that the public wanted to keep the African Americans in the Black Belt, an area in South Chicago. Reluctant lending agencies and realtors made it possible for speculators to operate. Speculators increased the cost of houses by 75 percent. All of these factors led to a housing shortage for

Conclusion ----- African Americans, which public housing filled.

Multiparagraph Answer

If the question is too complex to be handled in one paragraph, your opening paragraph should include your thesis statement and any essential background information. Begin your second paragraph by rephrasing one of the main points from your outline into a suitable topic sentence. Support this topic sentence with examples, reasons, or other appropriate details. Handle additional paragraphs in the same manner. If time permits, add a summary or concluding paragraph to bring all of your thoughts to a logical close.

Question: Explain the advantages and disadvantages of wind energy.

Thesis: Wind energy has an equal number of advantages and disadvantages.

> *Outline*
> I. *Advantages of wind energy*
>   A. *Renewable*
>   B. *Economical*
>   C. *Nonpolluting*
> II. *Disadvantages of wind energy*
>   A. *Intermittent*
>   B. *Unsightly*
>   C. *A danger to some wildlife*

The introductory paragraph sets up the essay's organization.

Each paragraph follows a point in the outline.

Wind energy has an equal number of advantages and disadvantages. [1] It is renewable, economical, and nonpolluting; but it is also intermittent, unsightly, and a danger to the bird population.

Wind energy is renewable. No matter how much wind energy is used [2] today, there will still be a supply tomorrow. As evidence indicates that wind energy was used to propel boats along the Nile River about 5000 B.C.E., it can be said that wind is an eternal, renewable resource.

Wind energy is economical. The fuel (wind) is free, but the initial cost [3] for wind turbines is higher than for fossil-fueled generators. However, wind energy costs do not include fuel purchases and only minimal operating expenses. Wind power reduces the amount of foreign oil the United States imports and reduces health and environmental costs caused by pollution. Is it possible to sell excess power? The Public Utilities Regulatory Policy Act of 1978 (PURPA) states that a local electric company must buy any excess power produced by a qualifying individual. This act encourages the use of wind power.

Wind energy does not pollute. Whether one wind turbine is used by an [4] individual or a wind farm supplies energy to many people, no air pollutants or greenhouse gases are emitted. California reports that 2.5 billion pounds of carbon dioxide and 15 million pounds of other pollutants have *not* entered the air thanks to wind energy.

How unfortunate is it that wind energy is intermittent? If a wind does not blow, there is little or no electrical power. One way to resolve this dilemma is to store the energy that wind produces in batteries. The word *intermittent* also refers to the fact that wind power is not always available at the places where it is most needed. Often the sites that offer the greatest winds are located in remote locations far from the cities that demand great electrical power.

Specific details explain the main point.

Are wind turbines unsightly? A home-sized wind machine rises about 30 feet with rotors between 8 and 25 feet in diameter. The largest machine in Hawaii stands about 20 stories high with rotors a little longer than the length of a football field. This machine supplies electricity to 1,400 homes. Does a single wind turbine upset the aesthetics of a community as much as a wind farm? The old adage "Beauty is in the eye of the beholder" holds up wherever wind turbines rotate. If ongoing electrical costs are almost nil, that wind turbine may look beautiful.

Questions help the reader understand the issue.

How serious is the issue of bird safety? The main questions are these: (1) Why do birds come near wind turbines? (2) What, if any, are the effects of wind development on bird populations? (3) What can be done to lessen the problem? If even one bird of a protected species is killed, the Endangered Species Act has been violated. If wind turbines kill migratory birds, the Migratory Bird Treaty Act has been violated. As a result, many countries and agencies are studying the problem carefully.

The ending makes a final conclusion.

The advantages of wind energy seem to outweigh the disadvantages. The wind-energy industry has been growing steadily in the United States and around the world. The new wind turbines are reliable and efficient. People's attitudes toward wind energy are mostly positive. Many manufacturers and government agencies are now cooperating to expand wind energy, making it the fastest-growing source of electricity in the world. ■

Reading for Better Writing

Working by yourself or with a group, answer these questions:

1. How does the writer provide a clear focus and logical organization in the essay answer? How soon are the focus and organization provided? What advantages does this approach offer the writer? The reader?

2. How do the sentences used to introduce the advantages differ from the sentences used to introduce the disadvantages? How does this technique aid the reader?

3. Why must the paragraphs in the body contain specific facts and examples? Which facts and examples does this writer use?

QUICK GUIDE
Writing Under Pressure: The Essay Test

■ **Make sure you are ready for the test both mentally and physically.**

- **Carefully listen to or read the instructions.**
  1. How much time do you have to complete the test?
  2. Do all the essay questions count equally?
  3. Can you use any aids, such as a dictionary or handbook?
  4. Are there any corrections, changes, or additions to the test?

- **Begin the test immediately and watch the time.** Don't spend so much time answering one question that you run out of time before answering the others.

- **Read all the essay questions carefullly,** paying special attention to the key words. (See pages 377–378.)

- **Ask the instructor for clarification** if you don't understand something.

- **Rephrase each question into a controlling idea for your essay answer.** (This idea becomes your thesis statement.)

- **Think before you write.** Jot down all the important information and work it into a brief outline. Do this on the back of the test sheet or on a piece of scrap paper.

- **Use a logical pattern of organization and a strong topic sentence for each paragraph.** Tie points together with clear, logical transitions.

- **Write concisely,** but don't use abbreviations or nonstandard language.

- **Be efficient.** Write about those areas of the subject of which you are most certain first; then work on other areas as time permits.

- **Keep your test paper neat and use reasonable margins.** Neatness is always important, and readability is a must, especially on an essay exam.

- **Revise and proofread.** Read through your essay as carefully and completely as time permits.

Note: Also see "Tips for coping with test anxiety," page 384.

Taking an Objective Test

Even though objective tests are generally straightforward and clear, following some tips can help you avoid making foolish mistakes.

True/False Test

- Read the entire question before answering. Often the first half of a statement will be true or false, while the second half is just the opposite. For an answer to be true, the entire statement must be true.
- Read each word and number. Pay special attention to names, dates, and numbers that are similar and could be easily confused.
- Beware of true/false statements that contain words such as *all, every, always,* and *never.* Very often these statements will be false.
- Watch for statements that contain more than one negative word. Remember: Two negatives make a positive. (*Example:* It is unlikely ice will not melt when the temperature rises above 32 degrees F.)

Matching Test

- Read through both lists quickly before you begin answering. Note any descriptions that are similar and pay special attention to the differences.
- When matching a word to a word, determine the part of speech of each word. If the word is a verb, for example, match it with another verb.
- When matching a word to a phrase, read the phrase first and look for the word it describes.
- Cross out each answer as you find it—unless you are told that the answer can be used more than once.
- Use capital letters rather than lowercase letters because they are less likely to be misread by the person correcting the test.

Multiple-Choice Test

- Read the directions to determine whether you are looking for the correct answer or the best answer. Also, check whether some questions can have two (or more) correct answers.
- Read the first part of the question, checking for negative words such as *not, never, except,* and *unless.*
- Try to answer the question in your mind before looking at the choices.
- Read all the choices before selecting your answer. This step is especially important on tests in which you must select the best answer, or on tests where one of your choices is a combination of two or more answers. (*Example:* d. Both a and b / e. All of the above / f. None of the above)

TIPS for coping with test anxiety

Consider the following advice:

- **Study smart.** Use a variety of study and memory techniques to help you see your coursework from several different angles.

- **Review with others.** Join a study group and prepare with the members. Also, ask a classmate or family member to put you to the test.

- **Prepare yourself both physically and mentally.** Get a good night's sleep and eat a healthful, light meal before the test (doughnuts and coffee are *not* a healthful, light meal).

- **Get some exercise.** Aerobic exercise (running, swimming, walking, aerobics) is a great way to relieve stress, and exercise has been proven to help you think more quickly and more clearly.

- **Hit the shower.** Hot water is relaxing, cold water is stimulating, and warm water is soothing. Take your pick.

- **Get to class early . . . but not too early!** Hurrying increases anxiety, but so does waiting.

- **Relax.** Take a few deep breaths, close your eyes, and think positive thoughts. The more relaxed you are, the better your memory will serve you.

- **Glance through the entire test.** Then plan your time, and pace yourself accordingly. You don't want to discover with only 5 minutes of class time left that the last question is an essay that counts for 50 percent of your grade.

- **Begin by filling in all the answers you know.** This process relieves anxiety and helps to trigger answers for other questions that you may not know immediately. Also, jot down important facts and formulas that you know you will need later on.

- **Don't panic.** If other people start handing in their papers long before you are finished, don't worry. They may have given up or rushed through the exam. The best students often finish last.

Bottom Line

The better you prepare for a test—mentally and physically—the less likely you'll be to suffer serious test anxiety.

WRITING FOR THE WORKPLACE

25

Audio

One thing you already know about writing in college is that you have to do a lot of it—and it has to be good. Nothing does more to help you make a good impression than writing well. You also know that college is very much like real life, in that you have to take care of business in and out of class. There are bills to pay, letters to write, memos to fax, and messages to e-mail. It's your personal responsibility to get each of these jobs done clearly, concisely, and on time.

This chapter should aid you in taking care of the business at hand. Sample letters and memos will help you communicate effectively with people ranging from the registrar to scholarship committees. The sample applications and resumés will help you make a favorable impression when you apply for a job or an internship. There's even a special set of guidelines to help you master e-mail messages so that you can "take care of business," no matter where in the world it may be.

Writing the Business Letter

Business letters do many things—for example, share ideas, promote products, or ask for help. Putting a message in writing gives you time to think about, organize, and edit what you want to say. In addition, a written message serves as a record of important details for both the sender and the recipient.

Parts of the Business Letter

1. **Heading** The heading gives the writer's complete address, either in the letterhead (company stationery) or typed out, followed by the date.

2. **Inside Address** The inside address gives the reader's name and address.
   - If you're not sure which person to address or how to spell someone's name, you could call the company or check their website for the information.
   - If the person's title is a single word, place it after the name and a comma (Mary Johnson, President). A longer title goes on a separate line.

3. **Salutation** The salutation begins with *Dear* and ends with a colon, not a comma.
   - Use *Mr.* or *Ms.* plus the person's last name, unless you are well acquainted. Do not guess at *Miss* or *Mrs.*
   - If you can't get the person's name, replace the salutation with *Dear* or *Attention* followed by the title of an appropriate reader.

     (*Examples:* Dear Dean of Students: or Attention: Personnel Manager)

     Note: See pages 104–106 for a complete list of "unbiased" ways to refer to an individual or a particular group.

4. **Body** The body should consist of single-spaced paragraphs with double-spacing between paragraphs. (Do not indent the paragraphs.)
   - If the body goes to a second page, put the reader's name at the top left, the number 2 in the center, and the date at the right margin.

5. **Complimentary Closing** For the complimentary closing, use *Sincerely, Yours sincerely,* or *Yours truly* followed by a comma; use *Best wishes* if you know the person well.

6. **Signature** The signature includes the writer's name both handwritten and typed.

7. **Initials** When someone types the letter for the writer, that person's initials appear (in lowercase) after the writer's initials (in capitals) and a colon.

8. **Enclosure** If a document (brochure, form, copy, or other form) is enclosed with the letter, the word *Enclosure* or *Encl.* appears below the initials.

9. **Copies** If a copy of the letter is sent elsewhere, type *cc:* beneath the enclosure line, followed by the person's or department's name.

Model Letter

Heading

Box 143
Balliole College
Eugene, OR 97440-5125
August 29, 2008

Four to Seven Spaces

Inside Address

Ms. Ada Overlie
Ogg Hall, Room 222
Balliole College
Eugene, OR 97440-0222

Double Space

Salutation

Dear Ms. Overlie:

Double Space

Body

As the president of the Earth Care Club, I welcome you to Balliole Community College. I hope the year will be a great learning experience both inside and outside the classroom.

Double Space

That learning experience is the reason I'm writing—to encourage you to join the Earth Care Club. As a member, you could participate in the educational and action-oriented mission of the club. The club has most recently been involved in the following:

- Organizing a reduce, reuse, recycle program on campus
- Promoting cloth rather than plastic bag use among students
- Giving input to the college administration on landscaping, renovating, and building for energy efficiency
- Putting together the annual Earth Day celebration

Double Space

Which environmental concerns and activities would you like to focus on? Bring them with you to the Earth Care Club. Simply complete the enclosed form and return it by September 8. Then watch the campus news for details on our first meeting.

Double Space

Complimentary Closing and Signature

Yours sincerely,

Four Spaces

Dave Wetland

Dave Wetland
President

Double Space

Initials Enclosure Copies

DW:kr
Encl. membership form
cc: Esther du Toit, membership committee

Writing Memos and E-mail

A memorandum is a written message sent from one person to one or more other people within the same organization. As such, it is less formal than a letter. A memo can vary in length from a sentence or two to a four- or five-page report. It can be delivered in person, dropped in a mailbox, or sent via e-mail.

Memos are written to create a flow of information within an organization—asking and answering questions, describing procedures and policies, or reminding people about appointments and meetings. Here are some guidelines:

- Write memos only when necessary, and only to those people who need them.
- Distribute them through the appropriate media—mail, fax, bulletin boards, kiosk, intranet, or e-mail.
- Make your subject line precise so that the topic is clear and the memo is easy to file.
- Get to the point: (1) state the subject, (2) give necessary details, and (3) state the response you want.

Date: September 26, 2008

To: All Users of the Bascom Hill Writing Lab

From: Kerri Kelley, Coordinator

The subject line clarifies the memo's purpose. --- Subject: New Hours/New Equipment

The main point is stated immediately. --- Beginning October 3, the Bascom Hill Writing Lab will expand its weekend hours as follows: Fridays, 7:00 A.M.–11:00 P.M.; Saturdays, 8:00 A.M.–11:00 P.M.

Also, six additional computers will be installed next week, making it easier to get computer time. We hope these changes will help meet the increased demand for time and assistance we've experienced this fall. Remember, it's still a good idea to sign up in advance. To reserve time, call the lab at 462-7722 or leave your request at bhill@madwis.edu.

Readers are asked to take note of a few final facts. Finally, long-range planners, mark your calendars. The lab will be closed on Thanksgiving Day morning and open from 1:00 P.M. to 11:00 P.M. We will also be closed on Christmas and New Year's Day. We will post our semester-break hours sometime next month.

Sending E-mail

With e-mail, people can correspond through computer networks around the globe. E-mail allows you to do the following:

- Send, forward, and receive many messages quickly and efficiently, making it ideal for group projects and other forms of collaboration
- Set up mailing lists (specific groups of e-mail addresses) so that you can easily send the same message to several people at the same time
- Organize messages in "folders" for later reference, and reply to messages

---

TIPS for e-mail
- **Revise and edit messages for clarity and correctness before sending them.** Confusing sentences, grammatical errors, and typos limit your ability to communicate on a computer screen just as they do on paper.
- **Use e-mail responsibly.** Sooner or later you will send e-mail to the wrong person, or a reader will forward your message to another person without your permission. Keep these possibilities in mind at all times, and never write anything that would embarrass you if the wrong party received it.
- **Make messages easy to read and understand.** (1) Provide a clear subject line so readers will scan it and decide whether to read or delete the message. (2) Type short paragraphs.

From:	"Sherry West" SWEST@stgeorge.edu
To:	outreach@stgeorge.edu
Date sent:	Mon, 22 Sept 2008 14:13:06 CST
Subject:	Agenda for Student Outreach Committee Meeting

Please remember that our next meeting is this Wednesday, Sept. 24, at 8:00 p.m. in SUB Room 201. We'll discuss the following agenda items:

1. The minutes of our Sept. 10 meeting
2. A proposal from SADD about Alcohol Awareness Week
3. A progress report on the Habitat for Humanity project

Before the meeting, please review the minutes and the SADD proposal attached to this message.

Applying for a Job

When you apply for some jobs, you have to do nothing more than fill out an application form. With other jobs, it's a different story. You may be required to write a letter of application, gather letters of recommendation, write an application essay, and put together a resumé. The following pages provide models to fit nearly every occasion.

Web Link

The Letter of Application

Your letter of application (or cover letter) introduces you to an employer and often highlights information on an accompanying resumé. Your goal in writing this letter is to convince the employer to invite you for an interview.

Ogg Hall, Room 222
Balliole College
Eugene, OR 97440-0222
April 17, 2008

Address a specific person, if possible.

Professor Edward Mahaffy
Greenhouse Coordinator
Balliole College
Eugene, OR 97440-0316

Dear Professor Mahaffy:

State the desired position and your chief qualification.

I recently talked with Ms. Sierra Arbor in the Financial Aid Office about work-study jobs for 2008–2009. She told me about the Greenhouse Assistant position and gave me a job description. As a full-time Balliole student, I'm writing to apply for this position. I believe that my experience qualifies me for the job.

Focus on how your skills meet the reader's needs.

As you can see from my resumé, I spent two summers working in a raspberry operation, doing basic plant care and carrying out quality-control lab tests on the fruit. Also, as I was growing up, I learned a great deal by helping with a large farm garden. In high school and college, I studied botany. Because of my interest in this field, I'm enrolled in the Environmental Studies program at Balliole.

Request an interview and thank the reader.

I am available for an interview. You may phone me any time at 341-3611 (and leave a message on my machine) or e-mail me at dvrl@balliole.edu. Thank you for considering my application.

Yours sincerely,

Ada Overlie

Ada Overlie

Encl. resumé

The Recommendation Request Letter

When you apply for a job or program, it helps to present references or recommendations to show your fitness for the position. To get the support you need from people familiar with your work (instructors and employers), you need to ask for that support. You can do so in person or by phone, but a courteous and clear letter or e-mail message makes your request official and helps the person complete the recommendation effectively. Here is a suggested outline:

Situation: Remind the reader of your relationship to him or her; then ask the person to write a recommendation or to serve as a reference for you.

Explanation: Describe the work you did for the reader and the type of job, position, or program for which you are applying.

Action: Explain what form the recommendation should take, to whom it should be addressed, and where and when it needs to be sent.

2456 Charles Street
Lexington, KY 40588-8321
March 21, 2008

Dr. Rosa Perez
271 University Boulevard
University of Kentucky
Lexington, KY 40506-1440

Dear Dr. Perez:

The situation

As we discussed on the phone, I would appreciate your writing a recommendation letter for me. You know the quality of my academic work, my qualities as a person, and my potential for working in the medical field.

The explanation

As my professor for Biology 201 and 202, you are familiar with my grades and work habits. As my adviser, you know my career plans and should have a good sense of whether I have the qualities needed to succeed in the medical profession. I am asking you for your recommendation because I am applying for summer employment with the Lexington Ambulance Service. I recently received my Emergency Medical Technician (Basic) license to prepare for such work.

The action

Please send your letter to Rick Falk, EMT Coordinator, at the University Placement Office by April 8. Thank you for your help. Let me know if you need any other information (phone 231-6700; e-mail jnwllms@ukentucky.edu).

Yours sincerely,

Jon Williams

Jon Williams

The Application Essay

For some applications, you may be asked to submit an essay, a personal statement, or a response paper. For example, you might be applying for admission to an academic program (social work, engineering, optometry school) or for an internship, a scholarship, or a research grant. Whatever the situation, what you write and how well you write it will be important factors in the success of your application.

On the facing page is a model application essay. Jessy Jezowski wrote this essay as part of her application to a college social work program.

TIPS for an application essay

- Understand what you are being asked to write and why. How does the essay fit into the entire application? Who will read your essay? What will they look for?

- Focus on the instructions for writing the essay. What type of question is it? What topics are you asked to write about? What hints do the directions give about possible organization, emphasis, style, length, and method of submitting the essay?

- Be honest with yourself and your readers. Don't try to write only what you think readers want to hear.

- Think about your purpose and audience:
  - What do you want to gain (internship, scholarship, job interview), and how could your writing help you gain it?
  - Who are your readers? What do they know about you? What should they know?

- Develop your essay using the following organization (if the instructions allow for it):
  - An introduction with a fresh, interesting opening statement and a clear focus or theme
  - A body that develops the focus or theme clearly and concisely— with some details and examples—in a way appropriate to the instructions
  - A conclusion that stresses a positive point and looks forward to participating in the program, internship, organization, or position

- Write in a style that is personal but professional. Use words that fit the subject and the readers. Avoid clichés, and balance generalizations with concrete examples and details.

- Refine your first draft into a polished piece. First, get feedback from another student or, if appropriate, a professor, and revise the essay. Second, edit the final version thoroughly: You don't want typos and grammar errors to derail your application.

Model Application Essay

Audio

February 28, 2008
Jessy Jezowski

Personal Statement

The opening provides a clear focus for the essay.

While growing up in Chicago, I would see people hanging   *1*
out on street corners, by grocery stores, and in parks—with
no home and barely any belongings. Poverty and its related
problems are all around us, and yet most people walk by
them with blinders on. I have found myself quick to assume
that someone else will help the poor man on the corner, the
woman trapped in an abusive relationship, or the teenager
struggling with an eating disorder. But I know in my heart
that all members of society are responsible to and for each
other. Social welfare issues affect every member of society—
including me.

The writer demonstrates knowledge of the field and explains what she hopes to learn.

Because these issues are serious and difficult to solve,   *2*
I wish to major in social work and eventually become a
social worker. In the major, I want to gain the knowledge,
skills, and attitudes that will make me part of the solution,
not part of the problem. By studying social work institutions,
the practices of social work, and the theory and history
behind social work, I hope to learn how to help people help
themselves. When that pregnant teenager comes to me, I
want to have strong, practical advice—and be part of an
effective social work agency that can help implement that
advice.

Two concrete examples help back up her general statements.

I am especially interested at this point in working with   *3*
families and teenagers, in either a community counseling or
school setting. Two experiences have created this interest.
First, a woman in my church who works for an adoption
agency, Ms. Lesage, has modeled for me what it means to
care for individuals and families within a community and
around the world. Second, I was involved in a peer counseling
program in high school. As counselors, we received training
in interpersonal relationships and the nature of helping. In a
concrete way, I experienced the complex challenges of helping
others.

The conclusion summarizes her goals for the future.

I believe strongly in the value of all people and am   *4*
interested in the well-being of others. As a social worker, I
would strive to make society better (for individuals, families,
and communities) by serving those in need, whatever their
problems.

Preparing a Resumé

A strong resumé isn't generic—a ho-hum fill-in-the-blanker. Rather, it's a vivid word picture of your skills, knowledge, and past responsibilities. It says exactly who you are by providing the kind of information listed below.

Personal Data: name, address, phone number, e-mail address (enough for the reader to identify you and reach you easily).

Job Objective: the type of position you want and the type of organization for which you want to work.

Skills Summary: the key qualities and skills you bring to a position, listed with supporting details. Here are some skill areas that you might consider for your own resumé:

- Communication
- Organization
- Problem solving
- Computer

- Management (people, money, other resources)
- Working with people, counseling, training
- Sales, marketing, public relations
- Languages

Experience: positions you've held (where and when), and your specific duties and your accomplishments.

Education: degrees, courses, and special projects.

Other Experiences: volunteer work, awards, achievements, tutoring jobs, extracurricular activities (related to your job objective), licenses, and certifications.

TIPS for resumé writing

- Design each resumé to fit the particular job.
- Be specific—use numbers, dates, and names.
- Present information first that is the most impressive and/or most important to the job for which you are applying. This guideline will help you determine whether to put your experience or your education first.
- Use everyday language and short, concise phrases.
- Be parallel—list similar items using similar structures.
- Use boldface type, underlining, white space, and indentations to make your resumé more readable.
- Get someone else's reaction; then revise and proofread.

Sample Resumé

Present contact information and employment objectives.

Feature skills with appropriate headings and lists.

List work and education chronologically, from most to least current.

Format for paper only: boldface, underlining, bulleted or indented lists, two columns.

Offer references.

Ada Overlie

Home	**School**
451 Wiser Lake Road	Ogg Hall, Room 222
Ferndale, WA 98248-8941	Balliole College
(360) 354-5916	Eugene, OR 97440-0222
	Phone: (503) 341-3611
	E-mail: dvrl@balliole.edu

Job Objective: Part-time assistant in a nursery or greenhouse.

Skills Summary:

Horticultural Skills: Familiar with garden planting, care, and harvesting practices—planning, timing, companion planting, fertilizing.

Lab Skills: Familiar with procedures for taking fruit samples, pureeing them, checking for foreign objects, and testing sugar content.

Experience:

Summers 2007 and 2008: Lab Technician.
Mayberry Farms and Processing Plant, Ferndale, WA.
Worked in Quality Control testing raspberries to make sure they met company standards.

Summers 2005 and 2006: Camp Counselor.
Emerald Lake Summer Camp, Hillsboro, WA.
Supervised 12-year-olds in many camp activities, including nature hikes in which we identified plants and trees.

Education:

August 2008 to present: Balliole College, Eugene, OR.
Environmental Studies and Communication major.
Courses completed and in progress include environmental studies and general botany. First semester GPA 3.7.

August 2004 to June 2008: Ferndale High School, Ferndale, WA.
Courses included biology, agriculture, U.S. government, and economics.

Special Projects: Completed research papers on clean-water legislation and organic farming practices.

References available upon request.

Sample Electronic Resumé

To find employees, companies often use computer programs to search electronic resumés for keywords (especially nouns) found in job descriptions or ads. Anticipating such a search, Jonathan Greenlind identified keywords and inserted them into his job description and resumé.

Present contact information and employment objective.

Jonathan L. Greenlind
806 5th Avenue
Waterloo, Iowa 50701
Telephone: 319.268.6955
E-mail: grnlnd@aol.com

OBJECTIVE
Position as hydraulics supervisor that calls for hydraulics expertise, technical skills, mechanical knowledge, reliability, and enthusiasm

List skills, experiences, and education using many keywords.

SKILLS
Operation and repair specialist in main and auxiliary power systems, subsystems, landing gears, brakes and pneumatic systems, hydraulic motors, reservoirs, actuators, pumps and cylinders from six types of hydraulic systems

Dependable, resourceful, strong leader, team worker

EXPERIENCE
Aviation Hydraulics Technician
United States Navy (2003–present)
* Repair, test, and maintain basic hydraulics, distribution systems, and aircraft structural hydraulics systems
* Manufacture low-, medium-, and high-pressure rubber and Teflon hydraulic hoses, and aluminum stainless-steel tubing
* Perform preflight, postflight, and other periodic aircraft inspections
* Operate ground-support equipment
* Supervise personnel
Aircraft Mechanic
Sioux Falls International Airport (2001–2003)
Sioux Falls, South Dakota
* Performed fueling, engine overhauls, minor repairs, and tire and oil changes of various aircraft

Format for e-mail:
• one column
• asterisks as bullets
• simple sans serif typeface
• flush-left margin
• no italics, boldface, or underlining
• ASCII or RTF text (readable by all computers)

EDUCATION
* United States Navy (2003–2007)
* Certificate in Hydraulic Technical School "A", GPA 3.8/4.0
* Certificate in Hydraulic, Pneumatic Test Stand School, GPA 3.9/4.0
* Courses in Corrosion Control, Hydraulic Tube Bender, Aviation Structural Mechanics
* Equivalent of 10 semester hours in Hydraulic Systems Maintenance and Structural Repair

Offer references.

References available upon request.

WRITING AND DESIGNING FOR THE WEB

26

A strong website depends on well-written, well-organized, and well-designed content. Above all, web content should be concise, focused, and visually appealing. After all, people don't read websites so much as they scan them, so information should be presented in short chunks of text. Webpages should be brief, designed to minimize scrolling and maximize the use of available screen space. Moreover, because online readers can be impatient, the writing must quickly and clearly address its intended purpose, audience, and topic. The chapter addresses the rhetorical fundamentals of creating a strong website and developing strong webpages.

Audio

Video

Webpage Elements and Functions

To design an effective website and develop dynamic webpages, you need to start with a basic understanding of webpage elements and functions. Because webpages use the same elements as printed pages, many of the same design principles apply. However, unlike printed pages, webpages are fluid (flowing their contents to match screen and browser settings), and they can include both elements and functions, as shown and discussed below and on the pages that follow.

Page Elements

On the web, page elements are defined primarily by purpose—headings, body text, image, and so forth. Before designing a webpage, it helps to understand the purpose of those elements.

1. **Headings** (also called headers) come in six levels and are used to separate different sections and subsections of web documents. Heading 1 is the largest; heading 6 is the smallest. All are bold black serif font by default.

2. **Body text** is organized into chunks, called paragraphs, which are separated by white space. Unlike printed text, paragraphs on the web do not generally have a first-line indentation. By default, body text is a black serif font roughly the same size as a heading level 4 (though not bold).

3. **Preformatted text** is "monospaced"; it displays all characters at the same width, like typewriter font. It is used primarily to show mathematical formulas, computer code, and the like.

4. **Lists** can be formatted in three types: Ordered lists are numbered, unordered lists are bulleted, and definition lists present pairs of information—usually terms alongside their definitions, which are indented. Because readers can scan them quickly, lists are an efficient way to present information.

5. **Images** can include photographs, clip art, graphs, line drawings, cartoon figures, icons, and animations. These can make a page much slower to display, so use them judiciously. Always be sure you have the legal right to use any images that you include in your pages. (See "Copyright violations," page 481.)

6. **Background color** for a webpage is white by default (medium gray in older browsers), which makes the standard headings and text easily legible.

7. **Tables** are a common tool for webpage layout. Simply put, tables are grids made up of rows and columns. By creating a table with no visible borders, a web designer can gain some control over where elements appear on a page.

Sample Webpage

Clear title —
Major sections —
Concise text —
Feature graphic —
Topic heading —
Feature heading —
Concise text —
Plain background for legibility —

Images courtesy of The Museum of Flight and Heath Moffett, photographer.

As seen above, not all webpages have black serif font on a white background. However, because web browsers are designed to flow content to suit each computer screen, changing the default styles can be problematic. It helps to keep the following tips in mind:

- **Simple is best.** Simple pages display the fastest and have the least chance of breaking. The more graphics you add, the longer a page takes to load. The more you change the default font settings, the more complicated the code becomes and the greater the chance of computer error.

- **Different computers display things differently.** Not every computer has the same font styles installed, and colors look different on different monitors. Always check your work on many different systems.

- **The user is king (or queen).** No matter which font style and size you choose, the reader can change how things display on her or his machine. So focus on useful content and clear organization instead of struggling to control graphic design.

Page Functions

Webpage functions set electronic pages apart from printed pages. On the web, readers can browse pages in almost any order, send and receive e-mail, send messages and files, post messages, and join live "chat" sessions. In short, readers can interact with webpages in ways they cannot with printed pages. Like webpage elements, webpage functions should serve your site's purpose.

1. **Hyperlinks** are strings of specially formatted text that enable readers to jump to another spot on the web. Internal hyperlinks (links for short) take you to another section of the same webpage or to another page on the same site. External links lead to pages on other websites. "Mail to" links allow readers to address e-mail to recipients, such as a professor or a classmate.

2. **Menus** offer structured lists of links that operate like a website's table of contents. Menus are typically presented in a column or row at the edge of a webpage. Good websites include a standard site menu on every page so readers don't get lost.

3. **Forms** enable the host of a website to interact with the site's readers. Web forms can be used for questionnaires, surveys, complaints and service requests, job applications, or suggestion boxes.

Developing a Website and Webpages

Regardless of the purpose, topic, and audience of your website, you can develop it by following the steps outlined on the next four pages.

Get focused.

Create an overview of the project—the purpose, the audience, and the topic. The questions below will help you get focused and develop fitting content for the site.

1. **What is the primary purpose of the website?** Am I creating a library of documents that my audience will reference? Am I going to present information and announcements about myself or my organization? Am I trying to promote a specific product or service?

2. **Who is the site's audience?** Which people will seek out this site? Why? What do they need? How often will they visit the site, and how often should it be updated? How comfortable is my audience with using computers and websites? What level of formality is appropriate for the language? Which graphics, colors, and design will appeal to them?

3. **What is the site's central topic?** What do I already know about the topic? What do I need to learn, and where can I find the information? How will I demonstrate that the information is credible and reliable? What will my audience want to know about the topic? How can I divide the information into brief segments? What visual elements would help present my message? Which other websites address this topic? Should my website link to them?

Establish your central message.

After you've made decisions about your purpose, audience, and topic, write out the main idea you want to communicate. You might call this the theme or "mission statement" of your website.

> The purpose of this website is to inform fellow students and the <u>general public</u> about <u>current research into hybrid-vehicle transportation.</u>

To help you stay on target with your project, post this mission statement in plain sight. Note, too, that you might modify your goal as the site develops, or add secondary goals for the site.

Create a site map.

As you gather content for your site, create a site map. Websites can be as simple as an elementary school bulletin board or as complex as a United States federal government site. Here are four principles to keep in mind:

1. **No one will read your entire site.** People curl up with books, not websites. If your audience is not asking for content, don't provide it.

2. **Your site will have many small audiences**—not one big audience. A site's audience may include anyone with a computer, an Internet connection, and an interest in your site's topic. Keep all potential readers in mind.

3. **Websites are not linear.** A single "home page" or "splash page" introduces the site, which branches out like tree limbs into pages with varied content. Websites "conclude" whenever the reader quits reading.

4. **You may need to build the site in phases.** You can add pages to a website after it has been published, so be careful that your site's organization does not limit future additions.

Sample Site Map

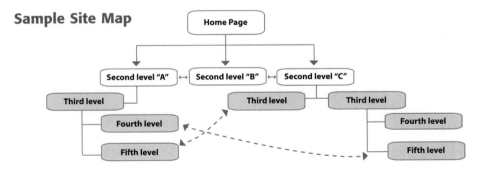

A map for a simple site might include only four items—a home page, page "A," page "B," and page "C" (as shown in white on the diagram). Users can "jump" between any of the secondary-level pages or back to the home page.

A more complex website typically needs more levels (as shown in green on the diagram). Likewise, its menu will offer more navigation choices. Related pages might be connected with links (as represented by the dotted lines).

Study similar sites.

Learn from successful sites, especially sites that serve a similar purpose—a campus club site, a department site, a personal job-search site. How do similar sites use elements: headings, body text, preformatted text, background color, lists, images, and tables? How do the sites use functions—links, menus, and forms? The seven traits (see pages 140–142) can also supply helpful benchmarks for evaluating sites.

1. **Ideas:** Does the site present clear ideas and information?
2. **Organization:** Is the content carefully and clearly structured?
3. **Voice:** Is the tone fitting for the audience?
4. **Words:** Is the language understandable? Is the wording concise?
5. **Sentences:** Are the sentences easy to read and generally short?
6. **Correctness:** Does the site avoid distracting errors?
7. **Design:** Are the pages user friendly? Is the site easy to navigate?

Gather and prioritize content.

Brainstorm and research the actual content, with the goal of creating an outline for your site. How many topics will the site address? How wide will your coverage of a topic be? How deep? Your outline can also be used to create the website's table of contents. Based on your research, discussions with others, and the deadlines for the project, select the content, features, and functions your site will offer.

Think about support materials.

List the documents (brochures, artworks, instructions, poems, reports) that will be presented on your site and note whether they will be displayed as webpages, made available for readers to download, or both. Construct a grid to keep track of how documents will be used.

List graphics that could make your pages more visual and informative and could help readers grasp the meaning of complex data or processes. Photographs may help "put a face" on your organization. Logos and icons will help brand your pages. Review the list below for electronic files that may be appropriate to your topic, audience, and purpose. (Remember: Use only graphics that are legally available. See the discussion of copyright on page 481.)

Images	**Audio**	**Video**
charts	music	animations
drawings	sound effects	film clips
graphs	spoken text	presentations
photographs		webcasts

Design and develop individual pages.

When you create individual pages for your site, consider both the design and the content—specifically, how to make the two work well together.

Design Principles

Most webpages—and the pages of most other publications—are designed on grids. Look at any newspaper or magazine page, and you should be able to draw horizontal and vertical lines denoting columns and rows of content. Some rows may span multiple columns, and some columns may overrun several rows.

Another fundamental design concept is balance. You might balance light elements with dark ones, text with images, and so forth. The balance of your page design should be driven by the purpose of your website, its audience, and its topic.

Websites may contain a variety of pages—each tailored to different purposes, audiences, and topics—to present some combination of informational and promotional content. Use each page's purpose to guide decisions about which elements and functions to include.

 Webpage design should follow fundamental document-design principles, including strategies for using color effectively. For more information, visit **www.thecollegewriter.com/3e.**

Drafting Principles

1. **Identify the site.** Working from your mission statement, write a brief introduction informing visitors about the site's purpose.

2. **Provide clear links.** Create links for your pages, using clear descriptors such as "Original Poetry." (Avoid phrases such as "Click here for poetry.") If necessary, add a descriptive sentence to further identify the link. Let visitors know precisely where each link will take them.

3. **Introduce each page.** Search sites may deliver some visitors to a page other than your home page. Give each page a brief introduction that clearly identifies it. Also, remember to provide a link back to your home page.

4. **Title each page.** Atop the browser window is a title bar where the current page should be identified. This title is used in browser bookmarks, search engine listings, and the like, so be sure to give every page on your website a descriptive title.

5. **Keep pages uncluttered.** Dense text is even more difficult to read on screen than on paper, so use short paragraphs when you can. Add headings to identify sections, and include visuals to help break up the text.

6. **Save the page as HTML.** To be viewed in a web browser, your pages must be formatted in Hypertext Markup Language (HTML). Your word processor may have a "Save as HTML" or "Save as Webpage" option. Many HTML editing programs are also available on the web.

Test, refine, and post your site.

Most websites are developed through the combined efforts of writers, graphic designers, and programmers. In such an environment, many content and layout ideas might be considered, rejected, and reformulated to produce and launch the site. Of course, the audience ultimately decides a website's success or failure. For that reason, test and refine your site before posting it.

1. **Check the site yourself.** Open your home page from your web browser. Does the site make sense? Can you navigate it easily?

2. **Get peer review.** Ask classmates—both experienced and inexperienced with the website's topic and with Internet searching—to use your site. Watch them navigate it, and take notes about any confusion they have.

3. **Check the text.** Reread all the text on your site. Trim wherever possible (the shorter, the better online), and check all spelling and punctuation.

4. **Check the graphics.** Do images load properly? Do they load quickly? Are menus and page headings in the same place on every page?

5. **Provide a feedback link.** Provide your e-mail address on the site, inviting visitors to contact you with any comments after the site goes "live."

6. **Post the site.** Upload the site to your hosting space. (Check your host's instructions for doing so.) Add the posting date to each page, and update it each time you change a page.

7. **Check for universality.** View the site on several different types of computers, using different browsers. Does the layout display well on all of them? Make any needed changes.

8. **Announce the site.** Advertise your site in e-mails. Submit it to search sites. Consider joining a "web ring" of similar sites to draw more traffic. Let your professors, classmates, friends, and family know about your site.

9. **Monitor the site.** After a site has been launched, its success may be measured by the amount of traffic it receives, feedback submitted by users, and any use of resources or services. (Check with your host for ways to measure traffic.)

10. **Make adjustments and updates.** A website should be a living thing. Update the content when possible to keep it fresh, and make any adjustments needed to adapt to changing technologies.

INSIGHT: Avoid using any features and functions that do not support your overall purpose for writing. If you find yourself distracted by the many bells and whistles of the web, remember that it's better to have a simple website that presents information clearly and effectively than a complex site that does not.

Sample Webpages

On the next two pages, you'll find sample pages from student and academic websites. Study each model for insights about what makes for strong web content and design.

For further analysis of webpages, including nonprofit and business sites, go to **www.thecollegewriter.com/3e.** There you'll also find tutorials on analyzing and evaluating websites.

Student-Designed Website

The following website was developed by undergraduate students from a Southwestern U.S. university who were studying abroad. Southwest Sojourners is a multiuser site with blogs and chat rooms that allow students to keep in touch with one another and with friends and family back home.

Purpose: This site is a gathering place for undergraduate students studying abroad. It describes itself as a "home away from home" for such students. The tone is light, conversational, and inviting, as befitting the purpose of connecting these students to one another and to the important people in their lives.

Audience: The site is meant for students, friends, and family members. By providing straight news, individualized blogs, and chat rooms and e-mail options, the site allows users to be as passive or as active as they wish. Membership is required for active participation, and members must "sign" a user's agreement before posting material.

Format: The golden background and sun icon visually convey the Southwestern theme, while the minimalist format makes the site easy to navigate. A large four-item toolbar on the left directs users to the linked pages, and brief text on the right gives a clear indication of what lies at the end of each link.

SOUTHWEST SOJOURNERS

Welcome to Southwest Sojourners! This site is meant to be a home away from home for students from Southwestern U.S. universities who are studying abroad. If you are such a student—or a friend or family member of such a student—this is the spot for you! Lurk, if you like, or log in and join the conversation.

Sojourners News   These pages are updated regularly with information about special events on this site—and in reality.

Click here for a list of students who are blogging about their studies abroad.

Student Blogs   For members only: Join the conversation with students in England, Germany, Italy, India, Japan—and elsewhere!

Chat Rooms   Membership is free, but we do need a little information and a digital signature on our posting agreement.

Log In!   Contact the Webmaster at: Webmaster@southsojourn.edu.
Site design: Mikayla Evans and Griffin Jenson

site launched: 29 January 2005
last updated: 29 July 2008

Academic Website

The Massachusetts Institute of Technology's Space Nanotechnology Laboratory website is an academic research site. It contains information about a specialized laboratory in the MIT Kavli Institute for Astrophysics and Space Research.

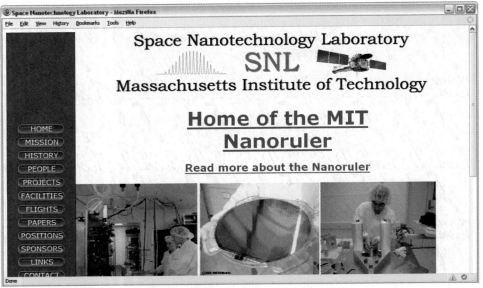

Courtesy of Space Nanotechnology Laboratory, Massachusetts Institute of Technology.

Purpose: This site aims to inform a very specific audience about a team of professors, graduate research assistants, and staff and their work to develop nanotechnology for space exploration. The site features the laboratory's creation of the "MIT Nanoruler," a device capable of measuring to the billionth of a meter. The site also provides pages that outline the laboratory's mission, history, people, projects, and facilities.

Audience: This website addresses "a consortium of microfabrication facilities with shared interests." In addition to providing articles of interest to this group, the site includes a list of available positions for professionals and students who may wish to join the laboratory. A sponsors page shows that the audience also includes funding agencies such as NASA and the National Science Foundation.

Format: The top of the home page announces the site and university, using iconic images of waveforms and a satellite to convey its central focus. Beneath this masthead, the page features the laboratory's current great achievement: "Home of the MIT Nanoruler" and "Read more about the Nanoruler." A selection of photos highlights work in the lab, and to the left, a list of pages makes navigation transparent.

Writing for Different Internet Environments

The Internet is a complex construct made up of much more than webpages. Other writing venues on the Net are described below, with writing tips for each.

OWLs Your university or college probably has a writing lab where you can seek help with your writing assignments. It might also have a web-based OWL (online writing lab) where you can access help. OWLs post answers to questions you may have about writing, and they often allow you to e-mail or send an instant message (see below) to a writing tutor. Before contacting an OWL tutor, carefully read any instructions posted on the site. *Example:* Purdue University OWL, owl.english.purdue.edu

Web Link

MUDs, MOOs, and MUSHes Some instructors hold classes or deliver lectures online in a MUD (multiuser dimension), a text-based "world" that people can share. (MOOs and MUSHes are variants of MUDs.) MUDs have virtual rooms to explore and virtual objects to examine and handle. To use a MUD, you must learn the text commands for interacting with it. Most MUDs require software for a telnet connection, but some are accessible via telnet-enabled webpages. *Example:* Diversity University MOO, www.marshall.edu/commdis/moo

Web Link

Message Boards Many websites have forms that allow visitors to post messages for public display. The messages and any replies are usually listed together so that readers can follow the message "thread."

Web Link

Mailing Lists Mailing lists allow users to send and receive text messages within a specific group of people interested in a particular subject. The software that maintains a mailing list is called a "list server." Some mailing lists are excellent resources of specialized information. *Example:* QUANTUMTEACHING-NMC <MTEACHING-NMC@LISTS.MAINE.EDU>

Web Link

Chat Servers A chat server provides a place on the Net where you can type a message that other people will see instantly. Those people can then respond with text messages of their own. Some teachers and tutors may use a chat room to confer with students or to hold a class discussion online. Although some chat servers require special software, many are available as webpages. *Example:* Yahoo! Chat, chat.yahoo.com

Web Link

Instant Messaging Services Instant messaging (IM) services allow you to send a text message instantaneously to friends and colleagues who use the same software. Most IMs also allow users to send computer files to one another. (Just be careful not to pass on a computer virus this way.) *Example:* ICQ, web.icq.com

Web Link

Blogs A blog (short for "weblog") is basically just an online journal posted to a webpage. In effect, it is a one-person message board (see above). For many people, blogging is more convenient than creating a webpage of their own, because it involves no design issues and requires no uploading of files.

Web Link

Writing Checklist

Use this checklist to review and revise your site and its pages:

_____ The purpose of the website is presented—or evident—on the home page and elsewhere on the site.

_____ The page elements—headlines, body text, preformatted text, background colors, lists, images, and tables—work together and are suited to the page's audience, topic, and purpose.

_____ The page functions, including navigation menus, are logically presented and enable readers to find what they need quickly.

_____ The content collected for the site (from brochures to reports) and support materials (images, audio, and video) are available, approved, accurate, and in the correct format for presentation or download.

_____ The site plan allows information to be presented and cross-referenced in logical and efficient pathways.

_____ The page design incorporates the design principles described on pages 403–404.

_____ The informational and promotional aspects of the site are appropriate to the audience, topic, and purpose.

Critical-Thinking and Writing Activities

As directed by your instructor, complete the following activities.

1. Research and study the content, style, and design of websites related to your particular major, field, or discipline. Then develop a report on those sites, incorporating three or four screen shots for analysis.

2. Go to the home page of your college or university and review the page elements and functions. Team up with a classmate to discuss how well the page addresses its purpose(s), audience(s), and topic(s). Then imagine you have been hired to revise and refine the page. Print out a copy and mark it up with your changes. Create a "mockup" of a new and improved home page. Draft a one-page overview that explains how your revision is better than the original.

3. Working with classmates, brainstorm a list of campus clubs and associations that currently do not have websites (or at least not quality websites). Using the guidelines from this chapter, develop a website for one of them. As another option, consider a nonprofit organization in your area. Collaborate and conduct research as needed.

◀ VISUALLY SPEAKING

Examine the photograph on page 397 and explain what it suggests about web design and web use.

PREPARING ORAL PRESENTATIONS 27

Throughout your career (including your college years), you will give many oral presentations—from brief introductions to lengthy reports. In each situation, the following basic steps will help you develop a strong message.

Audio

Video

State your purpose.

- Am I trying to persuade, inspire, inform, or teach?

Identify your audience.

- What are my listeners' ages, interests, and knowledge of the topic?
- What will their attitude be toward the topic and toward me?

Select and research your topic.

- Which topics will fulfill my assignment and achieve my purpose?
- Where can I find information about my topic?
- Which support materials would help me present my message?

Organizing Your Presentation

After you've gathered your information, you must organize and develop the message. How? Start by thinking about your presentation as having three distinct parts: (1) an introduction, (2) a body, and (3) a conclusion. The guidelines on this page and the following two pages will help you integrate, organize, and refine all the parts so they communicate the message and achieve your purpose.

Prepare an introduction.

For any speaking situation, you should develop an introduction that does the following things:

- Greets the audience and grabs their attention
- Communicates your interest in them
- Introduces your topic and main idea
- Shows that you have something worthwhile to say
- Establishes an appropriate tone

You may greet the audience in many ways, including introducing yourself or making appropriate comments about the occasion, the individuals present, or the setting. Following these comments, introduce your topic and main idea as quickly and as clearly as you can. For example, you could open with one of these attention-grabbing strategies:

- A little-known fact or statistic
- A series of questions
- A humorous story or anecdote
- An appropriate quotation
- A description of a serious problem
- A cartoon, picture, or drawing
- A short demonstration
- A statement about the topic's importance
- An eye-catching prop or display
- A video or an audio clip

Tip: As a matter of courtesy, audiences will generally give you their attention—but only for about thirty seconds. After that, you must *earn* it by presenting information that they believe is worth hearing.

Develop the body.

The body of your presentation should deliver the message—and supporting points—so clearly that the audience understands the presentation after hearing it only once. The key to developing such a clear message is choosing an organizational pattern that fits your purpose.

Before you outline the body, take a moment to review what you want your presentation to do: Explain a problem? Promote an idea? Teach a process? Be sure the organizational pattern will help you do that. For example, if you want to teach a process, the outline should list the process steps in chronological order. If your outline is clear, you may begin to write.

Organizational Patterns

Organizational patterns for explaining a process and other purposes are listed below.

- **Chronological order:** Arrange information according to the time order in which events (or steps in a process) take place.
- **Order of importance:** Arrange information according to its importance— greatest to least or least to greatest.
- **Comparison/contrast:** Give information about subjects by comparing and contrasting them.
- **Cause/effect:** Give information about a situation or problem by showing the causes and the effects.
- **Order of location:** Arrange information about subjects according to where things are located in relation to each other.
- **Problem/solution:** Describe a problem and then present a solution for it.

Writing an Outline or a Manuscript

After deciding how to organize your message, write it out in either outline or manuscript form. For help, see the tips below and the model on pages 414–415.

Body-Building Tips

- Build your presentation around several key ideas. (Don't try to cover too much ground.)
- Write with a personal, natural voice.
- Support your main points with reliable facts and clear examples.
- Present your information in short, easy-to-follow segments.
- Use positive, respectful language. (Avoid jargon.)
- Use graphic aids and handouts.

Come to a conclusion.

A strong introduction and conclusion work like bookends supporting the body of the presentation. The introduction gets the audience's attention, sets the tone, states the main idea, and identifies the key points of the message. Almost in reverse, the conclusion reviews those points, restates the main idea, reinforces the tone, and refocuses the audience on what it should think about or do. Together, those bookends emphasize and clarify the message so that listeners will understand and remember it.

Concluding Strategies

Here are some strategies—which you can use alone or in combination—for concluding a presentation:

- Review your main idea and key points.
- Issue a personal challenge.
- Come "full circle." (State those arguments or details that back up your original point.)
- Recommend a plan of action.
- Suggest additional sources of information.
- Thank the audience and ask for questions.

Hold a Q & A session.

After your presentation, you may want to invite your audience to ask questions. Very often, a Q & A session is the real payoff for participants. They can ask for clarification of points or inquire about how your message applies to their personal situations. Audience members may even offer their own insights or solutions to problems mentioned in the presentation.

Q & A Tips

The following suggestions will help you lead a good Q & A session:

- Listen carefully and think about each part of the question.
- Repeat or paraphrase questions for the benefit of the entire group.
- Answer the questions concisely and clearly.
- Respond honestly when you don't know the answer, and offer to find one.
- Ask for a follow-up question if someone seems confused after your answer.
- Look directly at the group when you answer.
- Be prepared to pose an important question or two if no one asks a question.
- Conclude by thanking the audience for their participation.

Writing Your Presentation

How much of your presentation you actually write out depends on your topic, audience, purpose, and—of course—personal style. The three most common forms to use when making a presentation are a list, an outline, and a manuscript.

List: Use a list for a short, informal speech such as an after-dinner introduction. Think about your purpose and then list the following:

- Your opening sentence (or two)
- A summary phrase for each of your main points
- Your closing sentence

Outline: Use an outline for a more complex or formal topic. You can organize your material in greater detail without tying yourself to a word-for-word presentation. Here's one way you can do it:

- Opening (complete sentences)
- All main points (sentences)
- Supporting points (phrases)
  quotations (written out)
  all supporting technical details,
  statistics, and sources (listed)
- Closing (complete sentences)

Wherever appropriate, include notes on visual aids (in caps or boldface).

Manuscript: Use the guidelines below if you plan to write out your presentation word for word:

- Double-space and number pages (or cards).
- Use complete sentences on a page (do not run sentences from one page to another).
- Mark difficult words for pronunciation.
- Mark the script for interpretation using symbols such as boldface or italics to signal emphasis or vocal color.

List

1. Opening sentence or two
2. Phrase 1
   Phrase 2
   Phrase 3
3. Closing sentence

Outline

I. Opening statement
   A. Point with support
   B. Point (purpose or goal) [VISUAL 1]
II. Body (with 3-5 main points)
   A. Main point
     1. Supporting details
     2. Supporting details
   B. Main point
     1. Supporting details
     2. Supporting details
   C. Main point
     1. Supporting details
     2. Supporting details
III. Closing statement
   A. Point, including restatement of purpose
   B. Point, possibly a call to action [VISUAL 2]

Student Model

Interactive

In her formal presentation below, student Burnette Sawyer argues that college students must begin a retirement savings plan today. Notice that she uses italics to mark words needing vocal color and boldface to mark words needing emphasis. She places all visual aid cues in color.

Save Now or Pay Later

The speaker begins with an anecdote.

Imagine that you've finished school, gotten a job, worked hard all week, *1* and this dollar bill represents your whole paycheck. [hold up dollar bill] As your employer, I'm about to hand you the check when I stop, tear off about 20 percent like this, give it to Uncle Sam, and say, "Here's my employee's income tax." Then I tear off another 30 percent like this, give that to Uncle Sam too, and say, "And here's her Medicare and Social Security tax."

She tears the dollar for emphasis.

Finally, I give you this half and say, "Here, hard worker, this is what's *2* left of your *whole paycheck.*"

Does that sound like science fiction? *3*

Senator Alan Simpson doesn't think so. In the magazine *Modern* *4* *Maturity,* he says that unless legislation changes the Social Security system, *our generation* will have to pay 20 percent [SLIDE 1] of our paychecks as income tax, and 30 percent [SLIDE 2] as Social Security tax. That means we can keep just **50 percent** [SLIDE 3] of what we earn.

But the news gets **worse.** Remember this 30 percent that we paid to *5* Social Security? [hold up piece of dollar bill] Well, that won't be enough money for retired people to live on in the year 2043. Remember that year, 2043—we'll come back to that soon.

The speaker asks questions to involve the audience.

What's the problem? The Social Security system can't ensure our *6* savings for retirement.

What's the solution? We have to start our own savings plans, and the *7* earlier, the better.

Ever since the Social Security system started back in 1935 [SLIDE 4], *8* it has never been secure. While the system has been "fixed" a number of times, these fix-it jobs haven't solved the problem. For example, writer Keith Carlson points out that in 1983 [SLIDE 5] Congress raised payroll taxes, extended the retirement age, and said that the system would be in good financial shape until 2056.

Throughout the speech, she uses 11 slides to give her listeners a clear understanding of the main points.

But then, says Carlson, *just nine years later,* a report came out saying *9* that Congress had been **wrong.** The report [SLIDE 6] said in 1992 that Social Security money wouldn't even last that long—it would run out by 2043. *Remember that year, 2043?* That's before many of us are supposed *to retire at age 67!*

Do you think this news is bad? The AARP Bulletin reported on the *10* Bipartisan Commission on Entitlement and Tax Reform. This commission warned that entitlement programs like Social Security [SLIDE 7] are growing so fast they could "bankrupt the country" by the year 2029—long before we retire!

So what should we do? This fall many of us will vote in a presidential *11* election for the first time. Both Democrats and Republicans say they have a plan to fix Social Security. What if we all vote for the presidential candidate with the best plan? Will that save our retirement funds? **Don't count on it!** As the track record for Social Security shows, one more fix-it job won't fix the system. We have to start *our own* retirement plans—and do it early in our careers.

In fact, in his book *Retirement 101,* Willard Enteman says that *12* we should start a personal savings plan the day we get our first paychecks. In sociology class last week, Mr. Christians made the same point. He gave us this bar graph [SLIDE 8] showing that if our goal is to save $500,000 by age 67, we had better *start early* before saving gets too expensive.

As you can see from the graph, if we start saving when we're 25, we *13* can reach $500,000 by saving just $121 a month. [SLIDE 9] If we wait until we're 35, we'll have to save $282 a month. [SLIDE 10] If we wait until we're 45, we'll have to put away $698 a month. [SLIDE 11] And if we wait until we're 55, we'll need $2,079 a month.

> The closing paragraphs help listeners reflect on the subject.

Look at the difference. To reach $500,000 by age 67 would cost $121 a *14* month if we start at 25, and $2,079 a month if we start at 55.

What's my point? The Social Security system *can't promise us* financial *15* security when we retire in 2050.

What's the solution? We have to start our own savings plans; and the *16* *earlier* we start, the *easier* it will be to reach our goals. ■

Note: Sample slides for this presentation are shown on page **416**.

Marking Your Presentation

As you rehearse your presentation, decide which words or phrases to emphasize, where to pause, and where to add visual aids. Then use the symbols and text enhancements below to mark the copy of your presentation.

Italic or boldface. . . . . for additional feeling or emotion
Underlining . . . . for greater volume or emphasis
Dash, diagonal, ellipsis . . . . . for a pause—or / a break in the flow
Brackets . . . . for actions or [visual aids]

Use visual aids.

While constructing your presentation, think about visual aids that would grab the audience's attention and help them understand the message. For example, in her speech, Burnette Sawyer used the computer-generated graphics below. (See pages 414–415.)

Sample Graphics

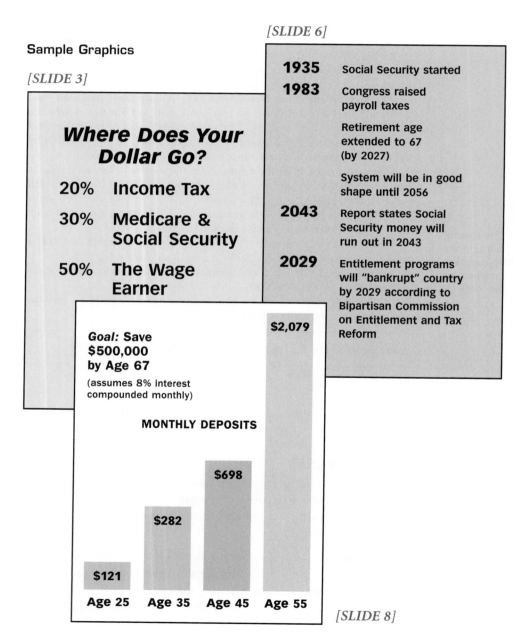

[SLIDE 6]

[SLIDE 3]

Where Does Your Dollar Go?

20% Income Tax

30% Medicare & Social Security

50% The Wage Earner

1935 Social Security started

1983 Congress raised payroll taxes

Retirement age extended to 67 (by 2027)

System will be in good shape until 2056

2043 Report states Social Security money will run out in 2043

2029 Entitlement programs will "bankrupt" country by 2029 according to Bipartisan Commission on Entitlement and Tax Reform

Goal: Save $500,000 by Age 67 (assumes 8% interest compounded monthly)

MONTHLY DEPOSITS

$2,079

$698

$282

$121

Age 25   Age 35   Age 45   Age 55

[SLIDE 8]

Developing Computer Presentations

To help you use presentation software effectively, follow the guidelines below.

1. **Develop a design.** Be sure your graphic design fits your topic and your audience—polished for a serious topic, casual for an informal topic.

2. **Create pages.** If a main idea has several parts, present each one on its own page. Each click of the mouse button (or computer key) should reveal a new detail.

3. **Use transitions.** Dissolves, fades, wipes, and other transitional effects refine a computer presentation and keep the audience's attention (as long as the devices don't detract from the message).

4. **Add sound.** Just as graphics and animation can enhance a presentation, so, too, can sound. Music can serve as an introduction or backdrop, and sound effects can add emphasis. Voice recording can add authority and help drive home key points.

TIP for speakers: Text can be animated to appear from off-screen at just the right moment. Graphics can be made to appear one element at a time, and illustrations can change before the viewer's eyes. Remember to use special effects—especially animation—wisely.

5. **Fine-tune your presentation.** Practice delivering your presentation while clicking through your pages. Try it with an audience of fellow students, if possible, and ask for their input.

6. **Check for word choice and style.** Make sure that the words on the screen are key words. Use these words as talking points—don't try to cover any point word for word. Also, check that transitions, animations, and sounds are smooth and not disruptive.

7. **Edit the final version.** Check spelling, punctuation, usage, and other mechanics. Remember: On-screen errors are glaringly obvious to everyone.

8. **Rehearse.** Perform your presentation for a friend or family member. Practice running the equipment until you can use it with confidence.

9. **Make a backup copy.** Protect all the effort you invested in your presentation.

TIP: Choose an easy-to-read font and type-size. In most situations, 36-point headings and 24-point text work well. However, the type-size needed depends on a number of variables, including the screen size, lens type, and audience's distance from the screen.

Overcoming Stage Fright Checklist

While it's okay to feel a little nervous before a presentation (the emotion keeps you alert), stage fright can limit your ability to communicate. The remedy for stage fright is confidence—confidence in what to say and how to say it. To develop that confidence, do the following:

Personal Preparation

_____ Know your subject well.

_____ Rehearse the presentation thoroughly, including the use of visuals.

_____ Schedule your time carefully, making sure to arrive early.

_____ Try to relax before the presentation by stretching or doing a deep-breathing exercise, remembering that your presentation can be successful without being perfect.

The Room and Equipment

_____ See that the room is clean, comfortable, and well lit.

_____ Make sure tables and chairs are set up and arranged correctly.

_____ Check that AV equipment is in place and working.

_____ Test the microphone volume.

_____ Position the screen and displays for good visibility.

Personal Details

_____ Check your clothing and hair.

_____ Arrange for drinking water to be available.

_____ Put your script and handouts in place.

Speaking Strategies

_____ Be confident, positive, and energetic.

_____ Maintain eye contact when speaking or listening.

_____ Use gestures naturally—don't force them.

_____ Provide for audience participation; survey the audience: "How many of you . . . ?"

_____ Maintain a comfortable, erect posture.

_____ Speak up and speak clearly—don't rush.

_____ Reword and clarify when necessary.

_____ After the presentation, ask for questions and answer them clearly.

_____ Thank the audience.

III

Research and writing

CONTENTS
Research and Writing

GETTING STARTED: FROM PLANNING RESEARCH TO EVALUATING SOURCES

28

At first glance, research looks like a dry-as-dust business carried out by obsessed scholars in dim libraries and mad scientists in cluttered laboratories. Research couldn't be further from the reality of your life.

But is it? Consider car tires. Before these were mounted, scientists researched which materials would resist wear and which adhesives would keep treads on steel belts. Sloppy research could cause blowouts; good research builds safe tires.

You want to do such good research in your college research assignments, which may be your toughest projects. They may take weeks to complete, including hours spent on the trail of facts, figures, and ideas. These projects demand that you organize your tasks carefully and digest the thinking of others while discovering your own perspective. However, the rewards of research projects can be great—new insights into a subject that really interests you, a deepened understanding of your major or profession, reliable knowledge to share with others, and sharpened thinking skills.

QUICK GUIDE

— Papers with Documented Research ——

Web Link

When you work on a research project, you ask important questions, look systematically for answers, and share your conclusions with readers. In other words, it's all about curiosity, discovery, and dialogue.

Starting Point: The assignment usually relates to a course concept, so consider what your instructor wants you to learn and how your project will be evaluated. Then take ownership of the project by looking for an angle that makes the writing relevant for you.

Purpose: The project requires you to conduct research and share results. Your main goal is to discover the complex truth about a topic and clarify that discovery for others.

Form: The traditional research paper is a fairly long essay (5 to 15 pages) complete with thesis, supporting paragraphs, integrated sources, and careful documentation. However, you may be asked to shape your research into a field report, a website, or a multimedia presentation.

Audience: Traditionally, research writing addresses "the academic community," a group made up mainly of instructors and students. However, your actual audience may be more specific: addicted smokers, all Floridians, fellow immigrants, and so on.

Voice: The tone is usually formal or semiformal, but check your instructor's expectations. In any research writing, maintain a thoughtful, confidently measured tone. After all, your research has made you somewhat of an authority on the topic.

Point of View: Generally, research writers avoid the pronouns "I" and "you" in an effort to remain properly objective and academic sounding. Unfortunately, this practice can result in an overuse of both the pronoun "one" and the passive voice. Some instructors encourage students to connect research with experience, meaning that you may use the pronouns "I" and "you" occasionally. Be careful, however, to keep the focus where it belongs— on the topic. Bottom line: Follow your instructor's requirements concerning pronoun use. For more on developing a strong academic style for your research writing, see pages 78–79.

INSIGHT: The best research writing centers on *your* ideas—ideas you develop through thoughtful engagement with sources. In poor research papers, the sources dominate, and the writer's perspective disappears.

The Research Process: A Flowchart

The research process involves getting started, planning, conducting the research, and organizing the results. This process is flexible enough to be adapted to diverse research projects. In fact, real research is typically dynamic: You might think during the planning phase that you've nailed down your topic, only to discover a surprising topical detour while conducting research. Generally, however, the research process maps out as shown below. When you get your assignment—whether to write a five-page paper on pasteurization or to develop a website on Middle Eastern political conflicts—review the process and tailor it to the task.

Getting Started
- Review the assignment.
- Consider your resources.
- Choose a subject.

List or cluster your current ideas and opinions.

Talk with others to learn opposing opinions.

Conduct preliminary research in reference works.

Planning Your Research
Narrow the topic, form a research question or working thesis, develop a research plan, and select keyword–searching terms.

Conducting Research

Conduct Primary Research

Take Careful Notes

Conduct Secondary Research

Observe, interview, survey, or experiment.

Reflect in your research journal.

Check books, articles, and websites.

Analyze primary documents and artifacts.

Create and add to a working bibliography.

Search catalogs, indexes, databases, and the Internet.

- Evaluate and take notes from sources.
- Summarize, para-phrase, and quote.

Organizing and Drafting
- Answer your research question or refine your thesis.
- Develop an outline.
- Write the research paper, integrating and documenting sources.

Video

Getting Started: Getting Focused

Early in your project, get focused by narrowing your topic, brainstorming research questions, and developing a working thesis. For help understanding assignments and selecting topics, as well as other prewriting strategies, see pages 30–31.

Establish a narrow, manageable topic.

To do good research, you need an engaging, manageable topic. Once you have a broad topic, narrow your focus to a specific feature or angle that allows for in-depth research. Try these strategies:

Video

- Check your topic in the Library of Congress subject headings, available in your library. Note "narrower terms" listed (see page 430).
- Read about your topic. By consulting specialized reference works, explore background that directs you to subtopics (see page 461).
- Check the Internet. For example, follow a subject directory to see where your topic leads (see pages 469–473).
- Freewrite to discover which aspect of the topic interests you most: a local angle, a connection with a group of people, or a personal concern.

Broad Topic	Manageable Focus
Homelessness	Homeless Families in Los Angeles
Bacteria and Viruses	Bacterial Resistance to Antibiotics
Alternative Energy Sources	Development of Hybrid-Electric Vehicles

Brainstorm research questions.

Good research questions help you find meaningful information and ideas about your topic. These questions sharpen your research goal, and the answers will become the focus of your writing. Brainstorm questions by following these guidelines:

List both simple and substantial questions. Basic questions aim for factual answers. More complex questions get at analysis, synthesis, and evaluation.

- **Question of fact:** When did Saddam Hussein gain power in Iraq?
- **Question of interpretation:** How did Saddam Hussein maintain power?

List main and secondary questions. Ask a primary question about your topic—the main issue that you want to get at. Then brainstorm secondary questions that you need to research to answer your primary question.

- **Main Question:** Should consumers embrace hybrid cars?
- **Secondary Questions** (*Who, What, When, Where, Why, How*): Who has developed hybrid cars? What is a hybrid car? When were hybrids developed? Where are hybrids currently used? Why are hybrids being developed? How does a hybrid work?

Testing Your Main Research Question

_____ Is the question so broad that I can't answer it in the project's time and page limits?

_____ Is the question so narrow that I won't be able to find sources?

_____ Is the question so simple that it will be too easy to answer?

_____ Will the question lead to significant sources and intellectual challenge?

_____ Am I committed to answering this question? Does it interest me?

_____ Will the question and answers interest my readers?

Develop a working thesis.

A working thesis offers a preliminary answer to your main research question. As your initial perspective on the topic, a good working thesis keeps you focused during research, helping you decide whether to carefully read a particular book or just skim it, fully explore a website or quickly surf through it. Make your working thesis a statement that demands "Prove it!" Don't settle for a simple statement of fact about your topic; instead, choose a working thesis that seems debatable or that requires some explanation. Try this formula:

Formula: Working Thesis =
limited topic + *tentative claim, statement, or hypothesis*

Examples: **E-communication technologies** *are eroding real communication skills.*

Downtown revitalization *will have distinct economic, environmental, and social benefits.*

Internet dating *is weakening long-term relationships.*

Working Thesis Checklist

_____ Does my working thesis focus on a single, limited topic?

_____ Is my working thesis stated in a clear, direct sentence?

_____ Does my working thesis convey my initial perspective about the topic?

_____ Do I have access to enough good information to support this working thesis?

_____ Does my working thesis direct me to write a paper that meets all assignment requirements?

INSIGHT: Your working thesis is written in sand, not stone. It may change as you research the topic because sources may push you in new directions. In fact, such change shows that you are engaging your sources and growing in your thinking.

Developing a Research Plan

It pays to plan your research. In fact, minutes spent planning research can save hours doing research. With your limited topic, main research question, and working thesis in front of you, plan your project more fully.

Choose research methods.

Consider these questions: What do you already know about the topic? What do you need to know? Which resources will help you answer your research question? Which resources does the assignment require? Based on your answers, map out a research plan that draws resources from fitting categories.

Background research: To find information about your topic's context, central concepts, and key terms, take these steps:

- Use the Library of Congress subject headings to find keywords for searching the library catalog, periodical databases, and the Internet (see page 430).
- Conduct a preliminary search of the library catalog, journal databases, and the Internet to confirm that good resources on your topic exist.
- Use specialized reference works to find background information, definitions, facts, and statistics (see page 461).

Field or primary research: If appropriate for your project, conduct field research:

- Use interviews (page 454) or surveys (page 450–451) to get key information from experts or others.
- Conduct observations or experiments (page 449) to obtain hard data.
- Analyze key documents or artifacts (pages 452–453).

Library research: Select important library resources:

- Use scholarly books to get in-depth, reliable material (pages 458–459).
- Use periodical articles (print or electronic) to get current, reliable information (pages 460–462). Select from news sources, popular magazines, scholarly journals, and trade journals.
- Consider other library resources, such as a documentary, recorded interview, pamphlet, marketing study, or government publication.

Internet research: Plan effective Internet searches using the following:

- Search engines and subject guides: Choose tools that will lead you to quality resources (pages 472–473).
- Expert guidance: Select reputable websites that librarians or other experts recommend (pages 468–471).
- Evaluation: Test all web resources for reliability (pages 432–435).
- Limitations: How many web resources are you allowed to use, if any?

Get organized to do research.

An organized approach to doing your research will save you time, help you work efficiently, and prevent frustration. Get organized by addressing these issues:

Establishing Priorities for Resources, Time, and Effort

- How much research material do you need?
- What range of resources will give you quality, reliable information?
- Which types of research does the assignment specify? Are you limited, for example, in the number of Internet sources you can use?
- What are the project's priorities: What must you do? Which tasks are secondary in nature?
- What weight does the project carry in the course? How should you match your time and effort with that weight?

INSIGHT: Gather more information than you could ever use in your paper. That richness gives you choices and allows you to sift for crucial information.

Selecting Research Methods and Systems

- Given the resources and technologies available, select methods that help you do research efficiently: signing out hard-copy library holdings or using interlibrary loan; photocopying book sections and journal articles; printing, saving, downloading, bookmarking, or e-mailing digital materials.
- Develop a note-taking system. Choose from the note-card, double-entry notebook, copy-and-annotate, and research-log methods (pages 438–441). In addition, set up a working bibliography (pages 436–437).
- Choose and review a documentation system. It's likely that your instructor will designate a system such as MLA (pages 493–534) or APA (pages 535–566). If he or she doesn't do so, then use a method that suits the subject matter and discipline. Review the system's basic rules and strategies.

Establishing a Schedule

Generally, you should spend about half your time on research and half on writing. Sketch out tentative deadlines for completing each phase of your work.

Web Link: A sample schedule is at **www.thecollegewriter.com/3e.**

Developing a Research Proposal

For some research projects (e.g., individual studies, field research, a senior thesis paper), you may have to formalize your plan by writing a research proposal. Such a proposal aims to show that the research is both valid and valuable; to communicate your enthusiasm for the project; to show that your plan is workable within the constraints of the assignment; and to gain your instructor's feedback and approval.

Web Link: A sample proposal is at **www.thecollegewriter.com/3e.**

Exploring Possible Information Resources and Sites

To conduct thorough, creative, but efficient research, you need a sense of which types of resources are available for your project and where to find them. Check the tables that follow.

Consider different information resources.

Examine the range of resources available: Which will give you the best information for your project? While one project (for example, a sociological report on airport behaviors) might require personal, direct sources, another project (for example, the effects of the September 11, 2001, terrorist attacks on the air transportation industry) might depend on government reports, business publications, and journal articles. Generally, a well-rounded research paper relies on a range of quality resources; in particular, it avoids relying on insubstantial web information.

Type of Resource	Examples
Personal, direct resources	Memories, diaries, journals, logs, experiments, tests, observations, interviews, surveys
Reference works (print and electronic)	Dictionaries, thesauruses, encyclopedias, almanacs, yearbooks, atlases, directories, guides, handbooks, indexes, abstracts, catalogs, bibliographies
Books (print and electronic)	Nonfiction, how-to, biographies, fiction, trade books, scholarly and scientific studies
Periodicals and news sources	Print newspapers, magazines, and journals; broadcast news and news magazines; online magazines, news sources, and discussion groups
Audiovisual, digital, and multimedia resources	Graphics (tables, graphs, charts, maps, drawings, photos), audiotapes, CDs, videos, DVDs, webpages, online databases
Government publications	Guides, programs, forms, legislation, regulations, reports, records, statistics
Business and nonprofit publications	Correspondence, reports, newsletters, pamphlets, brochures, ads, catalogs, instructions, handbooks, manuals, policies and procedures, seminar and training materials

Consider different information sites.

Where do you go to find the resources that you need? Consider the information "sites" listed below, remembering that many resources may be available in different forms in different locations. For example, a journal article may be available in library holdings or in an electronic database.

Information Location	Specific "Sites"
People	Experts (knowledge area, skill, occupation) Population segments or individuals (with representative or unusual experiences)
Libraries	General: public, college, online Specialized: legal, medical, government, business
Computer resources	Computers: software, CD-ROMs Networks: Internet and other online services (e-mail, limited-access databases, discussion groups, MUDs, chat rooms, websites, blogs, YouTube, image banks, wikis); intranets
Mass media	Radio (AM and FM) Television (network, public, cable, satellite) Print (newspapers, magazines, journals)
Testing, training, meeting, and observation sites	Plants, facilities, field sites, laboratories Research centers, universities, think tanks Conventions, conferences, seminars Museums, galleries, historical sites
Municipal, state, and federal government offices	Elected officials, representatives Offices and agencies, Government Printing Office Websites (GPO, www.gpoaccess.gov)
Business and nonprofit publications	Computer databases, company files Desktop reference materials Bulletin boards (physical and electronic) Company and department websites Departments and offices Associations, professional organizations Consulting, training, and business information services

Web Link

Conducting Effective Keyword Searches

Keyword searching can help you find information in electronic library catalogs, online databases that index periodical articles (for example, Lexis-Nexis, EBSCOhost), print indexes to periodical publications (for example, *Business Periodicals Index*), Internet resources, print books, and e-books.

Choose keywords carefully.

Keywords give you "compass points" for navigating through a sea of information. That's why choosing the best keywords is crucial. Consider these tips:

1. **Brainstorm a list of possible keywords**—topics, titles, and names—based on your current knowledge and/or background reading.

2. **Consult the Library of Congress subject headings.** These books contain the keywords librarians use when classifying materials. For example, if you looked up *immigrants,* you would find the entry below, indicating keywords to use, along with narrower, related, and broader terms. When you are conducting subject searches of catalogs and databases, these are the terms that will get you the best results.

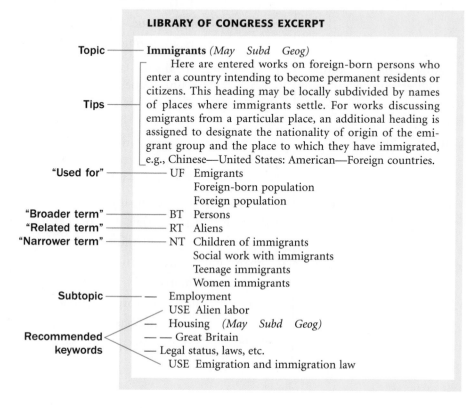

LIBRARY OF CONGRESS EXCERPT

Topic —— **Immigrants** *(May   Subd   Geog)*

Tips ——
Here are entered works on foreign-born persons who enter a country intending to become permanent residents or citizens. This heading may be locally subdivided by names of places where immigrants settle. For works discussing emigrants from a particular place, an additional heading is assigned to designate the nationality of origin of the emigrant group and the place to which they have immigrated, e.g., Chinese—United States: American—Foreign countries.

"Used for" —— UF   Emigrants
Foreign-born population
Foreign population

"Broader term" —— BT   Persons
"Related term" —— RT   Aliens
"Narrower term" —— NT   Children of immigrants
Social work with immigrants
Teenage immigrants
Women immigrants

Subtopic —— —   Employment
USE Alien labor
—   Housing   *(May   Subd   Geog)*
Recommended —— — Great Britain
keywords —— Legal status, laws, etc.
USE   Emigration and immigration law

Use keyword strategies.

The goal of a keyword search is to find quality research sources. To ensure that you identify the best resources available, follow these strategies:

Get to know the database. Look for answers to these questions:

- What material does the database contain? What time frames?
- What are you searching—authors, titles, subjects, full text?
- What are the search rules? How can you narrow the search?

Use a shotgun approach. Start with the most likely keyword. If you have no "hits," choose a related term. Once you get some hits, check the citations for clues regarding which words to use as you continue searching.

Use Boolean operators to refine your search. When you combine keywords with Boolean operators—such as those below—you will obtain better results.

Boolean Operators

Narrowing a Search **And, +, not, –** Use when one term gives you too many hits, especially irrelevant ones	**buffalo and bison** or **buffalo + bison**	Searches for citations containing both keywords
	buffalo not water **+buffalo –water**	Searches for "buffalo" but not "water," so that you eliminate material on water buffalo
Expanding a Search **Or** Combine a term providing few hits with a related word	**buffalo or bison**	Searches for citations containing either term
Specifying a Phrase **Quotation marks** Indicate that you wish to search for the exact phrase enclosed	**"reclamation project"**	Searches for the exact phrase "reclamation project"
Sequencing Operations **Parentheses** Indicate that the operation should be performed before other operations in the search string	**(buffalo or bison) and ranching**	Searches first for citations containing either "buffalo" or "bison" before checking the resulting citations for "ranching"
Finding Variations **Wild card symbols** Depending on the database, symbols such as $, ?, or # can find variations of a word	**ethic#** **ethic$**	Searches for terms like *ethics* and *ethical*

Engaging and Evaluating Sources

Using reliable benchmarks, you should test all sources before you rely on them in your writing. After all, credible sources help your own credibility; sources that aren't credible destroy it. The benchmarks on the next four pages will help you test your sources' usefulness and reliability.

Engage your sources.

Engaged reading is the opposite of passive reading—treating all sources equally, swallowing whole what's in the material, or looking only for information that supports your opinion. Full engagement involves these practices:

Test each source to see if it's worth reading. When reviewing source citations and generating a working bibliography, study titles, descriptions, lengths, and publication dates, asking these questions:

- How closely related to my topic is this source?
- Is this source too basic, overly complex, or just right?
- What could this source add to my overall balance of sources?

If you were writing about NASA's space shuttle program, for example, you might find a ten-page article in *Scientific American* more valuable and insightful than a brief news article on a specific flight or a *Star Trek* fan's blog on the topic.

INSIGHT: Don't reject a source simply because it disagrees with your perspective. Good research engages rather than ignores opposing points of view.

Skim sources before reading in-depth. Consider marking key pages or passages with sticky notes, tabs, or a digital bookmark.

- Review the author biography, preface, and/or introduction to discover the perspective, approach, scope, and research methods.
- Using your keywords, review any outline, abstract, table of contents, index, or home page to get a sense of coverage.

Read with an open but not an empty mind. Carry on a dialogue with the source, asking questions like "Why?" and "So what?"

- Note the purpose and audience. Was the piece written to inform or persuade? Is it aimed at the public, specialists, supporters, or opponents?
- Read to understand the source: What's clear and what's confusing?
- Relate the source to your research question: How does the source affirm or challenge your ideas? Synthesize what you read with what you know.
- Record your reactions to it—what it makes you think, feel, believe.
- Consider how you might use this source in your writing—key facts, important ideas, opposing perspectives, or examples.
- Check footnotes, references, appendices, and links for further leads.

Rate source reliability and depth.

You should judge each source on its own merit. Generally, however, types of sources can be rated for depth and reliability, as shown in the table below, based on their authorship, length, topic treatment, documentation, publication method, review process, distance from primary sources, allegiances, stability, and so on. Use the table to

1. Target sources that fit your project's goals,
2. Assess the approximate quality of the sources you're gathering, and
3. Build a strong bibliography that readers will respect.

DEEP, RELIABLE, CREDIBLE SOURCES

Scholarly Books and Articles: largely based on careful research; written by experts for experts; address topics in depth; involve peer review and careful editing; offer stable discussion of topic

Trade Books and Journal Articles: largely based on careful research; written by experts for educated general audience. *Sample periodicals: Atlantic Monthly, Scientific American, Nature, Orion*

Government Resources: books, reports, webpages, guides, statistics developed by experts at government agencies; provided as service to citizens; relatively objective. *Sample source: Statistical Abstract of the United States*

Reviewed Official Online Documents: Internet resources posted by legitimate institutions—colleges and universities, research institutes, service organizations; although offering a particular perspective, sources tend to be balanced

Reference Works and Textbooks: provide general and specialized information; carefully researched, reviewed, and edited; lack depth for focused research (e.g., general encyclopedia entry)

News and Topical Stories from Quality Sources: provide current affairs coverage (print and online), introduction-level articles of interest to general public; may lack depth and length. *Sample sources:* the *Washington Post,* the *New York Times; Time, Psychology Today;* NPR's *All Things Considered*

Popular Magazine Stories: short, introductory articles often distant from primary sources and without documentation; heavy advertising. *Sample sources: Glamour, Seventeen, Reader's Digest*

Business and Nonprofit Publications: pamphlets, reports, news releases, brochures, manuals; range from informative to sales-focused

List Server Discussions, Usenet Postings, Blog Articles, Talk Radio Discussions: highly open, fluid, undocumented, untested exchanges and publications; unstable resource

SHALLOW, UNRELIABLE, NOT CREDIBLE SOURCES

Unregulated Web Material: personal sites, joke sites, chat rooms, special-interest sites, advertising and junk e-mail (spam); no review process, little accountability, biased presentation

Tabloid Articles (print and web): contain exaggerated and untrue stories written to titillate and exploit. *Sample source:* the *National Enquirer,* the *Weekly World News*

Web Link

Evaluate print and online sources.

As you work with a source, you need to test its reliability. The benchmarks that follow apply to both print and online sources; note, however, the additional tests offered for web sources.

Credible author An expert is an authority—someone who has mastered a subject area. Is the author an expert on this topic? What are her or his credentials, and can you confirm them? For example, an automotive engineer would be an expert on hybrid-vehicle technology, whereas a celebrity in a commercial would not.

> *Web test:* Is an author indicated? If so, are the author's credentials noted and contact information offered (for example, an e-mail address)?

Reliable publication Has the source been published by a scholarly press, a peer-reviewed professional journal, a quality trade-book publisher, or a trusted news source? Did you find this resource through a reliable search tool (for example, a library catalog or database)?

> *Web test:* Which individual or group posted this page? Is the site rated by a subject directory or library organization? How stable is the site—has it been around for a while and does material remain available, or is the site "fly-by-night"? Check the site's home page, and read "About Us" pages and mission statements, looking for evidence of the organization's perspective, history, and trustworthiness.

Unbiased discussion While all sources come from a specific perspective and represent specific commitments, a biased source may be pushing an agenda in an unfair, unbalanced, incomplete manner. Watch for bias toward a certain region, country, political party, industry, gender, race, ethnic group, or religion. Be alert to connections among authors, financial backers, and the points of view shared. For example, if an author has functioned as a consultant to or a lobbyist for a particular industry or group (oil, animal rights), his or her allegiances may lead to a biased presentation of an issue.

> *Web test:* Is the online document one-sided? Is the site nonprofit (.org), government (.gov), commercial (.com), educational (.edu), business (.biz), informational (.info), network-related (.net), or military (.mil)? Is the site U.S. or international? Is this organization pushing a cause, product, service, or belief? How do advertising or special interests affect the site? You might suspect, for example, the scientific claims of a site sponsored by a pro-smoking organization.

> **Web Link:** Beware especially of masquerade sites—those that appear to be legitimate but are joke sites or, worse, propaganda lures. Check, for example, www.dhmo.org.

Current information A five-year-old book on computers may be outdated, but a forty-year-old book on Abraham Lincoln could still be the best source. Given what you need, is this source's discussion up-to-date?

Web test: When was the material originally posted and last updated? Are links live or dead?

Accurate information Bad research design, poor reporting, and sloppy documentation can lead to inaccurate information. Check the source for factual errors, statistical flaws, and conclusions that don't add up.

Web test: Is the site information-rich or -poor—filled with helpful, factual materials or fluffy with thin, unsubstantiated opinions? Can you trace and confirm sources by following links or conducting your own search?

Full, logical support Is the discussion of the topic reasonable, balanced, and complete? Are claims backed up with quality evidence? Does the source avoid faulty assumptions, twisted statistical analysis, logical fallacies, and unfair persuasion tactics? (See pages 267–270, for help.)

Web test: Does the webpage offer well-supported claims and helpful links to additional information?

Quality writing and design Is the source well written? Is it free of sarcasm, derogatory terms, clichés, catch phrases, mindless slogans, grammar slips, and spelling errors? Generally, poor writing correlates with sloppy thinking.

Web test: Are words neutral ("conservative perspective") or emotionally charged ("fascist agenda")? Are pages well designed—with clear rather than flashy, distracting multimedia elements? Is the site easy to navigate?

Positive relationship with other sources Does the source disagree with other sources? If yes, is the disagreement about the facts themselves or about how to interpret the facts? Which source seems more credible?

Web test: Is the site's information logically consistent with print sources? Do other reputable sites offer links to this site?

INSIGHT: Engage and evaluate visual resources as thoroughly as verbal materials. For example, ask yourself what tables, graphs, and photos really "say":

- Is the graphic informative or merely decorative?
- Does the graphic create a valid or manipulative central idea? For example, does the image seek to bypass logic by appealing to sexual impulses or to crude stereotypes?
- What does the graphic include and exclude in terms of information?
- Is the graphic well designed and easy to understand, or is it cluttered and distorted?
- Is a reliable source provided?

For more instruction on critical viewing, see pages 12–13.

Creating a Working Bibliography

A working bibliography lists sources you have used and intend to use. It helps you track your research, develop your final bibliography, and avoid plagiarism. Here's what to do:

Choose an orderly method.

Select an efficient approach for your project:

- **Paper note cards:** Use 3 × 5 inch cards, and record one source per card.
- **Paper notebook:** Use a small, spiral-bound book to record sources.
- **Computer program:** Record source information electronically, either by capturing citation details from online searches or by recording bibliographic information using word-processing software or research software such as TakeNote, EndNote Plus, or Bookends Pro.

Including Identifying Information for Sources

Start by giving each source a code number or letter: Doing so will help you when drafting and documenting your paper. Then include specific details for each kind of source listed below, shown on the facing page.

A. **Books:** author, title and subtitle, publication details (place, publisher, date)

B. **Periodicals:** author, article title, journal name, publication information (volume, number, date), page numbers

C. **Online sources:** author (if available), document title, site sponsor, database name, publication or posting date, access date, other publication information, URL

D. **Primary or field research:** date conducted, name and/or descriptive title of person interviewed, place observed, survey conducted, document analyzed

INSIGHT: Consider recording bibliographic details in the format of the documentation system you are using—MLA (pages 493–534) or APA (pages 535–566), for example. Doing so now will save time later. In addition, some research software allows you to record bibliographic information and then format it according to a specific system.

Adding Locating Information

Because you may need to retrace your research footsteps, include details about your research path:

A. **Books:** Include the Library of Congress or Dewey call number.

B. **Articles:** Note where and how you accessed them (stacks, current periodicals, microfilm, database)

C. **Webpages:** Record the complete URL, not just the broader site address.

D. **Field research:** Include a telephone number or e-mail address.

Annotating the Source

Add a note about the source's content, focus, reliability, and usefulness.

Sample Working Bibliography Entries

A. BOOK SOURCE NOTE:

> #2
>
> Howells, Coral Ann. Alice Munro. Contemporary World Writers. Manchester and New York: Manchester UP, 1998.
>
> PS 8576.U57 Z7 1998
>
> Book provides good introduction to Alice Munro's fiction, chapters arranged by Munro's works; contains intro, conclusion, and bibliography; 1998 date means author doesn't cover Munro's recent fiction

B. PERIODICAL SOURCE NOTE:

> #5
>
> Valdes, Marcela. "Some Stories Have to Be Told by Me: A Literary History of Alice Munro." Virginia Quarterly Review 82.3 (Summer 2006): 82-90.
>
> EBSCOhost Academic Search Premier http://web.ebscohost.com
>
> Article offers good introduction to Munro's life, her roots in Ontario, her writing career, and the key features of her stories

C. INTERNET SOURCE NOTE:

> #3
>
> "Alice Munro." Athabasca University Centre for Language and Literature: Canadian Writers. Updated 31 January 2008. Accessed 17 April 2008.
>
> http://www.athabascau.ca/writers/munro.html
> site offers good introduction to Munro's writing, along with links to bibliography and other resources

D. INTERVIEW SOURCE NOTE:

> #4
>
> Thacker, Robert. E-Mail interview. 7 March 2008.
>
> rthacker@mdu.edu
>
> author of critical biography on Munro, Alice Munro: Writing Her Lives, offered really helpful insights into her creative process, especially useful for story "Carried Away"

Developing a Note-Taking System

Accurate, thoughtful notes create a foundation for your research writing. The trick is to practice some sensible strategies and choose an efficient method.

Develop note-taking strategies.

What are you trying to do when you take notes on sources? What you are not doing is (a) collecting quotations to plunk in your project, (b) piling isolated grains of data into a large stack of disconnected facts, or (c) intensively reading and taking notes on every source you find. Instead, use these strategies:

Be selective. Guided by your research questions and working thesis, focus on sources that are central to your project. From these sources, record information clearly related to your limited topic, but also take notes on what surprises or puzzles you. Be selective, avoiding notes that are either too meager or too extensive. Suppose, for example, that you were writing a paper on the engineering problems facing NASA's space shuttle. If you were reading an article on the history and the future of this program, you might take careful notes on material describing the shuttle's technical details, but not on the astronauts' biographies.

Develop accurate, complete records. Your notes should . . .

- Accurately summarize, paraphrase, and quote sources (pages 442–444).
- Clearly show where you got your information.
- Cover all the research you've done—primary research (e.g., interviews, observations), books and periodical articles, and online sources.

Engage your sources. Evaluate what you are reading and develop your own responses. (See pages 4–11.) For example, with an article about NASA's space shuttle, you might test the author's biases, credentials, and logic; and you might respond with knowledge you have gained about other space programs.

INSIGHT: Take good notes on graphics in sources—tables, line graphs, photographs, maps, and so on. Such graphics are typically packed with information and powerfully convey ideas. (See "Critical Thinking Through Viewing," pages 12–17.)

Note-Taking Systems

A good note-taking system should help you do the following:

- Avoid unintentional plagiarism by developing accurate records, distinguishing among sources, and separating source material from your own ideas.
- Work efficiently at gathering what you need for the project.
- Work flexibly with a wide range of resources—primary and secondary, print and electronic, verbal and visual.
- Engage sources through creative and critical reflection.
- Record summaries, paraphrases, and quotations correctly.

- Be accurate and complete so that you need not reread sources.
- Efficiently develop your paper's outline and first draft.

INSIGHT: Different disciplines use different note-taking practices. In your major, learn these practices through courses that introduce you to the subject matter. Here are two examples:

- In literature studies, students conduct literary analyses by annotating print texts. Students may also take notes through keyword searches of e-books (for example, a Shakespeare play) and reviews of literary criticism.
- In environmental studies, students conduct research by (a) taking notes on published research to develop literature reviews, and (b) using a standard field notebook to collect data, make drawings, and reflect on results.

Four note-taking systems are outlined on the pages that follow. Choose the system that works best for your project, or combine elements to develop your own.

System 1: Paper or electronic note cards. Using paper note cards is the traditional method of note taking; however, note-taking software is now available with most word-processing programs and special programs like TakeNote, EndNote Plus, and Bookends Pro. Here's how a note-card system works:

1. Establish one set of cards (3 × 5 inches, if paper) for your bibliography.

2. On a second set of cards (4 × 6 inches, if paper), take notes on sources:
- Record one point from one source per card.
- Clarify the source: List the author's last name, a shortened title, or a code from the matching bibliography card. Include a page number.
- Provide a topic or heading: Called a slug, the topic helps you categorize and order information.
- Label the note as a summary, paraphrase, or quotation of the original.
- Distinguish between the source's information and your own thoughts.

	1
Slug ———————————	PROBLEMS WITH INTERNAL-COMBUSTION CARS
Quotation ———————	"In one year, the average gas-powered car produces five tons of carbon dioxide, which as it slowly builds up in the
Page Number —————	atmosphere causes global warming." (p. 43)
	-helpful fact about the extent of pollution caused by the traditional i-c engine
Comments —————————	-how does this number compare with what a hybrid produces?
Source —————————————	#7

Upside: Note cards are highly systematic, helping you categorize material and organize it for an outline and a first draft.

Downside: The method can be initially tedious and time-consuming.

System 2: Copy (or save) and annotate. The copy-and-annotate method involves working with photocopies, print versions, or digital texts of sources:

1. Selectively photocopy, print, and/or save important sources. Copy carefully, making sure you have full pages, including the page numbers.

2. As needed, add identifying information on the copy—author, publication details, and date. Each page should be easy to identify and trace. When working with books, simply copy the title and copyright pages and keep them with the rest of your notes.

3. As you read, mark up the copy and highlight key statements. In the margins or digital file, record your ideas:

- Ask questions. Insert a "?" in the margin, or write out the question.
- Make connections. Draw arrows to link ideas, or make notes like "see page 36."
- Add asides. Record what you think and feel while reading.
- Define terms. Note important words that you need to understand.
- Create a marginal index. Write keywords to identify themes and main parts.

Upside: Copying, printing, and/or saving helps you record sources accurately; annotating encourages careful reading and thinking.

Downside: Organizing material for drafting is inconvenient; when done poorly, annotating and highlighting involve skimming, not critical thinking.

 For a sample of annotation in action, see page 7.

System 3: The computer notebook or research log. The computer notebook or research log method involves taking notes on a computer or on sheets of paper. Here's how it works:

1. Establish a central location for your notes—a notebook, a file folder, a binder, or an electronic folder.

2. Take notes one source at a time, making sure to identify the source fully. Number your note pages.

3. Using your initials or some other symbol, distinguish your own thoughts from source material.

4. Use codes in your notes to identify which information in the notes relates to which topic in your outline. Then, under each topic in the outline, write the page number in your notes where that information is recorded. With a notebook or log, you may be able to rearrange your notes into an outline by using copy and paste—but don't lose source information in the process!

Upside: Taking notes feels natural without being overly systematic.
Downside: Outlining and drafting may require time-consuming paper shuffling.

System 4: The double-entry notebook. The double-entry notebook involves parallel note taking—notes from sources beside your own brainstorming, reaction, and reflection. Using a notebook or the columns feature of your word-processing program, do the following:

1. Divide pages in half vertically.

2. In the left column, record bibliographic information and take notes on sources.

3. In the right column, write your responses. Think about what the source is saying, why the point is important, whether you agree with it, and how the point relates to other ideas and other sources.

Upside: This method creates accurate source records while encouraging thoughtful responses; also, it can be done on a computer.

Downside: Organizing material for drafting may be a challenge.

Cudworth, Erika. <u>Environment and Society</u>. Routledge Introductions to Environment Series. London and New York: Routledge, 2003.	
Ch. 6 "Society, 'Culture' and 'Nature'— Human Relations with Animals"	*I've actually had a fair bit of personal experience with animals—the horses, ducks, dogs, and cats on our hobby farm. Will this chapter make trouble for my thinking?*
chapter looks at how social scientists have understood historically the relationship between people and animals (158)	
the word animal is itself a problem when we remember that people too are animals but the distinction is often sharply made by people themselves (159)	*Yes, what really are the connections and differences between people and animals? Is it a different level of intelligence? Is there something more basic or fundamental? Are we afraid to see ourselves as animals, as creatures?*
"In everyday life, people interact with animals continually." (159) – author gives many common examples	*Many examples—pets, food, TV programs, zoos—apply to me. Hadn't thought about how much my life is integrated with animal life! What does that integration look like? What does it mean for me, for the animals?*

Summarizing, Paraphrasing, and Quoting Source Material

As you work with sources, you must decide what to put in your notes and how to record it—as a summary, a paraphrase, or a quotation. Use these guidelines:

- How relevant is the passage to your research question or working thesis?
- How strong and important is the information offered?
- How unique or memorable is the thinking or phrasing?

The more relevant, the stronger, and the more memorable the material is, the more likely you should note it.

The passage below comes from an article on GM's development of fuel-cell technology. Review the passage; study how the researcher summarizes, paraphrases, and quotes from the source; and then practice these same strategies as you take notes on sources.

INSIGHT: Whenever possible, include a page number, paragraph number, or other locating detail with your paraphrase, summary, or quotation. Such identification at this stage is crucial to avoiding plagiarism down the road (see pages 486–489).

From Burns, L. D., McCormick, J. B., and Borroni-Bird, C. E. "Vehicle of Change." *Scientific American* 287:4 (October 2002): 10 pp.

When Karl Benz rolled his Patent Motorcar out of the barn in 1886, he literally set the wheels of change in motion. The advent of the automobile led to dramatic alterations in people's way of life as well as the global economy—transformations that no one expected at the time. The ever increasing availability of economical personal transportation remade the world into a more accessible place while spawning a complex industrial infrastructure that shaped modern society.

Now another revolution could be sparked by automotive technology: one fueled by hydrogen rather than petroleum. Fuel cells—which cleave hydrogen atoms into protons and electrons that drive electric motors while emitting nothing worse than water vapor—could make the automobile much more environmentally friendly. Not only could cars become cleaner, they could also become safer, more comfortable, more personalized—and even perhaps less expensive. Further, these fuel-cell vehicles could be instrumental in motivating a shift toward a "greener" energy economy based on hydrogen. As that occurs, energy use and production could change significantly. Thus, hydrogen fuel-cell cars and trucks could help ensure a future in which personal mobility—the freedom to travel independently— could be sustained indefinitely, without compromising the environment or depleting the earth's natural resources.

A confluence of factors makes the big change seem increasingly likely. For one, the petroleum-fueled internal-combustion engine (ICE), as highly refined, reliable and economical as it is, is finally reaching its limits. Despite steady improvements, today's ICE vehicles are only 20 to 25 percent efficient in converting the energy content of fuels into drive-wheel power. And although the U.S. auto industry has cut exhaust emissions substantially since the unregulated 1960s—hydrocarbons dropped by 99 percent, carbon monoxide by 96 percent and nitrogen oxides by 95 percent—the continued production of carbon dioxide causes concern because of its potential to change the planet's climate.

Summarize useful passages.

Summarizing condenses in your own words the main points in a passage. Summarize when the source provides relevant ideas and information on your topic.

1. Reread the passage, jotting down a few key words.

2. State the main point in your own words. Add key supporting points, leaving out examples, details, and long explanations. Be objective: Don't mix your reactions with the summary.

3. Check your summary against the original, making sure that you use quotation marks around any exact phrases you borrow.

Sample Summary:

While the introduction of the car in the late nineteenth century has led to dramatic changes in society and world economics, another dramatic change is now taking place in the shift from gas engines to hydrogen technologies. Fuel cells may make the car "greener," and perhaps even safer, cheaper, and more comfortable. These automotive changes will affect the energy industry by making it more environmentally friendly; as a result, people will continue to enjoy mobility while transportation moves to renewable energy. One factor leading to this technological shift is that the internal-combustion engine has reached the limits of its efficiency, potential, and development—while remaining problematic with respect to emissions, climate change, and health.

Paraphrase key passages.

Paraphrasing puts a whole passage in your own words. Paraphrase passages that present important points, explanations, or arguments but that don't contain memorable or straightforward wording. Follow these steps:

1. Quickly review the passage to get a sense of the whole, and then go through the passage carefully, sentence by sentence.
  - State the ideas in your own words, defining words as needed.
  - If necessary, edit for clarity, but don't change the meaning.
  - If you borrow phrases directly, put them in quotation marks.

2. Check your paraphrase against the original for accurate tone and meaning.

Sample Paraphrase of the Second Paragraph in the Passage:

Automobile technology may lead to another radical economic and social change through the shift from gasoline to hydrogen fuel. By breaking hydrogen into protons and electrons so that the electrons run an electric motor with only the by-product of water vapor, fuel cells could make the car a "green" machine. But this technology could also increase the automobile's safety, comfort, personal tailoring, and affordability. Moreover, this shift to fuel-cell engines in automobiles could lead to drastic, environmentally friendly changes in the broader energy industry, one that will be now tied to hydrogen rather than fossil fuels. The result from this shift will be radical changes in the way we use and produce energy. In other words, the shift to hydrogen-powered vehicles could promise to maintain society's valued mobility, while the clean technology would preserve the environment and its natural resources.

Web Link

Quote crucial phrases, sentences, and passages.

Quoting records statements or phrases in the original source word for word. Quote nuggets only—statements that are well phrased or authoritative:

1. Note the quotation's context—how it fits in the author's discussion.

2. Copy the passage word for word, enclosing it in quotation marks and checking its accuracy.

3. If you omit words, note that omission with an ellipsis. If you change any word for grammatical reasons, put changes in brackets. (See page 489).

Sample Quotations:

"[H]ydrogen fuel-cell cars and trucks could help ensure a future in which personal mobility . . . could be sustained indefinitely, without compromising the environment or depleting the earth's natural resources."

Note: This sentence captures the authors' main claim about the benefits and future of fuel-cell technology.

"[T]he petroleum-fueled internal-combustion engine (ICE), as highly refined, reliable and economical as it is, is finally reaching its limits."

Note: This quotation offers a well-phrased statement about the essential problem.

INSIGHT: Whether you are summarizing, paraphrasing, or quoting, aim to be true to the source by respecting the context and spirit of the original. Avoid shifting the focus or ripping material out of its context and forcing it into your own. For example, in the sample passage the authors discuss the limits of the internal-combustion engine. If you were to claim that these authors are arguing that the internal-combustion engine was an enormous engineering and environmental mistake, you would be twisting their comments to serve your own writing agenda.

For instruction on effectively integrating quotations, paraphrases, and summaries into your writing, see pages 486–489.

Avoiding Unintentional Plagiarism

Careful note taking helps prevent unintentional plagiarism. Plagiarism—using source material without giving credit—is treated more fully elsewhere (pages 476–479); essentially, however, unintentional plagiarism happens when you accidentally use a source's ideas, phrases, or information without documenting that material. At the planning stage of your project, you can prevent this problem from happening by adhering to principles of ethical research and following some practical guidelines.

Practice the principles of ethical research.

Because of the nature of information and the many challenges of working with it, conducting ethical research can be very complex and involved. To start with, however, commit to these principles of ethical research:

- Do the research and write the paper yourself.
- Adhere to the research practices approved in your discipline.
- Follow school- and discipline-related guidelines for working with people, resources, and technology.
- Avoid one-sided research that ignores or conceals opposition.
- Present real, accurate data and results—not "fudged" or twisted facts.
- Treat source material fairly in your writing.

Practices That Prevent Unintentional Plagiarism

The principles of ethical research above find expression when you prevent unintentional plagiarism. Do so by following these practices:

- Maintain an accurate working bibliography (pages 436–437).
- When taking notes, distinguish source material from your own reflection by using quotation marks, codes, and/or separate columns or note cards.
- When you draft your paper, transfer source material carefully by coding material that you integrate into your discussion, using quotation marks, double-checking your typing, or using copy and paste to ensure accuracy.
- Take time to do the project right—both research and writing. Avoid pulling an all-nighter during which you can't properly work with sources.

Practices That Prevent Internet Plagiarism

An especially thorny area related to unintentional plagiarism centers on the Internet. As with traditional print sources, Internet sources must be properly credited; in other words, web material cannot simply be transferred to your paper without acknowledgement. So treat web sources like print sources. And if you copy and paste digital material while taking notes and drafting, always track its origins with codes, abbreviations, or separate columns.

Checklist for Research

Use the checklist below to test how well you have gotten started on any given research project.

_____ I have clarified my assignment: the purpose, readers, and resources.

_____ I have selected an appropriate topic, conducted preliminary research, narrowed my focus, and developed a key research question or a clear working thesis.

_____ I have chosen research methods and gotten organized to do my research effectively.

_____ I have considered the range of resources and possible research sites available for my project.

_____ I have established and used a note-taking system that effectively keeps track of research resources, helps me gather key ideas and information from these sources, and encourages me to do my own thinking.

_____ I have carefully engaged and evaluated all my sources.

_____ I have sensibly summarized, paraphrased, and quoted useful sources.

_____ I have taken careful notes to prevent unintentional plagiarism.

Critical-Thinking and Writing Activities

As directed by your instructor, complete the following activities.

1. Write a research report about your major area of study. Discuss the types of knowledge the major explores and the professions to which it leads. Address the paper to students considering this major.

2. For a current research project, find and list fifteen to twenty available sources on your topic. Visit libraries to locate books, articles, and so forth. Use a search engine and locate sources on the web. Finally, list any interviews, observations, surveys, and questionnaires that you might set up.

3. Test the reliability of one of your Internet sources for a current research project. Refer to the "web test" questions on pages 434–435, and see if you can answer all of them. Based on your answers, decide whether the source is credible enough to strengthen your paper.

4. Choose a short article or a passage from one of your longer sources. Restate (paraphrase) what you have read using your own words. Put quotation marks around key words and phrases that you take directly from the text. Next, use the same materials to create a summary. Reduce what you just read to a few clear and important points using your own words.

◀ VISUALLY SPEAKING

Study the photograph at the beginning of this chapter (page 421). What does the collection of tools suggest about research and getting started on a research project?

CONDUCTING PRIMARY AND LIBRARY RESEARCH

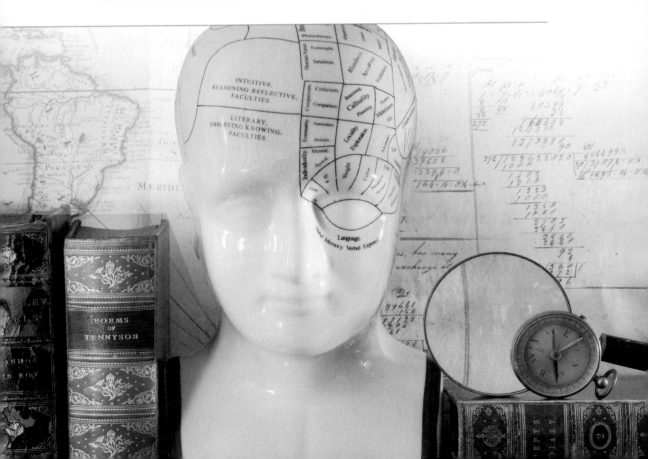

Today, conducting research is both easy and difficult. It's easy because research technology is powerful and many research methods are available. It's difficult because that technology and those methods provide access to so much information—the good, the bad, and the ugly.

How do you meet this challenge and conduct quality research? First, consider whether your project would benefit from primary research. When you engage in primary research, you gather information firsthand by observing sites, interviewing people, and analyzing documents. Second, learn how to use an expert resource—your college library. The library is your gateway to print and electronic materials.

Audio

Primary and Secondary Sources

Information sources for your research project can be either primary or secondary. Depending on your assignment, you may be expected to use one or both kinds of sources.

Consider primary sources.

A primary source is an original source, which gives firsthand information on a topic. This source (such as a diary, a person, or an event) informs you directly about the topic, rather than through another person's explanation or interpretation. The most common forms of primary research are observations, interviews, surveys, experiments, and analyses of original documents and artifacts.

Consider secondary sources.

Secondary sources present secondhand information on your topic—information at least once removed from the original. This information has been compiled, summarized, analyzed, synthesized, interpreted, or evaluated by someone studying primary sources. Journal articles, encyclopedia entries, documentaries, and nonfiction books are typical examples of such secondary sources.

Example: Below are possible primary and secondary sources for a research project exploring hybrid car technology and its viability. Note: Whether a source is primary or secondary depends on what you are studying. For example, if you were studying U.S. attitudes toward hybrid cars (and not hybrid car technology itself), the newspaper editorial and TV roundtable would be primary sources.

Primary Sources	Secondary Sources
E-mail interview with automotive engineer	Journal article discussing the development of hybrid car technology
Fuel-efficiency legislation	Newspaper editorial on fossil fuels
Visit and test-drive a car at a dealership	TV news roundtable discussion of hybrid car advantages and disadvantages
Published statistics about hybrid car sales	Promotional literature for a specific hybrid car

INSIGHT: Some resources are tertiary—that is, thirdhand. They are essentially reports of reports of research and, therefore, are distant from the original information. Examples of tertiary sources would include some articles in popular magazines and entries in Wikipedia. Aside from giving you ideas for focusing your topic, tertiary sources should generally not be used in college research projects and should not appear in works-cited or references lists.

Conducting Primary Research

When published sources can't give you the information that you need, consider conducting primary research. However, you must first weigh all its advantages and disadvantages.

Upside of Primary Research

- It produces information precisely tailored to your research needs.
- It gives you direct, hands-on access to your topic.

Downside of Primary Research

- It can take a lot of time and many resources to complete.
- It can require special skills, such as designing surveys and analyzing statistics and original documents.

Conduct primary research.

You need to choose the method of primary research that best suits your project. For help, review the following descriptions:

1. **Surveys and questionnaires** gather written responses you can review, tabulate, and analyze. These research tools pull together varied information—from simple facts to personal opinions and attitudes. See "Conduct surveys" on pages 450–451.

2. **Interviews** involve consulting two types of people. First, you can interview experts for their insights on your topic. Second, you can interview people whose direct experiences with the topic give you their personal insights. See "Conduct interviews," page 454, and "Interview Report," pages 331–338.

3. **Observations, inspections, and field research** require you to examine and analyze people, places, events, and so on. Whether you rely simply on your five senses or use scientific techniques, observing provides insights into the present state of your subject. For help with observation, field research, and writing reports based on this work, go to **www.thecollegewriter.com/3e**.

4. **Experiments** test hypotheses—predictions about why things do what they do—to arrive at conclusions that can be accepted and acted upon. Such testing often explores cause/effect relationships. See "Lab, Experiment, and Field Reports" on pages 339–352.

5. **Analysis of documents and artifacts** involves studying original reports, statistics, legislation, literature, artwork, and historical records. Such analysis provides unique, close-up interpretations of your topic. See "Analyze texts, documents, records, and artifacts" on pages 452–453, as well as "Writing About Literature and the Arts" on pages 355–372.

Conduct surveys.

One source of primary information that you can use for research projects is a survey or questionnaire. Surveys can collect facts and opinions from a wide range of people about virtually any topic. To get valid information, follow these guidelines:

1. **Find a focus.**
   - Limit the purpose of your survey.
   - Target a specific audience.

2. **Ask clear questions.**
   - Phrase questions so they can be easily understood.
   - Use words that are objective (not biased or slanted).

3. **Match your questions to your purpose.**
   - Closed questions give respondents easy-answer options, and the answers are easy to tabulate. Closed questions can provide two choices (*yes* or *no, true* or *false*), multiple choices, a rating scale (*poor 1 2 3 excellent*), or a blank to fill.
   - Open-ended questions bring in a wide variety of responses and more complex information, but they take time to complete, and the answers can be difficult to summarize.

4. **Organize your survey so that it's easy to complete.**
   - In the introduction, state who you are and why you need the information. Explain how to complete the survey and when and where to return it.
   - Guide readers by providing numbers, instructions, and headings.
   - Begin with basic questions and end with any complex, open-ended questions that are necessary. Move in a logical order from one topic to the next.

5. **Test your survey before using it.**
   - Ask a friend or classmate to read your survey and help you revise it, if necessary, before printing it.
   - Try out your survey with a small test group.

6. **Conduct your survey.**
   - Distribute the survey to a clearly defined group that won't prejudice the sampling (random or cross section).
   - Get responses from a good sample of your target group (10 percent if at all possible).
   - Tabulate responses carefully and objectively.
     Note: To develop statistically valid results, you may need expert help. Check with your instructor.

Sample Survey

The introduction includes the essential information about the survey.	Confidential Survey My name is Cho Lang, and I'm conducting research about the use of training supplements. I'd like to hear from you, Alfred University's athletes. Please answer the questions below by circling or writing out your responses. Return your survey to me, care of the Dept. of Psychology, through campus mail by Friday, April 5. Your responses will remain confidential.

<table>
<tr>
<td>The survey begins with clear, basic questions.</td>
<td>

1. Circle your gender. **Male   Female**

2. Circle your year.
   Freshman   Sophomore   Junior   Senior

3. List the sports that you play.

</td>
</tr>
<tr>
<td></td>
<td>

4. Are you presently using a training supplement?
   Yes   No
   Note: If you circled "no," you may turn in your survey at this point.

</td>
</tr>
<tr>
<td>The survey asks an open-ended question.</td>
<td>

5. Describe your supplement use (type, amount, and frequency).

</td>
</tr>
<tr>
<td></td>
<td>

6. Who supervises your use of this training supplement?
   Coach   Trainer   Self   Others

7. How long have you used it?
   **Less than 1 month   1–12 months
   12+ months**

</td>
</tr>
<tr>
<td>The survey covers the topic thoroughly.</td>
<td>

8. How many pounds have you gained while using this supplement?

9. How much has your athletic performance improved?
   None   1   2   3   4   5   Greatly

10. Circle any side effects you've experienced.
    Dehydration   Nausea   Diarrhea

</td>
</tr>
</table>

Analyze texts, documents, records, and artifacts.

An original document or record is one that relates directly to the event, issue, object, or phenomenon you are researching. Examining original documents and artifacts can involve studying letters, e-mail exchanges, case notes, literary texts, sales records, legislation, and material objects such as tools, sculptures, buildings, and tombs. As you analyze such documents and records, you examine evidence in an effort to understand a topic, arrive at a coherent conclusion about it, and support that judgment. How do you work with such diverse documents, records, and artifacts? Here are some guidelines:

Choose evidence close to your topic. Which texts, documents, records, and artifacts originated from or grew out of the topic you are researching? The closer to the topic, the more primary the source. Select materials that are directly related to your research questions and/or working thesis.

Example: If you were studying English labor riots of the 1830s, you could investigate these primary sources:

- To understand what rioters were demanding, copies of speeches given at demonstrations
- To know who the rioters were, names from police reports or union membership lists
- To learn the political response to the riots, political speeches or legislation
- To get at the attitudes of people from that time, newspaper reports, works of art, or novels from the period
- To find people's personal stories and private opinions related to the riots, personal letters, diaries, family albums, gravestones, and funeral eulogies

Frame your examination with questions. To make sense of the text, document, record, or artifact, understand what you are looking for and why. List the secondary questions that you want to answer in relation to the main question behind your research project.

Example: To study the legislative background behind the development of cleaner cars, such as the hybrid-fuel vehicle, you could access various documents on the Clean Air Act of 1990 (for example, *The Plain English Guide to the Clean Air Act*, an EPA publication). As you study this legislation, you could frame your reading with these additional questions:

- What are the requirements of the Clean Air Act?
- Specifically, how do those requirements affect automotive technology?
- Which private and public research projects will likely influence these requirements?
- Are schedules for change or deadlines written into the Clean Air Act?

Put the document or artifact in context. So that the material takes on meaning, clarify its external and internal natures. First, consider its external context—the five W's and H: What exactly is it? Who made it, when, where, why, and how? Second, consider its internal nature—what the document means, based on what it can and cannot show you: What does the language mean or refer to? What is the document's structure? What are the artifact's composition and style?

Example: If you were examining Mary Wollstonecraft's *A Vindication of the Rights of Woman* in a history or women's studies course, you would consider the following:

- **External Context:** who Mary Wollstonecraft was; when and why she wrote *A Vindication* and under what conditions; for whom she wrote it and their response; the type of document it is
- **Internal Context:** Wollstonecraft's essential argument and evidence; the nature of her views, their relationship to her times, and their relevance today

Draw coherent conclusions about meaning. Make sense of the source in relation to your research questions. What connections does the source reveal? What important changes or developments? What cause/effect relationships? What themes?

Example: A study of the Clean Air Act might lead you to a variety of conclusions regarding how environmental legislation relates to the development of hybrid technology—for example, that the United States must produce cleaner cars if it hopes to gain improved air quality.

INSIGHT: Studying primary documents and artifacts is central to many disciplines—history, literature, theology, philosophy, political studies, and archaeology, for example. Good analysis depends on asking research questions appropriate for the discipline. With the English labor riots of the 1830s again as an example, here's what three disciplines might ask:

- **Political science:** What role did political theories, structures, and processes play in the riots—both in causing and in responding to them?
- **Art:** How were the concerns of the rioters embodied in the new "realist" style of the mid-1800s? Did artists sympathize with and address an alienated working-class audience? How did art comment on the social structures of the time?
- **Sociology:** What type and quality of education did most workers have in the 1830s? How did that education affect their economic status and employment opportunities? Did issues related to the riots prompt changes in the English educational system? What changes and why?

With these examples in mind, consider your own major: What questions would this discipline ask of the English labor riots, of Mary Wollstonecraft's *A Vindication of the Rights of Woman,* or of the Clean Air Act of 1990?

Conduct interviews.

The purpose of an interview is simple: To get information, you talk with someone who has significant experience or someone who is an expert on your topic. Use the guidelines below whenever you conduct an interview. (See also pages 331–338.)

1. **Before the interview,** do your homework about the topic and the person you are planning to interview.

   - Arrange the interview in a thoughtful way. Explain to the interviewee your purpose and the topics to be covered.
   - Think about the specific ideas you want to cover in the interview and write questions for each. Addressing the 5 W's and H (*Who? What? Where? When? Why?* and *How?*) is important for good coverage.
   - Organize your questions in a logical order so the interview moves smoothly from one subject to the next.
   - Write the questions on the left side of a page. Leave room for quotations, information, and impressions on the right side.

2. **During the interview,** try to relax so that your conversation is natural and sincere.

   - Provide some background information about yourself, your project, and your plans for using the interview information.
   - Use recording equipment only with the interviewee's permission.
   - Jot down key facts and quotations.
   - Listen actively. Show that you're listening through your body language—eye contact, nods, smiles. Pay attention not only to what the person says, but also to how he or she says it.

   Based on the interviewee's responses, ask follow-up questions, and don't limit yourself to your planned questions only.

   - Be flexible. If the person looks puzzled by a question, rephrase it. If the discussion gets off track, redirect it. Based on the interviewee's responses, ask follow-up questions, and don't limit yourself to your planned questions only.

3. **After the interview,** do the appropriate follow-up work.

   - As soon as possible, review your notes. Fill in responses you remember but couldn't record at the time.
   - Thank the interviewee with a note, an e-mail, or a phone call.
   - If necessary, ask the interviewee to check whether your information and quotations are accurate.
   - Offer to send the interviewee a copy of your writing.

Using the Library

The library door is your gateway to information. Inside, the college library holds a wide range of research resources, from books to periodicals, from reference librarians to electronic databases.

Become familiar with the library.

To improve your ability to succeed at all your research assignments, become familiar with your college library system. Take advantage of tours and orientation sessions to learn its physical layout, resources, and services. Check your library's website for policies, tutorials, and research tools. The college library offers a variety of resources for your research projects.

Librarians: Librarians are information experts:

- Librarians manage the library's materials and guide you to resources.
- They help you perform online searches.

Collections: The library collects and houses a variety of materials:

- **Books and electronic materials**—CD-ROMs, CDs, and DVDs
- **Periodicals**—journals, magazines, and newspapers (print or microform)
- **Reference materials**—directories, indexes, handbooks, encyclopedias, and almanacs
- **Special collections**—government publications, historical documents, and original artifacts

Research tools: The library contains many tools that direct you to materials:

- The online catalog allows you to search everything in the library.
- Print indexes and subscription databases (Lexis-Nexis, EBSCOhost, ProQuest Direct) point you to abstracts and full-text articles.
- Internet access connects you with other library catalogs and online references.

Special services: Special services may also help you to complete research:

- Interlibrary loan allows you to obtain books and articles not available in your library.
- "Hold" allows you to request a book that is currently signed out.
- "Reserve" materials give you access to materials recommended by your instructors or heavily in demand.
- The reference desk can help you find information quickly, point you to the right resources, and help you with a search.
- Photocopiers, CD burners, scanners, and presentation software help you perform and share your research.

Search the catalog.

Library materials are catalogued so they are easy to find. In most college libraries, books, videos, and other holdings are catalogued in an electronic database. To find material, use book titles, author names, and related keyword searching. (See also pages 430–431.)

SAMPLE
ELECTRONIC
CATALOG

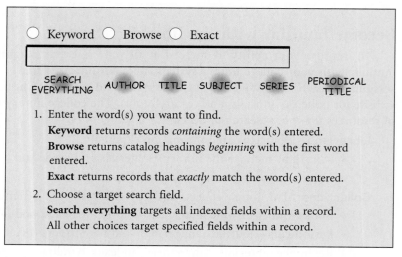

○ Keyword ○ Browse ○ Exact

SEARCH EVERYTHING   AUTHOR   TITLE   SUBJECT   SERIES   PERIODICAL TITLE

1. Enter the word(s) you want to find.
   Keyword returns records *containing* the word(s) entered.
   Browse returns catalog headings *beginning* with the first word entered.
   Exact returns records that *exactly* match the word(s) entered.
2. Choose a target search field.
   Search everything targets all indexed fields within a record.
   All other choices target specified fields within a record.

When you find a citation for a book or other resource, the result will provide some or all of the following information. Use that information to determine whether the resource is worth exploring further and to figure out other avenues of research. Note that a number of items appearing in blue, underlined type provide links to related books and other resources in the catalog.

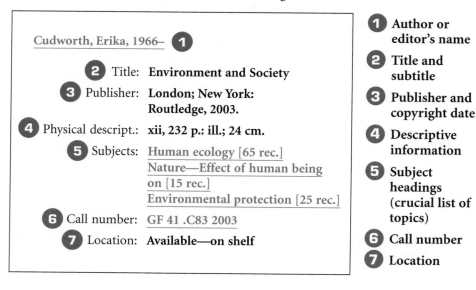

Cudworth, Erika, 1966– **1**

2 Title: **Environment and Society**

3 Publisher: **London; New York: Routledge, 2003.**

4 Physical descript.: **xii, 232 p.: ill.; 24 cm.**

5 Subjects: Human ecology [65 rec.]
Nature—Effect of human being on [15 rec.]
Environmental protection [25 rec.]

6 Call number: GF 41 .C83 2003

7 Location: **Available—on shelf**

1 Author or editor's name

2 Title and subtitle

3 Publisher and copyright date

4 Descriptive information

5 Subject headings (crucial list of topics)

6 Call number

7 Location

Web Link

Locating Resources by Call Numbers

Library of Congress (LC) call numbers combine letters and numbers to specify a resource's broad subject area, topic, and authorship or title. Finding a book, DVD, or other item involves combining both the alphabetical and the numerical order. Here is a sample call number for *Arctic Refuge: A Vanishing Wilderness?*:

VIDEO QH84.1.A72 1990

subject area (**QH**) topic number (**84**) subtopic number (**1**) cutter number (**A72**)

To find this resource in the library, first note the tab VIDEO. Although not part of the call number, this locator may send you to a specific area of the library. Once there, follow the parts of the call number one at a time:

1. Find the library section on natural history containing videos with the "QH" designation.

2. Follow the numbers until you reach "84."

3. Within the "84" items, find those with the subtopic "1."

4. Use the cutter "A72" to locate the resource alphabetically with "A," and numerically with "72."

Note: In the LC system, pay careful attention to the arrangement of subject area letters, topic numbers, and subtopic numbers: Q98 comes before QH84; QH84 before QH8245; QH84.A72 before QH84.1.A72.

Classification Systems

The LC classification system combines letters and numbers. The Dewey decimal system, which is used in some libraries, uses numbers only. Here is a list of the subject classes for both the LC and Dewey systems.

THE LIBRARY OF CONGRESS AND DEWEY DECIMAL SYSTEMS

LC Category		Dewey Decimal	LC Category		Dewey Decimal
A	General Works	000–999	K	Law	340–349
B	Philosophy	100–199	L	Education	370–379
	Psychology	150–159	M	Music	780–789
	Religion	200–299	N	Fine Arts	700–799
C	History: Auxiliary Sciences	910–929	P	Language	800–899
D	History: General and			Literature	400–499
	Old World	930–999	Q	Science	500–599
E–F	History: American	970–979	R	Medicine	610–619
G	Geography	910–919	S	Agriculture	630–639
	Anthropology	571–573	T	Technology	600–699
	Recreation	700–799	U	Military Science	355–359, 623
H	Social Sciences	300–399	V	Naval Science	359, 623
J	Political Science	320–329	Z	Bibliography and	010–0199
				Library Science	020–029

Using Books in Research

Your college library contains a whole range of books for you to use, from scholarly studies and reference works to trade books and biographies. Unfortunately, for most research projects you simply don't have time to read an entire book, and rarely do the entire contents relate to your topic. Instead, use the strategy outlined below to refine your research effort.

Approach the book systematically.

1. **Check out front and back information.**
   The title and copyright pages give the book's full title and subtitle; the author's name; and publication information, including publication date and Library of Congress subject headings. The back may contain a note on the author's credentials and other publications.

2. **Scan the table of contents.**
   Examine the contents page to see what the book covers and how it is organized. Ask yourself which chapters are relevant to your project.

3. **Using key words, search the index.**
   Check the index for coverage and page locations of the topics most closely related to your project. Are there plenty of pages, or just a few? Are these pages concentrated or scattered throughout the book?

4. **Skim the preface, foreword, or introduction.**
   Skimming the opening materials will often indicate the book's perspective, explain its origin, and preview its contents.

5. **Check appendices, glossaries, or bibliographies.**
   These special sections may be a good source of tables, graphics, definitions, statistics, and clues for further research.

6. **Carefully read appropriate chapters and sections.**
   Think through the material you've read and take good notes. (See pages 438–441.) Follow references to authors and other works to do further research on the topic. Study footnotes and endnotes for insights and leads.

Consider these options for working productively with books:

- When you find a helpful book, browse nearby shelves for more books.
- To confirm a book's quality, check the Internet, a periodical database, or *Book Review Digest* for a review.
- If your library subscribes to an e-book service such as NetLibrary, you have access to thousands of books in electronic form. You can conduct electronic searches, browse or check out promising books, and read them online.

Check reference works that supply information.

Encyclopedias supply facts and overviews for topics arranged alphabetically.

- General encyclopedias cover many fields of knowledge: *Encyclopedia Britannica, Collier's Encyclopedia.*
- Specialized encyclopedias focus on a single topic: *McGraw-Hill Encyclopedia of Science and Technology, Encyclopedia of American Film Comedy.*

Almanacs, yearbooks, and statistical resources, normally published annually, contain diverse facts.

- *The World Almanac and Book of Facts* presents information on politics, history, religion, business, social programs, education, and sports.
- *Statistical Abstract of the United States* provides data on population, geography, politics, employment, business, science, and industry.

Vocabulary resources supply information on languages.

- General dictionaries, such as *The American Heritage College Dictionary,* supply definitions and histories for a whole range of words.
- Specialized dictionaries define words common to a field, topic, or group: *Dictionary of Engineering, The New Harvard Dictionary of Music.*
- Bilingual dictionaries translate words from one language to another.

Biographical resources supply information about people. General biographies cover a broad range of people. Other biographies focus on people from a specific group. *Examples: Who's Who in America, Dictionary of Scientific Biography, World Artists 1980–1990.*

Directories supply contact information for people, groups, and organizations. *Examples: The National Directory of Addresses and Telephone Numbers, USPS ZIP Code Lookup and Address Information* (online), *Official Congressional Directory.*

Check reference works that are research tools.

Guides and handbooks help readers explore specific topics: *The Handbook of North American Indians, A Guide to Prairie Fauna.*

Indexes point you to useful resources. Some indexes are general, such as *Readers' Guide to Periodical Literature;* others are specific, such as *Environment Index* or *Business Periodicals Index.* (Many are now available online in databases your library subscribes to.)

Bibliographies list resources on a specific topic. A good, current bibliography can be used as an example when you compile your own bibliography on a topic.

Abstracts, like indexes, direct you to articles on a particular topic. But abstracts also summarize those materials so you learn whether a resource is relevant before you invest time in locating and reading it. Abstracts are usually organized into subject areas: *Computer Abstracts, Environmental Abstracts, Social Work Abstracts.* They are incorporated in many online subscription databases.

Web Link

Finding Periodical Articles

Periodicals are publications or broadcasts produced at regular intervals (daily, weekly, monthly, quarterly). Although some periodicals are broad in their subject matter and audience, as a rule they focus on a narrow range of topics geared toward a particular audience.

- **Daily newspapers and newscasts** provide up-to-date information on current events, opinions, and trends—from politics to natural disasters (*Wall Street Journal, USA Today, The NewsHour*).
- **Weekly and monthly magazines** generally provide more in-depth information on a wide range of topics (*Time, Newsweek, 60 Minutes*).
- **Journals,** generally published quarterly, provide specialized scholarly information for a narrowly focused audience (*English Journal*).

With thousands of periodicals available, how do you find helpful articles? Learn (a) which search tools your library offers, (b) which periodicals it has available in which forms, and (c) how to gain access to those periodicals.

Search online databases.

If your library subscribes to EBSCOhost, Lexis-Nexis, or another database service, use keyword searching (see pages 430–431) to find citations on your topic. You might start with the general version of such databases, such as EBSCOhost's Academic Search Elite, which provides access to more than 4,100 scholarly publications covering all disciplines.

Basic Search: The example below shows an EBSCOhost search screen for a search on hybrid electric cars. Notice how limiters, expanders, and other advanced features help you find the highest-quality materials.

Database list

Keyword field

Limiters available

Expanders available

Image courtesy of EBSCO Publishing

Advanced Search: A more focused research strategy would involve turning to specialized databases, which are available for virtually every discipline and are often an option within search services such as EBSCOhost (for example, Business Source Elite, PsycINFO, ERIC) and Lexis-Nexis (for example, Legal, Medical, and Business databases). If a basic search turns up little, turn to specialized databases, seeking help from a librarian if necessary. For a list of specialized databases, see page 463.

Particularly if you need articles published before 1985, you may need to go to the *Readers' Guide to Periodical Literature* or another print index. While databases are converting pre-1985 articles to digital form (for example, the JSTOR database), many excellent periodical articles are available only in print. To use the *Readers' Guide,* consult a librarian.

Generate citation lists of promising articles.

Your database search should generate lists of citations, brief descriptions of articles that were flagged through keywords in titles, subject terms, abstracts, and so on. For example, a search focused on hybrid electric cars leads to the results shown below. At this point, study the results and do the following:

- Refine the search by narrowing or expanding it.
- Mark specific citations for "capture" or further study.
- Re-sort the results.
- Follow links in a specific citation to further information.

Folder feature for "capturing" citations

"Sort" options

Numbered citations including titles, authors, journal information, length, location notes

Article links indicating article availability and format

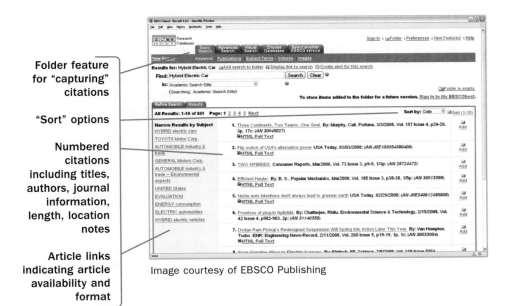

Image courtesy of EBSCO Publishing

Study citations and capture identifying information.

By studying citations (especially abstracts), you can determine three things:

- Is this article relevant to your research?
- Is an electronic, full-text version available?
- If not, does the library have this periodical?

To develop your working bibliography (see pages **436–437**), you should also "capture" the article's identifying details by using the save, print, or e-mail function, or by recording the periodical's title, the issue and date, and the article's title and page numbers. These functions are shown in the EBSCOhost citation below.

Save options

Source link for more details or full text

Subject links for further research

Summary with keywords highlighted

Image courtesy of EBSCO Publishing

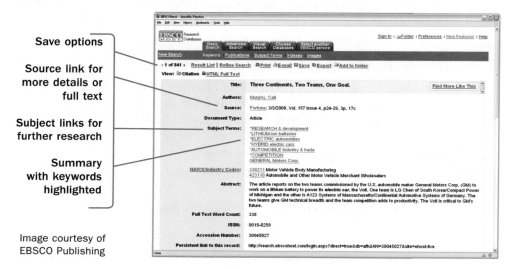

Find and retrieve the full text of the article.

When citations indicate that you have promising articles, access those articles efficiently, preferably through a direct link in the citation to an electronic copy. From there you can print, save, or e-mail the article. If the article is not available electronically, track down a print version:

- Check the online citation to see if your library has the article. If necessary, check your library's inventory of periodicals held; this list should be available online and/or in print. Examine especially closely the issues and dates available, the form (print or microfilm), and the location (bound or current shelves).

- To get the article, follow your library's procedure. You may have to submit a request slip so that a librarian can get the periodical, or you may be able to get it yourself in the current, bound, or microfilm collection. If the article is not available online or in your library, use interlibrary loan.

Databases for Disciplines

Most libraries offer access to databases from a wide range of disciplines. Check your library's website for access to databases like these:

Agricola offers citations from the National Agricultural Library group—with materials focused on issues from animal science to food and nutrition.

ARTbibliographies Modern abstracts articles, books, catalogs, and other resources on modern and contemporary art.

CAIRSS for Music offers bibliographic citations for articles on music-related topics, from music education to music therapy.

Communication & Mass Media Complete offers access to resources on topics like public speaking and TV broadcasting.

Engineering E-journal Search Engine offers free, full-text access to more than 150 online engineering journals.

ERIC offers citations, abstracts, and digests for more than 980 journals in the education field.

First Search, a fee-based information service, offers access to more than 30 scholarly databases in a range of disciplines.

GPO, the Government Printing Office, offers access to records for U.S. government documents (e.g., reports, hearings, judicial rules, addresses, and so on).

Health Source offers access to abstracts, indexing, and full-text material on health-related topics, from nutrition to sports medicine.

Ingenta offers citations for more than 25,000 journals, most in the sciences.

JSTOR offers full-text access to scholarly articles in a full range of disciplines, articles once available only in print.

Math Database offers article citations for international mathematics research.

Medline offers access to journals in medicine and medicine-related disciplines through references, citations, and abstracts.

MLA Bibliography provides bibliographic citations for articles addressing a range of modern-language and literature-related topics.

National Environmental Publications Internet Site (NEPIS) offers access to more than 6,000 EPA documents (full text, online).

PsycINFO offers access to materials in psychology and psychology-related fields (for example, social work, criminology, organizational behavior).

Scirus indexes science resources, citing article titles and authors, source publication information, and lines of text indicating the article's content.

Vocation and Career Collection offers full-text access to more than 400 trade- and industry-related periodicals.

Worldwide Political Science Abstracts offers bibliographic citations in politics-related fields, from public policy to international law.

Checklist for Research

Use the following checklist to monitor your primary and library research.

_____ I have chosen methods of primary research that fit the assignment.

_____ I have systematically, carefully, and ethically gathered and analyzed primary information.

_____ I have become familiar with my library's resources and services.

_____ Using solid keyword searching strategies, I have effectively searched the library's holdings for books and other items relevant to my topic.

_____ I have tapped print and electronic reference works for information.

_____ I have used my library's print and electronic periodical search tools and holdings to find relevant articles on my topic.

Critical-Thinking and Writing Activities

As directed by your instructor, complete the following activities.

1. Think about a research project that you have done or are doing now. How might primary research and library research (scholarly books and journals) strengthen your writing? Why not do all your research on the Free Web (see page **466**) using Google and resources like Wikipedia?

2. For the subject "Gender Differences in Toy Preferences," indicate whether the following sources would be considered primary or secondary (P or S):

_____ a. Observing children in a day-care setting

_____ b. Journal article about gender-based differences in the brain

_____ c. Magazine article about a hot new toy

_____ d. Survey of day-care workers

_____ e. *Boys' Toys of the Fifties and Sixties* (a book)

_____ f. Interviews with parents

3. By working with your library's website and its orientation tools, identify where you can physically and/or electronically locate books, reference resources, and journals.

4. Indicate which section of the library would house the following items:

_____ a. *JAMA (Journal of the American Medical Association)*

_____ b. *Places Rated Almanac*

_____ c. *Principles of Corporate Finance* (book)

◀ VISUALLY SPEAKING

Review the photograph on page **447**. What does the image suggest about doing research today? How does the image relate to your own research practices?

CONDUCTING RESEARCH ON THE INTERNET 30

Audio

For researchers, the Internet can be a great resource or a great waste of time. Consider the Internet's benefits and drawbacks:

Benefits

- The Internet contains a wealth of textual, audio, and video information.
- Information can be searched, copied, saved, and sent.

Drawbacks

- Finding useful information requires careful digging and evaluation.
- The Internet lacks quality control.
- Surfing can encourage shallow research practices and plagiarism.
- The Net changes rapidly—information vanishes or changes.

Understanding Internet Basics: A Primer

If you're familiar with the Internet, you already understand the basics of searching this medium. However, the following questions and answers may help you do quality research on the Net.

What is the Internet?

The Internet is a worldwide network of connected local computers and computer networks that allows computers to share information with one another. Your college's network likely gives you access to the library, local resources, and the Internet.

What is the World Wide Web?

The **web** provides access to much of the material on the Internet. Millions of webpages are available because of **hypertext links** that connect them. These links appear as clickable icons or highlighted web addresses. A **website** is a group of related webpages posted by the same sponsor or organization. A **home page** is a website's "entry" page. A **web browser** such as Safari, Internet Explorer, or Firefox gives you access to web resources through a variety of tools, such as directories and search engines. (**Directories** and **search engines** are special websites that provide a searchable listing of many services on the web.)

Sample Webpage:

Title bar

Navigation bar

Graphic link

Text links

Status bar

Reprinted by permission of CNN ImageSource.

INSIGHT: Distinguish between the Deep Web and the Free Web. The Deep Web includes material not generally accessible with popular search engines, such as all the scholarly research available through your library's subscription databases. The Free Web offers less reliable information.

What does an Internet address mean?

An Internet address is called a Uniform Resource Locator (URL). The address includes the protocol indicating how the computer file should be accessed—often *http:* or *ftp:* (followed by a double slash); a domain name—often beginning with *www;* and additional path information (following a single slash) to access other pages within a site.

http://www.nrcs.usda.gov/news/index.html#csp_watershed2

The domain name is a key part of the address because it indicates what type of organization created the site and gives you clues about its goal or purpose. Does the site aim to educate, inform, persuade, sell, and/or entertain? Most sites combine a primary purpose with secondary ones.

.com	a commercial organization or business
.gov	a government organization—federal, state, or local
.edu	an educational institution
.org	a nonprofit organization
.net	an organization that is part of the Internet's infrastructure
.mil	a military site
.biz	a business site
.info	any site primarily providing information

INSIGHT: International addresses generally include national abbreviations (for example, Canada = .ca). This clue helps you determine the origin of the information and communicate more sensitively on the Internet.

How can you save Internet information?

Accurately saving Internet addresses and material is an essential part of good research. Moreover, you may want to revisit sites and embed URLs in your research writing. Save Internet information through these methods:

Bookmark: Your browser can save a site's address through a "bookmark" or "favorites" function on your menu bar.

Printout: If a document looks promising, print a hard copy of it. Remember to write down all details needed for citing the source. (Although many details will automatically print with the document, some could be missing.)

Save or download: To keep an electronic copy of material, save the document to a specific drive on your computer. Beware of large files with many graphics: They take up a lot of space. To save just the text, highlight it, copy it, and then paste it into a word-processing program.

E-mail: If you're not at your own computer, you can e-mail the document's URL to your e-mail address through copy and paste.

 For instructions on writing for the web, see pages 397–408.

Locating Reliable Information

Because the Internet contains so much information of varying reliability, you need to become familiar with search tools that locate information you can trust. The key is knowing which search tool to use in which research situation.

Proceed with caution.

When it comes to doing Internet research, proceed with caution:

- Adhere to your assignment's restrictions on using websites (number and type). In fact, some instructors may not allow web resources for specific projects, limiting you to print sources and scholarly articles available in subscription databases.

- When you are using web resources, make sure the sites are sponsored by legitimate, recognizable organizations: government agencies, nonprofit groups, and educational institutions. For most projects, avoid relying on personal, commercial, and special-interest sites, as well as chat rooms, blogs, and news groups. Test the quality and reliability of online information by using the benchmarks outlined on pages **432–435**.

- Avoid developing your paper based on copying and pasting together chunks of webpages. By doing so, not only do you fail to engage your sources meaningfully, but you also commit plagiarism. For more on plagiarism, see pages **476–479**.

Use your library's website.

Your library may sponsor a website that gives you access to quality Internet resources. For example, it may provide the following assistance:

- Tutorials on using the Internet
- Guides to Internet resources in different disciplines
- Links to online document collections (Project Gutenberg, Etext Archives, New Bartleby Digital Library, and so on)
- Connections to virtual libraries, subscription databases, search engines, directories, government documents, and online reference works

Example: Your library may give you access to WorldCat, a global catalog. If you click on the "Internet" limiter, you'll be able to search specifically for websites and other Internet information recommended by librarians.

> **TIP:** If you need help doing electronic research, consider these options:
> - Ask a librarian for instructions.
> - Attend one of the library's training sessions on using library resources and conducting research.
> - Request instructions or a tutorial from your college writing center.

Work with URLs.

Finding useful Internet resources can be as easy as typing in a URL. If you don't have the exact URL, sometimes you can guess it, especially for an organization (company, government agency, or nonprofit group). Try the organization's name or a logical abbreviation to get the home page.

Follow helpful links.

Locating information on the Net can involve "surfing" leads:

- If you come across a helpful link (often highlighted in blue), click on the link to visit that new page. Note that the link may take you to another site.
- Your browser keeps a record of the pages you visit. Click the back arrow to go back one page or the forward arrow to move ahead again. Clicking the right mouse button on these arrows shows a list of recently visited pages.

INSIGHT: Note that "sponsored links" listed at a website are a form of advertising. Their purpose is primarily commercial, though they may contain useful information.

Follow the branches of a "subject tree."

Web Link

A *subject tree,* sometimes called a *subject guide* or *directory,* lists websites that have been organized into categories by experts who have reviewed those sites. Use subject trees or directories for the following reasons:

- You need to narrow down a broad topic.
- You want sites that have been evaluated, or you desire quality over quantity.

How does a subject tree work? Essentially, it allows you to select from a broad range of subjects or "branches." With each topic choice, you narrow down your selection until you arrive at a list of websites, or you can keyword-search a limited number of websites.

Check whether your library subscribes to a service such as NetFirst, a database in which subject experts have catalogued Internet resources by topic. Here are some other common subject directories that you can likely access at your library:

WWW Virtual Library	http://vlib.org/Overview.html
Argus	http://www.clearinghouse.net
Librarians' Index to the Internet	http://www.lii.org
Google Directory	http://www.google.com/dirhp
LookSmart	http://looksmart.com

A sample subject tree search is outlined on the pages that follow. Study the search, and then try one yourself with the subject trees available through your library.

> **TIP:** To get the best results from your search, avoid these problems: misspelling keywords; using vague or broad keywords (*education* or *business*); incorrectly combining Boolean operators; or shortening keywords too much.

Step 1: Select an appropriate broad category. Study the subject tree below provided by the Librarians' Index to the Internet (Lii). To find reviewed websites containing information on hybrid electric cars, you could select from this start page a range of categories, depending on the angle you want to explore: Arts & Humanities, Business, Computers, and so on. Each of these starting points will lead to a different listing of relevant sites. Another option would be to use the keyword search feature shown. *Hybrid cars* would likely appear under Science.

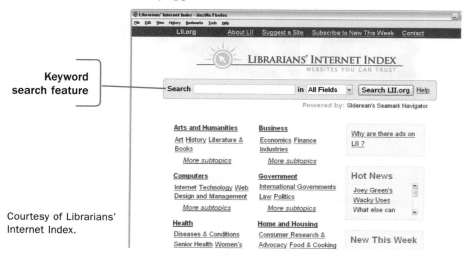

Keyword search feature

Courtesy of Librarians' Internet Index.

Step 2: Choose a fitting subcategory. If you chose Science, the subcategories shown below would appear. At this point, you would again have several choices: (1) to select Environment, (2) to follow Transportation, or (3) to do a keyword search of this now more limited grouping of websites. Each choice might lead to a distinct set of websites. In fact, your research may benefit by trying all three options.

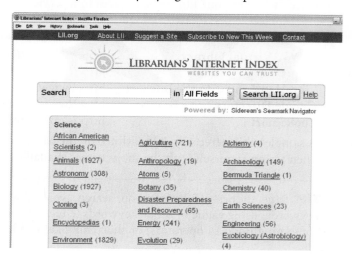

Courtesy of Librarians' Internet Index.

Step 3: Work toward a listing of websites. As you work down through narrower branches of the tree, you will arrive at a listing of relevant websites. Such sites, remember, have all been reviewed in terms of quality, though you still need to evaluate what you find. In the citation for a site, study the site title, the description of information available, site sponsorship, and the web address (particularly the domain name). Use that information to determine the site's relevance to your research. At this point, you can save the results (see page 467) and/or click on the site's web address and proceed to research the site.

Courtesy of Librarians' Internet Index.

Step 4: Visit, explore, and evaluate recommended sites. Once you have identified a promising site from the citation list, follow the links provided. Study and evaluate the site by asking questions such as these:

1. Who authored or sponsored the site? What is the author's or sponsor's perspective on the topic? Why did the author post these pages? What can you find out about the author through a broader Internet search?

2. What content does the site offer? What depth of information is available?

3. Does the website function as a primary, secondary, or tertiary source?

4. What external links does the site offer? Might these links take you to additional resources that are relevant and reliable?

INSIGHT: Careful investigation and evaluation of websites is even more important when you use search engines, like those discussed on the next pages. Use the resource evaluation guidelines on pages 434–435 for webpages that you find through either subject directories or search engines. Always proceed with caution, making sure that your research writing does not rely on unstable, shallow webpages.

Use search engines and metasearch tools.

Unlike a subject directory, which is constructed with human input, a search engine is a program that automatically scours a large amount of Internet material for keywords that you submit. A search engine is useful in the following circumstances:

- You have a very narrow topic in mind.
- You have a specific word or phrase to use in your search.
- You want a large number of results.
- You are looking for a specific type of Internet file.
- You have the time to sort through the material for reliability.

Be aware that not all search engines are the same. Some search citations of Internet materials, whereas others conduct full-text searches. Choose a search engine that covers a large portion of the Internet, offers quality indexing, and provides high-powered search capabilities. Here's an overview of some popular search engines.

Basic Search Engines: Search millions of webpages gathered automatically.

Alta Vista	http://www.altavista.com
AllTheWeb	http://www.alltheweb.com
Google	http://www.google.com
HotBot	http://www.hotbot.com
Vivísimo	http://www.vivisimo.com

Metasearch Tools: Search several basic search engines at once, saving you the time and effort of checking more than one search engine.

Ask	http://www.ask.com
Dog Pile	http://www.dogpile.com
Ixquick	http://www.ixquick.com
Northern Light	http://www.northernlight.com

"Deep Web" Tools: Check Internet databases and other sources not accessible to basic search engines.

Complete Planet	http://www.completeplanet.com

INSIGHT: One key to successfully using search engines lies in effective keyword searching (see pages 430–431). To ensure successful searches, it's best to become familiar with a few search engines—which areas of the Internet they search, whether they can access full text, and what rules you must follow.

A sample search: What would a search look like? If you were interested in information specifically on the Toyota hybrid-electric vehicles (a fairly narrow search term), you could conduct a search using the metasearch engine Ask Jeeves, following these steps:

Step 1: Begin your search with precise, narrow terms. Using Boolean operators and quotation marks, you might begin with the search terms "Toyota" and "hybrid electric vehicles." The more precise and narrow your terms are, the better your results will be.

Step 2: Study the results and refine your search as needed. The results of the initial search are shown below. At this point, you have several choices:

- Narrow or broaden your search by using the drop-down menus in the box.
- Follow the links (on the right) to related topics.
- Search the "Sponsored Web Results"—essentially advertising sites, such as Toyota's own website for the Prius.
- Search "Web Results"—sites that generally go beyond advertising into more in-depth information, although the site sponsorship is still important.
- Explore a related search of other topics and of other Internet resources.

For example, you might choose to check Toyota's pages on the Prius, to view Toyota's North America Environmental Report at its website, or to examine the "Honda Insight / Toyota Prius" comparison, which comes from an educational site (.edu). The key is to use sound judgment about where the information comes from, which sites provide the most reliable information, how the information relates to your research question, and what web graphics offer as potential resources for your research writing.

Refinement through search questions with drop-down lists

Results: sponsored sites (primarily advertising)

Results: other webpages

Revising search and advanced search option

Reprinted by permission of Google.

Checklist for Internet Research

As you conduct Internet research, use the following checklist to remind yourself of key principles to follow.

_____ I have avoided an over-reliance on free-web resources at the expense of more scholarly sources.

_____ By studying sites and their URLs, I understand where the information is coming from.

_____ I have used Internet search tools intelligently—from URL addresses to subject trees to search engines—to find quality, reliable information.

_____ I have carefully saved Internet information through bookmarking, printing, saving, or e-mailing.

_____ When copying and pasting material from Internet sources, I have carefully tracked that material so as to avoid plagiarism.

_____ I have carefully evaluated each Internet source for credible authorship, reliable sponsorship, lack of bias, currency, accuracy, logical support, and quality design. (See page 468 for more details on evaluating web resources.)

Critical-Thinking and Writing Activities

As directed by your instructor, complete the following activities.

1. Explore your library's handouts and website for information about Internet research. What services, support, and access does the library provide? Explore the various resources with your own major in mind, and draft an informal report to share with your instructor and classmates about web resources available in your discipline.

2. With a current research project in one of your classes as the focus, use one of the subject trees on page 469 to investigate and evaluate potential websites. After saving useful information in an appropriate fashion, conduct a search for this project using a search engine listed on page 472. Compare and contrast these two processes for finding Internet information.

3. Using the variety of methods outlined in this chapter, work with some classmates to search the Internet for information on a controversial topic, event, person, or place. Carefully analyze and evaluate the range of web information you find—the quality, perspective, depth, and reliability. Create a report on your findings for the rest of the class.

◄ VISUALLY SPEAKING

Study the photo montage on page 465 and explain what the image suggests about using the Internet for quality research.

Drafting a Paper with Documented Research

31

"That's incredible!" is normally a positive exclamation of amazement. But maybe it's an exclamation you *don't* want to hear about your writing, if incredible means unbelievable. Think about it:

- **A poor paper** reads like a recitation of unconnected facts, a set of unsupported opinions, or a string of undigested quotations. Sources are absent, or sources dominate and the writer disappears. At its worst, such writing is plagiarism.

- **A strong paper** centers on the writer's ideas, ideas advanced through thoughtful engagement with and crediting of sources.

Obviously, you want to draft a strongly documented paper—a credible discussion of your carefully researched topic. This chapter will help you achieve that goal.

Web Link

Video

Avoiding Plagiarism

The road to plagiarism may be paved with the best intentions—or the worst. Either way, the result is still a serious academic offense. As you write your research paper, do everything you can to stay off that road! Start by studying your school's and your instructor's guidelines on plagiarism and other academic offenses. Then study the following pages.

What is plagiarism?

Plagiarism is using someone else's words, ideas, or images (what's called intellectual property) so they appear to be your own. When you plagiarize, you use source material—whether published in print or online—without acknowledging the source. In this sense, plagiarism refers to a range of thefts:

- Submitting a paper you didn't write yourself.
- Pasting large chunks of a source into your paper and passing it off as your own work.
- Using summaries, paraphrases, or quotations without documentation.
- Using the exact phrasing of a source without quotation marks.
- Mixing up source material and your own ideas—failing to distinguish between the two.

 Plagiarism refers to more than "word theft." Because plagiarism is really about failing to credit ideas and information, the rules also apply to visual images, tables, graphs, charts, maps, music, videos, and so on.

In other words, plagiarism refers to a range of source abuses. What exactly do these violations look like? Read the passage below, and then review the five types of plagiarism that follow, noting how each misuses the source.

ORIGINAL ARTICLE

The passage below is from page 87 of "Some Stories Have to Be Told by Me: A Literary History of Alice Munro," by Marcela Valdes, published in the *Virginia Quarterly Review* 82.3 (Summer 2006).

What makes Munro's characters so enthralling is their inconsistency; like real people, at one moment they declare they will cover the house in new siding, at the next, they vomit on their way to the hospital. They fight against and seek refuge in the people they love. The technique that Munro has forged to get at such contradictions is a sort of pointillism, the setting of one bright scene against another, with little regard for chronology.

Submitting Another Writer's Paper

The most blatant plagiarism is taking an entire piece of writing and claiming it as your own work. Examples:

- Downloading, reformatting, and submitting an article as your own work.
- Buying a paper from a "paper mill" or taking a "free" paper off the Internet.
- Turning in another student's work as your own (see "Falstaffing" on page 481).

 Just as it's easy to plagiarize using the Internet, it's easy for your professors to recognize and track down plagiarism using Internet tools.

Using Copy and Paste

It is unethical to take chunks of material from another source and splice them into your paper without acknowledgment. In the example below, the writer pastes in a sentence from the original article (boldfaced) without using quotation marks or a citation. Even if the writer changed some words, it would still be plagiarism.

Life typically unfolds mysteriously for Munro's characters, with unexplained events and choices. **Like real people, at one moment they declare they will cover the house in new siding, at the next, they vomit on their way to the hospital.**

Failing to Cite a Source

Borrowed material must be documented. Even if you use information accurately and fairly, don't neglect to cite the source. Below, the writer correctly summarizes the passage's idea but offers no citation.

For the reader, the characters in Munro's stories are interesting because they are so changeable. Munro shows these changes by using a method of placing scenes side by side for contrast, without worrying about the chronological connections.

Neglecting Necessary Quotation Marks

Whether it's a paragraph or a phrase, if you use the exact wording of a source, that material must be enclosed in quotation marks. In the example below, the writer cites the source but doesn't use quotation marks around a phrase taken from the original (boldfaced).

What makes Munro's characters so typically human is that they **fight against and seek refuge in the people they love** (Valdes 87).

Confusing Borrowed Material with Your Own Ideas

Through carelessness (often in note taking), you may confuse source material with your own thinking. Below, the writer indicates that he borrowed material in the first sentence, but fails to indicate that he also borrowed the next sentence.

As Marcela Valdes explains, "[w]hat makes Munro's characters so enthralling is their inconsistency" (87). To achieve this sense of inconsistency, Munro places brightly lit scenes beside each other in a kind of pointillist technique.

Why is plagiarism serious?

Perhaps the answer is obvious. But some people operate with the notion that material on the Internet (whether text, graphics, or sound) is "free" and, therefore, fair game for research writing. After all, a lot of stuff on the web doesn't even list an author, so what's the harm? Here's some food for thought:

Academic Dishonesty

At its heart, plagiarism is cheating—stealing intellectual property and passing it off as one's own work. Colleges take such dishonesty seriously. Plagiarism, whether intentional or unintentional, will likely be punished in one or more ways:

- A failing grade for the assignment
- A failing grade for the course
- A note on your academic transcript (often seen by potential employers) that failure resulted from academic dishonesty
- Expulsion from college

Theft from the Academic Community

The research paper represents your dialogue with other members of the academic community—classmates, the instructor, others in your major, others who have researched the topics, and so on. When you plagiarize, you short-circuit the dialogue:

- You gain an unfair advantage over your classmates who follow the rules and earn their grades.
- You disrespect other writers, researchers, and scholars.
- You disrespect your readers by passing off others' ideas as your own.
- You insult your instructor, a person whose respect you need.
- You harm your college by risking its reputation and its academic integrity.

Now and in the Future

Because research projects help you master course-related concepts and writing skills, plagiarism robs you of an opportunity to learn either. Moreover, you rob yourself of your integrity and reputation. After all, as a student you are seeking to build your credibility within the broader academic community, your major, and your future profession.

In addition, research projects often train you for your future work in terms of research, thinking, and writing skills—skills that you will need to succeed in the workplace. If you do not learn the skills now, you will enter the workplace without them—a situation that your employer will, at some point, find out.

One tool to deter plagiarism is Turnitin.com. Students submit their papers for comparison against millions of webpages and other student papers. Students and instructors get reports about originality and matching text. For more on this tool, visit **www.thecollegewriter.com/3e**.

How do I avoid plagiarism?

Preventing plagiarism begins the moment you get an assignment. Essentially, prevention requires your commitment and diligence throughout the project.

Resist temptation. With the Internet, plagiarism is a mouse click away. Avoid last-minute all-nighters that make you desperate; start research projects early. *Note:* It's better to ask for an extension or accept a penalty for lateness than to plagiarize.

Play by the rules. Become familiar with your college's definition, guidelines, and policies regarding plagiarism so that you don't unknowingly violate them. When in doubt, ask your instructor for clarification.

Take orderly, accurate notes. From the start, carefully keep track of source material and distinguish it from your own thinking. Specifically, do the following:

- Maintain an accurate working bibliography (pages 436–437).
- Adopt a decent note-taking system (pages 438–441).
- Accurately summarize, paraphrase, and quote sources in your notes (pages 442–444).

Document borrowed material. Credit information that you have summarized, paraphrased, or quoted from any source, whether that information is statistics, facts, graphics, phrases, or ideas. Readers can then see what's borrowed and what's yours, understand your support, and do their own follow-up research.

Common Knowledge Exception: Common knowledge is information—a basic fact, for instance—that is generally known to readers or easily found in several sources, particularly reference works. Such knowledge need *not* be cited. However, when you go beyond common knowledge into research findings, interpretations of the facts, theories, explanations, claims, arguments, and graphics, you *must* document the source. Study the examples below, but whenever you are in doubt, document.

Examples:

- The fact that automakers are developing hybrid-electric cars is common knowledge, whereas the details of GM's AUTOnomy project are not.
- The fact that Shakespeare wrote *Hamlet* is common knowledge, whereas the details of his sources are not.

Work carefully with source material in your paper. See pages 486–489 for more on integrating and documenting sources, but here, briefly, are your responsibilities:

- Distinguish borrowed material from your own thinking by signaling where source material begins and ends.
- Indicate the source's origin with an attributive phrase and a citation (parenthetical reference or footnote).
- Provide full source information in a works-cited or references page.

Avoiding Other Source Abuses

Plagiarism, though the most serious offense, is not the only source abuse to avoid when writing a paper with documented research. Consider these pitfalls, which refer again to the sample passage on page 476.

Using Sources Inaccurately

When you get a quotation wrong, botch a summary, paraphrase poorly, or misstate a statistic, you misrepresent the original. *Example:* In this quotation, the writer carelessly uses several wrong words that change the meaning, as well as adding two words that are not in the original.

> As Marcela Valdes explains, "[w]hat makes Munro's characters so **appalling** is their **consistency**. . . . They fight against and seek **refuse** in the people **they say** they love" (87).

Using Source Material Out of Context

By ripping a statement out of its context and forcing it into yours, you can make a source seem to say something that it didn't really say. *Example:* This writer uses part of a statement to say the opposite of the original.

> According to Marcela Valdes, while Munro's characters are interesting, Munro's weakness as a fiction writer is that she shows "little regard for chronology" (87).

Overusing Source Material

When your paper reads like a string of references, especially quotations, your own thinking disappears. *Example:* The writer takes the source passage, chops it up, and splices it together.

> Anyone who has read her stories knows that "[w]hat makes Munro's characters so enthralling is their inconsistency." That is to say, "like real people, at one moment they declare they will cover the house in new siding, at the next, they vomit on their way to the hospital." Moreover, "[t]hey fight against and seek refuge in the people they love." This method "that Munro has forged to get at such contradictions is a sort of pointillism," meaning "the setting of one bright scene against another, with little regard for chronology" (Valdes 87)

"Plunking" Quotations

When you "plunk" quotations into your paper by failing to prepare the reader for them and follow them up, the discussion becomes choppy and disconnected. *Example:* The writer interrupts the flow of ideas with a quotation "out of the blue." In addition, the quotation hangs at the end of a paragraph with no follow-up.

> Typically, characters such as Del Jordan, Louisa Doud, and Almeda Roth experience a crisis through contact with particular men. "They fight against and seek refuge in the people they love" (Valdes 87).

Using "Blanket" Citations

Your reader shouldn't have to guess where borrowed material begins and ends. For example, if you place a parenthetical citation at the end of a paragraph, does that citation cover the whole paragraph or just the final sentence?

Relying Heavily on One Source

If your writing is dominated by one source, readers may doubt the depth and integrity of your research. Instead, your writing should show your reliance on a balanced diversity of sources.

Failing to Match In-Text Citations to Bibliographic Entries

All in-text citations must clearly refer to accurate entries in the works-cited, references, or endnotes page. Mismatching occurs in the following circumstances:

- An in-text citation refers to a source that is not listed in the bibliography.
- A bibliographic resource is never actually referenced anywhere in the paper.

Related Academic Offenses

Beyond plagiarism and related source abuses, steer clear of these academic offenses:

Double-dipping: When you submit one paper in two different classes without permission from both instructors, you take double credit for one project.

Falstaffing: This practice refers to a particular type of plagiarism in which one student submits another student's work. Know that you are guilty of Falstaffing if you let another student submit your paper.

Copyright violations: When you copy, distribute, and/or post in whole or in part any intellectual property without permission from or payment to the copyright holder, you commit a copyright infringement, especially when you profit from this use. To avoid copyright violations in your research projects, do the following:

- **Observe *fair use* guidelines:** Quote small portions of a document for limited purposes, such as education or research. Avoid copying large portions for your own gain.
- **Understand what's in the *public domain:*** You need not obtain permission to copy and use public domain materials—primarily documents created by the government, but also some material posted on the Internet as part of the "copy left" movement.
- **Observe *intellectual property and copyright laws:*** First, know your college's policies on copying documents. Second, realize that copyright protects the expression of ideas in a range of materials—writings, videos, songs, photographs, drawings, computer software, and so on. Always obtain permission to copy and distribute copyrighted materials.
- **Avoid changing a source** (e.g., a photo) without permission of the creator or copyright holder.

Organizing and Synthesizing Your Findings

Your research may generate a mass of notes, printouts, photocopies, electronic files, and more. The challenge is to move from this mass to a coherent structure for the paper you need to write. If you have systematically taken good notes (see pages 438–441), you are well on the way. In addition, the tips below and on the next page will help you move toward order.

Develop your ideas.

Good thinking is foundational to good research writing. To develop ideas for your research project, follow these steps:

Refocus on your research questions and working thesis. Has research changed your perspective and position?

Study the evidence. Review your materials once, twice, or more—as long as it takes for ideas to percolate and information to make sense. Consider these questions:

- Is the information complete or at least sufficient for the project?
- Does the information seem reliable and accurate?
- How does the information relate to the topic?
- What connections exist among different pieces of evidence?
- Does the information gathered fall naturally into patterns?

Develop sound conclusions through analysis and synthesis. Practice these strategies (and check pages 18–25 for more on sound thinking):

- Work against personal biases that create blind spots to what the evidence is saying. Be open to different angles provided by *all* the evidence. Think through both pros and cons.
- Practice logic in your analysis, but also tap into your intuition, creativity, and imagination.
- Interpret statistical data carefully and correctly.
- Logically distinguish between causes and effects; carefully link them.
- If you are comparing, make sure that the items can logically be compared, and make sure that you think through both similarities and differences.
- Avoid either/or and black-and-white thinking, as well as circular arguments, slippery slope claims, and sweeping generalizations. (See logical fallacies at pages 267–270.)
- Check your conclusions against counterarguments, your experience, and common sense. For example, what are the limits of hybrid-vehicle technology? What does your experience with cars and with culture tell you about how technological changes happen and get accepted?

Develop a structure for delivering research results.

Using your research questions and conclusions as guides, sift through and order your information. Consider these strategies:

Follow assignment recommendations. A pattern for your paper may be built into the assignment. For example, you may be asked to write a comparison/contrast paper. Shape your outline within that framework.

Clump and split. Using key ideas as main headings, arrange support and evidence under the most fitting heading. Depending on the note-taking system you used, separate and pile note cards, sketch out the structure on paper, use a graphic organizer (see pages 50–51), use a code system, copy and paste material electronically, or cut up your note pages. After categorizing information, decide how best to sequence the key ideas.

Rely on tested patterns. The patterns below offer sound methods for developing your thinking. Each choice offers a basic structure for your paper, but several patterns may be useful within your paper's body.

- **Argumentation** asserts and supports a claim, counters any opposition, and then reasserts the claim (perhaps in a modified form). See pages 259–312.
- **Cause/effect** can (1) explore the factors that led to an event or (2) explore the consequences of a specific event. See pages 183–198.
- **Chronological order** puts items in a sequence (order of events, steps in a process). See pages 229–242.
- **Classification** groups details based on their common traits or qualities. See pages 215–228.
- **Comparison/contrast** shows similarities and/or differences between specific elements of a topic. See pages 199–214.
- **Description** orders details in terms of spatial relationships, color, form, texture, and so on. See pages 145–180.
- **Explanation** clarifies how something works by breaking the object or phenomenon into parts or phases and then showing how they work together. See pages 229–242.
- **Order of importance** arranges items from most to least important, or least to most.
- **Partitioning** breaks down an object, a space, or a location into ordered parts, or a process into steps or phases.
- **Problem/solution** states a problem, explores its causes and effects, and presents solutions. See pages 313–328.
- **Question/answer** moves back and forth from questions to answers in a sequence that logically clarifies a topic

 For more help developing a structure, see pages 48–51.

Video

Developing Your First Draft

As you write your paper, your first goal is to develop and support your ideas—referring to sources, not being dominated by them. The discussion that follows will help you achieve this goal. Your second goal is to respect sources by integrating them naturally and providing correct documentation; that goal is addressed on pages 486–489.

Choose a drafting method.

Before starting your draft, choose a drafting method that makes sense for your project and your writing style. Consider these two options or something in between:

Writing Systematically

1. Develop a detailed outline, including supporting evidence.
2. Arrange your notes in precise order.
3. Write methodically, following your thesis, outline, and notes.
4. Cite your sources as you write.

Writing Freely

1. Review your working thesis and notes. Then set them aside.
2. If you need to, jot down a brief outline.
3. Write away—get all your research-based thinking down on paper.
4. Going back to your notes, develop your draft further and integrate citations.

Shape your first draft.

Develop the following parts in any order.

Draft an introduction. The introduction should do three things. First, it should say something interesting or surprising to gain your readers' attention. Second, the introduction should focus in on your topic by establishing some common ground. Third, your introduction should identify the issue or challenge related to your topic, and then offer your thesis. Consider these options:

- Begin with a revealing story or quotation.
- Give important background information.
- Offer a series of interesting or surprising facts.
- Cite details showing the topic's relevance.
- Provide important definitions.
- Introduce a problem issue, challenge, puzzle, or confusion about your topic.
- Identify the purpose and scope of your research.
- Identify your focus or thesis.
- Forecast how you will develop and support your thesis.

Draft the body. How do you develop a complete and insightful research paper? How do you add dimension and depth to your writing? For starters, you make sure that you have carefully explored and reflected on your specific topic. You also make sure that you have gathered plenty of compelling evidence to support your thesis.

It's in the main part of your paper—in the body—that you develop your thesis. The process usually works in this way: You present each main point supporting your thesis, expand on the points logically, include solid evidence such as facts or examples, and then offer additional analysis or documentation as needed.

Another way to approach your writing is to envision it as a series of paragraph clusters—one cluster of paragraphs for each main point. As you write, you imagine yourself conversing with your readers, telling them what they need to know, and communicating it as clearly and interestingly as you can.

Draft a conclusion. An effective closing adds to the reader's understanding of a research paper. The first part of the closing usually reviews (or ties together) important points in the paper, reinforces or reasserts the thesis, and/or draws a conclusion. The closing's final lines may expand the scope of the text by making a connection between the paper and the reader's experience, or between the paper and life in general.

Create a working title. At any point in the writing process, jot down possible titles that capture your paper's focused topic, research discoveries, and spirit. Consider key words and phrases that hint at your paper's thesis. For some papers, you may want to create a main title and a subtitle, separated by a colon.

TIPS for research writing

- As you draft your paper, keep the focus on your own thoughts. You don't want your paper to read like a strung-together series of references to other sources.
- Present your own ideas honestly and clearly. Although you will be considering the research of others, be sure to analyze this information yourself and relate your sources to one another. Work at offering your personal perspective on the topic.
- Your instructor may want your thesis in a specific location (perhaps in the last sentence of your first paragraph). Follow her or his wishes.
- Don't try to cram everything you've learned into your draft. Select material that is truly needed to develop your thesis.
- Avoid overusing one particular source; also avoid using too many direct quotations.
- To avoid accidental plagiarism, indicate the sources of all borrowed facts as you write your draft. (See "Avoiding Plagiarism," pages 476–479.)

Using Source Material in Your Writing

After you've found good sources and taken good notes on them, you want to use that research effectively in your writing. Specifically, you want to show (1) what information you are borrowing and (2) where you got it. By doing so, you create credibility. This section shows you how to develop credibility by integrating and documenting sources so as to avoid plagiarism and other abuses. *Note:* For a full treatment of documentation, see chapter 32 (MLA) and chapter 33 (APA).

Integrate source material carefully.

Source material—whether a summary, a paraphrase, or a quotation—should be integrated smoothly into your discussion. Follow these strategies:

The Right Reasons

Focus on what you want to say, not on all the source material you've collected. Use sources to do the following:

- Deepen and develop your point with the reasoning offered by a source.
- Support your point and your thinking about it with evidence—with facts, statistics, details, and so on.
- Give credibility to your point with an expert's supporting statement.
- Bring your point to life with an example, an observation, a case study, an anecdote, or an illustration.
- Address a counterargument or an alternative.

Quotation Restraint

In most research documents, restrict your quoting to nuggets:

- Key statements by authorities (e.g., the main point that a respected Shakespeare scholar makes about the role of Ophelia in *Hamlet*)
- Well-phrased claims and conclusions (e.g., a powerful conclusion by an ethicist about the problem with the media's coverage of cloning debates and technological developments)
- Passages where careful word-by-word analysis and interpretation are important to your argument (e.g., an excerpt from a speech made by a politician about the future of the NASA space shuttle program—a passage that requires a careful analysis for the between-the-lines message)

Quotations, especially long ones, must pull their weight, so generally paraphrase or summarize source material instead.

Primary Document Exception: When a primary text (a novel, a piece of legislation, a speech) is a key piece of evidence or the actual focus of your project, careful analysis of quoted excerpts is required. See pages 452–453 for more.

Smooth Integration

When you use quotations, work them into your writing as smoothly as possible. To do so, you need to pay attention to style, punctuation, and syntax. (See pages 488–489.)

Use enough of the quotation to make your point without changing the meaning of the original. Use quotation marks around key phrases taken from the source.

> *Example:* Ogden, Williams, and Larson also conclude that the hydrogen fuel-cell vehicle is "a strong candidate for becoming the Car of the Future," given the trend toward "tighter environmental constraints" and the "intense efforts underway" by automakers to develop commercially viable versions of such vehicles (25).

Integrate all sources thoughtfully. Fold source material into your discussion by relating it to your own thinking. Let your ideas guide the way, not your sources, by using this pattern:

1. State and explain your idea, creating a context for the source.
2. Identify and introduce the source, linking it to your discussion.
3. Summarize, paraphrase, or quote the source, providing a citation in an appropriate spot.
4. Use the source by explaining, expanding, or refuting it.
5. When appropriate, refer back to a source to further develop the ideas it contains.

Sample Passage: Note the integration of sources in the paragraph below.

Writer's ideas	The motivation and urgency to create and improve hybrid-electric technology comes from a range of complex forces. Some of these forces are economic, others environmental, and still others social. In "Societal Lifestyle Costs of Cars with Alternative Fuels/Engines," Joan Ogden, Robert Williams, and Eric Larson argue that "[c]ontinued reliance on current transportation fuels and technologies poses serious oil supply insecurity, climate change, and urban air pollution risks" (7). Because of the nonrenewable nature of fossil fuels as well as their negative side effects, the transportation industry is confronted with making the most radical changes since the introduction of the internal-combustion automobile more than 100 years ago. Hybrid-electric vehicles are one response to this pressure.
Attributive phrase	
Paraphrase, quotation, or summary	
Citation	
Commentary	
Conclusion	

Effectively document your sources.

Just as you need to integrate source material carefully into your writing, so you must also carefully document where that source material comes from. Readers should recognize which material is yours and which material is not.

Identify clearly where source material begins. Your discussion must offer a smooth transition to source material. Follow the guidelines below:

- For first references to a source, use an attributive statement that indicates some of the following: author's name and credentials, title of the source, nature of the study or research, and helpful background.

  Example: **Joan Ogden, Robert Williams, and Eric Larson, members of the Princeton Environmental Institute, explain** that modest improvements in energy efficiency and emissions reductions will not be enough over the next century because of anticipated transportation increases (7).

- For subsequent references to a source, use a simplified attributive phrase, such as the author's last name or a shortened version of the title.

  Example: **Ogden, Williams, and Larson go on to argue** that "[e]ffectively addressing environmental and oil supply concerns will probably require radical changes in automotive engine/fuel technologies" (7).

- In some situations, such as quoting straightforward facts, simply skip the attributive phrase. The parenthetical citation supplies sufficient attribution.

  Example: Various types of transportation are by far the main consumers of oil (three fourths of world oil imports); moreover, these same technologies are responsible for one fourth of all greenhouse gas sources (Ogden, Williams, and Larson 7).

- The verb you use to introduce source material is key. Use fitting verbs, such as those in the table below. Normally, use the present tense. Use the past tense only to stress the "pastness" of a source.

  Example: In their 2004 study, "Societal Lifecycle Costs of Cars with Alternative Fuels/Engines," Ogden, Williams, and Larson **present** a method for comparing and contrasting alternatives to internal-combustion engines. Earlier, these authors **made** preliminary steps . . .

accepts	considers	explains	rejects	acknowledges
contradicts	highlights	reminds	adds	contrasts
identifies	responds	affirms	criticizes	insists
shares	argues	declares	interprets	shows
asserts	defends	lists	states	believes
denies	maintains	stresses	cautions	describes
outlines	suggests	claims	disagrees	points out
supports	compares	discusses	praises	urges
concludes	emphasizes	proposes	verifies	confirms
enumerates	refutes	warns		

Indicate where source material ends. Closing quotation marks and a citation, as shown below, indicate the end of a source quotation. Generally, place the citation immediately after any quotation, paraphrase, or summary. However, you may also place the citation early in the sentence or at the end if the parenthetical note is obviously obtrusive. When you discuss several details from a page in a source, use an attributive phrase at the beginning of your discussion and a single citation at the end.

> *Example:* As the "Lifestyle Costs" study concludes, when greenhouse gases, air pollution, and oil insecurity are factored into the analysis, alternative-fuel vehicles "offer lower LCCs than typical new cars" (Ogden, Williams, and Larson 25).

Set off longer quotations. If a quotation is longer than four typed lines, set it off from the main text. Generally, introduce the quotation with a complete sentence and a colon. Indent the quotation one inch (10 spaces) and double-space it, but don't put quotation marks around it. Put the citation outside the final punctuation mark.

> *Example:* Toward the end of the study, Ogden, Williams, and Larson argue that changes to the fuel delivery system must be factored into planning:
>
> > In charting a course to the Car of the Future, societal LCC comparisons should be complemented by considerations of fuel infrastructure requirements. Because fuel infrastructure changes are costly, the number of major changes made over time should be minimized. The bifurcated strategy advanced here—of focusing on the H_2 FCV for the long term and advanced liquid hydrocarbon-fueled ICEVs and ICE/HEVs for the near term—would reduce the number of such infrastructure change to one (an eventual shift to H_2). (25)

Marking Changes to Quotations

You may shorten or change a quotation so that it fits more smoothly into your sentence—but don't alter the original meaning. Use an ellipsis within square brackets to indicate that you have omitted words from the original. An ellipsis is three periods with a space before and after each period.

> *Example:* In their projections of where fuel-cell vehicles are heading, Ogden, Williams, and Larson discuss GM's AUTOnomy vehicle, with its "radical redesign of the entire car. [. . .] In these cars, steering, braking, and other vehicle systems are controlled electronically rather than mechanically" (24).

Use square brackets to indicate a clarification or to change a pronoun or verb tense or to switch around uppercase and lowercase.

> *Example:* As Ogden, Williams, and Larson explain, "[e]ven if such barriers [the high cost of fuel cells and the lack of an H_2 fuel infrastructure] can be overcome, decades would be required before this embryonic technology could make major contributions in reducing the major externalities that characterize today's cars" (25).

 Chapters 2–7 contain additional tips. See pages 27–42 (beginning the writing process), pages 43–54 (planning), pages 55–70 (drafting), and pages 71–110 (revising, editing), and pages 111–116 (submitting/portfolio work).

Writing Checklist

Use the seven-traits checklist below to review documented research.

Ideas

_____ The thesis is clear and sharp; the support strong and balanced.
_____ Researched data are accurate, complete, and properly credited.

Organization

_____ The writing offers a structured chain of ideas built on evidence.
_____ The opening presents the purpose and scope of the research, the middle provides complete discussion, and the closing focuses on conclusions.

Voice

_____ The tone is confident but also sincere, measured, and objective.
_____ "I" and "you" are avoided unless allowed by the instructor.

Words

_____ Precise, clear phrasing is used throughout the paper.
_____ Terms are defined as needed.

Sentences

_____ The prose contains a good blend of sentence lengths and patterns.
_____ Source material is carefully integrated.

Copy

_____ Grammar, punctuation, mechanics, usage, and spelling are correct.
_____ Documentation is complete, correct, and consistent.

Design

_____ The format, page layout, and typography are all reader friendly.
_____ Data are effectively presented in discussion, lists, tables, graphs.

Critical-Thinking and Writing Activities

1. With some classmates, debate the seriousness of plagiarism and the use of tools such as Turnitin.com.

2. Closely examine one of your most recent research papers. Have you followed this chapter's guidelines? Where do you need to improve?

◀ VISUALLY SPEAKING

Review the photograph at the beginning of this chapter (page 475). What does the image suggest about research writing? How does the image relate to your research?

DOCUMENTATION AND FORMAT STYLES

Research-based writing—whether it is done in the humanities, social sciences, or natural and applied sciences—is assigned not only *to show* learning, but also *to share* learning. Careful and correct documentation of sources helps you do both. First, such documentation is a type of road map that *shows* your professor where you have gone and what you have done to learn about your topic and develop your thesis. But in addition, careful documentation *shares* your research results with all readers, enabling them to retrace your research steps, track the logic of your argument, and possibly study your sources for themselves.

The two chapters that follow will help you document your sources clearly and correctly. Chapter 32 explains how to document sources in accordance with the Modern Language Association's (MLA) style. The chapter includes "An American Hybrid," Katie Hughey's paper illustrating MLA formatting. Chapter 33 explains how to document sources in the American Psychological Association's (APA) style. This chapter includes "Our Roots Go Back to Roanoke . . . ," Renee Danielle Singh's paper illustrating APA formatting.

CONTENTS

Documentation and Format Styles

MLA DOCUMENTATION FORMAT

In research papers, it is commonly said, "You are commanded to borrow but forbidden to steal." To borrow ideas while avoiding plagiarism (see pages 476–479), you must not only mention the sources you borrow from but also document them completely and accurately. You must follow to the last dot the documentation conventions for papers written in your general subject area.

If you are composing a research paper in the humanities, your instructor will most likely require you to follow the conventions established in the style manual of the Modern Language Association (MLA). This chapter provides you with explanations and examples for citing sources in MLA format. An excellent way to learn MLA documentation is to see it in use, so turn to the sample paper demonstrating MLA form on pages 522–533. Additional information and MLA updates can be found on the website for this book: **www.thecollegewriter .com/3e.**

Video

MLA Research Paper Guidelines

Questions & Answers

IS A SEPARATE TITLE PAGE REQUIRED?

No. (unless your instructor requires one, in which case you would format it according to his or her instructions). On the first page of a research paper, type your name, your instructor's name, the course name and number, and the date, one below the other. The title comes next, centered. Then simply begin the text on the next line.

IS THE RESEARCH PAPER DOUBLE-SPACED?

Yes. Double-space everything, even tables, captions, long quotations, or works-cited entries.

WHAT ABOUT LONGER QUOTATIONS?

Verse quotations of more than three lines should be indented one inch (ten spaces) and double-spaced. Do not add quotation marks. Each line of a poem or play begins a new line of the quotation; do not run the lines together. When you are quoting prose that needs more than four typed lines, indent each line of the quotation one inch (ten spaces) from the left margin and double-space it; do not add quotation marks.

To quote two or more paragraphs—in addition to the one inch that you are already indenting for the lengthy quotation—you should indent the first line of each paragraph an extra quarter-inch (three spaces). However, if the first sentence quoted does not begin a paragraph in the source, do not include the additional indent. Indent only the first lines of the successive paragraphs.

ARE PAGE NUMBERS REQUIRED?

Yes. Pages should be numbered consecutively in the upper-right corner, one-half inch from the top and flush with the right margin (one inch). Your last name should precede the page number, and no abbreviations or other symbols should be included.

IS AN APPENDIX REQUIRED?

No. In MLA style, tables and illustrations are placed as close as possible to the related text.

IS AN ABSTRACT REQUIRED?	***No.*** An abstract, or summary of your research paper, is not an MLA requirement.
HOW WIDE SHOULD THE MARGINS BE?	Top, bottom, left, and right margins should be one inch (except for page numbering). The first word in a paragraph should be indented one-half inch (five spaces). Longer quotations should be set off one inch (ten spaces) from the left margin (see page 494).
ARE REFERENCES PLACED IN THE TEXT?	***Yes.*** Indicate only page numbers parenthetically if you identify the author in your text. Give the author's last name in a parenthetical reference if it is not mentioned in the text.
IS A LIST OF SOURCES USED IN THE PAPER REQUIRED?	***Yes.*** Full citations for all sources used (e.g., books, periodicals) are placed in an alphabetized list labeled "Works Cited" at the end of the paper. Whereas in-text parenthetical references generally indicate just the author's last name and a page number for the source material, the works-cited entry provides full publication details.
WHAT ABOUT HEADINGS?	MLA style does not specify a particular format for headings within the text; normally, headings are used only for separate sections of the paper ("Works Cited" or "Notes," for example).
HOW DO I INCORPORATE REFERENCE MARKERS IF I SUBMIT MY PAPER ELECTRONICALLY?	Numbering paragraphs is common in electronic publications. Place the paragraph number in brackets. Follow with a space and begin the paragraph. (For other electronic formatting guidelines, check with your instructor.)
ANY OTHER SPECIAL INSTRUCTIONS?	Always ask whether your school, department, or instructor has special requirements that may take precedence over those listed here.

Web Link: For additional questions and answers about MLA format, see the MLA Q&A page at http://www.mla.org/style_faq.

Web Link

Guidelines for In-Text Citations

The *MLA Handbook for Writers of Research Papers* suggests giving credit for your sources of information in the body of your research paper. One way to do so is by indicating the author and/or title in the text of your essay, and then putting a page reference in parentheses after the summary, paraphrase, or quotation, as needed. The simplest way to do so is to insert the appropriate information (usually the author and page number) in parentheses after the words or ideas taken from the source. To avoid disrupting your writing, place citations where a pause would naturally occur (usually at the end of a sentence but sometimes within a sentence, before internal punctuation such as a comma or semicolon). These in-text citations (often called "parenthetical references") refer to sources listed on the "Works Cited" page at the end of your paper. (See pages 532–533 for a sample works-cited list.)

General Guidelines for In-Text Citations

As you integrate citations into your paper, follow the guidelines below, referring to the sample citation as needed.

Sample In-Text Citation

As James Cuno, director of the Harvard University Art Museums, points out, the public, which subsidizes museums either directly through donations or indirectly via their status as tax-free nonprofit organizations, expects them to "carry out their duties professionally on its behalf" (164).

- Make sure each in-text citation clearly points to an entry in your list of works cited. The identifying information provided (usually the author's last name) must be the word or words by which the entry is alphabetized in that list.

- Keep citations brief, and integrate them smoothly into your writing.

- When paraphrasing or summarizing rather than quoting, make it clear where your borrowing begins and ends. Use stylistic cues to distinguish the source's thoughts ("Kalmbach points out . . . ," "Some critics argue . . .") from your own ("I believe . . . ," "It seems obvious, however"). See pages 486–487 for more on integrating sources.

- When using a shortened title of a work, begin with the word by which the work is alphabetized in your list of works cited (e.g., "Egyptian, Classical," not "Middle Eastern Art," for "Egyptian, Classical, and Middle Eastern Art").

- For inclusive page numbers larger than ninety-nine, give only the two digits of the second number (113–14, not 113–114).

- When including a parenthetical citation at the end of a sentence, place it before the end punctuation. (Citations for long, indented quotations are an exception. See pages 489, 494, 502, and 503.)

Special Guidelines for Sources Without Traditional Authorship and/or Pagination

Today many sources, especially electronic ones, have no stated authors and/or no pagination. For such sources, use these in-text citation strategies:

Source Without a Stated Author: In a signal phrase or in the parenthetical reference, identify the source as precisely as possible by indicating the sponsoring agency, the type of document, or the title (shortened in the parenthetical reference). See pages 499–500.

> While the Brooklyn Museum may be best known for the recent controversy over the Sensation exhibition, it does contain a strong collection of contemporary if less controversial art, "ranging from representational to abstract to conceptual" ("Contemporary Art").

Source with No Pagination: If no pagination exists within the document, use paragraph numbers (with the abbreviation *par.*), if the document provides them. If the document includes neither page nor paragraph numbers, cite the entire work. Do not create your own numbering system.

> The Museum's collection of Art of the Americas includes extensive holdings of works by the aboriginal peoples of North, Central, and South America, many of these gathered by archaeologist Herbert Spinden during at least seven expeditions between 1929 and 1950 ("Art of the Americas" par. 3).

Note: Because parenthetical notations are used to signal the end of an attribution, sources with no pagination or paragraph numbers offer a special challenge. When no parenthetical notation is possible, signal a shift back to your own discussion with a source-reflective statement indicating your thinking about the source.

> . . . indicated by his recording the audio tour of the exhibit, his supporting the show financially, and his promoting Sensation at his website. As Welland's discussion of David Bowie's participation indicates, the controversy over the Brooklyn Museum of Art's Sensation exhibit . . .

INSIGHT:

- Stable pagination for many electronic resources is available when you use the ".pdf" rather than the ".html" version of the source.
- For instruction on smoothly integrating source material into your paper, see pages 486–489.
- For cautions about sources without identified authors, see pages 499, 500, 506, and 512.

Sample In-Text Citations

The following entries illustrate the most common in-text citations.

Video

One Author: A Complete Work

You do not need an in-text citation if you identify the author in your text. (See the first entry below.) However, you must give the author's last name in an in-text citation if it is not mentioned in the text. (See the second entry.) When a source is listed in your works-cited page with an editor, a translator, a speaker, or an artist instead of the author, use that person's name in your citation.

With Author in Text: (This is the preferred way of citing a complete work.)

> In <u>No Need for Hunger</u>, Robert Spitzer recommends that the U.S.
> government develop a new foreign policy to help Third World
> countries overcome poverty and hunger.

Without Author in Text:

> <u>No Need for Hunger</u> recommends that the U.S. government develop
> a new foreign policy to help Third World countries overcome poverty
> and hunger (Spitzer).

Note: Do not offer page numbers when citing complete works, articles in alphabetized encyclopedias, one-page articles, and unpaginated sources.

One Author: Part of a Work

List the necessary page numbers in parentheses if you borrow words or ideas from a particular source. Leave a space between the author's last name and the page reference. No abbreviation or punctuation is needed.

With Author in Text:

> Bullough writes that genetic engineering was dubbed "eugenics" by a
> cousin of Darwin's, Sir Francis Galton, in 1885 (5).

Without Author in Text:

> Genetic engineering was dubbed "eugenics" by a cousin of Darwin's,
> Sir Francis Galton, in 1885 (Bullough 5).

A Work by Two or Three Authors

Give the last names of every author in the same order that they appear in the works-cited section. (The correct order of the authors' names can be found on the title page of the book.)

> Students learned more than a full year's Spanish in ten days using the
> complete supermemory method (Ostrander and Schroeder 51).

A Work by Four or More Authors

Give the first author's last name as it appears in the works-cited section followed by *et al.* (meaning "and others").

> **Communication on the job is more than talking; it is "inseparable from**
> **your total behavior" (Culligan et al. 111).**

Note: You may instead choose to list all of the authors' last names.

Two or More Works by the Same Author(s)

In addition to the author's last name(s) and page number(s), include a shortened version of the work's title when you cite two or more works by the same author(s).

> **With Author in Text:**
>
> > **Wallerstein and Blakeslee claim that divorce creates an enduring**
> > **identity for children of the marriage (Unexpected Legacy 62).**
>
> **Without Author in Text:**
>
> > **They are intensely lonely despite active social lives (Wallerstein and**
> > **Blakeslee, Second Chances 51).**

Note: When including both author(s) and title in a parenthetical reference, separate them with a comma, as shown above, but do not put a comma between the title and the page number.

Works by Authors with the Same Last Name

When citing different sources by authors with the same last name, it is best to use the authors' full names in the text to avoid confusion. However, if circumstances call for parenthetical references, add each author's first initial. If first initials are the same, use each author's full name.

> **Some critics think Titus Andronicus too abysmally melodramatic to be a**
> **work of Shakespeare (A. Parker 73). Others suggest that Shakespeare**
> **meant it as black comedy (D. Parker 486).**

A Work Authored by an Agency, a Committee, or an Organization

If a book or other work was written by an organization such as an agency, a committee, or a task force, it is said to have a corporate author. (See also page 506.) If the corporate name is long, include it in the text (rather than in parentheses) to avoid disrupting the flow of your writing. After the full name has been used at least once, use a shortened form of the name (common abbreviations are acceptable) in subsequent references. For example, *Task Force* may be used for *Task Force on Education for Economic Growth.*

> **The thesis of the Task Force's report is that economic success depends**
> **on our ability to improve large-scale education and training as quickly**
> **as possible (113–14).**

An Anonymous Work

When there is no author listed, give the title or a shortened version of the title as it appears in the works-cited section. (See page 506.)

Statistics indicate that drinking water can make up 20 percent of a person's total exposure to lead (Information 572).

Two or More Works Included in One Citation

To cite multiple works within a single parenthetical reference, separate the references with a semicolon.

In Medieval Europe, Latin translations of the works of Rhazes, a Persian scholar, were a primary source of medical knowledge (Albala 22; Lewis 266).

A Series of Citations from a Single Work

If no confusion is possible, it is not necessary to name a source repeatedly when making multiple parenthetical references to that source in a single paragraph. If all references are to the same page, identify that page in a parenthetical note after the last reference. If the references are to different pages within the same work, you need identify the work only once, and then use a parenthetical note with page number alone for the subsequent references.

Domesticating science meant not only spreading scientific knowledge, but also promoting it as a topic of public conversation (Heilbron 2). One way to enhance its charm was by depicting cherubic putti as "angelic research assistants" in book illustrations (5).

A Work Referred to in Another Work

If you must cite an indirect source—that is, information from a source that is quoted from another source—use the abbreviation *qtd. in* (quoted in) before the indirect source in your reference.

Paton improved the conditions in Diepkloof (a prison) by "removing all the more obvious aids to detention. The dormitories [were] open at night: the great barred gate [was] gone" (qtd. in Callan xviii).

A Work Without Page Numbers

If a work has no page numbers or paragraph numbers, treat it as you would a complete work. (See page 497.) This is commonly the case with electronic resources, for example. Do not count pages to create reference numbers of your own.

Antibiotics become ineffective against such organisms through two natural processes: first, genetic mutation; and second, the subsequent transfer of this mutated genetic material to other organisms (Davies par. 5).

A Work in an Anthology or a Collection

When citing the entirety of a work that is part of an anthology or a collection, if it is identified by author in your list of works cited, treat the citation as you would for any other complete work. (See page 498.)

> **In "The Canadian Postmodern," Linda Hutcheon offers a clear analysis of the self-reflexive nature of contemporary Canadian fiction.**

Similarly, if you are citing particular pages of such a work, follow the directions for citing part of a work. (See page 498.)

> **According to Hutcheon, "postmodernism seems to designate cultural practices that are fundamentally self-reflexive, in other words, art that is self-consciously artifice" (18).**

(To format this sort of entry in your list of works cited, see pages 506–507.)

An Item from a Reference Work

An entry from a reference work such as an encyclopedia or a dictionary should be cited similarly to a work from an anthology or a collection (see above). For a dictionary definition, include the abbreviation *def.* followed by the particular entry designation.

> **This message becomes a juggernaut in the truest sense, a belief that "elicits blind devotion or sacrifice" ("Juggernaut," def. 1).**

Note: While many such entries are identified only by title (as above), some reference works include an author's name for each entry (as below). Others may identify the entry author by initials, with a list of full names elsewhere in the work.

> **The decisions of the International Court of Justice are "based on principles of international law and cannot be appealed" (Pranger).**

(See page 508 for guidelines to formatting these entries in your works-cited list.)

A Part of a Multivolume Work

When citing only one volume of a multivolume work, if you identify the volume number in the works-cited list, there is no need to include it in your in-text citation. However, if you cite more than one volume of a work, each in-text reference must identify the appropriate volume. Give the volume number followed by page number, separated by a colon and a space.

> **"A human being asleep," says Spengler, ". . . is leading only a plantlike existence" (2: 4).**

When citing a whole volume, however, either identify the volume number in parentheses with the abbreviation *vol.* (using a comma to separate it from the author's name) or use the full word *volume* in your text.

> **The land of Wisconsin has shaped its many inhabitants more significantly than they ever shaped that land (Stephens, vol. 1).**

A One-Page Work

Cite a one-page work just as you would a complete work. (See page 498.)

As Samantha Adams argues in her editorial, it is time for NASA "to fully reevaluate the Space Shuttle's long-term viability for sending humans into space."

A Sacred Text or Famous Literary Work

Sacred texts and famous literary works are published in many different editions. For that reason, it is helpful to identify sections, parts, chapters, and such instead of or in addition to page numbers. If using page numbers, list them first, followed by an abbreviation for the type of division and the division number.

The more important a person's role in society—the more apparent power an individual has—the more that person is a slave to the forces of history (Tolstoy 690; bk. 9, ch. 1).

Books of the Bible and other well-known literary works may be abbreviated, if no confusion is possible.

"A generation goes, and a generation comes, but the earth remains forever" (The New Oxford Annotated Bible, Eccles. 1.4)

As Shakespeare's famous Danish prince observes, "One may smile, and smile, and be a villain" (Ham. 1.5.104).

Quoting Prose

To cite prose from fiction (novels, short stories), list more than the page number if the work is available in several editions. Give the page reference first, and then add a chapter, section, or book number in abbreviated form after a semicolon.

In The House of the Spirits, Isabel Allende describes Marcos, "dressed in mechanic's overalls, with huge racer's goggles" (13; ch. 1).

When you are quoting any sort of prose that takes more than four typed lines, indent each line of the quotation one inch (ten spaces) and double-space it; do not add quotation marks. In this case, you put the parenthetical citation (the pages and chapter numbers) outside the end punctuation mark of the quotation itself.

Allende describes the flying machine that Marcos has assembled:

The contraption lay with its stomach on terra firma, heavy and sluggish and looking more like a wounded duck than like one of those newfangled airplanes they were starting to produce in the United States. There was nothing in its appearance to suggest that it could move, much less take flight across the snowy peaks. (12; ch. 1)

Quoting Verse

Do not use page numbers when referencing classic verse plays and poems. Instead, cite them by division (act, scene, canto, book, part) and line, using Arabic numerals for the various divisions unless your instructor prefers Roman numerals. Use periods to separate the various numbers.

> **In the first act of the play named after him, Hamlet comments, "How weary, stale, flat and unprofitable, / Seem to me all the uses of this world" (1.2.133–134).**

Note: A slash, with a space on each side, shows where each new line of verse begins. If you are citing lines only, use the word *line* or *lines* in your first reference and numbers only in additional references.

> **At the beginning of the sestet in Robert Frost's "Design," the speaker asks this pointed question: "What had that flower to do with being white, / The wayside blue and innocent heal-all?" (lines 9–10).**

Verse quotations of more than three lines should be indented one inch (ten spaces) and double-spaced. Do not add quotation marks. Each line of the poem or play begins a new line of the quotation; do not run the lines together. If a line or lines of poetry are dropped from the quotation, ellipses that extend the width of the stanza should be used to indicate the omission.

> **Bin Ramke's poem "A Little Ovid Late in the Day" tells of reading by the last light of a summer day:**
>
> > **[T]ales of incest, corruption,**
> >
> > **any big, mythic vice**
> >
> > **against the color of the sun,**
> >
> > **the sweetness of the time of day—**
> >
> > **I know the story,**
> >
> > **it is the light I care about. (3–8)**

Listing an Internet Address

In printed documents, Internet addresses and e-mail addresses should always be enclosed in angle brackets. Without these brackets, these addresses might otherwise be confusing because of their internal punctuation.

> **<www.thecollegewriter.com/3e>**

Unfortunately, many modern word processors automatically convert such addresses to live hyperlinks, removing the angle brackets and adding an underline. To avoid this in your printed documents, either turn off the auto-formatting option in your word processor or cancel such formatting immediately after it occurs. If your instructor allows, you may use live links in electronic versions of your text.

QUICK GUIDE

MLA Works Cited

The works-cited section lists all of the sources you have cited (referred to) in your text. It does not include any sources you may have read or studied but did not refer to in your paper (that's a bibliography). Begin your list of works cited on a new page (the next page after the text), and number each page, continuing from the number of the last page of the text. A sample works-cited page is shown on pages 532–533; the guidelines here describe the format of the works-cited section.

1. Type the page number in the upper-right corner, one-half inch from the top of the page, with your last name before it.

2. Center the title *Works Cited* (not in italics or underlined) one inch from the top; then double-space before the first entry.

3. Begin each entry flush with the left margin. If the entry runs more than one line, indent additional lines one-half inch (five spaces) or use the hanging indent function on your computer.

4. End each element of the entry with a period. (Elements are separated by periods in most cases unless only a space is sufficient.) Use a single space after all punctuation.

5. Double-space lines within each entry and between entries.

6. List each entry alphabetically by the author's last name. If there is no author, use the first word of the title (disregard *A, An, The* as the first word). If there are multiple authors, alphabetize according to which author is listed first in the publication.

7. A basic entry for a book would be as follows:

    Black, Naomi. Virginia Woolf as Feminist. Ithaca: Cornell UP,
      2004.

8. A basic entry for a periodical (a journal or magazine) would be as follows:

    Stelmach, Kathryn. "From Text to Tableau: Ekphrastic
      Enchantment in Mrs. Dalloway and To the Lighthouse."
      Studies in the Novel 38.3 (Fall 2006): 304–26.

9. A basic entry for an online source would be as follows. (Note the URL in angle brackets followed by a period.)

    Clarke, S. N. "Virginia Woolf (1882-1941): A Short Biography."
      Virginia Woolf Society of Great Britain. 2000. 12 March 2008.
      <http://www.virginiawoolfsociety.co.uk/vw_res.biography.htm>

Video

Works-Cited Entries: Books and Other Documents

Components

The entries that follow illustrate the information needed to cite books, sections of a book, pamphlets, and government publications. The possible components of these entries are listed in order below:

1. Author's name
2. Title of a part of the book (an article in the book or a foreword)
3. Title of the book, underlined
4. Name of editor or translator
5. Edition
6. Number of volume
7. Name of series
8. Place of publication, publisher, year of publication
9. Page numbers, if citation is to only a part (For page spans, use a hyphen; if clarity is maintained, for pages above 100 you may also drop a digit from the second number—for example, 141–43, 201–334.)

Note: In general, if any of these components do not apply, they are not included in the works-cited entry. However, in the rare instance that a book does not state publication information, use the following abbreviations in place of information you cannot supply:

n.p.	No place of publication given
n.p.	No publisher given
n.d.	No date of publication given
n. pag.	No pagination given

Additional Guidelines

- List only the city for the place of publication if the city is in the United States. For cities outside the United States, add an abbreviation for the country if necessary for clarity. If several cities are listed, give only the first.
- Publishers' names should be shortened by omitting articles (*a, an, the*), business abbreviations (*Co., Inc.*), and descriptive words (*Books, Press*). For publishing houses that consist of the names of more than one person, cite only the first of the surnames. Abbreviate *University Press* as *UP*. Also use standard abbreviations whenever possible. See page 566 for more details.

A Book by One Author

> Green, Christopher. Picasso: Architecture and Vertigo. New Haven: Yale
> UP, 2005.

Two or More Books by the Same Author

List the books alphabetically according to title. After the first entry, substitute three hyphens for the author's name.

> Dershowitz, Alan M. Rights from Wrongs. New York: Basic Books, 2005.
>
> - - - . Supreme Injustice: How the High Court Hijacked Election 2000.
> Oxford: Oxford UP, 2001.

A Work by Two or Three Authors

> Bystydzienski, Jill M., and Estelle P. Resnik. Women in Cross-Cultural
> Transitions. Bloomington: Phi Delta Kappa Educational Foundation,
> 1994.

Note: List the authors in the same order as they appear on the title page. Reverse only the name of the first author.

A Work by Four or More Authors

> Schulte-Peevers, Andrea, et al. Germany. Victoria, Austral.: Lonely
> Planet, 2000.

Note: You may also choose to give all names in full in the order used on the title page.

A Work Authored by an Agency, a Committee, or an Organization

> Exxon Mobil Corporation. Great Plains 2000. Lincolnwood: Publications
> Intl., 2001.

An Anonymous Book

> Chase's Calendar of Events 2002. Chicago: Contemporary, 2002.

A Single Work from an Anthology

> Mitchell, Joseph. "The Bottom of the Harbor." American Sea Writing. Ed.
> Peter Neill. New York: Lib. of America, 2000. 584–608.

A Complete Anthology

If you cite a complete anthology, begin the entry with the editor(s).

> Neill, Peter, ed. American Sea Writing. New York: Lib. of America, 2000.
>
> Smith, Rochelle, and Sharon L. Jones, eds. The Prentice Hall Anthology of
> African American Literature. Upper Saddle River: Prentice, 2000.

Two or More Works from an Anthology or a Collection

To avoid unnecessary repetition when citing two or more entries from a larger collection, you may cite the collection once with complete publication information (see Rothfield, below). The individual entries (see Becker and Cuno, below) can then be cross-referenced by listing the author, title of the piece, editor of the collection, and page numbers.

> Becker, Carol. "The Brooklyn Controversy: A View from the Bridge."
> Rothfield 15–21.

> Cuno, James. "Sensation and the Ethics of Funding Exhibitions."
> Rothfield 162–170.

> Rothfield, Lawrence, Ed. <u>Unsettling Sensation: Arts-Policy Lessons from
> the Brooklyn Museum of Art Controversy.</u> Rutgers Series on the
> Public Life of the Arts. New Brunswick: Rutgers UP, 2001.

One Volume of a Multivolume Work

> Cooke, Jacob Ernest, and Milton M. Klein, eds. <u>North America in Colonial
> Times.</u> Vol. 2. New York: Scribner's, 1998.

Note: If you cite two or more volumes in a multivolume work, give the total number of volumes after each title. Offer specific references to volume and page numbers in the parenthetical reference in your text, like this: (8: 112–114).

> Salzman, Jack, David Lionel Smith, and Cornel West. <u>Encyclopedia of
> African-American Culture and History.</u> 5 vols. New York: Simon, 1996.

An Introduction, a Preface, a Foreword, or an Afterword

To cite the introduction, preface, foreword, or afterword of a book, list the author of the part first. Then identify the part by type, with no quotation marks or underlining, followed by the book title. Next, identify the author of the work, using the word *by.* (If the book's author and the part's author are the same person, give just the last name after *by.*) For a book that gives cover credit to an editor instead of an author, identify the editor as usual. Finally, list any page numbers for the part cited.

> Barry, Anne. Afterword. <u>Making Room for Students.</u> By Celia Oyler. New
> York: Teachers College, 1996.

> Proulx, Annie. Introduction. <u>Dance of the Happy Shades.</u> By Alice Munro.
> Toronto: Penguin Canada, 2005.

A Republished Book (Reprint)

Give the original publication date after the title.

> Atwood, Margaret. <u>Surfacing.</u> 1972. New York: Doubleday, 1998.

Note: After the original publication facts, cite new material added: Introd. C. Becker.

A Book with Multiple Publishers

When a book lists more than one publisher (not just different offices of the same publisher), include all of them in the order given on the book's title page, separated by a semicolon.

> Wells, H. G. The Complete Short Stories of H. G. Wells. New York: St. Martin's; London: A. & C. Black, 1987.

Second and Subsequent Editions

An edition refers to the particular publication you are citing, as in the third (3rd) edition.

> Joss, Molly W. Looking Good in Presentations. 3rd ed. Scottsdale: Coriolis, 1999.

An Edition with Author and Editor

The abbreviation *ed.* also refers to the work of one or more persons that is prepared by another person, an editor.

> Shakespeare, William. A Midsummer Night's Dream. Ed. Jane Bachman. Lincolnwood: NTC, 1994.

A Translation

> Lebert, Stephan, and Norbert Lebert. My Father's Keeper. Trans. Julian Evans. Boston: Little, 2001.

An Article in a Familiar Reference Book

It is not necessary to give full publication information for familiar reference works (encyclopedias and dictionaries). For these titles, list only the edition (if available) and the publication year. If an article is initialed, check the index of authors (in the opening section of each volume) for the author's full name.

> "Technical Education." Encyclopedia Americana. 2001 ed.

> Lum, P. Andrea. "Computed Tomography." World Book. 2000 ed.

When citing a single definition of several listed, add the abbreviation *Def.* and the particular number or letter for that definition.

> "Macaroni." Def. 2b. The American Heritage College Dictionary. 4th ed. 2002.

An Article in an Unfamiliar Reference Book

For citations of lesser-known reference works, give full publication information, as for any other sort of book.

> "S Corporation." The Portable MBA Desk Reference. Ed. Paul A. Argenti. New York: Wiley, 1994.

A Government Publication

State the name of the government (country, state, and so on) followed by the name of the agency. Most U.S. federal publications are published by the Government Printing Office (GPO).

> United States. Dept. of Labor. Bureau of Labor Statistics. <u>Occupational Outlook Handbook 2006-2007</u>. Indianapolis: Jist Works, 2006.

When citing the *Congressional Record*, the date and page numbers are all that is required for that source.

> Cong. Rec. 5 Feb. 2002: S311–15.

A Book in a Series

Give the series name and number (if any) before the publication information.

> Cudworth, Erika. <u>Environment and Society</u>. Routledge Introductions to Environment Series. London; New York: Routledge, 2003.

A Book with a Title Within Its Title

If the title contains a title normally in quotation marks, keep the quotation marks and underline the entire title.

> Stuckey-French, Elizabeth. <u>"The First Paper Girl in Red Oak, Iowa" and Other Stories</u>. New York: Doubleday, 2000.

Note: If the title contains a title that is normally underlined, do not underline that title in your entry:

> Beckwith, Charles E. <u>Twentieth Century Interpretations of</u> A Tale of Two Cities: <u>A Collection of Critical Essays</u>. Upper Saddle River: Prentice, 1972.

A Sacred Text

The Bible and other such sacred texts are treated as anonymous books. Documentation should read exactly as it is printed on the title page.

> <u>The Jerusalem Bible</u>. Garden City: Doubleday, 1966.

The Published Proceedings of a Conference

The published proceedings of a conference should be treated as a book. However, if the title of the publication does not identify the conference by title, date, and location, add the appropriate information immediately after the title.

> McIlwaine, Ia C., ed. <u>Advances in Knowledge Organization</u>. Vol. 9. Proc. of Eighth Intl. ISKO Conf., 13–16 July 2004, London. Wurzburg, Ger.: Ergon-Verlag, 2004.

To cite a particular presentation from the published proceedings of a conference, treat it as a work in an anthology.

> Vizine-Goetz, Diane, and Julianne Bea. "Using Literary Warrant to Define a Version of the DDC for Automated Classification Services." Advances in Knowledge Organization. Ed. Ia C. McIlwaine. Vol. 9. Proc. of Eighth Intl. ISKO Conf., 13–16 July 2004, London. Wurzburg, Ger.: Ergon-Verlag, 2004.

A Published Dissertation

An entry for a published dissertation contains the same information as a book entry, with a few added details. Add the abbreviation *Diss.* and the degree-granting institution before the publication facts. You may also add the order number at the end of the entry, if the work was published by University Microfilms International.

> Jansen, James Richard. Images of Dostoevsky in German Literary Expressionism. Diss. U of Utah, 2003. Ann Arbor: UMI, 2003. AAT 3084161.

An Unpublished Dissertation

The entry for an unpublished dissertation lists author, title in quotation marks, degree-granting institution, and year of acceptance. (For a master's thesis, use *MA thesis* or *MS thesis* rather than *Diss.*)

> Vaidhyanathan, Siva. "Unoriginal Sins: Copyright and American Culture." Diss. U Texas, 1999.

An Unpublished Essay

For an unpublished essay, list the author, the title of the work in quotation marks, the description *Unpublished essay*, and the year it was produced.

> Carmichael, F. "Bukowski's Faith." Unpublished essay, 2004.

A Pamphlet, Manual, or Other Workplace Document

Treat any such publication as you would a book.

> Grayson, George W. The North American Free Trade Agreement. New York: Foreign Policy Assn., 1993.

If publication information is missing, list the country of publication in brackets if known. Use *n.p.* (no place) if the country or the publisher is unknown and *n.d.* if the date is unknown, just as you would for a book.

> Pedestrian Safety. [United States]: n.p., n.d.

Works-Cited Entries:
Print Periodical Articles

Possible Components, in Order

1. Author's name, last name first
2. Title of article, in quotation marks and headline style capitalization
3. Name of periodical, underlined
4. Series number or name, if relevant (not preceded by period or comma)
5. Volume number (for a scholarly journal)
6. Issue number, separated from volume with a period but no space
7. Date of publication (abbreviate all months but May, June, July)
8. Page numbers, preceded by a colon, without "p." or "pp." (For articles continued nonconsecutively, add a plus sign after the first page number.)

If any of these components do not apply, they are not listed. The entries that follow illustrate the information and arrangement needed to cite periodicals.

An Article in a Weekly or Biweekly Magazine

List the author (if identified), article title (in quotation marks), publication title (underlined), full date of publication, and page numbers for the article. Do not include volume and issue numbers.

> Green, Andy. "U2, Neil Young Films Rock Sundance." Rolling Stone 7
>   Feb. 2008: 20.

An Article in a Monthly or Bimonthly Magazine

As for a weekly or biweekly magazine, list the author (if identified), article title (in quotation marks), and publication title (underlined). Then identify the month(s) and year of the issue, followed by page numbers for the article. Do not give volume and issue numbers.

> Mead, Walter Russell. "Born Again." Atlantic Monthly. March 2008: 21–24.

An Article in a Scholarly Journal Paginated by Issue

Rather than month or full date of publication, scholarly journals are identified by volume number. If each issue is numbered from page 1, your works-cited entry should identify the issue number as well. List the volume number immediately after the journal title, followed by a period and the issue number, and then the year of publication (in parentheses). End with the page numbers of the article, as usual.

> Sanchez, Melissa E. "Seduction and Service in The Tempest." Studies in
>   Philology 105.1 (Winter 2008): 50–82.

An Article in a Scholarly Journal with Continuous Pagination

For scholarly journals that continue pagination from issue to issue, no issue number is needed in the works-cited entry.

Frosch, Thomas R. "The Missing Child in A Midsummer Night's Dream." American Imago 64 (Winter 2007): 485–511.

An Unsigned Article in a Periodical

If no author is identified for an article, list the entry alphabetically by title among your works cited (ignoring any initial *A, An,* or *The*).

"Feeding the Hungry." Economist. 371.8374 (2004): 74.

A Printed Interview

Begin with the name of the person interviewed if that's who you are quoting.

Cantwell, Maria. "The New Technocrat." By Erika Rasmusson. Working Woman Apr. 2001: 20–21.

Note: If the interview is untitled, the word *Interview* (no italics) and a period follow the interviewee's name.

A Newspaper Article

Segal, Jeff, and Lauren Silva. "Case of Art Imitating Life?" Wall Street Journal 3 March 2008, Eastern ed.: C9.

Note: Cite the edition of a major daily newspaper (if given) after the date (1 May 1995, Midwest ed.: 1). If a local paper's name does not include the city of publication, add it in brackets (not underlined) after the name.

To cite an article in a lettered section of the newspaper, list the section and the page number. (For example, A4 would refer to page 4 in section A of the newspaper.) If the sections are numbered, however, use a comma after the year (or the edition); then indicate the section and follow with a colon and the page number (sec. 1: 20).

An unsigned newspaper article follows the same format:

"Bombs—Real and Threatened—Keep Northern Ireland Edgy." Chicago Tribune 6 Dec. 2001, sec. 1: 20.

A Newspaper Editorial or Letter to the Editor

If an article is an editorial, put *Editorial* (no italics) and a period after the title.

"Hospital Power." Editorial. Bangor Daily News 14 Sept. 2004: A6.

To identify a letter to the editor, put *Letter* (no italics) and a period after the author's name.

Sory, Forrest. Letter. Discover July 2001: 10.

A Review

Begin with the author (if identified) and title of the review. Use the notation *Rev. of* between the title of the review and that of the original work. Identify the author of the original work with the word *by*. Then follow with publication data for the review.

> Dillon, Brian. "Onion Pilfering." Rev. of Divisadero by Michael Ondaatje.
> London Review of Books 13 Dec. 2007: 19-20.

Note: If you cite the review of a work by an editor or a translator, use *ed.* or *trans.* instead of *by.*

An Abstract

An abstract is a summary of a work. To cite an abstract, first give the publication information for the original work (if any); then list the publication information for the abstract itself. Add the term *Abstract* and a period between these if the journal title does not include that word. If the journal identifies abstracts by item number, include the word *item* followed by the number. (Add the section identifier [A, B, or C] for those volumes of *Dissertation Abstracts [DA]* and *Dissertation Abstracts International [DAI]* that have one.) If no item number exists, list the page number(s).

> Faber, A. J. "Examining Remarried Couples Through a Bowenian Family
> System Lens." Journal of Divorce and Remarriage 40.3/4 (2004):
> 121–33. Social Work Abstracts 40 (2004): item 1298.

An Article with a Title or Quotation Within Its Title

> Morgenstern, Joe. "Sleeper of the Year: In the Bedroom Is Rich Tale of
> Tragic Love." Wall Street Journal 23 Nov. 2001: W1.

Note: Use single quotation marks around the shorter title if it is a title normally punctuated with quotation marks.

An Article Reprinted in a Loose-Leaf Collection

The entry begins with original publication information and ends with the name of the loose-leaf volume (Youth), editor, volume number, publication information including name of the information service (SIRS), and the article number. In the example below, the plus sign indicates continuing but nonconsecutive pages.

> O'Connell, Loraine. "Busy Teens Feel the Beep." Orlando Sentinel 7 Jan.
> 1993: E1+. Youth. Ed. Eleanor Goldstein. Vol. 4. Boca Raton: SIRS,
> 1993. Art. 41.

Video

Works-Cited Entries: Online Sources

Components

Citations for online sources follow the strategies used for print sources, with a few additions to reflect the changeable nature of the Internet. After the author's name and title of the document, include any print publication information (using the guidelines elsewhere in this chapter), then the electronic publication details and access information.

1. Author's name
2. Title of article or webpage
3. Print publication information
4. Title of Internet site, underlined
5. Site editor's name
6. Version (volume or issue) number
7. Date of electronic publication
8. Name of subscription service
9. Name of list or forum
10. Number range or total number of pages (or other sections)
11. Site sponsor's name
12. Date of access (most recent date on which you viewed the document)
13. URL in angle brackets (including access-mode identifiers such as http, ftp, and so on)

If any of these components do not apply, they are not listed. For documents with no listed date of electronic publication, use the site's posting date, date of update, or copyright date if available. MLA asks for page, paragraph, or section numbers if the document includes them.

A Personal Site

After the author's name, list the site title (underlined) or the words *Home page,* whichever is appropriate, followed by a period. Add the date of publication or most recent update (if available), your date of visit, and the URL.

> Mehuron, Kate. Home page. 30 Sept. 2008 <http://www.emich.edu/
> public/history/faculty/mehuron.html>.

A Professional Site

Generally, no author is identified for a professional site, so the entry begins with the site title. Use the copyright date if no date of update is given. A site sponsor can nearly always be found. Conclude with your date of access and the URL for the site's home page.

> Latimes.com. 1 Oct. 2004. <u>Los Angeles Times</u>. 1 Oct. 2008 <http://
> www.latimes.com/>.

A Site for a Department of a College or University

Begin with the name of the department, followed by a description such as *Dept. home page,* followed by a period. Then list the name of the institution, your date of access, and the URL. No date of publication or latest update is necessary.

> Department of Foreign Languages and Literatures. Dept. home page.
> Marquette U College of Arts & Sciences. 6 Nov. 2008 <http://
> www.marquette.edu/fola/>.

A Site for a Study Course

Start with the instructor's name, reversed as for an author. Then give the course title, without quotation marks, underlining, or italics. Follow with the phrase *Course home page,* followed by a period, the course dates, and the department and institution. End with your date of access and the URL, as usual.

> Strickland, Ron. Shakespeare on Stage. Course home page. 14 June
> 2004–4 Aug. 2004. Dept. of English. Illinois State U. 4 Oct. 2008
> <http://www.english.ilstu.edu/strickland/378/>.

A Site with a Long URL

If you must include a line break in a URL, do so only after a slash, and do not add a hyphen to indicate the break. For a URL that is long and complicated enough to invite errors in transcription, give the URL of the site's search page instead.

> MacLeod, Donald. "Shake-Up for Academic Publishing." <u>Guardian
> Unlimited</u>. 10 Nov. 2008 <http://www.guardian.co.uk/Archive/>.

If no search page is available, give the home page URL and path of links to the specific document.

> "Frederica: An 18th-Century Planned Community." <u>National Register
> of Historic Places</u>. National Parks Service. 27 Feb. 2008. <http://
> www.cr.nps.gov/nr/>. Path: Education; Hispanic Heritage Month;
> Frederica.

An Online Book

In general, follow the format for printed books. Include publication information for the original print version if available. Follow the date of publication with the access date and web address.

> Simon, Julian L. The Ultimate Resource II: People, Materials, and
>
> Environment. College Park: U of Maryland, 1996. 9 Apr. 2008
>
> <http://www.inform.umd.edu/EdRes/Colleges/BMGT/Faculty/
>
> JSimon/Ultimate_Resource/>.

When citing part of an online book, the title (or name of the part, such as Foreword) follows the author's name; the title of the book (underlined) is followed by its author's name if different from the first name listed.

> Untermeyer, Louis. "Author's Apology." The Donkey of God. 1999.
>
> iUniverse. 7 March 2008 <http://books.iuniverse.com/>.

An Article in an Online Periodical

The format for printed periodical matter applies here, with modifications. Begin with the author's name; the article title in quotation marks; and the underlined name of the periodical, its volume or issue number, and date of publication. Include page numbers (or other sections) if numbered. Close with the date of access and URL.

> Dickerson, John. "Nailing Jello." Time.com 5 Nov. 2001. 9 Dec. 2007
>
> <http://www.time.com/time/columnist/dickerson/>.

An Article in an Online Reference Work

Unless the author of the entry is identified, begin with the entry name in quotation marks. Follow with the usual online publication information.

> "Eakins, Thomas." Britannica Concise Encyclopedia 2004. Encyclopedia
>
> Britannica. 26 Sept. 2007 <http://concise.britannica.com/
>
> ebc/article?tocId=9363299>.

An Article in an Online Service

When you use a library to access a subscription service, add the name of the database if known (underlined), the service, and the library. Then give the date of access followed by the Internet address for the home page of the service (if known). If no Internet address is given for an entry, add a keyword or path statement in its place, if appropriate ("Keyword: Kiev" or "Path: World Events; Conflicts; Kiev").

> Davis, Jerome. "Massacre in Kiev." Washington Post 29 Nov. 1999,
>
> final ed.: C12. National Newspapers. ProQuest. Gateway Technical
>
> Coll. Elkhorn Campus Lib. 30 Nov. 2008
>
> <http://proquest.umi.com/pqdweb>.

A Scholarly Project or an Information Database

The title of the site is listed first, then the name of the editor (if given). Follow this with the version number (if relevant), the date of publication or update, name of the sponsor, date of access, and URL.

> Wired Style: Principles of English Usage in the Digital Age. 1994. Wired
> Digital Inc. 5 Nov. 2008 <http://hotwired.lycos.com/
> hardwired/wiredstyle/>.

If you are citing a book that is part of an online scholarly project, first list information about the printed book, followed by publication information for the project. End with the URL of the book and a period.

> Astell, Mary. Reflections on Marriage. London: Wilkin, 1706. Women
> Writers Project. Providence: Brown UP, 1999. 7 Feb. 2008 <http://
> www.wwp.brown.edu/texts/astell/marriage.html>.

An Online Government Publication

As with a governmental publication in print, begin with the name of the government (country, state, and so on) followed by the name of the agency. After the publication title, add the electronic publication information.

> United States. Dept. of Labor. Office of Disability Employment Policy.
> Emergency Preparedness for People with Disabilities. Apr. 2004. 12
> Sept. 2008 <http://www.dol.gov/odep/ep/eps.pdf>.

An Online Posting in a List Server

Begin the citation with the author's name and the document title (from the subject line). Follow this information with the description *Online posting* and a period, the date of posting, the name of the group, your date of access, and the URL of the list's Internet site (if any) or the e-mail address of the list's moderator. If possible, cite an archived version of the posting so that your readers can easily find the source.

> Moody, Ellen. "Alternate Persuasions." Online posting. 25 April 1998. The
> Austen-L Mailing List. 12 Jan. 2009 <http://lists.mcgill.ca>.

An Online Posting in a Web Forum

List the author's name and the title of the posting (in quotation marks), followed by *Online posting* and a period. Then give the posting date, the forum name, your date of access, and the URL of the posting.

> Cubby, J. "Re: Connecting Playwrights & Theatre Companies." Online
> posting. 27 May 2004. AACT Online Forums: Playwriting &
> Playwrights. 12 Jan. 2008 <http://www.aact.org/cgi-bin/yabb/
> YaBB.cgi>. Path: Public Boards; Playwriting & Playwrights;
> Connecting Playwrights & Theatre Companies.

An Online Posting in a Newsgroup

Start a newsgroup message as you would a posting to a list server or web forum, with the author's name, the posting title, the description *Online posting,* and a period. Then give the date of posting and your date of access, followed by the name and address of the group in angle brackets, with the prefix *news:*.

> Silverman, Neal. "Re: Perimeter of a Triangle." Online posting. 1 Oct.
>
> 2004. 12 Dec. 2007 <news:geometry.college>.

An Online Posting in a MUD, a MOO, an IRC, or Other Real-Time (Synchronous) Communication Forum

If you are citing a particular speaker, identify that person. Follow with the event description, the date of the event, the communication forum, the date of access, and the telnet URL.

> Del Rey, Juan Roberto. Online defense of dissertation "Chaos, Cadence,
>
> Tonality, Dissonance, and Meaning in the Music of Leonard
>
> Bernstein." 18 July 2005. Connections. 18 July 2005 <telnet://
>
> connections.moo.mud.org:3333>.

If possible, provide readers with a link to an archived version of the posting.

> Del Rey, Juan Roberto. Online defense of dissertation "Chaos, Cadence,
>
> Tonality, Dissonance, and Meaning in the Music of Leonard
>
> Bernstein." 18 July 2005. Connections. 3 Aug. 2008 <http://
>
> web.nwe.ufl.edu/~tari/connections/archives/delrey_phd_defense.txt>.

An Online Poem

List the poet's name, the title of the poem, and any print publication information before the electronic publication details.

> Nemerov, Howard. "Found Poem." War Stories. By Nemerov. U. of Chicago
>
> Press: 1987. Poets.org. 5 Oct. 2007 <http://www.poets.org/poems/
>
> poems.cfm?45442B7C000C040D0170>.

An Online Multimedia Resource: Painting, Photograph, Musical Composition, Film, or Film Clip

After the usual information for the type of work being cited, add electronic publication information.

> Goya, Francisco de. Saturn Devouring His Children. 1819–1823. Museo
>
> del Prado, Madrid. 13 Dec. 2008 <http://www.usc.edu/
>
> schools/annenberg/asc/projects/comm544/library/>.

A Publication in More Than One Medium

For a work that consists of more than one type of medium, either list all the media that make up the work or cite only the medium that contains the specific material cited in your paper.

>**CultureGrams**. **Book, CD-ROM. Lindon: Axiom, 2002.**

An Online Transcript of a Broadcast

Give the original publication information for the broadcast. Then add the description *Transcript,* followed by a period, and the electronic publication information for that document.

>**Lehrer, Jim. "Character Above All." Online NewsHour 29 May 1996.**
>
>>**Transcript. 23 Apr. 2007 <http://www.pbs.org/newshour/**
>>
>>**character/transcript/trans1.html>.**

A Document Accessed by FTP

Cite a document accessed by ftp as you would one accessed by http, but with "ftp://" in the URL.

>**Lewis, Winfred. "Three Translations of Rainer Rilke's 'Along the**
>
>>**sun-drenched roadside, from the great.'" 19 Feb. 2008 <ftp://**
>>
>>**english.saku.edu/writingprograms/documents/rilke_trans.rtf>.**

An E-mail Communication

Identify the author of the e-mail, then list the "Subject" line of the e-mail as a title, in quotation marks. Next, include a description of the entry, including the recipient—usually *E-mail to the author* (no italics), meaning you, the author of the paper. Finally, give the date of the message.

>**Barzinji, Atman. "Re: Frog Populations in Wisconsin Wetlands."**
>
>>**E-mail to the author. 1 Jan. 2009.**

Video

Works-Cited Entries: Other Sources (Primary, Personal, and Multimedia)

The following examples of works-cited entries illustrate how to cite sources such as television or radio programs, films, live performances, works of art, and other miscellaneous nonprint sources.

A Periodically Published Electronic Database

Citations for materials published on CD-ROM, diskette, or magnetic tape are similar to those for print sources, with these added considerations: (1) The contents of a work may vary from one medium to another; therefore, the citation should always identify the medium. (2) The publisher and vendor of the publication may be different, in which case both must be identified. (3) Because of periodic updates, multiple versions of the same database may exist, which calls for citation if possible of both the date of the document cited and the date of the database itself.

> Ackley, Patricia. "Jobs of the Twenty-First Century." New Rochelle
> Informer 15 (Apr. 1994): A4. New Rochelle Informer Ondisc. CD-
> ROM. Info-Line. Oct. 1994.

> Baker, Anthony. The New Earth Science. Diskette. Cincinnati: Freeman's
> P, 1991.

Reference Work on CD-ROM

If you use an encyclopedia or other reference book recorded on CD-ROM, use the form below. If available, include publication information for the printed source.

> The American Heritage Dictionary of the English Language. 3rd ed.
> Boston: Houghton-Mifflin, 1992. CD-ROM. Cambridge, MA: Softkey
> Intl., 1994.

A Television or Radio Program

> "U.S. Health Care Gets Boost from Charity." 60 Minutes. CBS. WBBM,
> Chicago. 28 Feb. 2008.

A Film

The director, distributor, and year of release follow the title. Other information may be included if pertinent.

> Atonement. Dir. Joe Wright. Perf. James McAvoy, Keira Knightley.
> Universal Pictures, 2007.

A Video Recording or an Audio Recording

Cite a filmstrip, slide program, videocassette, or DVD as you do a film, but include the medium before the name of the distributor.

> **Monet: Shadow & Light**. Videocassette. Devine Productions, 1999.

If you are not citing a CD, indicate *LP, Audiocassette,* or *Audiotape,* followed by a period. If you are citing a specific song on a musical recording, place its title in quotation marks before the title of the recording.

> O'Higgins, Michael B. **Beating the Dow with Bonds**. Audiocassette.
>   Harper Audio, 1999.

A Performance

Treat this similarly to a film, adding the location and date of the performance.

> **Chanticleer**. Young Auditorium, Whitewater, WI 23 Feb. 2003.

An Artwork on Display

> Titian. **The Entombment**. Louvre, Paris.

A Letter or Memo Received by the Author (You)

> Thomas, Bob. Letter to the author. 10 Jan. 2008.

An Interview by the Author (You)

> Brooks, Sarah. Personal interview. 15 Oct. 2008.

A Cartoon or Comic Strip (in Print)

> Luckovich, Mike. "The Drawing Board." Cartoon. **Time** 17 Sept. 2001:
>   18.

An Advertisement (In Print)

List the subject of the advertisement (product, company, organization, or such), followed by *Advertisement* and a period. Then give the usual publication information.

> Vaio Professional Notebooks. Advertisement. **Campus Technology** Oct.
>   2004: 45.

A Lecture, a Speech, an Address, or a Reading

If there is a title, use it instead of the descriptive label (for example, *Lecture*).

> Annan, Kofi. Lecture. Acceptance of Nobel Peace Prize. Oslo City Hall,
>   Oslo, Norw. 10 Dec. 2001.

A Legal or Historical Document

Familiar historical documents such as the U.S. Constitution and the United States code are typically not included in a works-cited list because they can so easily be abbreviated in a parenthetical note within the text of your paper: "(US Const., art. 4, sec. 1,)" and "(7 USC 308a, 1928)," for example. (Note that such documents are not underlined when referenced in this way.)

To list an act in your works cited, begin with the name of the act, then give its public law number (abbreviation *Pub. L.*), its date of enactment, and its Statutes at Large (abbreviation *Stat.*) cataloging number.

> **Do-Not-Call Implementation Act. Pub. L. 108–010. 11 Mar. 2003. Stat. 117–557.**

Abbreviate the names of law cases (spelling out the first important word of each party's name). Do not underline the name in your works cited (although it should be underlined within the body of your paper). Follow with the case number, the name of the court, and the date of the decision.

> **Missouri v. Seibert. No. 02–1371. Supreme Ct. of the US. 28 June 2004.**

A Map or Chart

Follow the format for an anonymous book, adding *Map* or *Chart* (without italics), followed by a period.

> **Wisconsin Territory. Map. Madison: Wisconsin Trails, 1988.**

Sample MLA Paper

Student writer Katie Hughey wrote the following research paper on the historical development of art museums in the United States and the challenges those museums now face. On the following pages, you will find the first two parts of Katie's paper excerpted to show you her research-based thinking and documentation. For the full version of Katie's paper, along with more information on the controversial case study that she focuses on in her paper, go to **www.thecollegewriter.com/3e**.

Because her paper focuses on an arts and humanities topic, Katie used MLA style for format and documentation. You can use Katie's paper in three ways:

1. To study how a well-written, major research paper develops careful thinking, builds a discussion, and orders supporting points and evidence.

2. To examine how source summaries, paraphrases, and quotations are carefully integrated into the writer's discussion to advance her thinking— a full-length example of the strategies addressed on pages 486–489.

3. To see in detail the format and documentation practices of MLA style, practices that allow the writer to share a professional-looking paper that fairly respects sources used.

Sample Paper: Format, In-Text Citation, and Works-Cited List

Note that MLA format requires that the paper be double-spaced throughout. That formatting is shown in the full version of the paper at the website: **www .thecollegewriter.com/3e.**

Hughey 1

> **The heading supplies identifying details.**

Katie Hughey
Professor E. K. Trump
Political Science 350
17 April 2008

> **The title (centered) indicates the paper's topic and theme.**

An American Hybrid:
The Art Museum as Public–Private Institution

> **The writer uses suggestive metaphors to create an engaging opening.**

> **The essential problem or issue is introduced.**

The American art museum suffers from a multiple personality disorder. It is a strange hybrid, both public and private in nature, and beholden to a constituency so varied in its interests that the function of the museum has become increasingly difficult to discern. Much of the confusion surrounding the nature and proper function of the art museum in the United States has to do with the unique form that arts patronage has taken in this country. There is a primary difficulty facing funding of the arts in America—namely, the fact that the benefits of art and art museums are not easily stated in the simple utilitarian terms that justify expenditures on things like roads and a police force. For this reason, cultural patronage has largely been a private venture. The first American museums were born of the private collections of robber barons, organized as not-for-profit corporations, and placed under the control of private boards of trustees. Only subsequently were municipal governments asked to contribute by way of funding construction costs for new buildings and providing maintenance expenses.

> **The introduction lists key questions that grow out of the writer's research and drive the paper forward.**

The involvement of the government in the funding of art museums raises several questions that serve to highlight the confusing hybrid nature of this uniquely American cultural institution. First, why do governments fund museums at all? The short answer involves the educational benefits conferred on the public by art museums. But once a municipality has taken on the task of paying for a public service that happens to be provided by an autonomous private institution, the real question becomes one of control. Who exactly "owns" the museum? If the stated goal of the museum enterprise is public in nature, while the works hanging on the walls and the programs offered by the museum are supported mainly by private funds, to whom is the museum accountable? Is it appropriate, for example, for a museum to accept support from individuals or corporations that stand to gain financially from the museum's exhibits? Further, if an art museum is perceived to

1

2

Hughey 2

be acting in a manner contrary to the public interest (whatever that may be), does the government, or an agent of that government, have the right to pull the plug on funding?

To begin to answer these questions, and thereby gain an understanding of the art museum's importance as a quasi-public American institution, one must examine the enterprise from all angles. A good place to start is with the inception of the art museum itself. From there, one may turn to the funding of art museums, discussing their public role and the ways in which this very role is compromised by the business of paying for public programs. Finally, to put the issues in perspective, this essay will focus on a contemporary museum controversy involving the Brooklyn Museum of Art. This case study hopes to show that when it comes to the arts in America, private and public interests need not be mutually exclusive. In fact, the public benefits from private commercial involvement in the museum enterprise via diversified museum collections and additional public programs.

I. The Birth of a Hybrid

Karl Meyer gives perhaps the best discussion of the emergence of the art museum in late nineteenth-century America. The notion of a public gallery accessible to all is, according to Meyer, a legacy of the French Revolution. On August 10, 1793, a year to the day after the overthrow of the French monarchy, the Louvre was proclaimed a musée révolutionnaire, open to all citizens of the Republic (Meyer 20). Wealthy, art-minded American travelers marveled at the treasures of the Louvre and dreamed of creating such a glorious monument to democracy in their own young country. To these men, "it seemed wholly proper that government should support art museums, in the same way that it assisted schools, libraries, and parks, all of which belonged to the fabric of civic-minded rule" (21).

It was not, however, the government that would lead the way in establishing the great public galleries of America, but rather well-to-do private citizens. The lack of governmental initiative in funding the arts is not surprising. Art museums have a far narrower appeal than public parks and are not as clearly utilitarian as public libraries, and the government has traditionally been loathe to spend taxpayers' money on ventures that are perceived as less than useful (Meyer 21-22).

The first public gallery was, in fact, founded in 1773 in Charlestown, South Carolina, by the city's Library Society, whose membership was largely drawn from the professional and landowning

Hughey 3

ranks. Soon, historical societies and colleges had gotten in on the
act, amassing their own collections of art and curiosities for public
display. As Meyer describes it, "each of these institutions was the
fruit of spontaneous citizen initiative" (24). Nearly all of these early
museums were organized as not-for-profit organizations controlled
by private boards of trustees, setting "a pattern of local initiative and
private control" that still prevails (25). It is not, Meyer contends, the
organization of the museum that has changed over the years, but rather
the ways in which they are funded.

Meyer uses the Metropolitan Museum of Art in New York to
illustrate the emergence of the public–private hybrid museum form.
The Metropolitan was the supreme undertaking of a Committee of Fifty
distinguished gentlemen, members of the prestigious Union League
Club and the Century Association, which, led by the lawyer John Jay
(grandson of the first Chief Justice of the Supreme Court), took "upon
itself the founding of a great museum in New York City" (Meyer 25).
Corporation lawyer Joseph H. Choate set the terms for the generous
municipal support that Metropolitan was to receive in the museum's
1870 charter. Under this charter, the museum was to be erected in
Central Park at a cost to the city of $500,000. The city was also to pay
for maintenance expenses. Control of the Metropolitan, however, was to
remain firmly in private hands, meaning, in effect, that "the city of New
York was being committed to support generously, if not munificently, a
museum over which it would have no real power" (Meyer 26).

Given that private interests kept control of the Metropolitan's day-
to-day functioning, how did the city justify the public cost of museum
sponsorship? Eugene Smolensky cites "education externality" as the
principal force driving municipal involvement in the museum movement
of the late nineteenth century (758). He identifies educational benefits
associated with the museum enterprise that help to explain government
support—specifically the role of the art museum in the "broad elevation
of the tastes among workers as a class" (761). This surely was what
motivated the City of New York to insist that the Metropolitan Museum
of Art remain open and free of charge on Sundays to allow the working
class to attend. In a small way, the city was able to exercise at least
some control, as funding was contingent on Sunday openings, "even
though various trustees saw in it blasphemy against either God or Art"
(Smolensky 763). Similarly, social reformers of the late 1800s viewed
establishing public art museums as just another means of spreading
social benefits broadly across the population; in that manner, these

When the author is named in an attributive phrase, the in-text citation includes only the page number.

The writer offers an extended illustration that shows the concepts being discussed at work.

Source material is correctly presented in terms of punctuation and mechanics.

7

8

Hughey 4

institutions were no different than settlement houses and public schools. The founding of these institutions represented what Germain Bazin, former curator of the Louvre, referred to as "construction charity," designed on the part of progressive activists to improve the general welfare of the public (qtd. in Smolensky 761).

Taken as a whole, however, public funding of art museums represented only a small portion of total museum expenditures. No matter how generous municipalities were in donating real estate and covering the cost of maintaining the new museums, a building and land on which to erect it do not a museum make. The galleries must be filled with works of art, and to this end private sponsors have carried most of the cost of the museum enterprise. Joseph Choate, beyond convincing Tammany Hall to pitch funds for the Metropolitan, was also able to sell the idea of art as investment to the nouveau riche. "Since often enough the new-rich found themselves burdened with the problem of how to spend their money," Meyer explains, "Choate's contention that art could yield dividends in pleasure, prestige, and public service fell on receptive ears" (27). Among those whom Choate converted to the art cause was financier J. P. Morgan, who between 1890 and his death in 1913 spent half of his fortune on works of art. Elected president of the Metropolitan Museum's board of trustees in 1904, Morgan packed the board full of fellow millionaires, thus ensuring that the "Metropolitan's board of trustees was not only the most exclusive club in New York, but also, without a doubt, the richest" (27–28).

By appealing to the particular pleasures of connoisseurship and collection building, the museum world was able to mobilize the support of the private sector with money to burn (Meyer 44). Ironically, however, it was government action that opened the floodgates to private donations to arts institutions. Meyer points to two fiscal measures that have been "indispensable to the rise of the art museum in the United States" (31). The first of these was the 1909 Payne–Aldrich Tariff, which allowed for the duty-free importation of original works of art more than twenty years old. The second was the introduction of the charitable deduction provisions in federal and state tax laws. "Without these legislative inducements," Meyer argues, "it is safe to say the museum explosion of this [the twentieth] century could never have occurred" (32).

II. Private Dollars, Public Interests

Few countries in the world have a system of cultural patronage like that of the United States. Far from being the planned creation

9

10

11

Hughey 5

A second
reference to a
source shortly
after the first
reference
cites just
the page
number in
parentheses—
the author's
last name
doesn't
need to be
repeated.

of a national government, the American art museum is, as we have
seen, a unique public–private hybrid, which indiscriminately "mingles
private and public monies, direct and indirect subsidies, and funding
by agencies at every level of government" (Meyer 64). One of the
inevitable difficulties arising under any form of patronage is the fact
that the patron, "wishing to be more than a passive conduit of money,"
seeks to influence the creative process (75). Meyer refers to this urge
as the "Medici Mentality," after the wealthy Florentine family that
bankrolled many of the great works of Italian Renaissance art. As James
Cuno, director of the Harvard University Art Museums, points out, the
public, which subsidizes museums either directly through donations or
indirectly via their status as tax-free nonprofit organizations, expects
them to "carry out their duties professionally on its behalf" (164).
Private individual and corporate donors, likewise, wish their interests to
be taken into account. These donors often exercise what theater director
Robert Brustein termed "coercive philanthropy" by restricting their gifts
to certain creative purposes (qtd. in Cuno 163).

The writer
effectively
integrates
multiple
sources to
advance her
discussion.

More often than not, funding controversies arise when the public   *12*
perceives a museum to be acting in a self-interested manner or for the
financial benefit of its private sponsors. Cuno argues that museums
are public institutions, even if they are privately funded and operated,
because they stand for a public good—specifically "easy if not equal
access to culture and learning" (162). As museum scholar Stephen
Weil sees it, the museum must learn to view itself as an instrument for
public service. Since the "cost of maintaining that instrument" is to a
considerable extent paid for by the community via direct and indirect
subsidy, Weil argues that the community ought to have some choice in
how the "instrument" is to be used (qtd. in Schuster 83).

The writer
uses cause-
effect thinking
to explain
the forces
at work in
art museum
changes.

American art institutions are, in fact, acutely aware of the public   *13*
expectations placed upon them. One of the ways that museums have
tried to fulfill their public purpose is by widening and diversifying their
audiences. These diversification efforts primarily involve reaching out
to previously under-served economic and racial minority segments of
the population. Museum consultant Teri Edelstein notes a "genuine
desire on the part of museums to reach out and include more people"
(110). Diversification and outreach have undoubtedly contributed to
the growing popularity of art museums, and in turn, higher attendance
figures have helped to legitimize public expenditures on the arts. Gilbert
Edelson, administrative vice president of the Art Dealers Association
of America, implicates the expanding public role of the museum in the

problem of funding. The art museum is no longer a "treasure house," Edelson contends, but a "cultural center, a people's palace of the arts, with educational programs, films, concerts, tours, lectures, classes," and so on (178). In light of the expansionist nature of the modern American museum, one cannot, in Cuno's opinion, underestimate the need to raise additional revenue, especially with the decline in recent years of governmental support (163). More and more, this much-needed support is commercial in nature.

Thus, another perverse consequence arises from the quasi-public nature of the American art museum: To fulfill what it views as a necessarily expanding public role, the museum world has immersed itself in private commercial ventures. It is not uncommon, for example, for a museum to exhibit works from a private collection that are likely to be sold during or put up for sale shortly after the exhibition (Edelson 175). Museums frequently enter into partnerships that may prove mutually beneficial. However, as Edelstein argues, "[e]xhibitions are not a zero-sum game." The interests of private museum sponsors are not necessarily at odds with the public interest (113).

This contention is not easy for the public to swallow. Drawing from Cuno, it must be borne in mind that a museum's reputation is built on trust. No matter how popular museums may become as a result of their diversification programs, they risk losing the public's trust if they appear to be serving their own or their patrons' interests rather than the interests of the people (Cuno 168). The public's wariness about museum involvement in commercial transactions is, according to Edelstein, largely a result of a lack of public understanding of the "mechanisms of exhibition organization" (112). In fact, this lack of understanding regarding the inner workings of museums (and arts funding organizations in general) is central to most contemporary public art controversies. Museums have, in a way, been forced to enter into partnerships with private individuals and corporations to better serve the public. "Museums have vigorously sought out acquisitions that mirror the cultural diversity of their communities," Edelstein explains, and have "actively created programs that attempt to attract larger and more diverse audiences" (111). These publicly beneficial exhibitions and programs require a lot of money and, in the absence of dependable government support, the private sector steps in to fill the void.

Besides merely accepting corporate sponsorship, art museums have now embarked on their own commercial enterprises. What self-respecting museum does not have a café, bookshop, gift shop, mail-order

14

15

16

Using sources fluently, the writer deepens her analysis of the forces at work in the world of art.

Sentence variety keeps the prose energetic and engaging.

Hughey 7

catalogue, or online outlet? Edelson also mentions the fact that many museum gift shops sell original jewelry, pottery, and even original signed prints. The next step is obvious: the museum as art dealer (179). In fact, in communities that are not major cultural centers, many museums have assumed this role, primarily to provide a much needed service. If not for the museum, Edelson argues, artists in these communities would have no outlet for displaying and selling their work, and the public would not have the opportunity to enjoy original, contemporary art (179).

In their drive to attract more income and larger audiences, art museums have also increasingly felt the impact of the over-stimulation of society by the media. Carol Becker argues that as a result of having to compete with television, film, the Internet, and so on, "museums now position art as entertainment" (17–18). Without some sort of dramatic hook, museums find it difficult to draw in the crowds they need to pay for the ever-expanding services they offer. Thus, museum exhibitions themselves have become increasingly commercial in nature. Shows featuring motorcycles, automobiles, the treasures of King Tutankhamen, the works of Van Gogh, and other blockbuster favorites not only have proven immensely popular, but have also offered the promise of corporate underwriting and ample commercial tie-ins (Meyer 116). To the extent that "access" is an adequate measure of museum performance, art as entertainment "has proven a resounding triumph" (268).

Contemporary observers, however, do not agree about the effects of commercialization on the American museum system. James Cuno, a believer in the principle of disinterested inquiry, frets over the potentially detrimental effects of commercialization on the educational aspect of the museum enterprise. Gilbert Edelson, by contrast, welcomes the diminishing prejudice against the involvement of museums in commercial activities (178). Teri Edelstein agrees. She contends that "as educational institutions, museums succeed when they bring thought-provoking art before the public," and this includes making available works owned by private collectors who may stand to benefit from the exposure offered by a museum exhibition (113). The issue turns, according to Edelson, on "reasonable perception." It is appropriate for museums to enter into mutually beneficial partnerships with private donors except on the occasion that a reasonable person would perceive market interests rather than art-historical importance as being the motivation behind a given exhibition (174–75).

The question remains, nonetheless, of who ultimately decides when the interests of the public have been violated. Certainly with

In her own words, the writer effectively paraphrases her source.

Specific examples make the discussion concrete.

The writer uses her sources effectively to address controversy and disagreement in a balanced way.

17

18

19

Hughey 8

growing museum attendance, more citizens and local interest groups have protested the policies and collections of museums. Edelstein notes that as a result of museums' diversification measures, works of art that once seemed to "transcend any kind of discord are increasingly read differently" by a new audience (111). Also, museums have come under heightened attack from minority groups for what is <u>not</u> present in their collections. But does the government, as distributor of public funds, have the right to intervene when it perceives that a museum has violated the terms of its charter by failing to serve the public interest? This question has been tackled primarily as a legal issue, and in this respect there are two opposing opinions—the majority view and the minority view.

> **The writer approaches a complex set of questions and then maps out both majority and minority views— showing attention to all sides of the issue.**

The majority view holds that art museums are engaged in a sort of speech protected by the First Amendment. To this end, once a municipality has endeavored to fund a museum, it may not then decide to pull funding simply because it objects to the content of the works exhibited (Strauss 44–45). According to David Ross, director of the San Francisco Museum of Modern Art, museums must serve the public good by serving "as broad a set of public interests as professionally possible" (97). This, of course, includes displaying works of art that many members of the public will appreciate but that others will find shocking or offensive. Excepting situations where questionable works may be proven to meet the strict constitutional standards for obscenity, the government may not mete out punishment by withholding public funds.

20

The minority view on this issue is presented by law professor Stephen B. Presser. Rather than emphasizing the constitutional questions raised by government funding of the arts (Presser, in fact, does not believe the First Amendment extends to the state and local levels at all), he considers the problem from the perspective of partnership law. Municipalities come to be involved in arts funding, he contends, because it is in the best interest of both the city and the museum to join forces: "The museum gets some essential funding from the city, and the city is able to perform its traditional function of education" (58). While the arrangement does not provide for direct involvement by the city in the day-to-day business of running the museum, the city may choose to withhold funding or cancel a lease in the event that the museum "shall cease to be maintained according to the true intent" of the legislation forging the partnership between the two parties (60). Therefore, if a museum exhibits works that offend certain members of the community or if it participates in

21

> **A key quotation is introduced with a full lead-in sentence and a colon.**

Hughey 9

questionable financial dealings, the municipality is completely within its rights to force compliance by withholding public money.

As can be seen, the American art museum represents a confusing melding of public and private interests. Without question, however, the primary function of the museum is to serve the public. This is, after all, the justification for government sponsorship of museums and largely explains the increasing expansion of public-oriented programs offered by art museums. In an ironic twist, museums have become increasingly commercialized in the effort to reach out to a broader audience and, in effect, have threatened their very legitimacy in the process. The public's apprehension regarding the commercialization of the museum is, in the minds of many experts, simply a matter of ignorance regarding the reality of museum operations. In fact, as the final section of this paper will seek to show, the public actually benefits from private commercial involvement in the museum enterprise. These benefits are wholly in line with the educational purpose of the museum and come in the form of more diversified museum collections and strengthened public programs.

22

III. The Brooklyn Museum Controversy

As the preceding discussion of the American art museum's past and present suggests, this public versus private tension may provoke significant controversy. In September 1999, the not-yet-opened Sensation exhibit of young British artists at the Brooklyn Museum of Art came under fierce attack. . . .

23

Conclusion

Art museums that have long suffered from their public–private hybrid nature may now take advantage of it. As the Brooklyn Museum controversy has shown, museums are best able to serve a broad audience if they are allowed to take risks and invite private sponsorship. While the risk for controversy increases as audiences expand, the very growth in attendance confers legitimacy upon the museum enterprise. Private dollars and public interests need not be at odds, as both parties reap the benefits of more programs and more diverse exhibitions. If museums are careful to choose their offerings based on aesthetic considerations rather than mere profit-making concerns, private commercial involvement may prove to be a public blessing.

24

Margin annotations:

The writer summarizes the second section of her analysis and forecasts the final section.

A heading and opening sentence transition from analysis in the first two parts to a concrete illustration in the third part.

After an in-depth analysis of the case study, the writer restates her reasonable, research-based conclusions.

Works-Cited List

The list of works cited begins on a separate page and includes the title, header, and page number.

Works Cited

Becker, Carol. "The Brooklyn Controversy: A View from the Bridge." Rothfield 15–21.

Bowie, David. BowieNet. 5 April 2008 <http://www.davidbowie.com>.

Cuno, James. "Sensation and the Ethics of Funding Exhibitions." Rothfield 162–170.

Edelson, Gilbert. "Some Sensational Reflections." Rothfield 171–180.

Edelstein, Teri. "Sensational or Status Quo: Museums and Public Perception." Rothfield 104–114.

Fraser, Andrea. "A Sensation Chronicle." Social Text 19.2 (2001): 127–156.

Halle, David, et al. "The Attitude of the Audience for 'Sensation' and of the General Public Toward Controversial Works of Art." Rothfield 134–152.

Levine, Peter. "Lessons from the Brooklyn Museum Controversy." Philosophy and Public Policy Quarterly 20.2/3 (2000). 7 April 2008 <http://www.puaf.umd.edu/IPPP/reports/vol20sum00/lessons.html>.

Meyer, Karl. The Art Museum: Power, Money, Ethics. New York: Morrow, 1979.

Presser, Stephen. "Reasons We Shouldn't Be Here: Things We Cannot Say." Rothfield 52–71.

Ross, David. "An All-Too-Predictable Sensation." Rothfield 96–103.

Rothfield, Lawrence, ed. Unsettling Sensation: Arts-Policy Lessons from the Brooklyn Museum of Art Controversy. Rutgers Series on the Public Life of the Arts. New Brunswick: Rutgers UP, 2001.

Sources are listed in alphabetical order by author (or by title if no author is given).

Titles are properly underlined (not italicized) or placed in quotation marks.

Correct abbreviations are used throughout.

Hughey 9

Schuster, J. Mark. "Who Should Pay (for the Arts and Culture)? Who
Should Decide? And What Difference Should It Make?" Rothfield
72–89.

Smolensky, Eugene. "Municipal Financing of the U.S. Fine Arts
Museum: A Historical Rationale." Journal of Economic History
46.3 (1986): 757–768.

Stántó, András. "Don't Shoot the Messenger: Why the Art World and the
Press Don't Get Along." Rothfield 181–198.

Steinfels, Margaret. "Virgins No More." Commonweal 19 May 2000:
23–24.

Strauss, David. "The False Promise of Free Speech." Rothfield 44–51.

Items are double-spaced throughout. Second and subsequent lines are indented (hanging indent).

Note: The works-cited page reflects the complete essay (available at www.thecollegewriter.com/3e). Some works (Bowie, Fraser, Halle, Levine, Stántó, and Steinfels) are not cited in the sections shown on pages 523–531.

Reading for Better Writing

Working by yourself or with a group, answer these questions:

1. What do you know about art museums? What experiences have you had with art? How did Hughey's paper on art museums in the United States change your understanding of these institutions?

2. Did you find her paper engaging? Why or why not?

3. Which types of evidence does Hughey use in her paper? Where has she gotten her evidence? Are her resources reliable?

4. How does Hughey distinguish her own thinking from source material? Why are these strategies necessary?

5. Hughey's complete paper, along with more information on the controversy over the Sensation exhibition at the Brooklyn Museum of Art, is available at **www.thecollegewriter.com/3e**. After reading the rest of Hughey's paper and reviewing the resources at the site, offer your own response to the controversy: What do you conclude about art and about art museums today?

Model

Checklist for MLA Format

As you format your paper and document your research according to MLA guidelines, use the checklist below to review your work.

_____ All borrowed material is acknowledged with an appropriate attributive phrase and/or in-text citation indicating author and page number, as appropriate.

_____ The works-cited list includes entries for all works referred to in the body of the paper: No sources are missing from the list; no extra sources are listed that have no reference within the paper.

_____ The entire works-cited list is properly alphabetized by authors' last names (or by the first main word in the title for anonymous works).

_____ Each works-cited entry contains the maximum amount of identifying and publication information, in the proper order, using all of the accepted abbreviations.

_____ The entire paper is properly formatted, from the first page heading and title to the final works-cited page entry.

_____ Placement, spacing, and margins are correct for the paper's header, the heading, the title, and "Works Cited."

_____ Pagination is correct and consistent.

_____ First lines of paragraphs and inset quotations are properly indented; works-cited entries are properly formatted with a hanging indent.

_____ The paper is cleanly printed single-sided on quality paper.

_____ The paper is properly bound with a paper clip in the upper-left corner.

Critical-Thinking and Writing Activities

1. The MLA style involves many rules about format and documentation. To make some sense of these rules, answer this question by yourself or with classmates: What is the essential logic of the MLA system?

2. Create MLA works-cited entries for the following publications:

   • An article in the May 27, 2002, issue (vol. 145, no. 11) of *Fortune* magazine by Joseph Nocera: "Return of the Raider" (pages 97–114)

   • Ernest Hemingway's novel *A Farewell to Arms,* published in 1986 by Collier Books, located in New York City

   • The webpage "Aruba," part of *The 2008 World Factbook,* sponsored by the Central Intelligence Agency. No author or publication date is listed. The site was last accessed March 8, 2008, at http://www.cia.gov/library/publications/the-world-factbook/index.html.

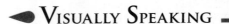
VISUALLY SPEAKING

What does the image on page 493 suggest about writing a research paper?

APA DOCUMENTATION FORMAT

Audio

Those who write papers in the social sciences—psychology, sociology, political science, and education, for example—usually follow the research-writing guidelines of the American Psychological Association (APA). Currently, those guidelines are contained in two publications: the fifth edition of the *Publication Manual of the American Psychological Association* (2001), and the *APA Style Guide to Electronic References* (2007). This chapter summarizes these two texts and helps you use APA format and documentation.

APA format is similar to MLA format in two ways: Both require (1) parenthetical citations within the text and (2) a final listing of all references cited in the paper. But in the social sciences, the date of publication is often much more crucial than it is in the humanities, so the date is highlighted in in-text citations. APA format also requires a cover page and an abstract.

Video

APA Research Paper Guidelines

Questions & Answers

IS A SEPARATE TITLE PAGE REQUIRED?

Yes. Include your paper's title, your name, and the name of your school on three separate lines, double-spaced, centered, and beginning approximately one-third of the way down from the top of the page. Place a shortened title and page number 1 in the upper-right corner. (See "What about paging?" on the next page.)

WHAT IS AN ABSTRACT AND WHERE DOES IT GO?

An abstract is required in APA format. An abstract is a 100- to 150-word paragraph summarizing your research paper. (See page **554**.) Place your abstract on a new page and label it "Abstract" (centered); type your short title and page number 2 flush right one-half inch from the top.

ARE REFERENCES PLACED IN THE TEXT?

Yes. Include the author and year, separated by a comma; for quotations, add the page number after a comma and "p."

DO YOU NEED A BIBLIOGRAPHY OF SOURCES USED IN THE PAPER?

Yes. Full citations for all sources used (books, periodicals, and so on) are placed in an alphabetized list labeled "References" at the end of the paper.

HOW ARE THE REFERENCE LISTS TO BE INDENTED?

Confusion sometimes arises over how the reference lists of APA manuscripts should be indented. Normal paragraph indentation has been called for by APA in the past. However, hanging indentation as shown in this chapter is currently the preferred manuscript form for APA documents, including student papers. As always, ask your instructor if you are in doubt.

DO YOU NEED AN APPENDIX?

Maybe. Ask your instructor. In student papers, charts, tables, and graphs may sometimes be incorporated at appropriate points in the text, making appendices unnecessary.

WHAT ABOUT LONGER QUOTATIONS?	Type quotations of 40 or more words in block style (all lines flush left) five spaces in from the left margin. Indent the first lines of any additional paragraphs in the long quotation five spaces in from the margin set for the quotation.
WHAT ABOUT MARGINS?	Leave a margin of at least one inch on all four sides (if you are binding your paper, leave one and one-half inches at the left margin); computer users may use a justified right margin, and end-of-line hyphens are acceptable in this format.
WHAT ABOUT PAGING?	Page numbers appear at the top-right margin, above the first line of text. Instead of your name, place the short title (first two or three words) either above or five spaces to the left of each page number.
WHAT ABOUT HEADINGS?	Headings, like an outline, show the organization of your paper and the importance of each topic. All topics of equal importance should have headings of the same level, or style. Below are the various levels of headings used in APA papers. (In most research papers, only levels 1, 3, and 4 are used.)

LEVEL 1: Centered Uppercase and Lowercase Heading

LEVEL 2: *Centered, Italicized, Uppercase and Lowercase Heading*

LEVEL 3: *Flush Left, Italicized, Uppercase and Lowercase Side Heading*

LEVEL 4: *Indented, italicized, lowercase paragraph heading ending with a period.*

ANY OTHER SPECIAL INSTRUCTIONS?	Always ask whether your school or department has special requirements that may take precedence over these guidelines.

Web Link

Video

Guidelines for In-Text Citations

The Form of an Entry

The APA documentation style is sometimes called the "author–date" system because both the author and the date of the publication must be mentioned in the text when citing a source. Both might appear in the flow of the sentence, like this:

> **Children in India are being trafficked for adoption, organ transplants, and labor such as prostitution, according to a 2007 article by Nilanjana Ray.**

If either name or date does not appear in the text, it must be mentioned within parentheses at the most convenient place, like this:

> **According to an article by Nilanjana Ray (2007), children in India . . .**

> **According to a recent article (Ray, 2007), children in India . . .**

Points to Remember

1. When paraphrasing rather than quoting, make it clear where your borrowing begins and ends. Use stylistic cues to distinguish the source's thoughts ("Kalmbach points out . . . ," "Some critics argue . . .") from your own ("I believe . . . ," "It seems obvious, however . . .").

2. When using a shortened title of a work, begin with the word by which the work is alphabetized in your references list (for example, for "Measurement of Stress in Fasting Man," use "Measurement of Stress," not "Fasting Man").

3. When including a parenthetical citation at the end of a sentence, place it before the end punctuation: *(Sacks, 1964)*.

Sample In-Text Citations

One Author: A Complete Work

The correct form for a parenthetical reference to a single source by a single author is parenthesis, last name, comma, space, year of publication, parenthesis. Also note that final punctuation should be placed outside the parentheses.

> **. . . in this way, the public began to connect certain childhood vaccinations with an autism epidemic (Baker, 2008).**

One Author: Part of a Work

When you cite a specific part of a source, give the page number, chapter, or section, using the appropriate abbreviations (*p.* or *pp., chap.,* or *sec.* For others, see pages 542 and 566). Always give the page number for a direct quotation.

> **. . . while a variety of political and scientific forces were at work in the developing crisis, it was parents who pressed the case "that autism had become epidemic and that vaccines were its cause" (Baker, 2008, p. 251).**

One Author: Several Publications in the Same Year

If the same author has published two or more articles in the same year, avoid confusion by placing a small letter *a* after the first work listed in the references list, *b* after the next one, and so on. Determine the order alphabetically by title.

Parenthetical Citation:

> Reefs harbor life forms heretofore unknown (Milius, 2001a, 2001b).

References:

> Milius, D. (2001a). Another world hides inside coral reefs. *Science News, 160*(16), 244.
>
> Milius, D. (2001b). Unknown squids—with elbows—tease science. *Science News, 160*(24), 390.

Works by Authors with the Same Last Name

When citing different sources by authors with the same last name, add the authors' initials to avoid confusion, even if the publication dates are different.

> While J. D. Wallace (2005) argued that privatizing social security would benefit only the wealthiest citizens, others such as E. S. Wallace (2006) supported greater control for individuals.

Two to Five Authors

In APA style, all authors—up to as many as five—must be mentioned in the first text citation, like this:

> Love changes not just who we are, but who we can become, as well (Lewis, Amini, & Lannon, 2000).

Note: The last two authors' names are always separated by a comma and an ampersand (&) when enclosed in parentheses.

For works with **two authors,** list both in every citation. For works with **three to five authors,** list all only the first time; after that, use only the name of the first author followed by "et al.," like this:

> These discoveries lead to the hypothesis that love actually alters the brain's structure (Lewis et al., 2000).

Six or More Authors

If your source has six or more authors, refer to the work by the first author's name followed by "et al.," both for the first reference in the text and all references after that. However, be sure to list all the authors (up to six) in your references list.

> According to a recent study, post-traumatic stress disorder (PTSD) continues to dominate the lives of Vietnam veterans, though in modified forms (Trembley et al., 2008).

A Work Authored by an Agency, a Committee, or Other Organization

Treat the name of the group as if it were the last name of the author. If the name is long and easily abbreviated, provide the abbreviation in square brackets. Use the abbreviation without brackets in subsequent references, as follows:

First Text Citation:

> A problem for many veterans continues to be heightened sensitivity
> to noise (National Institute of Mental Health [NIMH], 2005).

Subsequent Citations:

> In addition, veterans suffering from PTSD continue to have difficulty
> discussing their experiences (NIMH, 2005).

A Work with No Author Indicated

If your source lists no author, treat the first few words of the title (capitalized normally) as you would an author's last name. A title of an article or a chapter belongs in quotation marks; the titles of books or reports should be italicized:

> . . . including a guide to low-stress postures ("How to Do It," 2001).

A Work Referred to in Another Work

If you need to cite a source that you have found referred to in another source (a "secondary" source), mention the original source in your text. Then, in your parenthetical citation, cite the secondary source, using the words "as cited in."

> . . . theorem given by Ullman (as cited in Hoffman, 1998).

Note: In your references list at the end of the paper, you would write out a full citation for Hoffman (not Ullman).

A Work in an Anthology

When citing an article or a chapter in an anthology or a collection, use the authors' names for the specific article, not the names of the anthology's editors. (Similarly, the article should be listed by its authors' names in the references section. See page 543.)

> Phonological changes can be understood from a variationist perspective
> (Guy, 2005).

An Electronic or Other Internet Source

As with print sources, cite an electronic source by the author (or by shortened title if the author is unknown) and the publication date (not the date you accessed the source). If citing a specific part of the source, use an appropriate abbreviation: *p.* for page, ¶ (paragraph symbol) or *para.* for paragraph, and *chap.* for chapter.

> One study compared and contrasted the use of web and touch screen
> transaction log files in a hospital setting (Nicholas, Huntington, &
> Williams, 2001).

A Website

Whenever possible, cite a website by its author and posting date. In addition, refer to a specific page or document rather than to a home page or a menu page. If you are referring to a specific part of a webpage that does not have page numbers, direct your reader, if possible, with a section heading and a paragraph number.

> **According to the National Multiple Sclerosis Society (2003, "Complexities" section, para. 2), understanding of MS could not begin until scientists began to research nerve transmission in the 1920s.**

Two or More Works in a Parenthetical Reference

Sometimes it is necessary to lump several citations into one parenthetical reference. In that case, cite the sources as you usually would, separating the citations with semicolons. Place the citations in alphabetical order, just as they would be ordered in the references list:

> **Others report near-death experiences (Rommer, 2000; Sabom, 1998).**

A Sacred Text or Famous Literary Work

Sacred texts and famous literary works are published in many different editions. For that reason, the original date of publication may be unavailable or not pertinent. In these cases, use your edition's year of translation (for example, *trans. 2003*) or indicate your edition's year of publication (*2003 version*). When you are referring to specific sections of the work, it is best to identify parts, chapters, or other divisions instead of your version's page numbers.

> **An interesting literary case of such dysfunctional family behavior can be found in Franz Kafka's *The Metamorphosis,* where it becomes the commandment of family duty for Gregor's parents and sister to swallow their disgust and endure him (trans. 1972, part 3).**

Books of the Bible and other well-known literary works may be abbreviated, if no confusion is possible.

> **"Generations come and generations go, but the earth remains forever" (*The New International Version Study Bible,* 1985 version, Eccles. 1.4).**

Personal Communications

If you do the kind of personal research recommended elsewhere in *The College Writer,* you may have to cite personal communications that have provided you with some of your knowledge. Personal communications may include personal letters, phone calls, memos, and so forth. Because they are not published in a permanent form, APA style does not place them among the citations in your references list. Instead, cite them only in the text of your paper in parentheses, like this:

> **. . . according to M. T. Cann (personal communication, April 1, 2008).**
>
> **. . . by today (M. T. Cann, personal communication, April 1, 2008).**

QUICK GUIDE
APA References

The references section lists all the sources you have cited in your text (with the exception of personal communications such as phone calls and e-mails). Begin your references list on a new page after the last page of your paper. Number each references page, continuing the numbering from the text. Then format your references list by following the guidelines below.

1. Type the short title and page number in the upper-right corner, approximately one-half inch from the top of the page.

2. Center the title, *References,* approximately one inch from the top; then double-space before the first entry.

3. Begin each entry flush with the left margin. If the entry runs more than one line, indent additional lines approximately one-half inch (five to seven spaces) using a hanging indent.

4. Adhere to the following conventions about spacing, capitalization, and italics:

- Double-space between all lines on the references page.
- Use one space following each word and punctuation mark.
- With book and article titles, capitalize only the first letter of the title (and subtitle) and proper nouns. (Note that this practice differs from the presentation of titles in the body of the essay.)
  Example: The impact of the cold war on Asia.
- Use italics for titles of books and periodicals, not underlining.

5. List each entry alphabetically by the last name of the author, or, if no author is given, by the title (disregarding *A, An,* or *The*). For works with multiple authors, use the first author listed in the publication.

6. Follow these conventions with respect to abbreviations:

- With authors' names, generally shorten first and middle names to initials, leaving a space after the period. For a work with more than one author, use an ampersand (&) before the last author's name.
- For publisher locations, use the full city name plus the two-letter U.S. Postal Service abbreviation for the state. For international publishers, include a province and country name; for well-known publishing cities such as Boston and Amsterdam, whether U.S. or international, you may name the city only.
- Spell out "Press" in full, but for other publishing information, use the abbreviations below. Also see page 566.

Second edition	2nd ed.	Technical Report	Tech. Rep.
Part	Pt.	Supplement	Suppl.

Video

Reference Entries: Books and Other Documents

The general form for a book or brochure entry is this:

Author, A. (year). *Title*. Location: Publisher.

The entries that follow illustrate the information needed to cite books, sections of a book, brochures, and government publications.

A Book by One Author

Kuriansky, J. (2007). *Beyond bullets and bombs: Grassroots peacebuilding between Israelis and Palestinians.* Westport, CT: Praeger Press.

A Book by Two or More Authors

Hooyman, N., & Kramer, B. (2006). *Living through loss: Interventions across the life span.* New York: Columbia University Press.

An Anonymous Book

If an author is listed as "Anonymous," treat it as the author's name. Otherwise, follow this format:

Publication manual of the American Psychological Association (5th ed.). (2001). Washington, DC: American Psychological Association.

A Chapter from a Book

List the chapter title after the date of publication, followed by a period or appropriate end punctuation. Use *In* before the book title, and follow the book title with the inclusive page numbers of the chapter.

Tattersall, I. (2002). How did we achieve humanity? In *The monkey in the mirror* (pp. 138–168). New York: Harcourt.

A Single Work from an Anthology

Start with information about the individual work, followed by details about the collection in which it appears, including the page span. When editors' names come in the middle of an entry, follow the usual order: initial first, surname last. Note the placement of *Eds.* in parentheses.

Guy, G. R. (2005). Variationist approaches to phonological change. In B. D. Joseph & R. D. Janda (Eds.), *The handbook of historical linguistics* (pp. 369–400). Malden, MA: Blackwell.

One Volume of a Multivolume Edited Work

Indicate the volume in parentheses after the work's title.

Salzman, J., Smith, D. L., & West, C. (Eds.). (1996). *Encyclopedia of African-American culture and history* (Vol. 4). New York: Simon & Schuster Macmillan.

A Separately Titled Volume in a Multivolume Work

The Associated Press. (1995). *Twentieth-century America: Vol. 8. The crisis of national confidence: 1974–1980.* Danbury, CT: Grolier Educational Corp.

Note: When a work is part of a larger series or collection, as with this example, make a two-part title with the series and the particular volume you are citing.

An Edited Work, One in a Series

Start the entry with the work's author, publication date, and title. Then follow with publication details about the series.

Marshall, P. G. (2002). The impact of the cold war on Asia. In T. O'Neill (Ed.), *World history by era: Vol. 9. The nuclear age* (pp. 162–166). San Diego: Greenhaven Press.

A Group Author as Publisher

When the author is also the publisher, simply put *Author* in the spot where you would list the publisher's name.

Amnesty International. (2007). *Maze of injustice: The failure to protect indigenous women from sexual violence in the USA.* London: Author.

Note: If the publication is a brochure, identify it as such in brackets after the title.

An Edition Other Than the First

Trimmer, J. (2001). *Writing with a purpose* (13th ed.). Boston: Houghton Mifflin.

Two or More Books by the Same Author

When you are listing multiple works by the same author, arrange them by the year of publication, earliest first.

Sacks, O. (1995). *An Anthropologist on Mars: Seven paradoxical tales.* New York: Alfred A. Knopf.

Sacks, O. (2007). *Musicophilia: Tales of music and the brain.* New York: Alfred A. Knopf.

An English Translation

> Setha, R. (1998). *Unarmed* (R. Narasimhan, Trans.). Chennai, India:
>
> Macmillan. (Original work published 1995)

Note: If you use the original work, cite the original version; the non-English title is followed by its English translation, not italicized, in square brackets.

An Article in a Reference Book

Start the entry with the author of the article, if identified. If no author is listed, begin the entry with the title of the article.

> Lewer, N. (1999). Non-lethal weapons. In *World encyclopedia of peace*
>
> (pp. 279–280). Oxford: Pergamon Press.

A Reprint, Different Form

> Albanov, V. (2000). *In the land of white death: An epic story of survival*
>
> *in the Siberian Arctic.* New York: Modern Library. (Original work
>
> published 1917)

Note: This work was originally published in Russia in 1917; the 2000 reprint is the first English version. If you are citing a reprint from another source, the parentheses would contain "Reprinted from *Title*, pp. xx–xx, by A. Author, year, Location: Publisher."

A Technical or Research Report

> Taylor, B. G., Fitzgerald, N., Hunt, D., Reardon, J. A., & Brownstein, H.
>
> H. (2001). *ADAM preliminary 2000 findings on drug use and drug*
>
> *markets: Adult male arrestees.* Washington, DC: National Institute
>
> of Justice.

A Government Publication

Generally, refer to the government agency as the author. When possible, provide an identification number for the document after the title in parentheses.

> National Institute on Drug Abuse. (2000). *Inhalant abuse* (NIH
>
> Publication No. 00–3818). Rockville, MD: National Clearinghouse
>
> on Alcohol and Drug Information.

Note: If the document is not available from the Government Printing Office (GPO), the publisher would be either "Author" or the separate government department that published it.

Video

Reference Entries: Print Periodical Articles

The general form for a periodical entry is this:

Author, A. (year). Article title. *Periodical Title, volume number*(issue number), page numbers.

If the periodical does not use volume and issue numbers, include some other designation with the year, such as a date, a month, or a season. The entries that follow illustrate the information and arrangement needed to cite most types of print periodicals.

An Article in a Scholarly Journal

Benson, P., Karlof, K. L., & Siperstein, G. N. (2008). Maternal involvement in the education of young children with autism spectrum disorders. *Autism: The International Journal of Research & Practice, 12*(1), 47–63.

Note: Pay attention to the features of this basic reference to a scholarly journal:

1. Provide the authors' last names and initials, as for a book reference.
2. Place the year of publication in parentheses, followed by a period.
3. Format the article's title in lowercase, except for the first word of the main title and of a subtitle and except for proper nouns, acronyms, or initialisms; do not italicize the article title or place it in quotation marks.
4. Capitalize the first and all main words in the journal title; italicize it.
5. As recommended in the 2007 *APA Style Guide to Electronic References*, always include the volume number and the issue number for the journal, regardless of whether the journal is paginated consecutively throughout a volume or individually by issue. Italicize the volume number but not the issue number; place the issue in parentheses, without a space after the volume number.
6. Provide inclusive page numbers, without "pp." or "pages."

An Abstract of a Scholarly Article (from a Secondary Source)

When referencing an abstract published separately from an article, provide publication details of the article followed by information about where the abstract was published.

Shlipak, M. G., Simon, J. A., Grady, O., Lin, F., Wenger, N. K., & Furberg, C. D. (2001, September). Renal insufficiency and cardiovascular events in postmenopausal women with coronary heart disease. *Journal of the American College of Cardiology, 38*, 705–711. Abstract obtained from *Geriatrics*, 2001, 56(12), Abstract No. 5645351.

A Journal Article, More Than Six Authors

Yamada, A., Suzuki, M., Kato, M., Suzuki, M., Tanaka, S., Shindo, T., et
al. (2007). Emotional distress and its correlates among parents
of children with persuasive developmental disorders. *Psychiatry &
Clinical Neurosciences, 61*(6), 651–657.

Note: In the text, abbreviate the parenthetical citation: (Yamada et al., 2007).

A Review

To reference a book review or a review of another medium (film, exhibit, and so
on), indicate the review and the medium in brackets, along with the title of the work
being reviewed by the author listed.

Hutcheon, L., & Hutcheon, M. (2008). Turning into the mind. [Review
of the book *Musicophilia: Tales of music and the brain*]. *Canadian
Medical Association Journal, 178*(4), 441.

A Magazine Article

Weintraub, B. (2007, October). Unusual suspects. *Psychology Today,
40*(5), 80–87.

Note: If the article is unsigned, begin the entry with the title of the article.

Tomatoes target toughest cancer. (2002, February). *Prevention, 54*(2), 53.

A Newspaper Article

For newspaper articles, include the full publication date, year first followed by
a comma, the month (spelled out) and the day. Identify the article's location in the
newspaper using page numbers and section letters, as appropriate. If the article is a
letter to the editor, identify it as such in brackets following the title. For newspapers,
use *p.* or *pp.* before the page numbers; if the article is not on continuous pages, give
all the page numbers, separated by commas.

Schmitt, E., & Shanker, T. (2008, March 18). U.S. adapts cold-war idea
to fight terrorists. *The New York Times*, pp. 1A, 14A–15A.

Benderoff, E. (2008, March 14). Facebook sites face scrutiny for March
Madness pools. *Chicago Tribune*, 2C–3C.

A Newsletter Article

Newsletter article entries are similar to newspaper article entries; only a volume
number is added.

Teaching mainstreamed special education students. (2002, February).
The Council Chronicle, 11, 6–8.

Video

Reference Entries: Online Sources

When it comes to references for online sources, the 2007 *APA Style Guide to Electronic References* replaces the guidelines offered in the fifth edition of the *Publication Manual of the American Psychological Association* (2001):

1. Whenever possible, use the final version of an electronic resource. Typically, this is called the archival copy or the version of record, as opposed to a prepublished version. Right now, that final version is likely the same as the printed version of an article, though there is some movement toward the online publication being the final version (complete with additional data, graphics, and so on).

2. In the reference entry for an electronic source, start with the same elements in the same order for print or other fixed-media resources (author, title, and so on). Then add the most reliable electronic retrieval information that will (a) clarify what version of the source you used and (b) help your reader find the source him- or herself. Determine what you need to include based on these guidelines:

   • Whenever possible, use the electronic document's Digital Object Identifier (DOI). More and more, electronic publishers are using this registration code for the content of journal articles and other documents so that the document can be located on the Internet, even if the URL changes. The DOI will usually be published at the beginning of the article or be available in the article's citation.

   Author, A. A. (year). Title of article. *Title of Periodical, volume number*(issue number), pages. doi: code

   • If a DOI is not available for the electronic document, give the URL (without a period at the end). Generally, a database name is no longer needed, except for hard-to-find documents and those accessed through subscription-only databases. Use the home- or menu-page URL for subscription-only databases and online reference works.

   Author, A. A. (year). Title of article. *Title of Periodical, volume number*(issue number), pages. Retrieved from URL

   • If the content of the document is stable (e.g., archival copy or copy of record with DOI), do not include a retrieval date in your reference entry. However, if the content is likely to change or be updated, as is the case with a lot of the material on the free web, then offer a retrieval date. This would be the case with open-web material with no fixed publication date, edition, or version, or material that is prepublished (in preparation, in press).

   Author, A. A. (year). *Title of document.* Retrieved date from website: URL

A Journal Article with DOI

> Oberg, A., Blades, D., & Thom, J. S. (2007). Untying a dreamcatcher: Coming to understand possibilities for teaching students of aboriginal inheritance. *Educational Studies, 42*(2), 111–139. doi: 10.1080/00131940701513185

Note: Because the DOI references the final version of the article, the retrieval date, URL, and database name are not needed. If the online article is a preprint version, add "Advance online publication" and your retrieval date before the DOI.

A Journal Article Without DOI

> Bell, J. B., & Nye, E. C. (2007). Specific symptoms predict suicidal ideation in Vietnam combat veterans with Post-Traumatic Stress Disorder. *Military Medicine, 172*(11), 1144–1147. Retrieved from http://www.ebscohost.com

Note: Because this article has no DOI, the URL is provided for the subscription database search service. If you retrieved the article from the open web, you would supply the exact URL. If the version of the article you access is in press and you have retrieved it from the author's personal or institutional website, place "in press" in parentheses after the author's name and add a retrieval date before the URL.

A Newspaper Article

> Sengupta, S. (2008, March 18). Dalai Lama says he'll resign if violence escalates. *The New York Times.* Retrieved from http://www.nytimes.com

An Article in an Online Magazine (Ezine) not Published in Print

> Pike, D. L. (2008, February). A boy and his dog: On Will Smith, apocalypse, and I Am Legend [Online exclusive]. *Bright Lights Film Journal.* Retrieved April 17, 2008, from http://www.brightlightsfilm.com/59 /59legend.html

A Book Review

> Shapiro, K. (2007). Mystic chords. [Review of the book *Musicophilia: Tales of music and the brain*]. *Commentary, 124*(5), 73–77. Retrieved from http://web.ebscohost.com

An Electronic Book

> Kafka, F. (2002). *Metamorphosis.* D. Wylie (Trans.). Available from http://www.gutenberg.org/etext/5200

Note: If the URL goes directly to the ebook, use "Retrieved from."

Material from an Online Reference Work

> Agonism. (2008). In *Encyclopaedia Britannica*. Retrieved March 18,
> 2008, from http://search.eb.com

Note: Generally, do not use wikis such as Wikipedia for scholarly research.

Online Course Material

> Roderiguez, N. *Unit 3, Lecture 3: Sociological Theories of Deviance.*
> Retrieved from University of Houston Website: http://www.uh.edu
> /~nestor/lecturenotes/unit3lecture3.html

A Workplace Document or Other "Gray Literature."

"Gray Literature" refers to informative documents (e.g., brochures, fact sheets, white papers) produced by government agencies, corporations, and nonprofit groups. If possible, give a document number or identify the type of document in brackets.

> Foehr, U. G. (2006). *Media multitasking among American youth:*
> *Prevelance, predictors and pairings* (Publication No. 7592).
> Retrieved from the Kaiser Family Foundation: http://www.kff.org
> /entmedia/upload/7592.pdf

Undated Content on Website

> National Institute of Allergy and Infectious Diseases. (n.d.). *Antimicrobial*
> *(Drug) Resistance.* Retrieved June 19, 2008, from http://www3
> .niaid.nih.gov/topics/AntimicrobialResistance/default.htm

A Podcast

> Byrd, D., & Block, J. (Producers). (2008, February 5). Antonio Rangel:
> This is your brain on wine. *Earth & Sky: A Clear Voice for Science.*
> Podcast retrieved from http://www.earthsky.org/clear-voices/52199

Message on a Newsgroup, an Online Forum, or a Discussion Group

> Avnish, J. (2008, March 18). Sex education especially vital to teens
> nowadays. Message posted to AIDS Beyond Borders Group, archived
> at http://groups.google.ca/group/AIDS-Beyond-Borders/topics?hl=en

A Weblog Post

> Koyzis, D. (2007, June 27). Conservative environmentalists. Message posted
> to http://byzantinecalvinist.blogspot.com/2007_06_01_archive.html

Note about URLs: When necessary, break a URL before a slash or other punctuation mark. Do not underline or italicize the URL, place it in angle brackets, or end it with a period.

Video

Reference Entries: Other Sources (Primary, Personal, and Multimedia)

Cite audiovisual media sources and electronic sources as follows.

Specialized Computer Software with Limited Distribution

Standard nonspecialized computer software does not require a reference entry. Treat software as an unauthored work unless an individual has property rights to it.

> Carreau, Stéphane. (2001). Champfoot (Version 3.3) [Computer
> software]. Saint Mandé, France: Author.

Show the software version in parentheses after the title and the medium in brackets.

A Television or Radio Broadcast

List a broadcast by the show's producer or executive producer, and identify the type of broadcast in brackets after the show's title.

> Crystal, L. (Executive Producer). (2002, February 11). *The NewsHour
> with Jim Lehrer* [Television broadcast]. New York and Washington,
> DC: Public Broadcasting Service.

A Television or Radio Series or Episode

When referencing an entire series, identify the series producer and indicate the type of series in brackets after the title.

> Bloch, A. (Producer). (2002). *Thinking allowed* [Television series].
> Berkeley: Public Broadcasting Service.

When identifying a specific episode in a television or radio series, indicate the episode by writers, if possible. Then follow with the airing date, the episode title, and the type of series in brackets. Complete the entry with details about the series itself.

> Berger, Cynthia. (Writer). (2001, December 19). Feederwatch [Radio
> series program]. In D. Byrd & J. Block (Producers), *Earth & Sky*.
> Austin, TX: The Production Block.

An Audio Recording

Begin the entry with the speaker's or writer's name, not the producer. Indicate the type of recording in brackets.

> Kim, E. (Author, speaker). (2000). *Ten thousand sorrows* [CD]. New
> York: Random House.

A Music Recording

Give the name and function of the originators or primary contributors. Indicate the recording medium in brackets immediately following the title.

ARS Femina Ensemble. (Performers). (1998). *Musica de la puebla de Los Angeles: Music by women of baroque Mexico, Cuba, & Europe* [CD]. Louisville, KY: Nannerl Recordings.

A Motion Picture

Give the name and function of the director, producer, or both.

Cohn, J., & Cohn, E. (Directors). (2007). *No country for old men* [motion picture]. United States: Miramax Films.

A Published Interview, Titled, No Author

Start the entry with the interview's title, followed by publication details.

Stephen Harper: The Report interview. (2002, January 7). *The Report* (Alberta, BC), *29*, 10–11.

A Published Interview, Titled, Single Author

Start the entry with the interviewee's name, followed by the date and the title. Place the interviewer's name in brackets before other publication details.

Fussman, C. (2002, January). What I've learned [Interview with Robert McNamara]. *Esquire, 137*(1), 85.

An Unpublished Paper Presented at a Meeting

Indicate when the paper was presented, at what meeting, in what location.

Lycan, W. (2002, June). *The plurality of consciousness.* Paper presented at the meeting of the Society for Philosophy and Psychology, New York, NY.

An Unpublished Doctoral Dissertation

Place the dissertation's title in italics, even though the work is unpublished. Indicate the school at which the writer completed the dissertation.

Roberts, W. (2001). *Crime amidst suburban wealth.* Unpublished doctoral dissertation, Bowling Green State University, Bowling Green, OH.

Sample APA Paper

Student writer Renee Danielle Singh wrote the following research paper on the mystery of the lost colonists of Roanoke Island. In the paper, written for an anthropology class, she explores a range of historical, genetic, and linguistic evidence to resolve this mystery and to explain its continuing relevance. For more on Roanoke's lost colony and the Lumbee People of North Carolina, go to **www.thecollegewriter .com/3e.** You can use Renee's paper in three ways:

1. To study how a well-written research paper uses a range of resources to build a discussion or line of reasoning that answers a research question.

2. To examine how sources are used and integrated into social-sciences research writing—a full-length discussion of the strategies addressed on pages 486–489.

3. To see in detail the format and documentation practices of APA style.

Note: Often, a social-sciences research paper takes the form of an experiment report. For an example of such a report, go to **www.thecollegewriter.com/3e.**

Sample Title Page

Put five spaces between the header and number.

Our Roots   1

Running head: OUR ROOTS GO BACK TO ROANOKE

Type running head (abbreviated title in uppercase letters) flush left.

Our Roots Go Back to Roanoke:

Investigating the Link between

the Lost Colony and the Lumbee People of North Carolina

Renee Danielle Singh

University of California Davis

Full title, author(s), and school name are centered on the page, typed in uppercase and lowercase.

Sample Abstract

The abstract
summarizes
the paper's
central issue,
its main
conclusion,
the key
reasoning
and evidence
presented,
and the
study's
significance.

Abstract

While remaining something of a mystery, the disappearance in the
late sixteenth century of a group of colonists from Roanoke Island off
North Carolina is likely related to the mystery of the ancestry of the
North Carolina's Native American Lumbee tribe. Using evidence from
the parallel example of the Catawba Indians, as well as evidence related
to baldcypress tree rings, historical analysis, immunology, genetic
studies, and linguistic patterns, one can tentatively conclude that the lost
colonists were perhaps captured by, intermarried with, and were absorbed
by the sixteenth-century ancestors of the Lumbee. This conclusion points
to the need for further study, as the Lumbee People's status as Native
American is currently contested and needs to be resolved for them to be
recognized by the federal government.

Note: On the following pages, APA format for the body of the paper is shown
in general terms, without reproducing the actual appearance of the paper
as it would look on 8.5- by 11-inch sheets. That appearance is shown at the
book's website **www.thecollegewriter.com/3e**, but here are a few format
reminders to keep in mind as you study the sample paper:

- **Margins:** Leave a one-inch margin on all four sides of each page
  (with the exception of the running head and page number). You
  may use a justified right margin (not ragged) and end-of-line
  hyphens, if you wish.
- **Line Spacing:** Double-space your entire paper, unless your
  instructor allows single spacing for tables, titles, captions, and so
  on, for the sake of readability. Do not leave extra lines above or
  below titles and headings.

APA Research Paper: The Body

As you review the body of this paper, read the side notes and examine how the writer uses and documents her sources.

A running head and page number top each page.

The title is centered one inch from the top, and the paper is double-spaced.

After referencing multiple sources, the writer provides a narrative to put the main point in context.

The introduction focuses on the research question, suggests an answer, and forecasts a method for finding the answer.

Our Roots Go Back to Roanoke:
Investigating the Link between the Lost Colony
and the Lumbee People of North Carolina

Introduction: Something Is Terribly Wrong

Consider the following narrative, which features historical [1]
information from Kupperman (1984, 1985), Miller (2002), Oberg (1994),
and Quinn (1985):

Imagine yourself sailing across the warm waters of the Atlantic. It is a [2]
time before airplanes and automobiles, and our nation, which someday will
lie just a few miles ahead of you, is still called the "New World." You are
on your way to an island off the coast of what will one day be called North
Carolina, and you are anxious to see what a small group of colonists has
accomplished since their arrival there three years ago. Yes, this is the age of
colonization. This is the beginning of a nation.

As you draw closer to land, however, you get a strange feeling that [3]
something is terribly wrong. No fires are burning on the island, no greeters
waving. Instead, an eerie silence fills the air. At once, you cast your anchor
and row ashore, hoping that perhaps you've reached the wrong island by
mistake. Surely, this is not the island destined to be the first true settlement
in the New World? Surely, this is not Roanoke?

As you step ashore, your worst fears are confirmed. Pots and other [4]
artifacts lay unused on the ground and the shelters show signs of neglect.
Footprints and other marks are scattered about as well, but their makers are
nowhere in sight. The colonists of Roanoke have vanished.

For over four hundred years, the fate of the lost colonists of [5]
Roanoke has remained a mystery. While there are many theories to date
concerning what became of them, the most prevalent and well-supported
theory argues that the colonists were assimilated into the indigenous
tribes of North Carolina (Kupperman, 1984, 1985; Miller, 2002; Oberg,
1994; Quinn, 1985). If that is true, then the lost colonists of Roanoke

may be "found" in their suspected descendants: the Lumbee People of North Carolina. By examining the historical, genetic, and linguistic evidence concerning the origins of the Lumbee, we might yet shed light on one of history's greatest mysteries.

Who Are the Lumbee People?

A single tribe of over 50,000 individuals constitutes the Lumbee People, who currently live in Robeson County, North Carolina (Blu, 1980; Bryant & LaFromboise, 2005; Tobert, 2001). Historical records indicate that the Lumbee have been living near Robeson County's Lumber River since the early 1700s, taking their tribal name from this body of water (Blu, 1980; Bryant & LaFromboise, 2005; Tobert, 2001).

Many studies of the Lumbee characterize them as an eclectic tribe because their culture and biology have been highly influenced by non-native groups with whom the tribe has admixed (Blu, 1980; Bryant & LaFromboise, 2005; Tobert, 2001). For example, unlike most traditional tribes, the Lumbee are followers of the Southern Baptist faith. They also speak a dialect often referred to as a "variety of English," and many do not know their tribe's native language, which is Siouan in origin (Blu, 1980; Bryant & LaFromboise, 2005; Tobert, 2001). Additionally, many of the Lumbee exhibit physical characteristics such as blond hair and blue eyes (Blu, 1980; Bryant & LaFromboise, 2005).

How could this admixture have happened? Traditionally, most Native American groups have not been known to admix with outside parties. Indeed, the federal government discourages it by denying benefits to those who practice admixture (Blu, 1980; Bryant & LaFromboise, 2005). However, the Lumbee People are not alone in this respect. Other Native American tribes have also mixed with outsiders.

Admixture and Native American Groups:
The Catawba Indian Example

The Catawba Indians were a group of Native Americans living just outside Rock Hill, South Carolina. As Pollitzer et al. explain (1967), in 1962 the Catawba opted to terminate their reservation status, thus relinquishing all forms of federal recognition. Apparently, reservation life no longer met the needs of their newly acquired Mormon lifestyle. Around the same time, the Catawba allowed outside parties to study their blood types. Over 100 Catawba were typed for the ABO blood

---

The first section offers essential background for the mystery.

In-text citations list the multiple sources for the background information. Dates are featured.

The writer introduces a key concept (admixture) and then explores its relevance.

An attributive phrase for a source is followed by the publication year in parentheses. "Et al." indicates several authors.

6

7

8

9

Our Roots   5

groups. Physical features such as stature, cephalic index, facial index, and nasal index were also measured, and the data were studied in an attempt to better understand their current genetic composition. In other words, Pollitzer et al. conducted a study to see whether modern-day Catawba Indians were biologically more "white" or "Native American."

Despite centuries of admixing, a modern Catawba Indian was found to be, on average, 50% white and 50% Native American in genetic composition (Pollitzer et al., 1967). The results of the study surprised many who expected the percentage of white genetic attributes to be much higher (Pollitzer et al., 1967). Like the Lumbee, the Catawba were a nontraditional tribe. They practiced a non-native religion (Mormonism), abandoned their original Siouan dialect, and exhibited physical features that made some of them indistinguishable from Caucasians. Yet genetic data indicated they were still 50% Native American (Pollitzer et al., 1967).

10

The example of the Catawba Indians highlights the dangers of rushing to conclusions about a group's origins and biology based solely on their culture or physical features. The origins and biology of the Lumbee People cannot be studied, therefore, by merely observing modern-day members and associating them with whatever group they most closely resemble culturally and physically. To understand who the Lumbee People are today and from whom they came, we must go back to the beginning. We must go back to Roanoke.

11

A Mystery in History: The Story of the Lost Colony of Roanoke

Toward the end of the sixteenth century, Europeans had begun to set up the first permanent settlements in the New World (Kupperman, 1984, 1985; Miller, 2002; Oberg, 1994; Quinn, 1985). One participant was none other than Sir Walter Raleigh, the explorer after whom the capital of North Carolina is named. Raleigh had high hopes for the New World and, in June 1578, he was granted a patent by Queen Elizabeth I to explore and colonize North America. The patent would expire ten years after its issuance; thus, Raleigh had to move quickly. For the next nine years, Raleigh sent ships to and from the New World in search of a good spot to found the first settlement (Kupperman, 1984, 1985; Miller, 2002; Oberg, 1994; Quinn, 1985).

12

As Kupperman (1984, 1985), Miller (2002), Oberg (1994), and Quinn (1985) go on to explain, one particular expedition, launched

13

The writer offers conclusions about the genetic evidence, relating her illustration to her specific topic.

With the last sentence and the new heading, the writer makes a transition to the second part of the mystery.

Referencing multiple sources in attributive phrases and parenthetical citations, the writer provides extensive background on the Roanoke mystery.

in 1584, located a small island off the coast of North Carolina by mistake, after its ship struck a shoal in the sea. The island was later called Roanoke Island. As a result of damage to their ship, the crew of about 100 men was forced to remain on the island, and a fort and other structures were erected as shelters. When a relief ship arrived to rescue the crew, 15 men stayed behind to protect Raleigh's claim to the New World.

In 1587, with time running short, it was hastily agreed that the new settlement would be founded at Chesapeake Bay, Virginia (Kupperman, 1984, 1985; Miller, 2002; Oberg, 1994; Quinn, 1985). In July of that same year, a group of 117 men, women, and children embarked for the New World led by the Portuguese navigator Simon Fernandes. In addition to colonizing Chesapeake Bay, the colonists were given instructions to stop by Roanoke Island and retrieve the 15 volunteers from the previous expedition.   *14*

When the party arrived, however, on July 22, 1587, they found that all 15 men had vanished. It was later determined that the volunteer party had sailed back to England after losing six members during an Indian attack. Despite this discouraging news, the colonists persisted with their plan to found the first new settlement. Unfortunately, for reasons still not clearly understood, Fernandes was unable to deliver the colonists to Chesapeake Bay, and word reached England that the first settlement had been founded on Roanoke Island instead (Kupperman, 1984, 1985; Miller, 2002; Oberg, 1994; Quinn, 1985).   *15*

During August 1587, the colony's governor, John White, was forced to return to England to obtain more supplies. As Kupperman, Miller, Oberg, and Quinn explain, the trip was supposed to take no more than three months, but the arrival of the Spanish Armada prevented White from obtaining a ship for the journey back to Roanoke for three more years. In 1590, when White finally did return, he experienced a horrible fright: All 115 of the original colonists had vanished. Roanoke Island held nothing more than several unused pots and a few scattered footprints.   *16*

A series of questions links the two mysteries of the Lumbee and the Roanoke colonists.

Why would the colonists leave Roanoke? Why risk crossing paths with mainland natives, given what happened to the 15 volunteers who had fled before? And most importantly for our purposes, is there any evidence that they made contact with the indigenous groups of North Carolina?   *17*

Why Leave Roanoke?

Using a heading in the form of a question, the writer explores evidence explaining one part of the mystery.

Recently, scientists from the University of Arkansas and the College   *18*
of William and Mary discovered several individuals currently living in
North Carolina whose roots go back to Roanoke (Stahle et al., 1998).
According to Stahle et al., these individuals have been living in the
region since the colonists first landed in 1587, and therefore might well
be the only living "witnesses" to what occurred (1998).

Who are these "witnesses"? The ancient baldcypress trees (*Taxodium*   *19*
distichum) of North Carolina.

As Stahle et al. explain, most trees generate a single ring within   *20*
their trunks each time a year passes. By counting the rings in a cross
section of a tree's trunk, one can determine the age of the tree (1998).
Doing so, Stahle et al. confirmed that the baldcypresses were present
during the time of Roanoke. Yet tree rings can also provide information
on environmental conditions. For example, adequate water available
throughout the year results in a wider ring, whereas during a drought
the annual ring will be significantly narrower (Stahle et al., 1998). Tree
ring data collected from the baldcypress trees of North Carolina suggests
that the period between 1587 and 1589 was one of the driest in the area
in 800 years (Stahle et al., 1998). Such a severe drought probably led to
poor health and poor crop quality on Roanoke Island, thus forcing the
colonists to move to the mainland in search of food (Stahle et al., 1998).
Yet the question remains: Do we have any evidence of early contact
between colonists and Native Americans?

**Crossing Paths: Early Evidence of Contact Between
the Lost Colonists of Roanoke and Indigenous Peoples**

The writer adds to her overall argument by exploring another form of evidence related to illness and its effects.

As it turns out, historical records indicate that the lost colonists of   *21*
Roanoke may have been harboring a dangerous virus: influenza. Mainly
affecting the lungs, the influenza virus can easily be spread by simply
coming in contact with infected individuals (Mires, 1994). Historians
and biologists agree that the New World was free of the virus until the
arrival of Europeans during the late sixteenth century (Mires, 1994).
In fact, recent documents found by archaeologists from the University
of Minnesota indicate that an outbreak of influenza occurred on the
mainland of North Carolina at about the same time we speculate the

colonists left Roanoke Island (Mires, 1994). If the influenza virus was not present in the New World before the arrival of Europeans, and the only Europeans present in the area during the outbreak were those who arrived with the Roanoke expedition, then it is highly probable that the lost colonists of Roanoke made contact with the indigenous groups of North Carolina and served as vectors for influenza (Mires, 1994).

That being said, we must now turn to a different question, one that has remained unanswered for over four hundred years: What happened to those lost colonists?

22

Tracing Tribes:
A Theory of What Happened to the Lost Colonists

Building on the discussion of illness in the previous section, the writer explores evidence for the impact of European-borne illness on indigenous people.

As Kupperman (1984, 1985), Miller (2002), Oberg (1994), and Quinn (1985) all relate, centuries ago a group of natives known as the Eno inhabited North Carolina's wilderness. Archaeological evidence indicates that the Eno were a copper-mining people whose culture centered on this metal. For example, numerous copper ornaments have been found at Eno sites dating back to the sixteenth century, ornaments probably used to decorate Eno houses. As a Siouan-speaking tribe, the Eno were allied with the Occaneechi and other less well-defined Siouan groups dispersed throughout North Carolina. Historical records also suggest that the Eno participated in a slave trading market open to their fellow Siouan allies.

23

Yet historians believe the Eno's copper-based lifestyle was threatened after they lost several tribe members to an influenza epidemic in the late sixteenth century (Kupperman, 1984, 1985; Miller, 2002; Oberg, 1994; Quinn, 1985). Copper mining is not easy, requiring strong individuals to extract the metal sheets from rock formations. Kupperman, Oberg, Miller, and Quinn hypothesize that the Eno captured all 115 of the lost colonists, keeping the men to work the copper mines and selling the women and children to other Siouan-speaking groups involved in the slave market. Indeed, these other Siouan tribes would have been eager to obtain the lost women and children from Roanoke because their numbers would also have been reduced by the recent influenza epidemic. Eventually, the Roanoke women and children would have been assimilated into these other Siouan-speaking tribes (Kupperman, 1984, 1985; Miller, 2002; Oberg, 1994; Quinn, 1985).

24

All of this begs the question as to whether the Lumbee Pople are   *25*
descendants of the lost colonists of Roanoke. Answering that question
requires that we look not only at the historical evidence but also at the
genetic and linguistic evidence.

Are the Lumbee People Descendants
of the Lost Colonists of Roanoke?

Historical Clues

Unfortunately, seventeenth-century tribal records for the Eno, the   *26*
Occaneechi, and the other Siouan-speaking groups of North Carolina are
scarce, so these groups cannot be traced directly to the Lumbee People
(Kupperman, 1984, 1985; Miller, 2002; Oberg, 1994; Quinn, 1985).
However, a document dated 1725 does identify four Siouan-speaking
groups living near a river called the "Drowning River" in North Carolina
(Blu, 1980). Today, the "Drowning River" is known as the "Lumber
River," and tribal records for the Lumbee, which begin in the 1700s,
show that the four Siouan-speaking groups are, in fact, the earliest
documented ancestors of the Lumbee People (Blu, 1980).

Genetic Clues

During the late 1970s, the Lumbee People were typed for the human   *27*
leukocyte antigen (HLA) system in an attempt by Grier, Ruderman, and
Johnson (1979) to create an HLA profile for the tribe. The HLA system is a
group of genes that codes for antigens on the surfaces of cells and is part of
a complex known as the human major histocompatibility complex (MHC).
Scientists use the prefix "HLA" followed by a letter and a number to identify
the allele and HLA locus that is being studied (Grier et al., 1979).

Researchers note that most Native American groups have a high   *28*
frequency of HLA-B40 (Grier et al., 1979). However, Grier et al. (1979)
found that the Lumbee People have an unusually low frequency of HLA-
B40. This fact, along with other inconsistencies in the Lumbee HLA
profile, indicate that admixture, specifically with European groups, has
affected the current genetic composition of the Lumbee (Grier et al.,
1979).

Linguistic Clues

Although they originated in part from a Siouan-speaking tribe,   *29*
modern Lumbee People speak a modified form of English (Torbert,
2001). A linguistic study conducted by Benjamin Torbert from Duke

Using a new heading and a series of subheadings, the writer explores multiple forms of evidence to test her hypothesis.

The writer effectively draws on multiple sources for various types of evidence and reasoning.

University included a consonant cluster analysis of Lumbee speech. A consonant cluster is a group of consonants not separated by a vowel. For example, in the word "spring," the "spr-" group would be classified as a consonant cluster (Tobert, 2001).

Torbert compared the Lumbee dialect with that of other Native American groups in the region and found that, unlike most Native American tribes in North Carolina, the Lumbee speak a dialect that is saturated with consonant clusters. Thus, ancestors of the Lumbee People seem to have adopted consonant clusters after mixing with the lost colonists of Roanoke—whose own language, like that of most Europeans, included the frequent use of consonant clusters (Torbert, 2001).

30

Lumbee Origins and the Study of Human Variation: Ethnicity versus Biological Origins

Unfortunately, we may never know for certain what became of the lost colonists of Roanoke. However, we do know that some evidence suggests that the Lumbee People of North Carolina may be their modern-day descendants. As a result, the Lumbee People currently face a dilemma regarding the issue of racial classification (Blu, 1980; Bryant & LaFromboise, 2005). Unlike most native peoples in the United States, the Lumbee People have never been placed on a reservation, and thus have never been federally recognized as a Native American Group (Blu, 1980; Bryant & LaFromboise, 2005). They do not receive the same federal benefits as other indigenous groups in the country, a fact reflected in their poor health and living standards (Beltrane & McQueen, 1979; Bryant et al., 2004; Humphrey & Kupper, 1982). Simply put, they are a people with a confused identity (Blu, 1980; Bryant & LaFromboise, 2005). The Lumbee believe that they are Native Americans and would like to be considered as such, but the federal government has denied their requests for federal recognition (Blu, 1980; Bryant & LaFromboise, 2005). Stating that the Lumbee have "too open an enrollment policy," the federal government cites centuries of admixture that have significantly compromised the Lumbee identity as a tribe (Blu, 1980; Bryant & LaFromboise, 2005).

31

Is the federal government correct to assert that the Lumbee are no longer "Native Americans"? Recall that the Catawba Indians of South Carolina were similar to the Lumbee People in that they, too, frequently admixed throughout their history and did not look or act very Native

32

In the final section, the writer explores the relevance of the mystery the paper focuses on: the fate of the people involved.

American anymore (Blu, 1980; Bryant & LaFromboise, 2005). Unlike the Lumbee, however, the Catawba Indians were granted federal recognition even before they proved, genetically, that they were still 50% Native American (Pollitzer et al., 1967). Just how "Native American" does one have to be?

Conclusion: Something Is Still Terribly Wrong

Steps should be taken to answer the question concerning the origins of the Lumbee once and for all. The HLA profile study, conducted during the late 1970s by Grier et al., for example, is the only genetic study of the Lumbee to date. Modern mitochondrial DNA and possibly Y-chromosome DNA studies should be completed to further clarify the biological identity of the Lumbee tribe. At the same time, steps must be taken to protect the Lumbee People's ethnic identity. Recent cultural studies point out the high occurrence of alcoholism and suicide among the Lumbee as a result of their continuing identity crisis (Beltrane & McQueen, 1979; Bryant et al., 2004; Humphrey & Kupper, 1982). Just as John White found upon his belated return to the deserted colony over four hundred years ago, something is terribly wrong. We must ensure that the Lumbee People do not share the fate of the colonists who disappeared from that infamous island off the coast of North Carolina, the island of Roanoke.

> In the conclusion, the writer argues for additional research that will resolve the mystery and bring about justice.

33

Reading for Better Writing

Working by yourself or with a group, answer these questions.

1. Singh's paper focuses on a historical mystery with current relevance. What strategies make her readers care about the mystery?

2. What types of evidence does Singh use in her paper? Where has she gotten her evidence? Are her resources reliable?

3. How does Singh document her research? How does she distinguish her own thinking from source material? Why are these strategies necessary?

4. Follow-up: More information on the Roanoke mystery and the Lumbee People is available at this book's website, **www.thecollegewriter.com/3e.** After reviewing the resources at the site, offer your own response to the mystery: What do you conclude about what happened and how these developments should impact the current situation in North Carolina?

Our Roots   12

References

All works referred to in the paper appear on the references page, listed alphabetically by author (or title).

Beltrane, T., & McQueen, D. V. (1979). Urban and rural Indian drinking patterns: The special case of the Lumbee. *International Journal of the Addictions, 14*(4), 533–548.

Blu, K. I. (1980). *The Lumbee problem: The making of an American Indian People.* Cambridge: Cambridge University Press.

Bryant, A., Goins, R. T., Bell, R., Herrell, R., Manson, S. M., & Buchwald, D. (2004). Health differences among Lumbee Indians using public and private sources of care. *Journal of Rural Health, 20*(3), 231–236.

Bryant, A., & LaFromboise, T. D. (2005). The racial identity and cultural orientation of Lumbee American Indian high school students. *Cultural Diversity & Ethnic Minority Psychology, 11*(1), 82–89.

Each entry follows APA guidelines for listing authors, dates, titles, and publishing information.

Grier, J. O., Ruderman, R. J., & Johnson, A. H. (1979). HLA profile in the Lumbee Indians of North Carolina. *Transplant Proceedings, 11*(4), 1767–1769.

Humphrey, J. A., & Kupper, H. J. (1982). Homicide and suicide among the Cherokee and Lumbee Indians of North Carolina. *International Journal of Social Psychiatry, 28*(2), 121–128. doi: 10.1177/002076408202800210

Kupperman, K. O. (1984). *Roanoke, the abandoned colony.* New Jersey: Rowman & Allanheld.

Kupperman, K. O. (1985). Roanoke lost. *American Heritage, 36*(5), 81–96.

Miller, L. (2002). *Roanoke: solving the mystery of the lost colony.* New York: Penguin.

Capitalization, punctuation, and hanging indentation are consistent with APA format.

Mires, P. B. (1994). Contact and contagion: The Roanoke colony and influenza. *Historical Archaeology, 28*(3), 30–38.

Molnar, S. (2002). *Human variation: Races, types, and ethnic groups.* Englewood Cliffs, NJ: Prentice Hall.

Oberg, M. L. (1994). Indians and Englishmen at the first Roanoke colony: A note on Pemisapan's conspiracy, 1585–86. *American Indian Culture & Research Journal, 18*(2), 75–89.

Note: For the complete references list, go to **www.thecollegewriter.com/3e.**

Checklist for APA Format

When you are completing a paper in APA format, use the checklist below to ensure that you are following the format correctly.

_____ All borrowed material is acknowledged with an appropriate attributive phrase and/or in-text citation indicating author(s), publication date, and page number, as appropriate.

_____ All in-text citations effectively point readers to resources in the references list or to personal communication not listed.

_____ The references list includes entries for all works referred to in the body of the paper: No sources are missing from the list; no extra sources are listed that have no reference within the paper. Exception: Personal communications are identified with in-text citations but not in the references list.

_____ The entire references list is properly alphabetized by authors' last names (or by the first main word in the title for anonymous works).

_____ Each references entry (whether for an article, a book, an online document, or other source) contains the maximum amount of identifying and publication information, in the proper order, using the accepted abbreviations.

_____ The paper is properly formatted from the title page to any appendix.

Critical-Thinking and Writing Activities

1. To make sense of APA format rules, answer these questions by yourself or with classmates: What is the essential logic of the APA system? How does this logic reflect research practices and values in the Social Sciences?

2. Create references list entries in correct APA style for the following sources:

- An article in the October 2001 issue (vol. 29, no. 2) of *Learning & Leading with Technology* magazine by Bob Albrecht and Paul Davis titled "The Metric Backpack" (pages 29–31, 55)

- The book *The Playful World: How Technology Is Transforming Our Imagination,* by Mark Pesce, published in 2000 by Ballantine Books, located in New York City

- A webpage by Roger Fouts called "Frequently Asked Questions," part of the *Chimpanzee and Human Communication Institute* site, sponsored by Central Washington University; no publication date; site accessed May 8, 2008, at http://www.cwu.edu/~cwuchci/quanda.html.

◀ Visually Speaking

Review the photo montage at the beginning of this chapter (page 535). What does the image suggest about writing an APA research paper?

Research Paper Abbreviations

anon.	anonymous
bk.	book(s)
©	copyright
chap., ch.	chapter(s)
comp.	compiler, compiled, compiled by
ed.	edition(s), edited by
Ed.	editor(s)
e.g.	for example; *exempli gratia*
et al.	and others; *et alii, et aliae*
ex.	example
fig.	figure(s)
GPO	Government Printing Office, Washington, DC
ibid.	in the same place; *ibidem*
i.e.	that is; *id est*
illus.	illustration, illustrated by
introd.	introduction, introduced by
loc. cit.	in the place cited; *loco citato*
ms., mss.	manuscript(s)
narr.	narrated by, narrator(s)
n.d.	no date given
no.	number(s)
n.p.	no place of publication, no publisher given
n. pag.	no pagination
op. cit.	in the work cited; *opere citato*
p., pp.	page(s) (if necessary for clarity)
+	plus the pages that follow
pub. (or publ.)	published by, publication(s), publisher
rev.	revised by, revision, review, reviewed by
rpt.	reprinted by, reprint
sc.	scene
sec. (sect.)	section(s)
sic	thus in the source (used within brackets to indicate an error is that way in the original)
trans. (tr.)	translator, translation
viz.	namely; *videlicet*
vol.	volume(s): capitalize when used with numerals
vs. (v.)	versus (*v.* preferred in legal case titles)

IV

HANDBOOK

CONTENTS

■ Punctuation, Mechanics, Usage, and Grammar

■ Sentence Issues

■ Multilingual/ESL Issues

MARKING PUNCTUATION

Period

After Sentences

569.1

Use a **period** to end a sentence that makes a statement, requests something, or gives a mild command.

Statement: By 1997 almost 22 percent of females in the United States had received four or more years of college education**.**

Request: Please read the instructions carefully**.**

Mild command: If your topic sentence isn't clear, rewrite it**.**

Indirect question: The professor asked if we had completed the test**.**

Note: It is *not* necessary to place a period after a statement that has parentheses around it and is part of another sentence.

Think about joining a club **(the student affairs office has a list of organizations)** for fun and for leadership experience.

After Initials and Abbreviations

569.2

Use a period after an initial and some abbreviations.

Mr.	Mrs.	B.C.E.	Ph.D.	Sen. Daniel K. Inouye
Jr.	Sr.	D.D.S.	U.S.	Booker T. Washington
Dr.	M.A.	p.m.	B.A.	A. A. Milne

Some abbreviations (such as *pm*) also can be written without periods. Use no spacing in abbreviations except when providing a person's initials.

When an abbreviation is the last word in a sentence, use only one period at the end of the sentence.

Mikhail eyed each door until he found the name Rosa Lopez, **Ph.D.**

As Decimal Points

569.3

Use a period as a decimal point.

The government spends approximately **$15.5** million each year just to process student loan forms.

Ellipsis

570.1 ## To Show Omitted Words

Use an **ellipsis** (three periods) to show that one or more words have been omitted in a quotation. When typing, leave one space before and after each period.

(Original) We the people of the United States, in order to form a more perfect Union, establish justice, insure domestic tranquility, provide for the common defense, promote the general welfare, and secure the blessings of liberty to ourselves and our posterity, do ordain and establish this Constitution for the United States of America.

—Preamble, U.S. Constitution

(Quotation) "We the people . . . in order to form a more perfect Union . . . establish this Constitution for the United States of America."

Note: Omit internal punctuation (a comma, a semicolon, a colon, or a dash) on either side of the ellipsis marks unless it is needed for clarity.

570.2 ## To Use After Sentences

If words from a quotation are omitted at the end of a sentence, place the ellipsis after the period or other end punctuation.

(Quotation) "Five score years ago, a great American, in whose symbolic shadow we stand, signed the Emancipation Proclamation. . . . But one hundred years later, we must face the tragic fact that the Negro is still not free."

—Martin Luther King, Jr., "I Have a Dream"

The first word of a sentence following a period and an ellipsis may be capitalized, even though it was not capitalized in the original.

(Quotation) "Five score years ago, a great American . . . signed the Emancipation Proclamation. . . . One hundred years later, . . . the Negro is still not free."

Note: If the quoted material forms a complete sentence (even if it was not in the original), use a period, then an ellipsis.

(Original) I am tired; my heart is sick and sad. From where the sun now stands I will fight no more forever.

—Chief Joseph of the Nez Percé

(Quotation) "I am tired. . . . I will fight no more forever."

570.3 ## To Show Pauses

Use an ellipsis to indicate a pause or to show unfinished thoughts.

Listen . . . did you hear that?

I can't figure out . . . this number doesn't . . . just how do I apply the equation in this case?

Comma

Exercise
571.1

Between Independent Clauses

Use a **comma** between independent clauses that are joined by a coordinating conjunction (*and, but, or, nor, for, yet, so*). (See **644.2**.)

> The most expensive film ever made was *Titanic*, **but** the largest makeup budget for any film was $1 million for *Planet of the Apes.*

Note: Do not confuse a compound verb with a compound sentence.

> The $1 million makeup budget for *Planet of the Apes* <u>shocked</u> Hollywood **and** <u>made</u> producers uneasy. (compound verb)

> The $1 million makeup budget was 17 percent of the film's total production cost, **but** the film became a box-office hit and financial success. (compound sentence)

571.2

Between Items in a Series

Use commas to separate individual words, phrases, or clauses in a series. (A series contains at least three items.)

> Many college students must balance studying with **taking care of a family, working a job, getting exercise, and finding time to relax.**

Note: Do *not* use commas when all the items in a series are connected with *or, nor,* or *and.*

> Hmm . . . should I study **or** do laundry **or** go out?

571.3

To Separate Adjectives

Use commas to separate adjectives that *equally* modify the same noun. Notice in the examples below that no comma separates the last adjective from the noun.

> You should exercise regularly and follow a **sensible, healthful** diet.

> A good diet is one that includes lots of **high-protein, low-fat** foods.

Video

To Determine Equal Modifiers

To determine whether the adjectives in a sentence modify a noun *equally*, use these two tests.

1. Reverse the order of the adjectives; if the sentence is clear, the adjectives modify equally. (In the example below, *hot* and *crowded* can be reversed, and the sentence is still clear; *short* and *coffee* cannot.)

> Matt was tired of working in the **hot, crowded** lab and decided to take a **short coffee** break.

2. Insert *and* between the adjectives; if the sentence reads well, use a comma when *and* is omitted. (The word *and* can be inserted between *hot* and *crowded*, but *and* does not make sense between *short* and *coffee*.)

572.1

To Set Off Nonrestrictive Appositives

A specific kind of explanatory word or phrase called an **appositive** identifies or renames a preceding noun or pronoun.

> Albert Einstein, **the famous mathematician and physicist,** developed the theory of relativity.

Note: Do *not* use commas with *restrictive appositives.* A restrictive appositive is essential to the basic meaning of the sentence.

> The famous mathematician and physicist **Albert Einstein** developed the theory of relativity.

572.2

To Set Off Adverb Dependent Clauses

Use a comma after most introductory dependent clauses functioning as adverbs.

> **Although Charlemagne was a great patron of learning,** he never learned to write properly. (adverb dependent clause)

You may use a comma if the adverb dependent clause following the independent clause is not essential. Adverb clauses beginning with *even though, although, while,* or another conjunction expressing a contrast are usually not needed to complete the meaning of a sentence.

> Charlemagne never learned to write properly, **even though he continued to practice.**

Note: A comma is *not* used if the dependent clause following the independent clause is needed to complete the meaning of the sentence.

> Maybe Charlemagne didn't learn **because he had an empire to run.**

572.3

After Introductory Phrases

Use a comma after introductory phrases.

> **In spite of his practicing,** Charlemagne's handwriting remained poor.

Note: A comma is usually omitted if the phrase follows an independent clause.

> Charlemagne's handwriting remained poor **in spite of his practicing.**

Also Note: You may omit the comma after a short (four or fewer words) introductory phrase unless it is needed to ensure clarity.

> **At 6:00 a.m.** he would rise and practice his penmanship.

572.4

To Set Off Transitional Expressions

Use a comma to set off conjunctive adverbs and transitional phrases. (See 576.2–576.3.)

> Handwriting is not, **as a matter of fact,** easy to improve upon later in life; **however,** it can be done if you are determined enough.

Note: If a transitional expression blends smoothly with the rest of the sentence, it does not need to be set off. *Example:* If you are in fact coming, I'll see you there.

Video

Exercise

573.1

A Closer Look
at Nonrestrictive and Restrictive Clauses and Phrases

Use Commas with
Nonrestrictive Clauses and Phrases

Use commas to enclose **nonrestrictive** (unnecessary) phrases or dependent (adjective) clauses. A nonrestrictive phrase or dependent clause adds information that is not necessary to the basic meaning of the sentence. For example, if the clause or phrase (in **boldface**) were left out of the two examples below, the meaning of the sentences would remain clear. Therefore, commas are used to set off the nonrestrictive information.

> The locker rooms in Swain Hall**, which were painted and updated last summer,** give professors a place to shower. (nonrestrictive clause)

> Work-study programs**, offered on many campuses,** give students the opportunity to earn tuition money. (nonrestrictive phrase)

Don't Use Commas with
Restrictive Clauses and Phrases

573.2

Do *not* use commas to set off **restrictive** (necessary) adjective clauses and phrases. A restrictive clause or phrase adds information that the reader needs to understand the sentence. For example, if the adjective clause and phrase (in **boldface**) were dropped from the examples below, the meaning would be unclear.

> Only the professors **who run at noon** use the locker rooms in Swain Hall to shower. (restrictive clause)

> Using tuition money **earned through work-study programs** is the only way some students can afford to go to college. (restrictive phrase)

Using "That" or "Which"

573.3

Use *that* to introduce restrictive (necessary) adjective clauses; use *which* to introduce nonrestrictive (unnecessary) adjective clauses. When the two words are used in this way, the reader can quickly distinguish the necessary information from the unnecessary.

Video

> Campus jobs **that are funded by the university** are awarded to students only. (restrictive)

> The cafeteria**, which is run by an independent contractor,** can hire nonstudents. (nonrestrictive)

Note: Clauses beginning with *who* can be either restrictive or nonrestrictive.

> Students **who pay for their own education** are highly motivated. (restrictive)

> The admissions counselor**, who has studied student records,** said that many returning students earn high GPAs in spite of demanding family obligations. (nonrestrictive)

574.1 ## To Set Off Items in Addresses and Dates

Use commas to set off items in an address and the year in a date.

> Send your letter to **1600 Pennsylvania Avenue, Washington, DC 20006, before January 1, 2009,** or send an e-mail to president@whitehouse.gov.

Note: *No* comma is placed between the state and ZIP code. Also, *no* comma separates the items if only the month and year are given: January 2009.

574.2 ## To Set Off Dialogue

Use commas to set off the words of the speaker from the rest of the sentence.

> **"Never be afraid to ask for help,"** advised Ms. Kane.

> **"With the evidence that we now have,"** Professor Thom said**, "many scientists believe there is life on Mars."**

574.3 ## To Separate Nouns of Direct Address

Use a comma to separate a noun of direct address from the rest of the sentence.

> **Jamie,** would you please stop whistling while I'm trying to work?

574.4 ## To Separate Interjections

Use a comma to separate a mild interjection from the rest of the sentence.

> **Okay,** so now what do I do?

Note: Exclamation points are used after strong interjections: Wow! You're kidding!

574.5 ## To Set Off Interruptions

Use commas to set off a word, phrase, or clause that interrupts the movement of a sentence. Such expressions usually can be identified through the following tests: (1) They may be omitted without changing the meaning of a sentence; and (2) they may be placed nearly anywhere in the sentence without changing its meaning.

> For me, **well,** it was just a good job gone!   —Langston Hughes, "A Good Job Gone"

> Lela**, as a general rule,** always comes to class ready for a pop quiz.

574.6 ## To Separate Numbers

Use commas to separate a series of numbers to distinguish hundreds, thousands, millions, and so on.

> Do you know how to write the amount **$2,025** on a check?

> **25,000   973,240   18,620,197**

To Enclose Explanatory Words

575.1

Use commas to enclose an explanatory word or phrase.

> Time management, **according to many professionals,** is such an important skill that it should be taught in college.

To Separate Contrasted Elements

575.2

Use commas to separate contrasted elements within a sentence.

> We work to become, **not to acquire.**   —Eugene Delacroix

> Where all think alike, **no one thinks very much.**   —Walter Lippmann

Before Tags

575.3

Use a comma before tags, which are short statements or questions at the ends of sentences.

> You studied for the test, **right?**

To Enclose Titles or Initials

575.4

Use commas to enclose a title or initials and given names that follow a surname.

> Until Martin, **Sr.,** was 15, he never had more than three months of schooling in any one year.
> —Ed Clayton, *Martin Luther King: The Peaceful Warrior*

> The genealogical files included the names Sanders, **L. H.,** and Sanders, **Lucy Hale.**

Note: Some style manuals no longer require commas around titles.

For Clarity or Emphasis

575.5

Use a comma for clarity or for emphasis. There will be times when none of the traditional rules call for a comma, but one will be needed to prevent misreading or to emphasize an important idea.

> What she does, does matter to us. (clarity)

> It may be those who do most, dream most. (emphasis)   —Stephen Leacock

---

Avoid Overusing Commas

The commas (in red) below are used incorrectly. Do *not* use a comma between the subject and its verb or the verb and its object.

> Current periodicals on the subject of psychology, are available at nearly all bookstores.

> I think she should read, *Psychology Today.*

Do *not* use a comma before an indirect quotation.

> My roommate said, that she doesn't understand the notes I took.

Semicolon

To Join Two Independent Clauses

Use a **semicolon** to join two or more closely related independent clauses that are not connected with a coordinating conjunction. In other words, each of the clauses could stand alone as a separate sentence.

> I was thrown out of college for cheating on the metaphysics exam; I looked into the soul of the boy next to me.
>
> —Woody Allen

576.2

Before Conjunctive Adverbs

Use a semicolon before a conjunctive adverb when the word clarifies the relationship between two independent clauses in a compound sentence. A comma often follows the conjunctive adverb. Common conjunctive adverbs include *also, besides, however, instead, meanwhile, then,* and *therefore.*

> Many college freshmen are on their own for the first time; **however,** others are already independent and even have families.

576.3

Before Transitional Phrases

Use a semicolon before a transitional phrase when the phrase clarifies the relationship between two independent clauses in a compound sentence. A comma usually follows the transitional phrase.

> Pablo was born in the Andes; **as a result,** he loves mountains.

Transitional Phrases			
after all	at the same time	in addition	in the first place
as a matter of fact	even so	in conclusion	on the contrary
as a result	for example	in fact	on the other hand
at any rate	for instance	in other words	

576.4

To Separate Independent Clauses Containing Commas

Use a semicolon to separate independent clauses that contain internal commas, even when the independent clauses are connected by a coordinating conjunction.

> Make sure your CD player, computer, bike, and other valuables are covered by a homeowner's insurance policy; and be sure to use the locks on your door, bike, and storage area.

576.5

To Separate Items in a Series That Contain Commas

Use a semicolon to separate items in a series that already contain commas.

> My favorite foods are pizza with pepperoni, onions, and olives; peanut butter and banana sandwiches; and liver with bacon, peppers, and onions.

Colon

Exercise
577.1

After Salutations

Use a **colon** after the salutation of a business letter.

Dear Mr. Spielberg**:**   Dear Professor Higgins**:**   Dear Members**:**

577.2

Between Numbers Indicating Time or Ratios

Use a colon between the hours, minutes, and seconds of a number indicating time.

8**:**30 p.m.   9**:**45 a.m.   10**:**24**:**55

Use a colon between two numbers in a ratio.

The ratio of computers to students is 1**:**20. (one to twenty)

577.3

For Emphasis

Use a colon to emphasize a word, a phrase, a clause, or a sentence that explains or adds impact to the main clause.

I have one goal for myself: to become the first person in my family to graduate from college.

577.4

To Distinguish Parts of Publications

Use a colon between a title and a subtitle, volume and page, and chapter and verse.

*Ron Brown**:** An Uncommon Life*   *Britannica* 4**:** 211   Psalm 23**:**1–6

577.5

To Introduce Quotations

Use a colon to introduce a quotation following a complete sentence.

John Locke is credited with this prescription for a good life: "A sound mind in a sound body."

Lou Gottlieb, however, offered this version: "A sound mind or a sound body— take your pick."

577.6

To Introduce a List

Use a colon to introduce a list following a complete sentence.

A college student needs a number of things to succeed: basic skills, creativity, and determination.

Avoid Colon Errors

Do *not* use a colon between a verb and its object or complement.

Dave likes**:** comfortable space and time to think. (**Incorrect**)

Dave likes two things**:** comfortable space and time to think. (**Correct**)

Hyphen

In Compound Words

578.1

Use a **hyphen** to make some compound words.

     great-great-grandfather (noun)   starry-eyed (adjective)

     mother-in-law (noun)   three-year-old (adjective)

Writers sometimes combine words in new and unexpected ways. Such combinations are usually hyphenated.

     And they pried pieces of **baked-too-fast** sunshine cake from the roofs of their mouths and looked once more into the boy's eyes.

                                           —Toni Morrison, *Song of Solomon*

Note: Consult a dictionary to find how it lists a particular compound word. Some compound words (*living room*) do not use a hyphen and are written separately. Some are written solid (*bedroom*). Some do not use a hyphen when the word is a noun (*ice cream*) but do use a hyphen when it is a verb or an adjective (*ice-cream sundae*).

To Join Letters and Words

578.2

Use a hyphen to join a capital letter or a lowercase letter to a noun or a participle.

     T-shirt   U-turn   V-shaped   x-ray

To Join Words in Compound Numbers

578.3

Use a hyphen to join the words in compound numbers from *twenty-one* to *ninety-nine* when it is necessary to write them out. (See **595.1**.)

     Forty-two people found seats in the cramped classroom.

Between Numbers in Fractions

578.4

Use a hyphen between the numerator and the denominator of a fraction, but not when one or both of these elements are already hyphenated.

     four-tenths   five-sixteenths   seven thirty-seconds (7/32)

In a Special Series

578.5

Use a hyphen when two or more words have a common element that is omitted in all but the last term.

     We have cedar posts in **four-**, **six-**, and **eight**-inch widths.

To Create New Words

578.6

Use a hyphen to form new words beginning with the prefixes *self*, *ex*, *all*, and *half*. Also use a hyphen to join any prefix to a proper noun, a proper adjective, or the official name of an office.

     post-Depression   mid-May   ex-mayor

To Prevent Confusion

Use a hyphen with prefixes or suffixes to avoid confusion or awkward spelling.

re-cover (not *recover*) the sofa   **shell-like** (not *shelllike*) shape

To Join Numbers

Use a hyphen to join numbers indicating a range, a score, or a vote.

Students study **30-40** hours a week.   The final score was **84-82**.

To Divide Words

Use a hyphen to divide a word between syllables at the end of a line of print.

Guidelines for Word Division

1. Leave enough of the word at the end of the line to identify the word.

2. Never divide a one-syllable word: **rained, skills, through.**

3. Avoid dividing a word of five or fewer letters: **paper, study, July.**

4. Never divide a one-letter syllable from the rest of the word: **omit-ted**, not **o-mitted.**

5. Always divide a compound word between its basic units: **sister-in-law,** not **sis-ter-in-law.**

6. Never divide abbreviations or contractions: **shouldn't**, not **should-n't.**

7. When a vowel is a syllable by itself, divide the word after the vowel: **epi-sode**, not **ep-isode.**

8. Avoid dividing a numeral: **1,000,000**, not **1,000,-000.**

9. Avoid dividing the last word in a paragraph.

10. Never divide the last word in more than two lines in a row.

11. Check a dictionary for acceptable word divisions.

To Form Adjectives

Use a hyphen to join two or more words that serve as a single-thought adjective before a noun.

In real life I am a large, **big-boned** woman with rough, **man-working** hands.

—Alice Walker, "Everyday Use"

Most single-thought adjectives are not hyphenated when they come after the noun. (Check the dictionary to be sure.)

In real life, I am large and **big boned.**

Note: When the first of these words is an adverb ending in *ly*, do *not* use a hyphen. Also, do *not* use a hyphen when a number or a letter is the final element in a single-thought adjective.

fresh**ly** painted barn   grade **A** milk (letter is the final element)

Exercise

Dash

580.1 To Set Off Nonessential Elements

Use a **dash** to set off nonessential elements—explanations, examples, or definitions—when you want to emphasize them.

> Near the semester's end—**and this is not always due to poor planning**—some students may find themselves in academic trouble.

> The term *caveat emptor*—**let the buyer beware**—is especially appropriate to Internet shopping.

Note: A dash is indicated by two hyphens--with no spacing before or after--in typewriter-generated material. Don't use a single hyphen when a dash (two hyphens) is required.

580.2 To Set Off an Introductory Series

Use a dash to set off an introductory series from the clause that explains the series.

> **Cereal, coffee, and a newspaper**—without these I can't get going in the morning.

580.3 To Show Missing Text

Use a dash to show that words or letters are missing.

> **Mr. —** won't let us marry.
>
> —Alice Walker, *The Color Purple*

580.4 To Show Interrupted Speech

Use a dash (or an ellipsis) to show interrupted or faltering speech in dialogue. (Also see 570.1.)

> Well, I—ah—had this terrible case of the flu, **and—then—ah—the** library closed because of that flash flood, **and—well—the** high humidity jammed my printer.
>
> —Excuse No. 101

> "You told me to tell her about the—"
> "Oh, just stop."
>
> —Joyce Carol Oates,
> "Why Don't You Come Live with Me It's Time"

580.5 For Emphasis

Use a dash in place of a colon to introduce or to emphasize a word, a series, a phrase, or a clause.

> **Jogging**—that's what he lives for.

> **Life is like a grindstone**—whether it grinds you down or polishes you up depends on what you're made of.

> **This is how the world moves**—not like an arrow, but a boomerang.
>
> —Ralph Ellison

Question Mark

Exercise
581.1

After Direct Questions

Use a **question mark** at the end of a direct question.

What can I know**?** What ought I to do**?** What may I hope**?**   —Immanuel Kant

Since when do you have to agree with people to defend them from injustice**?**

          —Lillian Hellman

581.2

Not After Indirect Questions

No question mark is used after an indirect question.

After listening to Edgar sing, Mr. Noteworthy asked him if he had ever had formal voice training.

Note: When a single-word question like *how, when,* or *why* is woven into the flow of a sentence, capitalization and special punctuation are not usually required.

The questions we need to address at our next board meeting are not *why* or *whether,* but *how* and *when.*

581.3

After Quotations That Are Questions

When a question ends with a quotation that is also a question, use only one question mark, and place it within the quotation marks. (Also see 582.4.)

Do you often ask yourself, "What should I be**?**"

581.4

To Show Uncertainty

Use a question mark within parentheses to show uncertainty about a word or phrase within a sentence.

This July will be the 34th **(?)** anniversary of the first moon walk.

Note: Do *not* use a question mark in this manner for formal writing.

581.5

For Questions in Parentheses or Dashes

A question within parentheses—or a question set off by dashes—is punctuated with a question mark unless the sentence ends with a question mark.

You must consult your handbook **(what choice do you have?)** when you need to know a punctuation rule.

Should I use your charge card (you have one, don't you), or should I pay cash?

Maybe somewhere in the pasts of these humbled people, there were cases of bad mothering or absent fathering or emotional neglect—**what family surviving the '50s was exempt?**—but I couldn't believe these human errors brought the physical changes in Frank.   —Mary Kay Blakely, *Wake Me When It's Over*

Exercise

Quotation Marks

Exercise

582.1   To Punctuate Titles of Works Within Other Works

Use **quotation marks** to punctuate some titles. (Also see 584.2.)

"Two Friends" (short story)
"New Car Designs" (newspaper article)
"Desperado" (song)
"Multiculturalism and the Language Battle" (lecture title)
"The New Admissions Game" (magazine article)
"Reflections on Advertising" (chapter in a book)
"Force of Nature" (television episode from *Star Trek: The Next Generation*)
"Annabel Lee" (short poem)

582.2   For Special Words

Use quotation marks (1) to show that a word is being discussed as a word, (2) to indicate that a word or phrase is directly quoted, (3) to indicate that a word is slang, or (4) to point out that a word is being used in a humorous or ironic way.

1. A commentary on the times is that the word **"honesty"** is now preceded by **"old-fashioned."**

2. She said she was **"incensed."**

3. I drank a Dixie and ate bar peanuts and asked the bartender where I could hear **"chanky-chank,"** as Cajuns call their music.   —William Least Heat-Moon, *Blue Highways*

4. In an attempt to be popular, he works very hard at being **"cute."**

Note: A word used as a word can also be set off with italics.

582.3   Placement of Periods or Commas

Always place periods and commas inside quotation marks.

"Dr. Slaughter wants you to have liquids, Will," Mama said anxiously. "He said not to give you any solid food tonight."   —Olive Ann Burns, *Cold Sassy Tree*

582.4   Placement of Exclamation Points or Question Marks

Video

Place an exclamation point or a question mark inside quotation marks when it punctuates both the main sentence and the quotation *or* just the quotation; place it outside when it punctuates the main sentence.

Do you often ask yourself, "What should I be?"

I almost croaked when he asked, "That won't be a problem, will it?"

Did he really say, "Finish this by tomorrow"?

582.5   Placement of Semicolons or Colons

Always place semicolons or colons outside quotation marks.

I just read "Computers and Creativity"; I now have some different ideas about the role of computers in the arts.

A Closer Look at Marking Quoted Material

For Direct Quotations

583.1

Use quotation marks before and after a direct quotation—a person's exact words.

> Sitting in my one-room apartment, I remember Mom saying, **"Don't go to the party with him."**

Note: Do *not* use quotation marks for *indirect* quotations.

> I remember Mom saying **that I should not date him.** (These are not the speaker's exact words.)

For Quoted Passages

583.2

Use quotation marks before and after a quoted passage. Any word that is not part of the original quotation must be placed inside brackets.

> **(Original)** First of all, it must accept responsibility for providing shelter for the homeless.

> **(Quotation)** "First of all, it **[the federal government]** must accept responsibility for providing shelter for the homeless."

Note: If you quote only part of the original passage, be sure to construct a sentence that is both accurate and grammatically correct.

> The report goes on to say that the federal government **"must accept responsibility for providing shelter for the homeless."**

For Long Quotations

583.3

If more than one paragraph is quoted, quotation marks are placed before each paragraph and at the end of the last paragraph **(Example A).** Quotations that are five or more lines (MLA style) or forty words or more (APA style) are usually set off from the text by indenting ten spaces from the left margin (a style called "block form"). Do not use quotation marks before or after a block-form quotation **(Example B),** except in cases where quotation marks appear in the original passage **(Example C).**

Example A **Example B** **Example C**

For Quoting Quotations

583.4

Use single quotation marks to punctuate quoted material within a quotation.

> **"I was lucky,"** said Jane. **"The proctor announced, 'Put your pencils down,'** just as I was filling in the last answer."

Italics (Underlining)

584.1 In Handwritten and Printed Material

Italics is a printer's term for a style of type that is slightly slanted. In this sentence, the word *happiness* is printed in italics. In material that is handwritten or typed on a machine that cannot print in italics, underline each word or letter that should be in italics.

> In <u>The Road to Memphis</u>, racism is a contagious disease.
> (typed or handwritten)

> Mildred Taylor's *The Road to Memphis* exposes racism. (printed)

584.2 In Titles

Video

Use italics to indicate the titles of magazines, newspapers, books, pamphlets, full-length plays, films, videos, radio and television programs, book-length poems, ballets, operas, lengthy musical compositions, CDs, paintings and sculptures, legal cases, websites, and the names of ships and aircraft. (Also see **582.1**)

> *Newsweek* (magazine)　　　　　　　*The Nutcracker* (ballet)
> *New York Times* (newspaper)　　　　*Babe* (film)
> *Sister Carrie* (book)　　　　　　　*The Thinker* (sculpture)
> *Othello* (play)　　　　　　　　　　*Nightline* (television program)
> *Enola Gay* (airplane)　　　　　　　*GeoCities* (website)
> *The Joshua Tree* (CD)　　　　　　　*College Loans* (pamphlet)
> *ACLU v. State of Ohio* (legal case)

Exercise

When one title appears within another title, punctuate as follows:

> **"The *Fresh Prince of Bel-Air* Rings True"** is an article I read.
> (title of TV program in an article title)

> He wants to watch **Inside the *New York Times*** on PBS tonight.
> (title of newspaper in title of TV program)

584.3 For Key Terms

Italics are often used for a key term in a discussion or for a technical term, especially when it is accompanied by its definition. Italicize the term the first time it is used. Thereafter, put the term in Roman type.

> This flower has a ***zygomorphic*** (bilateral symmetry) structure.

584.4 For Foreign Words and Scientific Names

Use italics for foreign words that have not been adopted into the English language; italics are also used to denote scientific names.

> Say ***arrivederci*** to your fears and try new activities. (foreign word)

> The voyageurs discovered the shy ***Castor canadensis,*** or North American beaver.
> (scientific name)

Parentheses

To Enclose Explanatory or Supplementary Material

585.1

Use **parentheses** to enclose explanatory or supplementary material that interrupts the normal sentence structure.

> The RA **(resident assistant)** became my best friend.

To Set Off Numbers in a List

585.2

Use parentheses to set off numbers used with a series of words or phrases.

> Dr. Beck told us **(1)** plan ahead, **(2)** stay flexible, and **(3)** follow through.

For Parenthetical Sentences

585.3

When using a full "sentence" within another sentence, do not capitalize it or use a period inside the parentheses.

> Your friend doesn't have the assignment **(he was just thinking about calling you)**, so you'll have to make a few more calls.

When the parenthetical sentence comes after the main sentence, capitalize and punctuate it the same way you would any other complete sentence.

> But Mom doesn't say boo to Dad; she's always sweet to him. **(Actually she's sort of sweet to everybody.)**
> —Norma Fox Mazer, *Up on Fong Mountain*

To Set Off References

585.4

Use parentheses to set off references to authors, titles, pages, and years.

> The statistics are alarming **(see page 9)** and demand action.

Note: For unavoidable parentheses within parentheses (. . . [. . .] . . .), use brackets. Avoid overuse of parentheses by using commas instead.

Diagonal

To Form Fractions or Show Choices

585.5

Use a **diagonal** (also called a *slash*) to form a fraction. Also place a diagonal between two words to indicate that either is acceptable.

> My **walking/running** shoe size is **5 1/2**; my dress shoes are **6 1/2**.

When Quoting Poetry

585.6

When quoting poetry, use a diagonal (with one space before and after) to show where each line ends in the actual poem.

> A dryness is upon the house / My father loved and tended. / Beyond his firm and sculptured door / His light and lease have ended.
> —Gwendolyn Brooks, "In Honor of David Anderson Brooks, My Father"

Brackets

Exercise

586.1 <u>With Words That Clarify</u>

Video

Use **brackets** before and after words that are added to clarify what another person has said or written.

> "They'd [**the sweat bees**] get into your mouth, ears, eyes, nose. You'd feel them all over you."
> —Marilyn Johnson and Sasha Nyary, "Roosevelts in the Amazon"

Note: The brackets indicate that the words *the sweat bees* are not part of the original quotation but were added for clarification. (See 583.2.)

586.2 <u>Around Comments by Someone Other Than the Author</u>

Place brackets around comments that have been added by someone other than the author or speaker.

> "In conclusion, *docendo discimus*. Let the school year begin!" [**Huh?**]

586.3 <u>Around Editorial Corrections</u>

Place brackets around an editorial correction or addition.

> "Brooklyn alone has 8 percent of lead poisoning [**victims**] nationwide," said Marjorie Moore.
> —Donna Actie, student writer

586.4 <u>Around the Word *Sic*</u>

Brackets should be placed around the word *sic* (Latin for "so" or "thus") in quoted material; the word indicates that an error appearing in the quoted material was made by the original speaker or writer.

> "There is a higher principal *[sic]* at stake here: Is the school administration aware of the situation?"

Exclamation Point

586.5 <u>To Express Strong Feeling</u>

Exercise

Use an **exclamation point** to express strong feeling. It may be placed at the end of a sentence (or an elliptical expression that stands for a sentence). Use exclamation points sparingly.

> "That's not the point," said Wangero. "These are all pieces of dresses Grandma used to wear. She did all this stitching by hand. **Imagine!**"
> —Alice Walker, "Everyday Use"

> Su-su-something's crawling up the back of my neck!
> —Mark Twain, *Roughing It*

> She was on tiptoe, stretching for an orange, when they heard, "**HEY YOU!**"
> —Beverley Naidoo, *Journey to Jo'burg*

Apostrophe

☑
Exercise
587.1

In Contractions

Use an **apostrophe** to show that one or more letters have been left out of two words joined to form a contraction.

don't → o is left out   **she'd** → **woul** is left out   **it's** → i is left out

Note: An apostrophe is also used to show that one or more numerals or letters have been left out of numbers or words.

class of **'02** → **20** is left out   good **mornin'** → **g** is left out

To Form Plurals

587.2

Use an apostrophe and an *s* to form the plural of a letter, a number, a sign, or a word discussed as a word.

A → **A's**   8 → **8's**   + → **+'s**
You use too many **and's** in your writing.

Note: If two apostrophes are called for in the same word, omit the second one.
Follow closely the do's and **don'ts** (not **don't's**) on the checklist.

To Form Singular Possessives

587.3

(( ))
Video

The possessive form of singular nouns is usually made by adding an apostrophe and an *s*.

Spock's ears   my **computer's** memory

Note: When a singular noun of more than one syllable ends with an *s* or a *z* sound, the possessive may be formed by adding just an apostrophe—or an apostrophe and an *s*. When the singular noun is a one-syllable word, however, the possessive is usually formed by adding both an apostrophe and an *s*.

Dallas' sports teams *or* **Dallas's** sports teams (two-syllable word)

Kiss's last concert   my **boss's** generosity (one-syllable words)

To Form Plural Possessives

587.4

The possessive form of plural nouns ending in *s* is made by adding just an apostrophe.

the **Joneses'** great-grandfather   **bosses'** offices

Note: For plural nouns not ending in *s*, add an apostrophe and *s*.

women's health issues   **children's** program

To Determine Ownership

You will punctuate possessives correctly if you remember that the word that comes immediately before the apostrophe is the owner.

girl's guitar (*girl* is the owner)   **girls'** guitar (*girls* are the owners)
boss's office (*boss* is the owner)   **bosses'** office (*bosses* are the owners)

588.1

Video

To Show Shared Possession

When possession is shared by more than one noun, use the possessive form for the last noun in the series.

Jason, Kamil, and **Elana's** sound system
(All three own the same system.)

Jason's, Kamil's, and Elana's sound systems
(Each owns a separate system.)

588.2

In Compound Nouns

The possessive of a compound noun is formed by placing the possessive ending after the last word.

his **mother-in-law's** name (singular)
the **secretary of state's** career (singular)

their **mothers-in-law's** names (plural)
the **secretaries of state's** careers (plural)

588.3

With Indefinite Pronouns

The possessive form of an indefinite pronoun is made by adding an apostrophe and an *s* to the pronoun. (See **623.4**.)

everybody's grades   **no one's** mistake   **one's** choice

In expressions using *else*, add the apostrophe and *s* after the last word.

anyone else's   **somebody else's**

588.4

To Show Time or Amount

Use an apostrophe and an *s* with an adjective that is part of an expression indicating time or amount.

yesterday's news   a **day's** wage   a **month's** pay

588.5

Punctuation Marks

´ (é)	Accent, acute	:	Colon	¶	Paragraph
` (è)	Accent, grave	,	Comma	( )	Parentheses
< >	Angle brackets	†	Dagger	.	Period
'	Apostrophe	—	Dash	?	Question mark
*	Asterisk	¨ (ä)	Dieresis	" "	Quotation marks
{ }	Braces	/	Diagonal/slash	§	Section
[ ]	Brackets	...	Ellipsis	;	Semicolon
^	Caret	!	Exclamation point	˜ (ñ)	Tilde
ç	Cedilla	-	Hyphen	___	Underscore
^ (â)	Circumflex	.....	Leaders		

CHECKING MECHANICS

Audio

Exercise

Capitalization

Proper Nouns and Adjectives

Capitalize all proper nouns and all proper adjectives (adjectives derived from proper nouns). The chart below provides a quick overview of capitalization rules. The pages following explain specific or special uses of capitalization.

Capitalization at a Glance

Days of the week . . . . **Sunday, Monday, Tuesday**
Months . . . . **June, July, August**
Holidays, holy days . . . . **Thanksgiving, Easter, Hanukkah**
Periods, events in history . . . . **Middle Ages, World War I**
Special events . . . . **Tate Memorial Dedication Ceremony**
Political parties. . . . . **Republican Party, Socialist Party**
Official documents . . . . **the Declaration of Independence**
Trade names . . . . **Oscar Mayer hot dogs, Pontiac Firebird**
Formal epithets . . . . **Alexander the Great**
Official titles. **Mayor John Spitzer, Senator Feinstein**
Official state nicknames . . . . **the Badger State, the Aloha State**
Geographical names
    Planets, heavenly bodies . . . .**Earth, Jupiter, the Milky Way**
    Continents . . . . **Australia, South America**
    Countries . . . . **Ireland, Grenada, Sri Lanka**
    States, provinces . . . . **Ohio, Utah, Nova Scotia**
    Cities, towns, villages . . . . **El Paso, Burlington, Wonewoc**
    Streets, roads, highways . . . .**Park Avenue, Route 66, Interstate 90**
    Sections of the United States
    and the world . . . .**the Southwest, the Far East**
    Landforms . . . . **the Rocky Mountains, the Kalahari Desert**
    Bodies of water . . . . **the Nile River, Lake Superior, Bee Creek**
    Public areas . . . . **Central Park, Yellowstone National Park**

590.1   First Words

Capitalize the first word in every sentence and the first word in a full-sentence direct quotation. (Also see 583.1.)

> **Attending** the orientation for new students is a good idea.
>
> Max suggested, "**Let's** take the guided tour of the campus first."

590.2   Sentences in Parentheses

Capitalize the first word in a sentence that is enclosed in parentheses if that sentence is not contained within another complete sentence.

> The bookstore has the software. (**Now** all I need is the computer.)

Note: Do *not* capitalize a sentence that is enclosed in parentheses and is located in the middle of another sentence. (Also see 585.3.)

> Your college will probably offer everything (**this** includes general access to a computer) that you'll need for a successful year.

590.3   Sentences Following Colons

Capitalize a complete sentence that follows a colon when that sentence is a formal statement, a quotation, or a sentence that you want to emphasize. (Also see 577.5.)

> Sydney Harris had this to say about computers: "**The** real danger is not that computers will begin to think like people, but that people will begin to think like computers."

590.4   Salutation and Complimentary Closing

In a letter, capitalize the first and all major words of the salutation. Capitalize only the first word of the complimentary closing.

> **Dear Personnel Director:**   **Sincerely** yours,

590.5   Sections of the Country

Words that indicate sections of the country are proper nouns and should be capitalized; words that simply indicate direction are not proper nouns.

> Many businesses move to the **South**. (section of the country)
>
> They move **south** to cut fuel costs and other expenses. (direction)

590.6   Languages, Ethnic Groups, Nationalities, and Religions

Capitalize languages, ethnic groups, nationalities, and religions.

> **African American   Latino   Navajo   French   Islam**

Nouns that refer to the Supreme Being and holy books are capitalized.

> **God   Allah   Jehovah   the Koran   Exodus   the Bible**

Titles

Capitalize the first word of a title, the last word, and every word in between except articles (*a, an, the*), short prepositions, *to* in an infinitive, and coordinating conjunctions. Follow this rule for titles of books, newspapers, magazines, poems, plays, songs, articles, films, works of art, and stories.

Going to Meet the Man	*Chicago Tribune*
"Nothing Gold Can Stay"	"Jobs in the Cyber Arena"
A Midsummer Night's Dream	*The War of the Roses*

Note: When citing titles in a bibliography, check the style manual you've been asked to follow. For example, in APA style, only the first word of a title is capitalized.

Organizations

Capitalize the name of an organization or a team and its members.

American Indian Movement	Democratic Party
Tampa Bay Buccaneers	Tucson Drama Club

Abbreviations

Capitalize abbreviations of titles and organizations. (Some other abbreviations are also capitalized. See pages 597–598.) (Also see 569.2.)

M.D.   Ph.D.   NAACP   C.E.   B.C.E.   GPA

Letters

Capitalize letters used to indicate a form or shape.

U-turn   **I**-beam   **S**-curve   **V**-shaped   **T**-shirt

Words Used as Names

Capitalize words like *father, mother, uncle, senator,* and *professor* when they are parts of titles that include a personal name or when they are substituted for proper nouns (especially in direct address). (Also see 574.3.)

Hello, **Senator** Feingold. (*Senator* is part of the name.)
Our **senator** is an environmentalist.

Who was your chemistry **professor** last quarter?
I had **Professor** Williams for Chemistry 101.

Note: To test whether a word is being substituted for a proper noun, simply read the sentence with a proper noun in place of the word. If the proper noun fits in the sentence, the word being tested should be capitalized. Usually the word is not capitalized if it follows a possessive—*my, his, our, your,* and so on.

Did **Dad (Brad)** pack the stereo in the trailer? (*Brad* works in this sentence.)

Did your **dad (Brad)** pack the stereo in the trailer? (*Brad* does not work in this sentence; the word *dad* follows the possessive *your.*)

592.1   ## Titles of Courses

Words such as *technology, history,* and *science* are proper nouns when they are included in the titles of specific courses; they are common nouns when they name a field of study.

> Who teaches **Art History 202?** (title of a specific course)
>
> Professor Bunker loves teaching **history.** (a field of study)

Note: The words *freshman, sophomore, junior,* and *senior* are not capitalized unless they are part of an official title.

> The **seniors** who maintained high GPAs were honored at the **Mount Mary Senior Honors Banquet.**

592.2   ## Internet and E-mail

The words *Internet* and *World Wide Web* are always capitalized because they are considered proper nouns. When your writing includes a web address (URL), capitalize any letters that the site's owner does (on printed materials or on the site itself). Not only is it respectful to reprint a web address exactly as it appears elsewhere, but, in fact, some web addresses are case-sensitive and must be entered into a browser's address bar exactly as presented.

> When doing research on the **Internet**, be sure to record each site's **web** address (**URL**) and each contact's **e-mail** address.

Note: Some people include capital letters in their e-mail addresses to make certain features evident. Although e-mail addresses are not case-sensitive, repeat each letter in print just as its owner uses it.

592.3

Avoid Capitalization Errors

Do not capitalize any of the following:

- A prefix attached to a proper noun
- Seasons of the year
- Words used to indicate direction or position
- Common nouns and titles that appear near, but are not part of, a proper noun

Capitalize	Do Not Capitalize
American	un-American
January, February	winter, spring
The South is quite conservative.	Turn south at the stop sign.
Duluth City College	a Duluth college
Chancellor John Bohm	John Bohm, our chancellor
President Bush	the president of the United States
Earth (the planet)	earthmover
Internet	e-mail

Plurals

✓
Exercise
593.1

Nouns Ending in a Consonant

Some nouns remain unchanged when used as plurals (*species, moose, halibut,* and so on), but the plurals of most nouns are formed by adding an *s* to the singular form.

>   dorm—**dorms**   credit—**credits**   midterm—**midterms**

The plurals of nouns ending in *sh, ch, x, s,* and *z* are made by adding *es* to the singular form.

>   lunch—**lunches**   wish—**wishes**   class—**classes**

Nouns Ending in *y*

593.2

The plurals of common nouns that end in *y* (preceded by a consonant) are formed by changing the *y* to *i* and adding *es*.

>   dormitory—**dormitories**   sorority—**sororities**   duty—**duties**

The plurals of common nouns that end in *y* (preceded by a vowel) are formed by adding only an *s*.

>   attorney—**attorneys**   monkey—**monkeys**   toy—**toys**

The plurals of all proper nouns ending in *y* (whether preceded by a consonant or a vowel) are formed by adding an *s*.

>   the three **Kathys**   the five **Faheys**

Nouns Ending in *o*

593.3

The plurals of words ending in *o* (preceded by a vowel) are formed by adding an *s*.

>   radio—**radios**   cameo—**cameos**   studio—**studios**

The plurals of most nouns ending in *o* (preceded by a consonant) are formed by adding *es*.

>   echo—**echoes**   hero—**heroes**   tomato—**tomatoes**

Musical terms always form plurals by adding an *s*; check a dictionary for other words of this type.

>   alto—**altos**   banjo—**banjos**   solo—**solos**   piano—**pianos**

Nouns Ending in *f* or *fe*

593.4

The plurals of nouns that end in *f* or *fe* are formed in one of two ways: If the final *f* sound is still heard in the plural form of the word, simply add *s*; if the final sound is a *v* sound, change the *f* to *ve* and add an *s*.

>   **Plural ends with *f* sound:** roof—**roofs**   chief—**chiefs**
>   **Plural ends with *v* sound:** wife—**wives**   loaf—**loaves**

Note: The plurals of some nouns that end in *f* or *fe* can be formed by either adding *s* or changing the *f* to *ve* and adding an *s*.

>   **Plural ends with either sound:** hoof—**hoofs, hooves**

594.1

Irregular Spelling

Many foreign words (as well as some of English origin) form a plural by taking on an irregular spelling; others are now acceptable with the commonly used *s* or *es* ending. Take time to check a dictionary.

child—**children**	alumnus—**alumni**	syllabus—**syllabi, syllabuses**
goose—**geese**	datum—**data**	radius—**radii, radiuses**

594.2

Words Discussed as Words

The plurals of symbols, letters, figures, and words discussed as words are formed by adding an apostrophe and an *s*.

Many colleges have now added **A/B's** and **B/C's** as standard grades.

Note: You can choose to omit the apostrophe when the omission does not cause confusion.

YMCA's or YMCAs   CD's or CDs

594.3

Nouns Ending in *ful*

The plurals of nouns that end with *ful* are formed by adding an *s* at the end of the word.

three **teaspoonfuls**   two **tankfuls**   four **bagfuls**

594.4

Compound Nouns

The plurals of compound nouns are usually formed by adding an *s* or an *es* to the important word in the compound. (Also see **578.1**.)

brothers-in-law   **maids** of honor   **secretaries** of state

594.5

Collective Nouns

Collective nouns do not change in form when they are used as plurals.

class (a unit—singular form)

class (individual members—plural form)

Because the spelling of the collective noun does not change, it is often the pronoun used in place of the collective noun that indicates whether the noun is singular or plural. Use a singular pronoun (**its**) to show that the collective noun is singular. Use a plural pronoun (**their**) to show that the collective noun is plural.

The class needs to change **its** motto.
(The writer is thinking of the group as a unit.)

The class brainstormed with **their** professor.
(The writer is thinking of the group as individuals.)

esl Note: To determine whether a plural requires the article *the*, you must first determine whether it is definite or indefinite. Definite plurals use *the*, whereas indefinite plurals do not require any article. (See **658.3–659.1**.)

Numbers

Exercise
595.1

Numerals or Words

Numbers from one to one hundred are usually written as words; numbers 101 and greater are usually written as numerals. (APA style uses numerals for numbers 10 and higher.) Hyphenate numbers written as two words if less than one hundred.

two   seven   ten   twenty-five   106   1,079

The same rule applies to the use of ordinal numbers.

second   tenth   twenty-fifth   ninety-eighth   106th   333rd

If numbers greater than 101 are used infrequently in a piece of writing, you may spell out those that can be written in one or two words.

two hundred   fifty thousand   six billion

You may use a combination of numerals and words for very large numbers.

1.5 million   3 billion to 3.2 billion   6 trillion

Numbers being compared or contrasted should be kept in the same style.

8 to **11** years old *or* **eight** to **eleven** years old

Particular decades may be spelled out or written as numerals.

the **'80s** and **'90s** *or* the **eighties** and **nineties**

Numerals Only

595.2

Use numerals for the following forms: decimals, percentages, pages, chapters (and other parts of a book), addresses, dates, telephone numbers, identification numbers, and statistics.

26.2	**8** percent	Chapter **7**
pages **287–289**	Highway **36**	**(212) 555–1234**
398-55-0000	a vote of **23** to **4**	May **8, 2007**

Note: Abbreviations and symbols are often used in charts, graphs, footnotes, and so forth, but typically they are not used in texts.

He is **five feet one inch** tall and **ten years old.**

She walked **three and one-half miles** to work through **twelve inches** of snow.

However, abbreviations and symbols may be used in scientific, mathematical, statistical, and technical texts (APA style).

Between **20%** and **23%** of the cultures yielded positive results.

Your **245B** model requires **220V.**

Always use numerals with abbreviations and symbols.

5'4"   8%   10 in.   **3** tbsp.   **6** lb. **8** oz.   **90°F**

Use numerals after the name of local branches of labor unions.

The Office and Professional Employees International Union, Local **8**

596.1   <u>Hyphenated Numbers</u>

Hyphens are used to form compound modifiers indicating measurement. They are also used for inclusive numbers and written-out fractions.

a **three-mile** trip	the **2001–2005** presidential term
a **2,500-mile** road trip	**one-sixth** of the pie
a **thirteen-foot** clearance	**three-eighths** of the book

596.2   <u>Time and Money</u>

If time is expressed with an abbreviation, use numerals; if it is expressed in words, spell out the number.

> **4:00** a.m. *or* **four** o'clock (not 4 o'clock)
>
> the **5:15** p.m. train
>
> a **seven o'clock** wake-up call

If money is expressed with a symbol, use numerals; if the currency is expressed in words, spell out the number.

> **$20** or **twenty** dollars (not 20 dollars)

Abbreviations of time and of money may be used in text.

> The concert begins at **7:00** p.m., and tickets cost **$30**.

596.3   <u>Words Only</u>

Use words to express numbers that begin a sentence.

> **Fourteen** students "forgot" their assignments.
>
> **Three hundred** contest entries were received.

Note: Change the sentence structure if this rule creates a clumsy construction.

> **Six hundred thirty-nine** students are new to the campus this fall. (Clumsy)
>
> This fall, **639** students are new to the campus. (Better)

Use words for numbers that precede a compound modifier that includes a numeral. (If the compound modifier uses a spelled-out number, use numerals in front of it.)

> She sold **twenty 35-millimeter** cameras in one day.
>
> The chef prepared **24 eight-ounce** filets.

Use words for the names of numbered streets of one hundred or less.

> **Ninth** Avenue
>
> **123 Forty-fourth** Street

Use words for the names of buildings if that name is also its address.

> **One Thousand State Street**   **Two Fifty Park Avenue**

Use words for references to particular centuries.

> **the twenty-first century**   **the fourth century B.C.E.**

Abbreviations

An **abbreviation** is the shortened form of a word or a phrase. These abbreviations are always acceptable in both formal and informal writing:

Mr.   Mrs.   Ms.   Dr.   Jr.   a.m. (A.M.)   p.m. (P.M.)

Exercise

Note: In formal writing, do not abbreviate the names of states, countries, months, days, units of measure, or courses of study. Do not abbreviate the words *Street, Road, Avenue, Company,* and similar words when they are part of a proper name. Also, do not use signs or symbols (%, &, #, @) in place of words. (The dollar sign, however, is appropriate when numerals are used to express an amount of money. See 596.2.)

Also Note: When abbreviations are called for (in charts, lists, bibliographies, notes, and indexes, for example), standard abbreviations are preferred. Reserve the postal abbreviations for ZIP code addresses.

Correspondence Abbreviations

States/Territories

	Standard	Postal
Alabama	Ala.	AL
Alaska	Alaska	AK
Arizona	Ariz.	AZ
Arkansas	Ark.	AR
California	Cal.	CA
Colorado	Colo.	CO
Connecticut	Conn.	CT
Delaware	Del.	DE
District of Columbia	D.C.	DC
Florida	Fla.	FL
Georgia	Ga.	GA
Guam	Guam	GU
Hawaii	Hawaii	HI
Idaho	Idaho	ID
Illinois	Ill.	IL
Indiana	Ind.	IN
Iowa	Ia.	IA
Kansas	Kans.	KS
Kentucky	Ky.	KY
Louisiana	La.	LA
Maine	Me.	ME
Maryland	Md.	MD
Massachusetts	Mass.	MA
Michigan	Mich.	MI
Minnesota	Minn.	MN
Mississippi	Miss.	MS
Missouri	Mo.	MO
Montana	Mont.	MT
Nebraska	Neb.	NE
Nevada	Nev.	NV
New Hampshire	N.H.	NH
New Jersey	N.J.	NJ
New Mexico	N. Mex.	NM
New York	N.Y.	NY
North Carolina	N.C.	NC
North Dakota	N. Dak.	ND
Ohio	Ohio	OH

	Standard	Postal
Oklahoma	Okla.	OK
Oregon	Ore.	OR
Pennsylvania	Pa.	PA
Puerto Rico	P.R.	PR
Rhode Island	R.I.	RI
South Carolina	S.C.	SC
South Dakota	S. Dak.	SD
Tennessee	Tenn.	TN
Texas	Tex.	TX
Utah	Utah	UT
Vermont	Vt.	VT
Virginia	Va.	VA
Virgin Islands	V.I.	VI
Washington	Wash.	WA
West Virginia	W. Va.	WV
Wisconsin	Wis.	WI
Wyoming	Wyo.	WY

Canadian Provinces

	Standard	Postal
Alberta	Alta.	AB
British Columbia	B.C.	BC
Labrador	Lab.	LB
Manitoba	Man.	MB
New Brunswick	N.B.	NB
Newfoundland	N.F.	NF
Northwest Territories	N.W.T.	NT
Nova Scotia	N.S.	NS
Nunavut		NU
Ontario	Ont.	ON
Prince Edward Island	P.E.I.	PE
Quebec	Que.	PQ
Saskatchewan	Sask.	SK
Yukon Territory	Y.T.	YT

Address Abbreviations

	Standard	Postal
Apartment	Apt.	APT
Avenue	Ave.	AVE
Boulevard	Blvd.	BLVD
Circle	Cir.	CIR
Court	Ct.	CT
Drive	Dr.	DR
East	E.	E
Expressway	Expy.	EXPY
Freeway	Frwy.	FWY
Heights	Hts.	HTS
Highway	Hwy.	HWY
Hospital	Hosp.	HOSP
Junction	Junc.	JCT
Lake	L.	LK
Lakes	Ls.	LKS
Lane	Ln.	LN
Meadows	Mdws.	MDWS
North	N.	N
Palms	Palms	PLMS
Park	Pk.	PK
Parkway	Pky.	PKY
Place	Pl.	PL
Plaza	Plaza	PLZ
Post Office Box	P.O. Box	PO BOX
Ridge	Rdg.	RDG
River	R.	RV
Road	Rd.	RD
Room	Rm.	RM
Rural	R.	R
Rural Route	R.R.	RR
Shore	Sh.	SH
South	S.	S
Square	Sq.	SQ
Station	Sta.	STA
Street	St.	ST
Suite	Ste.	STE
Terrace	Ter.	TER
Turnpike	Tpke.	TPKE
Union	Un.	UN
View	View	VW
Village	Vil.	VLG
West	W.	W

Common Abbreviations

abr. abridged, abridgment

AC, ac alternating current, air-conditioning

ack. acknowledgment

AM amplitude modulation

A.M., a.m. before noon (Latin *ante meridiem*)

AP advanced placement

ASAP as soon as possible

avg., av. average

B.A. bachelor of arts degree

BBB Better Business Bureau

B.C.E. before common era

bibliog. bibliography

biog. biographer, biographical, biography

B.S. bachelor of science degree

C 1. Celsius **2.** centigrade **3.** coulomb

c. 1. *circa* (about) **2.** cup(s)

cc 1. cubic centimeter **2.** carbon copy **3.** community college

CDT, C.D.T. central daylight time

C.E. common era

CEEB College Entrance Examination Board

chap. chapter(s)

cm centimeter(s)

c/o care of

COD, c.o.d. 1. cash on delivery **2.** collect on delivery

co-op cooperative

CST, C.S.T. central standard time

cu 1. cubic **2.** cumulative

D.A. district attorney

d.b.a., d/b/a doing business as

DC, dc direct current

dec. deceased

dept. department

disc. discount

DST, D.S.T. daylight saving time

dup. duplicate

ed. edition, editor

e.g. for example (Latin *exempli gratia*)

EST, E.S.T. eastern standard time

etc. and so forth (Latin *et cetera*)

F Fahrenheit, French, Friday

FM frequency modulation

F.O.B., f.o.b. free on board

FYI for your information

g 1. gravity **2.** gram(s)

gal. gallon(s)

gds. goods

gloss. glossary

GNP gross national product

GPA grade point average

hdqrs. headquarters

HIV human immunodeficiency virus

hp horsepower

Hz hertz

ibid. in the same place (Latin *ibidem*)

id. the same (Latin *idem*)

i.e. that is (Latin *id est*)

illus. illustration

inc. incorporated

IQ, I.Q. intelligence quotient

IRS Internal Revenue Service

ISBN International Standard Book Number

JP, J.P. justice of the peace

K 1. kelvin (temperature unit) **2.** Kelvin (temperature scale)

kc kilocycle(s)

kg kilogram(s)

km kilometer(s)

kn knot(s)

kw kilowatt(s)

L liter(s), lake

lat. latitude

l.c. lowercase

lit. literary; literature

log logarithm, logic

long. longitude

Ltd., ltd. limited

m meter(s)

M.A. master of arts degree

man. manual

Mc, mc megacycle

MC master of ceremonies

M.D. doctor of medicine (Latin *medicinae doctor*)

mdse. merchandise

mfg. manufacture, manufacturing

mg milligram(s)

mi. 1. mile(s) **2.** mill(s) (monetary unit)

misc. miscellaneous

mL milliliter(s)

mm millimeter(s)

mpg, m.p.g. miles per gallon

mph, m.p.h. miles per hour

MS 1. manuscript **2.** multiple sclerosis

Ms. title of courtesy for a woman

M.S. master of science degree

MST, M.S.T. mountain standard time

NE northeast

neg. negative

N.S.F., n.s.f. not sufficient funds

NW northwest

oz, oz. ounce(s)

PA public-address system

pct. percent

pd. paid

PDT, P.D.T. Pacific daylight time

PFC, Pfc. private first class

pg., p. page

Ph.D. doctor of philosophy

P.M., p.m. after noon (Latin *post meridiem*)

POW, P.O.W. prisoner of war

pp. pages

ppd. 1. postpaid **2.** prepaid

PR, P.R. public relations

PSAT Preliminary Scholastic Aptitude Test

psi, p.s.i. pounds per square inch

PST, P.S.T. Pacific standard time

PTA, P.T.A. Parent-Teacher Association

R.A. residence assistant

RF radio frequency

R.P.M., rpm revolutions per minute

R.S.V.P., r.s.v.p. please reply (French *répondez s'il vous plaît*)

SAT Scholastic Aptitude Test

SE southeast

SOS 1. international distress signal **2.** any call for help

Sr. 1. senior (after surname) **2.** sister (religious)

SRO, S.R.O. standing room only

std. standard

SW southwest

syn. synonymous, synonym

tbs., tbsp. tablespoon(s)

TM trademark

UHF, uhf ultrahigh frequency

v 1. physics: velocity **2.** volume

V electricity: volt

VA Veterans Administration

VHF, vhf very high frequency

VIP informal: very important person

vol. 1. volume **2.** volunteer

vs. versus, verse

W 1. electricity: watt(s) **2.** physics: (also **w**) work **3.** west

whse., whs. warehouse

whsle. wholesale

wkly. weekly

w/o without

wt. weight

www World Wide Web

Acronyms and Initialisms

Acronyms

An **acronym** is a word formed from the first (or first few) letters of words in a set phrase. Even though acronyms are abbreviations, they require no periods.

radar	radio detecting and ranging
CARE	Cooperative for Assistance and Relief Everywhere
NASA	National Aeronautics and Space Administration
VISTA	Volunteers in Service to America
FICA	Federal Insurance Contributions Act

Initialisms

An **initialism** is similar to an acronym except that the initials used to form this abbreviation are pronounced individually.

CIA	Central Intelligence Agency
FBI	Federal Bureau of Investigation
FHA	Federal Housing Administration

Common Acronyms and Initialisms

AIDS	acquired immune deficiency syndrome	**OSHA**	Occupational Safety and Health Administration
APR	annual percentage rate	**PAC**	political action committee
CAD	computer-aided design	**PIN**	personal identification number
CAM	computer-aided manufacturing	**POP**	point of purchase
CETA	Comprehensive Employment and Training Act	**PSA**	public service announcement
FAA	Federal Aviation Administration	**REA**	Rural Electrification Administration
FCC	Federal Communications Commission	**RICO**	Racketeer Influenced and Corrupt Organizations (Act)
FDA	Food and Drug Administration	**ROTC**	Reserve Officers' Training Corps
FDIC	Federal Deposit Insurance Corporation	**SADD**	Students Against Destructive Decisions
		SASE	self-addressed stamped envelope
FEMA	Federal Emergency Management Agency	**SPOT**	satellite positioning and tracking
FHA	Federal Housing Administration	**SSA**	Social Security Administration
FTC	Federal Trade Commission	**SUV**	sport-utility vehicle
IRS	Internal Revenue Service	**SWAT**	Special Weapons and Tactics
MADD	Mothers Against Drunk Driving	**TDD**	telecommunications device for the deaf
NAFTA	North American Free Trade Agreement	**TMJ**	temporomandibular joint
		TVA	Tennessee Valley Authority
NATO	North Atlantic Treaty Organization	**VA**	Veterans Administration
OEO	Office of Economic Opportunity	**WHO**	World Health Organization
ORV	off-road vehicle		

Exercise

Basic Spelling Rules

600.1 Write *i* Before *e*

Write *i* before *e* except after *c*, or when sounded like *a* as in *neighbor* and *weigh*.

believe **relief** **receive** **eight**

Note: This sentence contains eight exceptions:

Neither sheik dared **leisurely seize either weird species** of **financiers.**

600.2 Words with Consonant Endings

When a one-syllable word (*bat*) ends in a consonant (*t*) preceded by one vowel (*a*), double the final consonant before adding a suffix that begins with a vowel (*batting*).

sum—**summary** god—**goddess**

Note: When a multisyllable word (*control*) ends in a consonant (*l*) preceded by one vowel (*o*), the accent is on the last syllable (*con trol´*), and the suffix begins with a vowel (*ing*)—the same rule holds true: Double the final consonant (*controlling*).

prefer—**preferred** begin—**beginning**
forget—**forgettable** admit—**admittance**

600.3 Words with a Final Silent *e*

If a word ends with a silent *e*, drop the *e* before adding a suffix that begins with a vowel. Do *not* drop the *e* when the suffix begins with a consonant.

state—**stating**—**statement** like—**liking**—**likeness**
use—**using**—**useful** nine—**ninety**—**nineteen**

Note: Exceptions are **judgment, truly, argument, ninth.**

600.4 Words Ending in *y*

When *y* is the last letter in a word and the *y* is preceded by a consonant, change the *y* to *i* before adding any suffix except those beginning with *i*.

fry—**fries, frying** hurry—**hurried, hurrying**
lady—**ladies** ply—**pliable**
happy—**happiness** beauty—**beautiful**

Note: When forming the plural of a word that ends with a *y* that is preceded by a vowel, add *s*.

toy—**toys** play—**plays** monkey—**monkeys**

TIP: Never trust your spelling to even the best spell checker. Carefully proofread and use a dictionary for words you know your spell checker does not cover.

Commonly Misspelled Words

The commonly misspelled words that follow are hyphenated to show where they would logically be broken at the end of a line.

A

ab-bre-vi-ate
a-brupt
ab-scess
ab-sence
ab-so-lute (-ly)
ab-sorb-ent
ab-surd
a-bun-dance
ac-a-dem-ic
ac-cede
ac-cel-er-ate
ac-cept (-ance)
ac-ces-si-ble
ac-ces-so-ry
ac-ci-den-tal-ly
ac-com-mo-date
ac-com-pa-ny
ac-com-plice
ac-com-plish
ac-cor-dance
ac-cord-ing
ac-count
ac-crued
ac-cu-mu-late
ac-cu-rate
ac-cus-tom (-ed)
ache
a-chieve (-ment)
ac-knowl-edge
ac-quaint-ance
ac-qui-esce
ac-quired
ac-tu-al
a-dapt
ad-di-tion (-al)
ad-dress
ad-e-quate
ad-journed
ad-just-ment
ad-mi-ra-ble
ad-mis-si-ble
ad-mit-tance
ad-van-ta-geous
ad-ver-tise-ment

ad-ver-tis-ing
ad-vice (n.)
ad-vis-able
ad-vise (v.)
ad-vis-er
ae-ri-al
af-fect
af-fi-da-vit
a-gainst
ag-gra-vate
ag-gres-sion
a-gree-able
a-gree-ment
aisle
al-co-hol
a-lign-ment
al-ley
al-lot-ted
al-low-ance
all right
al-most
al-ready
al-though
al-to-geth-er
a-lu-mi-num
al-um-nus
al-ways
am-a-teur
a-mend-ment
a-mong
a-mount
a-nal-y-sis
an-a-lyze
an-cient
an-ec-dote
an-es-thet-ic
an-gle
an-ni-hi-late
an-ni-ver-sa-ry
an-nounce
an-noy-ance
an-nu-al
a-noint
a-non-y-mous
an-swer
ant-arc-tic

an-tic-i-pate
anx-i-ety
anx-ious
a-part-ment
a-pol-o-gize
ap-pa-ra-tus
ap-par-ent (-ly)
ap-peal
ap-pear-ance
ap-pe-tite
ap-pli-ance
ap-pli-ca-ble
ap-pli-ca-tion
ap-point-ment
ap-prais-al
ap-pre-ci-ate
ap-proach
ap-pro-pri-ate
ap-prov-al
ap-prox-i-mate-ly
ap-ti-tude
ar-chi-tect
arc-tic
ar-gu-ment
a-rith-me-tic
a-rouse
ar-range-ment
ar-riv-al
ar-ti-cle
ar-ti-fi-cial
as-cend
as-cer-tain
as-i-nine
as-sas-sin
as-sess (-ment)
as-sign-ment
as-sist-ance
as-so-ci-ate
as-so-ci-a-tion
as-sume
as-sur-ance
as-ter-isk
ath-lete
ath-let-ic
at-tach
at-tack (-ed)

at-tempt
at-tend-ance
at-ten-tion
at-ti-tude
at-tor-ney
at-trac-tive
au-di-ble
au-di-ence
au-dit
au-thor-i-ty
au-to-mo-bile
au-tumn
aux-il-ia-ry
a-vail-a-ble
av-er-age
aw-ful
aw-ful-ly
awk-ward

B

bac-ca-lau-re-ate
bach-e-lor
bag-gage
bal-ance
bal-loon
bal-lot
ba-nan-a
ban-dage
bank-rupt
bar-gain
bar-rel
base-ment
ba-sis
bat-tery
beau-ti-ful
beau-ty
be-com-ing
beg-gar
be-gin-ning
be-hav-ior
be-ing
be-lief
be-lieve
ben-e-fi-cial
ben-e-fit (-ed)
be-tween

bi-cy-cle
bis-cuit
bliz-zard
book-keep-er
bought
bouil-lon
bound-a-ry
break-fast
breath (n.)
breathe (v.)
brief
bril-liant
Brit-ain
bro-chure
brought
bruise
bud-get
bul-le-tin
buoy-ant
bu-reau
bur-glar
bury
busi-ness
busy

C

caf-e-te-ria
caf-feine
cal-en-dar
cam-paign
can-celed
can-di-date
can-is-ter
ca-noe
ca-pac-i-ty
cap-i-tal
cap-i-tol
cap-tain
car-bu-ret-or
ca-reer
car-i-ca-ture
car-riage
cash-ier
cas-se-role
cas-u-al-ty
cat-a-log

ca-tas-tro-phe
caught
cav-al-ry
cel-e-bra-tion
cem-e-ter-y
cen-sus
cen-tu-ry
cer-tain
cer-tif-i-cate
ces-sa-tion
chal-lenge
chan-cel-lor
change-a-ble
char-ac-ter (-is-tic)
chauf-feur
chief
chim-ney
choc-o-late
choice
choose
Chris-tian
cir-cuit
cir-cu-lar
cir-cum-stance
civ-i-li-za-tion
cli-en-tele
cli-mate
climb
clothes
coach
co-coa
co-er-cion
col-lar
col-lat-er-al
col-lege
col-le-giate
col-lo-qui-al
colo-nel
col-or
co-los-sal
col-umn
com-e-dy
com-ing
com-mence
com-mer-cial
com-mis-sion
com-mit
com-mit-ment
com-mit-ted
com-mit-tee
com-mu-ni-cate

com-mu-ni-ty
com-par-a-tive
com-par-i-son
com-pel
com-pe-tent
com-pe-ti-tion
com-pet-i-tive-ly
com-plain
com-ple-ment
com-plete-ly
com-plex-ion
com-pli-ment
com-pro-mise
con-cede
con-ceive
con-cern-ing
con-cert
con-ces-sion
con-clude
con-crete
con-curred
con-cur-rence
con-demn
con-de-scend
con-di-tion
con-fer-ence
con-ferred
con-fi-dence
con-fi-den-tial
con-grat-u-late
con-science
con-sci-en-tious
con-scious
con-sen-sus
con-se-quence
con-ser-va-tive
con-sid-er-ably
con-sign-ment
con-sis-tent
con-sti-tu-tion
con-tempt-ible
con-tin-u-al-ly
con-tin-ue
con-tin-u-ous
con-trol
con-tro-ver-sy
con-ven-ience
con-vince
cool-ly
co-op-er-ate
cor-dial

cor-po-ra-tion
cor-re-late
cor-re-spond
cor-re-spond-
    ence
cor-rob-o-rate
cough
coun-cil
coun-sel
coun-ter-feit
coun-try
cour-age
cou-ra-geous
cour-te-ous
cour-te-sy
cous-in
cov-er-age
cred-i-tor
cri-sis
crit-i-cism
crit-i-cize
cru-el
cu-ri-os-i-ty
cu-ri-ous
cur-rent
cur-ric-u-lum
cus-tom
cus-tom-ary
cus-tom-er
cyl-in-der

D

dai-ly
dair-y
dealt
debt-or
de-ceased
de-ceit-ful
de-ceive
de-cid-ed
de-ci-sion
dec-la-ra-tion
dec-o-rate
de-duct-i-ble
de-fend-ant
de-fense
de-ferred
def-i-cit
def-i-nite (-ly)
def-i-ni-tion

del-e-gate
de-li-cious
de-pend-ent
de-pos-i-tor
de-pot
de-scend
de-scribe
de-scrip-tion
de-sert
de-serve
de-sign
de-sir-able
de-sir-ous
de-spair
des-per-ate
de-spise
des-sert
de-te-ri-o-rate
de-ter-mine
de-vel-op
de-vel-op-ment
de-vice
de-vise
di-a-mond
di-a-phragm
di-ar-rhe-a
dic-tio-nary
dif-fer-ence
dif-fer-ent
dif-fi-cul-ty
di-lap-i-dat-ed
di-lem-ma
din-ing
di-plo-ma
di-rec-tor
dis-agree-able
dis-ap-pear
dis-ap-point
dis-ap-prove
dis-as-trous
dis-ci-pline
dis-cov-er
dis-crep-an-cy
dis-cuss
dis-cus-sion
dis-ease
dis-sat-is-fied
dis-si-pate
dis-tin-guish
dis-trib-ute
di-vide

di-vis-i-ble
di-vi-sion
doc-tor
doesn't
dom-i-nant
dor-mi-to-ry
doubt
drudg-ery
du-pli-cate
dye-ing
dy-ing

E

ea-ger-ly
ear-nest
eco-nom-i-cal
econ-o-my
ec-sta-sy
e-di-tion
ef-fer-ves-cent
ef-fi-ca-cy
ef-fi-cien-cy
eighth
ei-ther
e-lab-o-rate
e-lec-tric-i-ty
el-e-phant
el-i-gi-ble
e-lim-i-nate
el-lipse
em-bar-rass
e-mer-gen-cy
em-i-nent
em-pha-size
em-ploy-ee
em-ploy-ment
e-mul-sion
en-close
en-cour-age
en-deav-or
en-dorse-ment
en-gi-neer
En-glish
e-nor-mous
e-nough
en-ter-prise
en-ter-tain
en-thu-si-as-tic
en-tire-ly
en-trance

en-vel-op (v.)
en-ve-lope (n.)
en-vi-ron-ment
equip-ment
equipped
e-quiv-a-lent
es-pe-cial-ly
es-sen-tial
es-tab-lish
es-teemed
et-i-quette
ev-i-dence
ex-ag-ger-ate
ex-ceed
ex-cel-lent
ex-cept
ex-cep-tion-al-ly
ex-ces-sive
ex-cite
ex-ec-u-tive
ex-er-cise
ex-haust (-ed)
ex-hi-bi-tion
ex-hil-a-ra-tion
ex-is-tence
ex-or-bi-tant
ex-pect
ex-pe-di-tion
ex-pend-i-ture
ex-pen-sive
ex-pe-ri-ence
ex-plain
ex-pla-na-tion
ex-pres-sion
ex-qui-site
ex-ten-sion
ex-tinct
ex-traor-di-nar-y
ex-treme-ly

F

fa-cil-i-ties
fal-la-cy
fa-mil-iar
fa-mous
fas-ci-nate
fash-ion
fa-tigue (-d)
fau-cet
fa-vor-ite

fea-si-ble
fea-ture
Feb-ru-ar-y
fed-er-al
fem-i-nine
fer-tile
fic-ti-tious
field
fierce
fi-ery
fi-nal-ly
fi-nan-cial-ly
fo-li-age
for-ci-ble
for-eign
for-feit
for-go
for-mal-ly
for-mer-ly
for-tu-nate
for-ty
for-ward
foun-tain
fourth
frag-ile
fran-ti-cal-ly
freight
friend
ful-fill
fun-da-men-tal
fur-ther-more
fu-tile

G

gad-get
gan-grene
ga-rage
gas-o-line
gauge
ge-ne-al-o-gy
gen-er-al-ly
gen-er-ous
ge-nius
gen-u-ine
ge-og-ra-phy
ghet-to
ghost
glo-ri-ous
gnaw
go-ril-la

gov-ern-ment
gov-er-nor
gra-cious
grad-u-a-tion
gram-mar
grate-ful
grat-i-tude
grease
grief
griev-ous
gro-cery
grudge
grue-some
guar-an-tee
guard
guard-i-an
guer-ril-la
guess
guid-ance
guide
guilty
gym-na-si-um
gyp-sy
gy-ro-scope

H

hab-i-tat
ham-mer
hand-ker-chief
han-dle (-d)
hand-some
hap-haz-ard
hap-pen
hap-pi-ness
ha-rass
har-bor
hast-i-ly
hav-ing
haz-ard-ous
height
hem-or-rhage
hes-i-tate
hin-drance
his-to-ry
hoarse
hol-i-day
hon-or
hop-ing
hop-ping
horde

hor-ri-ble
hos-pi-tal
hu-mor-ous
hur-ried-ly
hy-drau-lic
hy-giene

I

i-am-bic
i-ci-cle
i-den-ti-cal
id-io-syn-cra-sy
il-leg-i-ble
il-lit-er-ate
il-lus-trate
im-ag-i-nary
im-ag-i-na-tive
im-ag-ine
im-i-ta-tion
im-me-di-ate-ly
im-mense
im-mi-grant
im-mor-tal
im-pa-tient
im-per-a-tive
im-por-tance
im-pos-si-ble
im-promp-tu
im-prove-ment
in-al-ien-able
in-ci-den-tal-ly
in-con-ve-nience
in-cred-i-ble
in-curred
in-def-i-nite-ly
in-del-ible
in-de-pend-ence
in-de-pend-ent
in-dict-ment
in-dis-pens-able
in-di-vid-u-al
in-duce-ment
in-dus-tri-al
in-dus-tri-ous
in-ev-i-ta-ble
in-fe-ri-or
in-ferred
in-fi-nite
in-flam-ma-ble
in-flu-en-tial

in-ge-nious
in-gen-u-ous
in-im-i-ta-ble
in-i-tial
ini-ti-a-tion
in-no-cence
in-no-cent
in-oc-u-la-tion
in-quir-y
in-stal-la-tion
in-stance
in-stead
in-sti-tute
in-struc-tor
in-sur-ance
in-tel-lec-tu-al
in-tel-li-gence
in-ten-tion
in-ter-cede
in-ter-est-ing
in-ter-fere
in-ter-mit-tent
in-ter-pret (-ed)
in-ter-rupt
in-ter-view
in-ti-mate
in-va-lid
in-ves-ti-gate
in-ves-tor
in-vi-ta-tion
ir-i-des-cent
ir-rel-e-vant
ir-re-sis-ti-ble
ir-rev-er-ent
ir-ri-gate
is-land
is-sue
i-tem-ized
i-tin-er-ar-y

J

jan-i-tor
jeal-ous (-y)
jeop-ar-dize
jew-el-ry
jour-nal
jour-ney
judg-ment
jus-tice
jus-ti-fi-able

K

kitch-en
knowl-edge
knuck-le

L

la-bel
lab-o-ra-to-ry
lac-quer
lan-guage
laugh
laun-dry
law-yer
league
lec-ture
le-gal
leg-i-ble
leg-is-la-ture
le-git-i-mate
lei-sure
length
let-ter-head
li-a-bil-i-ty
li-a-ble
li-ai-son
lib-er-al
li-brar-y
li-cense
lieu-ten-ant
light-ning
lik-able
like-ly
lin-eage
liq-ue-fy
liq-uid
lis-ten
lit-er-ary
lit-er-a-ture
live-li-hood
log-a-rithm
lone-li-ness
loose
lose
los-ing
lov-able
love-ly
lun-cheon
lux-u-ry

M

ma-chine
mag-a-zine
mag-nif-i-cent
main-tain
main-te-nance
ma-jor-i-ty
mak-ing
man-age-ment
ma-neu-ver
man-u-al
man-u-fac-ture
man-u-script
mar-riage
mar-shal
ma-te-ri-al
math-e-mat-ics
max-i-mum
may-or
mean-ness
meant
mea-sure
med-i-cine
me-di-eval
me-di-o-cre
me-di-um
mem-o-ran-dum
men-us
mer-chan-dise
mer-it
mes-sage
mile-age
mil-lion-aire
min-i-a-ture
min-i-mum
min-ute
mir-ror
mis-cel-la-neous
mis-chief
mis-chie-vous
mis-er-a-ble
mis-ery
mis-sile
mis-sion-ary
mis-spell
mois-ture
mol-e-cule
mo-men-tous
mo-not-o-nous

mon-u-ment
mort-gage
mu-nic-i-pal
mus-cle
mu-si-cian
mus-tache
mys-te-ri-ous

N

na-ive
nat-u-ral-ly
nec-es-sary
ne-ces-si-ty
neg-li-gi-ble
ne-go-ti-ate
neigh-bor-hood
nev-er-the-less
nick-el
niece
nine-teenth
nine-ty
no-tice-able
no-to-ri-ety
nu-cle-ar
nui-sance

O

o-be-di-ence
o-bey
o-blige
ob-sta-cle
oc-ca-sion
oc-ca-sion-al-ly
oc-cu-pant
oc-cur
oc-curred
oc-cur-rence
of-fense
of-fi-cial
of-ten
o-mis-sion
o-mit-ted
op-er-ate
o-pin-ion
op-po-nent
op-por-tu-ni-ty
op-po-site
op-ti-mism
or-di-nance
or-di-nar-i-ly

orig-i-nal
out-ra-geous

P

pag-eant
pam-phlet
par-a-dise
para-graph
par-al-lel
par-a-lyze
pa-ren-the-ses
pa-ren-the-sis
par-lia-ment
par-tial
par-tic-i-pant
par-tic-i-pate
par-tic-u-lar-ly
pas-time
pa-tience
pa-tron-age
pe-cu-liar
per-ceive
per-haps
per-il
per-ma-nent
per-mis-si-ble
per-pen-dic-u-lar
per-se-ver-ance
per-sis-tent
per-son-al (-ly)
per-son-nel
per-spi-ra-tion
per-suade
phase
phe-nom-e-non
phi-los-o-phy
phy-si-cian
piece
planned
pla-teau
plau-si-ble
play-wright
pleas-ant
plea-sure
pneu-mo-nia
pol-i-ti-cian
pos-sess
pos-ses-sion
pos-si-ble
prac-ti-cal-ly

prai-rie
pre-cede
pre-ce-dence
pre-ced-ing
pre-cious
pre-cise-ly
pre-ci-sion
pre-de-ces-sor
pref-er-a-ble
pref-er-ence
pre-ferred
prej-u-dice
pre-lim-i-nar-y
pre-mi-um
prep-a-ra-tion
pres-ence
prev-a-lent
pre-vi-ous
prim-i-tive
prin-ci-pal
prin-ci-ple
pri-or-i-ty
pris-on-er
priv-i-lege
prob-a-bly
pro-ce-dure
pro-ceed
pro-fes-sor
prom-i-nent
pro-nounce
pro-nun-ci-a-tion
pro-pa-gan-da
pros-e-cute
pro-tein
psy-chol-o-gy
pub-lic-ly
pump-kin
pur-chase
pur-sue
pur-su-ing
pur-suit

Q

qual-i-fied
qual-i-ty
quan-ti-ty
quar-ter
ques-tion-naire
quite
quo-tient

R

raise
rap-port
re-al-ize
re-al-ly
re-cede
re-ceipt
re-ceive
re-ceived
rec-i-pe
re-cip-i-ent
rec-og-ni-tion
rec-og-nize
rec-om-mend
re-cur-rence
ref-er-ence
re-ferred
reg-is-tra-tion
re-hearse
reign
re-im-burse
rel-e-vant
re-lieve
re-li-gious
re-mem-ber
re-mem-brance
rem-i-nisce
ren-dez-vous
re-new-al
rep-e-ti-tion
rep-re-sen-ta-tive
req-ui-si-tion
res-er-voir
re-sis-tance
re-spect-a-bly
re-spect-ful-ly
re-spec-tive-ly
re-spon-si-bil-i-ty
res-tau-rant
rheu-ma-tism
rhyme
rhythm
ri-dic-u-lous
route

S

sac-ri-le-gious
safe-ty
sal-a-ry

sand-wich
sat-is-fac-to-ry
Sat-ur-day
scarce-ly
scene
scen-er-y
sched-ule
schol-ar-ship
sci-ence
scis-sors
sec-re-tary
seize
sen-si-ble
sen-tence
sen-ti-nel
sep-a-rate
ser-geant
sev-er-al
se-vere-ly
shep-herd
sher-iff
shin-ing
siege
sig-nif-i-cance
sim-i-lar
si-mul-ta-ne-ous
since
sin-cere-ly
ski-ing
sol-dier
sol-emn
so-phis-ti-cat-ed
soph-o-more
so-ror-i-ty
source
sou-ve-nir
spa-ghet-ti
spe-cif-ic
spec-i-men
speech
sphere
spon-sor
spon-ta-ne-ous
sta-tion-ary
sta-tion-ery
sta-tis-tic
stat-ue
stat-ure
stat-ute
stom-ach
stopped

straight
strat-e-gy
strength
stretched
study-ing
sub-si-dize
sub-stan-tial
sub-sti-tute
sub-tle
suc-ceed
suc-cess
suf-fi-cient
sum-ma-rize
su-per-fi-cial
su-per-in-tend-ent
su-pe-ri-or-i-ty
su-per-sede
sup-ple-ment
sup-pose
sure-ly
sur-prise
sur-veil-lance
sur-vey
sus-cep-ti-ble
sus-pi-cious
sus-te-nance
syl-la-ble
sym-met-ri-cal
sym-pa-thy
sym-pho-ny
symp-tom
syn-chro-nous

T

tar-iff
tech-nique
tele-gram
tem-per-a-ment
tem-per-a-ture
tem-po-rary
ten-den-cy
ten-ta-tive
ter-res-tri-al
ter-ri-ble
ter-ri-to-ry
the-ater
their
there-fore
thief
thor-ough (-ly)

though
through-out
tired
to-bac-co
to-geth-er
to-mor-row
tongue
to-night
touch
tour-na-ment
tour-ni-quet
to-ward
trag-e-dy
trai-tor
tran-quil-iz-er
trans-ferred
trea-sur-er
tru-ly
Tues-day
tu-i-tion
typ-i-cal
typ-ing

U

unan-i-mous
un-con-scious
un-doubt-ed-ly
un-for-tu-nate-ly
unique
u-ni-son
uni-ver-si-ty
un-nec-es-sary
un-prec-e-dent-ed
un-til
up-per
ur-gent
us-able
use-ful
using
usu-al-ly
u-ten-sil
u-til-ize

V

va-can-cies
va-ca-tion
vac-u-um
vague
valu-able
va-ri-ety

var-i-ous
veg-e-ta-ble
ve-hi-cle
veil
ve-loc-i-ty
ven-geance
vi-cin-i-ty
view
vig-i-lance
vil-lain
vi-o-lence
vis-i-bil-i-ty
vis-i-ble
vis-i-tor
voice
vol-ume
vol-un-tary
vol-un-teer

W

wan-der
war-rant
weath-er
Wednes-day
weird
wel-come
wel-fare
where
wheth-er
which
whole
whol-ly
whose
width
wom-en
worth-while
wor-thy
wreck-age
wres-tler
writ-ing
writ-ten
wrought

Y

yel-low
yes-ter-day
yield

Steps to Becoming a Better Speller

1. **Be patient.** Becoming a good speller takes time.

2. **Check the correct pronunciation of each word you are attempting to spell.**

   Knowing the correct pronunciation of each word can help you to remember its spelling.

3. **Note the meaning and history of each word as you are checking the dictionary for the pronunciation.**

   Knowing the meaning and history of a word provides you with a better notion of how the word is properly used, and it can help you remember the word's spelling.

4. **Before you close the dictionary, practice spelling the word.**

   You can do so by looking away from the page and trying to "see" the word in your "mind's eye." Write the word on a piece of paper. Check the spelling in the dictionary and repeat the process until you are able to spell the word correctly.

5. **Learn some spelling rules.**

   The four rules in this handbook (page 600) are four of the most useful—although there are others.

6. **Make a list of the words that you misspell.**

   Select the first ten words and practice spelling them.

   First: Read each word carefully; then write it on a piece of paper. Look at the written word to see that it's spelled correctly. Repeat the process for those words that you misspelled.

   Then: Ask someone to read the words to you so you can write them again. Then check for misspellings. Repeat both steps with your next ten words.

7. **Write often.**

   As noted educator Frank Smith said,

   "There is little point in learning to spell
   if you have little intention of writing."

USING THE RIGHT WORD

a, an Use *a* as the article before words that begin with consonant sounds and before words that begin with the long vowel sound *u* (yü). Use *an* before words that begin with other vowel sounds.

> **An** older student showed Kris **an** easier way to get to class.
>
> **A** uniform is required attire for **a** cafeteria worker.

607.1

a lot, alot, allot *Alot* is not a word; *a lot* (two words) is a vague descriptive phrase that should be used sparingly, especially in formal writing. *Allot* means to give someone a share.

> Prof Dubi **allots** each of us five spelling errors per semester, and he thinks that's **a lot**.

607.2

accept, except The verb *accept* means "to receive or believe"; the preposition *except* means "other than."

> The instructor **accepted** the student's story about being late, but she wondered why no one **except** him had forgotten about the change to daylight saving time.

607.3

adapt, adopt, adept *Adapt* means "to adjust or change to fit"; *adopt* means "to choose and treat as your own" (a child, an idea). *Adept* is an adjective meaning "proficient or well trained."

> After much thought and deliberation, we agreed to **adopt** the black Lab from the shelter. Now we have to agree on how to **adapt** our lifestyle to fit our new roommate.

607.4

adverse, averse *Adverse* means "hostile, unfavorable, or harmful." *Averse* means "to have a definite feeling of distaste—disinclined."

> Groans and other **adverse** reactions were noted as the new students, **averse** to strenuous exercise, were ushered past the X-5000 pump-and-crunch machine.

607.5

advice, advise *Advice* is a noun meaning "information or recommendation"; *advise* is a verb meaning "to recommend."

> Successful people will often give you sound **advice**, so I **advise** you to listen.

607.6

affect, effect *Affect* means "to influence"; the noun *effect* means "the result."

> The employment growth in a field will **affect** your chances of getting a job. The **effect** may be a new career choice.

607.7

608.1 **aid, aide** As a verb, *aid* means "to help"; as a noun, *aid* means "the help given." An *aide* is a person who acts as an assistant.

608.2 **all, of** *Of* is seldom needed after *all.*

☑ Exercise

> **All** the reports had an error in them.
> **All** the speakers spoke English.
> **All of** us voted to reschedule the meeting.
> (Here *of* is needed for the sentence to make sense.)

608.3 **all right, alright** *Alright* is the incorrect form of *all right.* (**Note:** The following are spelled correctly: *always, altogether, already, almost.*)

608.4 **allude, elude** *Allude* means "to indirectly refer to or hint at something"; *elude* means "to escape attention or understanding altogether."

> Ravi often **alluded** to wanting a supper invitation by mentioning the "awfully good" smells from the kitchen. These hints never **eluded** Ma's good heart.

608.5 **allusion, illusion** *Allusion* is an indirect reference to something or someone, especially in literature; *illusion* is a false picture or idea.

> Did you recognize the **allusion** to David in the reading assignment? Until I read that part, I was under the **illusion** that the young boy would run away from the bully.

608.6 **already, all ready** *Already* is an adverb meaning "before this time" or "by this time." *All ready* is an adjective form meaning "fully prepared." (**Note:** Use *all ready* if you can substitute *ready* alone in the sentence.)

> By the time I was a junior in high school, I had **already** taken my SATs. That way, I was **all ready** to apply early to college.

608.7 **altogether, all together** *Altogether* means "entirely." *All together* means "in a group" or "all at once." (**Note:** Use *all together* if you can substitute *together* alone in the sentence.)

> **All together** there are 35,000 job titles to choose from. That's **altogether** too many to even think about.

608.8 **among, between** *Among* is used when emphasizing distribution throughout a body or a group of three or more; *between* is used when emphasizing distribution to two individuals.

> There was discontent **among** the relatives after learning that their aunt had divided her entire fortune **between** a canary and a favorite waitress at the local cafe.

608.9 **amoral, immoral** *Amoral* means "neither moral (right) nor immoral (wrong)"; *immoral* means "wrong, or in conflict with traditional values."

> Carnivores are **amoral** in their hunt; poachers are **immoral** in theirs.

608.10 **amount, number** *Amount* is used for bulk measurement. *Number* is used to count separate units. (See also **fewer.**)

> The **number** of new instructors hired next year will depend on the **amount** of revenue raised by the new sales tax.

and etc. Don't use *and* before *etc.* since *et cetera* means "and the rest."

Did you remember your textbook, notebook, handout, **etc.**?

annual, biannual, semiannual, biennial, perennial An *annual* event happens once every year. A *biannual* event happens twice a year (*semiannual* is the same as *biannual*). A *biennial* event happens every two years. A *perennial* event happens throughout the year, every year.

anxious, eager Both words mean "looking forward to," but *anxious* also connotes fear or concern.

The professor is **eager** to move into the new building, but she's a little **anxious** that students won't be able to find her new office.

anymore, any more *Anymore* (an adverb) means "any longer"; *any more* means "any additional."

We won't use that textbook **anymore**; call if you have **any more** questions.

any one (of), anyone *Any one* means "any one of a number of people, places, or things"; *anyone* is a pronoun meaning "any person."

Choose **any one** of the proposed weekend schedules. **Anyone** wishing to work on Saturday instead of Sunday may do so.

appraise, apprise *Appraise* means "to determine value." *Apprise* means "to inform."

Because of the tax assessor's recent **appraisal** of our home, we were **apprised** of an increase in our property tax.

as Don't use *as* in place of *whether* or *if.*

I don't know **as** I'll accept the offer. (Incorrect)

I don't know **whether** I'll accept the offer. (Correct)

Don't use *as* when it is unclear whether it means *because* or *when.*

We rowed toward shore **as** it started raining. (Unclear)

We rowed toward shore **because** it started raining. (Correct)

assure, ensure, insure (See insure.)

bad, badly *Bad* is an adjective, used both before nouns and as a predicate adjective after linking verbs. *Badly* is an adverb.

Christina felt **bad** about serving us **bad** food.

Larisa played **badly** today.

beside, besides *Beside* means "by the side of." *Besides* means "in addition to."

Besides the two suitcases you've already loaded into the trunk, remember the smaller one **beside** the van.

between, among (See among.)

bring, take *Bring* suggests the action is directed toward the speaker; *take* suggests the action is directed away from the speaker.

If you're not going to **bring** the video to class, **take** it back to the resource center.

610.1   **can, may** In formal contexts, *can* is used to mean "being able to do"; *may* is used to mean "having permission to do."

> **May** I borrow your bicycle to get to the library? Then I **can** start working on our group project.

610.2   **capital, capitol** The noun *capital* refers to a city or to money. The adjective *capital* means "major or important" or "seat of government." *Capitol* refers to a building.

> The **capitol** is in the **capital** city for a **capital** reason. The city government contributed **capital** for the building expense.

610.3   **cent, sent, scent** *Cent* is a coin; *sent* is the past tense of the verb "send"; *scent* is an odor or a smell.

> For forty-one **cents**, I **sent** my friend a love poem in a perfumed envelope. She adored the **scent** but hated the poem.

610.4   **chord, cord** *Chord* may mean "an emotion or a feeling," but it also may mean "the combination of three or more tones sounded at the same time," as with a guitar *chord*. A *cord* is a string or a rope.

> The guitar player strummed the opening **chord**, which struck a responsive **chord** with the audience.

610.5   **chose, choose** *Chose* (chōz) is the past tense of the verb *choose* (chüz). (See 631.)

> For generations, people **chose** their careers based on their parents' careers; now people **choose** their careers based on the job market.

610.6   **climactic, climatic** *Climactic* refers to the climax, or high point, of an event; *climatic* refers to the climate, or weather conditions.

Exercise

> Because we are using the open-air amphitheater, **climatic** conditions will just about guarantee the wind gusts we need for the **climactic** third act.

610.7   **coarse, course** *Coarse* means "of inferior quality, rough, or crude"; *course* means "a direction or a path taken." *Course* also means "a class or a series of studies."

> A basic writing **course** is required of all students.
> Due to years of woodworking, the instructor's hands are rather **coarse**.

610.8   **compare with, compare to** Things in the same category are *compared with* each other; things in different categories are *compared to* each other.

> **Compare** Christopher Marlowe's plays **with** William Shakespeare's plays.
> My brother **compared** reading *The Tempest* **to** visiting another country.

610.9   **complement, compliment** *Complement* means "to complete or go well with." *Compliment* means "to offer an expression of admiration or praise."

> We wanted to **compliment** Zach on his decorating efforts; the bright yellow walls **complement** the purple carpet.

610.10   **comprehensible, comprehensive** *Comprehensible* means "capable of being understood"; *comprehensive* means "covering a broad range, or inclusive."

> The theory is **comprehensible** only to those who have a **comprehensive** knowledge of physics.

comprise, compose *Comprise* means "to contain or consist of"; *compose* means "to create or form by bringing parts together." 611.1

Fruitcake **comprises** a variety of nuts, candied fruit, and spice.

Fruitcake is **composed** of (not *comprised of*) a variety of ingredients.

conscience, conscious A *conscience* gives one the capacity to know right from wrong. *Conscious* means "awake or alert, not sleeping or comatose." 611.2

Your **conscience** will guide you, but you have to be **conscious** to hear what it's "saying."

continual, continuous *Continual* often implies that something is happening often, recurring; *continuous* usually implies that something keeps happening, uninterrupted. 611.3

The **continuous** loud music during the night gave the building manager not only a headache but also **continual** phone calls.

counsel, council, consul When used as a noun, *counsel* means "advice"; when used as a verb, *counsel* means "to advise." *Council* refers to a group that advises. A *consul* is a government official appointed to reside in a foreign country. 611.4

The city **council** was asked to **counsel** our student **council** on running an efficient meeting. Their **counsel** was very helpful.

decent, descent, dissent *Decent* means "good." *Descent* is the process of going or stepping downward. *Dissent* means "disagreement." 611.5

The food was **decent**.

The elevator's fast **descent** clogged my ears.

Their **dissent** over the decisions was obvious in their sullen expressions.

desert, dessert *Desert* is barren wilderness. *Dessert* is food served at the end of a meal. The verb *desert* means "to abandon." 611.6

different from, different than Use *different from* in formal writing; use either form in informal or colloquial settings. 611.7

Rafael's interpretation was **different from** Andrea's.

discreet, discrete *Discreet* means "showing good judgment, unobtrusive, modest"; *discrete* means "distinct, separate." 611.8

The essay question had three **discrete** parts.

Her roommate had apparently never heard of quiet, **discreet** conversation.

disinterested, uninterested Both words mean "not interested." However, *disinterested* is also used to mean "unbiased or impartial." 611.9

A person chosen as an arbitrator must be a **disinterested** party.

Professor Eldridge was **uninterested** in our complaints about the assignment.

effect, affect (See affect.)

elicit, illicit *Elicit* is a verb meaning "to bring out." *Illicit* is an adjective meaning "unlawful." 611.10

It took a hand signal to **elicit** the **illicit** exchange of cash for drugs.

612.1   **eminent, imminent** *Eminent* means "prominent, conspicuous, or famous"; *imminent* means "ready or threatening to happen."

> With the island's government about to collapse, assassination attempts on several **eminent** officials seemed **imminent**.

ensure, insure, assure (See insure.)

except, accept (See accept.)

612.2   **explicit, implicit** *Explicit* means "expressed directly or clearly defined"; *implicit* means "implied or unstated."

> The professor **explicitly** asked that the experiment be wrapped up on Monday, **implicitly** demanding that her lab assistants work on the weekend.

612.3   **farther, further** *Farther* refers to a physical distance; *further* refers to additional time, quantity, or degree.

> **Further** research showed that walking **farther** rather than faster would improve his health.

612.4   **fewer, less** *Fewer* refers to the number of separate units; *less* refers to bulk quantity.

> Because of spell checkers, students can produce papers containing **fewer** errors in **less** time.

612.5   **figuratively, literally** *Figuratively* means "in a metaphorical or analogous way—describing something by comparing it to something else"; *literally* means "actually."

> The lab was **literally** filled with sulfurous gases—**figuratively** speaking, dragon's breath.

612.6   **first, firstly** Both words are adverbs meaning "before another in time" or "in the first place." However, do not use *firstly*, which is stiff and unnatural sounding.

☑
Exercise

> **Firstly** I want to see the manager. (Incorrect)
>
> **First** I want to see the manager. (Correct)

Note: When enumerating, use the forms *first, second, third, next, last*—without the *ly*.

612.7   **fiscal, physical** *Fiscal* means "related to financial matters"; *physical* means "related to material things."

> The school's **fiscal** work is handled by its accounting staff.
>
> The **physical** work is handled by its maintenance staff.

612.8   **for, fore, four** *For* is a conjunction meaning "because" or is a preposition used to indicate the object or recipient of something; *fore* means "earlier" or "the front"; *four* is the word for the number *4*.

> The crew brought treats **for** the barge's **four** dogs, who always enjoy the breeze at the **fore** of the vessel.

612.9   **former, latter** When two things are being discussed, *former* refers to the first thing, and *latter* to the second.

> Our choices are going to a movie or eating at the Pizza Palace: The **former** is too expensive, and the **latter** too fattening.

good, well *Good* is an adjective; *well* is nearly always an adverb. (When used to indicate state of health, *well* is an adjective.)

> A **good** job offers opportunities for advancement, especially for those who do their jobs **well.**

613.1

heal, heel *Heal* (a verb) means "to mend or restore to health"; a *heel* (noun) is the back part of a human foot.

613.2

healthful, healthy *Healthful* means "causing or improving health"; *healthy* means "possessing health."

> **Healthful** foods and regular exercise build **healthy** bodies.

613.3

I, me *I* is a subject pronoun; *me* is used as an object of a preposition, a direct object, or an indirect object. (See 625.1.) (A good way to know if *I* or *me* should be used in a compound subject is to eliminate the other subject; the sentence should make sense with the pronoun—*I* or *me*—alone.)

> My roommate and **me** went to the library last night. (Incorrect)
>
> My roommate and **I** went to the library last night. (Correct: Eliminate "my roommate and"; the sentence still makes sense.)
>
> Rasheed gave the concert tickets to Erick and **I.** (Incorrect)
>
> Rasheed gave the concert tickets to Erick and **me.** (Correct: Eliminate "Erick and"; the sentence still makes sense.)

613.4

Video

illusion, allusion (See allusion.)

immigrate (to), emigrate (from) *Immigrate* means "to come into a new country or environment." *Emigrate* means "to go out of one country to live in another."

> **Immigrating** to a new country is a challenging experience.
>
> People **emigrating** from their homelands face unknown challenges.

613.5

imminent, eminent (See eminent.)

imply, infer *Imply* means "to suggest without saying outright"; *infer* means "to draw a conclusion from facts." (A writer or a speaker *implies*; a reader or a listener *infers*.)

> Dr. Rufus **implied** I should study more; I **inferred** he meant my grades had to improve, or I'd be repeating the class.

613.6

ingenious, ingenuous *Ingenious* means "intelligent, discerning, clever"; *ingenuous* means "unassuming, natural, showing childlike innocence and candidness."

> Gretchen devised an **ingenious** plan to work and receive college credit for it.
>
> Ramón displays an **ingenuous** quality that attracts others.

613.7

insure, ensure, assure *Insure* means "to secure from financial harm or loss," *ensure* means "to make certain of something," and *assure* means "to put someone's mind at rest."

> Plenty of studying generally **ensures** academic success.
>
> Nicole **assured** her father that she had **insured** her new car.

613.8

interstate, intrastate *Interstate* means "existing between two or more states"; *intrastate* means "existing within a state."

613.9

614.1 **irregardless, regardless** *Irregardless* is a nonstandard synonym for *regardless*.

> **Irregardless** of his circumstance, José is cheerful. (Incorrect)
> **Regardless** of his circumstance, José is cheerful. (Correct)

614.2 **it's, its** *It's* is the contraction of "it is." *Its* is the possessive form of "it."

> **It's** not hard to see why my husband feeds that alley cat; **its** pitiful limp and mournful mewing would melt any heart.

614.3 **later, latter** *Later* means "after a period of time." *Latter* refers to the second of two things mentioned.

> The **latter** of the two restaurants you mentioned sounds good.
> Let's meet there **later**.

614.4 **lay, lie** *Lay* means "to place." *Lay* is a transitive verb. (See **626.2**.) Its principal parts are *lay, laid, laid*. (See **631**.)

> If you **lay** another book on my table, I won't have room for anything else.
> Yesterday, you **laid** two books on the table.
> Over the last few days, you must have **laid** at least 20 books there.

Exercise

Lie means "to recline." *Lie* is an intransitive verb. (See **626.2**.) Its principal parts are *lie, lay, lain*.

> The cat **lies** down anywhere it pleases.
> It **lay** down yesterday on my tax forms.
> It has **lain** down many times on the kitchen table.

614.5 **learn, teach** *Learn* means "to acquire information"; *teach* means "to give information."

> Sometimes it's easier to **teach** someone else a lesson than it is to **learn** one yourself.

614.6 **leave, let** *Leave* means "to allow something to remain behind." *Let* means "to permit."

> Please **let** me help you carry that chair; otherwise, **leave** it for the movers to pick up.

614.7 **lend, borrow** *Lend* means "to give for temporary use"; *borrow* means "to receive for temporary use."

> I asked Haddad to **lend** me $15 for a CD, but he said I'd have to find someone else to **borrow** the money from.

less, fewer (See *fewer*.)

614.8 **liable, libel** *Liable* is an adjective meaning "responsible according to the law" or "exposed to an adverse action"; the noun *libel* is a written defamatory statement about someone, and the verb *libel* means "to publish or make such a statement."

> Supermarket tabloids, **liable** for ruining many a reputation, make a practice of **libeling** the rich and the famous.

614.9 **liable, likely** *Liable* means "responsible according to the law" or "exposed to an adverse action"; *likely* means "in all probability."

> Rain seems **likely** today, but if we cancel the game, we are still **liable** for paying the referees.

like, as *Like* should not be used in place of *as*. *Like* is a preposition, which is followed by its object (a noun, a pronoun, or a noun phrase). *As* is a subordinating conjunction, which introduces a clause. Do not use *like* as a subordinating conjunction. Use *as* instead.   **615.1**

> You don't know her **like** I do. (Incorrect)

> You don't know her **as** I do. (Correct)

> **Like** the others in my study group, I do my work **as** any serious student would—carefully and thoroughly. (Correct)

literally, figuratively (See figuratively.)

loose, lose, loss The adjective *loose* (lüs) means "free, untied, unrestricted"; the verb *lose* (lüz) means "to misplace or fail to find or control"; the noun *loss* (lòs) means "something that is misplaced and cannot be found."   **615.2**

> Her sadness at the **loss** of her longtime companion caused her to **lose** weight, and her clothes felt uncomfortably **loose**.

may, can (See can.)

maybe, may be Use *maybe* as an adverb meaning "perhaps;" use *may be* as a verb phrase.   **615.3**

> She **may be** the computer technician we've been looking for. **Maybe** she will upgrade the software and memory.

miner, minor A *miner* digs in the ground for ore. A *minor* is a person who is not legally an adult. The adjective *minor* means "of no great importance."   **615.4**

> The use of **minors** as coal **miners** is no **minor** problem.

number, amount (See amount.)

OK, okay This expression, spelled either way, is appropriate in informal writing; however, avoid using it in papers, reports, or formal correspondence of any kind.   **615.5**

> Your proposal is satisfactory [not *okay*] on most levels.

oral, verbal *Oral* means "uttered with the mouth"; *verbal* means "relating to or consisting of words and the comprehension of words."   **615.6**

> The actor's **oral** abilities were outstanding, her pronunciation and intonation impeccable, but I doubted the playwright's **verbal** skills after trying to decipher the play's meaning.

passed, past *Passed* is a verb. *Past* can be used as a noun, an adjective, or a preposition.   **615.7**

> That little pickup truck **passed** my 'Vette! (verb)

> My stepchildren hold on dearly to the **past**. (noun)

> I'm sorry, but my **past** life is not your business. (adjective)

> The officer drove **past** us, not noticing our flat tire. (preposition)

peace, piece *Peace* means "tranquility or freedom from war." A *piece* is a part or fragment.   **615.8**

> Someone once observed that **peace** is not a condition, but a process—a process of building goodwill one **piece** at a time.

616.1   **people, person** Use *people* to refer to human populations, races, or groups; use *person* to refer to an individual or the physical body.

> What the American **people** need is a good insect repellent.
>
> The forest ranger recommends that we check our **persons** for wood ticks when we leave the woods.

616.2   **percent, percentage** *Percent* means "per hundred"; for example, 60 percent of 100 jelly beans would be 60 jelly beans. *Percentage* refers to a portion of the whole. Generally, use the word *percent* when it is preceded by a number. Use *percentage* when no number is used.

Exercise

> Each person's **percentage** of the reward amounted to $125—25 **percent** of the $500 offered by Crime Stoppers.

616.3   **personal, personnel** *Personal* (an adjective) means "private." *Personnel* (a noun) are people working at a particular job.

> Although choosing a major is a **personal** decision, it can be helpful to consult with guidance **personnel**.

616.4   **perspective, prospective** *Perspective* (a noun) is a point of view or the capacity to view things realistically; *prospective* is an adjective meaning "expected in or related to the future."

> From my immigrant neighbor's **perspective**, any job is a good job.
>
> **Prospective** students wandered the campus on visitors' day.

616.5   **pore, pour, poor** The noun *pore* is an opening in the skin; the verb *pore* means "to gaze intently." *Pour* means "to move with a continuous flow." *Poor* means "needy or pitiable."

> **Pour** hot water into a bowl, put your face over it, and let the steam open your **pores**. Your **poor** skin will thank you.

616.6   **precede, proceed** To *precede* means "to go or come before"; *proceed* means "to move on after having stopped" or "go ahead."

> Our biology instructor often **preceded** his lecture with these words:
>
> "OK, sponges, **proceed** to soak up more fascinating facts!"

616.7   **principal, principle** As an adjective, *principal* means "primary." As a noun, it can mean "a school administrator" or "a sum of money." A *principle* (noun) is an idea or a doctrine.

> His **principal** gripe is lack of freedom. (adjective)
>
> My son's **principal** expressed his concerns to the teachers. (noun)
>
> After 20 years, the amount of interest was higher than the **principal**. (noun)
>
> The **principle** of *caveat emptor* guides most consumer groups. (noun)

616.8   **quiet, quit, quite** *Quiet* is the opposite of noisy. *Quit* means "to stop or give up." *Quite* (an adverb) means "completely" or "to a considerable extent."

> The meeting remained **quite quiet** when the boss told us he'd **quit**.

616.9   **quote, quotation** *Quote* is a verb; *quotation* is a noun.

> The **quotation** I used was from Woody Allen. You may **quote** me on that.

616.10   **real, very, really** Do not use the adjective *real* in place of the adverbs *very* or *really*.

> My friend's cake is usually **very** [not *real*] fresh, but this cake is **really** stale.

right, write, wright, rite *Right* means "correct or proper"; it also refers to that which   617.1
a person has a legal claim to, as in *copyright*. *Write* means "to inscribe or record." A *wright*
is a person who makes or builds something. *Rite* is a ritual or ceremonial act.

> Did you **write** that it is the **right** of the **shipwright** to perform the **rite** of
> christening—breaking a bottle of champagne on the bow of the ship?

scene, seen *Scene* refers to the setting or location where something happens; it also may   617.2
mean "sight or spectacle." *Seen* is the past participle of the verb "see."

> An exhibitionist likes to be **seen** making a **scene**.

set, sit *Set* means "to place." *Sit* means "to put the body in a seated position." *Set* is a   617.3
transitive verb; *sit* is an intransitive verb (See 626.2.).

> How can you just **sit** there and watch as I **set** the table?

sight, cite, site *Sight* means "the act of seeing" (a verb) or "something that is seen" (a   617.4
noun). *Cite* (a verb) means "to quote" or "to summon to court." *Site* means "a place or
location" (noun) or "to place on a site" (verb).

> After **sighting** the faulty wiring, the inspector **cited** the building contractor for
> breaking two city codes at a downtown work **site**.

some, sum *Some* refers to an unknown thing, an unspecified number, or a part of   617.5
something. *Sum* is a certain amount of money or the result of adding numbers together.

> **Some** of the students answered too quickly and came up with the wrong **sum**.

stationary, stationery *Stationary* means "not movable"; *stationery* refers to the paper   617.6
and envelopes used to write letters.

> Odina uses **stationery** that she can feed through her portable printer. Then she
> drops the mail into a **stationary** mail receptacle at the mall.

take, bring (See bring.)

teach, learn (See learn.)

than, then *Than* is used in a comparison; *then* is an adverb that tells when.   617.7

> Study more **than** you think you need to. **Then** you will probably be satisfied with
> your grades.

their, there, they're *Their* is a possessive personal pronoun. *There* is an adverb used as   617.8
a filler word or to point out location. *They're* is the contraction for "they are."

> Look over **there**. **There** is a comfortable place for students to study for **their**
> exams, so **they're** more likely to do a good job.

threw, through *Threw* is the past tense of "throw." *Through* (a preposition) means   617.9
"from one side of something to the other."

> In a fit of frustration, Sachiko **threw** his cell phone right **through** the window.

to, too, two *To* is a preposition that can mean "in the direction of." *To* is also used to   617.10
form an infinitive. *Too* (an adverb) means "also" or "very." *Two* is the number 2.

> **Two** causes of eye problems among students are lights that fail **to** illuminate
> properly and computer screens with **too** much glare.

618.1 **vain, vane, vein** *Vain* means "valueless or fruitless"; it may also mean "holding a high regard for oneself." *Vane* is a flat piece of material set up to show which way the wind blows. *Vein* refers to a blood vessel or a mineral deposit.

> The weather **vane** indicates the direction of the wind; the blood **vein** determines the direction of flowing blood; and the **vain** mind moves in no particular direction, content to think only about itself.

618.2 **vary, very** The verb *vary* means "to change"; the adverb *very* means "to a high degree."

> To ensure the **very** best employee relations, the workloads should not **vary** greatly from worker to worker.

verbal, oral (See oral.)

618.3 **waist, waste** The noun *waist* refers to the part of the body just above the hips. The verb *waste* means "to squander" or "to wear away, decay"; the noun *waste* refers to material that is unused or useless.

> His **waist** is small because he **wastes** no opportunity to exercise.

618.4 **wait, weight** *Wait* means "to stay somewhere expecting something." *Weight* refers to a degree or unit of heaviness.

> The **weight** of sadness eventually lessens; one must simply **wait** for the pain to dissipate.

618.5 **ware, wear, where** The noun *ware* refers to a product that is sold; the verb *wear* means "to have on or to carry on one's body"; the adverb *where* asks the question "In what place?" or "In what situation?"

> The designer boasted, "**Where** can one **wear** my **wares**? Anywhere."

618.6 **weather, whether** *Weather* refers to the condition of the atmosphere. *Whether* refers to a possibility.

> **Weather** conditions affect all of us, **whether** we are farmers or plumbers.

well, good (See good.)

which, that (See 573.3.)

618.7 **who, which, that** *Who* refers to people. *Which* refers to nonliving objects or to animals. (*Which* should never refer to people.) *That* may refer to animals, people, or nonliving objects. (See also 573.3.)

618.8 **who, whom** *Who* is used as the subject of a verb; *whom* is used as the object of a preposition or as a direct object.

> Captain Mather, to **whom** the survivors owe their lives, is the man **who** is being honored today.

618.9 **who's, whose** *Who's* is the contraction for "who is." *Whose* is a possessive pronoun.

> **Whose** car are we using, and **who's** going to pay for the gas?

618.10 **your, you're** *Your* is a possessive pronoun. *You're* is the contraction for "you are."

> If **you're** like most Americans, you will have held eight jobs by **your** fortieth birthday.

Understanding Grammar

Grammar is the study of the structure and features of the language, consisting of rules and standards that are to be followed to produce acceptable writing and speaking. **Parts of speech** refers to the eight different categories that indicate how words are used in the English language—as *nouns, pronouns, verbs, adjectives, adverbs, prepositions, conjunctions,* or *interjections.*

Audio

Noun

A **noun** is a word that names something: a person, a place, a thing, or an idea.

619.1

Toni Morrison/author	*Lone Star*/**film**	**Renaissance/era**
UC-Davis/university	*A Congress of Wonders*/**book**	

esl **Note:** See 657.1–658.2 for information on count and noncount nouns.

Exercise

Classes of Nouns

All nouns are either *proper nouns* or *common nouns.* Nouns may also be classified as *individual* or *collective,* or *concrete* or *abstract.*

Proper Nouns

619.2

A **proper noun,** which is always capitalized, names a specific person, place, thing, or idea.

Rembrandt, Bertrand Russell (people)

Stratford-upon-Avon, Tower of London (places)

The Night Watch, **Rosetta stone** (things)

New Deal, Christianity (ideas)

Common Nouns

619.3

A **common noun** is a general name for a person, a place, a thing, or an idea. Common nouns are not capitalized.

optimist, instructor (people)	**cafeteria, park** (places)
computer, chair (things)	**freedom, love** (ideas)

620.1   ## Collective Nouns

A **collective noun** names a group or a unit.

> family   audience   crowd   committee   team   class

620.2   ## Concrete Nouns

A **concrete noun** names a thing that is tangible (can be seen, touched, heard, smelled, or tasted).

> child   The White Stripes   gym   village   microwave oven   pizza

620.3   ## Abstract Nouns

An **abstract noun** names an idea, a condition, or a feeling—in other words, something that cannot be seen, touched, heard, smelled, or tasted.

> beauty   Jungian psychology   anxiety   agoraphobia   trust

Forms of Nouns

Nouns are grouped according to their *number, gender,* and *case.*

620.4   ## Number of Nouns

Number indicates whether a noun is singular or plural.

A singular noun refers to one person, place, thing, or idea.

> student   laboratory   lecture   note   grade   result

A plural noun refers to more than one person, place, thing, or idea.

> students   laboratories   lectures   notes   grades   results

620.5   ## Gender of Nouns

Gender indicates whether a noun is masculine, feminine, neuter, or indefinite.

Masculine:
> father   king   brother   men   colt   rooster

Feminine:
> mother   queen   sister   women   filly   hen

Neuter (without sex):
> notebook   monitor   car   printer

Indefinite or common (masculine or feminine):
> professor   customer   children   doctor   people

Case of Nouns

The **case** of a noun tells what role the noun plays in a sentence. There are three cases: *nominative, possessive, and objective.*

A noun in the **nominative case** is used as a subject. The subject of a sentence tells who or what the sentence is about.

> **Dean Henning** manages the College of Arts and Communication.

Note: A noun is also in the nominative case when it is used as a predicate noun (or predicate nominative). A predicate noun follows a linking verb, usually a form of the *be* verb (such as *am, is, are, was, were, be, being, been*), and repeats or renames the subject.

> Ms. Yokum is the **person** to talk to about the college's impact in our community.

A noun in the **possessive case** shows possession or ownership. In this form, it acts as an adjective.

> Our **president's** willingness to discuss concerns with students has boosted campus morale.

A noun in the **objective case** serves as an object of the preposition, a direct object, an indirect object, or an object complement.

> To survive, institutions of higher **learning** sometimes cut **budgets** in spite of **protests** from **students** and **instructors**. (*Learning* is the object of the preposition *of, protests* is the object of the preposition *in spite of, budgets* is the direct object of the verb *cut,* and *students* and *instructors* are the objects of the preposition *from.*)

A Closer Look
at Direct and Indirect Objects

A **direct object** is a noun (or pronoun) that identifies what or who receives the action of the verb.

> Budget cutbacks reduced class **choices**. (*Choices* is the direct object of the active verb *reduced.*)

An **indirect object** is a noun (or pronoun) that identifies the person *to whom* or *for whom* something is done, or the thing *to which* or *for which* something is done. An indirect object is always accompanied by a direct object.

> Recent budget cuts have given **students** fewer class choices. (*Choices* is the direct object of *have given; students* is the indirect object.)

esl Note: Not every transitive verb is followed by *both* a direct object and an indirect object. Both can, however, follow *give, send, show, tell, teach, find, sell, ask, offer, pay, pass,* and *hand.*

622.1   Pronoun

Exercise

A **pronoun** is a word that is used in place of a noun.

> Roger was the most interesting 10-year-old I ever taught. **He** was a good thinker and thus a good writer. I remember **his** paragraph about the cowboy hat **he** received from **his** grandparents. **It** was "too new looking." The brim was not rolled properly. But the hat's imperfections were not the main idea in Roger's writing. No, the main idea was how **he** was fixing the hat **himself** by wearing **it** when **he** showered.

622.2   Antecedents

An **antecedent** is the noun or pronoun that the pronoun refers to or replaces. Most pronouns have antecedents, but not all do. (See 623.4.)

> As the wellness **counselor** checked *her* chart, several **students** *who* were waiting *their* turns shifted uncomfortably. (*Counselor* is the antecedent of *her; students* is the antecedent of *who* and *their.*)

Note: Each pronoun must agree with its antecedent in number, person, and gender. (See pages 624–625 and 649.)

622.3

Classes of Pronouns

Personal

I, me, my, mine / we, us, our, ours / you, your, yours
they, them, their, theirs / he, him, his, she, her, hers, it, its

Reflexive and Intensive

myself, yourself, himself, herself, itself, ourselves, yourselves, themselves

Relative

who, whose, whom, which, that

Indefinite

all	anything	everybody	most	no one	some
another	both	everyone	much	nothing	somebody
any	each	everything	neither	one	someone
anybody	each one	few	nobody	other	something
anyone	either	many	none	several	such

Interrogative

who, whose, whom, which, what

Demonstrative

this, that, these, those

Reciprocal

each other, one another

Classes of Pronouns

There are several classes of pronouns: *personal, reflexive and intensive, relative, indefinite, interrogative,* and *demonstrative.*

Personal Pronouns

A **personal pronoun** refers to a specific person or thing.

> *Marge* started **her** car; **she** drove the antique *convertible* to Monterey, where **she** hoped to sell **it** at an auction.

623.1

Reflexive and Intensive Pronouns

A **reflexive pronoun** is formed by adding *-self* or *-selves* to a personal pronoun. A reflexive pronoun can act as a direct object or an indirect object of a verb, an object of a preposition, or a predicate nominative.

> Charles loves **himself.** (direct object of *loves*)
> Charles gives **himself** A's for fashion sense. (indirect object of *gives*)
> Charles smiles at **himself** in store windows. (object of preposition *at*)
> Charles can be **himself** anywhere. (predicate nominative)

An **intensive pronoun** intensifies, or emphasizes, the noun or pronoun it refers to.

> Leo **himself** taught his children to invest their lives in others.
> The lesson was sometimes painful—but they learned it **themselves.**

623.2

Relative Pronouns

A **relative pronoun** relates an adjective dependent (relative) clause to the noun or pronoun it modifies. (The noun is italicized in each example below; the relative pronoun is in bold.)

> *Freshmen* **who** believe they have a lot to learn are absolutely right.
> Just navigating this *campus,* **which** is huge, can be challenging.

Make sure you know when to use the relative pronouns *who* or *whom* and *that* or *which.* (See 573.3, 618.7, 618.8, and 642.3.)

623.3

Indefinite Pronouns

An **indefinite pronoun** refers to unnamed or unknown people, places, or things.

> **Everyone** seemed amused when I was searching for my classroom in the student center. (The antecedent of *everyone* is unnamed.)
> **Nothing** is more unnerving than rushing at the last minute into the wrong room for the wrong class. (The antecedent of *nothing* is unknown.)

Most indefinite pronouns are singular, so when they are used as subjects, they should have singular verbs. (See pages 645–648.)

623.4

624.1 <u>Interrogative Pronouns</u>

An **interrogative pronoun** asks a question.

> So **which** will it be—highlighting and attaching a campus map to the inside of your backpack, or being lost and late for the first two weeks?

Note: When an interrogative pronoun modifies a noun, it functions as an adjective.

624.2 <u>Demonstrative Pronouns</u>

A **demonstrative pronoun** points out people, places, or things.

> We advise **this:** Bring along as many maps and schedules as you need. **Those** are useful tools. **That** is the solution.

Note: When a demonstrative pronoun modifies a noun, it functions as an adjective.

Forms of Personal Pronouns

The **form** of a personal pronoun indicates its *number* (singular or plural), its *person* (first, second, or third), its *case* (nominative, possessive, or objective), and its *gender* (masculine, feminine, neuter, or indefinite).

624.3 <u>Number of Pronouns</u>

A **personal pronoun** is either singular (*I, you, he, she, it*) or plural (*we, you, they*).

> **He** should have a budget and stick to it. (singular)
> **We** can help new students learn about budgeting. (plural)

624.4 <u>Person of Pronouns</u>

The **person** of a pronoun indicates whether the person is speaking (first person), is spoken to (second person), or is spoken about (third person).

> **First person** is used to name the speaker(s).
>
> > **I** know **I** need to handle **my** stress in a healthful way, especially during exam week; **my** usual chips-and-doughnuts binge isn't helping. (singular)
> >
> > **We** all decided to bike to the tennis court. (plural)
>
> **Second person** is used to name the person(s) spoken to.
>
> > Maria, **you** grab the rackets, okay? (singular)
> >
> > John and Tanya, can **you** find the water bottles? (plural)
>
> **Third person** is used to name the person(s) or thing(s) spoken about.
>
> > Today's students are interested in wellness issues. **They** are concerned about **their** health, fitness, and nutrition. (plural)
> >
> > Maria practices yoga and feels **she** is calmer for **her** choice. (singular)
> >
> > One of the advantages of regular exercise is that **it** raises one's energy level. (singular)

Case of Pronouns
625.1

The **case** of each pronoun tells what role it plays in a sentence. There are three cases: *nominative, possessive,* and *objective.*

A pronoun in the **nominative case** is used as a subject. The following are nominative forms: *I, you, he, she, it, we, they.*

> **He** found an old map in the trunk.
>
> My friend and **I** went biking. (not *me*)

A pronoun is also in the nominative case when it is used as a predicate nominative, following a linking verb (*am, is, are, was, were, seems*) and renaming the subject.

> It was **he** who discovered electricity. (not *him*)

A pronoun in the **possessive case** shows possession or ownership: *my, mine, our, ours, his, her, hers, their, theirs, its, your, yours.* A possessive pronoun before a noun acts as an adjective: *your* coat.

> That coat is **hers.**   This coat is **mine.**   **Your** coat is lost.

A pronoun in the **objective case** can be used as the direct object, indirect object, object of a preposition, or object complement: *me, you, him, her, it, us, them.*

> Professor Adler hired **her.** (*Her* is the direct object of the verb *hired.*)
>
> He showed Mary and **me** the language lab. (*Me* is the indirect object of the verb *showed.*)
>
> He introduced the three of **us**—Mary, Shavonn, and **me**—to the faculty.
> (*Us* is the object of the preposition *of; me* is part of the appositive renaming *us.*)

Gender of Pronouns
625.2

The **gender** of a pronoun indicates whether the pronoun is masculine, feminine, neuter, or indefinite. (See page 106.)

Masculine:
he, him, his

Feminine:
she, her, hers

Neuter (without sex):
it, its

Indefinite (masculine or feminine):
they, them, their

Number, Person, and Case of Personal Pronouns
625.3

	Nominative Case	Possessive Case	Objective Case
First Person Singular	I	my, mine	me
Second Person Singular	you	your, yours	you
Third Person Singular	he, she, it	his, her, hers, its	him, her, it
First Person Plural	we	our, ours	us
Second Person Plural	you	your, yours	you
Third Person Plural	they	their, theirs	them

626.1

Exercise

Verb

A **verb** shows action (*pondered, grins*), links words (*is, seemed*), or accompanies another action verb as an auxiliary or helping verb (*can, does*).

> Harry **honked** the horn. (shows action)
> Harry **is** impatient. (links words)
> Harry **was** honking the truck's horn. (accompanies the verb *honking*)

Classes of Verbs

Verbs are classified as action, auxiliary (helping), or linking (state of being).

626.2

Action Verbs: Transitive and Intransitive

As its name implies, an **action verb** shows action. Some action verbs are *transitive;* others are *intransitive.* (The term *action* does not always refer to a physical activity.)

> Rain **splashed** the windshield. (transitive verb)
> Josie **drove** off the road. (intransitive verb)

Transitive verbs have direct objects that receive the action (621.2, 639.5).

> The health care industry **employs** more than 7 million **workers** in the United States. (*Workers* is the direct object of the action verb *employs.*)

Intransitive verbs communicate action that is complete in itself. They do not need an object to receive the action.

> My new college roommate **smiles** and **laughs** a lot.

Note: Some verbs can be either transitive or intransitive.

> Ms. Hull **teaches** physiology and microbiology. (transitive)
> She **teaches** well. (intransitive)

626.3

Auxiliary (Helping) Verbs

Auxiliary verbs (helping verbs) help to form some of the *tenses* (628.1), the *mood* (629.2), and the *voice* (629.1) of the main verb. In the following example, the auxiliary verbs are in **bold,** and the main verbs are in *italics.*

> I *believe,* I **have** always *believed,* and I **will** always *believe* in private enterprise as the backbone of economic well-being in America.
> —Franklin D. Roosevelt

Common Auxiliary Verbs							
am	been	could	does	have	might	should	will
are	being	did	had	is	must	was	would
be	can	do	has	may	shall	were	

esl Note: "Be" auxiliary verbs are always followed by either a verb ending in *ing* or a past participle. Also see "Common Modal Auxiliary Verbs" (662.2).

Linking (State of Being) Verbs

A **linking verb** is a special form of intransitive verb that links the subject of a sentence to a noun, a pronoun, or an adjective in the predicate. (See the chart below.)

The streets **are** flooded. (adjective)   The streets **are** rivers! (noun)

Common Linking Verbs
am are be become been being is was were
Additional Linking Verbs
appear feel look seem sound grow remain smell taste

Note: The verbs listed as "additional linking verbs" above function as linking verbs when they do not show actual action. An adjective usually follows these linking verbs.

The thunder **sounded** ominous. (adjective)

My little brother **grew** frightened. (adjective)

Note: When these same words are used as action verbs, an adverb or a direct object may follow them.

I **looked** carefully at him. (adverb)

My little brother **grew** corn for a science project. (direct object)

Forms of Verbs

A verb's **form** differs depending on its *number* (singular, plural), *person* (first, second, third), *tense* (present, past, future, present perfect, past perfect, future perfect), *voice* (active, passive), and *mood* (indicative, imperative, subjunctive).

Number of a Verb

Number indicates whether a verb is singular or plural. The verb and its subject both must be singular, or they both must be plural. (See "Subject–Verb Agreement," pages 645–648.)

My college **enrolls** high schoolers in summer programs. (singular)

Many colleges **enroll** high schoolers in summer courses. (plural)

Person of a Verb

Person indicates whether the subject of the verb is *first, second,* or *third person.* The verb and its subject must be in the same person. Verbs usually have a different form only in **third person singular of the present tense.**

	First Person	**Second Person**	**Third Person**
Singular	I think	you think	he/she/it thinks
Plural	we think	you think	they think

628.1 <u>Tense of a Verb</u>

Tense indicates the time of an action or state of being. There are three basic tenses (*past, present, and future*) and three verbal aspects (*progressive, perfect, and perfect progressive*).

628.2 <u>Present Tense</u>

Present tense expresses action happening at the present time or regularly.

In the United States, more than 75 percent of workers **hold** service jobs.

Present progressive tense also expresses action that is happening continually, in an ongoing fashion at the present time, but it is formed by combining *am, are,* or *is* and the present participle (ending in *ing*) of the main verb.

More women than ever before **are working** outside the home.

Present perfect tense expresses action that began in the past and has recently been completed or that continues up to the present time.

My sister **has taken** four years of swimming lessons.

Present perfect progressive tense also expresses an action that began in the past but stresses the continuing nature of the action. Like the present progressive tense, it is formed by combining auxiliary verbs (*have been* or *has been*) and present participles.

She **has been taking** them since she was six years old.

628.3 <u>Past Tense</u>

Past tense expresses action that was completed at a particular time in the past.

A hundred years ago, more than 75 percent of laborers **worked** in agriculture.

Past progressive tense expresses past action that continued over an interval of time. It is formed by combining *was* or *were* with the present participle of the main verb.

A century ago, my great-grandparents **were farming.**

Past perfect tense expresses an action in the past that was completed at a specific time before another past action occurred.

By the time we sat down for dinner, my cousins **had eaten** all the olives.

Past perfect progressive tense expresses a past action but stresses the continuing nature of the action. It is formed by using *had been* along with the present participle.

They **had been eating** the olives all afternoon.

628.4 <u>Future Tense</u>

Future tense expresses action that will take place in the future.

Next summer I **will work** as a lifeguard.

Future progressive tense expresses an action that will be continuous in the future.

I **will be working** for the park district at North Beach.

Future perfect tense expresses future action that will be completed by a specific time.

By 10:00 p.m., I **will have completed** my research project.

Future perfect progressive tense also expresses future action that will be completed by a specific time but (as with other perfect progressive tenses) stresses the action's continuous nature. It is formed using *will have been* along with the present participle.

I **will have been researching** the project for three weeks by the time it's due.

Voice of a Verb

629.1

Voice indicates whether the subject is acting or being acted upon.

Active voice indicates that the subject of the verb is performing the action.

> People **update** their resumés on a regular basis. (The subject, *People*, is acting; *resumés* is the direct object.)

Passive voice indicates that the subject of the verb is being acted upon or is receiving the action. A passive verb is formed by combining a *be* verb with a past participle.

> Your resumé **should be updated** on a regular basis. (The subject, *resumé*, is receiving the action.)

Using Active Voice

Generally, use active voice rather than passive voice for more direct, energetic writing. To change your passive sentences to active ones, do the following: First, find the noun that is doing the action and make it the subject. Then find the word that had been the subject and use it as the direct object.

Passive: The winning goal **was scored** by Eva. (The subject, *goal*, is not acting.)

Active: Eva **scored** the winning goal. (The subject, *Eva*, is acting.)

Note: When you want to emphasize the receiver more than the doer—or when the doer is unknown—use the passive voice. (Much technical and scientific writing regularly uses the passive voice.)

Mood of a Verb

629.2

The **mood** of a verb indicates the tone or attitude with which a statement is made.

Indicative mood, the most common, is used to state a fact or to ask a question.

> **Can** any theme **capture** the essence of the complex 1960s culture? President John F. Kennedy's directive [stated below] **represents** one ideal popular during that decade.

Imperative mood is used to give a command. (The subject of an imperative sentence is *you*, which is usually understood and not stated in the sentence.)

> **Ask** not what your country can do for you—**ask** what you can do for your country.
> —John F. Kennedy

Subjunctive mood is used to express a wish, an impossibility or unlikely condition, or a necessity. The subjunctive mood is often used with *if* or *that*. The verb forms below create an atypical subject–verb agreement, forming the subjunctive mood.

> If I **were** rich, I would travel for the rest of my life. (a wish)

> If each of your brain cells **were** one person, there would be enough people to populate 25 planets. (an impossibility)

> The English Department requires that every student **pass** a proficiency test. (a necessity)

630.1 Verbals

A **verbal** is a word that is made from a verb, but it functions as a noun, an adjective, or an adverb. There are three types of verbals: *gerunds, infinitives,* and *participles.*

630.2 Gerunds

A **gerund** ends in *ing* and is used as a noun.

Waking each morning is the first challenge. (subject)

I start **moving** at about seven o'clock. (direct object)

I work at **jump-starting** my weary system. (object of the preposition)

As Woody Allen once said, "Eighty percent of life is **showing up**."
(predicate nominative)

630.3 Infinitives

An **infinitive** is *to* and the base form of the verb. The infinitive may be used as a noun, an adjective, or an adverb.

To succeed is not easy. (noun)

That is the most important thing **to remember**. (adjective)

Students are wise **to work** hard. (adverb)

esl **Note:** It can be difficult to know whether a gerund or an infinitive should follow a verb. It's helpful to become familiar with lists of specific verbs that can be followed by one but not the other. (See **661.2–662.1**.)

630.4 Participles

A **present participle** ends in *ing* and functions as an adjective. A **past participle** ends in *ed* (or another past tense form) and also functions as an adjective.

The **studying** students were annoyed by the **partying** ones.
The students **playing** loud music were **annoying**.
(These participles function as adjectives: *studying* students and *partying* students. Notice, however, that *playing* has a direct object: *music*. All three types of verbals may have direct objects. See **640.3**.)

Using Verbals

Make sure that you use verbals correctly; look carefully at the examples below.

Verbal: **Diving** is a popular Olympic sport.
(*Diving* is a gerund used as a subject.)

Diving gracefully, the Olympian hoped to get high marks.
(*Diving* is a participle modifying *Olympian*.)

Verb: The next competitor was **diving** in the practice pool.
(Here, *diving* is a verb, not a verbal.)

Irregular Verbs

Irregular verbs can often be confusing. That's because the past tense and past participle of irregular verbs are formed by changing the word itself, not merely by adding *d* or *ed*. The following list contains the most troublesome irregular verbs.

Common Irregular Verbs and Their Principal Parts

Present Tense	Past Tense	Past Participle	Present Tense	Past Tense	Past Participle	Present Tense	Past Tense	Past Participle
am, be	was, were	been	fly	flew	flown	see	saw	seen
arise	arose	arisen	forget	forgot	forgotten, forgot	set	set	set
awake	awoke, awaked	awoken, awaked	freeze	froze	frozen	shake	shook	shaken
beat	beat	beaten	get	got	gotten	shine (light)	shone	shone
become	became	become	give	gave	given	shine (polish)	shined	shined
begin	began	begun	go	went	gone	show	showed	shown
bite	bit	bitten, bit	grow	grew	grown	shrink	shrank	shrunk
blow	blew	blown	hang (execute)	hanged	hanged	sing	sang	sung
break	broke	broken	hang (suspend)	hung	hung	sink	sank	sunk
bring	brought	brought	have	had	had	sit	sat	sat
build	built	built	hear	heard	heard	sleep	slept	slept
burn	burnt, burned	burnt, burned	hide	hid	hidden	speak	spoke	spoken
			hit	hit	hit	spend	spent	spent
burst	burst	burst	keep	kept	kept	spring	sprang	sprung
buy	bought	bought	know	knew	known	stand	stood	stood
catch	caught	caught	lay	laid	laid	steal	stole	stolen
choose	chose	chosen	lead	led	led	strike	struck	struck, stricken
come	came	come	leave	left	left			
cost	cost	cost	lend	lent	lent	strive	strove	striven
cut	cut	cut	let	let	let	swear	swore	sworn
dig	dug	dug	lie (deceive)	lied	lied	swim	swam	swum
dive	dived, dove	dived	lie (recline)	lay	lain	swing	swung	swung
do	did	done	make	made	made	take	took	taken
draw	drew	drawn	mean	meant	meant	teach	taught	taught
dream	dreamed, dreamt	dreamed, dreamt	meet	met	met	tear	tore	torn
			pay	paid	paid	tell	told	told
drink	drank	drunk	prove	proved	proved, proven	think	thought	thought
drive	drove	driven				throw	threw	thrown
eat	ate	eaten	put	put	put	wake	woke, waked	woken, waked
fall	fell	fallen	read	read	read			
feel	felt	felt	ride	rode	ridden	wear	wore	worn
fight	fought	fought	ring	rang	rung	weave	wove	woven
find	found	found	rise	rose	risen	wind	wound	wound
flee	fled	fled	run	ran	run	wring	wrung	wrung
						write	wrote	written

Adjective

632.1 An **adjective** describes or modifies a noun or pronoun. The articles *a, an,* and *the* are adjectives.

> Advertising is **a big** and **powerful** industry. (*A*, *big*, and *powerful* modify the noun *industry*.)

Numbers are also adjectives.

> **Fifty-three** relatives came to my party.

632.2 *Note:* Many demonstrative, indefinite, and interrogative forms may be used as either adjectives or pronouns (*that, these, many, some, whose,* and so on). These words are adjectives if they come before a noun and modify it; they are pronouns if they stand alone.

> **Some** advertisements are less than truthful. (*Some* modifies *advertisements* and is an adjective.)

> **Many** cause us to chuckle at their outrageous claims. (*Many* stands alone; it is a pronoun and replaces the noun *advertisements*.)

632.3 ## Proper Adjectives

Proper adjectives are created from proper nouns and are capitalized.

> **English** has been influenced by advertising slogans. (proper noun)
> The **English** language is constantly changing. (proper adjective)

632.4 ## Predicate Adjectives

A **predicate adjective** follows a form of the *be* verb (or other linking verb) and describes the subject. (See **627.1**.)

> At its best, advertising is **useful;** at its worst, **deceptive.** (*Useful* and *deceptive* modify the noun *advertising*.)

632.5 ## Forms of Adjectives

Adjectives have three forms: *positive, comparative,* and *superlative*.

The **positive form** is the adjective in its regular form. It describes a noun or a pronoun without comparing it to anyone or anything else.

> Joysport walking shoes are **strong** and **comfortable.**

The **comparative form** (*-er, more,* or *less*) compares two things. (*More* and *less* are used generally with adjectives of two or more syllables.)

> Air soles make Mile Eaters **stronger** and **more comfortable** than Joysports.

The **superlative form** (*-est, most,* or *least*) compares three or more things. (*Most* and *least* are used most often with adjectives of two or more syllables.)

> My old Canvas Wonders are the **strongest, most comfortable** shoes of all!

esl *Note:* Two or more adjectives before a noun should have a certain order when they do not modify the noun equally. (See **571.3**.)

Adverb

An **adverb** describes or modifies a verb, an adjective, another adverb, or a whole sentence. An adverb answers questions such as *how, when, where, why, how often,* or *how much.*

> The temperature fell **sharply.** (*Sharply* modifies the verb *fell.*)

> The temperature was **quite** low. (*Quite* modifies the adjective *low.*)

> The temperature dropped **very quickly.** (*Very* modifies the adverb *quickly,* which modifies the verb *dropped.*)

> **Unfortunately,** the temperature stayed cool. (*Unfortunately* modifies the whole sentence.)

Types of Adverbs

Adverbs can be grouped in four ways: *time, place, manner,* and *degree.*

Time (These adverbs tell *when, how often,* and *how long.*)
   today, yesterday   daily, weekly   briefly, eternally

Place (These adverbs tell *where, to where,* and *from where.*)
   here, there   nearby, beyond   backward, forward

Manner (These adverbs often end in *ly* and tell *how* something is done.)
   precisely   regularly   regally   smoothly   well

Degree (These adverbs tell *how much* or *how little.*)
   substantially   greatly   entirely   partly   too

Forms of Adverbs

Adverbs have three forms: *positive, comparative,* and *superlative.*

The **positive form** is the adverb in its regular form. It describes a verb, an adjective, or another adverb without comparing it to anyone or anything else.

> With Joysport shoes, you'll walk **fast.** They support your feet **well.**

The **comparative form** (*-er, more,* or *less*) compares two things. (*More* and *less* are used generally with adverbs of two or more syllables.)

> Wear Jockos instead of Joysports, and you'll walk **faster.** Jockos' special soles support your feet **better** than the Joysports do.

The **superlative form** (*-est, most,* or *least*) compares three or more things. (*Most* and *least* are used most often with adverbs of two or more syllables.)

> Really, I walk **fastest** wearing my old Canvas Wonders. They seem to support my feet, my knees, and my pocketbook **best** of all.

Regular Adverbs			Irregular Adverbs		
positive	comparative	superlative	positive	comparative	superlative
fast	faster	fastest	well	better	best
effectively	more effectively	most effectively	badly	worse	worst

634.1

Exercise

Preposition

A **preposition** is a word (or group of words) that shows the relationship between its object (a noun or pronoun following the preposition) and another word in the sentence.

> **Regarding** your reasons **for** going **to** college, do they all hinge **on** getting a good job **after** graduation? (In this sentence, *reasons, going, college, getting,* and *graduation* are objects of their preceding prepositions *regarding, for, to, on,* and *after.*)

634.2

Prepositional Phrases

A **prepositional phrase** includes the preposition, the object of the preposition, and the modifiers of the object. A prepositional phrase may function as an adverb or an adjective.

> A broader knowledge **of the world** is one benefit **of higher education.** (The two phrases function as adjectives modifying the nouns *knowledge* and *benefit* respectively.)

> He placed the flower **in the window.** (The phrase functions as an adverb modifying the verb *placed.*)

634.3

Prepositions				
aboard	back of	except for	near to	round
about	because of	excepting	notwithstanding	save
above	before	for	of	since
according to	behind	from	off	subsequent to
across	below	from among	on	through
across from	beneath	from between	on account of	throughout
after	beside	from under	on behalf of	'til
against	besides	in	onto	to
along	between	in addition to	on top of	together with
alongside	beyond	in behalf of	opposite	toward
alongside of	but	in front of	out	under
along with	by	in place of	out of	underneath
amid	by means of	in regard to	outside	until
among	concerning	inside	outside of	unto
apart from	considering	inside of	over	up
around	despite	in spite of	over to	upon
as far as	down	instead of	owing to	up to
aside from	down from	into	past	with
at	during	like	prior to	within
away from	except	near	regarding	without

esl **Note:** Prepositions often pair up with a verb and become part of an idiom, a slang expression, or a two-word verb. (See pages **663** and **674–676.**)

Conjunction

635.1

A **conjunction** connects individual words or groups of words.

> **When** we came back to Paris, it was clear **and** cold **and** lovely.
>
> —Ernest Hemingway

Coordinating Conjunctions

635.2

Coordinating conjunctions usually connect a word to a word, a phrase to a phrase, or a clause to a clause. The words, phrases, or clauses joined by a coordinating conjunction are equal in importance or are of the same type.

> Civilization is a race between education **and** catastrophe.
>
> —H. G. Wells

Correlative Conjunctions

635.3

Correlative conjunctions are a type of coordinating conjunction used in pairs.

> There are two inadvisable ways to think: **either** believe everything **or** doubt everything.

Subordinating Conjunctions

635.4

Subordinating conjunctions connect two clauses that are not equally important. A subordinating conjunction connects a dependent clause to an independent clause. The conjunction is part of the dependent clause.

> Experience is the worst teacher; it gives the test **before** it presents the lesson.
> (The clause *before it presents the lesson* is dependent. It connects to the independent clause *it gives the test.*)

Conjunctions

635.5

Coordinating: and, but, or, nor, for, so, yet

Correlative: either, or; neither, nor; not only, but (but also); both, and; whether, or

Subordinating: after, although, as, as if, as long as, because, before, even though, if, in order that, provided that, since, so that, than, that, though, unless, until, when, whenever, where, while

---

Note: Relative pronouns (623.3) can also connect clauses.

Interjection

635.6

An **interjection** communicates strong emotion or surprise (*oh, ouch, hey,* and so on). Punctuation (often a comma or an exclamation point) is used to set off an interjection.

> **Hey!   Wait!   Well,** so much for catching the bus.

A Closer Look
at the Parts of Speech

Noun

A **noun** is a word that names something: a person, a place, a thing, or an idea.

Toni Morrison/author   *Lone Star*/film
UC–Davis/university   Renaissance/era
A Congress of Wonders/book

Pronoun

A **pronoun** is a word used in place of a noun.

| I | my | that | themselves | which |
| it | ours | they | everybody | you |

Verb

A **verb** is a word that expresses action, links words, or acts as an auxiliary verb to the main verb.

| are | break | drag | fly | run | sit | was |
| bite | catch | eat | is | see | tear | were |

Adjective

An **adjective** describes or modifies a noun or pronoun. (The articles *a, an,* and *the* are adjectives.)

The carbonated drink went down easy on **that hot, dry** day. (*The* and *carbonated* modify *drink; that, hot,* and *dry* modify *day.*)

Adverb

An **adverb** describes or modifies a verb, an adjective, another adverb, or a whole sentence. An adverb generally answers questions such as *how, when, where, how often,* or *how much.*

greatly	precisely	regularly	there
here	today	partly	quickly
slowly	yesterday	nearly	loudly

Preposition

A **preposition** is a word (or group of words) that shows the relationship between its object (a noun or pronoun that follows the preposition) and another word in the sentence. Prepositions introduce prepositional phrases, which are modifiers.

| across | for | with | out | to | of |

Conjunction

A **conjunction** connects individual words or groups of words.

| and | because | but | for | or | since | so | yet |

Interjection

An **interjection** is a word that communicates strong emotion or surprise. Punctuation (often a comma or an exclamation point) is used to set off an interjection from the rest of the sentence.

Stop! No! What, am I invisible?

Audio

Exercise

CONSTRUCTING SENTENCES

A **sentence** is made up of at least a subject (sometimes understood) and a verb and expresses a complete thought. Sentences can make statements, ask questions, give commands, or express feelings.

The web delivers the universe in a box.

Using Subjects and Predicates

637.1

Sentences have two main parts: a **subject** and a **predicate**.

Technology frustrates many people.

Exercise

Note: In the sentence above, *technology* is the subject—the sentence talks about technology. *Frustrates many people* is the complete predicate—it tells what the subject is doing.

The Subject

637.2

The **subject** names the person or thing either performing the action, receiving the action, or being described or renamed. The subject is most often a noun or a pronoun.

Technology is an integral part of almost every business.

Manufacturers need technology to compete in the world market.

They could not go far without it.

A verbal phrase or a noun dependent clause may also function as a subject.

To survive without technology is difficult. (infinitive phrase)

Downloading information from the web is easy. (gerund phrase)

That the information age would arrive was inevitable. (noun dependent clause)

Note: To determine the subject of a sentence, ask yourself *who* or *what* performs or receives the action or is described.

In most sentences, the subject comes before the verb; however, in many questions and some other instances, that order is reversed. (See 643.2, 643.3, 646.1, and 669.)

esl Note: Some languages permit the omission of a subject in a sentence; English does not. A subject must be included in every sentence. (The only exception is an "understood subject," which is discussed at 638.4.)

638.1   <u>Simple Subject</u>

A **simple subject** is the subject without the words that describe or modify it.

> Thirty years ago, reasonably well-trained **mechanics** could fix any car on the road.

638.2   <u>Complete Subject</u>

A **complete subject** is the simple subject *and* the words that describe or modify it.

> Thirty years ago, **reasonably well-trained mechanics** could fix any car on the road.

638.3   <u>Compound Subject</u>

A **compound subject** is composed of two or more simple subjects joined by a conjunction and sharing the same predicate(s).

> Today, **mechanics** and **technicians** would need to master a half million manual pages to fix every car on the road.

> **Dealerships** and their service **departments** must sometimes explain that situation to the customers.

638.4   <u>Understood Subject</u>

Sometimes a subject is **understood.** This means it is not stated in the sentence, but a reader clearly understands what the subject is. An understood subject occurs in a command (imperative sentence). (See 643.3.)

> **(You)** Park on this side of the street. (The subject *you* is understood.)

> Put the CD player in the trunk.

638.5   <u>Delayed Subject</u>

In sentences that begin with *There is, There was,* or *Here is,* the subject follows the verb.

> There are 70,000 **fans** in the stadium. (The subject is *fans; are* is the verb. *There* is an expletive, an empty word.)

> Here is a **problem** for stadium security. (*Problem* is the subject. *Here* is an adverb.)

The subject is also delayed in questions.

> Where was the **event**? (*Event* is the subject.)

> Was **Dave Matthews** playing? (*Dave Matthews* is the subject.)

The Predicate (Verb)

The **predicate,** which contains the verb, is the part of the sentence that either tells what the subject is doing, tells what is being done to the subject, or describes or renames the subject.

> Students **need technical skills as well as basic academic skills.**

Simple Predicate

A **simple predicate** is the complete verb without the words that describe or modify it. (The complete verb can consist of more that one word.)

> Today's workplace **requires** employees to have a range of skills.

Complete Predicate

A **complete predicate** is the verb, all the words that modify or explain it, and any objects or complements.

> Today's workplace **requires employees to have a range of skills.**

Compound Predicate

A **compound predicate** is composed of two or more verbs, all the words that modify or explain them, and any objects or complements.

> Engineers **analyze problems** and **calculate solutions.**

Direct Object

A **direct object** is the part of the predicate that receives the action of an active transitive verb. A direct object makes the meaning of the verb complete.

> Marcos visited several **campuses.** (The direct object *campuses* receives the action of the verb *visited* by answering the question "Marcos visited what?")

Note: A direct object may be compound.

> A counselor explained the academic **programs** and the application **process.**

Indirect Object

An **indirect object** is the word(s) that tells *to whom/to what* or *for whom/for what* something is done. A sentence must have a direct object before it can have an indirect object.

> I showed our **children** my new school.

> Use these questions to find an indirect object:
> - What is the verb?   *showed*
> - *Showed* what?   school (direct object)
> - Showed *school* to whom?   children (indirect object)

> I wrote **them** a note.

Note: An indirect object may be compound.

> I gave the **instructor** and a few **classmates** my e-mail address.

Using Phrases

640.1

A **phrase** is a group of related words that functions as a single part of speech. A phrase lacks a subject, a predicate, or both. There are three phrases in the following sentence:

Examples of technology can be found in ancient civilizations.

of technology
(prepositional phrase that functions as an adjective; no subject or predicate)

can be found
(verb phrase—all of the words of the verb; no subject)

in ancient civilizations
(prepositional phrase that functions as an adverb; no subject or predicate)

Types of Phrases

There are several types of phrases: *verb, verbal, prepositional, appositive,* and *absolute*.

640.2

Verb Phrase

A **verb phrase** consists of a main verb and its helping verbs.

Students, worried about exams, **have camped** at the library all week.

640.3

Verbal Phrase

A **verbal phrase** is a phrase that expands on one of the three types of verbals: *gerund, infinitive,* or *participle*. (See **630.1–630.4**.)

A **gerund phrase** consists of a gerund and its modifiers and objects. The whole phrase functions as a noun. (See **630.2**.)

Becoming a marine biologist is Rashanda's dream. (The gerund phrase is used as the subject of the sentence.)

She has acquainted herself with the various methods for **collecting sea-life samples.** (The gerund phrase is the object of the preposition *for*.)

An **infinitive phrase** consists of an infinitive and its modifiers and objects. The whole phrase functions as a noun, an adjective, or an adverb.

To dream is the first step in any endeavor. (The infinitive phrase functions as a noun used as the subject.)

Remember **to make a plan to realize your dream.** (The infinitive phrase *to make a plan* functions as a noun used as a direct object; *to realize your dream* functions as an adjective modifying plan.)

Finally, apply all of your talents and skills **to achieve your goals.** (The infinitive phrase functions as an adverb modifying *apply*.)

A **participial phrase** consists of a present or past participle (a verb form ending in *ing* or *ed*) and its modifiers. The phrase functions as an adjective.

Doing poorly in biology, Theo signed up for a tutor. (The participial phrase modifies the noun *Theo*.)

Some students **frustrated by difficult course work** don't seek help. (The participial phrase modifies the noun *students*.)

Functions of Verbal Phrases			
	Noun	**Adjective**	**Adverb**
Gerund	■		
Infinitive	■	■	■
Participial		■	

641.1

Prepositional Phrase

641.2

A **prepositional phrase** is a group of words beginning with a preposition and ending with its object, a noun or a pronoun. Prepositional phrases are used mainly as adjectives and adverbs. See 634.3 for a list of prepositions.

> Denying the existence **of exam week** hasn't worked **for anyone** yet.
> (The prepositional phrase *of exam week* is used as an adjective modifying the noun *existence*; *for anyone* is used as an adverb modifying the verb *has worked*.)

> Test days still dawn and GPAs still plummet **for the unprepared student.**
> (The prepositional phrase *for the unprepared student* is used as an adverb modifying the verbs *dawn* and *plummet*.)

esl **Note:** Do not mistake the following adverbs for nouns and incorrectly use them as objects of prepostions: *here, there, everywhere.*

Appositive Phrase

641.3

An **appositive phrase,** which follows a noun or a pronoun and renames it, consists of a noun and its modifiers. An appositive adds new information about the noun or pronoun it follows.

> The Olympic-size pool, **a prized addition to the physical education building,** gets plenty of use. (The appositive phrase renames *pool*.)

Absolute Phrase

641.4

An **absolute phrase** consists of a noun and a participle (plus the participle's object, if there is one, and any modifiers). It usually modifies the entire sentence.

> Their enthusiasm sometimes waning, the students who cannot swim are required to take lessons. (The noun *enthusiasm* is modified by the present participle *waning*; the entire phrase modifies *students*.)

Phrases can add valuable information to sentences, but some phrases add nothing but "fat" to your writing. For a list of phrases to avoid, see page 103.

Exercise

Using Clauses

A **clause** is a group of related words that has both a subject and a verb.

642.1 ## Independent/Dependent Clauses

An **independent clause** contains at least one subject and one verb, presents a complete thought, and can stand alone as a sentence; a **dependent clause** (also called a subordinate clause) does not present a complete thought and cannot stand alone (make sense) as a sentence.

> Though airplanes are twentieth-century inventions (dependent clause), people have always dreamed of flying (independent clause).

Exercise

Types of Clauses

There are three basic types of dependent, or subordinate, clauses: *adverb, adjective,* and *noun.* These dependent clauses are combined with independent clauses to form complex and compound-complex sentences.

642.2 ### Adverb Clause

An **adverb clause** is used like an adverb to modify a verb, an adjective, or an adverb. All adverb clauses begin with subordinating conjunctions. (See **635.4**.)

> **Because Orville won a coin toss,** he got to fly the power-driven air machine first. (The adverb clause modifies the verb *got.*)

642.3 ### Adjective Clause

An **adjective clause** is used like an adjective to modify a noun or a pronoun. Adjective clauses begin with relative pronouns (*which, that, who*). (See **623.3**.)

> The men **who invented the first airplane** were brothers, Orville and Wilbur Wright. (The adjective clause modifies the noun *men. Who* is the subject of the adjective clause.)

> The first flight, **which took place December 17, 1903,** was made by Orville. (The adjective clause modifies the noun *flight. Which* is the subject of the adjective clause.)

642.4 ### Noun Clause

A **noun clause** is used in place of a noun. Noun clauses can appear as subjects, as direct or indirect objects, as predicate nominatives, or as objects of prepositions. Noun clauses can also play a role in the independent clause. They are introduced by subordinating words such as *what, that, when, why, how, whatever, who, whom, whoever,* and *whomever.*

> He wants to know **what made modern aviation possible.** (The noun clause functions as the object of the infinitive.)

> **Whoever invents an airplane with vertical takeoff ability** will be a hero. (The noun clause functions as the subject.)

Note: If you can replace a whole clause with the pronoun *something* or *someone,* it is a noun clause.

Exercise

Using Sentence Variety

A sentence can be classified according to the kind of statement it makes and according to the way it is constructed.

Kinds of Sentences

Sentences can make five basic kinds of statements: *declarative, interrogative, imperative, exclamatory,* or *conditional.*

Declarative Sentence

Declarative sentences make statements. They tell us something about a person, a place, a thing, or an idea.

> In 1955, Rosa Parks refused to follow segregation rules on a bus in Montgomery, Alabama.

643.1

Interrogative Sentence

Interrogative sentences ask questions.

> Do you think Ms. Parks knew she was making history?
>
> Would you have had the courage to do what she did?

643.2

Imperative Sentence

Imperative sentences give commands. They often contain an understood subject (you). (See **638.4**.)

> Read chapters 6 through 10 for tomorrow.

esl **Note:** Imperative sentences with an understood subject are the only sentences in which it is acceptable to have no subjects stated.

643.3

Exclamatory Sentence

Exclamatory sentences communicate strong emotion or surprise. They are punctuated with exclamation points.

> I simply can't keep up with these long reading assignments!
>
> Oh my gosh, you scared me!

643.4

Conditional Sentence

Conditional sentences express two circumstances. One of the circumstances depends on the other circumstance. The words *if, when,* or *unless* are often used in the dependent clause in conditional sentences.

> **If** you practice a few study-reading techniques, college reading loads will be manageable.
>
> **When** I manage my time, it seems I have more of it.
>
> Don't ask me to help you **unless** you are willing to do the reading first.

643.5

Exercise

Structure of Sentences

A sentence may be *simple, compound, complex,* or *compound-complex,* depending on how the independent and dependent clauses are combined.

644.1

Simple Sentence

A **simple sentence** contains one independent clause. The independent clause may have compound subjects and verbs, and it may also contain phrases.

My **back aches.**
(single subject: *back;* single verb: *aches*)

My **teeth** and my **eyes hurt.**
(compound subject: *teeth* and *eyes;* single verb: *hurt*)

My **memory** and my **logic come** and **go.**
(compound subject: *memory* and *logic;* compound verb: *come* and *go*)

I **must need** a vacation.
(single subject: *I;* single verb: *must need;* direct object: *vacation*)

644.2

Compound Sentence

A **compound sentence** consists of two independent clauses. The clauses must be joined by a semicolon, by a comma and a coordinating conjunction (*and, but, or, nor, so, for, yet*), or by a semicolon followed by a conjunctive adverb (*besides, however, instead, meanwhile, then, therefore*) and a comma.

I had eight hours of sleep**, so** why am I so exhausted?

I take good care of myself**;** I get enough sleep.

I still feel fatigued**; therefore,** I must need more exercise.

644.3

Complex Sentence

A **complex sentence** contains one independent clause (in bold) and one or more dependent clauses (underlined).

When I can, **I get eight hours of sleep.** (dependent clause; independent clause)

When I get up on time, and if someone hasn't used up all the milk,

I eat breakfast. (two dependent clauses; independent clause)

When the dependent clause comes before the independent clause, use a comma.

644.4

Compound-Complex Sentence

A **compound-complex sentence** contains two or more independent clauses (in bold type) and one or more dependent clauses (underlined).

If I'm not in a hurry, **I take leisurely walks,** and **I try to spot some wildlife.**

(dependent clause; two independent clauses)

I saw a hawk when I was walking, and **other smaller birds were chasing it.**

(independent clause, dependent clause; independent clause)

Audio

AVOIDING SENTENCE ERRORS

Subject–Verb Agreement

645.1

The subject and verb of any clause must agree in both *person* and *number*. *Person* indicates whether the subject of the verb is *first, second,* or *third person*. *Number* indicates whether the subject and verb are *singular* or *plural*. (See 627.2, 627.3.)

Exercise

	Singular	**Plural**
First Person	I think	we think
Second Person	you think	you think
Third Person	he/she/it thinks	they think

Agreement in Number

645.2

A verb must agree in number (singular or plural) with its subject.

> The **student was** rewarded for her hard work. (Both the subject *student* and the verb *was* are singular; they agree in number.)

Note: Do not be confused by phrases that come between the subject and the verb. Such phrases may begin with words like *in addition to, as well as,* or *together with.*

> The **instructor,** as well as the students, **is** expected to attend the orientation. (*Instructor,* not *students,* is the subject.)

Compound Subjects

645.3

Compound subjects connected with *and* usually require a plural verb.

> **Dedication and creativity are** trademarks of successful students.

Note: If a compound subject joined by *and* is thought of as a unit, use a singular verb.

> **Macaroni and cheese is** always available in the cafeteria.

(Also see 646.3 and 646.4.)

646.1   ## Delayed Subjects

Delayed subjects occur when the verb comes *before* the subject in a sentence. In these inverted sentences, the true (delayed) subject must still agree with the verb.

> There **are** many nontraditional **students** on our campus.
> Here **is** the **syllabus** you need.
> (*Students* and *syllabus* are the subjects of these sentences, not the adverbs *there* and *here*.)

Note: Using an inverted sentence, on occasion, will lend variety to your writing style. Simply remember to make the delayed subjects agree with the verbs.

> However, included among the list's topmost items **was "revise research paper."**
> (Because the true subject here is singular—one item—the singular verb *was* is correct.)

646.2   ## Titles as Subjects

When the subject of a sentence is the title of a work of art, literature, or music, the verb should be singular. This is also true of a word (or phrase) being used as a word (or phrase).

> *Lyrical Ballads* **was** published in 1798 by two of England's greatest poets, Wordsworth and Coleridge. (Even though the title of the book, *Lyrical Ballads,* is plural in form, it is still a single title being used as the subject, correctly taking the singular verb *was.*)

> **"Over-the-counter drugs" is** a phrase that means nonprescription medications. (Even though the phrase is plural in form, it is still a single phrase being used as the subject, correctly taking the singular verb *is.*)

646.3   ## Singular Subjects with *Or* or *Nor*

Singular subjects joined by *or* or *nor* take a singular verb.

> Neither a **textbook** nor a **notebook is required** for this class.

Note: When the subject nearer a present-tense verb is the singular pronoun *I* or *you,* the correct singular verb does not end in *s.* (See the chart on page **645.**)

> Neither **Marcus** nor **I feel** (not *feels*) right about this.

> Either **Rosa** or **you have** (not *has*) to take notes for me.

> Either **you** or **Rosa has** to take notes for me.

646.4   ## Singular/Plural Subjects

When one of the subjects joined by *or* or *nor* is singular and one is plural, the verb must agree with the subject nearer the verb.

> Neither the **professor** nor her **students were** in the lab. (The plural subject *students* is nearer the verb; therefore, the plural verb *were* agrees with *students.*)

> Neither the **students** nor the **professor was** in the lab. (The singular subject *professor* is nearer the verb; therefore, the singular verb *was* is used to agree with *professor.*)

Collective Nouns 647.1

Generally, **collective nouns** (*faculty, pair, crew, assembly, congress, species, crowd, army, team, committee,* and so on) take a singular verb. However, if you want to emphasize differences among individuals in the group or are referring to the group as individuals, you can use a plural verb.

> My lab **team takes** its work very seriously. (*Team* refers to the group as a unit; it requires a singular verb, *takes*.)

> The **team assume** separate responsibilities for each study they undertake. (In this example, *team* refers to individuals within the group; it requires a plural verb, *assume*.)

Note: Collective nouns such as (the) *police, poor, elderly,* and *young* use plural verbs.

> The **police direct** traffic here between 7:00 and 9:00 a.m.

Plural Nouns with Singular Meaning 647.2

Some nouns that are plural in form but singular in meaning take a singular verb: *mumps, measles, news, mathematics, economics, robotics,* and so on.

> **Economics is** sometimes called "the dismal science."

> The economic **news is** not very good.

Note: The most common exceptions are *scissors, trousers, tidings,* and *pliers.*

> The **scissors are** missing again.

> **Are** these **trousers** prewashed?

With Linking Verbs 647.3

When a sentence contains a linking verb (usually a form of *be*)—and a noun or pronoun comes before and after that verb—the verb must agree with the subject, not the predicate nominative (the noun or pronoun coming after the verb).

> The cause of his problem **was** poor study habits. (*Cause* requires a singular verb, even though the predicate nominative, *habits,* is plural.)

> His poor study habits **were** the cause of his problem. (*Habits* requires a plural verb, even though the predicate nominative, *cause,* is singular.)

Nouns Showing Measurement, Time, and Money 647.4

Mathematical phrases and phrases that name a period of time, a unit of measurement, or an amount of money take a singular verb.

> Three and three **is** six.

> Eight pages **is** a long paper on this topic.

> In my opinion, two dollars is a high price for a cup of coffee.

648.1 Relative Pronouns

When a **relative pronoun** (*who, which, that*) is used as the subject of a dependent clause, the number of the verb is determined by that pronoun's antecedent. (The *antecedent* is the word to which the pronoun refers.)

> This is one of the **books that are** required for English class.
> (The relative pronoun *that* requires the plural verb *are* because its antecedent is *books,* not the word *one.* To test this type of sentence for agreement, read the *of* phrase first: *Of the books that are . . .*)

Note: Generally, the antecedent is the nearest noun or pronoun to the relative pronoun and is often the object of a preposition. Sometimes, however, the antecedent is not the nearest noun or pronoun, especially in sentences with the phrase "the only one of."

> Dr. Graciosa wondered why Claire was the only **one** of her students **who was** not attending lectures regularly. (In this case, the addition of the modifiers *the only* changes the meaning of the sentence. The antecedent of *who* is *one,* not *students.* Only one student was not attending.)

648.2 Indefinite Pronoun with Singular Verb

Many indefinite pronouns (*someone, somebody, something; anyone, anybody, anything; no one, nobody, nothing; everyone, everybody, everything; each, either, neither, one, this*) serving as subjects require a singular verb.

> **Everybody is** welcome to attend the chancellor's reception.
> **No one was** sent an invitation.

Note: Although it may seem to indicate more than one, *each* is a singular pronoun and requires a singular verb. Do not be confused by words or phrases that come between the indefinite pronoun and the verb.

> **Each** of the new students **is** (not *are*) encouraged to attend the reception.

648.3 Indefinite Pronoun with Plural Verb

Some indefinite pronouns (*both, few, many, most,* and *several*) are plural; they require a plural verb.

> **Few are** offered the opportunity to study abroad.
> **Most take** advantage of opportunities closer to home.

648.4 Indefinite Pronoun or Quantity Word with Singular/Plural Verb

Some indefinite pronouns or quantity words (*all, any, most, part, half, none,* and *some*) may be either singular or plural, depending on the nouns they refer to. Look inside the prepositional phrase to see what the antecedent is.

> **Some** of the students **were** missing. (*Students,* the noun that *some* refers to, is plural; therefore, the pronoun *some* is considered plural, and the plural verb *were* is used to agree with it.)

> **Most** of the lecture **was** over by the time we arrived. (Because *lecture* is singular, *most* is also singular, requiring the singular verb *was.*)

Pronoun–Antecedent Agreement

A pronoun must agree in number, person, and gender (sex) with its *antecedent*. The antecedent is the word to which the pronoun refers.

> **Yoshi** brought **his** laptop computer and e-book to school. (The pronoun *his* refers to the antecedent *Yoshi*. Both the pronoun and its antecedent are singular, third person, and masculine; therefore, the pronoun is said to agree with its antecedent.)

Singular Pronoun

Use a singular pronoun to refer to such antecedents as *each, either, neither, one, anyone, anybody, everyone, everybody, somebody, another, nobody,* and *a person.*

> **Each** of the maintenance vehicles has **their** doors locked at night. (Incorrect)
>
> **Each** of the maintenance vehicles has **its** doors locked at night. (Correct: Both *Each* and *its* are singular.)
>
> **Somebody** left **his or her** (not *their*) vehicle unlocked. (Correct)

Plural Pronoun

When a plural pronoun (*they, their*) is mistakenly used with a singular indefinite pronoun (such as *everyone* or *everybody*), you may correct the sentence by replacing *their* or *they* with optional pronouns (*her or his* or *he or she*), or make the antecedent plural.

> **Everyone** must learn to wait **their** turn. (Incorrect)
>
> **Everyone** must learn to wait **her or his** turn. (Correct: Optional pronouns *her* or *his* are used.)
>
> **People** must learn to wait **their** turns. (Correct: The singular antecedent, *Everyone,* is changed to the plural antecedent, *People.*)

Two or More Antecedents

When two or more antecedents are joined by *and,* they are considered plural.

> **Tomas** and **Jamal** are finishing **their** assignments.

When two or more singular antecedents are joined by *or* or *nor,* they are considered singular.

> **Connie** or **Shavonn** left **her** headset in the library.

Note: If one of the antecedents is masculine and one feminine, the pronouns should likewise be masculine and feminine.

> Is **Ahmad** or **Phyllis** bringing **his or her** laptop computer?

Note: If one of the antecedents joined by *or* or *nor* is singular and one is plural, the pronoun is made to agree with the nearer antecedent.

> Neither **Ravi** nor **his friends** want to spend **their** time studying.
>
> Neither **his friends** nor **Ravi** wants to spend **his** time studying.

Shifts in Sentence Construction

A shift is an improper change in structure midway through a sentence. The following examples will help you identify and fix several different kinds of shifts.

650.1

Shift in Person

Shift in person is mixing first, second, or third person within a sentence. (See 624.4, 627.3.)

> **Shift:** One may get spring fever unless **you** live in California or Florida. (The sentence shifts from third person, *one*, to second person, *you*.)
>
> **Corrected:** **You** may get spring fever unless **you** live in California or Florida. (Stays in second person)
>
> **Corrected:** **People** may get spring fever unless **they** live in California or Florida. (*People*, a third person plural noun, requires a third person plural pronoun, *they*.)

650.2

Shift in Tense

Shift in tense is using more than one tense in a sentence when only one is needed.

> **Shift:** Sheila **looked** at nine apartments in one weekend before she **had chosen** one. (Tense shifts from past to past perfect for no reason.)
>
> **Corrected:** Sheila **looked** at nine apartments in one weekend before she **chose** one. (Tense stays in past.)

650.3

Shift in Voice

Shift in voice is mixing active with passive voice. Usually, a sentence beginning in active voice should remain so to the end.

> **Shift:** As you look (active voice) for just the right place, many interesting apartments will probably be seen. (passive voice)
>
> **Corrected** As you look (active voice) for just the right place, **you will probably see** (active voice) many interesting apartments.

650.4

Unparallel Construction

Unparallel construction occurs when the kind of words or phrases being used shifts or changes in the middle of a sentence.

> **Shift:** In my hometown, people pass the time shooting pool, pitching horseshoes, and at softball games. (Sentence shifts from a series of general phrases, *shooting pool* and *pitching horseshoes*, to the prepositional phrase *at softball games*.)
>
> **Parallel:** In my hometown, people pass the time **shooting pool, pitching horseshoes, and playing softball.** (Now all three activities are gerund phrases—they are consistent, or parallel.)

Fragments, Comma Splices, and Run-Ons

Except in a few special situations, you should use complete sentences when you write. By definition, a complete sentence expresses a complete thought. However, a sentence may actually contain several ideas, not just one. The trick is getting those ideas to work together to form a clear, interesting sentence that expresses your exact meaning. Among the most common sentence errors that writers make are fragments, comma splices, and run-ons.

Fragments

A **fragment** is a phrase or dependent clause used as a sentence. It is not a sentence, however, because a phrase lacks a subject, a verb, or some other essential part, and a dependent clause must be connected to an independent clause to complete its meaning.

651.1

Exercise

> *Fragment:* Pete gunned the engine. Forgetting that the boat was hooked to the truck. (This is a sentence followed by a fragment. This error can be corrected by combining the fragment with the sentence.)
>
> Corrected: Pete gunned the engine, forgetting that the boat was hooked to the truck.
>
> *Fragment:* Even though my best friend had a little boy last year. (This clause does not convey a complete thought. We need to know what is happening despite the birth of the little boy.)
>
> Corrected: Even though my best friend had a little boy last year, **I do not comprehend the full meaning of "motherhood."**

Comma Splices

A **comma splice** is a mistake made when two independent clauses are connected ("spliced") with only a comma. The comma is not enough: A period, semicolon, or conjunction is needed.

651.2

Video

Exercise

> *Splice:* People say that being a stay-at-home mom or dad is an important job, their actions tell a different story.
>
> Corrected: People say that being a stay-at-home mom or dad is an important job, **but** their actions tell a different story. (The coordinating conjunction *but,* added after the comma, corrects the splice.)
>
> Corrected: People say that being a stay-at-home mom or dad is an important job; their actions tell a different story. (A semicolon—rather than just a comma—makes the sentence correct.)
>
> Corrected: People say that being a stay-at-home mom or dad is an important job. **Their** actions tell a different story. (A period creates two sentences and corrects the splice.)

652.1 Run-Ons

Exercise

A **run-on sentence** is actually two sentences (two independent clauses) joined without adequate punctuation or a connecting word.

Run-on: The Alamo holds a special place in American history it was the site of an important battle between the United States and Mexico.

Corrected: **The Alamo holds a special place in American history because it was the site of an important battle between the United States and Mexico.** (A subordinating conjunction is added to fix the run-on by making the second clause dependent.)

Run-on: Antonio de Santa Anna, the president of Mexico who once held a funeral for his amputated leg, is the same Santa Anna who stormed the Alamo he led his troops to victory over the Texan rebels defending that fort. Two famous American frontiersmen died they were James Bowie and Davy Crockett. Santa Anna enjoyed fame, power, and respect among his followers. He died in 1876 he was poor, blind, and ignored.

Corrected: Antonio de Santa Anna, the president of Mexico who once held a funeral for his amputated leg, is the same Santa Anna who stormed the Alamo. He led his troops to victory over the Texan rebels defending that fort. Two famous American frontiersmen were killed in the battle; they were James Bowie and Davy Crockett. Santa Anna enjoyed fame, power, and respect among his followers. When he died in 1876, he was poor, blind, and ignored.

652.2

The writer corrected the run-on sentences in the paragraph above by adding punctuation and making one sentence a dependent clause. While doing so, the writer also made a few changes to improve the ideas. The writer makes further improvements in the paragraph below by revising one sentence and by combining two sets of short sentences into one stronger sentence.

Improved: Antonio de Santa Anna, the president of Mexico who once held a funeral for his amputated leg, is the same Santa Anna who stormed the Alamo. He led his troops to victory over Texan rebels defending that fort. Two famous American frontiersmen, **James Bowie and Davy Crockett, were killed in the battle.** Santa Anna enjoyed fame, power, and respect among his followers; **but when** he died in 1876, he was poor, blind, and ignored.

Once you make a correction, you may see an opportunity to add, cut, or improve something else. Correcting and editing sentences can be frustrating at times, but with practice, these processes can become some of the more enjoyable parts of the writing process.

Misplaced and Dangling Modifiers

Writing is thinking. Before you can write clearly, you must think clearly. Nothing is more frustrating for the reader than having to reread writing just to understand its basic meaning. Look carefully at the common errors that follow. Then use this section as a checklist when you revise. Always avoid leaving misplaced or dangling modifiers in your finished work.

Misplaced Modifiers

653.1

Misplaced modifiers are descriptive words or phrases so separated from what they are describing that the reader is confused.

Misplaced: The neighbor's dog has nearly been barking nonstop for two hours. (*Nearly* been barking?)

Corrected: The neighbor's dog has been barking nonstop **for nearly two hours.** (Watch your placement of *only, just, nearly, barely,* and so on.)

Misplaced: The commercial advertised an assortment of combs for active people with unbreakable teeth. (*People* with unbreakable teeth?)

Corrected: The commercial advertised an assortment of combs **with unbreakable teeth for active people.** (*Combs* with unbreakable teeth)

Misplaced: The pool staff gave large beach towels to the students marked with chlorine-resistant ID numbers. (*Students* marked with chlorine-resistant ID numbers?)

Corrected: The pool staff gave large beach towels **marked with chlorine-resistant ID numbers to the students.** (*Towels* marked with chlorine-resistant ID numbers)

Dangling Modifiers

653.2

Dangling modifiers are descriptive phrases that tell about a subject that isn't stated in the sentence. These often occur as participial phrases containing *ing* or *ed* words.

Dangling: After standing in line all afternoon, the manager informed us that all the tickets had been sold. (It sounds as if the manager has been *standing in line all afternoon.*)

Corrected: **After we had stood in line all afternoon,** the manager informed us that all the tickets had been sold.

Dangling: After living in the house for one month, the electrician recommended we update all the wiring. (It sounds as if the electrician has been *living in the house.*)

Corrected: After living in the house for one month, **we hired an electrician, who recommended we update all the wiring.**

Exercise

Ambiguous Wording

Sloppy sentences confuse readers. No one should have to wonder, "What does this writer mean?" When you revise and edit, check for indefinite pronoun references, incomplete comparisons, and unclear wording.

654.1 Indefinite Pronoun References

An **indefinite reference** is a problem caused by careless use of pronouns. There must always be a word or phrase nearby (its antecedent) that a pronoun clearly replaces.

Indefinite: When Tonya attempted to put her dictionary on the shelf, it fell to the floor. (The pronoun *it* could refer to either the dictionary or the shelf since both are singular nouns.)

Corrected: When Tonya attempted to put her dictionary on the shelf, **the shelf** fell to the floor.

Indefinite: Juanita reminded Kerri that she needed to photocopy her resumé before going to her interview. (Who *needed to photocopy her resumé*—Juanita or Kerri?)

Corrected: Juanita reminded Kerri **to photocopy her resumé before going to her interview.**

654.2 Incomplete Comparisons

Incomplete comparisons—leaving out words that show exactly what is being compared to what—can confuse readers.

Incomplete: After completing our lab experiment, we concluded that helium is lighter. (*Lighter* than what?)

Corrected: After completing our lab experiment, we concluded that helium is lighter **than oxygen.**

654.3 Unclear Wording

One type of ambiguous writing is wording that has two or more possible meanings due to an unclear reference to something elsewhere in the sentence. (See **654.1**.)

Unclear: I couldn't believe that my sister bought a cat with all those allergy problems. (Who has the *allergy problems*—the cat or the sister?)

Corrected: I couldn't believe that my sister, **who is very allergic, bought a cat.**

Unclear: Dao intended to wash the car when he finished his homework, but he never did. (It is unclear which he *never did*—wash the car or finish his homework.)

Corrected: Dao intended to wash the car when he finished his homework, **but he never did manage to wash the car.**

Nonstandard Language

Nonstandard language is language that does not conform to the standards set by schools, media, and public institutions. It is often acceptable in everyday conversation and in fictional writing but seldom is used in formal speech or other forms of writing.

Exercise

Colloquial Language

655.1

Colloquial language is wording used in informal conversation that is unacceptable in formal writing.

> *Colloquial:*   Hey, wait up! Cal wants to go with.
>
> **Standard:**   **Hey, wait!** Cal wants to go with us.

Double Preposition

655.2

The use of certain **double prepositions**—*off of, off to, from off*—is unacceptable.

> *Double
> Preposition:*   Pick up the dirty clothes from off the floor.
>
> **Standard:**   Pick up the dirty clothes **from the floor.**

Substitution

655.3

Avoid substituting *and* for *to.*

> *Substitution:*   Try and get to class on time.
>
> **Standard:**   **Try to** get to class on time.

Avoid substituting *of* for *have* when combining with *could, would, should,* or *might.*

> *Substitution:*   I should of studied for that exam.
>
> **Standard:**   **I should have** studied for that exam.

Double Negative

655.4

A **double negative** is a sentence that contains two negative words used to express a single negative idea. Double negatives are unacceptable in academic writing.

> *Double
> Negative:*   After paying for essentials, I haven't got no money left.
>
> **Standard:**   **I haven't got** any money left. **/** **I have no** money left.

Slang

655.5

Avoid the use of **slang** or any "in" words in formal writing.

> *Slang:*   The way the stadium roof opened was way cool.
>
> **Standard:**   The way the stadium roof opened **was remarkable.**

QUICK GUIDE

Avoiding Sentence Problems

■ **Does every subject agree with its verb?** (See pages 645–648.)
- In person and number?
- When a word or phrase comes between the subject and the verb?
- When the subject is delayed?
- When the subject is a title?
- When a compound subject is connected with *or*?
- When the subject is a collective noun (*faculty, team,* or *crowd*)?
- When the subject is a relative pronoun (*who, which, that*)?
- When the subject is an indefinite pronoun (*everyone, anybody,* or *many*)?

■ **Does every pronoun agree with its antecedent?** (See page 649.)
- When the pronoun is a singular indefinite pronoun such as *each, either,* or *another*?
- When two antecedents are joined with *and*?
- When two antecedents are joined with *or*?

■ **Did you unintentionally create inappropriate shifts?** (See page 650.)
- In person?
- In tense?
- From active voice to passive voice?
- In another unparallel construction?

■ **Are all your sentences complete?** (See pages 651–652.)
- Have you used sentence fragments?
- Are some sentences "spliced" or run together?

■ **Did you use any misplaced modifiers or ambiguous wording?**
(See pages 653–654.)
- Have you used misplaced or dangling modifiers?
- Have you used incomplete comparisons or indefinite references?

■ **Did you use any nonstandard language?** (See page 655.)
- Have you used slang or colloquial language?
- Have you used double negatives or double prepositions?

MULTILINGUAL AND ESL GUIDELINES

Audio

English may be your second, third, or fifth language. As a multilingual learner, you bring to your writing the culture and knowledge of the languages you use. This broader perspective enables you to draw on many experiences and greater knowledge as you write and speak. Whether you are an international student or someone who has lived in North America a long time and is now learning more about English, this chapter provides you with important information about writing in English.

Five Parts of Speech

Noun

Count Nouns

Exercise

657.1

Count nouns refer to things that can be counted. They can have *a, an, the,* or *one* in front of them. One or more adjectives can come between the articles *a, an, the,* or *one* and the singular count noun.

> **an apple, one orange, a plum, a purple plum**

Count nouns can be singular, as in the examples above, or plural, as in the examples below.

> **plums, apples, oranges**

Note: When count nouns are plural, they can have the article *the,* a number, or a demonstrative adjective in front of them. (See **659.1** and **659.3**.)

> I used **the** plums to make a pie.
>
> He placed **five** apples on my desk.
>
> **These** oranges are so juicy!

The *number* of a noun refers to whether it names a single thing (*book*), in which case its number is *singular,* or whether it names more than one thing (*books*), in which case the number of the noun is *plural.*

Note: There are different ways in which the plural form of nouns is created. For more information, see pages **593–594**.

Web Link

658.1   ## Noncount Nouns

Noncount nouns refer to things that cannot be counted. Do not use *a, an,* or *one* in front of them. They have no plural form, so they always take a singular verb. Some nouns that end in *s* are not plural; they are noncount nouns.

fruit, furniture, rain, thunder, advice, mathematics, news

Abstract nouns name ideas or conditions rather than people, places, or objects. Many abstract nouns are noncount nouns.

The students had **fun** at the party. Good **health** is a wonderful gift.

Collective nouns name a whole category or group and are often noncount nouns.

homework, furniture, money, faculty, committee, flock

Note: The parts or components of a group or category named by a noncount noun are often count nouns. For example, *report* and *assignment* are count nouns that are parts of the collective, noncount noun *homework.*

658.2   ## Two-Way Nouns

Some nouns can be used as either count or noncount nouns, depending on what they refer to.

I would like a **glass** of water. (count noun)

Glass is used to make windows. (noncount noun)

Articles and Other Noun Markers

658.3   ## Specific Articles

Use articles and other noun markers or modifiers to give more information about nouns. The **specific** (or **definite**) **article** *the* is used to refer to a specific noun.

I found **the** book I misplaced yesterday.

658.4   ## Indefinite Articles and Indefinite Adjectives

Exercise

Use the **indefinite article** *a* or *an* to refer to a nonspecific noun. Use *an* before singular nouns beginning with the vowels *a, e, i, o,* and *u.* Use *a* before nouns beginning with all other letters of the alphabet, the consonants. Exceptions do occur: *a* unit; *a* university.

I always take **an** apple to work.

It is good to have **a** book with you when you travel.

Indefinite adjectives can also mark nonspecific nouns—*all, any, each, either, every, few, many, more, most, neither, several, some* (for singular and plural count nouns); *all, any, more, most, much, some* (for noncount nouns).

Every student is encouraged to register early.

Most classes fill quickly.

Determining Whether to Use Articles

Listed below are a number of guidelines to help you determine whether to use an article and which one to use.

Use *a* or *an* with singular count nouns that do not refer to one specific item.

A zebra has black and white stripes. **An apple** is good for you.

Do not use *a* or *an* with plural count nouns.

Zebras have black and white stripes. **Apples** are good for you.

Do not use *a* or *an* with noncount nouns.

Homework needs to be done promptly.

Use *the* with singular count nouns that refer to one specific item.

The apple you gave me was delicious.

Use *the* with plural count nouns.

The zebras at Brookfield Zoo were healthy.

Use *the* with noncount nouns.

The money from my uncle is a gift.

Do not use *the* with most singular proper nouns.

Mother Theresa loved the poor and downcast.

Note: There are many exceptions: the Sahara Desert, the University of Minnesota, the Fourth of July

Use *the* with plural nouns.

the Joneses (both Mr. and Mrs. Jones), **the Rocky Mountains, the United States**

Possessive Adjectives

The possessive case of nouns and pronouns can be used as adjectives to mark nouns.

possessive nouns: *Tanya's, father's, store's*
The car is **Tanya's,** not her **father's.**

possessive pronouns: *my, your, his, her, its, our*
My hat is purple.

Demonstrative Adjectives

Demonstrative pronouns can be used as adjectives to mark nouns.

Demonstrative adjectives: *this, that, these, those* (for singular and plural count nouns); *this, that* (for noncount nouns)
Those chairs are lovely. Where did you buy **that** furniture?

660.1   ## Quantifiers

Expressions of quantity and measure are often used with nouns. Below are some of these expressions and guidelines for using them.

The following expressions of quantity can be used with count nouns: *each, every, both, a couple of, a few, several, many, a number of.*

> We enjoyed **both** concerts we attended. **A couple of** songs performed were familiar to us.

Use a number to indicate a specific quantity of a continuum.

> I saw **fifteen** cardinals in the park.

To indicate a specific quantity of a noncount noun, use *a* + quantity (such as *bag, bottle, bowl, carton, glass,* or *piece*) + *of* + noun.

> I bought **a carton of milk, a head of lettuce, a piece of cheese,** and **a bag of flour** at the grocery store.

The following expressions can be used with noncount nouns: *a little, much, a great deal of.*

> We had **much** wind and **a little** rain as the storm passed through yesterday.

The following expressions of quantity can be used with both count and noncount nouns: *no/not any, some, a lot of, lots of, plenty of, most, all, this, that.*

> I would like **some** apples *(count noun)* and **some** rice *(noncount noun)*, please.

Exercise

Verb

As the main part of the predicate, a verb conveys much of a sentence's meaning. Using verb tenses and forms correctly ensures that your readers will understand your sentences as you intend them to. For a more thorough review of verbs, see pages **626–631**.

660.2   ## Progressive (Continuous) Tenses

Progressive or continuous tense verbs express action in progress (see page **628**).

To form the **present progressive** tense, use the helping verb *am, is,* or *are* with the *ing* form of the main verb.

> He **is washing** the car right now.
> Kent and Chen **are studying** for a test.

To form the **past progressive** tense, use the helping verb *was* or *were* with the *ing* form of the main verb.

> Yesterday he **was working** in the garden all day.
> Julia and Juan **were watching** a movie.

To form the **future progressive** tense, use *will* or a phrase that indicates the future, the helping verb *be,* and the *ing* form of the main verb.

> Next week he **will be painting** the house.
> He **plans to be painting** the house soon.

Exercise

661.1

Note that some verbs are generally not used in the progressive tenses, such as the following groups of frequently used verbs:

- Verbs that express thoughts, attitudes, and desires: *know, understand, want, prefer*
- Verbs that describe appearances: *seem, resemble*
- Verbs that indicate possession: *belong, have, own, possess*
- Verbs that signify inclusion: *contain, hold*
  Kala **knows** how to ride a motorcycle.
  NOT THIS: Kala **is knowing** how to ride a motorcycle.

Objects and Complements of Verbs

661.2

Active transitive verbs take objects. These can be direct objects, indirect objects, or object complements. Linking verbs take subject complements—predicate nominatives or predicate adjectives—that rename or describe the subject.

Infinitives as Objects

661.3

Infinitives can follow many verbs, including these: *agree, appear, attempt, consent, decide, demand, deserve, endeavor, fail, hesitate, hope, intend, need, offer, plan, prepare, promise, refuse, seem, tend, volunteer, wish.* (See **630.3** for more on infinitives.)

He **promised to bring** some samples.

The following verbs are among those that can be followed by a noun or pronoun plus the infinitive: *ask, beg, choose, expect, intend, need, prepare, promise, want.*

I **expect you to be** there on time.

Note: Except in the passive voice, the following verbs must have a noun or pronoun before the infinitive: *advise, allow, appoint, authorize, cause, challenge, command, convince, encourage, forbid, force, hire, instruct, invite, order, permit, remind, require, select, teach, tell, tempt, trust.*

I will **authorize Emily to use** my credit card.

Unmarked infinitives (no *to*) can follow these verbs: *have, help, let, make.*

These glasses **help me see** the board.

Gerunds as Objects

661.4

Gerunds can follow these verbs: *admit, avoid, consider, deny, discuss, dislike, enjoy, finish, imagine, miss, postpone, quit, recall, recommend, regret.* (Also see **630.2**.)

I **recommended hiring** Ian for the job.

Here *hiring* is the direct object of the active verb *recommended*, and *Ian* is the object of the gerund.

662.1 Infinitives or Gerunds as Objects

Either **gerunds** or **infinitives** can follow these verbs: *begin, continue, hate, like, love, prefer, remember, start, stop, try.*

> **I hate having** cold feet. **I hate to have** cold feet. (In either form, the verbal phrase is the direct object of the verb *hate*.)

Note: Sometimes the meaning of a sentence will change depending on whether you use a gerund or an infinitive.

> **I stopped to smoke.** (I *stopped* weeding the garden *to smoke* a cigarette.)

> **I stopped smoking.** (I no longer smoke.)

662.2 Common Modal Auxiliary Verbs

Modal auxiliary verbs are a kind of auxiliary verb. (See **626.3.**) They help the main verb express meaning. Modals are sometimes grouped with other helping or auxiliary verbs.

Modal verbs must be followed by the base form of a verb without *to* (not by a gerund or an infinitive). Also, modal verbs do not change form; they are always used as they appear in the following chart.

Modal	Expresses	Sample Sentence
can	ability	I *can* program a VCR.
could	ability	I *could* babysit Tuesday.
	possibility	He *could* be sick.
might	possibility	I *might* be early.
may, might	possibility	I *may* sleep late Saturday.
	request	*May* I be excused?
must	strong need	I *must* study more.
have to	strong need	I *have to* (have got to) exercise.
ought to	feeling of duty	I *ought to* (should) help Dad.
should	advisabillity	She *should* retire.
	expectation	I *should* have caught that train.
shall	intent	*Shall* I stay longer?
will	intent	I *will* visit my grandma soon.
would	intent	I *would* live to regret my offer.
	repeated action	He *would* walk in the meadow.
would + you	polite request	*Would you* help me?
could + you	polite request	*Could you* type this letter?
will + you	polite request	*Will you* give me a ride?
can + you	polite request	*Can you* make supper tonight?

Common Two-Word Verbs

This chart lists some common verbs in which two words—a verb and a preposition—work together to express a specific action. A noun or pronoun is often inserted between the parts of the two-word verb when it is used in a sentence: break *it* down, call *it* off.

break down	to take apart or fall apart
call off	cancel
call up	make a phone call
clear out	leave a place quickly
cross out	draw a line through
do over	repeat
figure out	find a solution
fill in/out	complete a form or an application
fill up	fill a container or tank
* **find out**	discover
* **get in**	enter a vehicle or building
* **get out of**	leave a car, a house, or a situation
* **get over**	recover from a sickness or a problem
give back	return something
give in/up	surrender or quit
hand in	give homework to a teacher
hand out	give someone something
hang up	put down a phone receiver
leave out	omit or don't use
let in/out	allow someone or something to enter or go out
look up	find information
mix up	confuse
pay back	return money or a favor
pick out	choose
point out	call attention to
put away	return something to its proper place
put down	place something on a table, the floor, and so on.
put off	delay doing something
shut off	turn off a machine or light
* **take part**	participate
talk over	discuss
think over	consider carefully
try on	put on clothing to see if it fits
turn down	lower the volume
turn up	raise the volume
write down	write on a piece of paper

* These two-word verbs should *not* have a noun or pronoun inserted between their parts.

Spelling Guidelines for Verb Forms

Exercise

The same spelling rules that apply when adding a suffix to other words apply to verbs as well. Most verbs need a suffix to indicate tense or form. The third-person singular form of a verb, for example, usually ends in *s*, but it can also end in *es*. Formation of *ing* and *ed* forms of verbs and verbals needs careful attention, too. Consult the rules below to determine which spelling is correct for each verb. (For general spelling guidelines, see page **600**.)

fyi There may be exceptions to these rules when forming the past tense of irregular verbs because the verbs are formed by changing the word itself, not merely by adding *d* or *ed*. (See the chart of irregular verbs on page **631**.)

664.1

Past Tense: Adding *ed*

Add *ed* . . .

- When a verb ends with two consonants:

    touch—**touched**   ask—**asked**   pass—**passed**

- When a verb ends with a consonant preceded by two vowels:

    heal—**healed**   gain—**gained**

- When a verb ends in *y* preceded by a vowel:

    annoy—**annoyed**   flay—**flayed**

- When a multisyllable verb's last syllable is not stressed (even when the last syllable ends with a consonant preceded by a vowel):

    budget—**budgeted**   enter—**entered**   interpret—**interpreted**

Change *y* to *i* and add *ed* when a verb ends in a consonant followed by *y:*

    liquefy—**liquefied**   worry—**worried**

Double the final consonant and add *ed* . . .

- When a verb has one syllable and ends with a consonant preceded by a vowel:

    wrap—**wrapped**   drop—**dropped**

- When a multisyllable verb's last syllable (ending in a consonant preceded by a vowel) is stressed:

    admit—**admitted**   confer—**conferred**   abut—**abutted**

664.2

Past Tense: Adding *d*

Add *d* . . .

- When a verb ends with *e:*

    chime—**chimed**   tape—**taped**

- When a verb ends with *ie:*

    tie—**tied**   die—**died**   lie—**lied**

Present Tense: Adding *s* or *es*

Add *es* . . .

- When a verb ends in *ch, sh, s, x,* or *z:*

    watch—**watches**   fix—**fixes**

- To *do* and *go:*

    do—**does**   go—**goes**

Change *y* to *i* and add *es* when the verb ends in a consonant followed by *y:*

    liquefy—**liquefies**   quantify—**quantifies**

Add *s* to most other verbs, including those already ending in *e* and those that end in a vowel followed by *y:*

    write—**writes**   buy—**buys**

Present Tense: Adding *ing*

Drop the *e* and add *ing* when the verb ends in *e:*

    drive—**driving**   rise—**rising**

Double the final consonant and add *ing* . . .

- When a verb has one syllable and ends with a consonant preceded by a vowel:

    wrap—**wrapping**   sit—**sitting**

- When a multisyllable verb's last syllable (ending in a consonant preceded by a vowel) is stressed:

    forget—**forgetting**   begin—**beginning**   abut—**abutting**

Change *ie* to *y* and add *ing* when a verb ends with *ie:*

    tie—**tying**   die—**dying**   lie—**lying**

Add *ing* . . .

- When a verb ends with two consonants:

    touch—**touching**   ask—**asking**   pass—**passing**

- When a verb ends with a consonant preceded by two vowels:

    heal—**healing**   gain—**gaining**

- When a verb ends in *y:*

    buy—**buying**   study—**studying**   cry—**crying**

- When a multisyllable verb's last syllable is not stressed (even when the last syllable ends with a consonant preceded by a vowel):

    budget—**budgeting**   enter—**entering**   interpret—**interpreting**

Note: Never trust your spelling to even the best computer spell checker. Carefully proofread. Use a dictionary for questionable words your spell checker may miss.

Adjective

Placing Adjectives

You probably know that an adjective often comes before the noun it modifies. When several adjectives are used in a row to modify a single noun, it is important to arrange the adjectives in the well-established sequence used in English writing and speaking. The following list shows the usual order of adjectives. (Also see **571.3**.)

First, place . . .

1. articles .... **a, an, the**
   demonstrative adjectives .... **that, those**
   possessives .... **my, her, Misha's**

Then place words that . . .

2. indicate time .... **first, next, final**
3. tell how many .... **one, few, some**
4. evaluate .... **beautiful, dignified, graceful**
5. tell what size .... **big, small, short, tall**
6. tell what shape .... **round, square**
7. describe a condition .... **messy, clean, dark**
8. tell what age .... **old, young, new, antique**
9. tell what color .... **blue, red, yellow**
10. tell what nationality .... **English, Chinese, Mexican**
11. tell what religion .... **Buddhist, Jewish, Protestant**
12. tell what material .... **satin, velvet, wooden**

Finally, place nouns . . .

13. used as adjectives .... **computer [monitor], spice [rack]**

      my second try (1 + 2 + noun)

      gorgeous young white swans (4 + 8 + 9 + noun)

Present and Past Participles as Adjectives

Both the **present participle** and the **past participle** can be used as adjectives. (Also see **630.4**.) Exercise care in choosing whether to use the present participle or the past participle. A participle can come either before a noun or after a linking verb.

A **present participle** used as an adjective should describe a person or thing that is causing a feeling or situation.

    His **annoying** comments made me angry.

A **past participle** should describe a person or thing that experiences a feeling or situation.

    He was **annoyed** because he had to wait so long.

Note: Within each of the following pairs, the present (*ing* form) and past (*ed* form) participles have different meanings.

annoying/annoyed	depressing/depressed	fascinating/fascinated
boring/bored	exciting/excited	surprising/surprised
confusing/confused	exhausting/exhausted	

Nouns as Adjectives
667.1

Nouns sometimes function as adjectives by modifying another noun. When a noun is used as an adjective, it is always singular.

> Many European cities have **rose** gardens.

> Marta recently joined a **book** club.

TIP: Try to avoid using more than two nouns as adjectives for another noun. These "noun compounds" can get confusing. Prepositional phrases may get the meaning across better than long noun strings.

> *Correct:* Omar is a **crew** member in the **restaurant** kitchen during **second** shift.

> *Not correct:* Omar is a **second-shift restaurant kitchen crew** member.

Adverb

Placing Adverbs
Exercise
667.2

Consider the following guidelines for placing adverbs correctly. See page 633 for more information about adverbs.

Place adverbs that tell how often (*frequently, seldom, never, always, sometimes*) after a helping (auxiliary) verb and before the main verb. In a sentence without a helping verb, adverbs that tell *how often* are placed before an action verb but after a linking verb.

> The salesclerk will **usually** help me.

Place adverbs that tell when (*yesterday, now, at five o'clock*) at the end of a sentence.

> Auntie El came home **yesterday.**

Adverbs that tell where (*upside-down, around, downstairs*) usually follow the verb they modify. Many prepositional phrases (*at the beach, under the stairs, below the water*) function as adverbs that tell *where.*

> We waited **on the porch.**

Adverbs that tell how (*quickly, slowly, loudly*) can be placed either at the beginning, in the middle, or at the end of a sentence—but not between a verb and its direct object.

> **Softly** he called my name. He **softly** called my name. He called my name **softly.**

Place adverbs that modify adjectives directly before the adjective.

> That is a **most** unusual dress.

Adverbs that modify clauses are most often placed in front of the clause, but they can also go inside or at the end of the clause.

> **Fortunately,** we were not involved in the accident.
> We were not involved, **fortunately,** in the accident.
> We were not involved in the accident, **fortunately.**

Note: Adverbs that are used with verbs that have direct objects must *not* be placed between the verb and its object.

> *Correct:* Luis **usually** catches the most fish.   **Usually,** Luis catches the most fish.

> *Not correct:* Luis catches **usually** the most fish.

Exercise

Preposition

A **preposition** combines with a noun to form a prepositional phrase, which acts as a modifier—an adverb or an adjective. See pages 634 and 636 for a list of common prepositions and for more information about prepositions.

668.1

Using *in*, *on*, *at*, and *by*

In, *on*, *at*, and *by* are four common prepositions that refer to time and place. Here are some examples of how these prepositions are used in each case.

To show time

> **on** a specific day or date: *on* June 7, *on* Wednesday
>
> **in** part of a day: *in* the afternoon
>
> **in** a year or month: *in* 2008, *in* April
>
> **in** a period of time: completed *in* an hour
>
> **by** a specific time or date: *by* noon, *by* the fifth of May
>
> **at** a specific time of day or night: *at* 3:30 this afternoon

To show place

> **at** a meeting place or location: *at* school, *at* the park
>
> **at** the edge of something: standing *at* the bar
>
> **at** the corner of something: turning *at* the intersection
>
> **at** a target: throwing a dart *at* the target
>
> **on** a surface: left *on* the floor
>
> **on** an electronic medium: *on* the Internet, *on* television
>
> **in** an enclosed space: *in* the box, *in* the room
>
> **in** a geographic location: *in* New York City, *in* Germany
>
> **in** a print medium: *in* a journal
>
> **by** a landmark: *by* the fountain

TIP: Do not insert a preposition between a transitive verb and its direct object. Intransitive verbs, however, are often followed by a prepositional phrase (a phrase that begins with a preposition).

> I **cooked** hot dogs on the grill. (transitive verb)
>
> I **ate** in the park. (intransitive verb)

668.2

Phrasal Prepositions

Some prepositional phrases begin with more than one preposition. These **phrasal prepositions** are commonly used in both written and spoken communication. A list of common phrasal prepositions follows:

according to	because of	in case of	on the side of
across from	by way of	in spite of	up to
along with	except for	instead of	with respect to

Understanding Sentence Basics

Simple sentences in the English language follow the five basic patterns shown below. (See pages **637–644** for more information.)

Subject + Verb

┌─ S ─┐┌─ V ─┐
Naomie winked.

Some verbs like *winked* are intransitive. Intransitive verbs *do not* need a direct object to express a complete thought. (See **626.2**.)

Subject + Verb + Direct Object

┌ S ┐┌ V ┐┌─ DO ─┐
Harris grinds his teeth.

Some verbs like *grinds* are transitive. Transitive verbs *do* need a direct object to express a complete thought. (See **626.2**.)

Subject + Verb + Indirect Object + Direct Object

┌ S ┐┌ V ┐┌ IO ┐┌ DO ┐
Elena offered her friend an anchovy.

The direct object names who or what receives the action; the indirect object names to whom or for whom the action was done.

Subject + Verb + Direct Object + Object Complement

┌──── S ────┐┌ V ┐ DO ┌──── OC ────┐
The chancellor named Ravi the outstanding student of 2007.

The object complement renames or describes the direct object.

Subject + Linking Verb + Predicate Nominative (or Predicate Adjective)

┌ S ┐ LV ┌──── PN ────┐   ┌ S ┐ LV ┌── PA ──┐
Paula is a computer programmer.   **Paula is very intelligent.**

A linking verb connects the subject to the predicate noun or predicate adjective. The predicate noun renames the subject; the predicate adjective describes the subject.

Inverted Order

In the sentence patterns above, the subject comes before the verb. In a few types of sentences, such as those below, the subject comes *after* the verb.

LV ┌ S ┐ ┌ PN ┐   LV ┌── S ──┐
Is Larisa a poet?   **There was a meeting.**
(A question)   (A sentence beginning with "there")

Sentence Problems

This section looks at potential trouble spots and sentence problems. For more information about English sentences, their parts, and how to construct them see pages 637 through 644 in the handbook. Pages 645 through 656 cover the types of problems and errors found in English writing. The guide to avoiding sentence problems found on page 656 is an excellent editing tool.

670.1   ## Double Negatives

When making a sentence negative, use *not* or another negative adverb (*never, rarely, hardly, seldom,* and so on), but not both. Using both results in a double negative (see 655.4).

670.2   ## Subject–Verb Agreement

Be sure the subject and verb in every clause agree in person and number. (See pages 645–648.)

The **student was** rewarded for her hard work.

The **students were** rewarded for their hard work.

The **instructor,** as well as the students, **is** expected to attend the orientation.

The **students,** as well as the instructor, **are** expected to attend the orientation.

670.3   ## Omitted Words

Do not omit subjects or the expletives *there* or *here*. In all English clauses and sentences (except imperatives in which the subject *you* is understood), there must be a subject.

    Correct: Your mother was very quiet; **she** seemed to be upset.
Not correct: Your mother was very quiet; seemed to be upset.

    Correct: **There** is not much time left.
Not correct: Not much time left.

670.4   ## Repeated Words

Do not repeat the subject of a clause or sentence.

    Correct: The doctor prescribed an antibiotic.
Not correct: The doctor, **she** prescribed an antibiotic.

Do not repeat an object in an adjective dependent clause.

    Correct: I forgot the flowers that I intended to give to my hosts.
Not correct: I forgot the flowers that I intended to give **them** to my hosts.

Note: Sometimes the relative pronoun that begins the adjective dependent clause is omitted but understood.

    I forgot the flowers I intended to give to my hosts.
    (The relative pronoun *that* is omitted.)

Conditional Sentences

Conditional sentences express a situation requiring that a condition be met in order to be true. Selecting the correct verb tense for use in the two clauses of a conditional sentence can be problematic. Below you will find an explanation of the three types of conditional sentences and the verb tenses that are needed to form them.

1. **Factual conditionals:** The conditional clause begins with *if, when, whenever,* or a similar expression. Furthermore, the verbs in the conditional clause and the main clause should be in the same tense.

   Whenever we **had** time, we **took** a break and **went** for a swim.

2. **Predictive conditionals** express future conditions and possible results. The conditional clause begins with *if* or *unless* and has a present tense verb. The main clause uses a modal (*will, can, should, may, might*) plus the base form of the verb.

   Unless we **find** a better deal, we **will buy** this sound system.

3. **Hypothetical past conditionals** describe a situation that is unlikely to happen or that is contrary to fact. To describe situations in the past, the verb in the conditional clause is in the past perfect tense, and the verb in the main clause is formed from *would have, could have,* or *might have* plus the past participle.

   If we **had started out** earlier, we **would have arrived** on time.

Note: If the hypothetical situation is a present or future one, the verb in the conditional clause is in the past tense, and the verb in the main clause is formed from *would, could,* or *might* plus the base form of the verb.

   If we **bought** groceries once a week, we **would** not **have** to go to the store so often.

Quoted and Reported Speech

Quoted speech is the use of exact words from another source in your own writing; you must enclose these words in quotation marks. It is also possible to report nearly exact words without quotation marks. This is called **reported speech,** or indirect quotation. (See pages 582–583 for a review of the use of quotation marks.)

   Direct quotation: Felicia said, "Don't worry about tomorrow."

   Indirect quotation: Felicia said that you don't have to worry about tomorrow.

In the case of a question, when a direct quotation is changed to an indirect quotation, the question mark is not needed.

   Direct quotation: Ahmad asked, "Which of you will give me a hand?"

   Indirect quotation: Ahmad asked which of us would give him a hand.

Notice how pronouns are often changed in indirect quotations.

   Direct quotation: My friends said, "**You**'re crazy."

   Indirect quotation: My friends said that **I** was crazy.

Note: In academic writing, the use of another source's spoken or written words in one's own writing without proper acknowledgment is called *plagiarism.* Plagiarism is severely penalized in academic situations. (See pages 476–479.)

671.1

671.2

Numbers, Word Parts, and Idioms

Exercise

Numbers

As a multilingual/ESL learner, you may be accustomed to a way of writing numbers that is different than the way it is done in North America. Become familiar with the North American conventions for writing numbers. Pages **595** and **596** show you how numbers are written and punctuated in both word and numeral form.

672.1

Using Punctuation with Numerals

Note that the **period** is used to express percentages (5.5%, 75.9%) and the **comma** is used to organize large numbers into units (7,000; 23,100; 231,990,000). Commas are not used, however, in writing the year (2002). (Also see **574.1** and **574.6**.)

672.2

Cardinal Numbers

Cardinal numbers are used when counting a number of parts or objects. Cardinal numbers can be used as nouns (she counted to **ten**), pronouns (I invited many guests, but only **three** came), or adjectives (there are **ten** boys here).

Write out in words the numbers one through one hundred. Numbers 101 and greater are often written as numerals. (See **595.1**.)

672.3

Ordinal Numbers

Ordinal numbers show place or succession in a series: the fourth row, the twenty-first century, the tenth time, and so on. Ordinal numbers are used to talk about the parts into which a whole can be divided, such as a fourth or a tenth, and as the denominator in fractions, such as one-fourth or three-fifths. Written fractions can also be used as nouns (I gave him **four-fifths**) or as adjectives (a **four-fifths** majority).

Note: See the list below for names and symbols of the first twenty-five ordinal numbers. Consult a college dictionary for a complete list of cardinal and ordinal numbers.

First	1st	Tenth	10th	Nineteenth	19th
Second	2nd	Eleventh	11th	Twentieth	20th
Third	3rd	Twelfth	12th	Twenty-first	21st
Fourth	4th	Thirteenth	13th	Twenty-second	22nd
Fifth	5th	Fourteenth	14th	Twenty-third	23rd
Sixth	6th	Fifteenth	15th	Twenty-fourth	24th
Seventh	7th	Sixteenth	16th	Twenty-fifth	25th
Eighth	8th	Seventeenth	17th		
Ninth	9th	Eighteenth	18th		

Exercise

Prefixes, Suffixes, and Roots

Following is a list of many common word parts and their meanings. Learning them can help you determine the meaning of unfamiliar words as you come across them in your reading. For instance, if you know that *hemi* means "half," you can conclude that *hemisphere* means "half of a sphere."

Prefixes	Meaning	Suffixes	Meaning
a, an	not, without	able, ible	able, can do
anti, ant	against	age	act of, state of
co, con, com	together, with	al	relating to
di	two, twice	ate	cause, make
dis, dif	apart, away	en	made of
ex, e, ec, ef	out	ence, ency	action, quality
hemi, semi	half	esis, osis	action, process
il, ir, in, im	not	ice	condition, quality
inter	between	ile	relating to
intra	within	ish	resembling
multi	many	ment	act of, state of
non	not	ology	study, theory
ob, of, op, oc	toward, against	ous	full of, having
per	throughout	sion, tion	act of, state of
post	after	some	like, tending to
super, supr	above, more	tude	state of
trans, tra	across, beyond	ward	in the direction of
tri	three		
uni	one		

Roots	Meaning	Roots	Meaning
acu	sharp	ject	throw
am, amor	love, liking	log, ology	word, study, speech
anthrop	man	man	hand
aster, astr	star	micro	small
auto	self	mit, miss	send
biblio	book	nom	law, order
bio	life	onym	name
capit, capt	head	path, pathy	feeling, suffering
chron	time	rupt	break
cit	to call, start	scrib, script	write
cred	believe	spec, spect, spic	look
dem	people	tele	far
dict	say, speak	tempo	time
erg	work	tox	poison
fid, feder	faith, trust	vac	empty
fract, frag	break	ver, veri	true
graph, gram	write, written	zo	animal

Exercise

Web Link

Idioms

Idioms are phrases that are used in a special way. An idiom can't be understood just by knowing the meaning of each word in the phrase. It must be learned as a whole. For example, the idiom *to bury the hatchet* means "to settle an argument," even though the individual words in the phrase mean something much different. These pages list some of the common idioms in American English.

a bad apple	• One troublemaker on a team may be called **a bad apple.** *(a bad influence)*
an axe to grind	• Mom has **an axe to grind** with the owners of the dog that dug up her flower garden. *(a problem to settle)*
as the crow flies	• She lives only two miles from here **as the crow flies.** *(in a straight line)*
beat around the bush	• Dad said, "Where were you? Don't **beat around the bush.**" *(avoid getting to the point)*
benefit of the doubt	• Ms. Hy gave Henri the **benefit of the doubt** when he explained why he fell asleep in class. *(another chance)*
beyond the shadow of a doubt	• Salvatore won the 50-yard dash **beyond the shadow of a doubt.** *(for certain)*
blew my top	• When my money got stolen, I **blew my top.** *(showed great anger)*
bone to pick	• Nick had a **bone to pick** with Adrian when he learned they both liked the same girl. *(problem to settle)*
break the ice	• Shanta was the first to **break the ice** in the room full of new students. *(start a conversation)*
burn the midnight oil	• Carmen had to **burn the midnight oil** the day before the big test. *(work late into the night)*
chomping at the bit	• Dwayne was **chomping at the bit** when it was his turn to bat. *(eager, excited)*
cold shoulder	• Alicia always gives me the **cold shoulder** after our disagreements. *(ignores me)*
cry wolf	• If you **cry wolf** too often, no one will come when you really need help. *(say you are in trouble when you aren't)*
drop in the bucket	• My donation was a **drop in the bucket.** *(a small amount compared with what's needed)*
face the music	• José had to **face the music** when he got caught cheating on the test. *(deal with the punishment)*
flew off the handle	• Tramayne **flew off the handle** when he saw his little brother playing with matches. *(became very angry)*

floating on air	• Teresa was **floating on air** when she read the letter. *(feeling very happy)*
food for thought	• The coach gave us some **food for thought** when she said that winning isn't everything. *(something to think about)*
get down to business	• In five minutes you need to **get down to business** on this assignment. *(start working)*
get the upper hand	• The other team will **get the upper hand** if we don't play better in the second half. *(probably win)*
hit the ceiling	• Rosa **hit the ceiling** when she saw her sister painting the television. *(was very angry)*
hit the hay	• Patrice **hit the hay** early because she was tired. *(went to bed)*
in a nutshell	• **In a nutshell,** Coach Roby told us to play our best. *(to summarize)*
in the nick of time	• Zong grabbed his little brother's hand **in the nick of time** before he touched the hot pan. *(just in time)*
in the same boat	• My friend and I are **in the same boat** when it comes to doing Saturday chores. *(have the same problem)*
iron out	• Jamil and his brother were told to **iron out** their differences about cleaning their room. *(solve, work out)*
it stands to reason	• **It stands to reason** that if you keep lifting weights, you will get stronger. *(it makes sense)*
knuckle down	• Grandpa told me to **knuckle down** at school if I want to be a doctor. *(work hard)*
learn the ropes	• Being new in school, I knew it would take some time to **learn the ropes.** *(get to know how things are done)*
let's face it	• **"Let's face it!"** said Mr. Sills. "You're a better long distance runner than you are a sprinter." *(let's admit it)*
let the cat out of the bag	• Tia **let the cat out of the bag** and got her sister in trouble. *(told a secret)*
lose face	• If I strike out again, I will **lose face.** *(be embarrassed)*
nose to the grindstone	• If I keep my **nose to the grindstone,** I will finish my homework in one hour. *(working hard)*
on cloud nine	• Walking home from the party, I was **on cloud nine.** *(feeling very happy)*
on pins and needles	• I was **on pins and needles** as I waited to see the doctor. *(feeling nervous)*

over and above	• **Over and above** the assigned reading, I read two library books. *(in addition to)*
put his foot in his mouth	• Chivas **put his foot in his mouth** when he called his teacher by the wrong name. *(said something embarrassing)*
put your best foot forward	• Grandpa said that whenever you do something, you should **put your best foot forward.** *(do the best that you can do)*
rock the boat	• The coach said, "Don't **rock the boat** if you want to stay on the team." *(cause trouble)*
rude awakening	• I had a **rude awakening** when I saw the letter F at the top of my Spanish quiz. *(sudden, unpleasant surprise)*
save face	• Grant tried to **save face** when he said he was sorry for making fun of me in class. *(fix an embarrassing situation)*
see eye to eye	• My sister and I finally **see eye to eye** about who gets to use the phone first after school. *(are in agreement)*
sight unseen	• Grandma bought the television **sight unseen.** *(without seeing it first)*
take a dim view	• My brother will **take a dim view** if I don't help him at the store. *(disapprove)*
take it with a grain of salt	• If my sister tells you she has no homework, **take it with a grain of salt.** *(don't believe everything you're told)*
take the bull by the horns	• This team needs to **take the bull by the horns** to win the game. *(take control)*
through thick and thin	• Max and I will be friends **through thick and thin.** *(in good times and in bad times)*
time flies	• When you're having fun, **time flies.** *(time passes quickly)*
time to kill	• We had **time to kill** before the ballpark gates would open. *(extra time)*
to go overboard	• The teacher told us not **to go overboard** with fancy lettering on our posters. *(to do too much)*
under the weather	• I was feeling **under the weather,** so I didn't go to school. *(sick)*
word of mouth	• We found out who the new teacher was by **word of mouth.** *(talking to other people)*

Web Link

Note: Like idioms, **collocations** are groups of words that often appear together. They may help you identify different senses of a word; for example, *old* means slightly different things in these collocations: *old* man, *old* friends. You will find sentence construction easier if you check for collocations.

Targeting Trouble Spots

A sentence that is perfectly acceptable in one language may be unacceptable when directly translated into English. For example, many East Asian languages do not use articles, so using these words can be a challenge to learners of English. The following pages will help you target trouble spots for your general language group.

Help for Speakers of Latin American Languages

Advice	DO NOT Write . . .	DO Write . . .
Study the use of count and noncount nouns (657.1–658.2).	I have three homeworks.	I have three homework assignments. *or* I have three types of homework.
Do not omit the subject, *it* as subject, or *there* with delayed subjects (638.5, 670.3).	Is hot sitting in this room. Are going to the theater.	It is hot sitting in this room. We are going to the theater.
Place most subjects before the verb (669).	Gave I the tutor my thanks.	I gave the tutor my thanks.
Avoid using *the* with certain generalizations (659.1).	The business is a difficult major.	Business is a difficult major.
Avoid using *the* with singular proper nouns (659.1).	The April is the cruelest month.	April is the cruelest month.
Avoid double subjects (670.4).	My mother she is a nurse.	My mother is a nurse.
Learn whether to use a gerund or an infinitive after a verb (661.2–662.1).	The professor wants finishing the paperwork. She regrets to wait until the last minute.	The professor wants to finish the paperwork. She regrets waiting until the last minute.
Do not use *which* to refer to people (618.7).	The professors which teach English are here.	The professors who teach English are here. *or* The professors that teach English are here.
Avoid double negatives (655.4).	I never got no assignment.	I never got the assignment. *or* I got no assignment.

Help for Speakers of European Languages

Advice	DO NOT Write . . .	DO Write . . .
Do not omit the subject, *it* as a subject, or *there* with delayed subjects (638.5, 670.3).	Are thousands of books in the library. Is okay to talk.	There are thousands of books in the library. It is okay to talk.
Avoid using *the* with certain generalizations and singular proper nouns (659.1).	I excel at the physics. The Professor Smith marks grammar errors.	I excel at physics. Professor Smith marks grammar errors.
Learn to use progressive verb tenses (660.2).	I still work on my term paper.	I am working on my term paper.
Learn whether to use a gerund or an infinitive after a verb (661.2–662.1).	The students need finishing their projects. The professors finished to grade the papers.	The students need to finish their projects. The professors finished grading the papers.
Avoid placing adverbs between verbs and direct objects (667.2).	I wrote very quickly the first draft.	I wrote the first draft very quickly.
Do not use *which* to refer to people (618.7).	I am one of the students which sing in the choir.	I am one of the students who sing in the choir.

Help for Speakers of African and Caribbean Languages

Advice	DO NOT Write . . .	DO Write . . .
Avoid double subjects (670.4).	The professor she gave us an assignment.	The professor gave us an assignment.
Use plural nouns after plural numbers (660.1).	The class has two professor.	The class has two professors.
Use the correct form of the *be* verb (627.1).	The union be having a blood drive. We be going.	The union is having a blood drive. We are going.
Make subjects and verbs agree in number (645.2).	She have her own notes. They finishes on time.	She has her own notes. They finish on time.
Use past tense verbs correctly (628.1–628.4).	When the semester began, I study hard.	When the semester began, I studied hard.
Study the rules for article use (658.3–659.1).	I need to buy computer. Entrance exam is required.	I need to buy a computer. An entrance exam is required.

Help for Speakers of East Asian Languages

Advice	DO NOT Write . . .	DO Write . . .
Use plural forms of nouns (657.1–658.2).	I have three difficult class.	I have three difficult classes.
Learn to use adjectival forms (666.1–667.1).	He is a very intelligence professor.	He is a very intelligent professor.
Use the objective case of pronouns (625.1).	The tutor helps I with homework.	The tutor helps me with homework.
Include a subject (or *there*) (646.1, 670.3).	Is good to be here. Are many parts.	It is good to be here. There are many parts.
Study subject–verb agreement (670.2).	The course have a long reading list.	The course has a long reading list.
Study past tenses (628.1–628.4).	We study yesterday. At first, I don't get it.	We studied yesterday. At first, I didn't get it.
Use articles—*a, an,* and *the* (658.3–659.1).	I want to be nurse.	I want to be a nurse.
Study conjunction use (635.1–635.5).	Though she studies, but she struggles.	Though she studies, she struggles.
Learn whether to use a gerund or an infinitive (661.2–662.1).	The students need helping each other study.	The students need to help each other study.

Help for Speakers of Middle–Eastern Languages

Advice	DO NOT Write . . .	DO Write . . .
Study pronoun gender and case (625.1–625.3).	My mother works hard at his job. Give she credit.	My mother works hard at her job. Give her credit.
Don't include a pronoun after a relative clause (642.3, 670.4).	The study space that I share with two others it is too small.	The study space that I share with two others is too small.
Place most subjects before the verb (669).	Received the freshmen the assignment.	The freshmen received the assignment.
Don't overuse progressive verb tenses (660.2).	I am needing a nap. I am wanting food.	I need a nap. I want food.
Use the definite article *the* correctly (659.1).	Union is closed during the July.	The union is closed during July.

Index